ISRAEL

People | Land | State

ISRAEL
People | Land | State
A Nation and its Homeland

Editor: Avigdor Shinan

Co-editors: Aharon Oppenheimer   Avraham Grossman   Yehoshua Kaniel

YAD IZHAK BEN-ZVI · JERUSALEM

IN MEMORY OF

MEYER-HIRSCH GOLDSCHMIDT, *1887–1982*
and GERMAINE-SARAH GOLDSCHMIDT, *1892–1982 of Capetown, South Africa*
and their grandson LOUIS ARIEL GOLDSCHMIDT, *1952–1971 of Haifa*

THEY ALL LOVED ISRAEL

Translation: Eliyahu Green

Editorial coordinator and copy editor: Yohai Goell

Book Design: Nomi Morag

Maps: Tamar Sofer

Pre-press, color separations, printing, and binding:

  Keterpress Enterprises, Jerusalem

ISBN 965-217-239-1

Preface

This volume is devoted to the ages-long, ongoing, and unbroken connection of the People of Israel to its ancient homeland, the Land of Israel, from the biblical period to the first two decades of the State of Israel. Yad Izhak Ben-Zvi initiated the writing of this work by leading scholars at Israeli universities specializing in the various periods. The results were first published in Hebrew, and are now presented to readers of English.

The Directorate of Yad Izhak Ben-Zvi and the volume's chief editor, Prof. Avigdor Shinan, wish to thank the many without whose help this project could not have been undertaken and brought to fruition.

Our thanks to members of Yad Izhak Ben-Zvi's Editorial Committee who contributed their expertise and devoted much energy to getting the project underway: Professors Israel Ef'al, David Rosenthal, and Efraim Stern, and Dr. Zvi Zameret.

The volume's editorial board, whose members bore the brunt of the effort, was comprised of Prof. Avigdor Shinan, Prof. Aaron Oppenheimer, Israel Prize Laureate Prof. Avraham Grossman, and the late Prof. Yehoshua Kaniel. The latter three edited all chapters in the Ancient Period, the Middle Ages, and the Modern Period, respectively, and also contributed chapters of their own. Our heartfelt thanks also go to the other authors for their outstanding contributions to the book. We are extremely grateful to Israel Prize Laureate Professor Eliezer Schweid for his important essay that appears as the Epilogue to this volume.

Special thanks to Prof. Zeev Safrai whose efforts resulted in many of the maps accompanying the chapters, and to Prof. Shalom Sabar who placed items from his photo collection and his great knowledge of Jewish and other art at our disposal. To these we must add the many institutions, curators, photographers, and production staff members – too numerous to be cited here – who enabled us to produce this handsome volume.

The English edition would have been impossible without the efforts of Yohai Goell, editorial coordinator and copy editor of English publications at Yad Izhak Ben-Zvi; Eliyahu Green, who prepared the translation that served as the basis for the chapters; Tamar Sofer, who prepared the maps; Nomi Morag, the graphic designer whose good taste is evident on every page; and the staff at Keterpress Enterprises Ltd., responsible for production, especially Tal Zeidani and Alexandra Klemper.

To all of them we are most grateful.

Jerusalem, 2005

Contents

INTRODUCTION

Avigdor Shinan

The Land of Israel is the accepted appellation for a territory along the eastern coast of the Mediterranean Sea, a location which may be described as the crossroads of three continents: Asia, Europe, and Africa. Its names (such as Canaan and Palestine) as well as its real and utopian borders have changed over the ages. **The People of Israel** is a national entity with various names (Hebrews, Jews), a tortuous history of more than three thousand years, a religion, a culture, a common historical memory, and diverse hopes for the future. **The State of Israel** is the fifty-seven-year-old state of that ancient people, only part of which lives in the land that bears its name, together with a not inconsiderable number of other peoples. The object of this volume is to present in broad outline the ties, relationships, and points of contact between the three entities bearing the name Israel: people, land, and (much later) state. What emerges from these essays is that the People of Israel, both as individuals and as a collective unit, exhibits astoundingly diverse forms of relationships and links to the land that bears its name: immigration to it, striking roots and settling within its borders, exile and return, voluntary abandonment, longing for it – and even living a full life without it.

Let us begin from the beginning which, surprisingly, already embodies all those aspects. Through vignettes it draws of biblical personalities, the Bible presents us with all possible patterns of the relationship of the People of Israel to the Land of Israel (the modern state, as already indicated, is a new phenomenon and we shall not deal with it at this stage). We shall discuss seven such personages from Abraham, the first immigrant to the Land of Israel who came body and soul from the East to the West, to one of the last of the biblical heroes, Mordecai, who lived in the East and whose soul did not exactly yearn for the Land of Israel in the West.

Abraham was seventy-five when he heard the call from Heaven that demanded of him to exchange the land of his residence for another country: "The Lord said to Abram, Go forth from your native land and from your father's house to the land that I will show you. I will make of you a great nation..." (Gen 12:1–2). And when he came to the Land of Canaan, God appeared to him and made him a promise concerning the link between the land and man: "I will assign this land to your offspring" (Gen 12:7). This ancient tradition relating to the first believer and the land promised to his descendants underlies the entire history of the people and of the land, combining them into one saga. However, Abraham, the first man to ascend (i.e., to immigrate) to the Land of Israel only passed through it, constantly wandering from place to place, and even abandoning it at a time of distress: "There was a famine in the land, and Abram went down to Egypt to sojourn there, for the famine was severe in the land" (Gen 12:10). We have here, all in a few verses, immigration to the land, temporary residence there, and departure from it on account of difficult conditions. Abraham also exemplifies the return to the land after absence from it: "From Egypt, Abram went up... And he proceeded by stages... to the place where his tent had been formerly" (Gen 13:1–3). From this point on, the story of Abraham tells us about his wanderings from place to place, diverse relations with the non-Hebrew inhabitants of the country, battles fought against foreign invaders, planting trees and digging wells, establishing holy places and the purchase of land and burial caves, begetting offspring, and the burial of those who passed away at an advanced age. In the story of how Rebecca was brought for Isaac we also read how relatives living outside the country were encouraged to immigrate to it. A reading of the essays collected in this volume, which deal with the history of the People of Israel and the Land of Israel from antiquity to our own times, shows that Nahmanides' well-known dictum: "The acts of the fathers are a sign for the sons and for the sons of the sons" also holds true for the history of Israel.

In the biblical account, **Isaac**, the son of Abraham, personifies the native-born person who never left the country, not even in difficult times. There was he born and there, too, did he die. "Do not go down to Egypt," he was told by the Lord when he sought to emulate his father and go down to Egypt at a time of famine (Gen 26:2). He was also told: "Reside in this land, and I will be with you and bless you; I will assign all these lands to you and your offspring, fulfilling the oath I swore to your father Abraham" (Gen 26:3). The Bible stories about Isaac, too, are replete with wandering from place to place, relations with the inhabitants of the country, digging wells, and establishing bountiful agriculture, reaping "a hundredfold." We learn, too, about parents who encourage their son to leave the land for a fixed period of time in order to seek and bring back a wife, as well as about the aspiration to be buried in the family tomb.

The third Hebrew patriarch, **Jacob**, presents us with another type, one different from his forefathers. Jacob is a native of the Land of Israel who left it at a relatively young age to rise in status and standing, and to seek a family and property abroad. When his father sent him away he told him: "Up, go to Paddan-Aram... and take a wife there... May El Shaddai bless you, make you fertile and numerous, so that you become an assembly of peoples" (Gen 28:2–3). Isaac then went on to say: "May He grant the blessing of Abraham to you and your offspring, that you may possess the land where you are sojourning, which God assigned to Abraham" (Gen 28:4). After a lengthy sojourn in Haran, Jacob-Israel returned to his homeland, now possessing a family and property, and emulated the deeds of his fathers. He wandered throughout the land while struggling with its inhabitants, established holy sites, purchased land, and set up tombstones. He even sent his sons to seek food from abroad during a period of famine. Finally, Jacob left the Land of Israel to pass away in a foreign country, but not before he demanded of his sons: "Please do not bury me in Egypt. When I lie down with my fathers, take me up from Egypt and bury me in their burial place" (Gen 47:29–30). And so it came to pass. The remains of Jacob were brought back to the Land of Israel accompanied by a multitude.

Another relationship between a man and the Land of Israel is personified in the life of **Moses**. A native of Egypt, he aspired all his lifetime to bring his people and himself to the Promised Land, but he was not destined to set his foot upon it. When God sent him to Pharaoh, He said: "I have marked well the plight of My people... I have come down to rescue them from the Egyptians and to bring them out of that land to a good and spacious land, a land flowing with milk and honey.... " (Ex 3:7–8). And, in another instance, the Lord said: "I will bring you into the land which I swore to give to Abraham, Isaac, and Jacob" (Ex 6:8). After forty years of leading the People of Israel as lawgiver, warrior, and prophet, Moses brought it within a stone's throw of the Land of Israel. It was destined that he himself would not enter the land but, at the end of his life, he was allowed to see it and to hear: "This is the land of which I swore to Abraham, Isaac, and Jacob, 'I will assign it to your offspring'" (Deut 34:4).

These four heroes of the Pentateuch – the three Patriarchs and Moses – embody in the biblical narratives that record their biographies the wealth of possible mutual relationships between a land and its people: immigration to the land as the outcome of a mission or a call, and forced emigration from it; permanent or temporary residence; settling down in one spot or wandering the length and breadth of the land; an unfulfilled aspiration to come to the land; temporary, voluntary emigration from it in order to prosper abroad; wells and holy places; agriculture and tombs; a time of war and a time of peace with the other inhabitants of the land.

Let us now jump over several centuries to the end of the biblical period, skipping over the conquest of the Land of Israel, its division among the tribes and into ancestral estates, the establishment of a kingdom and its split into two, the battles fought against the inhabitants of the country and wars waged to expand its borders, or warfare against those who sought to encroach upon it and invade the land. We shall also pass over traditions about the beginnings of Jewish communities outside the Land of Israel after the destruction of the northern kingdom and the saga of the destruction of the First Temple, as well as the painful departure for exile in Babylon. We shall return to the biblical narrative when three more personages appear on the scene, and they too – each in his own way – shaped patterns that would be adopted and followed by future generations throughout the ages.

It is related of **Daniel**, who was exiled in his childhood from Judea as a child, that he rose to greatness in the courts of Babylon and Persia. Even if he was given a foreign name, he never forgot his homeland. It is said of him that he used to pray three times a day facing Jerusalem (Dan 6:11), and there is even a report of a long prayer that he uttered for the sake of the Land of Israel and the site of the Temple (Dan 9:4–20). As far as we know, he never returned to the land, but maintained its memory in his heart and envisioned it at all times.

Ezra the Scribe (of priestly descent), who was a high-ranking official in the Persian Empire, also sought – like Moses before him – to bring his brethren to the Land of Israel with the authorization of a foreign king. In this case the wish was granted. The book that bears his name narrates at length the economic, political, and administrative preparations for immigration made on alien soil and the journey of the returnees to the Land of Israel. Thus we read about the difficulties of acclimatization in the land, and from the Book of Nehemiah, which complements that of Ezra, we gain a harsh picture of struggles with the inhabitants of the country, of construction pursued under armed guard: "doing work with one hand while the other held a weapon" (Neh 4:11), and of a tremendous effort to restore and reconstruct the ruins of buildings and heal breaches in society and in religious practice.

The last of the biblical personalities to whom we shall refer is **Mordecai**, who "had been exiled from Jerusalem in the group that was carried into exile along with King Jeconiah of Judah, which had been driven into exile by King Nebuchadnezzar of Babylon" (Esther 2:6). Mordecai rose to greatness in the court of King Ahasuerus, "he sought the good of his people" who were dispersed throughout the kingdom, sent dispatches "to all the Jews throughout the provinces of King Ahasuerus, near and far" (Esther 9:20), but did not return to his homeland, nor is it even mentioned in descriptions of his achievements and deeds. The Book of Esther describes a Jewish society living in exile, struggling to maintain itself in a hostile world, but the Land of Israel plays no role in the book. Mordecai, unlike Daniel or Ezra, was much at home in the life of the capital city of Shushan, while Zion was for him no more than his birthplace, not a cherished destination. True, in the *midrashim* (homiletic interpretations of the Bible) the Sages did much to correct this impression, but that is not what emerges from the narrative itself.

Abraham, the first immigrant to the Land of Israel, and Isaac, the first native-born son, Jacob who left the country because of famine and was brought back to be buried there, Moses who wanted to reach the land but failed to do so, Daniel who longed for the land from which he had been taken, Ezra who restored its ruins, and Mordecai who felt at ease on foreign soil – all these embody in the biblical narrative which deals with them what has happened to the Jewish People as a group, as sub-groups, and as individuals throughout the ages until our own time. And it is not difficult to discern even today – in the State of Israel and in the Diaspora – those who resemble these biblical heroes. These are joined, regrettably, by another type who has no prototype in the Bible – a Jew born in the Diaspora who takes no interest in the Land of Israel, its inhabitants, or what happens there.

The object of the present collection of essays is to recount the history of the Land of Israel through its encounter with the People of Israel, and the history of the People of Israel through its relationship to the Land of Israel. We begin with the archaeological evidence from the period of settlement in the land and the literary traditions about the era of the three Patriarchs (Abraham, Isaac, and Jacob), and end with the Six Day War in 1967, a turning point in the history of the State, the People, and the Land of Israel. We do not as yet have the historical perspective for a scholarly study of the past three or four decades. The volume is structured chronologically, comprising essays written by different scholars. Each wrote his contribution from his own perspective, emphasizing the topics that interest him or are most relevant for the period with which he is dealing, without a uniform standard framework being imposed upon the authors.

Nevertheless, an overview of the history of the relationship between the People of Israel and its land reveals that one may divide it into three periods which do not necessarily coincide with the accepted historiographical periodization of Jewish history into the ancient, medieval, and modern eras. What distinguishes the three periods we suggest one from the other is the proportional distribution of the Jewish People between the Land of Israel and the Diaspora, and how this distribution influenced the role that the Land of Israel played in the consciousness, creative works, and deeds of the People of Israel.

The First Period: "To the Land and on the Soil"

These are the two traits of the period from the beginning of the history of the People of Israel until after the destruction of the Second Temple. It is founded on a deep inner consciousness of the fact that though the People of Israel came to the land under Divine guidance, its origins were elsewhere. The father of the nation, Abraham, traveled "to the land that I will show you" and his progeny did the same thing several generations later, at the time of their exodus from Egypt. Alongside these traditions are those relating to the conquest and taking possession of the Land of Canaan, culminating in settlement "on the soil that the Lord your God gave you." Most of the People of Israel – until a certain period the vast majority – lived in the Land of Israel. And even if important Jewish centers began to arise outside its borders as well from the end of the First Temple period onwards, such as Babylon and Persia (as a consequence of the First Exile) or later in Egyptian Alexandria, they still considered themselves in principle as being subordinate to the center in the Land of Israel and as its representatives in the Diaspora. Torah would still "come forth from Zion" (Isaiah 2:3).

The Second Period: "On Foreign Soil with the Land in Our Hearts"

The destruction of the Second Temple and the Bar Kokhba Revolt which soon followed altered the historical scene. Most of the people now lived in foreign lands, with the Land of Israel transformed only into a historical memory, a splendid hope, or a place of temporary residence for a small part of the nation. The Jewish centers outside the Land of Israel constantly increased in size and strength, whereas the Jewish population within it was dwindling and becoming weaker. The center of power slowly passed to Babylon and the East after a continuous, sometimes bitter, struggle. Later, the cleavage became much more severe with the rise of many additional centers in Spain, Provence, northern France and Germany, Italy, North Africa, and Yemen. Even later, centers rose and flourished in Eastern Europe and finally on the American continent as well. From our sources we know that the Jewish population of the Land of Israel never completely disappeared. However, in the years between the Bar Kokhba Revolt and the end of the Ottoman period it underwent lengthy periods of decline and wretchedness alongside short periods of vigorous growth and splendor. The Land of Israel became a vital ideal, diversely expressed in thought, prayer, and various customs. The Torah of the Land of Israel declined in status, while many centers now saw themselves as that "Zion" from which the Torah "came forth."

The Third Period: "From the Lands of the Nations to the Soil of the Homeland"

Not much more than a century ago began the return of the People of Israel to the Land of Israel. They came from East and West, North and South. Jews abandoned the lands which they had inhabited for hundreds of years and returned to their spiritual homeland, at first in a trickle and afterwards – during the period of the British Mandate, and especially after the Holocaust, the establishment of the State of Israel and the collapse of the Soviet Union – in very great numbers. The story of their absorption and integration in Israel, a saga of which we are still in the midst and which seems to be without counterpart in world history, is full of wonderful manifestations of brotherhood, devotion, and steadfastness alongside hardships and pain.

Thus, over the past century we have witnessed Abraham arriving in "the land that I will show you," and the native-born Isaac who voluntarily makes concessions so that he can receive those who come to the land. We have seen more than once Jacob leaving the land for the outside world to fill his needs there, to marry, acquire property, or avoid the hardships of life in the

Land of Israel, and have also seen Jacob dying in a foreign land and being brought for burial in the land of his forefathers. Nor will it be difficult to discern around us Moses, the leader who toils for his people, but does not succeed in fulfilling his greatest wish during his lifetime, or Daniel, who constantly bears in his heart the memory of the Land of Israel of yesteryear. Mordecai, too, who lives peacefully in the Diaspora and leads his people, is no stranger to us. The Book of Books, as we intimated, is a reflection of almost everything.

A reflection of "almost everything" and not of "everything," for our century has witnessed another event, the likes of which the Jewish People had never before experienced during its lengthy history. This episode is so unique that it is impossible to deal with it together with anything else. We refer of course to the Holocaust, that manifestation of human baseness that descended to its ugliest depths in the atrocious attempt to wipe the Jewish People off the face of the Earth. The massacre of almost a third of the Jewish People, inhabitants of Europe and adjacent areas who believed that they could live peacefully in those countries, and the destruction of these millions of people led to a dramatic rise in the importance and status of American Jewry, hastened the establishment of the State of Israel, and made a decisive contribution to generating waves of immigration to the Land of Israel.

To be sure, we are still far from claiming that most of the People of Israel lives in the Land of Israel; after all, less than half the Jews in the world are citizens of the State of Israel. Yet, even among those who have chosen to remain outside the state there are many who are torn between loyalty to the country of their residence and devotion to the land where the Jewish People was born. Alongside all these we can today discern new phenomena, heretofore unknown in Jewish history, such as Jews who show no interest in the Land of Israel or the State of Israel, or Jews who live within its borders but do not find the state to their liking. All these make for an extremely complex fabric of contemporary Jewish society. Only time will tell what new shape the relationship between the People, the State, and the Land of Israel will assume.

We cannot foresee the future, but we may hope that it will be like the beginnings in the distant past, and that most of the People of Israel will reside on the soil on which it was created. And of course, we must do everything in our power so that the words of the prophet shall be fulfilled: "Torah shall go forth from Zion."

In this schematic presentation we have not elaborated upon the well-known fact that other peoples and religions aspired to gain a foothold in the Land of Israel, and even actually settled there. These included, for example, Samaritan Israelites,

12

Hellenistic pagans, Christians, and Muslims. Their ties and relationship with the country and with their Jewish neighbors is a complex story, at times sad and painful, but it is not the subject of this volume and is dealt with only sporadically, primarily from the Ottoman period onwards. The principal issues which we have set out to present to the reader concern the expansion and spread of the Jewish population throughout the country, its livelihoods, and governing and leadership institutions. Other topics are immigration to and emigration from the Land of Israel and their causes, the struggle for hegemony between the center in the Land of Israel and other Jewish centers in the Diaspora, and how the Jewish communities in the Land of Israel and in the Diaspora related to one another. Thus, we have also sought to understand the nature of the mechanisms that helped to preserve the bond between the Land of Israel and Diaspora Jewry. What emerges from these essays in this respect is a relationship that was preserved by diverse means. On the physical, material level we find, among others, pilgrimage, financial support, emissaries to the Diaspora, and bringing the deceased for burial in the Land of Israel, while some spiritual manifestations of this relationship are mentioning the Land of Israel in prayer and philosophical literature, or the important role it and its traditions played in the shaping of *halakhah* (Jewish law) or in the development of *kabbalah* (Jewish mysticism).

On the spiritual level, the literature of the Sages – the Mishnah, the two Talmuds, the *midrashim* (homiletical interpretations of the Bible), and the prayer book – is of special importance, particularly since it is the link connecting the Bible to the *aggadic*, halakhic, and philosophical literature produced by later generations. This corpus of literature reinterpreted the biblical narrative that preceded it while shaping – due to its special standing – the conceptions that would be characteristic of the Jewish People from those days on. Here was the concept of the Land of Israel as the Holy Land (which, of course, had its origins in the Bible) developed in its most forceful form, and here were cast several of the practical frameworks for preserving the bond between the People of Israel and its land. Two examples are mention of the land in the "Eighteen Benedictions" prayer on weekdays ("And may You gather us from the four corners of the earth to our land," and so forth) as well as in the Grace recited after meals ("We thank You ... for granting to our forefathers a good and broad land of delight"). In this context we should also bear in mind the special status which Jewish law affords to the Land of Israel (special commandments such as a tithe for the priests, which can only be observed in the land) and the exaggerated celebration of the splendor and praises of the Land of Israel, such as "The Land of Israel is lacking in nothing" (Babylonian Talmud, *Berakhot*, 36b). To this can be added the various manners in which the Jewish People has throughout the ages kept alive the memory of the destruction of the Temple (different ways of "remembering the destruction"), and the custom of citing the Land of Israel in general and Jerusalem in particular at all Jewish celebrations. The unique relationship between the Land, the People, and the God of Israel was expressed, for example, in these two sayings: "A man shall always dwell in the Land of Israel, even in a city where the majority are non-Jews. And he shall not dwell outside the land, even in a city where the majority are Jews. For everyone who dwells in the Land of Israel is like someone who has God with him, and everyone who dwells outside the land is like someone who does not have God with him" (Babylonian Talmud, *Ketubbot*, 110b); "Living in the Land of Israel is equal to all the commandments in the Torah" (*Sifrei*, Deuteronomy, Re'eh, Paragraph 70). Development of the concept of the Chosen People and the Chosen Land led the Sages to attribute the following statement to the Lord: "I shall bring Israel, since they are beloved by Me, into the land, since it is beloved by Me" (*Numbers Rabbah*, 23:7), and thus the People and the Land of Israel become as one with He who has chosen them both.

I would like to express my heartfelt thanks to all those who lent their support to the creation of this volume, first and foremost to the authors who generously shared with us their knowledge and scholarship, proving that the Sages did not err when they claimed: "Ten measures of wisdom came down to the world; the Land of Israel took nine and all the rest of the world took one" (Babylonian Talmud, *Kiddushin*, 49b).

And may it be His will that what the Torah promised be fulfilled for us all: "And you shall... dwell securely in your land" (Lev 26:5).

Avigdor Shinan
Jerusalem 2005

The Ancient Period

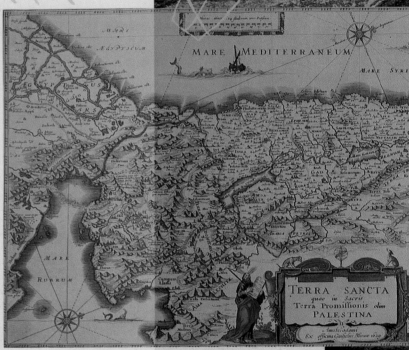

From Settlement in the Land of Israel to the Muslim Conquest

Aharon Oppenheimer

The Land of Israel is the national homeland of the Jewish People. During several periods in antiquity there was an independent Jewish state in the country. This was the case with the kingdoms during the biblical period, the later Hasmonean state, and the brief episode of the Bar Kokhba Revolt. However, during most of antiquity, even when the Land of Israel was subject to foreign rule, the Jewish People enjoyed social and religious autonomy, and was generally allowed to conduct its own affairs and live as it wished, although many continued to hope for full independence.

The Land of Israel is richly variegated in its physical features. There are a number of climatic zones and an abundant variety of fauna and flora. However, it is not these physical features which define its territory, but the unique historical, religious, and ideological consciousness which developed among the members of one of the peoples who lived there.

In the second millenium BCE the Land of Israel was part of a larger entity, the Land of Canaan, its territory divided among many city-states, both small and large, each of which claimed possession of the surrounding area. At the beginning of the first millenium BCE these Canaanite states were replaced by a new array of kingdoms, Israel and Judah. Each kingdom had its own borders and system of internal administration, and each saw in the territory demarcated by its borders its own land, and those residing within them its own people.

The transformation in the consciousness of nation and territory began only after the Kingdom of Israel was annexed by the Assyrian Empire and ceased to exist as an independent state. It was then that a new concept began to emerge in the Kingdom of Judah, one which viewed the inhabitants of Israel and Judah as a single people with a common past and origin, possessing a bond to a specific territory which it had been promised at the dawn of history. The historical narrative of the Hebrew Bible, which chronicled the history of the Israelites from the beginning until the time of the Bible's compilation, played a decisive role in molding and crystallizing the new conception of the People of Israel and the Land of Israel. The process of internalizing this historical and ideological concept which was centered around the God of Israel, the People of Israel, and the Land of Israel continued for many generations, culminating in the period of the Return to Zion under the leadership of Ezra and Nehemiah. Thus it is possible to trace the development of the consciousness of the continuity and identity of a specific people, a consciousness which developed against the specific political, religious, and ideological background of a defined historical period and is inseparably linked to a particular territory. This is what fixed the relationship of the people and the land in the consciousness of the Jewish People throughout the ages.

During the period of Persian rule in the Land of Israel, the Jews were part of a multi-national empire. In this context too they saw themselves as a people. At this time Jewish identity centered round the Temple. A new leadership gradually emerged in the Land of Israel based on the link between those with the most distinguished pedigree – the hereditary priests – and the Temple. Following the conquests of Alexander the Great in 312 BCE, the Land of Israel came under the influence of a non-Oriental civilization. The Hellenistic period was characterized by supra-nationalism, rather than multi-nationalism, for Greek language and culture united the Hellenistic world. As this concept took hold, the Jews began to define their identity in terms of their culture and religion. Over time, they learned to take good advantage of the decline of the Hellenistic states, and as a result of the revolt that was a consequence of Antiochos Epiphanes' religious decrees they united all the Land of Israel within the independent Hasmonean state.

From the beginning of the Hasmonean period that part of the Land of Israel inhabited by Jews was continually expanded. During the reign of Aristobulos in the late second century BCE, almost all the Jewish inhabitants of the Land of Israel were under Jewish sovereign rule for the first time since the days of the First Temple. Many non-Jewish inhabitants of the country were converted to Judaism, with the result that the Land of Israel became a state with a dominant Jewish component. The newly-created identity between the Jewish population and the territory of the Land of Israel was also noted by outsiders.

The end of the Hasmonean state came in 63 BCE when the Roman commander Pompey and his legions conquered the Land of Israel, turning it into a Roman province. However the name Iudaea (Judea) given it by the Romans is evidence of the decisive ethnic preponderance of the Jewish element in the population. This was one expression of the unique character of the country as compared with neighboring Roman provinces.

The destruction of the Second Temple in 70 CE during the Jewish War (First Revolt) against the Romans was a traumatic event which has left its mark on Jewish history to this day. Nevertheless, the destruction did not bring about the end of Jewish social and religious autonomy in the Land of Israel. The Jewish leadership institutions which were created in Yavneh to a great extent filled the void left after the destruction. They molded Judaism anew, without Jerusalem and the Temple. Study of the Torah was given the highest priority, replacing the sacrifices, and even to some extent the commandments, which were performed mainly in relation to the Temple and its rites.

The intensity of the Bar Kokhba Revolt (132–135 CE) shows that even after the destruction of the Temple not only did the Jewish People conduct its religious and social life under its own leadership institutions, but it was also capable of impressive political and military action. The destruction wreaked upon Judea as a consequence of the revolt was so great that the leadership institutions moved to Galilee, together with many refugees from all social classes. Thus the center of gravity of Jewish life in the Land of Israel shifted to Galilee. The times of R. Judah ha-Nasi (ca. 180–220) were a golden age for Jewish life in the Land of Israel during the period of the Mishnah and the Talmud. They left their impression on later generations as a result of the redaction of the Mishnah by R. Judah ha-Nasi. Thus was created a work, second only to the Bible in importance

for Jewish culture, which laid a single, common foundation for Jewish law (*halakhah*). Both the Talmud of the Land of Israel (also knows as the Jerusalem Talmud) and the Babylonian Talmud developed on the basis of the Mishnah.

The halakhic boundaries of the Land of Israel were set in accordance with a religious principle. They defined the territory within which certain commandments applied. Only within the Land of Israel were Jews obliged to set aside a tithe for the priests in the Temple and to refrain from working the land in a sabbatical year. In setting these boundaries mundane secular considerations were also involved which had to do with society, the economy, and relations with the Roman authorities.

After the glorious days of R. Judah ha-Nasi, a series of events led to the gradual decline of the Jewish population in the Land of Israel. These included economic pressures and heavy taxes during the period of imperial crisis (235–284), the recognition of Christianity as the imperial religion (313), and abolition of the office of patriarch (*nasi*) by the authorities (429). In the Byzantine period, the history of the Land of Israel and that of the People of Israel gradually followed different paths. Most Jews were then concentrated in part of Galilee, although there were also active Jewish centers at Lod and Caesarea. The Land of Israel became the focus of Christian interest, and with imperial support the Christians turned their religious vision into reality. Nevertheless, by elevating those who studied the Torah and by stressing the spiritual aspect of Judaism instead of the Temple and its worship, the People of Israel was able to function and preserve its identity, even in the Diaspora. Thus the ground was prepared for the consolidation of Babylonian Jewry until it took over from the Land of Israel, grasping the reins of world Jewish leadership in its hands.

The sages, who had constituted the leadership of Jewish society since the destruction of the Second Temple, took steps to strengthen the Jewish bond to the Land of Israel, precisely because of the problems there during the Roman and Byzantine periods. In the period following the Bar Kokhba Revolt, and even more during the imperial crisis of the third century, religious laws were enacted and declarations made which sought to prevent Jews from leaving the Land of Israel and praised its merits.

Archaeological finds show that despite the upheavals that were the lot of the Jewish population in the Land of Israel there was still a significant Jewish population in the country during the Roman and Byzantine periods. The best evidence for the vitality of Jewish life in the Land of Israel is demonstrated by the growing number of synagogues discovered wherever Jews lived in the Land of Israel at that time.

Aerial view of Megiddo, the biblical Armageddon

Map of the Land
of Israel, by
Robert Seaton,
showing its
division among
the tribes,
London 1835
(JNUL, Laor 712)

From the Settlement of the Land to the Destruction of the Temple

Nadav Na'aman

Between History and Historiography

We may easily sum up the biblical narrative of the history of Israel. According to the Bible the Children of Israel originated from one father, who, migrating from the land of his birth, settled in Canaan. Two generations later, his descendants migrated to Egypt, where they multiplied and became a nation. The tribal structure of the People of Israel was the result of natural reproduction in Egypt. After the Exodus the twelve tribes, joined together under the leadership of one man, received in the desert the Torah, the commandments, and the laws, which from now on would regulate their religion and dictate their way of life. The process of consolidation continued in the desert for some forty years, after which, with the disappearance of the desert generation, the people of Israel were ready to conquer and settle the land promised to their forefathers.

The Bible further relates that the land was already settled by a people which, by all its characteristics, was the very opposite of the People of Israel. This was an ancient nation which had inhabited the land from of old, in contrast to young Israel which had been forged into a nation in another country. Canaanite society was urban and settled, unlike the Israelite nomadic tribal society. The Canaanites were divided into states, each with its own king, in contrast to unified Israelite society which was headed by a leader to whom all deferred. Most important, the religion and culture of the Canaanites were completely contradictory to the Torah, the commandments, and the laws that the Israelites had received in Sinai. Therefore, the Children of Israel were commanded to erase the Canaanites; to completely wipe out their culture, and to inherit their land. And indeed, after crossing the Jordan the Israelites fulfilled their divine commandment: they laid waste the Canaanite cities pursuing their inhabitants to the very borders of the land. After which they divided the conquered land between the twelve tribes, settling it throughout, thus continuing and preserving their tribal structure.

It is also related in the Bible that in the period of the Judges, the People of Israel still preserved its tribal structure and ethnic cohesion, while norms relating to faith and worship remained etched in their collective memory. True, inter-tribal unity declined and the People of Israel occasionally even violated their covenant with the God of Israel, for which they were punished with subjugation by their neighbors until they mended their ways. After which, a savior would arise from their ranks and their fortunes would be restored. The return to the path of righteousness proves that the religious norms had never been fully forgotten, while the rallying around the judge-saviors indicates that their fundamental national cohesion had not been essentially altered.

Letter on clay tablet from Tel el-Amarna, Egypt, describing conditions in Canaan in the first half of the 14th cent. BCE

21

The establishment of the monarchy changed the leadership structure of the People of Israel, restoring the unity and cohesiveness which had declined since the settlement of the country. Although the unity of earlier times was restored by a new supra tribal system, the inhabitants of the new kingdom (kings as well as subjects) were still as bound to the Laws of the Torah as their forefathers in the past had been.

In the biblical narrative the first stage in the establishment of the monarchy was marked by the struggle against the Philistines and their expulsion from the mountain region. This was followed by a period of expansion and aggrandizement in which a great kingdom was founded spanning both sides of the Jordan, and surrounded by a series of vassal kingdoms. One generation later, the Temple and the palace were erected in all their splendor and glory. Jerusalem became the capital of a large kingdom, and additional administrative centers were built throughout the country. Even the later division of the monarchy did not destroy the all-Israelite consciousness, and although the two kingdoms existed side by side for about 200 years, a sense of belonging to one people was preserved in them both. When the northern kingdom came to an end, much of the People of Israel was lost in the process. However, those who remained, in the kingdom of Judah, preserved a sense of unity and of common origin, continuing to observe the laws and commandments – the heritage of the period of Israel's wandering in the desert. Finally, both these elements were also maintained after the destruction of the Temple and the exile from the Land of Judah.

The biblical account briefly summarized above stands in contradiction to the history of Israel as conventionally accepted by modern-day scholars, who maintain that the complex and prolonged process of shaping the Israelite nation took place inside the Land of Israel, with the role played by the establishment of the monarchy being decisive. The Israelites originated from the primeval inhabitants of the land, including remnants of the urban-rural society of early Canaan and the nomads who roamed its peripheral areas, as well as groups of migrants who had come to Canaan in the wake of the large-scale migration of the "Sea Peoples" with its consequent destruction of states throughout the eastern Mediterranean basin.

In the wake of the destruction of the Canaanite kingdoms a process of settlement and gradual consolidation began, which – about two centuries later – led to the establishment of a kingdom possessing well-defined and demarcated borders, with all who lived within them its subjects: the descendants of the old

Egyptian administrative center ●
City mentioned in el-Amarna letters ◆
Capital of a kingdom ★

0   10   20   30 km

Canaan in the el-Amarna period

**Right:
The Land of
Canaan and the
allotments of the
twelve tribes**

**Left:
The allotments of
the twelve tribes**

inhabitants of the country (the Canaanites), of the West Semitic nomads on its periphery, and of the migrants who had arrived in the territory from the north and the south. They were subject to a military draft, obligated to perform various kinds of labor for the state, to pay taxes and bring gifts to the royal court and,

"[Belonging] to Shema, slave of Jeroboam," seal found at Megiddo, probably referring to Jeroboam II, 8ᵗʰ cent. BCE

further, to worship the national God of the kingdom in the temple built for him. After the schism in the monarchy, the definition of "who is an Israelite?" was clear: an "Israelite" is someone who lives in the territory of the kingdom of Israel (as distinct from Judah), who benefits from its defense and protection, and fulfills all the duties and obligations that it imposes upon its subjects.

Conversely, a "Judahite" is an inhabitant of the kingdom of Judah. We do not know how the inhabitants defined themselves in the periods preceding the establishment of the monarchy or during its early years, but from the division of the monarchy there was a clear distinction between "Israelites" and "Judahites."

Finally, it should be noted that most researchers are convinced that a not inconsiderable part of the laws, commandments, and ordinances emerged at the end of the First Temple period, and another part only during the period of exile and return to Zion. Furthermore, these prescriptions were not as yet the accepted norm in the First Temple period. The Israelite nation, as it is described in biblical historiography, was shaped and colored by the ideological and didactic objectives of the historians who wrote their works late

23

in the First Temple period and afterwards. Indeed, the biblical image of the People of Israel as described in the early histories of Israel influenced its coalescence, its organizational structure, and the norms that it adopted during the period of the exile and that of the Return to Zion.

It would appear, therefore, that there is an unbridgeable abyss

also emerged within the Land of Israel. Thus, it is only proper to try to create a new picture to explain how and under which circumstances the biblical concepts of the Land and People as we know them actually developed, asking for example, what do the biblical descriptions of the Land of Canaan with its borders, and those of the Twelve Tribes of Israel reflect in reality? When

"The other events of Ahab's reign ... and all the towns that he fortified..." (1 Kings 22:39).
Fragment of ivory ornamentation from palace of the Kings of Israel in Samaria

between the biblical account of the growth and consolidation of Israel and the historical reality as it has been reconstructed in scholarly research. All the elements which formed the identity of the Israelite nation that – according to the biblical account – had already existed during the forty years' wandering in the desert and which were brought to the Land during its conquest, emerged in fact on the soil of the Land of Israel, taking shape during a prolonged historical process. Further, the concept of borders and territory that form an integral part of the ancient history of Israel,

and against what background did the concept of the Promised Land from the Euphrates to the River of Egypt emerge? From which period did the inhabitants of the kingdom of Judah begin to be called "Israelites"? Against what background did the concept of the unity of the Israelite nation within the Land of Israel emerge? An analysis of "Israel – People and Land" during the First Temple period must try to address these fundamental questions. Needless to say, the answers are complex and intricate, and often subject to academic controversy.

. . . .

Canaan and Canaanites in Historical Reality and in Biblical Historiography

As already noted, the People of Israel emerged on the ruins of a network of Canaanite kingdoms, and many elements of Israelite government, society, economy, cult and culture are of Canaanite origin. A description of Late Bronze Age Canaanite kingdoms shows not only the similarities and differences between them and the kingdoms emerging in the First Temple period, but also whether ethnic and territorial concepts from this earlier epoch are reflected in the biblical text.

In the Late Bronze Age (1550 to 1150 BCE), the term "Land of Canaan" indicated the area of Egyptian rule in Asia. This territorial-political designation appears in letters sent by the rulers of the great powers of the day (Babylon, Egypt, and Hatti). Moreover, in those letters despatched from Byblos and Tyre (two kingdoms on the Lebanese coast, within the territory of the Land of Canaan), this designation serves as a synonym for the expression "the king's land" (the king = pharaoh). Most references

Joshua's capture of Jericho. From psalter of Louis IX,
France, 1256 (BN, MS. Lat. 10525, fol. 42)

24

Aerial view of the City of David, the slope from which Jerusalem developed, and the Temple Mount to the north

The Exodus from Egypt, from a Hebrew manuscript prayer book, Germany, 15th cent. (SUH, Cod. Hebr. 37, fol. 29v)

to Canaan are carried by documents originating from outside the land, while those written inside it carry few. Since the subjects of Egyptian rule were divided into citizens of various kingdoms, both large and small, the use of an overall territorial term is therefore in need of clarification. Hence, we may ask: Besides being citizens of these kingdoms, did the inhabitants consider themselves to be "Canaanites," that is, as belonging to the broader territorial entity of the Land of Canaan?

To this day, no document has turned up wherein any local inhabitant calls himself a "Canaanite." However, it is significant that in legal and administrative documents discovered in neighboring countries (Egypt, as well as Ugarit and Alalakh in northern Syria), persons are mentioned with the accompanying designation of "Canaanite." It would seem that those persons presented themselves as Canaanites and were therefore so registered in the documents. Thus, it may be that in contacts with neighboring kingdoms, inhabitants of Canaan sometimes used the better known broader territorial-political name rather than that of their specific kingdom. In this way, they expressed the fact that they belonged to a territory that was ruled by one of the major powers (Egypt). Herodotos (VIII:144) presented

pan-Hellenism (the concept of the unity of Hellas = Greece) as being based on the consciousness of common origin, common language, and common worship, culture and customs, distinct from those of other peoples who are called barbarians. However, in most of these elements (perhaps in all) the Canaanites were no different from their neighbors. It would seem that the name "Canaanite" had the principal connotation of belonging to a specific political-territorial space. It is doubtful whether it had any other implications.

The destruction of the Canaanite kingdoms, and the withdrawal of the Egyptians in the second half of the twelfth century BCE, did not mean the disappearance of the terms "Canaan" and "Canaanite," as they continued to appear in Phoenician and Punic texts, in biblical historiography, as well as later in the New Testament. The use of archaic terms to indicate existing territorial-political or ethnic units is well known in the ancient East. Nevertheless, the biblical use of the words "Canaan" and "Canaanite" goes far beyond this. The previous political-territorial connotation was exchanged in the Bible for a new ethnic-religious-cultural one. The authors were, of course, aware that the historical Canaan had been divided into kindgoms, each with its ruler; but in their works they attached little importance to belonging to a specific place. Instead, they chose to portray the ancient inhabitants of the land as people whose origin was from a fully developed entity possessing a uniform ethnic, religious, and cultural character.

Biblical historiography makes an exception, however, in the use of "Canaan" as a general territorial description. Numbers 34 and Ezekiel 47 contain detailed descriptions of the boundaries of the Land of Canaan. Included within its bounds are the districts of the Bashan, Damascus, the Valley of Lebanon (up to Lebo-Hamath), and the coast of Lebanon (nearly up to Nahr al-Kabir), as well as desert regions down to Kadesh-Barnea. In contrast,

Painted Canaanite vessels, First Middle Bronze Age (3500–3000 BCE)

Caravan of Canaanite nomads on the way to Egypt. Reproduced from wall painting in Beni Hassan, Egypt, 19th cent. BCE

the areas east of the Jordan are outside its boundaries. The borders of the Land of Canaan are sometimes also described by the short formula: "from ... to..." (Numbers 13:21; I Kings 8:65; I Chronicles 13:5).

Comparison of the region described in the Bible with the borders of the Egyptian province in Asia displays a great measure of conformity with the exception of the southern border where the biblical Land of Canaan extends far to the south of the area of the historical Canaan. The demarcations of the biblical Land of Canaan do not match the boundaries that the People of Israel inhabited at any period: on the north they encompass areas that were never included within the bounds of Israelite settlement; on the east, on the other hand, Israelite settlement spread far beyond the Jordan River, touching the borders of the kingdoms of Moab, Ammon, and Aram.

We should note how the borders of the Land of Canaan are described in various books of the Bible. In Numbers, Canaan is presented as the land destined for the Children of Israel. After the districts west of the Jordan were conquered, they were divided among nine and one-half tribes; however, the Philistine coast and the northern districts, which were part of the Land of Canaan but had not yet been conquered and not included within the bounds of settlement of the tribes of Israel, were designated as "the land that remains" (Joshua 13:2-6). Ezekiel, in contrast, disregarded (or was unaware of) the concept of "the land that remains" as that which had not been conquered and settled by the Israelites, also disregarding the complex of tribal allotments. For him, the entire Land of Canaan was the land destined for the Twelve Tribes of Israel.

There is no need to point out how greatly the biblical account diverges from ancient reality as described in scholarly research, and how wide the gap is between the biblical usage of the terms Canaan and Canaanites and the actual use made of them in the Late Bronze Age.

The United Monarchy: Between History and Historiography

The name "Israel" appears once, in an inscription from the fifth year of the reign of Merenptah, king of Egypt (1208 BCE). However, the identity of that "Israel" is subject to controversy that cannot be resolved. The inscription refers to a tribal group which fought the Egyptians. The fact that the name "Israel" appears in such an ancient non-biblical source is of great importance, although nothing is known of the size, location, origin, or nature of this group. All the opinions expressed on this issue are no more than conjecture, as there is no evidence to support any of them. For this reason, it is best to avoid basing any conjecture as to the growth or consolidation of the Israelite nationality on this inscription.

From the Early Iron Age (twelfth and eleventh centuries BCE) as well, we have absolutely no information about the identity of the groups that settled and established themselves in the mountain districts on both sides of the Jordan, where the

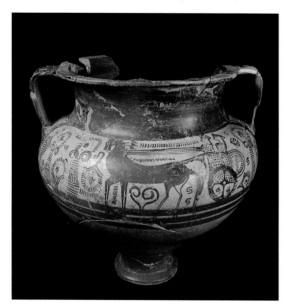

Mycenean jar discovered at Tel Dan, 14th cent. BCE

27

kingdoms of Israel and Judah were later to arise. Archaeology is of no help in defining the identity of these settlers, nor can it indicate traits of any substance that distinguish these groups from others that settled near them. The history of the People of Israel was written hundreds of years later, at a time when only dim memories, at most, survived from the primordial stages of the Israelite nation. Of course, it may be that various details mentioned in the biblical tradition reflect something of the reality of the earlier period, but we are unable to isolate them and base our historical research upon them. It is also apparent that an entity named "Israel" existed then in the mountain districts, but we cannot neither identify those who comprised it nor apprehend its size, institutions,

The four-celled gate at Hazor, ascribed by some to King Solomon

rituals or culture. We may refer to the Israelite entity only from that moment when it took shape within a defined territorial framework which we can delimit, and when we can describe its organizational features and forms of cult and culture. The pre-monarchic period belongs to the proto-historic age in the history of Israel and the biblical accounts of that period cannot serve as a basis for historical reconstruction.

The biblical evidence on the period of the United Monarchy is the subject of extreme controversy among conptemporary scholars. Many agree that historical writing began in the kingdoms of Israel and Judah no earlier than the eighth century BCE, and that the comprehensive history of Israel was written – at the earliest – towards the end of the seventh century BCE, not long before the destruction of the Temple. Were these ancient historians able to use documents from the tenth century BCE as a reliable basis for their description of the development of the monarchial process in Israelite society? Could it have been that only a few such documents survived, and that the authors depended mainly on oral traditions to reconstruct the historical narrative, as they attempted to use the past to transmit religious and ideological messages to their own contemporaries? Unfortunately, even now there is no consensus among archaeologists as to the dating of settlement strata from the Iron I–IIA periods, making it difficult to determine the scope of urbanization, fortifications, and public

building in the tenth century BCE, and to what extent relations had developed with neighboring kingdoms. Some researchers accept the biblical tradition at face value and assume that the United Monarchy existed, in all its glory and splendor, as is described in the biblical narrative. Other scholars totally reject the assumption that a United Monarchy ever existed, and believe that the biblical account of the period is no more than a retrospective reconstruction, motivated by a desire to embellish the primeval stages of the Israelite monarchy and to present them as an ideal model worthy of aspiring to return to – a seeming "restoration of ancient glory."

In my opinion, it is possible that King David conquered extensive territories holding them for a certain period of time, and that after his death many of these territories were lost (I Kings 11:14-25; see 9:11). However, it is very doubtful whether he was able to establish a proper administrative system in the conquered territories or whether the borders of his kingdom were so firmly delineated in his time as to justify reference to the "the border of Israel" for that period. It should be emphasized that on the ideological level the very presence of a king in a far-off land is sufficient to argue that he ruled there. A raid or a short-term conquest is enough to provide grounds for a "historic" claim to that area. Although David's conquests, whatever their exact scope, were short-term and of only minor historic importance, it seems

**Episodes in the life of David; Psalter of the Emperor Basil II (976–1025), a Byzantine manuscript, Constantinople
(BNM cod. marc. Gr. Z. 17(=421), fol. 4v)**

to me that they left an ideological imprint for generations to come, influencing the biblical descriptions of the boundaries according to the ideological pattern of "David's conquests."

The account of the events of Solomon's times includes a list of the districts within his kingdom, together with a list of governors or prefects appointed to rule them (I Kings 4:7-19). Was the list already set down during Solomon's times and preserved for hundreds of years until it finally reached the later historian who incorporated it into his work? Why was such a list drawn up and how did it survive for such a prolonged period of time? The area that emerges from the list of Solomon's districts corresponds to a great extent to the combined area of the kingdoms of Israel and Judah after the schism. Did Solomon control all those territories, and does the list faithfully reflect the reality of his time? Or is it a retrospective reconstruction, influenced by the reality of later periods in the history of Israel? There is no clear answer to any of these questions. Hence, it is difficult to take an unambiguous position on either the issue of dating the system of borders, or the date of the list's composition.

Another problem has to do with determining the combined

Administrative divisions of Solomon's kingdom

Ceramic vessel from First Temple period (late 8th cent. BCE) bearing the word *kadesh* in ancient Hebrew script, found at Tel Beer-Sheba

range of the districts described. We may recall that such a reconstruction rests to a great extent on other, later sources, and there is no certainty as to whether the author of the list in I Kings used such sources. For example, it has been proposed that "the second district" mentioned in the list (verse 9) is identical in area with the tribal territory of Dan referred to in Joshua 19:40-46. But from the plain meaning of the text it emerges that "the second district" encompassed only a limited area west of Bet-Shemesh, and that it in no way resembles the tribal territory of Dan. Likewise, we do not know with certainty which territories were included in the district of Mahanaim (verse 14) or in that of Ramoth-Gilead (verse 13a). There is much academic debate over the interpretation and scope of "in Asher and Bealoth" (verse 16). On the other hand, the territory of Judah is not mentioned in the list, and there is some controversy as to whether it was included in the network of Solomonic districts. The list was slightly revised in a later period, probably by the author of the history of Solomon's times, and verses 13b and 19 were not part of the original list. It seems that the list was drawn up at a relatively early period, but it is doubtful as to whether it reflects Solomon's reign or whether the borders of the kingdom had by then become stabilized to the extent that one might speak of a fully-formed network of districts that served the kingdom's administration.

On the whole, the biblical account of the period of the United Monarchy as the golden age of Israel is neither historically reliable nor compatible with the early stages of the establishment of the monarchy in Israel. For that reason, we cannot rely on this account as a starting point for studying the history of the kingdoms of Israel and Judah.

The Kingdoms of Israel and Judah

The network of kingdoms that emerged during the ninth and eighth centuries BCE was much different from the one found during the Late Bronze Age. The many city-states that had divided the country into scores of political entities, both small and large, were now replaced by a few kingdoms spread over the area of the earlier ones. At the center was the kingdom of Israel, whose territory encompassed the lands of many Canaanite kingdoms that had formerly been situated in the mountain area, the valleys, the Shephelah, and along the seacoast. The kingdom of Judah included within its borders the territories of several former Canaanite kingdoms in the mountain and Shephelah districts. Settlement in the east grew and spread to the semi-arid areas on the fringes of the desert, while the trans-Jordanian kingdoms (Ammon, Moab, and Edom) were established in an area that had not previously been included in the network of Canaanite city-states. Only the Philistine and Phoenician states preserved the configuration of the Canaanite city-states that had preceded them, and there is a clear continuum between Canaanite civilization and the Philistine and Phoenician civilizations that rose on its ruins. Indeed, the biblical narrative sometimes refers to the inhabitants of these districts as Canaanites (Genesis 10:15, 17-18a; Numbers 13:29; Deuteronomy 1:7; Joshua 5:1; Isaiah 23:11; Ovadiah 1:20; Zephaniah 2:5). Likewise, in an Egyptian inscription from the era of the Twelfth Dynasty (945–713 BCE), the author of the inscription (who apparently was an Egyptian envoy sent to Philistia) is referred to as "the emissary of Canaan of Philist(ines)," (compare Zephaniah 2:5). In contrast, Philo of Byblos mentions Canaan (Chna) as "the first one who changed his name to Phoenicia (Phoenix)."

The new kingdoms differed from their predecessors not only in size, but also in the disposition and number of their settlements. There was very little rural settlement in Canaan during the Late Bronze Age, in contrast to the many hundreds of settlements that sprang up throughout the country from the twelfth century BCE on. The mountain and desert frontier districts, that had been almost completely unpopulated in the Late Bronze Age, were gradually settled and important urban centers emerged. The center of gravity of the new hinterland states was located in the mountain region or east of the Jordan, while the important Canaanite centers in the Late Bronze Age had been located mainly in the coastal zones, the Shephelah, and the northern valleys. We can safely state, therefore, that the network of kingdoms that emerged at the beginning of the first millenium BCE differed in many of its components from its predecessor, and that the

kingdoms of Israel and Judah were new political and social entities in the history of the Land of Canaan.

Lastly, it should be noted that in the Late Bronze Age, one power (Egypt) ruled the entire territory of Canaan. At the beginning of the first millenium BCE, on the other hand, there was no major state in the region, and the balance of power was determined by the relative strength of the new kingdoms that had arisen and on the basis of their interests.

Research of the period following the division of the monarchy stands on a rather solid foundation. The territorial extent of the kingdom of Israel (the northern kingdom) can be determined by means of biblical citations which mention sites on and within its borders, as well as through extra-biblical inscriptions (i.e., the

Monumental inscription in basalt rock found at Tel Dan commemorating the conflict between Aram and Israel, second half of 9ᵗʰ cent. BCE

Mesha stele, the Tel Dan inscription, and Assyrian royal inscriptions). The territory of the kingdom of Judah can be determined exactly thanks to the list of cities and districts in the Book of Joshua (15; 18:11-28) which apparently reflects the extent of the kingdom during the reign of Josiah (639–609 BCE).

There is no doubt that the kingdom of Israel was considerably larger than the kingdom of Judah, and included extensive mountain districts (Samaria, Galilee, and the Gilead), fertile valleys (the Jezreel and Bet-Shean valleys), certain areas in the northern Shephelah, the seacoast between Mount Carmel and the Yarkon River, and the plain south of the Gilead. Its northern border reached Dan and Ijon while the kingdom's southern boundary stretched from the northern Dead Sea to Bethel, Bet-Horon and along wadi Aijalon. The kingdom of Judah

31

Right: The kingdom of Judah during the reign of Josiah

Left: The kingdoms of Israel and Judah, 8th cent. BCE

encompassed the districts of Benjamin (except for the Jericho area which was included in the northern kingdom), the Judean highlands, the Shephelah, and the Negev (the Beer-Sheba Valley). Most of the settled districts in the tenth and ninth centuries were included in the kingdom of Israel, whereas the kingdom of Judah mainly included the thinly-populated marginal areas. The kingdom of Israel comprised a mosaic of districts and ethnic groups, each one of which had a history and cultural tradition of its own, showing that its population too was of varied origin. The territory of the kingdom of Judah, on the other hand, included mainly rural settlements and groups of nomads, which made it possible for the central authority to fashion fairly uniform modes of worship and culture. The kingdom of Israel shared a common border with a series of neighboring kingdoms (Philistia, Tyre, Aram, Moab and Ammon) and was susceptible to outside influences, whereas Judah bordered only on the kingdoms of Philistia and Edom (which became a kingdom only from the middle of the ninth century BCE). The kingdom of Israel was much the stronger and more influential of the two, and as long as both existed, the kingdom of Judah was overshadowed by its northern neighbor.

In the ninth and eighth centuries BCE, the pace of settlement and establishment of new settlements greatly increased. Likewise, the existing settlements expanded in area and their population gradually increased. The two kingdoms enjoyed many peaceful years with established monarchial institutions and well-organized governments. This led to prosperity and increasing strength, which reached a peak in the second half of the eighth century, on the eve of the Assyrian conquest. According to one estimate, about 350,000 persons then lived in the kingdom of Israel on both sides of the Jordan, while the population of the kingdom of Judah numbered about 125,000. The estimated population of the two kingdoms, then, totalled about 475,000 in contrast to about 150,000 who had lived in the country on the eve of the establishment of the monarchy – an average annual increase of 0.4%.

• • • • • • • • • •

The Fall of the Kingdoms of Israel and Judah

The Assyrian conquests with the destruction and mass deportations that followed in their wake were a watershed for both political conditions in the country and the size of its population. The kingdom of Israel was annexed to Assyria in two stages (in the years 733/732 and 720), its districts becoming a part of the network of Assyrian administrative districts. Assyrian governors ruled from the administrative centers of the newly-founded provinces (Samaria, Megiddo, Dor, and perhaps Gilead as well),

32

whose inhabitants were now citizens of Assyria and subject to all the duties and obligations imposed on the entire population of the empire. Many towns and villages throughout the kingdom were destroyed and abandoned, or suffered a sharp decline in the quality of their building infrastructure and the number of their inhabitants. Some were exiled to far-off countries and replaced by people brought from other lands. These newcomers were generally made to settle in the province of Samaria and along the border with Egypt. However, it should be stressed that most inhabitants of the northern kingdom remained in the country, and that the forced exile was selective and planned, in accordance with decisions taken by the new masters of the land.

Sennacherib's campaign against Judah in 701 BCE destroyed many of the kingdom's fortified towns and villages, especially in the Shephelah, the southern Judean hill country and the Beer-Sheba Valley. Since many of its inhabitants were exiled, the kingdom could not rebuild the ruined and abandoned areas for lack of manpower. As for the kingdom of Judah, in the seventh century it had declined both in the number of settlements and in economic power in relation to the previous century. However, unlike the kingdom of Israel which was annexed by Assyria, Judah continued to exist as an Assyrian vassal. After the Assyrian withdrawal from the arena, Judah attained independence for a short while, but was quickly subjugated again – first by Egypt and then by Babylon.

In the wake of the Babylonian campaign against Judah and the conquest of Jerusalem in 587/586, Judah became a Babylonian province. Jerusalem was totally destroyed and its population deported to Babylon, together with some other inhabitants of the kingdom. Mizpah was the administrative center of the new province which contained mainly the districts of Benjamin and northern Judah, most of whose inhabitants remained in the country following the Babylonian campaigns. The Negev and southern Judah gradually fell into the hands of nomads who lived in the vicinity and maintained close contact with the kingdom of Edom. Following the destruction wreaked upon the settled areas and the southern line of fortresses of the kingdom of Judah, groups of Edomites migrated into the southern districts of Judah. From the mid-sixth century, Judah's former territory was divided into two districts: that of Yehud in the north (including a limited area of the northern Shephelah) and that of Idumaea in the south.

There were three principal deportations in the wake of the Assyrian conquest of the Land of Israel. The first occurred during the reign of Tiglath-pileser III, when the Gilead, the Galilee, and the coastal plain were annexed to Assyria (II Kings 15:29). We do not know where the exiles were settled. The second took place in the time of Sargon II, after the Assyrian conquest and annexation of the Samarian hill country. According to the Assyrian source 22,290 persons were exiled at that time, while the biblical narrative (II Kings 17:6) informs us that they were settled "in Halah, at the [River] Habor, at the River Gozan, and in the towns of Media." This is popularly referred to as "the exile of the Ten Tribes." The third deportation, executed by Sennacherib after his campaign against Judah, resulted in the uprooting of tens of thousands of the kingdom's inhabitants (the number of exiles specified by Sennacherib in his inscription – 200,150 – is universally considered to be an exaggeration). As in the case of the first wave of exiles from Israel, we do not know where they were settled.

The names of some Israelite exiles have been discovered in Assyrian documents. Palṭiyahu, Neriyahu, and "Ḥalbishu of Samaria," for instance, are mentioned in a letter sent from Gozan. In other documents there is mention of "the Samarians," as well

Detail from relief in palace of Sennacherib, King of Assyria, in Nineveh, depicting the capture of Lachish (701 BCE)

as persons bearing Yahwistic names (Yōga'a, AḤiyō, Ḥilkiyahu, Geriyahu, and Hosea). But there is no evidence of the formation of Israelite or Judahite communities which preserved their distinct identity within the Assyrian empire. Since the Assyrians adopted a deliberate policy of commixing the exiles and "blending" them into "Assyrians," they did not allow members of ethnic minorities to organize in groupings based on ethnic-geographic origin. In this they differed from the Babylonians who enabled the exiles to preserve their national identity. The exiles from Israel (the "Ten Tribes") thus were put through the "melting pot" of the Assyrian empire, losing their former identity.

We have no direct evidence of the stages in the establishment of the Jewish communities in Egypt which, by the beginning of the sixth century BCE, were already settled "in Migdol, in Tahpanhes, and Noph, and in the land of Pathros" (Jeremiah, 44:1). In all probability, during every period there was a migration of individuals and families from Judah and Israel to Egypt, in search of a livelihood, and this movement was greatly accelerated during times of political crisis, particularly after the Assyrian and Babylonian conquests. One example is the migration of a group of people – including Jeremiah – that had gathered around Gedaliah, son of Ahikam, in Mizpah, and then fled to Egypt after the murder of Gedaliah and the Babylonian garrison stationed at Mizpah, lest they should be accused of the deed (II Kings 25:23-26; Jeremiah 40-43).

. . . .

The Development of the Biblical Account of Israel and its Land

When did the historical polarization between Israel and Judah disappear and the inhabitants of both kingdoms, including those who resided in Judah, begin to be called "Israelites"? This seems to be connected with the annexation of the kingdom of Israel to Assyria, when the historical "Israel" ceased to exist.

One cannot know just how vivid was the historical memory of a past common to the two kingdoms at that time nor to what degree did it influence the sense of unity. Both kingdoms worshipped the same national god, and perhaps even held forms of worship in common, a state of events that certainly would have created a not inconsiderable sense of unity. Furthermore, we know that after the Assyrian conquest, people from Israel migrated to Judah, especially to Jerusalem, bringing with them northern traditions and ideological conceptions (and perhaps scrolls as well) to the southern kingdom. In this way, the admonitions of the northern prophets – in particular that of

Hosea – penetrated the southern kingdom, leading to the formation of what scholars term the Deuteronomistic movement and influencing the composition of the Book of Deuteronomy, the commandments of which were a guiding light for this ideological movement. Thus, the concept of Judah as the legitimate heir of historical Israel began to develop.

A decisive role in forming the concept of one people was played, I believe, by this book, recording the history of Israel from its beginnings until the author's own times. The work created an image of a single people with a long history of unified existence and cooperation between all its parts, a people which though temporarily divided, had preserved its traits and unity in later times. Against this background emerged (once again?) the ideal of a united kingdom which had existed at the dawn of the history of the kingdoms of Israel and Judah, before "Ephraim turned away from Judah" (Isaiah 7:17). For this reason, the period of the United Monarchy assumed greater importance in Israelite history, with its glorification of the ancient kings who had ruled over the whole of Israel at the beginning of the monarchic period. The historical account of Israel in the era of their nomadic wanderings and subsequently, was disseminated by these cultural agents of culture who were devoted to the new ideology – scribes, priests, and prophets. In the course of time, this account came to be accepted as the official history of the People of Israel, becoming firmly fixed in the minds of all parts of the nation. This composition was, I believe, an extremely significant act. It marked the genesis of a unified historical consciousness among the members of the Israelite community and was a central factor in shaping the conception of the primordial unity of the People of Israel. We do not know whether this concept of Israel as a people with a common past and a definite identity going back to its early days was widely accepted in Judah even before the exile, or whether it grew and developed mainly during the period of exile, serving as

Stele of Sennacherib recording his campaigns, including that against the kingdom of Judah

an important lever for the ideology of the Return to the Land. The historical evidence on this point is not clear, and we lack any data by which we may determine the spread of beliefs and opinions among broad circles of the inhabitants of Israel and Judah in the First Temple period.

There is controversy as to whether the first comprehensive written work on the history of Israel (the Deuteronomic history) was composed at the end of the First Temple period and completed after the destruction of the Temple, or whether it was first set down after the destruction. However, there is no doubt that it was composed no earlier than the late seventh century BCE. It seems likely that the author(s) of the history had access to earlier works which related various stages of the history of Israel. Yet, these compositions, too, were written at a rather late date, either in the eighth century or during the seventh century. This relative late date of the sources accounts for the unbridgeable gap between the academic view of the history of Israel and the account of Israel's history in biblical historiography.

While the depiction of the course of Israel's history as presented by biblical historiography is clear and well formed, that which emerges from the prophetic writings is much less uniform and coherent. The concept of "the one nation that came from outside the borders of the Land" appears among the early Israelite prophets (Amos and Hosea), but is lacking in the works of prophets from Judah who were active at the end of the eighth century BCE (Isaiah and Micah). In their prophecies, the distinctions between Israel and Judah are still prominent. These distinctions begin to wane with those prophets active at the end of the First Temple period, especially during the period of Babylonian exile and afterwards. In the Book of Jeremiah, particularly its first chapters, there is still a clear distinction between Israel and Judah, expressed in the hope that Ephraim/Israel would return from exile and be united with Zion/Judah (Jeremiah 30-31). An opposite conception is expressed in the prophecies of Ezekiel in which Israel is one people associated with one land. Even when referring to the two kingdoms, he stresses their close mutual relationship. Likewise, in his description of the Promised Land, Ezekiel envisions the settlement of the Twelve Tribes in all parts of the Land of Canaan, from Lebo-Hamath to Kadesh-Barnea.

In the accounts of a unified Israelite nation, inhabiting the Land of Israel before the foundation of the monarchy and in the period of the United Monarchy, the formulaic description of the borders is often: "from Dan to Beer-Sheba" (Judges 20:1; I Samuel 3:20; II Samuel 3:10; 17:11; 24:2 and 15; I Kings 4:25 [MT 5:5]; the reversed formula, "from Beer-Sheba to Dan" only

appears in late historiography). This formulaic description combines the most nothern site of the kingdom of Israel with the southernmost one of the kingdom of Judah, with the purpose of defining the boundaries of settlement of Israel before the schism in the kingdom.

• • • • • • • • • •

The Concept of Tribal Boundaries

To complement the concept of a unified nation under a single leadership which had conquered the entire Land of Israel, there emerged another, geographical, concept of the borders within which the people of Israel lived. No biblical text exists which provides a continuous description of the external boundary of the tribal territories, such as that which delimits the borders of the Land of Canaan. The boundaries of all tribal territories taken together can be determined only by reference to the external borders of the individual tribal allotments as described in Joshua 13-19, as well as by references to these all-inclusive boundaries elsewhere in the Bible.

One of these complementing descriptions is "the land that remains" which includes references to borders by the means of which the biblical author defined the territorial discrepancy between the area covered by the tribal territories and the boundaries of the Land of Canaan (Joshua 13:2-6). For example, "From the Shihor, which is close to Egypt, to the territory of Ekron on the north," "From Baal-Gad at the foot of Mount Hermon to Lebo-Hamath," "From the Lebanon to Misrephot-Maim." Such formulaic phrases relating to the borders of the tribal territories appear in the story of the conquest (Joshua 10:41; 11:8, 17; 12:7). The borders of the area conquered in trans-Jordan also appear in a brief formulaic phrasing (Deuteronomy 3:8; Joshua 12:1) or in a broader combination (Deuteronomy 4:48).

The borders on the east and north, too, within which David's census was conducted (II Samuel 24:5-7), are congruous with the boundaries of the allotments of the Israelite tribes. The border points mentioned in this description are Aroer, Jazer, the land at the foot of the Hermon (this is the proper interpretation instead of "the region of Tahtim-Hodshi"), Dan, Ijon, ("Jaan" with a transposition of letters), and the fortress of Tyre.

By combining all the data at our disposal, the following description of the border emerges: in the south it reached the Brook of Egypt (Nahal Besor) and Kadesh-Barnea, and on the east it touched – along the Arabah Valley – the border of the kingdom of Edom. From there it continued to the Arnon River which was the border with Moab; it passed along the borders of Ammon and

35

Aram, and reached the foothills of Mount Hermon. From Dan the border crossed over to the Mizpah Valley (the valley of Marj ʿAyyun), from where it continued along the Litani River, north of which lay the kingdom of Sidon. Before reaching the sea the border turned south and passed along the eastern border of the kingdom of Tyre until it turned westward to the sea somewhere near Rosh ha-Niqra. From there it followed the seacoast down to the border of Philistia. As for the coast of Philistia, there is a duality in the descriptions: in one it is included in the tribal allotment of Judah and in another it is within the bounds of "the land that remains."

Decorated Philistine pottery, found at Ekron, 11th–10th cent. BCE

Thin silver plaque from 7th cent. BCE found at Kettef Hinnom, Jerusalem, bearing the "Priestly Benediction." This is the earliest extant example of a written biblical text

The tribal territorial allotments do not reflect any historical situation in the history of Israel. They contained areas that were never included in the kingdoms of Israel and Judah. For example, the area north of the Arnon River was part of the kingdom of Moab from the very beginning. After all, the dynasty of Mesha, king of Moab, originated in the city of Dibon north of the Arnon. It is also very doubtful whether the districts of the Bashan, inhabited by Arameans and forming part of the territory of Aram-Damascus, ever belonged to the domain of Israel. Further, it is dubious whether the plain of Acre, which was Canaanite from the outset and was included in the territory of the kingdom of Tyre, ever belonged to Israel. Needless to say, the coast of Philistia was never part of the domain of Israel. The external borders of the tribal territories emerged as a kind of retrospective reconstruction of the conquests of David who, according to the Bible, defeated all of Israel's neighbors and annexed all the adjacent territories. In biblical historiography, this reconstruction was integrated into the story of the conquest and served as a basis for the description of the scope of Joshua's conquests and for the subsequent allotment of tribal territories.

This description of the allotments of the Twelve Tribes that divided all the conquered territory among themselves – each tribal allotment touching upon the next without any empty space between them – is also basically a literary-ideological one. The very existence of the tribes and their role in the history of the Israelite nation is a matter of controversy among scholars. It is clear that tribes per se did not exist in much of the country in the pre-monarchic period, and that these areas were inhabited by various and sundry groups of people who united in one framework for the first time when the monarchy was established. The entire system, with its external and internal borders, is a literary and ideological one, and was intended to present a harmonious scene of the tribes of Israel living throughout the kingdom that was to be later conquered by David. It was the tribes' presence throughout the Land that provided the People of Israel with the legitimate right of possession of it during the days of the later author, and forever thereafter.

The sources upon which the late author (who belonged to the priestly school, which was active in the periods of Exile and the Return to Zion) relied call for a detailed discussion which is outside the scope of this chapter.

Finally, we should not overlook the maximal borders mentioned in the Bible, that may be called "the borders of the Patriarchs." These borders are specified in the promise to Abraham (Genesis 15:18): "To your offspring I assign this land, from the river of Egypt to the great river, the river Euphrates." And in the story of Moses in the wilderness (Deuteronomy 11:24): "Every spot on which your foot treads shall be yours; your territory shall extend from the wilderness to the Lebanon and from the River – the Euphrates – to the Western Sea." This promise is repeated in God's words to Joshua (Joshua 1:3-4) and in other biblical passages (Exodus 23:31; Deuteronomy 1:7). It also appears in an abbreviated formula both in prophecy (Micah 7:12; Zechariah 9:10) and in Psalms (72:8; 80:12; 89:25 [MT 89:26]).

The southern border of the territory encompassed by these boundaries is on the Nile ("the River of Egypt") while its northern border is on the Euphrates. On the east it is demarcated by the Syrian desert ("the desert" or "the wilderness") and on the west by the Mediterranean Sea ("the Western Sea," "the Great Sea where the sun goes down"). The phrase "borders of the Patriarchs" encompasses a region much broader than that enclosed within other descriptons of borders in the Bible, and it is delineated only through its outermost border points, in contrast to the two other arrays of borders (of the Land of Canaan and of the Israelite tribal allotments) which can be reconstructed by means of a series of points along them.

Obviously, the Kingdom of Israel never extended to those maximal borders. In the early first millenium BCE this broad region was divided among many kingdoms, and was first united under the rule of the Assyrian Empire at the beginning of the seventh century BCE. At the end of the eighth century a new territorial term had emerged to mark this region: *ebir-nari* or *ᶜEver ha-Nahar* (= Beyond the River; that is, beyond the Euphrates from the vantage point of someone to the east of it). Over the course of time ᶜEver ha-Nahar became the accepted term for the combined territory of Syria and the Land of Israel. In the Persian Empire the Aramaic form of this name, *ᶜAbar Nahara*, became the official name for the Fifth Satrapy which included the entire territory of this region (see Ezra 4-7). The "border of the Patriarchs" overlaps the territory of the ᶜEver ha-Nahar satrapy, and it embodies the divine promise that at the End of Days the borders of Israel will be enhanced to match the extent of that territory, from the Nile to the Euphrates, and thus to transform Israel into a power that rules over an extensive region.

The domain of ᶜEver ha-Nahar is also reflected in accounts of Solomon's times, according to which "Solomon's rule extended over all the kingdoms from the Euphrates to the land of the Philistines and the boundary of Egypt" (I Kings 4:21 [MT5:1]); and furthermore, "For he controlled the whole region west of the Euphrates – all the kings west of the Euphrates, from Tiphsah to Gaza" (I Kings 4:24 [MT 5:4]). Verses 1-4 in this chapter were written by a later editor who intended to glorify the reign of Solomon and present him as a ruler over all the territory "beyond the river," like the rulers of the great powers of his time. This late tendency to glorify Solomon was also expressed in a few passages in Psalms (72:8; 89:25 [MT 89:26]). Needless to say, experts have judged these writings to have no historical basis, their whole purpose being to present the times of Solomon as the golden age of the history of Israel.

Biblical history combines real and legendary, literary and theological, early and late elements. Sifting history from story, and reality from legend, is extremely complicated and necessitates a critical approach and a combinaton of various disciplines. A critical approach recognizing the late date in which biblical history was written is the only way in which we can analyze the sources at hand and try, with all due caution, to reconstruct the history of early Israel, its land, and culture.

Stele of Mesha, King of Moab, discovered in 1868 at Dibon in trans-Jordan, commemorating the freeing of Moab from the yoke of Israel (Louvre AO 5066)

"Restore our fortunes, O Lord,
like watercourses in the Negev"
(Psalms 126:4)

. . . .

From the Return to Zion
Until the Hasmonean Revolt

Daniel R. Schwartz

With the final downfall of the kingdom of Judah an historical period began similar to one that the People of Israel had previously experienced. In the eighth century BCE the kingdom of Israel had been conquered and ruined, its inhabitants exiled. That event brought irreversible changes. The destruction and exile by the Assyrians did not give rise to a Jewish community in a foreign land. Rather, they led the exiled northern tribes to lose their identity as Israelites and become foreigners. In this chapter, we shall survey the divergent results of the destruction of the kingdom of Judah and of the Babylonian Exile. This was a period of transition between the monarchy of the House of David and that of the Hasmoneans. It initiated (if we disregard the traditions about the Patriarchal era) the People of Israel's successful contention with Exile in the two arenas of the nation's existence: within and without the Land of Israel. For Exile is not only, or even primarily, a geographic condition. Rather it is a political situation in which Jews are ruled by non-Jews. Thus, our period begins the age of Jewish existence in exile.

However, the Second Temple Period is unique in that it was marked not only by foreign domination but also by an institution which intrinsically bespoke Jewish sovereignty – the Temple. The Temple was more than a special, large synagogue, a place where Jews congregated to worship their God; rather it was the **House** of the Lord, in which He resided. Now, since in the Bible the Lord is the King of Israel, the kings of the House of David (in their time) being considered merely His covenantal agents, the Temple was actually a kind of royal palace. And this concept became even more relevant in the period with

Depiction of the Temple in a 14th cent. manuscript (SNM, Sarajevo Haggadah, fol. 32)

which we are dealing, when the Jews did not have other kings or palaces. But a palace indicates the existence of a capital city and a state, thus engendering the paramount contradiction that distinguished the Second Temple Period: in apparent contradiction to foreign domination stood an institution that seemingly pointed to the existence of a sovereign Jewish state. Indeed, we may sum up the history of the Second Temple Period as a series of attempts by the Jews and their foreign rulers to simultaneously maintain the two elements of this contradictory equation. These attempts ultimately failed and, therefore, one of those elements had to be destroyed.

Logically, there are only two ways to undo a contradiction: either one removes one of the opposing forces (either by the elimination of foreign rule in the Hasmonean period or by the destruction of the Temple at the end of the Second Temple epoch), or one limits the demands of the parties so that they do not compete for the same spheres. For example, the Jews in the Diaspora succeeded in living under the conditions of exile: by defining two spheres – "state" and "religion" – and limiting the claims of the ruler to the first domain and those of God to the second domain, they could avoid, or hope to avoid, clashing one with another. In the Second Temple Period, since Jewish synagogues in the Diaspora were considered by their congregants to be no more than religious and communal meeting places without any political connotation, their existence did not clash with the state's demands, and they were usually respected and protected by the authorities. Correspondingly, the foreign rulers expected and required that their Jewish subjects see the Temple, too, as merely a place of worship, rather than as a royal palace, and as such they generally protected and respected it. It was the way the Jews responded to this expectation and demand that dictated the course of their history during this period, until the destruction of the Second Temple.

However, the issue of how the Temple was construed was a part of a wider one, that of "Who is a Jew?" For the Temple was not only the central institution of a territory deemed to be a Jewish state; it was also central to the concept that identified the Jews as belonging to that state. If, during the monarchy – now destroyed – the kings of Judah were looked upon as agents of the God resident in the sanctuary, then "the Children of Israel" or "the Jews" were considered first and foremost to be inhabitants of His state. The term "the Children of Israel" was then mainly applied to the inhabitants of the Kingdom of Israel, while "Jews"

(or "Judeans") were the inhabitants of the Kingdom of Judah. For example, the Torah reiterates (Exodus 12:49; Numbers 15:15-16, etc.) that one body of law, one Torah, was binding on both "the citizen" and "the stranger who **dwells** among you"; the place of residence was decisive. In this vein, David complains that those pursuing him and forcing him to leave the country are driving him away from "the Lord's estate" and thereby telling him: "Go and worship other gods" (I Samuel 26:19). It seems that the ten northern tribes saw things the same way: since identity was closely linked to territory, they had to join other peoples in the lands of their exile, and this they did indeed (perhaps after several generations of nostalgia).

It might have been expected that something similar would happen after the destruction of Judah too. For instance, the poets of the Temple remembered those bleak days:

By the rivers of Babylon

there we sat,

sat and wept,

as we thought of Zion...

for our captors asked us there for songs,

our tormentors, for amusement,

"Sing us one of the songs of Zion."

How can we sing a song of the Lord

on alien soil? (Psalms 137:1-4)

This response of the poets, with its elements of astonishment, was quite natural for those who equated "a song of Zion" with "a song of the Lord." If the Lord dwells in Zion, there is no reason to sing His songs outside of Zion, just as there is no reason to wave one country's flag within the borders of another.

But if a man defines himself, and is defined by others by his residence in a certain country, then his prolonged sojourn in another country will make him a different man. Therefore, contending with a state of exile involved not only facing up to the significance of the Temple, but also to the issue of Jewish identity. Now, there were two alternatives to the territorial-political definition: if not defined as a "Judean" (because the country did not belong to him or because he did not reside in it), a man was likely to be a Jew on the basis of his **people** or according to his **culture** (or his religion – that is, according to a system of values, norms, and so forth). The two natural sub-divisions of the epoch we are discussing are, from a political vantage point, the age of Persian rule from Cyrus to Alexander the

Map of Yehud

40

Cyrus orders the rebuilding of the Temple. From a manuscript of Josephus Flavius' *Jewish Antiquities*, **France, early 15ᵗʰ cent. (BN, MS. 6446, fol. 152)**

Great, and then the subsequent Hellenistic period (Alexander annexed Judea to his empire in the year 332/1 BCE). The two sub-periods are distinguished one from the other in that each tended to the adoption of a different alternative. In the Persian age, the Jews were ruled by a great multi-national empire: "each province in its own script, and each people in its own language" (Esther 3:12, etc.). In such a context it was only natural that the Jews, too, would view themselves as members of a people. In contrast, the Hellenistic period was not so much multi-national as it was – at least ideally – supra-national, a world united by Greek language and culture. In a setting of this nature, it was natural that the Jews too began to view themselves as being supra-national, as being defined by their culture which, due to its link to faith in the Lord, we would today term a "religion."

. . . .

The Persian Period: Between "The Holy Seed" and "The Congregation of the Returning Exiles"

A short while after Cyrus gained control over Babylon, in 539 BCE, he allowed the Jews to restore their ruined Temple. A reading of his proclamation, which has come down to us in two principal versions, immediately brings to light the problematic issues above.

The Hebrew version (Ezra 1:2-4):

Thus said King Cyrus of Persia:
The Lord God of Heaven has given me all the kingdoms of the earth and has charged me with building Him a house in Jerusalem, which is in Judah. Anyone of you of all His people — may his God be with him, and let him go up to Jerusalem that is in Judah and build the House of the Lord God of Israel, the God that is in Jerusalem; and all who stay behind, wherever he may be living, let the people of his place assist him with silver, gold, goods, and livestock, besides the freewill offering to the House of God that is in Jerusalem.

The Aramaic version (Ezra 6:3-5):

In the first year of King Cyrus, King Cyrus issued an order concerning the House of God in Jerusalem: "Let the house be rebuilt, a place for offering sacrifices, with a base built up high. Let it be sixty cubits high and sixty cubits wide, with a course of unused timber for each three courses of hewn stone. The expenses shall be paid by the palace. And the gold and silver vessels of the House of God which Nebuchadnezzar had taken away from the temple in Jerusalem and transported to Babylon shall be returned, and let each go back to the temple in Jerusalem where it belongs; you shall deposit it in the House of God."

Illustration by E.M. Lilien (1874–1925) of the verses "By the rivers of Babylon, there we sat, sat and wept, as we thought of Zion. There on the poplars we hung up our lyres..." (Psalms 137:1–2) (IMJ 2469–9–74 OS)

On one hand, the Aramaic version is clearly more authentic, not only on account of its being written in the official language of the empire but also because it avoids mentioning the Jewish god. It is also an indication of the attitude of the empire to the Jewish temple: the new king was making a gesture towards the Jews in that he was making it possible to right the wrong that had been perpetrated by one of his predecessors. Nebuchadnezzar had destroyed the Temple and sacked its vessels, whereas Cyrus ordered the restoration of the Temple and the return of its vessels. This wise and conciliatory policy on the part of the new king is also evident in Cyrus' clay cylinder inscription (illustration on the next page).

On the other hand, it is clear that the Hebrew version is a Jewish document: Cyrus says that he is doing what he is doing because the God of the Jews **commanded** him to do so. Only a

Jew could have written in such a vein. But now comes the element most relevant to our discussion: the Hebrew document reveals a certain indecisiveness as to the location of the Lord. True, the passage deals with building the Temple in Jerusalem, but alongside God's identification as "the God that is in Jerusalem," He appears here as the "God of Heaven" as well. If He is in Heaven, how can one say He is in Jerusalem and speak of His house that is in Jerusalem? As it is put by one of the prophets of the Exile, perhaps not long after Cyrus' time and not far from where were those who could not decide whether to accept his offer that they return to Judah:

Thus said the Lord:
The heaven is My throne
And the earth is My footstool:
Where could you build a house for Me,

What place could serve as My abode?
All this was made by My hand,
And thus it all came into being
— declares the Lord (Isaiah 66:1-2).

Thus, already Cyrus' proclamation – the founding document of Judea in Second Temple times – reveals a certain tension between two conceptions: that of the citizens of a land whose sovereign was among them, as He had been in the past; and that of members of a people whose sovereign was in the heavens which extend over the entire earth.

the sons of Ater: Hezekiah — 98;
the sons of Bezai — 323;
the sons of Jorah — 112 (Ezra 2:13-18)

In other words, during their first generations of exile in Babylonia, many Jews were accustomed to identifying themselves as such according to a territorial definition: they were Jews because they had come from Judea. Moreover, as the basis of this territorial identity they preserved their affinity to their places of origin in Judea. There is also evidence that other peoples in that period did likewise despite their exile, just as in our own days, in countries

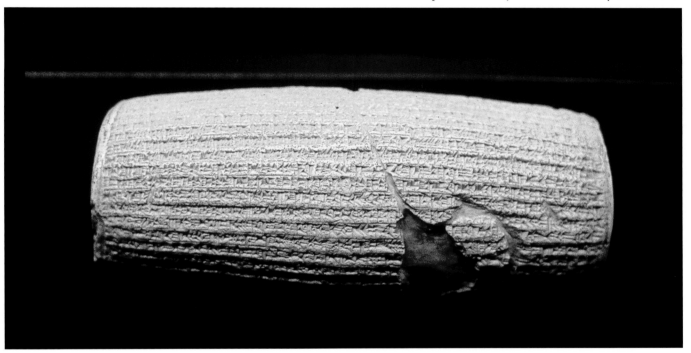

Inscription on a clay cylinder in which Cyrus presents himself as the emissary of Marduk, god of Babylon. The inscription includes an authorization by Cyrus to various peoples to restore their temples

This duality also comes to light in the second chapter of the Book of Ezra, which lists those who returned to Judea in the time of Cyrus. This long list identifies the Jews included in it in two manners. On one hand there are notations according to place of origin in the Land of Israel, such as:

the sons of Kiriath-Arim: Chephirah and Beeroth — 743;
the sons of Ramah and Geba — 621;
the men of Michmas — 122;
the men of Bethel and Ai — 223;
the men of Nebo — 52 (Ezra 2:25-29)

On the other hand there are notations according to family, such as:

the sons of Adonikam — 666:
the sons of Bigvai — 2,056;
the sons of Adin — 454;

receiving many immigrants, there is a widespread phenomenon of immigrants forming, in their new homes, associations based on their city or country of origin (*Landsmannschaften*). It seems, however, that over time this form of self-identification dissipated and lost its significance. Obviously, as time passed it became more difficult to define a person who lived in Babylon as "a man of Geba" or "a man of Michmas." Furthermore, such identification fulfilled no function. It was important to know that a certain family was Jewish, but the family's exact territorial origin was of no importance. Hence, over time, families simply became known as Jewish families. As we have seen, a few such families already appear in the list in Ezra Chapter 2; in the one in Chapter 8, which lists those who returned to Judea with Ezra in the mid-fifth century BCE, **all** are identified only by the family to which they belong:

43

Ezra the Scribe (or Moses). A fresco in the synagogue at Dura-Europos, mid-3ʳᵈ cent. CE

Of the sons of Phinehas, Gershom; of the sons of Ithamar, Daniel; of the sons of David, Hattush. Of the sons of Shecaniah: of the sons of Parosh, Zechariah; through him the genealogy of 150 males was registered. Eliehoenai son of Zerahiah, of the sons of Pahath-moab, and with him 200 males. Of the sons of Shecaniah son of Jahaziel; and with him 300 males... (Ezra 8:2-5).

Thus, we see that self-identification as members of a people – that is, as a group defined by common lineage – increasingly replaced, among the Jews in Babylon, self-identification based upon a particular place of origin. This conception reached its peak in the episode of the forced divorce of foreign wives during the time of Ezra. The story is important not only because of its content, but also because of the very way it is formulated:

When this was over, the officers approached me, saying: "The people of Israel and the priests and Levites have not separated themselves from the peoples of the land and their abhorrent practices – the Canaanites, the Hittites, the Perizzites, the Jebusites, the Ammonites, the Moabites, the Egyptians, and the Amorites. They have taken their daughters as wives for themselves and for their sons, so that the holy seed has become intermingled with the peoples of the land" (Ezra 9:1-2).

This formulation says everything. Today we refer to mixed marriages between Jews and non-Jews; a Jew living in the Persian period, the period of "every people in its own language," individually refers to each and every one of seven distinct peoples. What was common to them all is that they were "peoples of the land," that is, other peoples inhabiting the Land of Israel. Perhaps those who had intermarried with them believed that the fact of their being inhabitants of the Land of Israel in and of itself made them part of the community, as in the phrase "the stranger who dwells among you." Then Ezra came along, a man accustomed to the usages of the Diaspora, and taught that not only in the Diaspora, but in the Land of Israel too, what defined a group was its lineage. But who comprises this group? Here too the formulation is interesting. Ezra speaks not of plain "Jews" but rather of "the people of Israel and the priests and the Levites" – three separate genealogical categories. Correspondingly, it was only to be expected that Ezra – himself descended, as Chapter 7 of his book takes pains to tell us, through fifteen generations from Phinehas son of Eleazar son of Aaron the priest – who already imparted great importance to lineage by the very formulation he used, could conceive of only one solution: to send away the foreign wives, together with their offspring. And that, precisely, is what they did, as the continuation of the story informs us, and no one proposed converting the women. After all, if descent is the criterion, conversion is ruled out. It is impossible to convert seed, just as a simple Israelite can never be a *kohen*, a priest, even if he learns all there is to know about service in the Temple.

What has just been said about Israelites and priests brings us to another aspect of the enhanced importance of lineage in this period. The status of the priesthood was at its highest at this time. Thus, for instance, says the Prophet Malachi:

A coin of Yehezkiah the *Pehah* (satrap), second half of the 4ᵗʰ cent. BCE

44

Know then that I have sent this charge to you that My covenant with Levi may endure – said the Lord of Hosts. I had with him a covenant of life and well-being, which I gave to him, and of reverence, which he showed Me. For he stood in awe of My name.

Proper rulings [lit.: true Torah] were in his mouth,

And nothing perverse on his lips;

He served Me with complete loyalty

And held the many back from iniquity.

For the lips of a priest guard knowledge,

And men seek rulings from his mouth;

For he is a messenger of the Lord of Hosts.   (Malachi 2:4-7)

The preeminence afforded to the priestly class had a clear institutional basis. We should bear in mind that Cyrus did not grant the Jews the right to build a state, but only a temple. The small Jewish community in the country, Yehud as the Persians called it, that was mainly limited to the area around Jerusalem (from Bethel in the north to Bet-Zur in the south, and from Jericho in the east to the edge of the Shephelah, the Lowlands, in the west), was to serve only as a basis for the Temple, as its periphery. And that is what it continued to be. Therefore, the priests, the administrators of the Temple, became the most important class in the society that emerged in Judea, and the High Priest was its most important single personality. During the time of the monarchy, he had stood in the king's shadow, but now there was no king. True, at the beginning of the period under discussion, leading the "returnees to Zion" were "two sons of olive oil" (Zechariah 4:14), i.e., two anointed dignitaries, Jeshua son of Jozadak, the

The name "Yerushalem" (Jerusalem) stamped on a jar found in the City of David, 4ᵗʰ cent. BCE

High Priest, and Zerubbabel son of Shealtiel, a scion of the royal dynasty. However, despite the great hopes that the visionary seers placed on Zerubbabel (Haggai 2:2-23) – or, perhaps, because of them – he vanished from the scene; the House of David now became only the object of expectations for the End of Days, leaving center stage to the High Priests alone. When Nehemiah arrived in Judea as Persian satrap in the middle of the fifth century BCE, his opposite number and partner as head of the community was Eliashib the High Priest (Nehemiah 3:1 ff.; 13:4 ff., 28). From the Elephantine papyri we learn that Jewish soldiers in the Persian army in Egypt sent letters to Johanan, the High Priest

(grandson of Eliashib – Nehemiah 12:10-11, 22) in Jerusalem. High Priests minted coins in the fourth century BCE, and conducted – at least according to legend – the negotiations between the Jews and Alexander the Great.

Thus, if until this stage the condition of exile was the only cause mentioned for giving priority to lineage in this period, and hence genealogical identification was only a kind of easy "default option" after it had become impossible to continue to maintain the territorial definition, we now add in the importance of the priesthood, which constituted another, positive factor contributing to the same result. A society which holds the priesthood in esteem also values lineage, because a priest can only be one if he is descended from a line of priests. Note well that according to the biblical assumptions, that continued to prevail during the Second Temple Period, there are several concentric circles in Israel. Out of the twelve tribes of Israel, the children of

the Patriarch Jacob, one tribe was chosen to be the Lord's servants. This was the tribe of Levi, whose sons were called "Levites." They served in various capacities in the Temple. Out of the tribe of Levi, one son, Aaron the brother of Moses, was selected. He and his sons were chosen to be *kohanim*, priests, and to perform the main tasks in the Temple. From among the priests, the sons of Aaron, one descendant was selected, Zadok, who lived in the time of King Solomon, and his sons became High Priests; between the Bible and the writings of Josephus we are able to assemble a list of Zadokite High Priests from the time of Solomon until the Hasmonean revolt. In the Second Temple Period, in

45

A golden menorah between two olive trees which are emptying their oil into it through golden tubes (according to Zechariah's vision). Cervera Bible, Spain 1300 (BNL, MS. 72, fol. 316v)

the absence of a monarch, they became in fact the leaders of the Jewish community. It would seem that vision and reality were joined together by the author who, as the period under discussion drew to a close, wrote:

Give thanks to Him Who exalts the House of David
Because His benevolence is forever
Give thanks to Him Who chooses the sons of Zadok to be Priest
Because His benevolence is forever   (Ben Sira 51:28-29)

This is the time to add a significant demographic fact: according to a reasonable evaluation (by archaeologist Magen Broshi), based on the size of Jerusalem, it seems that its population during the Persian period was less than five thousand souls. A very high percentage – about one-sixth, or 4,000 persons – of those returning to Zion listed in the second chapter of the Book of Ezra were priests. It is reasonable to assume that many of them settled in Jerusalem, near the Temple. Hence, the priests must have made up a very considerable part, perhaps a majority, of Jerusalem's population at that time.

Now, a Jew who lives in a colony which surrounds a temple – a colony in which the most important functionaries, who reside in the capital alongside the temple, are chosen and distinguished one from

another according to their lineage – surely such a Jew will conclude and believe that lineage is extremely significant. And if that be the case, it is also a sufficiently significant criterion by which to distinguish between himself and a gentile. Thus, a simple, uniform world view was created, one that added another concentric circle: the circle of Israel which is located between the Levites on one hand, and the gentile nations on the other. In this way, the central status of the priests during this period helped to instill in the People of Israel its generic self-identification as sons of the "Jewish seed" in the words of Zeresh and Haman's advisors in the Book of Esther (6:13), as sons of "the holy seed" in those of Ezra (9:2).

To conclude, defining the Jews as members of a certain stock, as a people – if indeed the roots of this definition went back as far as the Patriarchal Age – became ever more significant and central during the period of the Return to Zion, because now it could also define the Jewish collectivity in a state of exile, when sovereignty in the Land of Israel had been lost and the majority of that collectivity resided outside its borders. This conception became quite firmly linked in Judea with the old territorial conception, and together they created an establishment based on the connection between the members of the most exalted lineage, the *kohanim* (priests), and the elect place where they ruled, the Temple.

All this applies only to Judea; obviously, in the Diaspora, self-

In the fifth and fourth centuries BCE, Athenian coinage dominated international trade. This coin imitates an Athenian coin in every way, but instead of "Athens," the Hebrew inscription "Yehud" appears in the old Hebrew script. The original Athenian coin is on the right

identification on the basis of descent functioned **instead** of the territorial conception, rather than together with it. We have already seen the dilemma in the Jewish version of Cyrus' proclamation – is the Lord "the God of Heaven" or "the God Who is in Jerusalem"? – and we have noted the way the exilic prophet decided this issue: "The heaven is My throne, And the earth is My footstool: Where could you build a house for Me…?" The very appellation "God of Heaven" which often appears in the Persian period in both Hebrew and Aramaic, in the Bible and in the Elephantine papyri, while almost completely lacking in earlier times, now fills a need. A state of exile requires that the Lord be in Heaven, for if He were only in the Land of Israel then someone going abroad would actually lose his God and would have to worship other gods, as in the phrase attributed to King David (I Samuel 26:19).

But the heavens lie above the gentiles as well, and Jews who resided outside the Land of Israel also came into contact with gentiles in daily life and may have noticed that the difference in lineage between Jews and gentiles has no clearly evident expressions. Moreover, the concept of a direct line of descent does not allow room for conversion, a rather unpleasant situation for Jews who live in the Diaspora among a gentile population. For whoever says of himself that it is good to be a Jew, that this entitles him to a special covenant with God and the unique providence of the Creator, as is written in the Torah and promised by the prophets, finds it difficult – both for himself and in relation to his non-Jewish neighbors – to shut the doors of his community before them. This would involve a measure of arrogance, or at least his neighbors might see it that way. Jews living abroad, as a minority, have generally felt constrained to avoid arrogance.

True, such problems were not overly critical during the Persian period, since it was the norm in those days that each and every person belonged to a certain people defined by ethnic origin. Nevertheless, the Jews were exceptional in that they also identified their national god as being the Creator of the world and "the God of Heaven." Therefore, it is no wonder that already in this

The bringing of the first fruits to the Temple in an etching by Auguste Calmet (1725), based on the Mishnah, Tractate *Bikkurim* (3:3): "… and the ox walks before them and its horns are gilded with gold and an olive wreath crowns its head. The flute plays before them… The governors, the deputies, and the treasury officials come out towards them…" (Courtesy of M. Pollak Gallery, Tel Aviv)

47

period another approach began to develop instead of the genealogical approach, one likely in the final analysis to open the doors of Israel to gentiles as well. We refer to the religious approach, whose beginnings can already be discerned in the Persian period.

We have already noted how shocked Ezra was when he learned about the mixed marriages, and in that context we stressed the genealogical orientation of the problem and its solution. However, this narrative sounds another note as well:

Then a proclamation was issued in Judah and Jerusalem that all who had returned from the exile should assemble in Jerusalem, and that anyone who did not come in three days would, by decision of the officers and elders, have his property confiscated and himself excluded from the congregation of the returning exiles. (Ezra 10:7-8)

In other words, we have before us a group of people, each one of whom is required to make a choice: whether he considers himself as part of the group or as an outsider. Accordingly, the appellation used to denote this group is not "the holy seed," but

rather "the sons of the exile," or "the congregation of the returning exiles." These are people who returned from abroad, but continued to identify themselves as "sons of the exile," in contrast to "the peoples of the land." Furthermore, they defined themselves as a voluntary community in the sense that anyone may leave it if such is his desire. Likewise, anyone who so desires may join the community. Further on in the narrative, people affix their names to a document in which they commit themselves to divorce their wives, just as a few years later Jews would sign a covenant requiring them to observe various commandments, of which it was written: "We have laid upon ourselves obligations..." (Nehemiah 10:33). This is just like any association that constitutes itself, draws up a constitution, and accepts or rejects members on that basis.

All these developments greatly impinged upon the genealogical concept. After all, according to a concept based solely on descent, one cannot change his identity and withdraw from his group, just as a man cannot stop being a man even if he stops acting like a man. On the other hand, with Ezra and Nehemiah things are different: we read about membership – which can be cancelled – in a group, "the congregation of the returning exiles," and about a commitment that the members of the group take upon themselves. Yet, we should not exaggerate the importance of this matter in the period under discussion. We have no knowledge of conversion in the Persian period (though some do believe that the Book of Ruth, which reflects a positive attitude towards conversion, and the Book of Judith, which tells about a convert [14:10], were composed in this period, whereas others advance the former in time and relegate the latter to a later period). It seems that as a rule the voluntaristic religious approach, whose beginnings we have witnessed, functioned only within the bounds of the main concept – identity by lineage. This was to change in the next historical period.

· · · · · · · · · ·

The Hellenistic Period:
The Rise of the Cultural Definition of Identity

At the beginning of the Hellenistic age, with the fall of the Persian Empire to Alexander the Great, and when almost all Jews came under the influence of Hellenistic states and culture, both the genealogical and territorial conceptions were weakened. A situation was now created that encouraged defining a person by his commitments and his deeds. In the Hellenistic age, the world known to the Greeks (*oecumene*) which extended from Macedonia to India and to Egypt had been conquered by tens

Rhyton (vessel for drinking wine), from Sepphoris, 4th cent. BCE

48

of thousands of men from Macedonia and Greece. They had settled in the Orient, married Eastern women, and produced offspring who continued to live in these countries. But their children were called "Greeks" – and were indeed Greeks – despite their mixed lineage and place of residence. They were Greeks because their culture was Greek.

Of course, as pointed out by W. W. Tarn, the distinguished historian of the Hellenistic world, the Greeks did not conquer the world with a cultural mission in mind but, rather, in order to amass riches. Likewise, one should not view too positively the willingness of the Greeks to absorb "barbarians" into their ranks, and should bear in mind that more than a few Orientals rejected Greek openness and tried to preserve their own uniqueness. Nevertheless, despite all these reservations, the basic truth is that the Greek culture continued to define the Greeks even when they had departed from their places of origin and their ancestry. Moreover, this culture could be learned and adopted by non-Greeks, who thereby became Greeks. Institutions for instilling Greek culture (*gymnasia*) were established wherever Greeks settled. The most distinguished Greeks prided themselves on this openness and saw in it something desirable in itself, rather than as merely a state of affairs dictated by events. For example, as early as the fourth century BCE, Isocrates – philosopher, orator and one of the mentors of Philip II, Alexander's father – praised Athens in these words:

And so far behind did our city leave the rest of mankind, in everything having to do with thinking and speaking, that its [the city's] pupils have become teachers of others, and thereby brought it about that the name of the Greeks no longer implies a race (*genos*) but, rather, a type of thought (*dianoia*), and [therefore] those who share our culture (*paideusis*) are more appropriately called "Greeks" than are those who share our physical nature (*physis*). (Isocrates, *Panegyrikos* 50)

The willingness of the Greeks to accept barbarians as Greeks, as a result of their education, was an outcome of a deeply rooted Greek inclination to seek the nature of things, the invisible inner character. Just as the Platonic dialogues strove to see behind the visible example of a certain category in order to discover the invisible quality common to all related objects, so did the Greeks strive to discover the invisible qualities of man. What is important is not his place of origin or his lineage, but what is inside him, his spirit, and this can be influenced by education. Thus, for example, Josephus preserves a fragment in which one of Aristotle's disciples, Clearchos of Soli (in Cilicia), reports his master's remarks about his encounter with a Jewish sage:

"Well," said Aristotle, "in accordance with the precepts of rhetoric, let us begin by describing his race...." "Well," he replied, "the man was a Jew of

Alexander the Great

Coele-Syria. These people are descended from the Indian philosophers. The philosophers, they say, are in India called Calani, in Syria by the territorial name of Jews; for the district which they inhabit is known as Judea. Their city has a remarkably odd name: they call it Hierusaleme. Now this man, who was entertained by a large circle of friends and was on his way down from the interior to the coasts, not only spoke Greek, but had the soul of a Greek. During my stay in Asia, he visited the same places as I did, and came to converse with me and some other scholars, to test our learning. But as one who had been intimate with many cultivated persons, it was rather he who imparted to us something of his own." (Josephus, *Against Apion*, I:178–181, tr. Thackeray)

By distinguishing between racial origin (*genos*) – which is not of the essence and is referred to only because the rhetoricians are accustomed to doing so – and the "soul" (*psyche*), which is the essence of man and reflects "culture" which is a result of education (*paideia*), Aristotle well demonstrated the approach that stressed a man's inward nature as opposed to his outer, physical features.

49

Wall painting in the Sidonian cave at Maresha, whose inhabitants were Hellenist by culture

And like the words of Isocrates, who also distinguished between racial origin, which was of secondary importance, and culture, which was significant, this fragment presents the universal potential of such an approach. According to Aristotle, a **man** stood before him, who – despite the insignificant detail of his Jewish origin – was in fact, on the basis of the significant criterion, a Greek, and as wise as himself.

Hence, when the Jews came into the Hellenistic world they entered a world that was a creation of people who had left their native land and began to do away with the importance of lineage and base everything on culture. The Jews were invited to join this world, or, at least to start considering themselves in a similar manner. This "invitation" was not expressed merely in books, but was presented to the Jews in very real life settings.

At the outset of the Hellenistic period we are also witness to the beginnings, more or less, of an important Jewish Diaspora community in the West. It is an interesting fact that during the

Persian period, as once again in the Talmudic period, the main Jewish exilic community – both in size and in cultural vitality – was in Babylon. However, from the time of Alexander until Trajan, that is, from the end of the fourth century BCE until the beginning of the second century CE, it was located in the cities around the Mediterranean, first and foremost – especially in the period with which we are dealing – in Alexandria. We do not know exactly how that great Jewish community was founded. The *Letter of Aristeas* relates that Jews were exiled to Alexandria by Ptolemy I (one of the successors of Alexander), whereas other sources speak of voluntary immigration of Jews to that city. Both versions may contain some truth. In any event, what is certain is that Jews lived in such places, and were therefore in daily intercourse with Greeks and Hellenism and, by virtue of the ports, also in contact with the greater Hellenistic world. Hence, they were intensely exposed to Greek concepts and began to internalize them into their own Jewish world. As early as the third century

BCE, the Torah was translated into Greek (the "Septuagint") and Jews began to compose literature in Greek on Jewish topics, following the accepted Greek models.

But we are concerned principally with the Jews in the Land of Israel. Scholars are divided as to the pace and scope of Hellenization among them. Some date its beginnings earlier than others; some believe that it was widespread, while others minimize its extent. It is especially difficult to provide clear-cut answers to these questions for the period now under consideration, that preceding the Maccabean revolt. Nevertheless, we do know several facts. First of all, more than twenty Greek cities (*poleis*) were established in the Land of Israel during that time. True, they were mainly founded in areas with few Jewish inhabitants, especially along the coast from Rafiah and Gaza in the south to Straton's Tower (later Caesarea) and Ptolemais (Acre) in the north. Likewise, Greek cities flourished in Trans-Jordan, such as Gerasa, Gadara, and Hippos (Susita), and in Galilee – Paneas (Banyas) and Scythopolis (Bet-Shean). But these areas were not completely void of Jewish inhabitants, as we know from several stories from early Hasmonean times (i.e. II Maccabees 12:3-9, 30-31 about Jews in Jaffa, Jamnia, and Bet-Shean). In any case, we must assume that many ties existed between inhabitants of these cities and the Jews in Judea and Jerusalem.

Moreover, the Land of Israel was not a backwards, tranquil corner of the Hellenistic world at that time. Rather, it was the scene of important international events. As early as the first generation after the death of Alexander (323 BCE), several wars were fought on the soil of the Holy Land. We need only mention that Ptolemy I conquered the country four times, being driven out again on three occasions, until he was finally able to establish a firm rule over it in 301 BCE. And in the third century BCE, another five "Syrian Wars" were waged between Ptolemaic Egypt and Seleucid Syria. Egypt won the first four, thus retaining control of the country, whereas in the Fifth Syrian War it was taken by the Seleucid Empire after the victory of Antiochus III ("the Great") in the battle of Paneas (200 BCE). Though these wars had various specific causes and pretexts, from a geopolitical viewpoint they had one root: the nature of empires to try to extend their borders. Since the Land of Israel was a link connecting Africa to Asia and as such was located on the border between the Ptolemaic and the Seleucid empires, control over it was the first step towards

Dedicatory inscription in Aramaic and Greek found at Tel Dan, early 2ⁿᵈ cent. BCE: "To the god who is in Dan to whom Zoilos made a vow." The nature of the "god who is in Dan" is not clear

realization of the aspirations of both sides. Hence these wars repeatedly brought tens of thousands of soldiers of both powers to the Land of Israel. For example, in the Fourth Syrian War, which ended with a Ptolemaic victory at the battle of Rafiah (217 BCE), more than sixty thousand troops took part on each side. These soldiers needed supplies and services of all sorts, and, of course,

A fragment from the Book of Ben Sira, discovered at Masada. Until the discovery of the Cairo geniza about a century ago, the Book of Ben Sira was known only in translation, though it had originally been written in Hebrew early in the second century BCE. Sizable fragments of the original, the very existence of which had been disputed until then, were discovered in the Cairo geniza. Additional fragments were discovered at Masada, shedding new light on the original Hebrew text

51

The Codex Sinaiticus of the Septuagint. This 4th-cent. manuscript was discovered in St. Catherine's Monastery in Sinai (hence its name) in the middle of the 19th cent.

married her uncle Joseph after the latter had earlier lusted after a gentile dancer. We may assume that there were many and sundry ties that were not recorded in the few sources we have for this period.

Anyone seeking literary evidence of the encounter with Hellenism in Judea during this period will generally come upon chronological and geographical uncertainties, it not always being clear whether a certain work was written in the Land of Israel or elsewhere, in the third century or the second century, or perhaps even later. Nevertheless, there is one book that was certainly composed in the country towards the end of the Hellenistic era – the Book of Ben Sira (or Ecclesiasticus). We can date the book's composition in general terms – the beginning of the second century BCE – on the basis of two facts: chapter 50 presents a vivid description of the High Priest Simon son of Onias, who is known to us from Josephus as High Priest at the time of transition to Seleucid rule; the

this burden was imposed on the local population.

Therefore, the territories around Judea knew the heavy presence of Greek and Hellenized foreigners – as permanent residents, soldiers or various kinds of travelers – during the 150 years between Alexander the Great and Antiochus Epiphanes. The Jews of the Land of Israel also had links with their brothers in the Hellenistic Diaspora, and although it is very difficult for us to quantify and document them, these connections surely played their role. Josephus, in one of the few examples known to us, tells about Joseph son of Tobiah, a scion of one of the most prestigious families in Judea (the son of the High Priest's sister), whose brother took his daughter to Alexandria to marry her to the son of one the leading Jewish families there (*Jewish Antiquities*, 12:187). The cultural atmosphere that the bride found in Alexandria, the Hellenistic metropolis, was surely not totally foreign to her. This example of a living link between the Jews of the Land of Israel and the Jews of Alexandria has been preserved only because of its piquant ending, which relates how the brother's daughter actually

translator, who was the author's grandson, writes in his introduction that he himself immigrated to Egypt in 132 BCE, and we may assume that he was not a child at the time. Let us, then, examine the Book of Ben Sira, keeping in mind our questions as to the status of the people and the country.

We should find this book extremely interesting, since it was written by a priest of Jerusalem, a man whose personal status as a priest resembled that of Ezra. However, while Ezra was a man of the Exile who came to the Land of Israel, Jeshua Ben Sira was born and educated in Jerusalem. As such, we would expect to hear from him, too, the old priestly attitudes that exalt geographical origin and lineage. And if we do not hear them, then this would attest to the influence of 150 years of Hellenistic rule and culture.

As one might expect, a mixed picture emerges from the book. On one hand, it contains statements that would warm the heart of any priest. For example, if Malachi likened the priests to angels of the Lord, Ben Sira goes farther and actually places them on

52

the same plane as the Lord himself:

Honor the Lord with all your soul,

And revere his priests.

Love Him who made you with all your strength,

And do not forsake His ministers.

Fear the Lord and honor the priest,

And give him his portion, as you were commanded:

The first fruits, and the sin offering, and the gift of the shoulders,

And the sacrifice of consecration, and the first fruits of holy things.

(Ben Sira, 7:29-31, Goodspeed tr.)

More in the same vein emerges from the enthusiastic description of the High Priest at the conclusion of his service in the Temple:

How glorious he was, surrounded by the people,

As he came out of the sanctuary!

Like the morning star among the clouds,

Like the moon when it is full;

Like the sun shining forth upon the sanctuary of the Most High;

Like the rainbow, showing itself among glorious clouds...

When he assumed his glorious robe, and put on glorious perfection,

And when he went up to the holy altar,

He made the court of the sanctuary glorious...

And when he finished the service at the altars,

To adorn the offering of the Most High. (Ben Sira, 50:5-14; Goodspeed tr.)

There is much more of the same in Ben Sira, and this is not surprising, for its author was a Jerusalemite priest, as we have noted. What is surprising, and attests to the "Hellenistic" gap that separates him from Ezra, is his openness towards gentiles. For example, we may point to the name used in this book for God, e.g. at the end of the above quotation: "the Most High." This appellation allows for gods of other peoples, even if it assigns them a status inferior to that of the God of Israel. Moreover, the famous section which begins "Let us now praise distinguished men, our forefathers before us" (Ben Sira, Chapters 44-50) and lauds the heroes of the past

The name Tobiah inscribed on a structure in the area

In 'Araq al-Amir in Jordan, the name Tobiah was found inscribed over the openings of two chambers. Qasr al-'Abed (The Fortress of the Slave) was also found at this site. Some identify this structure with Tobiah the Ammonite (Nehemiah 2:10)

53

Abraham – a woodcut by E.M. Lilien (1874–1925) illustrating the verse: He took him outside and said, "Look toward heaven and count the stars, if you are able to count them." And He added, "So shall your offspring be" (Genesis 15:5)

And, when he was tested, he proved faithful.
For that reason He assured him with an oath
That nations would be blessed through his
    posterity,
And that He would make him as numerous as the
    dust of the earth,
And would raise his posterity as high as the stars,
And that they should possess from sea to sea,
And from the river to the end of the earth.
(Ben Sira, 44:19-21; Goodspeed tr.)

Of course, the author is not creating anything new here; it is all in the Book of Genesis. However, his editing – the inclusions, the omissions, and the order of precedence – demonstrates his outlook. The first detail reported about Abraham is that he was the "father of a multitude of nations," and the first detail mentioned in God's oath to him is "that nations would be blessed through his posterity." In between, Ben Sira refers to the binding of Isaac ("when he was tested, he proved faithful") and to the oath after that trial. It is interesting to compare Ben Sira's text to the biblical version of this oath (Genesis 22:16-18).

The blessing for all the other nations, which in Genesis comes last, has been moved up in Ben Sira to the first line, where it is also placed next to the explanation that Abraham was considered the "father of a multitude of nations." True, this phrase too is based on a verse: "Your name shall be Abraham, for I make you the father of a multitude of nations" (Genesis 17:5). But how great and significant is the difference between Ben Sira's words and what was deemed important to remember and to affirm when, in the days of Nehemiah, the time came to review the early history of the nation!

You alone are the Lord. You made the heavens, the highest heavens, and all their host, the earth and everything upon it, the seas and everything in them. You keep them all alive, and the host of heaven prostrate themselves before You. You are the Lord God, who chose Abram, who brought him out of Ur of the Chaldeans and changed his name to Abraham. Finding his heart true to You, You made a covenant with him to give the land of the Canaanite, the Hittite, the Amorite, the Perizzite, the Jebusite, and the Girgashite — to give it to his descendants. And You kept Your word, for You are righteous.

one by one, begins precisely with lofty descriptions of primeval non-Jews, such as Enoch and Noah (44:16-18), although most of the figures mentioned are of Israel, and although it is Aaron the priest who receives the lengthiest praises (45:6-22). Similarly, the section concludes with exalted affirmations about Enoch and the rest of the primeval non-Jews (49:14–16: "No one was ever created on earth like Enoch... But above every living thing was Adam in his creation" [Goodspeed tr.]).

Especially interesting in this connection are Ben Sira's remarks about Abraham:

Abraham was the great father of a multitude of nations,
And no one has been found equal to him in glory,
He observed the Law of the Most High,
And entered into an agreement with Him.
He certified the agreement in his flesh,

54

You took note of our fathers' affliction in Egypt... (Nehemiah 9:6-9; the discourse continues until the end of the chapter.)

The differences are striking. First, this oration from the Persian period uses the Tetragrammaton ("Lord") rather than "Most High" (an appellation that does not appear at all in the books of Ezra or Nehemiah). Next, it contains a summary of Genesis 1 without any mention of those who were created, and from there it skips (passing over Adam, Enoch, Noah, and the others) directly to Chapter 12 and God's covenant with Abraham. Here, finally, Abram's name is changed to Abraham without giving the reason ("father of a multitude of nations"), and we are given a summary of the covenant that completely overlooks the blessing of the nations (which is repeated in Genesis in several other places, in addition to Chapter 12). That is, what the text of Genesis put at the end and the oration from Nehemiah's time omitted altogether, Ben Sira emphasizes. This difference between Ben Sira and his forerunners reflects the difference between the Persian and the Hellenistic periods, since what Ben Sira stressed in relation to Abraham is exactly what Isocrates emphasized concerning Athens.

In 161 BCE, twenty or thirty years after Ben Sira wrote his book, Judah the Maccabee sent two envoys to Rome: Eupolemos son of Johanan son of Hakkoz and Jason son of Eleazar (I Maccabees 8:17). The first was surely a priest (since Hakkoz was the name of a priestly family [I Chronicles 24:10]; it seems that Ben Sira, too, belonged to this family, since *sira* in Aramaic means *koz* [thorn-bush] in Hebrew). There is also reason to believe that Jason, too, was a priest. In any event, what is most significant for our discussion is that one generation before the Maccabean revolt, Jerusalemite fathers named Johanan and Eleazar saw fit to call their sons by Greek names such as Eupolemos and Jason. These sons received a Greek education befitting their names, at least a basic Greek education which enabled them to function as diplomats in the international world. Ideas such as those that we find in the book Jeshua ben Sira, who was a teacher in Jerusalem, wrote for his disciples demonstrate the deeper context of that education.

For the moment, in the Hellenistic period, no one sensed an urgent necessity to choose between the various approaches. A man like Ben Sira could grasp the rope at both ends: he could hold on to the old, priestly values that placed such high esteem on lineage and place of origin, yet at the same time grasp the universalist approach that undermined the importance of these elements, as had the Greeks since Alexander. Nevertheless, in the end, profound contradictions such as these must unravel. The crisis was to come in the next era; a crisis which would demand that every Jew take a position on one side or the other. And even when that crisis had passed, and the Jews and their leaders could once again grasp one end without letting go of the other, it would always be done against the background of the memory of that crisis. Thus, each of the coming periods would be distinguished from that of the innocent, tranquil encounter described in this chapter.

Jason's Tomb, a splendid burial complex from the Hasmonean period that was discovered in the Rehavia neighborhood in Jerusalem and named after one of those buried there

The Herodion fortress and palace, named after Herod, who built it within an artificial earthwork mound that he erected atop a hill. Near the fortress Herod also established a town. During the Great Revolt and the Bar Kokhba uprising, the site served as a stronghold for the insurgents. According to Josephus, this was also Herod's burial place

From the Hasmonean Revolt to the Destruction of the Second Temple

Isaiah M. Gafni

The Second Temple period witnessed the return of the People of Israel to their land. This return was multi-faceted, for it occurred not only within a specific time-frame and physical context, but also on a spiritual level, accompanied by the gradual emergence of a revitalized national self-identity. To be sure, the nation had never completely abandoned its links to the Land of Israel, even while residing abroad. Just as the exiles of Judah remembered Zion while situated "by the rivers of Babylon," so too did the Jewish residents of Elephantine in Egypt turn, in their time of need, to "Jehohanan the High Priest" and his fellow priests in Jerusalem with a request for aid in restoring their own temple. Memories and images of the Land of Israel can be found throughout the Jewish literature of the Second Temple period. The following pages, however, are not concerned with what

many scholars have designated as the "spiritualization" of Eretz Israel – the Land of Israel – and its transformation into a disembodied and abstract concept, adding thereby to memories of biblical times that were surely preserved in the hearts of many Jews. Rather, we shall concentrate on the practical and physical return of the Jewish people to Zion, a process that began under the Persians and gradually developed in very clear stages.

Cyrus' declaration permitted and even encouraged a return "to Jerusalem which is in Judah" (Ezra 1:3) and the building of a temple within its precincts. But this permission was never meant to

Graphic ornamentation entitled "Remembrance of the Destruction" on the wall of a building in Jerusalem, illustrating the scripture in Psalms 137:1–2: "By the rivers of Babylon, there we sat and wept, as we remembered Zion. There on the poplars we hung up our lyres"

57

be taken as the establishment of a "national homeland" for the Jewish people, nor was it intended to bring about a mass return of Jews to the many portions of the Land of Israel that had been vacated by its Israelite inhabitants during the last years of the First Temple. Consequently, while enclaves of Jewish settlement were in fact added in areas outside the narrow boundaries of Judah during Persian and Hellenistic times, their numbers remained a small minority within the total population of the country, and even a minority of its Jewish residents. Beginning with the "Return to Zion" (538 BCE) and the dedication of the Second Temple (516 BCE), almost all Jewish activity was confined to the limited borders of the *pahava* of Yehud. This territory stretched from Bet-El (Bethel) in the north to Bet-Zur (north of Hebron) in the south, and from Jericho (with the addition of certain Jewish settlements east of the Jordan River) in the east to the *shephela* (lowlands) around Lod (Lydda) in the west. These boundaries, with minor modifications, demarcated the main areas of Jewish settlement in the Land of Israel for 350 years, until the conquests of the Hasmoneans.

. . . .

Changing Borders and National Self–Consciousness

Beginning with the Hasmonean period, and even in the early stages of the revolt and prior to the achievement of full political independence, the links between the spread of Jewish settlements throughout the Land of Israel and the responsibility assumed by Hasmonean leaders for their safety on the one hand, and the role of the Land of Israel in the national consciousness and collective memory of the nation on the other, became increasingly apparent. A significant and enduring change was effected both in the history of Jewish settlement in the Land of Israel as well as in the demarcation of its borders, and these would play a profound role in the history of Israel far beyond the Second Temple period.

Within one generation from the outbreak of the Hasmonean revolt in 167 BCE, the map of Jewish settlement had changed radically, and with it the self-identity of the inhabitants of the Land of Israel was also transformed beyond recognition. The decrees of Antiochus IV against the Jewish religion apparently affected the lives of Jews living outside the narrow confines of Judea, whether by forcing them to participate in idol worship or through decrees that undermined the status and security of those Jews who resided in or near Hellenistic cities throughout the Land of Israel. This situation contributed to a closer relationship between the Hasmoneans and the entire Jewish population of the country. The fifth chapter of I Maccabees describes how "the gentiles all around took counsel to destroy the seed of Jacob among them," and how Judah the Maccabee and his brothers crossed beyond the borders of Judea to defend their threatened countrymen in Idumea, western Galilee, and the Gilead. That the Jews of Gilead and Galilee appealed to Judah (I Maccabees 5:9–15) is most instructive, for this indicates for the first time that they considered the Hasmonean warriors to be the guardians of the entire Jewish community in the Land of Israel, and not

The island of Elephantine in the Nile and the ruins of Syene (Aswan) on the river bank. Syene and Elephantine, located near the southern border of Egypt, were of great strategic and economic importance beginning in the seventh century BCE. Jewish troops formed part of the garrison that defended them in the fifth century BCE. Engraving from David Roberts, *Egypt & Nubia...*, II, London 1849, no. 28 (JNUL, Laor)

merely those struggling to liberate Jerusalem and restore the worship of the Lord to the Temple.

Under Judah's leadership of the revolt (167–160 BCE), efforts were made primarily to defend Jews throughout the country, but following his death his two surviving brothers, Jonathan (160–142 BCE) and Simon (142–135 BCE) proceeded with the annexation of territories adjacent to Judea, thereby attaching them to an area that had long been populated primarily by Jews. By the time Judea became an independent state under the leadership of Simon (142 BCE), Jewish control had expanded beyond the limited confines of Judea and now included southern districts of Samaria as well as the cities of Jaffa and Gezer. As the Seleucid Empire grew increasingly weaker, even greater possibilities presented themselves to Simon's son, John Hyrcanus (134–104 BCE). Under his rule the regions of Idumea and Samaria were added to the Jewish state, as well as districts east of the Jordan River. With the annexation of the Galilee to the Hasmonean state during the brief reign of John's son Aristobolus (104–103 BCE), almost all the Jewish inhabitants of the Land of Israel were subjects of a sovereign Jewish ruler, a situation that had not existed since the days of the First Temple. Moreover, there was by now a far greater congruence between the population of the Land of Israel and the historic boundaries of Eretz Israel, following the conversion to Judaism of many additional segments of the local gentile population, primarily in Idumea but also in

several Hellenistic cities and in the Galilee. The Land of Israel was thus transformed into a primarily Jewish state, and it is noteworthy that at least some of the districts in which these converts were concentrated would be considered "Jewish" territories by the time the country was eventually occupied by the Romans.

To be sure, not all the territories conquered by the various Hasmonean rulers merged entirely into the new Jewish political enterprise. The conquests of Alexander Jannaeus (103–76 BCE), both along the coastal strip as well as in the vicinity of the Greek cities east of the Jordan, did not effect an ethnic or cultural transformation among the Greek residents who formed the majority of residents within those conquered areas. With the Roman conquest of the Hasmonean state, those districts reassumed their Gentile character, and to a great extent this also occurred in the Samaritan country around Mount Gerizim. These, however, were the exceptions to the general process of Judaization that enveloped much of the Land of Israel under the Hasmoneans. The legacy of the Hasmonean state may be found not only in its success at checking the spread and domination of an urban Hellenistic culture throughout the entire country, but also in its molding

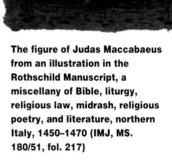

The figure of Judas Maccabaeus from an illustration in the Rothschild Manuscript, a miscellany of Bible, liturgy, religious law, midrash, religious poetry, and literature, northern Italy, 1450–1470 (IMJ, MS. 180/51, fol. 217)

of the majority of the country's population into one national-cultural entity. The predominantly Jewish character of this body was so apparent that for both Jews and Gentiles the identification of the geographical reality of the Land of Israel with its Jewish character became self evident. For the renowned geographer Strabo (1st century BCE–1st century CE) the entire country "between Gaza and the Anti-Lebanon mountains is called Judea" (*Geography* 16:2:21). This name – Judea – was to serve as the common designation of the Land of Israel, signifying its national-ethnic character as well, even after it had become a Roman

Greek inscription found in the fields of Kibbutz Hephzibah in the Jezreel Valley. The inscription includes letters from the Seleucid King Antiochus III, who conquered the Land of Israel from the Ptolemies in 202–198 BCE. The letters were sent to Antiochus' governor in the country, Ptolemy son of Thraseas, and discuss matters of landed property in the Jezreel Valley (IMJ)

59

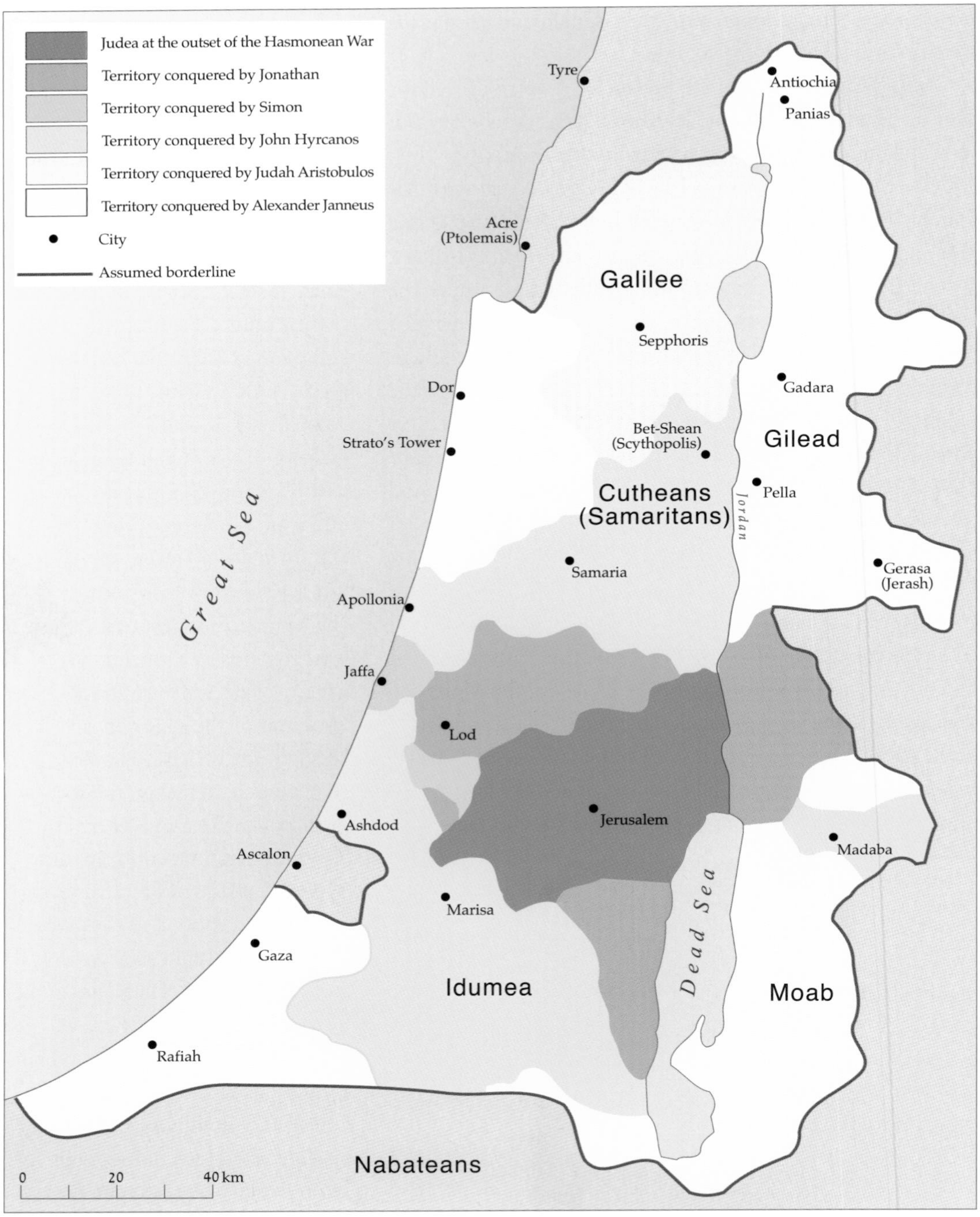

Map Legend:

- Judea at the outset of the Hasmonean War
- Territory conquered by Jonathan
- Territory conquered by Simon
- Territory conquered by John Hyrcanos
- Territory conquered by Judah Aristobulos
- Territory conquered by Alexander Janneus
- ● City
- —— Assumed borderline

Map labels:

Tyre, Antiochia, Panias, Acre (Ptolemais), Galilee, Sepphoris, Dor, Gadara, Strato's Tower, Bet-Shean (Scythopolis), Gilead, Great Sea, Cutheans (Samaritans), Pella, Jordan, Samaria, Gerasa (Jerash), Apollonia, Jaffa, Lod, Jerusalem, Madaba, Ashdod, Dead Sea, Ascalon, Marisa, Idumea, Moab, Gaza, Rafiah, Nabateans

0   20   40 km

Stages in the geographic expansion of the Hasmonean State

province. In fact the Romans continued to employ this name (JUDAEA) as their official designation of the province for decades after the destruction of the Second Temple in 70 CE, and it was only the Bar Kokhba uprising that finally led to the renaming of the country.

The unification and gradual liberation of the Jewish population of the Land of Israel from foreign rule were thus accompanied during the Hasmonean period by a growing awareness that this process did not merely encompass a local population with shared interests. It was, rather, the reemergence of a community harboring a national-religious and historical attachment to the regions it settled, some of which came into its possession only under the reign of the Hasmonean dynasty. The outstanding expression of this historic link can be found in Simon's response to the demands of the Seleucid King Antiochus VII Sidetes, that he return those "cities of my kingdom" captured

60

Scenes of the Maccabean Revolt; frontispiece to the Book of Maccabees from a manuscript of the Bible prepared in Acre, 13ᵗʰ cent. (BA, MS. 5211, fol. 339r)

contributed there as well to a renewed perception of the role of the Land of Israel as one component in Jewish self-identity. At least one Jewish author in the Hellenistic diaspora, Jason of Cyrene, saw fit to compose his own version of the events in Judea that preceded the outbreak of the revolt and took place there in the days of Judah Maccabee. His work would serve as the basis for the Second Book of Maccabees in our possession today, and while its emphasis and per-spective frequently differ from those embraced in I Maccabees, it nevertheless testifies to the keen interest of diaspora Jewry in what was happening in Jerusalem and the Temple. II Maccabees begins with letters purportedly written by Jews in the Land of Israel to their brethren in Egypt, encouraging them to join their co-religionists in celebrating the liberation of the Temple by the Hasmoneans, a celebration we recognize as the Feast of Hannukah. Although we are not absolutely certain as to the identity of the

by the Hasmonean forces (I Maccabees 15:29). Simon's reply, as recorded in I Maccabees, indicates to what extent the formulators of Hasmonean ideology were bent on justifying their endeavor, at least in its more advanced stages, on the basis of a collective national memory that rendered the Land of Israel a defining component of the national self-mage:

And Simon said to him in reply: "We have neither taken other men's land, nor are we in possession of other men's property, but of the inheritance of our forefathers; it was wrongfully usurped by our enemies at one time, but we, grasping our opportunity, hold firmly the inheritance of our forefathers" (I Maccabees 15:33–34).

· · · · · · · · · · ·

Diaspora Jewry

Reports of the developments in the Land of Israel under the Hasmoneans surely reached the Jews of the various diasporas, and it is likely that the achievements of the sons of Mattathias

authors of those letters, their theme is clear: the holidays of Judean Jews are likewise the festivals of diaspora Jewry. And therefore

We [the Jews of Eretz Israel] write to you. You would do rightly to celebrate these days. It is God who has saved all his people and given his estate to all of us and dominion and the priesthood and the Temple… [May God] speedily have mercy on us, and gather us together from all the earth under heaven to the holy place… (II Maccabees 2:16–18).

Was this invitation addressed to a community of convinced Jews, or might it reflect the fear that the Jews of Egypt do not consider themselves full partners in the rejoicing of their Judean brethren, and therefore need to be urged into joining a common celebration? The letterwriters surely knew that a Jewish temple existed on foreign soil from the middle of the 2ⁿᵈ century BCE, namely the Temple of Onias in Egypt. In their letter they emphasized that the high priest Jason sinned by not keeping faith with "the Holy Land" (ἁγία γῆ; II Maccabees 1:7). We should

61

![Remnants of the Hasmonean fortress of Hyrcania]

Remnants of the Hasmonean fortress of Hyrcania, in the northern Judean desert. The fortress was built by John Hyrcanus, hence its name. In the fifth century a monastery was erected on the site.

pilgrimage to Jerusalem, nor do we have reliable information regarding the extent of the financial support for the city and its temple by means of the annual contribution of shekels. The information we do possess for these phenomena derives primarily from the period following the Roman conquest of the country in 63 BCE. Nevertheless we do have some evidence for the practical involvement of diaspora Jews in the affairs of the Land of Israel prior to the Roman conquest, and these bits of information do not derive necessarily from the fanciful exaggerations found in certain literary works of the Hellenistic period, such as the Letter of Aristeas or the fragments attributed to Greek authors of that early period such as Hecataeus of Abdera, which in fact may have actually been written, or at least influenced, by Jews.

note that this seems to be the first use of the term "Holy Land" as a designation for the Land of Israel, and certainly the first Greek appearance of the phrase, although a general reference to "sacred land" or "sacred ground" (*admat ha-kodesh*) does appear in the Book of Zechariah (2:16).

The establishment of the Hasmonean state opened a new chapter in the interest and active involvement of diaspora Jewry in the affairs of the Land of Israel. Manifestations of this partnership would become even more apparent with the Roman conquest of Judea and the fall of the independent Jewish state. We can reasonably assume that the intensive foreign policy evinced by the Hasmoneans contributed considerably to the links of diaspora Jews to the Land of Israel. The Hasmoneans fostered ties with Rome, Egypt, Sparta, Pergamon, Parthia, and other territories, and beyond their obvious diplomatic goals these relations surely enhanced the status of local Jewish communities in each of these lands.

The Hasmonean state maintained its independence for some eighty years, beginning with the days of Simon's leadership (142 BCE) and until the conquest of Judea by the Roman general Pompey (63 BCE). Surprisingly, while this period produced a variety of literary sources that reflect the social ferment of the time, precious little has survived to provide a concrete and reliable description of the full extent of Jewish ties to the Land of Israel. Precisely for the time that the Jewish state was flourishing and expanding geographically we possess no descriptions of mass

An early example of the increasing involvement of diaspora Jewry in the events of Judea, rendering it something of a political lobby in support of the Jewish state, transpired during the early years of Alexander Jannaeus' reign. Jannaeus, it appears, had gotten off to a bad start: during his very first year as ruler of Judea the land was invaded by Ptolemy Lathyrus, son of Cleopatra queen of Egypt and a rival for her throne. Ptolemy conquered

Silver Hannukah lamp from the Austro-Hungarian Empire, second half of the 19th century. Eight vials for oil in front of a spread-tailed peacock. The festival of Hannukah serves Jews throughout the dispersion as a reminder of the Temple and of hopes for redemption

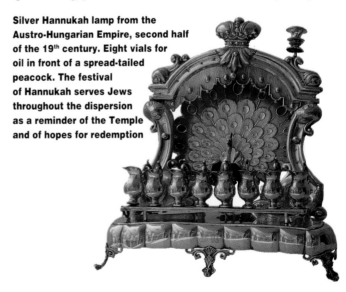

62

The "Sidonian cave" at Maresha. The Hellenistic city in Idumea was conquered by John Hyrcanus I (111 BCE). Josephus reports that the Idumeans were given the choice of conversion to Judaism or expulsion, and most chose to convert

extensive parts of the land, and it soon became clear that these successes were intended to serve as a staging area for his ultimate goal, which was the invasion and conquest of Egypt. Cleopatra advanced naval and ground forces to thwart this threat, with her army under the command of two Jewish generals, Chelkias (Hilqiyah) and Ananias (Hananiah). The queen's efforts succeeded, but after repelling her son she entertained the idea of capturing the Jewish state herself.

Ananias, however, gave the opposite advice, saying that she would commit an injustice if she deprived an ally of his own possessions, "**especially one who is our kinsman. For I would have you know that an injustice done to this man will make all us Jews your enemies**" (Josephus, *Antiquities* 13:354).

The Jews of Egypt continued their involvement in the affairs of the Land of Israel even after the independent Hasmonean state ceased to exist. Josephus recounts how Julius Caesar was aided by the Jews of "the district of Onias" after they had received letters from the High Priest John Hyrcanus II urging them "to be friendly to Caesar and receive his army hospitably and furnish it with all things necessary" (*Antiquities* 14:131). According to Josephus this aid was in fact tendered and contributed considerably to Caesar's victory.

These were not isolated events, but the beginning of a series of expressions of diaspora Jewry's growing interest in the affairs of the Land of Israel, and of their willingness to become actively involved in these affairs – even at some risk to themselves – with the purpose of influencing the policies of the various powers

towards Judea and its Jewish inhabitants. This phenomenon increased with the onset of Roman rule in the Land of Israel. Thus we read that eight thousand Jews of Rome joined emissaries dispatched from Judea after the death of Herod (4 BCE), sent to plead before Augustus for the cessation of Herodian rule in the country (*Antiquities* 17:300). Another picturesque example is the story of a Jew from Sidon who managed to reach Rome, where he claimed to be Alexander, Herod's son, who had ostensibly been put to death by his father. On his way to Rome the imposter succeeded in winning the support of various Jewish communities, among them those of Crete and Delos, while in Rome itself "the whole Jewish population went out to meet him, regarding his extraordinary escape from death as an act of God, and giving him a joyful welcome because of their racial tie with his mother" (i.e., Mariamme the Hasmonean; *Antiquities* 17:331).

Under totally different circumstances, when Gaius Caligula intended to erect an idol in the Jerusalem Temple, it was the fear of a violent reaction

Bronze coin struck by the last Hasmonean king, Mattathias Antigonus (40–37 BCE)

63

Portion of the Habakkuk Commentary, one of the Dead Sea Scrolls discovered in the Judean Desert, probably written in the first century BCE.
The author quotes scripture from Habakkuk and adds his own *pesher* (commentary), suggesting the fulfillment of the prophecy in his own days.
Other literary works of the same period project an era of cultural ferment

throughout the Jewish diaspora that deterred the Roman governor Petronius from carrying out the emperor's decree:

He took into account the vast numbers of our people, that cannot be contained by the confines of one country like all the other peoples…they are spread abroad over all the continents and islands…. To draw all these myriads into enmity against him was surely very dangerous. Heaven forbid, indeed, that the Jews in all their places should come by common agreement to the defense. The result would be something too stupendous to be combatted (Philo, *The Embassy to Gaius*, 214–215).

What we encounter here would seem to be a unique phenomenon in the ancient world: the members of a nation disbursed over countries and continents cultivated a practical involvement in the affairs of their historic land of origin, and even exploited their numbers and potential strength for the purpose of influencing the policies of various rulers towards that country. The other side of the same coin, of course, was the recognition, perceived by Jews and gentiles alike, that such ties between Jews throughout the world and their brethren in Judea did in fact exist, thereby justifying punishment of the former for the sins of the latter. The author of the Book of Tobit (1:18) took it for granted that King Sennacherib, after his setback in Jerusalem, might vent his wrath upon the Jews of Nineveh. Likewise, the author of III Maccabees saw no difficulty in pointing to the humiliation of the Egyptian King Ptolemy Philopator in Jerusalem (III Maccabees 2:21–24) as the principal motive for the harsh decrees that he imposed on the Jews of Egypt. The most striking example of a perceived connection between the Jews of the Land of Israel and their brethren in the diaspora, a connection that justified imposing punishment on the latter

for the sins of the former, was the tax placed by the Emperor Vespasian on all Jews throughout the empire after suppression of the great Jewish insurrection in Judea, a war that ended with the destruction of Jerusalem and the Temple (Josephus, *The Jewish War*, 7:218).

The Temple as a Factor in the Life of the Nation

The relationship of world Jewry to the Land of Israel and to the events that took place there during the Second Temple period did not derive solely from faint biblical memories – a sort of collective national nostalgia. Rather, there were additional ties between the Jews of the Land of Israel and their diaspora kinsmen that created a sense of mutual responsibility. Without a doubt the most outstanding unifying factor, and one that led Jews everywhere to turn their hearts towards the Land of Israel, was the Temple in Jerusalem. For Jews the Temple served as the principal focal point for their worship of God, although we should bear in mind that there was also a "Temple of Onias" in Leontopolis in Egypt, which undoubtedly served the needs of some local Jews from its establishment in the middle of the second century BCE and until its closure by order of Vespasian in 73 CE. But the uniqueness of the Jerusalem Temple lay in the fact that it fostered among the entire Jewish nation a sense of belonging and of mutual responsibility. Information on the dispatching of shekels from all over the Jewish world to the Temple has come down to us from various and sundry sources, and these testimonies suggest a temple that sought to highlight its belonging to all believers, rather than being the possession of a restricted caste of priests. Philo relates that "every year they [the Jews] send emissaries for the sacred purpose of conveying to the Temple a great quantity of silver and gold that has been accumulated through their generosity" (Philo, *Embassy to Gaius*, 216). Josephus reports in a similar vein: "No one should wonder that there was such wealth in our Temple. For all the Jews in the world, and all the worshippers of God, even from Asia and Europe, used to donate generously to it for a great many years" (*Antiquities* 14:110).

Philo has furnished us with a vivid description of how the shekels were brought to Jerusalem:

Since the [Jewish] nation is plentiful in population, the offerings are likewise plentiful and abundant. Indeed, a depository for these sacred funds can be found in almost every city, and people regularly come and give their offerings. And at fixed times escorts are appointed for these sacred funds. They are selected on their merit, from each city men of the highest repute, and they escort the hopes of each and every one safely. For it is on the offerings ordained by the Torah that the hopes of the Heaven-fearers rest (Philo, *On the Special Laws*, 1:78).

funds, and the decrees were issued in order to confirm their right to do so and to warn against any interference on the part of local authorities. The best known instance of such interference occurred in 59BCE, when the Roman proconsul of Asia Minor, Flaccus, tried to confiscate Jewish monies intended for dispatch to Jerusalem. We know of this incident because the renowned orator Cicero was engaged to defend Flaccus at his trial in Rome and we possess his oration for the defense. From Cicero's remarks it appears that very considerable sums intended for transfer to Jerusalem had been seized in various cities throughout Asia Minor: "At Apamea a little less than a hundred pounds [*pondo* in the Latin source] of gold was openly seized…at Laodicea a little more than twenty pounds…at Adramyttium a hunderd pounds…"(Cicero, *In Defense of Flacco*, 28:68).

Cicero actually tried to justify the confiscation of these funds from the Jews by claiming that only a few years earlier their brethren in Judea had fought against Pompey's armies. He also hinted at the close ties between the various Jewish communities: the Jews of Rome, he feared, might exert pressure on behalf of their brethren in Asia Minor, who in turn were determined to send funds to their kinsmen in Jerusalem. It is hardly surprising, therefore, that some years later Tacitus would claim that "wretches

Drawing of a ship on a wall in the "Tomb of Jason," discovered in the Jerusalem neighborhood of Rehavia

Josephus quotes a lengthy series of imperial decrees on this practice (*Antiquities* 16:162–171), such as the following one issued by Augustus: "Caesar to Norbanus Flaccus, greetings: The Jews wherever they may be, who are accustomed according to ancient custom to gather and transmit dedicated funds to Jerusalem, may do this without interference" (ibid., 16:166). From the texts of several of these decrees, it is also apparent that there were indeed attempts to prevent Jews from sending these

from among other peoples, having abandoned the religion of their fathers, continue to send monies to Jerusalem, thereby adding to the wealth of the Jews" (Tacitus, *The Histories*, 5:5:1).

Early talmudic tradition also describes how the shekels arrived from all over the diaspora, and how from these monies offerings were made on behalf of the various diaspora communities at specified times:

He removed the first offering (i.e., removed an amount of money from all

Inscription on a stone tablet, first century BCE or CE, attesting to a synagogue in late Second Temple Jerusalem: "Theodotos son of Vatinos, priest and archisynagogos (=head of the congregation), son of an archisynagogos, grandson of an archisynagogos, built the synagogue for the reading of the Torah and the study of the commandments, and the lodging house and the rooms and the water system for the purpose of hosting the needy of foreign lands. It was founded by his forefathers and the elders and Simonides"

the funds that had arrived until that moment) and proclaimed: "Behold, this is from Eretz Israel"…(at a later stage) he removed a second offering and proclaimed: "Behold this is from Ammon and Moab and from the cities around the periphery of Eretz Israel"…(yet later) he removed a third offering and proclaimed: "Behold this is from Babylonia and from Media and from lands far from Eretz Israel" (Tosefta, *Shekalim* 2:3-4).

The shekels were earmarked, first and foremost, for the purchase of all the public sacrifices offered up at the Temple, thereby emphasizing the relationship of all of world Jewry to the Temple service. But the sources also note that the "remainders" of the funds (i.e., those not used to purchase sacrifices) were utilized to cover the cost of maintaining "the water conduit and the city wall and its towers and all the needs of the city" (Mishnah, *Shekalim* 4:2). The outlay of these funds for the maintenance of the entire city, and not just its ritual requirements, enhanced the perception of Jerusalem as part of the national domain, owned by the people of Israel at large and not just the local residents.

· · · · · · · · · ·

Pilgrimage and Immigration to Eretz Israel

It was pilgrimage, more than anything else, that fostered a sense of national partnership in the affairs of Jerusalem and the Temple. In the course of their pilgrimages, Diaspora Jews gained firsthand knowledge of the Land of Israel. Philo provides us with an emotional description of pilgrimage, characterized by a spiritual exaltation for both the individual and the community:

Countless multitudes from countless cities come, some over land, others over sea, from east and west and north and south, at every feast. They arrive at the Temple as to a common haven, a safe harbor from the storms and turmoil of life. There they seek to find tranquility, to be released from worries whose yoke has weighed heavily upon them from their earliest childhood, and to enjoy a brief breathing space in scenes of gladness and joy. Thus, their hearts filled with satisfying hopes, they devote this vital leisure to holiness and giving glory to God. They also form ties of friendship with people whom they did not know before. And in the blending of hearts over feasting and libations, they find convincing proof of the unity of minds (Philo, *On the Special Laws*, 1:69–70).

This stirring account, however, set down in a state of exaltation, did not reflect what often also occurred precisely during pilgrimage seasons. It was only to be expected that the very fact of masses assembling at the nation's holiest site, and especially during holidays, would arouse sentiments of national pride. Indeed Josephus explicitly attests to this phenomenon, from which it was only a short step to enhanced national expectations on the one hand, and a sense of bitterness over the continuing state of occupation and repression on the other.

The relationship of world Jewry to the Land of Israel is manifest not only in regard to pilgrimage and the Temple. The first signs of Jewish immigration to the Land of Israel from the diaspora appear during the reign of Herod (37–4 BCE), and strangely enough there is no evidence for the phenomen during the Hasmonean era that preceded Herodian rule. Also noteworthy from the age of Herod is the support provided by the Jews of the Land of Israel for their brethren of the diaspora,

Coins dating from the time of the Great Revolt, found at Silwan in Jerusalem

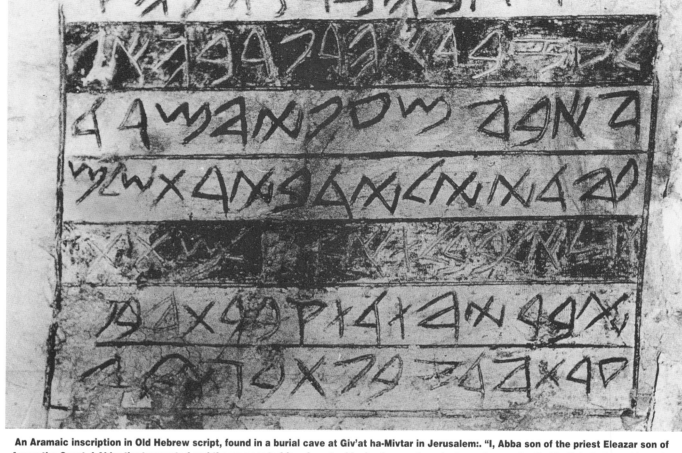

An Aramaic inscription in Old Hebrew script, found in a burial cave at Giv'at ha-Mivtar in Jerusalem:. "I, Abba son of the priest Eleazar son of Aaron the Great, I Abba the tormented and the persecuted (or: downtrodden), who was born in Jerusalem and exiled to Babylonia and brought Mattathi[as] son of Judah up [to the Land of Israel] and buried him in the cave that I bought by contract"

thus projecting a two-way relationship between diaspora Jewry and the Judean center. The very same Herod who was considered a tyrant and "puppet king" by the Jews of the Land of Israel, nevertheless intervened on behalf of Jewish communities in the diaspora who had been suffereng at the hands of their Greek neighbors (Josephus, *Antiquities* 16:27–63). Herod also seems to have made special efforts to encourage Jewish immigration to the Land of Israel. His aim in this was to establish a more diverse local aristocracy that was not closely linked to the Hasmoneans, the royal dynasty upon whose ruins Herod had established his own regime, with the considerable help of the Romans. One outstanding example of this policy was Herod's introduction of Jewish priests from the diaspora – both Babylonia and Egypt – into the ranks of the Jerusalem priesthood, and their appointment as High Priests. Herod also invited a group of military settlers from Babylonia, led by one Zamaris (Zimri), to come and settle in the Bashan (the eastern Golan Heights), and to assume responsibility for security in the region (*Antiquities* 17:24–26).

Jews from the diaspora began to arrive and settle in the Land of Israel even without the direct intervention of Herod. For the first time since the days of Ezra the Scribe, we encounter the arrival of respected sages from the diaspora, the greatest among them, of course, being Hillel the Babylonian. Even after the establishment of direct Roman rule in Judea in 6 CE, noted personalities from the diaspora continued to make their way to the Land of Israel and to settle therein. The best known instance of such *aliya* (literally "ascent" to the Land of Israel) was that of Queen Helena of Adiabene, together with part of her family, after their earlier conversion to Judaism in their homeland (*Antiquities* 20:49–53; ibid. 95). Both the queen and her son Izates were

The "Tombs of the Kings," a magnificent burial complex from the 1st century CE, ascribed to the royal family of Adiabene, some of whom were buried in Jerusalem. Etching from Louis François Cassas, *Voyage pittoresque de la Syrie, de la Phénicie, de la Palestine et de la Basse Égypte*, Paris [1798], III, no. 25

buried in Jerusalem in a magnificent burial complex, and it is likely that this was but one of many such imposing structures – including synagogues – erected in Jerusalem by representatives of Jewish communities from abroad. Moreover, numerous tombs of diaspora Jews have been discovered in the environs of Jerusalem. Some of these Jews had already immigrated to the Land of Israel, like the family of "Nikanor, the maker of the gates" whose grave was discovered on Mt. Scopus, while others may have died there while on pilgrimage. Thus, towards the end of the Second Temple period the Land of Israel was increasingly transformed into a microcosm of the Jewish nation as a whole. Jews from various countries came there, some for the moment and others to stay. The latter settled in the country and sometimes filled key positions in its religious and spiritual life as priests, sages, courtiers, and intimates of royal personages.

Homeland, Exile, Diaspora

All the above raises an interesting question: Did the existence of an extensive Jewish presence in most of the Land of Israel lead to demands upon the Jews of the diaspora to also immigrate there, and were aspersions cast on those continuing to live abroad? At the same time, did the Jews of the diaspora feel any discomfort in not pulling up roots and immigrating – especially in light of their avowed attachment to the Land of Israel and their

69

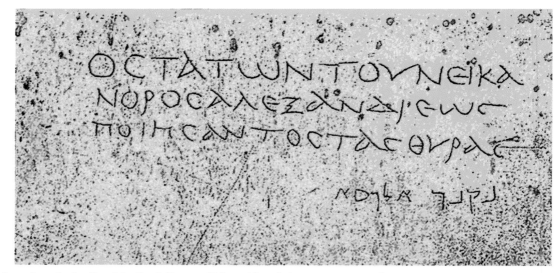

Evidence in Jerusalem of a family originating in Egypt: a bi-lingual inscription on an ossuary discovered in a splendid family burial-cave on Mount Scopus. The cave belonged to the family of a man who donated gates to the Temple: "These are the bones of Nikanor (or; 'of the people of Nikanor') of Alexandria who made the doors Nikanor Aleksa." This inscription may be connected to the reference in the Mishnah (*Yoma* 3:6) to the miracles connected with "the gates of Nikanor"

involvement in its affairs? This duality of Jewish existence that we have described – a large and prosperous Jewish diaspora existing alongside a large, and for a time independent, Jewish center – has occurred only twice in Jewish history: the first example was during Second Temple times, while the second appeared only in recent generations, with the fulfillment of modern Zionist aspirations. And just as our own contemporaries – in Israel and the diaspora – have formulated a variety of positions on this state of affairs, drawing from it at various times radically different conclusions, so, it appears, was the case in the Second Temple era as well. For most of that period we do not encounter explicit demands directed by the Jews of the Land of Israel towards their diaspora brethren, demanding that the latter immigrate to the Land. This is also the case for the first years following the destruction of the Second Temple. Demands for *aliya*, and the concommitant aspersions cast on those Jews remaining in the diaspora, would begin to appear only in the aftermath of the Bar Kokhba uprising (132–135 CE), when fears were first raised about the viability of maintaining the predominant Jewish character of the Land of Israel.

To be sure, throughout the Second Temple period there were always expectations for a future "ingathering of exiles." These hopes are expressed not only at the beginning of the Second Book of Maccabees, but in the writings of Philo as well:

For even though they dwell in the uttermost parts of the earth, in slavery to those who led them away captive, one signal as it were, will one day bring liberty to all…. When they have gained this unexpected liberty, those who

but now were scattered in Greece and the barbarian lands, over islands and continents, will arise and flow, each one from his place, out of a single impulse to arrive at the appointed place, guided by a divine, superhuman vision unseen by others but manifest to them at their time of redemption… (Philo, *On Reward and Punishment,* 164–165)

The very same Philo, however, was able to distinguish between this ingathering to the homeland, destined for some future but as yet unknown date, and the present loyalties evinced by Jews towards the Land of Israel as well as their current lands of residence:

While they hold their Holy City, where stands the Temple of the most high God, to be their mother city [metropolis], yet all those places where they dwell, where they were born and reared, they treat as a homeland, places which fell to their lot as an inheritance from their fathers, grandfathers, and ancestors even farther back. They came to some of those places when they were founded – as if they had been sent to establish a colony – to the satisfaction of the founders (Philo, *Against Flaccus,* 46).

Consequently, alongside his recognition of the virtues of the Land of Israel and the fact that it had come down to the Jewish nation as a legacy, Philo was also ready to proclaim that "[Jewish] settlers abroad and residents of other places are not sinners" (Philo, *Life of Moses,* 2:232).

Something quite different emerges from the pages of Josephus' writings. He, of course, experienced firsthand the events of the Great War and the destruction of the Second Temple, and for him that war effectively concluded the "Land of Israel" chapter of Jewish history. Consequently, Josephus did not hesitate to put the following words into Balaam's "blessing" of Israel (ironically a paraphrase of the verse describing Israel as "a people that dwells alone and not counted among the nations" – Numbers 23:9):

You will also succeed in supplying inhabitants of your stock to all the countries of the world. Do you wonder, O blessed army, that you have become such a large people from this one father? Indeed it is still small at this time and the Land of Canaan can contain it. But you should know that the whole world lies before you as a dwelling place forever, and you shall surely dwell on the islands and the mainland in your multitudes" (*Antiquities* 4:115-116).

As noted by Abraham Schalit, Josephus did not consider this

to be the end of Jewish history. On the contrary, his is "a song of praise to the people of Israel as a nation living in the diaspora…not only does the diaspora not represent a disaster for the ongoing existence of the nation, but rather it was a mission imposed on it by God" (A. Schalit's Hebrew translation of *Antiquities*, vol. 2, p. xliii, note 295a).

Within one generation it was to become clear – with great poignancy – how mistaken Josephus had been in his reading of events (at least for the moment), and how a portion of the Jewish nation living in the Land of Israel had not reconciled itself to the loss of Jerusalem and the Temple. That segment of the population would still be prepared to make enormous sacrifices in order to realize its hopes for "the freedom of Jerusalem" and "the redemption of Israel."

A coin struck by Bar Kokhba in the first year of the revolt. On the left – a palm tree and beneath it the inscription: "Simon Nasi of Israel." On the right the reverse of the same coin, bearing the inscription: "Year One of the redemption of Israel"

Aerial view of ancient Caesarea
and its Roman theater

From the Destruction of the Second Temple to the Christianization of the Empire

Aharon Oppenheimer

The Destruction of the Temple and its Consequences

The destruction of the Second Temple led to one of the most difficult crises in Jewish history, and endangered the religious and national existence of the Jewish people in the Land of Israel. They had lost Jerusalem and the Temple which had been the center for Jews in the Land of Israel and in the Diaspora for nearly six hundred years. In Second Temple times, Judaism had increasingly centered on Jerusalem and the Temple. The worship of God in the Temple was the central focus of Judaism and all manifestations of national life. The Temple was the only cult site and hence many of the central commandments were connected to it, such as individual and communal sacrifices, purity and purification from severe defilement, setting aside of gifts for the priests and Levites who served in the Sanctuary, and paying the half-*sheqel* tax. Moreover, the central festive ceremonies were also conducted there. These included the special sacrifices for each festival, blowing the *shofar* (ram's horn) on the New Year (*Rosh ha-Shanah*) while the Additional Offerings (*Musaf*) were being made, the High Priest's ritual on the Day of Atonement (*Yom Kippur*) intended to atone for himself and for his people, the procession around the altar with the Four Species on the Feast of Tabernacles (*Sukkot*),

The candelabrum and utensils from the Temple, borne in a Roman triumphal procession. A bas relief on the Arch of Titus, Rome

offering the paschal sacrifice and then eating it in a company within the Temple courtyards, bringing the First Fruits, and so forth. The commandment of pilgrimage to the Temple on Passover, Pentecost (*Shavuot*), and Sukkot, was one of the means by which ties were strengthened between Jerusalem and many of the Jews all over the country, and even the Diaspora. Many pilgrims for the Sukkot festival advanced their arrival in Jerusalem to Rosh ha-Shanah or at least to Yom Kippur, thus bringing about a considerable concentration of Jews in Jerusalem on the holidays. The Romans, too, were aware of the national significance of Jerusalem and the Temple, and instead of the half-sheqel tax that the Jews had been accustomed to bringing to Jerusalem, the Romans imposed a two-*dinar* tax which had to be sent to Rome. The sum was not large, and since the Romans could have increased one of the existing levies instead, it is clear that their intention in levying this tax was to humiliate the Jews and underline their defeat.

73

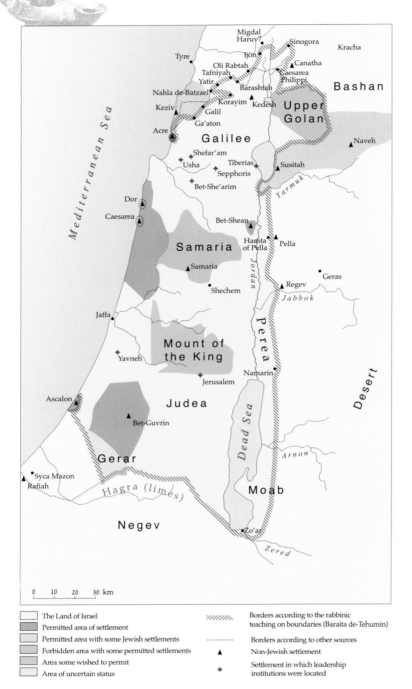

Legend:
- The Land of Israel
- Permitted area of settlement
- Permitted area with some Jewish settlements
- Forbidden area with some permitted settlements
- Area some wished to permit
- Area of uncertain status
- Borders according to the rabbinic teaching on boundaries (Baraita de-Tehumin)
- Borders according to other sources
- ▲ Non-Jewish settlement
- ◆ Settlement in which leadership institutions were located

The territory of the Land of Israel according to the *halakhah*

The failure of the First Revolt against the Romans had harsh consequences. The number of Jews killed, wounded and taken captive was immense. The captives were sold into slavery, as was the practice in those days. The Romans expropriated land in various places throughout the country, especially the lands of communities whose inhabitants had participated in the revolt. Some of these lands were transferred to lessees, who in turn employed tenant farmers. In this way, a man might find himself as a tenant farmer working on confiscated land which had been

in his family's possession for generations. However, the deepest crisis, the most dangerous of all for the existence of the people in its land, was the spiritual crisis. Whereas after the destruction of the First Temple Jews could find an explanation as to why the great disaster had befallen them in the preaching of the prophets, now, for those who witnessed the destruction of the Second Temple, that question remained unanswered. The unsatisfactory answer provided by the talmudic *aggadah* about Qamtsa and Bar Qamtsa – that their senseless hatred had led to the destruction of the Second Temple – only served to underline the mental distress that plagued those who lived in that age.

Talmudic literature well reflects the feelings of the people whose world had collapsed around them. We find sayings such as, "Since the day that the Temple was destroyed, a wall of iron has intervened between Israel and their Father in Heaven" (Babylonian Talmud, *Berakhot* 32b). The assertion that, "It were better for a man not to have been created than to have been created" (Babylonian Talmud, *Eruvin*, 13b), should be ascribed to the era of the Destruction; this statement expressed a pessimistic view as whether human life was at all worthwhile, considering it to be of no value. Among the apocryphal writings are two books – IV Ezra and the Syriac Apocalypse of Baruch – that reflect the despair and bewilderment that gripped the people after the destruction of the Temple. In a vein similar to the talmudic assertion, Baruch is portrayed as lamenting among the ruins of Zion and saying:

Happy is he who was not born or who was born and died. And we who live, woe to us that we see the calamities of Zion and what happened to Jerusalem… You, O farmers, sow no longer. And you, O soil, to whom shall you give the fruits of your produce? Keep within you the sweetness of your fruit. And you, O vine, why shall you continue to give your wine since none of it will any longer come close to Zion, and the first fruits will no longer be brought [to the Temple] …? (*Syriac Apocalypse of Baruch*, 10:6-10).

We learn from a *baraita* (a Tannaitic source) that mourning was expressed not only in speech and poems of lamentation, but for some of the people it also manifested itself in everyday life:

Our rabbis taught: When the Temple was destroyed for the second time, large numbers in Israel became ascetics, binding themselves neither to eat meat nor to drink wine, and their argument was: "Shall we eat meat which used to be brought as an offering on the altar, now that the altar is in abeyance? Shall we drink wine which used to be poured as a libation on the altar but is not longer?" (Babylonian Talmud, *Bava Batra* 60b, and parallels).

There are those who see the failure of the revolt, the loss of Jerusalem, and the destruction of the Temple as signifying the physical separation of the Jewish People from its land and the beginning of its tormented life of exile in the Diaspora, a life of persecution and tribulations. The common expression referring to "two thousand years of exile" of the Jewish People indicates in round numbers the period between the destruction of the Second Temple and the establishment of the State of Israel. This expression also found its way into the national anthem of the State of Israel, expressing "the two-thousand-year-old hope, to be a free people in our Land, the Land of Zion and Jerusalem." The attitude that sees in the destruction of the Temple the beginning of the Exile has a certain apologetic background that stems from the approach of Protestant Christian scholars of the nineteenth and early twentieth centuries. They viewed the destruction of the Second Temple as divine punishment of the Jewish people, and concomitantly saw nascent Christianity as the true successor of Judaism. Jewish scholars, beginning with the school of *Wissenschaft des Judentums* (the scientific study of Judaism) and the period of the *Haskalah* (Jewish Enlightenment), such as Heinrich Graetz, blindly followed in the footsteps of their Christian counterparts without sensing their apologetic motives.

Yet, despite the profound crisis of the Jewish People that resulted from the failure of the revolt, the destruction of Jerusalem and of the Temple, in 70 CE should neither be seen as the dividing line between independence and Exile nor as the date after which the nation was cut off from its homeland. First of all, it should be pointed out that independence did not come to an end in the year 70. In fact the Jews had only been independent under the Hasmoneans for a short period of time in the Second Temple era. Prior to the Hasmoneans, the Land of Israel was ruled by Persians, Ptolemies and Seleucids, and the destruction of the Temple itself occurred 133 years after the Roman conquest of the country. Furthermore, throughout the

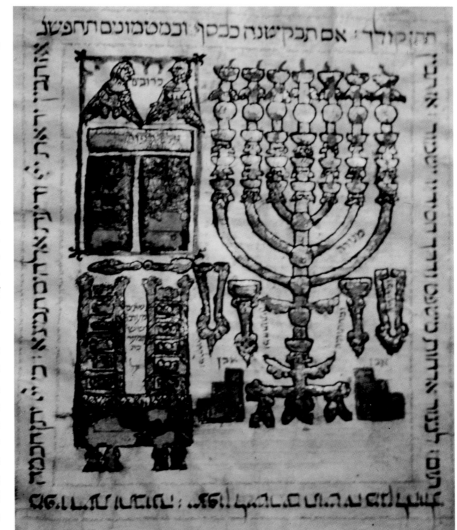

Page ornamented with Temple utensils from the Toledo Bible, 1277 (BP, MS. Parma 2668, fol. 7r)

entire Second Temple period many Jews resided in the Diaspora; in fact, some believe that more Jews lived in Egypt alone than in the Land of Israel. Even more important, the year 70 did not bring an end to a significant Jewish presence in the country. Many Jews stayed put; many rural properties remained in their owners' possession in spite of everything; the economic situation gradually stabilized after the economic crisis caused by the defeat; and most important of all, Rome allowed the Jewish people a great measure of autonomy and did not intervene in their conduct of religious life – this at a time when religious life was the most important of national values. The major manifestation of that autonomy were the leadership institutions comprised of the sages, at whose head, in time, stood a dynasty of *nesi'im* who claimed descent from Hillel the Elder. These institutions of self-government continued the tradition of the Pharisees of Second Temple times, and replaced the High Priest and the Great

75

חתנים ועל הארוס בפולמוס שלקיטס
גזרו על עטרות הכלה ושלא ילמד
אדם את בנו יוונית בפולמוס האחרון
גזרו שלא תצא הכלה בפיריון בתוך
העיר ורבותינו התירו שתצא הכלה
בפיריון בתוך העיר יח משמת
רבן יוחנן בן זכיי בטל זיו החכמה
משמת רבן גמלא הזקן בטל כבוד
התורה ומתה טהרה ופרישות משמת
ישמעא. בן פיאבי בטל זיו הכהונה
משמת רבי בטלה ענוה ויראת
חטא יט משמתר מאיר בטלו
משלי משלות משמת ר עקיבה
בטלו הדור שונים משמת בן עזיי בטלו
השוקדנים משמת בן זומא בטלו
משמת ר יהושע בטלרה
טובה מן העולם משמת רבן שמעון
בן גמליא בא וגביי ערות משמת ר
אלעזר בן עזריה פסקה העושרמן
החכמים משמת ר חנניה בן דוסא
בטלו אנשי מעשה משמת ר יוסה
קטונתן פסקו החסידים ולמה נקרא
שמו קטונתא שהיה קטנן שלחסידים
ג ר פינחס בן יאיר אומ מיום שחרב
בית המקדש בושו חבירים ובני חב
חבירין וחפו ראשן וידללו אנשי
מעשה במעשיהם וגברו בעלי זרוע
וגברו בעלי לשון הרע ואין דורש
ואין מבקש על מה לנו להישען על

אבינו שבשמים כא ר אליעזר הגדול
אומ מיום שחרב בית המקדש שרין
חכמיה למהוי כספריה וספריה
כתלמידיה ותלמידיה כעמא ועמא
כעמי אזלה ודלה ואין דורש ואין
מבקש ועל מה לנו להשען על אבינו
שבשמים כב בעיקבות המשיח
חוצפה יסגא ויקר יאמיר הגפן תתן
פריה והיין ביוקר והמלכות תהא
מינות ואין תוכחת כג בית ועער
יהיה לזנות והגליל יחרב והגבלן י
יישום ואנשי הגבל יסובבו מעיר
לעיר ולא יתחננו וחכמת סופרים
תיסרח ויראי חטא ימאסו והאמת
תהא נעדרת כד נערים ילבינו
וזקנים יעמידו מן הקטנים בן מנבל
אב בת קמה באימה כלה בחמותה
איבי איש אנשי ביתו דור שפניו
דומות כלב וגל מה לנו להישען על
אבינו שבשמים כה ר פינחס בן
יאיר אומ זריזות מביאה לידי נקיות
נקיות מביאה לידי טהרה טהרה לידי
קדושה לידי ענוה ענוה לידי יראת
חטא חסידות חסידות לידי רוח הזה
הקודש רוח הקדש ליה לידי תחיית
המיתים ותחיית המיתים באה לידי
אליהו זכור לטוב חסל סוטה
פר ט

Mishnah, Tractate *Sotah,* end of Ch. 9, Kaufmann Manuscript, HAS, Ms. A 50

**Section of mosaic floor of the synagogue at Hulda from the Byzantine period bearing a Greek inscription: "Blessing to the people,"
and a candelabrum, shofar (ram's horm), incense shovel, *etrog* (citron), and a *lulav* decorated with myrtle leaves**

Sanhedrin that had convened in the Chamber of Hewn Stone in the Temple. These institutions became so powerful that they had authority not only over the Jews of the Land of Israel, but also over those living in the Diaspora. Hence it is clear that though the destruction of the Temple did indeed constitute, from certain points of view, the end of a period in the history of the Jewish people in its land, it did not signify the beginning of the era of Exile in Jewish history.

. . . .

Rabban Yohanan ben Zakkai and His Work

Rabban Yohanan ben Zakkai established these institutions of self-government. Even during the First Revolt he had tried to conduct a rational policy and curb the zealots for whom the end justified the means. When he saw the coming defeat, he fled from Jerusalem at the height of the rebellion and conducted negotiations with the Romans. As a result, he was sent to Yavneh in the coastal plain, an area where most of the inhabitants were pagans, which was the usual Roman practice for people who had

come to terms with them. The Roman attitude towards him was apparently one of "Respect him and suspect him." They were quite pleased that an important figure had abandoned rebellious Jerusalem. However, they preferred to have him reside in an area where he would not have the Jewish-populated hinterland necessary for raising the banner of revolt, should he wish to do so for any reason. Rabban Yohanan ben Zakkai, together with some of his disciples, succeeded in establishing a center of leadership in Yavneh that served to a certain extent as a substitute for Jerusalem. This made it possible to partially fill the vacuum created by the destruction of the Temple, and enabled the continued maintenance of Jewish religious and national life in the Land of Israel. For example, setting the calendar – that is, proclamation of the new moon and calculating leap years, which had been performed by the Great Sanhedrin in Second Temple times – was now transferred to Yavneh. The calendar played a particularly important role in setting the cycle of Jewish life. Thus, whenever any group seceded from the mainstream of Judaism, this was also expressed in the establishment of its own calendar. The fact that the new moon was proclaimed, and leap years were calculated in Yavneh reflects the authority of the leadership institutions there. It also reflects the extent of their hegemony over Jewry both inside and outside the Land of Israel.

R. Joshua ben Hananiah, one of the outstanding disciples of Rabban Yohanan ben Zakkai, stood up in opposition to those despairing Jews who abstained from meat and wine and lived their lives – if it could be called living – in the shadow of the destruction of the Temple. In the continuation of the passage cited above from *Bava Batra* is a dialogue of sorts that he conducted with them to show them that the path they had chosen was hopeless, and it could only lead to personal and national oblivion:

מקדש אור חמדתי זכור וכרתיהו

ומכתלי ביתי
נבר כי שחתיהו

ועל ראש שמחתי
בין עיני שמתהו

A memorial of the Destruction at the entrance to a building on David Yellin Street in Jerusalem

He [Rabbi Joshua] said to them: "If that is so, we should not eat bread either, because the meal offerings have ceased." They said: "We can manage with fruit." "We should not eat fruit either," [he said], because there is no longer an offering of firstfruits." "Then we can manage with other fruits" [they said]. "But, [he said], we should not drink water, because there is no longer any ceremony of the pouring of water." To this they could find no answer, so he said to them: "My sons, come and listen to me. Not to mourn at all is impossible, because the blow has fallen. To mourn overmuch is also impossible, because we do not impose on the community a hardship which the majority cannot endure... The sages therefore have ordained thus: A man may stucco his house, but he should leave a little bare... A man can prepare a full-course banquet, but he should leave out an item or two... A woman can put on all her ornaments, but leave off one or two (Babylonian Talmud, *Bava Batra*, 60b).

Thus did Rabbi Joshua bring the claims of those ascetic Pharisees *ad absurdum*, by following with them their own line of reasoning, that a man cannot enjoy something that ostensibly fell into abeyance with the destruction of the Temple. His final point was that if they wished to abstain from any food or beverage

that had formerly served in the Temple form of service, then they should not even drink water, for when the Temple stood in all its grandeur, the ceremony of libation with water was celebrated during the festival of Sukkot. Therefore, R. Joshua set the trend that exists in Judaism until our own times: a man must indeed "Exalt Jerusalem over all his joys," and he must constantly bear in mind the destruction of the Temple. This, however, must be done in degree, symbolically, without smothering the joy of life. This mode of conduct was without doubt a means for coping with despair; however, it still did not provide a solution for the vacuum created with the destruction of the Temple.

The problem of ensuring the continuation of Jewish national life without Jerusalem and without the Temple was resolved by the ordinances enacted by Rabban Yohanan ben Zakkai and his successor, Rabban Gamaliel, with the participation of all members of the leadership institution of the Yavneh sages. These ordinances were rulings of *halakhah* made to cope with specific circumstances. In this case they were guided by two principles: the first, elements of Divine worship in the Temple should be transferred to Yavneh or to any Jewish community; and second, new content should be cast into religious frameworks that had been emptied of their substance. In this manner, the sages of Yavneh sought to avoid breaking off from the line followed by Pharisaic Judaism of Second Temple times, while simultaneously making it possible to maintain the fullness of Jewish life without Jerusalem and without the Temple.

This can be easily demonstrated through the following ordinance relating to the Four Species on the festival of Sukkot: "Originally, the *lulav* [palm fronds] was waved in the Temple for seven days and throughout the country for one day; after the Temple was destroyed, Rabban Yohanan ben Zakkai ordained that the lulav be waved throughout the country for seven days in memory of the Temple" (Mishnah, *Rosh ha-Shanah* 4:3; *Sukkah*, 3:12). In other words, while the Temple stood, the lulav was waved in the Temple on every day of Sukkot, while elsewhere only on the first day of the festival. A study of the origins of the commandment dealing with the Four Species leads to the conclusion that waving them apparently formed part of the ceremony of offering sacrifices, as the people circled the altar with their lulavim. Waving the Four Species outside the Temple on the first day of Sukkot was done principally as a counterpart to the main ceremony inside the Temple. After the Temple was destroyed, one might have argued that in the absence of the sacrifices, waving the lulav should no longer be practiced at all, even on the first day of the holiday. Rabban Yohanan ben Zakkai, however, ordained that after the destruction of the Temple, this commandment applied to every one of the seven days of Sukkot and should be done everywhere, on the grounds that this practice was "in commemoration of the Temple."

This ruling characterized the general approach of the leadership institutions in Yavneh towards reconstructing Judaism after the destruction of the Temple. It reflected a desire to have the best of both worlds: on one hand, Rabban Yohanan ben Zakkai severed the connection between the waving of the lulav and the Temple, allowing its performance anywhere, and this is the practice observed to this very day. On the other hand, he stressed that the change was being made "in commemoration of the Temple," as if proclaiming that this was not a new commandment but rather a continuation of Temple times and a remembrance of them, in the hope that "the Temple will soon be rebuilt" and that everything would be as it was. It should be pointed out that waving the Four Species on Sukkot is part of the public rejoicing that characterizes this holiday. A wreath as a sign of rejoicing was common throughout the Hellenistic-Roman world too, while among the Jews the Four Species were customary not only on Sukkot, but also constituted a symbol of public joy in general and rejoicing at a victory in particular. For example, both Judah the Maccabee, when he rededicated the Temple, and his brother Shimeon, when he conquered the Akra, waved a version of the Four Species. No wonder, therefore, that the Four Species were stamped on Jewish coins, and were also a major motif on reliefs and in synagogue mosaic floors.

Coin of the Bar Kokhba revolt, bearing the Four Species

Nor does it come as a surprise that Bar Kokhba himself organized a supply of the Four Species for his warriors. The Romans were well aware of the national significance of this commandment and banned it, as part of their persecutory decrees.

Likewise, Rabban Yohanan ben Zakkai ordained that the shofar should be blown in Yavneh on Rosh ha-Shanah (New Year) when that day fell on the Sabbath, just as had been done in the Temple. In this case too, the major element of this commandment had been performed in the Temple. The shofar had been blown over the sacrifices as they were offered. It had already been ordained, while the Temple still stood, that when the New Year fell on a weekday, the shofar would be blown everywhere, in parallel to the blowing in the Temple. Rabban Yohanan ben Zakkai now ruled that when Rosh ha-Shanah fell on a weekday the shofar would continue to be blown, just as during Temple times, even though the Temple had been destroyed and sacrifices were no longer offered. When Rosh ha-Shanah fell on the Sabbath, the shofar would be blown only at Yavneh, the seat of the leadership institutions. In this case, Rabban Yohanan ben Zakkai surely had an additional motive – to enhance the status of Yavneh as the center that to some extent replaced Jerusalem.

The following baraita preserves a discussion that relates to the enactment of this ordinance, reflecting something of the process by which Rabban Yohanan ben Zakkai instituted ordinances:

Our Rabbis taught: Once, New Year fell on a Sabbath and all the towns assembled, Rabban Yohanan ben Zakkai said to the Bene Bathyra: "Let us blow [the shofar]." They said to him: "Let us discuss the matter." He said to them: "Let us blow and afterwards discuss." After they had blown, they said to him: "Let us now discuss the question." He said to them: "The horn has already been heard in Yavneh, and what has been done is no longer open to

Head phylactery found at Qumran, 1ˢᵗ cent. CE

discussion" (Babylonian Talmud, *Rosh ha-Shanah*, 29b).

That is, in order to establish the ordinance, Rabban Yohanan ben Zakkai was forced to use his diplomatic skill and enact the ordinance by means of creating a precedent (*ma'aseh* in the vocabulary of the sages).

Rabban Gamaliel and His Work

One generation later, when Rabban Gamaliel was at the head of the Yavneh leadership institutions, their authority was further enhanced. Rabban Gamaliel himself belonged to the dynasty of Hillel the Elder, and his sons and their descendants served as nesi'im until the abolition of that office at the beginning of the fifth century. He won a measure of recognition from the Roman authorities as well, meeting with their officials in Palestine and in Syria, and set sail for Rome on more than one occasion.

In his ordinances, Rabban Gamaliel continued to transfer elements of the Temple service to every place. However, he also cast new content into the existing forms of the holidays. One ordinance enacted by Rabban Gamaliel appears in the Passover Haggadah, and is also in the Mishnah: "Rabban Gamaliel used to say: Whoever has not mentioned these

Ship in a floor mosaic from a villa in Lod, 3rd or 4th cent.

three things on Passover has not done his duty, and they are: *pessah* [the paschal sacrifice], *matzah* [the unleavened bread] and *maror* [bitter herbs]" (Mishnah, *Pesahim*, 10:5). In Second Temple times, people ate the paschal lamb in company in the courtyards of the Temple after the sacrifice, together with matzah and maror, according to the verse: "They shall eat the flesh that same night ... with unleavened bread and with bitter herbs" (Exodus, 12:8). After the destruction of the Temple, one might have said that since sacrifices were in abeyance, there was no reason to eat matzah and maror in the context of performing the Passover commandments. Now came Rabban Gamaliel and elevated matzah and maror to the same level of significance formerly given to the paschal sacrifice. True, the sacrifice itself could only be referred to, and therefore the Passover Haggadah says: "Whoever has not mentioned these three rulings" etc. But matzah and maror could be eaten while reciting the blessing: "... Who sanctified us

with His commandments and commanded us to eat matzah / maror...," just as is customary on the Passover Eve to this very day. However, eating matzah and maror could not of themselves be a proper solution to how to preserve the status of Passover. After all, in Second Temple times this festival focussed on pilgrimage and the paschal sacrifice, the only one that an ordinary Jew, and not a priest alone, was authorized to offer. Rabban Gamaliel and his contemporaries transferred the focal point of Passover from a public ceremony in the courtyards of the Temple to one celebrated within the family, wherever it may be, a ritual that also included reciting the story of the Exodus from Egypt and transmitting its lessons from generation to generation. From these developed the *seder* (the ritual ceremony and meal on Passover Eve) and its central element, the Passover Haggadah. The Day of Atonement (*Yom Kippur*) underwent a similar process. Rabban Gamaliel and his colleagues ordained that, whereas in the time of the Temple, the central element of this festival had been the service of the high priest in the Sanctuary, which reached its peak when he entered the Holy of Holies; now, in the absence of the Temple, the way to obtain atonement for sins would be through full repentance on the part of every individual Jew, no matter where he be.

The central element in Judaism that was meant to replace the Temple and its ritual was Torah study. It was at Yavneh that the principle, "Study of the Torah outweighs everything," was established. This, of course, also derived in great measure from the fact that the nation was led by a body of Torah sages. In Second Temple times a man was assigned his place on the social scale depending upon how fastidious he was about keeping the laws of purity and tithing – someone who strictly respected them was called a *haver* (fellow, associate), whereas those who made light of them were called by the pejorative term *ʿam ha-aretz*. After the destruction of the Temple the term *ʿam ha-aretz* was applied to those who did not study Torah, who did not turn up to hear the Sabbath sermons in the synagogues, who were lax in sending their sons to school and did not strictly fulfil commandments that reminded Jews of Torah study and its importance, such as *tefillin* (phylacteries), *mezuzah* or *tzitzit* (ritual fringes).

Rabban Gamaliel, unlike Rabban Yohanan ben Zakkai, did not limit himself to ordinances dealing with religious practice, which, as we have noted, was at the very center of national life in that era. He was also active in the areas of economics and society. An important ruling that was meant to preserve the physical connection to the Land of Israel and to restore agriculture, which was in dire straits following the revolt and the Roman repression, was the prohibition of raising small cattle (sheep and goats) in the settled parts of the country. After the destruction of the Temple, many left agriculture for pastoral stock-raising, some because their land had been confiscated by the Romans, others because of the economic crisis in the wake of the revolt and the prospect of easier profits from raising sheep and goats, not to mention less exposure to Roman taxation. However, what seemed advantageous had a flaw: sheep, and particularly goats, intensified the damage that had already been caused to agriculture, since they destroyed farm crops. Quite simply, a concrete danger was posed to the Jewish settlement in the Land of Israel. For this reason, a ruling was enacted that limited sheep- and goat-raising to arid zones and to groves of trees that did not bear fruit, where those animals could not cause any tangible damage. The following story about R. Judah ben Bava, who lived in the period when communal leadership was concentrated in Yavneh, exemplifies the importance of this ruling:

Passover *seder* from a manuscript Haggadah, Germany, 15ᵗʰ cent. (HLH, Cod. or. 8, fol. 37v)

They tell about Judah ben Bava that all of his deeds were directed for the glory of Heaven, except that he raised small cattle. It happened that he fell ill, and a physician came to him. He said to him: "There is no remedy for you except for boiling milk." He got himself a goat and tied it to the legs of his bed, and he would suck hot milk from it, and groan. One time sages wanted to come in to him. But they said: "How is it possible to come to him when there is a robber with him in the house?" And when he died, sages examined carefully all his deeds, and they found in him no sin except for that one. And he too said, when he was dying: "I know that I have no sin except for that one which I have done in transgressing the opinion of my colleagues" (Tosefta, *Bava Qamma*, 8:13).

Rabban Gamaliel and his colleagues began to formulate a system of ordinances with the object of keeping the lands of the Land of Israel in Jewish hands (these ordinances were reinforced after the Bar Kokhba revolt, and will all be discussed below), and invested great efforts in uniting the people. They understood that

81

after the traumatic destruction of the Temple, the factionalism that had characterized the nation at the end of the Second Temple era could no longer be tolerated. Therefore, whoever was willing to follow the path set by the Yavneh sages, the heirs of the Pharisees, was welcome, but whoever still opted for factionalism was expelled from the normative Jewish community. This explains several post-Destruction phenomena: the disappearance of the Sadducees from the Jewish social fabric; the choice made in the Yavneh period between the two schools of Pharisees and the decision that the halakhah would be according to the school of Hillel; repudiation of ʿamei ha-aretz who did not attend the synagogue and showed no interest in the Torah and its study; and rejection of Christianity by means of "the blessing of the *minim*" cursing the Christians, which became part of the Eighteen Benedictions prayer, as well as through various halakhic rulings and sayings.

The Bar Kokhba Insurrection and Its Aftermath

There were still some elderly persons alive, who had been youngsters in Second Temple times, when another revolt broke out, greater in intensity than any other Jewish uprising in antiquity, including the First Revolt that had culminated in the destruction of the Temple, even though the latter is often called "the Great Revolt." The more intense uprising was that of Bar Koziba (better known as Bar Kokhba), which was waged between 132–135 CE. This insurrection was the climax and the undoing of resistance to Roman rule in the Land of Israel. It was the last

Coin from Aelia Capitolina, struck by Hadrian

serious attempt, until Israel's War of Independence in 1947–48, to restore political independence to the Jewish people in the Land of Israel in order to establish there some form of a Jewish state.

The efforts of the institutions of leadership headed by Rabban Gamaliel to unite the nation laid the ground for national unity at the time of the revolt. We cannot assume that everyone joined in the revolt. Nevertheless, this was the only uprising during which no counter-movement emerged within the nation to oppose it, as had been the case when the Hellenized Jews rose up against the Maccabees, or the "Pursuers of Peace" (*rodfei shalom*) against the zealots when the Second Temple still stood. Some indication of the great number of rebels can be gained from the magnitude of the Roman forces that were required to suppress the revolt. The two legions stationed in Judea – the Tenth Legion *Fretensis*, garrisoned in Jerusalem, and the Sixth Legion *Ferrata*, stationed in Legio near Megiddo – could not quell the revolt. Even the reinforcements that came to their aid from the neighboring provinces – Syria, Arabia, and Egypt – were defeated by the insurgents. Some scholars believe this to have been the reason for the disappearance of the Twenty-Second Legion *Deiotariana* (garrisoned in Egypt) from the muster of the Roman legions. The Romans were forced to put the best general they had at that time – Julius Severus, governor of Britain – at the head of their troops. He mobilized entire legions and units of others from Europe (e.g., from Pannonia, in present-day Hungary). Quite justly, the revolt is named after its leader, because all the insurgents rallied together under the banner of Bar Kokhba, who also operated a quasi-state, minting coins, leasing lands, and so forth.

The main reason for the insurrection was apparently Hadrian's decision to rebuild Jerusalem as a Roman *colonia* (a city with the status of a colony), building a pagan temple in the city, and changing its name to Aelia Capitolina. "Aelia" was derived from the emperor's own name (Aelius Hadrianus) and "Capitolina," was in honor of Zeus, the chief of the Greek gods (Jupiter by his Roman name), whose seat in Rome was the Capitoline Hill. There may have been another motive for the insurrection, considered by some to be the only one: the Roman prohibition of the practice of circumcision.

Even a combination of the evidence provided by the literary sources and archaeological findings does not enable us to draw the full picture of the course of the insurrection. Most of the written testimony and the archaeological findings relate to the area of Judah, and it seems that this was the major arena of the revolt. It is reasonable to assume that Jerusalem fell to the insurgents, although there is no clear-cut proof. Perhaps they

Letter from Shimeon ben Koziba to the commander of one of the camps, Yesh a ben Galgula, threatening punishment ("I'll tie your legs") if his commands were not carried out

even began to rebuild the Temple, though there is no concrete evidence for this either. There certainly were those who wanted to restore the Temple, but perhaps the short time that Jerusalem was under their control, and this in the midst of warfare, did not enable them to begin that important task.

Various details about Bar Kokhba's activities as commander of the rebels and as director of the daily life of a quasi-state can be gleaned from contemporary documents that were preserved in the Judean desert caves. These documents have gained renown chiefly due to letters signed in the name of Bar Kokhba addressed to commanders of rebel units; land lease documents also signed in his name; and a family archive of legal documents brought to the caves by a woman named Babatha, a resident of Zoar to the south of the Dead Sea, who fled there at the time of the defeat. These documents cannot furnish us with a full description of the course of the revolt, as does Josephus Flavius' *War of the Jews* for the First Revolt. However, they contain random information of great value in various fields.

The talmudic literature often depicts the horrors of defeat in

bleak hues, dwelling especially upon the bitter fate of the Jews besieged at Betar. The last stronghold of the rebels, Betar lies just over ten kilometers southwest of Jerusalem. The Arab village of Battir preserves the ancient name. Near its ancient well were found remnants of inscriptions of the Roman legions that were brought to Judea to suppress the insurrection. The Arabs call a nearby hill Khirbat al-Yahud (the ruin of the Jews), and remains of the Roman siege encampments can still be identified around it. Talmudic legend attributes the fall of Betar to an act of treachery by the Samaritans, just as it points to their behavior as a cause for the outbreak of the revolt. In fact there were good relations between Samaritans and Jews at that time, for the Samaritans had suffered a fate similar to that of the Jews: in Shechem (Neapolis), too, the Romans had set up a pagan temple in the heart of the area populated by Samaritans, and perhaps they, too, were forbidden to practice circumcision. We do not know whether the Samaritans actively participated in the insurrection. However, it is inconceivable that they caused the revolt by instigating conflict between the Jews and the Romans,

83

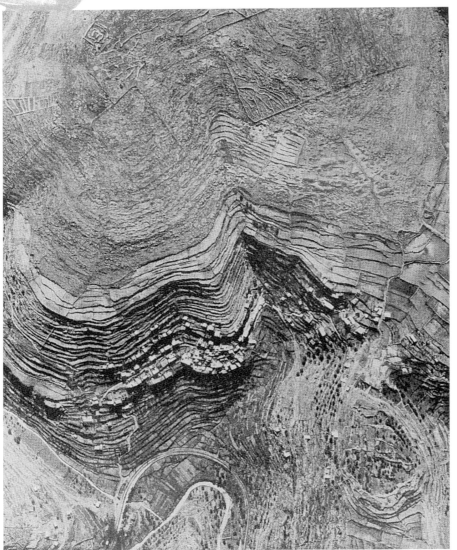

Aerial photograph showing part of the walls that surrounded the Roman encampments (at the top) above the ruins of Betar (lower right), Bar Kokhba's last stronghold

a snake was found coiled around him, indicating that history is merely a tool in the hands of the Creator. Some of the refugees from the revolt found their way to the Judean Desert caves. They eventually died under siege, but they left behind the documents mentioned above. The number of dead, of captives sold into slavery, and of refugees who abandoned the country was greater than after the First Revolt. Hadrian changed the name of the province from *Iudaea* to *Syria-Palaestina*. For the first time in history, the name Palestine was used to denote the geographical area of the Land of Israel. The Romans imposed a series of edicts on the Jews that are known in Jewish historiography as "The Decrees of Persecution." These struck at various aspects of religious life around which national existence revolved in that era. The purpose of the edicts was not to suppress the Jewish religion as such; rather they were meant to undermine those elements with national significance. Hence, the decrees did not compel Jews to violate prohibitory commandments, such as those that proscribed idol worship or eating forbidden foods. They were only prohibitions on fulfillment of positive commandments: the practice of circumcision; having recourse to rabbinical courts; ordaining sages; and assembling in synagogues. Also prohibited were tefillin, the mezuzah, waving the lulav on Sukkot, eating matzah on Passover, lighting lamps on Hanukkah, and so on. The picture that emerges is quite clear. It indicates that the Romans wanted to rule out the very possibility of any further insurrections as well as to punish the nation and strike at its religious and national substance.

The response of the people and the sages to the Decrees of Persecution was not a uniform one. A few complied and were even ready to abandon Judaism, the most famous among them being Elisha ben Avuyah, whom the sages called *Aher* (the Other) because of his apostasy. The majority, however, tried to carry on performing the now-forbidden commandments, but in secrecy and with modifications, so as not to be caught. Others openly

or that they led to the fall of Betar by promoting division among the Jews during its siege. The accusation leveled against the Samaritans by the talmudic sources reflects the relationship between Jews and Samaritans in the period of the *amoraim* in the third century. The strained relations resulted from the outcome of the Bar Kokhba revolt, since the Samaritans spread out to settlements beyond the hills of Samaria, both in the south of the country and in the coastal plain, taking over settlements that had been abandoned by the Jews in the wake of the revolt. The physical proximity between Samaritans and Jews created tensions due to religious differences and economic competition, leading to mutual estrangement and to the increasingly held view that the Samaritans were totally non-Jewish.

Bar Kokhba was killed in the fall of Betar. Legend has it that

Left – pair of sandals found in a basket in caves used by Bar Kokhba's men at Ein-Gedi
Right – a similar pair found at Masada which was destroyed in the First Revolt, about sixty years before the Bar Kokhba revolt

violated the Roman decrees, prepared to be martyrs for the sake of "the sanctification of the Name" (of God). The best known of the latter was Rabbi Akiva who, while in prison, disobeyed the prohibition to recite the Shem⸗a prayer and did not stop doing so even when he was being tortured and his flesh scourged with iron combs until he died. These acts created the norms of Jewish reaction to persecution and harsh decrees for many generations to come.

In the wake of the Bar Kokhba revolt, the national existence of the Jewish people in the Land of Israel was once again jeopardized. The number of captives sold into slavery was so great that the price of slaves fell sharply in all the markets of the Empire,

and in Judah a slave could be bought for the price of a horse's feed.

Between the Land of Israel and Babylon

Very many refugees abandoned the Land of Israel and migrated to Babylon. The Jews there were the only large Jewish community in the Diaspora at that time that was not under Roman rule. The Parthians, a Persian dynasty then ruling over Babylon, maintained a quasi-feudal system of government in which they gave the Jews much autonomy. This marked the beginning of the rise of the Babylonian Diaspora that eventually took over from the Land of Israel to a great extent. The first manifestations of two institutions that typified Babylonian Jewry throughout the age of the Talmud and the *geonim* – the exilarchate and the great *yeshivot* – already appeared in this early period.

A Babylonian sage named Hananiah, the nephew of R. Joshua ben Hananiah, tried to intercalate the years in Babylon. He believed that in view of the Decrees of Persecution and the turmoil prevailing in the Land of Israel, there was no body there that could deal with this important matter. On the other hand, the strength of the community in Babylon and the authority of its sages were sufficient, in his opinion, to determine the calendar there. In the meantime, however, with the rise of the Antonines to the imperial throne in Rome, the Decrees of Persecution were no longer enforced and the leadership institutions were gradually restored. The sages of the Land of Israel sent him a sharp message through two of their number – a clear warning that by

The anointing of David, a fresco from the synagogue at Dura-Europos (now in Syria)

85

his action, he was severing the Babylonian community from the Jewish People. In the end, Hananiah backed down and agreed that the calendar would be fixed in the Land of Israel. Nonetheless, the very attempt indicates what a blow the Land of Israel had suffered when the revolt failed, no less than it points

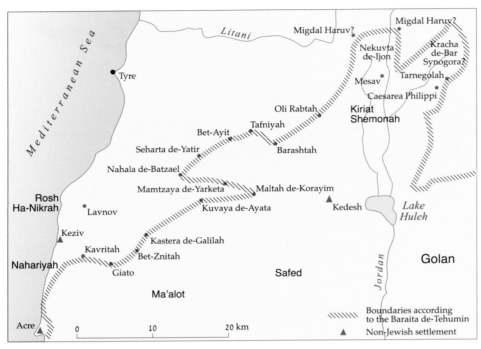

The borders of Jewish settlement in the Galilee

to the rising importance of Babylonian Jewry.

• • • • • • • • • • •

From Judah to Galilee

As a result of the failure of the Bar Kokhba revolt, the center of Jewish life in the Land of Israel shifted from Judah to Galilee. As we recall, Galilee had been less involved in the revolt than had Judah and therefore it suffered less from the Decrees of Persecution and could serve as a refuge for some of those fleeing them. A ruling was made in the Yavneh period, that a Jew was forbidden to purchase from the Roman authorities land that had been confiscated from another Jew. Following the Bar Kokhba revolt, as an ad-hoc ordinance in a time of national emergency, the sages annulled that ruling in regard to Judah and determined that a Jew could purchase land there without restriction. In contrast, the original ruling remained in effect in Galilee. We may make several important deductions about the history of the Land of Israel from the historical development of that ordinance, which the sources call "the Law of the Siqariqon." The first is that Galilee did in fact suffer less from the failure of the revolt.

The second is that the extent of lands sequestered from Jews in Galilee was not great enough to justify a change in the ordinance that would be harmful to the rights of the original landowner. As for Judah, however, we may infer that Jewish ownership of land there was so jeopardized as to justify putting the Law of the Siqariqon temporarily in abeyance. Nevertheless, the very fact that the sages dealt with these regulations indicates that there were Jewish buyers even for lands in Judah, indicating that Judah was not totally abandoned by its Jewish inhabitants, nor was it totally desolate, as more than a few scholars have claimed.

An illustration of the migration of refugees from Judah to Galilee may be found in synagogue inscriptions as well as talmudic traditions and early liturgical poems which show a connection between *mishmarot ha-kehunah* ("priestly courses") and Galilean villages. During Second Temple times, the priests serving in the Temple were divided into twenty-four courses that rotated among themselves. It was only natural for these to settle in Jerusalem and its vicinity. The connection of the priestly courses – without exception – to settlements in Galilee clearly demonstrates that refugees from the revolt migrated there.

The outstanding expression of the transfer of the Jewish center of gravity from Judah to Galilee after the Bar Kokhba revolt was the relocation of the leadership institutions to the north. The main step in the rehabilitation of the Jewish community after the revolt was the setting up anew of these institutions in Ushah. This occurred after a one-time sort of emergency conclave had been held in the Bet Rimmon Valley (which many researchers identify with the present-day Arab village of Rummana, located in the south of the Bet Netofa Valley). A unique testimony survived in the sources about the "constituent assembly" at Ushah:

At the end of the great persecution our teachers met together at Ushah, namely, R. Judah and R. Nehemiah, R. Meir, R. Yose, R. Shimeon bar Yohai, R. Eliezer, the son of R. Yose the Galilean, and R. Eliezer ben Jacob. They sent to the elders of Galilee saying: "Whoever has learnt let him come and teach, and whoever has not learnt, let him come and learn." They came together and studied and took all necessary steps (*Song of Songs Rabbah* 2:5).

The call issued by the sages of Ushah that was directed to the sages of Galilee at the end of the Decrees of Persecution indicates that they followed the policy set at Yavneh – placing study of the Torah at the center of Jewish life. Despite the economic crisis, the waves of emigration, and other dangers, they called on sages and their potential disciples to come join the leadership center in its role as a central academy for Torah study.

Together with their efforts to rehabilitate the leadership organs and restore their hegemony in fixing the calendar and other matters, the sages of Ushah devoted great efforts to extricating the economy from the crisis caused by the consequences of the revolt, and to restoring the status of the Land of Israel as the center of Jewish religious and national life. In this context, the sages of Ushah extended a series of ordinances aimed quite simply at preserving Jewish ownership of land. The original ordinances had already been laid down during the crisis after the First Revolt. They had forbidden selling land to non-Jews; even more, it was also forbidden to sell to non-Jews – or even to Jews who lived abroad – slaves or large cattle that provided labor for agriculture.

A marble fragment found in Caesarea with part of the list of the "priestly courses"

Strengthening the Jewish Community in the Land of Israel and Preventing Emigration

The sages of Ushah took great pains to curb emigration from the Land of Israel. The following passage may reflect upon their efforts:
A person should not go to settle abroad unless wheat goes at the price of two *seah*s [a dry measure] for a *sela* [a coin]. Said R. Shimeon: "Under what circumstances? Only in a case in which he does not find any to buy even at that price. But if he finds some to buy at that price, even [if] a *seah* [goes] for a *sela*, lo, he shall not go abroad." And so did R. Shimeon say: "Elimelech was one of the great men of his generation and one of the leaders of the community. And because he went abroad, he and his sons died of famine. But all the Israelites survived on their own land..." (Tosefta, *Avodah Zarah*, IV:4).

R. Shimeon ben Yohai, one of the most important sages in Ushah and Rabbi Akiva's outstanding disciple, who on another occasion came out in favor of migration from Judah to the Galilee, sharply opposed leaving the Land of Israel. He sought to institute a ruling that as long as one was capable of buying food, however high its price might be, he must not go abroad. With no little irony, R. Shimeon ben Yohai connects his ruling with what befell Elimelech, in the Book of Ruth. There is more than a hint here of the fate of wealthy men and communal leaders who leave the country, in contrast to the simple folk who stay behind and will experience the revival on their land. A legendary tradition graphically describes the efforts of R. Shimeon ben Yohai to stop

his disciples from even considering emigration:
There is a story concerning a disciple of R. Shimeon ben Yohai who went to India and came back laden with wealth. When he came in to visit R. Shimeon ben Yohai, and the disciples saw the profits he had made, they were envious. What did R. Shimeon do? He took his disciples and went out with them to a certain valley, and he charged the valley: "O valley, valley, fill up with golden denarii," and it filled up with them. He then said to his disciples: "Let each one of you take up his portion – all that you wish. But know ye, that by as much as each man takes up, he takes away from his reward in the world-to-come..." (*Midrash Tehilim*, 92:8).

It is during these years that we encounter, for the first time, persons who went abroad to study Torah there. This derived, of course, from a combination of the difficult conditions in the Land of Israel and the first flourishing of Babylonian yeshivot. One tradition about two sages of that time – R. Eleazar ben Shammuᶜa and R. Yohanan ha-Sandlar – reports that they sought to go to Babylon to study Torah at the *bet midrash* of R. Judah ben Batyra in Nisibin (this apparently refers to a town near Nehardeᶜa). But while they were on their way they had a change of heart and returned to the Land of Israel, saying: "Dwelling in the Land of Israel is equivalent to all the other commandments of the Torah put together" (*Sifre Deuteronomy* 80).

Rabbi Meir, another of the most important sages of Ushah, promises eternal life to everyone who fulfilled certain conditions, including living in the Land of Israel: "It was taught in the name

87

of Rabbi Meir, Whoever is fixed [in place] in the Land of Israel... will receive the good tidings that he has a place in the world to come" (Talmud Yerushalmi, *Sheqalim*, iii:47c). Clearly, this promise in itself reflects the extent to which the phenomenon of emigration caused concern to the sages, and to what extent they felt a powerful desire to curb it in any way possible.

The tendency to strengthen the Jewish community in the Land of Israel was also manifested in ordinances enacted by the sages of Ushah in regard to redeeming captives. For example, "Captives should not be ransomed for more than their value, as a precaution for the general good. Captives should not be helped to escape, as a precaution for the general good. R. Shimeon ben Gamaliel says: 'As a precaution for the good of the captives'." (Mishnah, *Gittin*, IV:6). It transpires, therefore, that despite their encouragement of the redemption of captives, the sages of Ushah took care that exorbitant ransoms should not be paid to redeem them, for in that case the opposite would be achieved since it would cause a rise in ransom fees and make it difficult to continue redeeming captives.

This corpus of ordinances, aggadot, and sayings attests that the concern of the sages of Ushah for the Jewish community in the Land of Israel – as a consequence of the Bar Kokhba revolt – led to a change in their attitude towards the Land. For the first time, an unambiguous position was taken and expressed in

A Jewish inscription in Greek found at Qatzyun in Galilee, in honor and for the welfare of the Roman emperors

the halakhah condemning emigration abroad and residence in the Diaspora, and extolling living in the Land of Israel. This reveals a kind of inverse ratio that, as will become clear below, became even more pronounced in the period of the amoraim: as the Jewish community declined in numbers and became weak in the Land of Israel, the importance of the Land of Israel increased in the Jewish *Weltanschauung*. In this connection, the

turning point was the aftermath of the Bar Kokhba revolt.

Rabbi Judah ha-Nasi and His Work

The time of R. Judah ha-Nasi was the golden age of Jewish life in the Land of Israel during the era of the Mishnah and the Talmud. It was a time of good relations with the Roman authorities and a flourishing economy. The autonomous leadership was invested in a *nasi* who wielded broad authority, a unique and commanding personality who brought the work of redacting the Mishnah to an end. Contemporaries of R. Judah ha-Nasi – to whom the written sources at times refer simply as "Rabbi", or "our holy master" – conceived of their days as being a sort of "beginning of redemption." Such a view emerges, for example, from the following anecdote:

It happened that R. Hiyya Rabba and R. Shimeon ben Halafta were walking in the Valley of Arbel at daybreak and they saw the light of dawn begin to shine. R. Hiyya Rabba said to R. Shimeon ben Halafta be-Rabbi: The redemption of Israel is like this; at first little by little, the more it progresses the larger it grows (Talmud Yerushalmi, *Berakhot*, I: 2c).

The Arbel Valley near Lake Kinneret (the Sea of Galilee) generally appears in traditions that emphasize the difficulties in times of crisis. Here it serves as a promise of hope, when R. Hiyya, one of the most important sages of Rabbi's time, compares the redemption to the dawn: both move so slowly that it is difficult to discern them, and suddenly they are overwhelming in the fullness of their intensity. We may draw parallels between the sages' image of R. Judah ha-Nasi and Bar Kokhba. They ascribed political messianism to them both, and the genealogy of both was ascribed to the royal House of David. They placed hopes for redemption in both, but Bar Kokhba wanted to attain instant redemption, through an uprising against Rome, while R. Judah ha-Nasi adopted a policy of one step at a time, while buttressing his leadership in contacts with the authorities and by drawing nearer to the urban Jewish aristocracy.

We do not know the exact dates of R. Judah ha-Nasi's lifetime. However, most of the period of his activity, which continued at least until 219 CE, coincided with the rule of the Severan dynasty (193–235). One of the factors accounting for the good relations that prevailed between Rabbi and the authorities may have been Jewish support of the founder of the dynasty, Septimius Severus, in his struggle for the imperial throne against Pescennius Niger, governor of Syria. After his victory,

Bet She⸗arim, on the border between the Jezreel Valley and Lower Galilee, was the seat of R. Judah ha-Nasi for a period of years. After his death it became a necropolis to which Jews were brought for burial from all over the country and the Diaspora

Septimius Severus withdrew the status of *polis* from Neapolis (Shechem), the city of the Samaritans, who had supported Niger. In contrast, he granted a series of privileges to the Jews, whose gratitude can be seen from a unique inscription from Qatzyun in the eastern Upper Galilee (near present-day Rosh Pinah) which is dated to 197 and may have been taken from a synagogue. The inscription blesses Septimius Severus and his sons and also mentions the emperor's wife by name.

One expression of the increased authority of the autonomous leadership under R. Judah ha-Nasi was their transfer, first to Bet She⸗arim and from there to Sepphoris. As already noted, they had first been reconstituted in Ushah when the Decrees of Persecution were no longer enforced. Sages had been active in the Jewish settlement of Ushah even before the Bar Kokhba revolt. R. Judah ben Ilai, who was pro-Roman to a certain extent, lived there. The traditions relating to the migrations of the Sanhedrin report a move from Ushah to Shefar⸗am, a place similar to its predecessor. Rabbi, for his part, first transferred the leadership institutions to Bet She⸗arim, whose lands had been in the possession of the authorities as early as the Hasmonean period. They were then transferred to the Herodian kings and then to the Romans. The latter bestowed the lands of Bet She⸗arim on Rabbi as a gift or through lease, just as he obtained lands from them in other regions of the Land of Israel. Transfer of the leadership

institutions to Bet She⸗arim reflected Roman recognition of their authority and devolvement of powers to them. Some years later, R. Judah ha-Nasi once more transferred the leadership institutions, this time to Sepphoris, one of the most important cities in Galilee, if not the most important at that time. Their location in a central polis was, of course, an indication of their enhanced authority in general and of the subordination of urban government institutions – which were controlled by the local Jewish aristocracy – in particular. Sepphoris had apparently already been awarded the status of polis by Hadrian early in his reign. The Severan emperors, who adopted a policy of urbanization in the eastern part of the Empire, granted such

A seven-branched candelabrum on a clay lamp from Summaqa, on the Carmel range

89

status to additional cities in Palestine. Thus, Septimius Severus conferred it on Lod (Diospolis) and on Bet Guvrin (Eleutheropolis). Under the Severans, Sebaste – and apparently Tiberias too – received the status of *colonia*. It may be that R. Judah ha-Nasi himself was connected with the conversion of Tiberias into a colonia, and in any case this can explain the transfer of the leadership institutions in stages from Sepphoris to Tiberias later on in the third century, in the time of his descendants. Thus was the process of putting the leadership institutions in the Galilee on a firm footing completed, one that had begun when enforcement of the Decrees of Persecution had ended. This development started with their reconstitution in Ushah and continued as they gradually gained strength while being transferred to Shefar°am, to Bet She°arim and to Sepphoris, and finally to Tiberias, which had now become a sort of capital of the Galilee.

R. Judah ha-Nasi issued many ordinances meant to bring about normalization of Jewish life in the Land of Israel and to strengthen Jewish presence there. An important group of such ordinances were those in which R. Judah's aims were compatible with the Roman authorities' policy of urbanization. These exempted Jewish residents of cities where most residents were non-Jews from performing the "commandments dependent on residence in the Land of Israel." These cities included Caesarea, Bet Shean, Bet Guvrin, and Ascalon. Nevertheless, he made it clear that the rulings did not remove these or other places from "the boundaries of the Land of Israel," and that "the impurity of the land of the non-Jewish nations" does not apply to them. It seems obvious that Rabbi's intention was to encourage Jews to

settle in these cities by granting them incentives, thus making it easier for them to compete economically with the non-Jewish residents. All this indicates a substantive transformation in the character and status of the cities of the Land of Israel in the time of R. Judah ha-Nasi, during the reign of the Severans. This was a tangible change from the policy of Hadrian which had been to encourage the Hellenization of the cities where Jews were dominant, including Tiberias and Sepphoris, and to transfer urban government to the pagan elements of the population.

· · · · · · · · · ·

The Crisis of the Third Century

The idyll of R. Judah ha-Nasi's time was cut short at the beginning of the period of the Land of Israel amoraim. This was due to the crisis in the Roman Empire that lasted from the end of the Severan period until the rise of Diocletian to the imperial throne (235-284). Though the crisis was principally an internal affair marked by instability and endless struggles for power in Rome, it naturally had an impact throughout the empire as well. Its greatest impact on the Land of Israel was a considerable increase in the burden of taxation that caused a profound economic crisis. This in turn led to deterioration in the status of the Jewish community in the country. The tax burden grew considerably when taxes levied ad hoc gradually became permanent. For example, the *annona militaris*, called *arnona* in talmudic literature, which was mainly a tax on crops, was imposed for the benefit of the army after permission had been granted by the central authorities. The instability of the regime and the many struggles connected to rivalry for the throne led to untrammeled collection of this tax until it was converted into a permanent one and was extended to livestock, clothing, and other basic commodities. Biblical commandment had forbidden cultivation of the land in the sabbatical year. Now conditions reached a point where R. Yannai, one of the most important of the first generation of amoraim in the Land of Israel, permitted sowing in a sabbatical year because of the burden of the arnona.

In similar fashion, the officials and the legions often imposed *angareia* (compulsory duties) and *akhsaniah* (billeting of troops) in an unrestrained manner. Angareia entailed placing men or beasts at the service of the authorities or the army, performing duties such as hauling loads or paving roads and maintaining them in good condition. Akhsaniah was an obligation imposed on a certain settlement, or on innkeepers, to lodge and feed passing government functionaries or army personnel in their homes. Another extraordinary tax of this period in the Roman

A fox on a mosaic found in Bet Guvrin, a Roman polis with a Jewish community in the talmudic period

Mosaic floor displaying the zodiac from the synagogue in Sepphoris, 5th cent

Empire – to what extent it applied to the Jews of the Land of Israel is not clear – was the *tironia*. It was the duty to provide soldiers for the Roman army or to redeem potential recruits with money. To all these should be added the regular annual taxes, the most notable of which were the poll tax and the land tax.

New waves of emigration from the Land of Israel to the Diaspora, particularly to Babylon, were the almost inevitable result of the continuing economic crisis. Once again, as in the Ushah period, the sages sought to curb emigration by condemning it through sayings and homilies, as well as by enacting oprdinances. Exemplifying the forceful stance of the amoraim in condemnation of emigration is an episode related by R. Hanina, the head of the Sanhedrin (court) in the first generation of the Land of Israel amoraim:

A priest came to R. Hanina. He said to him: "What is the law as to going to

Tyre to carry out a religious duty, namely, to perform the rite of *halitza* [releasing a widow from the obligation to marry her late childless husband's brother] or to enter into levirate marriage?" He said to him: "Your brother went abroad. Blessed is the Omnipresent Who has smitten him. And now you want to do the same thing?" (Talmud Yerushalmi, *Mo'ed Qatan*, iii:71c).

Side by side with a threatening tone toward the emigrants – in this case even the danger of death from Heaven – were other sayings and rulings that included various promises for whoever refrained from emigration, or for whoever immigrated to the Land of Israel. For example: "R. Yohanan said: Whoever walks four cubits in the Land of Israel is assured of a place in the world-to-come" (Babylonian Talmud, *Ketubot*, 111a). Nevertheless, that very R. Yohanan, head of the Sanhedrin in Tiberias in the second generation of the Land of Israel amoraim, advised those whose situation was hopeless to leave the country: "If your name is

91

mentioned for service on the city council, let the Jordan be your border" (Talmud Yerushalmi, *Mo'ed Qatan*, ii:81b). In other words, he whose name has come up as a candidate for the *boule* (city council) – a post that was desirable in normal times – would do well to cross the Jordan and go abroad. Otherwise, he would

A stone capital with a sculpted candelabrum, from the synagogue at Capernaum

end up impoverished because of his debts to the authorities and due to his responsibility for collecting taxes. In the eastern provinces of the Roman Empire during this period of crisis, it was common practice to abandon a place of residence on account of the tax burden – sometimes even by all the inhabitants.

Many maxims of the sages who lived during the imperial crisis of the third century focus on praise of burial in the Land of Israel, stressing its importance. According to these sayings, burial in the Land of Israel can atone for sins; furthermore, the deceased in the Land of Israel will be the first to arise from the dead when the Messiah comes, whereas those buried in the Diaspora will undergo the ordeal of rolling through tunnels to the Land of Israel. What lay behind this concept, which had its origins in the period after the Bar Kokhba revolt, is the desire to encourage the people to be in the Land of Israel, to increase immigration to the country, and to prevent emigration.

From this concept developed the practice – prevalent to the present day – of bringing deceased Jews from the Diaspora for burial in the Land of Israel. Thus Jews sought the best of both worlds: life in Babylon that freed them from the heavy burden of taxation that was then common in the Roman Empire, and atonement for sins that would ensure resurrection of the dead at the End of Days without undergoing the torments of rolling through tunnels. That the sages' attitude to such a phenomenon was ambivalent is indicated, for example, by a discussion conducted by amoraim in Tiberias in the third century, as they witnessed the arrival of corpses from abroad that were designated for burial in the city:

R. ben Qurya and R. Leazar were sitting and studying in a glass factory by Tiberias, when they saw coffins coming from abroad. Said R. Qurya to R. Leazar: "To these I apply the verse, in your lifetime 'Ye made My heritage an abomination' (Jeremiah 2:7), and in your death 'Ye entered and defiled My Land' (ibid.)." "It is not so," he replied, "for as soon as they reach the Land of Israel a clod of earth is placed on them which makes atonement for them. What is the proof? 'And His land maketh expiation for His people' (Deuteronomy 32:43)" (*Genesis Rabbah*, 96:30, p. 1240).

One of the speakers was openly critical of those who did not draw the proper conclusion from the words of the sages – to remain in the country or to immigrate to it during their lifetime. His colleague evinced satisfaction from the transfer of corpses from the Diaspora for burial in the Land of Israel, since this was undoubtedly economically beneficial; a whole industry had apparently developed around the cemeteries such as the necropolis in Bet She'arim or the burial places in Tiberias itself.

Despite the blow dealt to the Jewish community by the imperial crisis of the third century, there was still a considerable and significant number of Jews residing in the Land of Israel. Evidence of this are the Jewish settlements and their synagogues, dating from the talmudic period, that continued to be discovered in recent decades, particularly in Galilee but in Judah as well. Moreover, various anecdotes in the written sources unintentionally indicate that the Jews accounted for the great majority of the inhabitants of the Land of Israel, at least in certain areas of Galilee. For example:

R. Hanina once found a slaughtered kid between Tiberias and Sepphoris and he was permitted [to appropriate] it ... seeing that it was permitted to appropriate in the regard of the method of slaughter, the majority [in the area] must have consisted of Israelites… R. Ami found slaughtered chickens between Tiberias and Sepphoris; he came before R. Assi, while some say before R. Yohanan, and some say to the house of study; and they said to him: "Go, take for yourself" (Babylonian Talmud, *Bava Metzia*, 24b).

What emerges from such passages is that most of the travelers on the roads between Tiberias and Sepphoris were Jews, so much so that R. Hanina bar Hama, whom we have already encountered, was permitted to eat a slaughtered kid that he found there, on the presumption that it had been ritually slaughtered by Jews. Likewise, R. Ami, a third-generation *amora,* was permitted to eat slaughtered chickens that he had found between Tiberias and Sepphoris. In fact R. Yohanan ruled: "If a dead person [is found] between Tiberias and Sepphoris, it is taken for granted that he was an Israelite" (Talmud Yerushalmi, *Sanhedrin*, v:22c). That is to say, the Jewish majority in that region in the third century was so obvious that it was presumed that a dead person found in this area was a Jew. Similar conclusions emerge from testimony in the Jerusalem Talmud:

A roast kid was found on the road to Gofta, and it was permitted [to be eaten] because of two things, because it was found [in a Jewish area] and because most of the travelers on the roads [were Jews] ... and it was found

that it was from the house of Rabbi.... A round of cheese was found in the inn of a Levite and it was permitted [to be eaten] because of two things, because it was found [in a Jewish area] and because most of the travelers on the roads [were Jews] ... and it was found that it was from [the house of] R. Eleazar of the house of R. Yose (Talmud Yerushalmi, *Sheqalim*, vii:50c).

In the first case it was permitted to eat a roast kid that had been found on the road passing through Gofta, near Sepphoris, on the assumption that the travelers on the road were Jews, and indeed it was established that the kid had come from the house of Rabbi. In the second case, which occurred towards the end of the period of the amoraim, a round of cheese was permitted to be eaten that had been found in the inn of a Levite (in some of the versions: "the inn of Lavi", that is, an inn in a place called Lavi, near modern Lavi in Galilee) without fear of the ban on cheeses produced by non-Jews. Here too it emerged in the end that the cheese belonged to a Jew, to R. Eleazar of the house of R. Yose, of the fifth generation of amoraim of the Land of Israel, in the second half of the fourth century.

**The synagogue in Baram in Upper Galilee, built toward the end of the Roman period.
The facade and the impressive entrance face south toward Jerusalem**

Gilded glass saucer depicting the Temple utensils, the Holy Ark, and lions from the catacombs in Rome, 4th cent.

· · · · · · · · · · · · · · · · · · · ·

The Byzantine Period

Oded Irshai

The period between the fourth and the seventh centuries CE was one of momentous change for the history of the Land of Israel and its inhabitants. Increasingly during that period, the history of the country was no longer one with the history of the people that had lived there for hundreds of years. Gradually, the Land of Israel was no longer predominantly settled by Jews, most of whom were still concentrated in Galilee (though not all of it) and on its environs (in the Golan), while most of the country's territory and much of its non-Jewish population were won over by Christianity, now master of the land under the aegis of the Roman empire. The Jews had lost their institution of central leadership, the *nesiut* (patriarchate), their copious literary legacy was redacted and completed, and the status of the centers of their spiritual creativity – the *yeshivot* – was in decline. In their stead a strong movement of decentralization occurred in which the status of local communities was enhanced, communities whose public life was centered around their synagogues where liturgical poets, preachers, and interpreters from Hebrew into Aramaic were active. In the words of the *midrash* (homily): "A small city, that is a synagogue, and the few people there – that is a community" (*Ecclesiastes Rabbah* 9:14). The void created among Diaspora Jewry which until then had been under the leadership of the Land of Israel was increasingly being filled by the Jewish center in Babylon, which from the end of the Byzantine period was to lead the world of Jewry for many generations. The saga of the Land of Israel and its Jews in that period is therefore one of how its Jewish center was stripped of the forces and institutions that had unified it and been the source of its strength for a lengthy span of time.

The status of Christianity, on the other hand, and its hold upon the country changed beyond recognition. From the fourth century onwards, Palestine became a focus of interest for many Christians who, with the help of emperors and kings, transformed the utopian religious vision into reality. The barren country was imbued with sanctity and became *Terra Sancta* (the Holy Land). This transformation is reflected in the fact that most of our knowledge about the history of the Holy Land and its inhabitants, both Jewish and non-Jewish, has come down to us from Christians, who are represented in this period as victors. In the words of an anonymous contemporary Jewish liturgical poet: "We do not have the splendid attire of the *kohen* [priest], and the wearers of sackcloth [monks] rule over us." The writings of Church Fathers active in Palestine (Biblical commentaries, polemics, and letters galore), together with the travel itineraries of pilgrims from East and West, liturgical texts and rites narrate the history of that era. True, some of the everyday experiences of the Jews of the Land of Israel and their spiritual world are also presented to us in Jewish sources: fragmentary collections of rabbinic legal *midrashic* texts (homiletic interpretations of the Bible) and *piyyutim* (liturgical poetry) as well as in apocalyptic works.

95

A tombstone from Zo'ar at the south end of the Dead Sea, early 5th cent. The inscription is in Aramaic and Hebrew: "... Three hundred and eighty-six years since the Destruction of the Temple... Peace upon Israel"

"The Empire Converts to Heresy"

The second half of the third century CE was a difficult period for the Roman Empire, especially in the Near East. There it faced a regional superpower in the form of Sassanid Persia which from the fourth decade of that century encroached upon the territory of Rome's eastern provinces and dealt it severe defeats. External difficulties were compounded by many domestic problems: the declining authority of the traditional institutions of government, paralleled by the ushering in of an age of soldier-emperors reflecting the increasing power of the legions, who for several decades crowned and dethroned numerous rulers in Rome, not to mention many attempts at usurpation. The deep political crisis was accompanied by a no less severe economic one which intensified the sense of utter futility on the part of the Empire's citizens. These feelings were especially intense in the East, creating a wave of apocalyptic expectations for the approaching demise of Rome.

Such hopes, and the great resentment against Rome's desert client kingdoms that came to her defense, were also echoed in the Jewish academies in the Land of Israel. A dialogue from the close of that century, quoted in a midrash in *Genesis Rabbah*, illustrates that point:

A *hegemon* [a Roman military officer] asked a man of the House of Silena [a respected Jewish family in Tiberias]: "Who will seize [power] after us?" He [of the House of Silena] brought a piece of paper, took a pen and wrote on it: "Then his brother emerged, holding on to the heel of Esau; they said: See old things from a new old man" (*Genesis Rabbah* 63:9).

In many of the homilies created in that period, future redemption was seen as dependent on the various internal conditions and external forces that would hasten Rome's collapse. The period indeed was characterized by the Jews' further distancing themselves from messianic activism. The memory of the unsuccessful past revolts against Rome had not yet faded away. Political realism was combined with existing apocalyptic schemes of various dimensions, and the Sages put their trust in the mighty power struggles being waged in the East. The primeval mythological tension between East and West and its corollary in the form of the somewhat prevalent apocalyptic tradition that the downfall of Rome would come from the East was combined

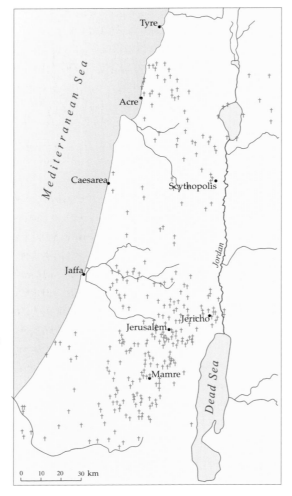

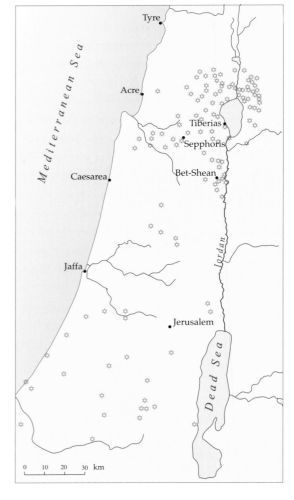

Left: Dispersion of Christian settlements in Palestine in the Roman- Byzantine period

Right: Dispersion of Jewish settlements in Palestine in the Roman-Byzantine period

with (or should we say, underlay) this geopolitical reality. Indeed, some of the political and military events of the period reinforced this feeling. For example, in the late sixties of the third century the Palmyrene desert princes rebelled against Rome and, led by their legendary queen Zenobia whose fame had spread far and wide, conquered extensive regions of the Roman East, even reaching distant Egypt. This episode of revolt against Edom (a designation for Rome in the Sages' vocabulary) was in fact quelled fairly quickly. However, it surely awakened the secret hopes of people in the region. The connection thus created by the Sages between their realistic outlook and their messianic expectations imparted to many events an extraordinary historic imagery and transformed them into important links in the process of redemption which focussed on bringing down the Fourth Kingdom, that is Edom – the evil Roman Empire. Not surprisingly, similar sentiments were held by pagan circles, as can be gleaned from the Thirteenth Sybillic Oracle.

Towards the end of the third century, it seemed that conditions had ripened for Rome's complete collapse. It was then that a Dalmatian cavalry officer, Diocletian, seized power late in November 284 under somewhat suspicious circumstances. People thought that he, like his predecessors, would not last long. In a Land of Israel midrash he is portrayed as the "last king of Edom."

However, much to the chagrin of the Sages precisely this emperor, whom they mockingly called "swineherd" in order to stress his lowly origin, succeeded in maintaining his rule for some two decades, finally relinquishing it of his own free will. Diocletian demanded that his subjects receive him with rituals of adoration of a quasi-divine nature. He set the empire on a new path by presenting a new political model of orderly, planned succession to power. His steps were intended to give the Empire political, defensive, and economic stability. As to the affairs of the Roman Orient, he redistributed territories among the provinces: those south of Provincia Arabia (southern Transjordan, including the Petra area) were transferred to the authority of Provincia Syria-Palaestina. This new division made the latter province the largest and most important of those in proximity to the Arabian desert which bordered on Sassanid territory.

In addition to these quite significant administrative changes, Diocletian created a unifying religio-political mechanism through which he led the entire empire towards a monarchy under the exclusive aegis of two of the prominent gods of the Roman pantheon, Hercules and Jupiter. At the core of the

Diocletianic revival stood the emphatic introduction of a new imperial theology by which the Tetrarchic rule represented a system of divine cooperation with the temporal monarch, which in essence extremely resembled Christian theological constructs.

The ruins of Palmyra, painting by Margaret Thomas, early 20ᵗʰ cent.

It was precisely these far-reaching steps, taken with the objective of creating governmental stability and renewing the ancient Hellenistic ideal of a monarchy representing a god, that in fact prepared the ground for the revolutionary measures of the first Christian emperor, Constantine the Great, who joined the imperial leadership in 306 at the height of the great persecutions of the Church and its believers. It was the growing affinity of ideas between the pagans and the Christians that seems to have led to increasing pagan-Christian tension.

Pagan animosity towards Christians broke out in full force throughout the Empire when imperial decrees were enacted early in the fourth century, between 305 and 312, enforcing above all public display of cultic sacrifice. The exact scope of the persecutions is not known. However, an important, detailed source documenting these acts of persecution was compiled precisely in Palestine by a man subsequently known as "the father of Christian historiography," Eusebius, bishop of Caesarea. In his *Martyrs of Palestine* he recorded at length the lives, and especially the trials, of Christians, both those from throughout the country and those brought from Egypt to stand trial, those who were executed and those who were sentenced to banishment and hard labor. This Christian ordeal which, according to Eusebius, surpassed any similar event elsewhere in the Empire, where the Christians were more than once exposed in their weakness, can be said with hindsight to have been a kind of sacrificial altar on which the country was presented to the Christians. For the Jews,

97

Remains of the Roman hippodrome on the outskirts of Tyre

transformation in the character of Rome have not come down to us, found some consolation in the change, and the form of their expectations of Redemption adjusted to the new reality. They were no longer faced with the difficulties of Rome's *Realpolitik* at home and abroad; they were now concerned with the religious changes in the Roman Empire which had not yet been completed. The conversion of the emperor foreshadowed the Christianization of the Empire as a whole, now conceived of as part of the process of redemption. The description of the eschatological scheme in the process of Redemption in an interpolation to Mishnah *Sotah* (9:15): "And the Empire will be converted to the heresy" [i.e., Christianity], was reformulated by a contemporary sage: "Rabbi Isaac said: Until the **whole** Empire is converted to the heresy" (Babylonian Talmud, *Sanhedrin*, 97a). By this textual emendation not only was the estimated time of the End of Days postponed, but, paradoxically, the Jews joined with the Christians in seeking to hasten the transformation, though for opposing motives. After all, prominent Church Fathers (such as the Caesarean Origen) also believed that salvation would come about only as a consequence of the spread of the Christian faith among the nations of the world. Christianization of the empire presented Constantine with an extraordinary opportunity to harness the imperial system – politically, militarily, and economically centralized as it was – which had undergone an organizational transformation, in the service of a universal religion possessing a heritage, authority, and a well-established missionary apparatus. In the eyes of the Sages, this radical change apparently symbolized the transition of Rome from a nation and a state which placed a heavy yoke on the Jews but at the same time tolerated them to the utterly polar opposite to Judaism. Under such conditions hostility intensified between Caesarea (the seat of the Roman governor) and Jerusalem, of which it was said that they could not endure together under one roof. "That Caesarea is laid waste and Jerusalem flourishing, or that Jerusalem is laid waste and Caesarea flourishing, believe it" (Babylonian Talmud, *Megillah*, 6a).

Therefore, when the empire (pagan Rome) was delivered into the tight grip of the (Christian) heresy, this was apprehended as a step from which there was no going back. The situation urgently called for Redemption. With this in mind we can understand the phrase of R. Isaac quoted above, that there still remained some delay since the Son of David does not come until the **whole**

the internal tension that accompanied the persecutions may have added another dimension to the wobbly image of the state and to their sense of its approaching end, but they were to be disappointed. Rome did not collapse, it merely changed its appearance. The young pagan emperor, Constantine the Great, emperor of the West during the years of the "great persecution," undertook at that very same time a policy of appeasement and tolerance towards the Christians in the area under his control. Quite dramatically (according to later traditions), at the end of the persecutions (312), when he had already risen in the hierarchy, he became a Christian. This act continues to this very day to perturb and astonish scholars.

The conversion of Constantine, who would ten years later become the sole, unchallenged ruler of the empire, was to have a decisive influence on the nature and character of Palestine. The Land of Israel sages, whose explicit reactions to this great

Empire has converted to the heresy (i.e., Christianity). R. Isaac was followed in this by the renowned fourth-century Babylonian sage Rava who adopted terminology taken from the biblical laws of leprosy: "What is the meaning of the verse, He has turned **all white**" (Leviticus 13:13; *Sanhedrin*, loc. cit.). Thus, Rava's explanation compared heresy and leprosy in the following manner: that just as when leprosy has completed its spread throughout the body, then – quite paradoxically – it is healed and purified, so too when heresy (i.e. Christianity) has completed its takeover of the Empire, then the time of Redemption has finally come. It was apparently no coincidence that use was made of this simile, which was probably part of the polemical aura that adhered to the image of Constantine. For among the legendary traditions that sprouted up around the emperor, prominent was the one about Constantine's encounter with the Bishop of Rome, Sylvester, describing the circumstances of Constantine's conversion. According to this legend, while the Christians were being hounded to death and Sylvester had gone into exile, Constantine became severely afflicted with leprosy. Whereas his physicians and other savants failed to find a cure for his illness, priests of the Capitoline temple in Rome proposed that he come to their temple and immerse his body in the blood of infants. Constantine, horrified by this proposal, stopped his chariot on the way to the temple and in an address to the masses resolutely declared that it was unfitting for a warrior such as himself to be healed in that manner. He immediately commanded that the babies that had already been brought to the temple be returned to their mothers' bosoms. That very night the important saints of Rome, Peter and Paul, appeared to the emperor in his dream and promised him salvation and healing by means of the immersion (baptism) that the exiled Sylvester would conduct for him, and so it happened. Following his cure, the emperor tied his fate to that of the Church, promulgated decrees for its benefit, and was personally involved in the renovation and renewal of the Church of Rome. Could it be that this legend found its way, at least as an allusion, into the midrash?

For this reason it was said, When a person has on the skin of his body a swelling, a rash, or a discoloration, and it develops into a scaly infection on the skin of his body; and so forth (Leviticus 13:2). The text speaks of [four] kingdoms. A swelling is Babylon... a rash is the kingdom of the Medes... a discoloration is the kingdom of Greece... a scaly infection is the kingdom of evil, Edom [= Rome], that the Holy One Blessed Be He afflicts with leprosy, and likewise its prince [= the emperor] (*Midrash Tanhuma, Tazri'a*, 11)

From now on, apparently, the "Fourth Kingdom" was

Red marble statue discovered at Caesarea. It was apparently a complete figure representing Hadrian, and stood in the temple erected in his honor in the second century

identified with the Church and not with pagan Rome, as in the earlier sources.

Immediately after Constantine gained control over the whole empire, he began to put into practice his plan to convert Palestine to Christianity.

· · · · · · · · · ·

The Creation of the "Holy Land" – the Appropriation of Palestine by the Church

Palestine and Its Population

While Constantine was conceiving his plan Palestine was inhabited by various ethnic groups. The earliest inhabitants, who also claimed ownership to it – the Jews – were densely settled

99

only in part of the country. The overwhelming majority of the Jewish population had for some time been concentrated in Galilee (mostly in Lower Galilee, others in Upper Galilee and the Golan Heights). Groups of Jews also lived in the areas of the *Darom*, the south (sometimes demarcated as the area between the *Shephelah* – the Lowlands – of Lod [Lydda] and the northern Negev, however, more often it signified the vicinity of Bet-Guvrin and the northern Judean Desert), some of them in cities and towns of mixed population, and some in villages of their own, as recorded in the *Onomasticon* (a book of biblical and post-biblical place names drawn up by Eusebius, bishop of Caesarea, for the benefit of students of the Bible). Of course, Jews also inhabited the coastal plain, living in the Hellenized cities with their mixed population of pagans and Christians, such as Caesarea, Ascalon, and Gaza. Nevertheless, the greatest change that the Jewish community of the Land of Israel underwent following the Bar Kokhba Revolt was its so-called "exile" from Judea to Galilee, though its scope is not entirely clear. It was precisely that region of the country in which the Gospel to the Gentiles had begun that was now inhabited by those who rejected

Ramat Mamre near Hebron. Christian sources from the Byzantine period relate that Jews were sold into slavery here after the Bar Kokhba Revolt for the price of a portion of horse's feed

it, and in the past had even persecuted its bearers. This was surely a difficult state of affairs for Eusebius and his contemporaries.

The void left behind in Judea was filled to only a limited extent by pagans. This can be ascertained by the dissemination of cultic activities in the region. Examples are the site dedicated to Adonis, in the vicinity of Bethlehem, or the lively pagan fair at Mamre, near Hebron, in which Jews also took part; and especially

Jerusalem, named Aelia Capitolina by Emperor Hadrian. Aside from these famous centers, there was a significant population void in Judea, the nature and scope of which have not yet been sufficiently clarified. Over the course of the fourth and fifth centuries, it was filled by Christians. It is difficult to ascertain with certainty the composition and origin of the new inhabitants. Were they mostly local pagans who converted to Christianity, or were they also Christian pilgrims who were drawn to Judea and settled there, or did they also include Judeo-Christians or even Jews who had converted to Christianity?

We may learn from works that predate the formulation of the concept of "the Christian Holy Land" about the deep aspirations that might have motivated hopes for a Christian hold on Palestine at the beginning of the Byzantine period. These elements are notable in the early works of Eusebius, the *Onomasticon* and the *Martyrs of Palestine*. The first, more than fulfilling the immediate needs of Paulinus, bishop of Tyre (ca. 313–329), for aid in interpreting the Bible (as he himself had requested from Eusebius), was the consummation of the tacit wishes of its author to record the successful Christian efforts to settle in the Holy Land, and perhaps also to sketch the outlines of future Christian settlement while basing it on the appropriation of local historical traditions. Thus, for example, Eusebius commented that the city of Jericho – which had been privileged to have the presence of the Savior – had been destroyed, like Jerusalem, because of the lack of faith of its inhabitants, and had been rebuilt a third time. The age-old historical and symbolic connection between Jerusalem and Jericho was fostered through Jewish traditions. It is easy therefore to discern, through Eusebius' hints, a desire to continue this connection, albeit in a new wrapping. For later Christian clerics as well as pilgrims, the territory between the Jordan, Jericho, and Jerusalem would become a new Christian terrain, perhaps in no small measure by virtue of the image that had taken shape in works like the *Onomasticon*.

Though less clearly, this concept also emerges from the second work, which was mainly an attempt to draw the map of Palestinian Christian martyrology at the beginning of the fourth

The Fount of David waterfall near Ein Gedi, an important Jewish settlement in the Byzantine period

101

century. Indeed, Galilee is missing from Eusebius' accounts. However, the scene of Christian martyrdom stretched from Bet-Shean to Gaza. Thus, this territorial span was sanctified not only by virtue of the early traditions describing events that had transpired there but also by virtue of the warm, spurting blood of the martyrs.

The Christianization of Palestine: The Process and Its Implications

The Christians who came to Palestine found there, of course, a wealth of elements that together shaped their collective memory. Palestine in general and Judea in particular were strewn with places and sites where biblical stories and episodes in the life and death of Jesus had occurred. In late third-century Jerusalem, the destroyed Jewish Temple (there is doubt as to whether an actual pagan compound had stood on its site) faced the temple of the goddess Venus-Aphrodite. On the ruined foundations of the city with a past common to both Jews and Christians alike, a pagan city lacking historical roots had arisen which sought to obliterate this historical memory. However, rootless pagan Jerusalem, just like similar places elsewhere in the country, could not overcome the vivid, deeply rooted memory. Thus, faced by the process described earlier, it was not difficult for the Palestinian Christian establishment to dispossess the centers of pagan worship. Unlike other parts of the empire, the Christianization of Palestine did not begin with the conversion of its inhabitants to Christianity, but with annexation of the traditionally hallowed areas. The process of shaping the sacred topography of the Holy Land and settlement within it was accompanied by theological disputes over the sanctity of various places and the presence of God at certain sites. Nevertheless, Church Fathers such as Cyril of Jerusalem and Jerome (translator of and commentator on the Bible who had immigrated from Italy to Palestine and settled in Bethlehem) gave great priority to gatherings at the holy places. Jerome even asserted that honoring the place where the Lord's feet had trod was part of the faith (Epistle 46:7 to Desiderius). The Christian establishment took energetic steps to appropriate the Holy Land by erecting magnificent churches in central locations which had been carefully chosen on account of the

102

"Peace upon Israel" – an inscription in a mosaic in the synagogue at Jericho, Byzantine period

St. George's Monastery on a cliff in the Perath Valley (Wadi Qelt) overlooking Jericho. Built in the fifth century, it was expanded in the sixth and seventh centuries

memories connected to those sites, while, concomitantly, the Christian leaders encouraged the consolidation and broadening of the popular movement of Christian pilgrimage to the country.

The forerunners of the fourth-century pilgrims who had begun to arrive in the Holy Land had conceived of the link between historical events and the places where they had occurred, especially (but not exclusively) as a means of understanding the Holy Scriptures. This may have been what prompted Eusebius to compile his *Onomasticon* (catalogue of names). This associative-interpretive basis for the visit was replaced by a rising tide of longing for physical contact with the sites where these events had transpired and to sense at first hand the result or surviving traces of important moments in the collective memory. This phenomenon gave rise, from the fourth and into the seventh centuries, to the wide distribution of holy relics (*reliquiae*) and even to trading in them. Thus, the Latin pilgrim monk Paulinus of Nola (late fourth century) stated that nothing attracted people to Jerusalem other than their need to touch places where Jesus had been physically present (Epistle 49, 4). This phenomenon had great importance for the Christians of the Holy Land in that it renewed the stable image of the country as the historical cradle of Christianity, and because it enhanced the political and religious status of the Palestinian leadership.

However, the process of appropriation and sanctification of Palestine did not stop there. The leaders of the Palestinian Church – above all the bishops of Jerusalem – quickly realized the deeper foundations inherent in the connection between a holy, historical site and the memory that was linked to it as an instrument par excellence for spiritual exaltation, for the creation of an unmediated link between the believing pilgrim and the object of his adoration, and for the forging of as sense of emulation by walking in the paths of kings and prophets, and particularly of the Savior – what they called *imitatio Christi* (emulation of Christ). Such sensations reached a height when the passionate pilgrim arrived at the scene of the historic event precisely on the day of the year that had been fixed as its anniversary. This led those engaged in shaping the above-mentioned link to create a ceremonial atmosphere through which the connection of time and place would be made substantial over the continuum of history. The Christian calendar, with its central foci and holy days, was now dramatically strewn with additional dates having an obviously local historical basis. This phenomenon merely intensified what was common knowledge, that in fact even the major Church holy days were grounded in clearly local historical events. These processes had already been perfected over the course of the fourth century, and particularly during its second half.

They are to be associated primarily with the bishop of Jerusalem, Cyril (ca. 315–386), who shaped them, and with the pilgrim Egeria who visited the Holy Land and surrounding areas in the years 382–384 and was the first to report them, profoundly sensing the special virtues inherent in this development and so documented it. Her fascinating, detailed account reveals the inner nature of Christian pilgrimage, not only what met the eye at every site. She succeeded in presenting the intimate dimension of the pilgrim's encounter with the events of the past, thus illustrating how the time gap between the historic events and the renewed experience of the visitor was narrowed. This experience reached its peak with a ceremony conducted on site, at any site, in which Scriptural texts were read and prayers recited that had been carefully chosen "befitting the time and place." The country was being increasingly overwhelmed by rising waves of pilgrims who crossed its length and breadth on foot, some of them even taking up residence there. This phenomenon to a great extent shaped the face and appearance of Palestine in that period, as the country was increasingly appropriated by the Church.

The site attributed to Jesus' birthplace in Bethlehem

An oil lamp of the Byzantine period with prayer inscriptions – a souvenir from the Holy Land

103

The question may be asked, upon which conceptual foundations rested that elaborate ceremonial framework which stood at the center of the Christian's world, whether he was a local resident or a pilgrim? There were two outstanding guidelines that shaped the local Christian tradition, and both stemmed from the

Imaginary depiction of Jerusalem: Detail from "Jesus in the Garden of Olives" by Andrea Mantegna, 15th cent. (Musée des Beaux-Arts de Tours)

profound need of the Church to take root in the Holy Land despite the indifference or criticism that it met within its own camp on one hand, and the conflict with the earlier Judaic tradition on the other hand. From the generation after the crucifixion of Jesus onwards, when the Church turned to the Gentiles and set salvation in the name of and on behalf of the Lord Jesus as a central tenet, the relationship to the earthly, physical nature of Jesus had been increasingly weakened and the landscape of his historic memory correspondingly neglected. Consequently, Palestine's status as the arena of events as described in the New and Old Testaments faded. This was especially notable in regard to Jerusalem whose ruin was perceived as being eternal, a testimony to the punishment of those who had crucified the Savior and ill-treated his apostles. More than a tangible, physical city, albeit in ruins, Jerusalem had become an abstract concept adopted from the description of the End of Days, when its resurgence would be realized in utopian dimensions, as described in the Apocalypse of John (Revelation: 21). Even if this book was only slowly accepted and disseminated, more than a few of its ideas were adopted by leading Christian thinkers. Thus, in the pre-Constantine period Palestine in general and Jerusalem in particular were very far from being at the center of the Christian experience. This situation

needed to be remedied. The intervention of the Christian royal family did much to help those who took the initiative to create powerful foci that perpetuated once again the remembrance of local traditions which had grown dim. The endeavors of the royal house, however, should perhaps be seen in a broader political context of creating a balance between the new, rising world of Christianity and the old order of the pagan world. After all, during the very years in which the new Christian Jerusalem was being built, the Emperor dedicated his new-old capital of Byzantium (Constantinople) on foundations exhibiting a clearly pagan hue. Establishing equality and balance between these two poles exemplified the cautious steps of the first Christian emperor. However, in the local Palestinian context the transformation was mainly expressed in the shaping of a conceptual framework that connected the large churches that were increasingly being built in Judea and Jerusalem. The great achievement of the ambitious building program was epitomized by the relationship created among the Church of the Nativity in Bethlehem, the Church of the Holy Sepulcher and the Resurrection (Anastasis) in Jerusalem, and the Church of the Ascension on the Mount of Olives. Indeed, the common denominator of these sites was that they were caves dedicated to local rites, but they also symbolized the three most important episodes in the earthly life of the Savior. Thus Jerusalem – and Palestine – returned to the center of Christian consciousness. However, something was needed that would impart to this step a timeless, mythic status and image by virtue of which Jerusalem would restore to itself its historic, central preeminence. It seems that the appearance, at the end of that century, of the legend of the finding of the True Cross by Constantine's mother, Queen Helena, filled the void. True, the involvement of the emperor's mother in finding the holy relic had long been known. Yet the miraculous circumstances of this discovery (the identification of its location by a Jew named Judah and the miraculous verification of the True Cross, after which the Jew converted) had slowly undergone change and taken shape, apparently over the course of the century, until they burst forth at its end, just when the legendary tradition of the leprous Constantine and his miraculous cure and baptism was obtaining fame at Rome. The renewed

104

The Jordan, photograph by Felix Bonfils (active in the Middle East, 1867-1885). The photograph was later colored, apparently by his son Adrien

recognition of the preeminence of Jerusalem matured in the fifth century, when it was proclaimed a patriarchate – one of the five most important centers of Christianity alongside Rome, Antioch, Alexandria, and Constantinople.

The appearance of a Jew named Judah (unquestionably a highly symbolic name) as the central figure of the legendary tale of finding the cross directs our attention to the other pole in the process of creating a new, Christian guise for the Holy Land, one that developed through conflict with the Jewish heritage and its exploitation. In this process, the map of Christian sacral places in the Holy Land was made to correspond with the map of biblical and post-biblical sites, accompanied by an array of commentaries and symbols that were meant to impart to the Christian holy places a new, symbolic meaning drawing upon the ancient events that had occurred there. In this manner, the sacred status of the Jordan River crossing as the holy site of the baptism took on added significance when it was identified with the place where the Children of Israel had entered the Land of Israel under the leadership of Joshua (who symbolized another, later Joshua, that is, Jesus); and the twelve stones that Joshua had set up at Gilgal when he entered the country now became symbols not only of the twelve tribes but of Jesus' twelve apostles as well. This method

105

of using a biblical event and biblical narrative as the prototype for a later tale or event from the time of Jesus and his disciples was already known and widespread, and had transformed the Hebrew Bible into a kind of mirror reflecting the ever more important reality embodied in the New Testament account. Now it was being used for the more practical purposes of creating a sense of identity based on sacred geography. For example, the contrast, charged with messianic symbolism, between King David's barefoot ascent of the Mount of Olives, weeping and disgraced, with Jesus' descent down the same slope and his entry into Jerusalem as a savior mounted on a young donkey and a she-ass. This is not the place to point out the abundance of ways in which the local Christian tradition carried on a polemic with the Jewish past that underlay it, but this tendency can be demonstrated by actions on the ground. These were especially

Jews lamenting near the Temple Mount on the Ninth of Av, painting by A. Sochovolsky

evident in Jerusalem where the Christians, the new lords of the city, emphasized the contrast between the city being rebuilt around the basilica of the Church of the Holy Sepulcher and other churches, and the ruined, desolate site of the Temple Mount. An ancient Christian tradition held that Hadrian had prohibited Jews from entering the city, and some held – on the basis of flimsy evidence – that Constantine had renewed the prohibition. It is doubtful whether this was actually so, although there are grounds to believe that Jews were forbidden by a local provincial order (perhaps inspired by the Jerusalem Church) to enter the city except for one day a year, the Ninth of Av, the day of bitter mourning over the destruction of the Temple. Jerome's harsh description of the procession of Jewish mourners and

lamenters on that day is especially caustic, presenting with full force the blatant contrast between the victorious Christian and the defeated Jew:

On the day that Jerusalem was conquered and destroyed by the Romans, one could see this people, the women dressed in rags and the old bearing their tatters and their years, gather for a time of mourning, proving by their bodies and their dress the meaning of the wrath of the Lord ... and while the wood of the crucifix of the Lord shines and glows ... and the symbol of the Cross is glowing on the Mount of Olives, the children of this wretched nation are bemoaning the destruction of their temple ... the weeping still continues in fear and trembling, with pale arms and with a wild shudder, and the soldier is already demanding his charge so that they be allowed to weep some more (Jerome, *Commentary on Zephaniah*, 1:15).

Despite all this, here too an event was needed that would set the stamp on the Christian achievement, and it was not long in coming. In 363 the pagan emperor, Julian (who had seized power from his uncle, Emperor Constantius II, son of Constantine the Great), sought to restore the Jews to their privileged status in the Land of Israel by rebuilding their destroyed Temple. What lay behind Julian's scheme was the recognition that it was necessary to undermine the Christian belief in the eternity of the Destruction, which was based on a statement attributed to Jesus: "Verily I say unto you, There shall not be left here one stone upon another that shall not be thrown down" (Matthew, 24:2). The restoration of the Temple was part and parcel of Julian's ambitious plan to establish a pagan empire that would be founded on the political-organizational principles of the Christian empire. Preparations for rebuilding the Temple were in high gear and the new foundations were about to be laid when suddenly – for reasons insufficiently clear (due to an earthquake according to several traditions) – construction ceased, and soon afterwards Julian himself died on the Persian front in circumstances which also elicited a wave of rumors, most of them legendary. One may easily imagine how the failure of the plan was received by the Church leaders who interpreted it as divine intervention on their behalf. Some went so far as to see the episode as a kind of prelude to the concluding episode of the Christian vision of the End of Days, in the context of which the Anti-Christ, the benefactor and defender of the Jews – symbolized by the historic Julian – would be vanquished for ever. This episode not only placed

Jerusalem at the center of Jewish-Christian conflict in the past, but also at the core of the future, decisive arena of struggle at the End of Days. Thus did the Christian concept of "the Holy Land" take shape, carried on the waves of a profound transformation in Christian thought, and fed by the ruin of the Jews who claimed to be the true owners of the Promised Land, yet had lost hold of it on account of their sins. Was this true in fact? Did Christianity gain control of the entire country? It seems that this was not so. Galilee remained overwhelmingly under Jewish domination, which continued throughout the period under discussion despite the decline of the Jewish presence in the Land of Israel.

'Galilee of the Gentiles': Galilee as a Jewish Center

Not only did the Christians seek to dispossess the Jews of their hold on their country, but also to undermine their social fabric and institutions. To that purpose, in the fourth century they began to undermine the public status of the Jewish leadership, at whose head stood the *nasi* (Patriarch). The exalted status of the nasi was grounded in his lineage, as a descendant of the House of David. This lineage and the concomitant status were a thorn in the flesh of the Church, which ascribed a similar descent to Jesus, its Savior. The rising status of the Church in general and the Palestinian Church in particular was the opening signal for a campaign to harass the nasi and his leadership in an attempt to also undermine the Jewish society which was under his sway. Christian incitement intensified, and the *nesiut* ceased to exist during the course of the first third of the fifth century.

The following tradition well illustrates the content of the conflict and the methods adopted to enhance it. About the year 375, the fanatical Church Father Epiphanius of Salamis (on Cyprus), who had previously lived in the Bet-Guvrin area, recorded a testimony that he had heard some two decades earlier from a Jew named Joseph, a frequent visitor to the home of the Jewish nasi. Joseph, who subsequently converted to Christianity and became close to the Emperor Constantine, was actually relating the story of his own life and the circumstances of his

Bet-Shean, a city of commercial and military importance during almost every period

conversion, but he spun his tale around his intimate acquaintance with the nasi. Among other things, he recounted the ailing nasi's conversion to Christianity on his death bed, and that he had secretly received the sign of Jesus (i.e. baptism) from the bishop of Tiberias. As if this were not enough, Joseph continued to supply Epiphanius with additional tales about the lifestyle in the household of the nasi, while elaborating on the wretchedness of his sons "who acted like reckless good-for-nothings." The premise underlying this wretched image of the nesiut was that those who accepted this leadership deserved a new patronage, that of the Church. Thus was the way opened for Christianizing Jewish Galilee. The convert Joseph took this mission upon himself under imperial sponsorship:

Josephus asked only this very great favor from the emperor, permission by imperial rescript to build Christ's churches in the Jewish towns and villages where no one had even been able to found churches since there are no Greeks, Samaritans or Christians among the population. This [rule] of having no gentiles among them is observed especially at Tiberias, Diocaesarea, Sepphoris, Nazareth, and Capernaum (Epiphanius, *Panarion*, 30,11,9-10).

107

Caesarea, site of an ancient Sidonian city (Migdal Sharshon, Straton's Tower) conquered by Alexander Jannaeus in 90 BCE. In the Byzantine period Caesarea was an important Christian center, and also had a Jewish community

From the continuation of the tale it transpires that Joseph was not successful and was forced to leave Galilee and settle in Bet-Shean, a city of mixed population where the Christians had a real foothold. Various scholars have pointed out that the entire tale – or at least much of it – lacks historical value. Yet, that is not what is pertinent. This episode, besides being adorned with indirect allusions from the Christian polemic against Judaism and in addition to its intention to provide the Christian believer with an acknowledgement by the leaders of Judaism as to the superiority of Christianity and the failure of the line of hereditary leadership in which the Jews took so much pride, may also include a messianic element. For the end of Jewish leadership symbolized the total victory of the Church and its salvation. However, as shall become clear below, the Galilean atmosphere that emerges from this story encapsulates some central components of Jewish history in the Land of Israel at that time.

Lod, Caesarea, and Galilee – Center and Periphery

The Jews that had migrated to Galilee after the failure of the Bar Kokhba Revolt, taking with them their institutional foci of power (the Sanhedrin and the nesiut in its early stages), did not create there a totally new Jewish center. After all, outstanding Jewish spiritual leaders of great repute had already been active in Galilee. However, the institutional move did shift the center of gravity of Jewish population in the Land of Israel to this region to a considerable extent. Yet, alongside the major centers of Jewish creativity in Galilee – Tiberias and Sepphoris – there were others elsewhere: in Lod (Diospolis), and a more renowned one in Caesarea. The latter city was distinctive in that it had produced a unique social and religious fabric, one that reflected the cosmopolitan ambiance in which the Jews of the Land of Israel lived in Late Antiquity. Caesarea was the city with the most mixed population in Palestine in those days. Samaritans, Jews, pagans, and Christians lived side by side in a situation that fluctuated

Part of the mosaic in the "House of the Nile Festival" in Sepphoris, the Byzantine period. Egypt is personified in the form of a woman

between reserved neighborliness and constant friction. From its founding, the city had a mixed, cosmopolitan character which was shaped by its being both an administrative and military center of Roman (and later, Byzantine) rule, as well as a center for trade and an important international port.

An ever-growing Jewish community developed in Caesarea, and it was there, more than anywhere else in Palestine, that a common fabric of life was created among the different religions. Thus it was possible in fourth-century Caesarea to hear Jews (who may have immigrated from the Diaspora and settled in that city) reciting the daily prayer *Shema* in Greek. Although this astonished the sages they accepted it nonetheless. In the same city one might come upon a Jew who was a stagehand and maintenance man in the local theater. R. Abbahu of Caesarea, who was acquainted with the Greek tongue and its culture, provided his daughters with a Greek education and was a constant visitor to the home of the Roman governor. He was the man best suited to serve as the main Jewish spokesman in the

developing conflict between Judaism and Christianity that was very much alive in Caesarea. After all, the intellectual elite of Palestinian Christian society had established itself in this city, led by the Church Father, preacher, and commentator Origen (died ca. 253 CE), and his successor, the most prominent bishop in the Christian leadership at that time, Eusebius (died in 339). R. Abbahu, like Origen, understood that at the heart of the conflict between the two camps also lay the element that connected them – the Bible. R. Abbahu proclaimed to the *minim* (heretics, that is, Judeo-Christians or Gentile Christians) of his city that on account of their being neighbors, the local Jews had the responsibility of studying the Bible in order to respond to their arguments, just as Origen a few decades earlier had remarked the same to a close friend. Caesarea therefore became an important post on the frontline of the Jewish-Christian encounter. The administrative status of Caesarea indeed underwent a certain transformation from the fourth century on. This change entailed the division of the province into two, or even three,

administrative regions, leading to the growing importance of other cities (such as Bet-Shean) in the areas of administration and justice. Nonetheless, Caesarea preserved its senior status in Palestine and in one area, that of Church administration, it struggled forcefully to preserve its primacy against the rising power of the bishopric of Jerusalem, which in the first half of the fifth century was made a patriarchate, as noted above.

Even though Caesarea and Lod were outstanding centers of Torah study in their own right, the threads of spiritual creativity woven in them were drawn to and from Galilee, where most of religious literature –Talmud, *midrash,* and apparently the wealth of early liturgical poetry too – took their final shape. These works, most of which were redacted in this

period and some were even compiled then, do not tell us about their authors, and only careful reading between the lines teaches us something about the circumstances of their creation. Major and minor events such as those that stirred the Jewish population as early as the fourth century and others that occurred later, were not substantially documented here. For example, we have almost no mention of the violent outburst against the Romans in the mid-fourth century (known as the Gallus Revolt) that centered on Sepphoris. What is even more glaring is the lack of any reference to the unsuccessful plan of Emperor Julian "the Apostate" to rebuild the Temple in Jerusalem. This should not

Lions, a panther, an antelope (oryx), and partridges from a mosaic discovered at Lod, 3rd–4th cent.?

be ascribed to the early redaction of the Jerusalem Talmud, since allusions to later events were in fact incorporated into the text by its redactors. Therefore it is more reasonable to assume that the terrible failure and the unfulfilled dream, which many in the nation shared even if their leaders did not look favorably upon it, led the redactors to play it down. However, that very calamity might have had an even deeper influence on the Jews in that period, for it encouraged messianic calculations of the End of Days. There is a hint of this both in the joy displayed by Christians when the plan failed, and in later testimonies as to the messianic expectations of Jews in that generation. Even if it is hard to find in the Hebrew sources actual records of events, they remain an immense store of knowledge concerning the

110

atmosphere within contemporary Jewish society. It is quite likely that what lies behind the paucity of historical information or its concealment reflects a rearguard action mounted by the Jewish community in the Land of Israel – and particularly in Galilee – at the end of the fourth century against the developing hegemony of the Church.

An especially interesting example, indicative of the process of dwindling numbers and self-isolation that was the lot of the Jewish community, emerges from what has been described in recent research as the creation of a local Galilean Jewish identity. By weaving expressions of place and time into an extensive fabric, the Galilean Jews created a local myth which supplied them with the frame of their own self-image. Though this myth appears in its full, detailed form in the High Middle Ages as part of the Jewish polemic against the Christian-Crusader world, its foundations were laid in Late Antiquity. In this manner, for instance, the Galilean Jews transferred to their region many of the biblical narrative traditions which were set in other areas of the country. Thus, metaphorically speaking, the whole Land of Israel was folded up under the Galileans' footsteps. Through this intricate endeavor, exemplified by the transferal of personages, tombs, and events (thereby making clear polemical statements, in some cases), did Galilean Jewish society seek to challenge the new, unwelcome inheritors of the land who trampled it underfoot. Hence it is not surprising that, for their part, those who molded Christian sacred traditions transferred narratives connected to Jesus from Galilee to the terrain of Judea and Jerusalem, while simultaneously downplaying the image of other Galilean sites. In this cultural atmosphere Christians found it difficult to penetrate the region which had been the site of their Savior's deeds, a condition that continued throughout the Byzantine era (except in Western Galilee). Therefore it seems as if each side, in drawing the demarcation line between them, sought to tell the other that the part of the country they controlled was like the entire land. The centrality of Galilee in the Land of Israel Jewish consciousness was also obvious in the creation of a central necropolis at Bet-She'arim on the fringe of Lower Galilee. Not only were the dead of Galilee laid to rest in this cemetery (close to the important center in Sepphoris), but the bodies of deceased Jews were brought from abroad on the basis of a tradition renewed in the third century. Thereby, past and present merged in the everyday life of Galilee and increased its importance.

The Son of David and the Sons of Aaron – Transmutations in the Leadership

Side by side with the fierce, but to a great extent concealed, conflict over the image and the cultural world of Jewish society and its Galilean stronghold, as hinted above a bitter struggle was waged, overtly and with far-reaching implications, over the future

The "Rehov Inscription" from the synagogue in Rehov, southern Bet-Shean Valley, detailing regions as well as agricultural crops forbidden or permitted in the sabbatical (*shmittah*) year in these regions. Also detailed are the regions of the Land of Israel that were held by those who returned from Babylon, and their implications for the commandments that applied only in the Land of Israel

of the Jewish leadership, that of the nesiut. If the early third century is considered the golden age of the nesiut (whatever its real status may have been), and the Hebrew sources abound in descriptions of its ties with the highest Roman authorities, then over the course of the fourth century we are witness to the decline of this institution. At the beginning of the third century, R. Judah ha-Nasi was still the leader for both the people and the sages. But in the fourth century there are signs that the status of the nasi had declined vis-à-vis the sages and, it is nearly certain, as far as non-Jewish society, too, was concerned, so much so that the emperors had to enact a law forbidding disgracing the nasi in public. The *nesi'im* (pl. of nasi) who held office in the third century are known by their names and their deeds even if they were not always to the taste of some contemporary sages, whereas for those who filled this post in the fourth century we do not always have clear information as to their names or their terms in

111

Rabban Gamaliel and his disciples, from the Sarajevo Haggadah, second half of the 14th cent. (SNM, Sarajevo Haggadah)

office. In fact, more than the Jewish sources provide us with data about them, Christian sources denigrate them. The later nesi''im lacked the spiritual stature and the level of learning of their forerunners, and they became not a little alienated from the community over whom they were entrusted.

We know of cases in which the sages pleaded with the nasi to take up the public's burden. However, unfortunate appointments of nesi'im, appointments that were tainted by corruption, and the heavy tax burden that they levied were not to the liking of the Jews who resided in the Land of Israel and in the Diaspora. It was not without reason that the Emperor Julian sent a letter "To the Community of the Jews" in the spring of 363 in which he scolded the nasi Julus (Hillel the Second) for the heavy tax burden which he had imposed, and demanded that the taxes be annulled. One of the main occupations of the nasi was revealed in this letter – collecting taxes for his own needs and those of his office, something that weighed heavily on the Jewish public and

greatly annoyed many of the Church Fathers. The nasi at that time kept somewhat aloof from public, political, and cultural activity. This may explain why there is no mention of his involvement in events that agitated the country in the middle of the the fourth century: the clash with Rome in 351/352 (the Gallus Revolt) and Emperor Julian's plan to rebuild the Temple. The revolt, the causes of which are not known and of which we have but a few details, erupted in Sepphoris and spread to other parts of Galilee. It was led by a man named Patricius, and during the revolt (according to one of the traditions) both Christians and pagans were killed. However, it was quickly suppressed. The Jewish sources tell of several acts of repression against the Jewish population (burning a Torah scroll in Sennabris near the Sea of Galilee, and so on) in which Ursicinus, military commander and right-hand man of Emperor Gallus, was involved. Political agitation apparently waned in the wake of a visit by two of the most important sages of that period, R. Jonah and R. Yose, to

112

Ursicinus' headquarters in Antioch. The Roman general, according to a tradition colored by legend, received them with great honor, rising to greet them – to the astonishment of those around him. This attests that they came not as representatives of someone else (that is, the nasi) but perhaps as the self-appointed leaders of the community. We should not deduce from this that the political power of the nasi had declined. After all, another famous Antioch personage, the orator Libanius (second half of the fourth century), attests to the contrary. He reports of the nasi's involvement in administrative appointments made by the authorities, as well as his intervention in the affairs of the Diaspora Jewish communities. The nasi's political influence was so great that at least in one case, towards the end of the century, a conflict between the nasi Gamaliel VI and a senior administrative official led to the latter's execution.

The imperial authorities' view of the status of the nesi'im contrasted with the wretched image of them held by their own community, whom they treated with aloofness and haughtiness. As early as the beginning of the fourth century, matters had reached a state in which a prominent sage, R. Jeremiah, sent a letter to the patriarch containing an especially insulting sentence: "To hate those who love you and to love those who hate you" (Jerusalem Talmud, *Megillah*, 3:2b). This may have been what led to the legislation mentioned above that forbade public displays of contempt for the nesi'im. It is no wonder then that in such an atmosphere the most zealous defamers of the nesiut – Church circles led by Epiphanius of Salamis – swooped down on the prey. Actually, we do not know whether bishops such as Epiphanius were additionally motivated by the force of Jewish public criticism of the nesiut, but it is hard to ignore the fact that most attacks on this institution originated with the Palestinian Church. Though it is doubtful whether there were any among the Jews who wanted to abolish the nesiut, it is difficult to overlook the simultaneous timing of criticism from within the community and attacks from without. Although the historical value of the tales recounted to Epiphanius by Joseph is meager, they played a significant role in the battle of disinformation and polemics that was part of the inter-religious conflict. This was because, in addition to dispossessing the Jews from their age-old patrimony, the Christians also wanted to dispossess them of the elements of their national leadership, especially those that perpetuated their historic eminence. The dynasty of nesi'im, that traced its descent from the House of David, was wont to display regal manners and claimed a messianic status. As already noted, they stood in glaring contradiction to Church doctrine which claimed that its one and only Savior had sprung from the stock of Jesse. Attempting to present the members of the family of nesi'im as unworthy of their eminent rank, or efforts to disprove their genealogical claim, as undertaken by some other Church Fathers, was a fitting backdrop to Joseph's libelous tale about the nasi who converted, thereby providing proof of which side possessed the truth.

In contrast to this inheritance of the flesh that passed from father to son the Christians posed an alternative in the form of inheritance of the spirit. Hence the nesi'im symbolized the leadership of the vanishing past, whereas the Church's leadership symbolized that of the felicitous present and future. However, this issue created an obvious conflict of interest between the Church leadership, that scorned the nesiut and what it signified, and the imperial authorities, who wanted to preserve the power of the nesiut, recognizing it as a representative body very much apt for monitoring and controlling their relations with the Jewish community. Though official imperial policy did indeed lag behind the hidden or overt wishes of the Church leaders, it was not by much. The Church's intensifying agitation against the religious and social elements that, in its opinion, endangered the unity of Christendom, won out in the end. The growing influence of the bishops within various government circles (in matters of imperial legislation, among others) also left its mark in regard to the nesiut. The first noticeable signs appeared towards the end of the fourth century when

Ceramic lamp, 3rd–4th cent., found in Jerusalem, decorated with a relief of a candelabrum, an incense burning shovel, and a shofar (ram's horn)

the nesi'im were no longer looked upon with favor, not even by the emperors. In 415, after imposing limitations on the nasi's activity, Emperors Honorius and Theodosius II signed a law that diminished the standing of Gamaliel VI and limited his authority. From here it was but a short step to the abolition of the nesiut as an institution, although a law of this sort was not explicitly enacted. Therefore, some now see the nesiut's disappearance as a natural fading away due to the death of Gamaliel VI and the lack

113

of an heir. However, a law of 429 arranged for the transfer of the *aurum coronarium* (the yearly tax paid to the nasi) to the state treasury, rather than to the councils of Jewish leaders (*sanhedriyot*) which arose to replace the traditional institution. The downfall of this important institutional symbol represented the moral triumph of the Church, a victory accompanied by expressions of mockery and humiliation.

A candelabrum on basalt from Yahudiyyah, on the Golan Heights, Byzantine period

Nothing is known of the methods and character of the new leadership. However, if we may judge from contemporary inscriptions and later evidence, something of the patterns of nesiut leadership was preserved, especially in matters having to do with the ties between the community in the Land of Israel and those in the Diaspora. For example, the funerary inscription of the daughter of a Jewish municipal leader in Venosa in southern Italy (sixth century) mentions the presence and eulogies of two emissary-sages ("*Rebbites-Apostoles*") from the Land of Israel. As in the days of the nesi'im, these emissaries may have also been sent to collect contributions, despite the legal limitations imposed by the authorities on fundraising at the end of the fourth century. But their primary objective was to guide the Diaspora communities in spiritual matters. In any event, we know very little about the composition and character of the leadership of the Land of Israel Jewish community from the fifth century onwards.

The decline in status of the nesiut occurred around the time when Jewish literary works produced in the Land of Israel were assuming their final shape (the Jerusalem Talmud was completed

and redacted in that period, as well as the early *midrashei aggadah* - homilies on passages of the Bible incorporating legendary materials), such as *Genesis Rabbah*, *Leviticus Rabbah*, and *Pesikta de-Rav Kahana*, which were apparently redacted during the fifth century. Indeed the preponderant part of the canon of works for the study of the Law was compiled, edited, and completed then. Hence it seems that the two leading elements of the Jewish leadership until then had finally completed their historical role at that moment. These were the intellectual elite represented by the fellowship of scholars in the house of study (i.e. the "sages"), which lacked defined social stratification, and the dynastic leadership of illustrious lineage, the nesi'ut. Although there is meager proof, it seems that compilation of the literature of Jewish Law (*halakhah*) created in the house of study continued even afterwards. This is indicated by the development of a genre of compendia of rabbinic halakhic dictas known as "*The Ma'asim* (The Book of Rulings)." This literature, extensive sections of which have survived in the Cairo Genizah, reflects everyday life in the Land of Israel during the sixth and seventh centuries. The setting of these rabbinic judgments which, according to one opinion, originated in the registers of the rabbinic court in Tiberias, is that of the late Hellenistic culture, and it was suffused with the legal and economic terminology of its surroundings. Especially fascinating is what we can learn about the lives of women. For instance, one passage reads: "And it is forbidden for a woman to adorn her daughter and take her out to the marketplace because she is risking her life, and a woman who has perfumed herself and goes to [houses of i]dol worship is to be flogged and her hair shaved off..."

Greek inscription from the synagogue at Hammath, 3ʳᵈ–4ᵗʰ cent.: "May Propotoros the Mizotoros be remembered for good and blessing. He made this stoa of the holy place. Blessing upon him. Amen. Shalom"

In addition to learning about aspects of social behavior described here and the proposed punishments, we discern an objective: to preserve feminine modesty at all costs. This was also highly compatible with what Church leaders demanded of members of Christian society. The Jews sought to adopt something of the practices current in the surrounding society, fearing the social proximity between the societies. Indeed, questions that emerged in the wake of instances of conversion make up much of this collection of rabbinic rulings. It is tempting to envisage in the compilation of this practical compendium –

seemingly, presented with their moment of opportunity.

Without any special intent on their part, time and again Christian authors of the fifth and sixth centuries supply information about the leading priests in Tiberias, in some cases sent on diplomatic missions to other lands in the southern Mediterranean region. Thus we learn that a man named Pinhas (the Priest) from Tiberias participated in a Christian assembly that convened in Alexandria in 552 as an expert on the calendar. According to another sixth-century tradition priests sent by the Jewish authorities in Tiberias were involved in agitation against

"The Season of Tishrei" (Fall) from the zodiac in the synagogue mosaic at Hammath-Tiberias, 3rd–4th cent.

which cannot be defined as an original work – and the earlier redaction of the Talmud a rabbinical version of the widespread trends of codification manifested in collections of Church canonical and Byzantine imperial laws that were compiled during the fifth and sixth centuries.

It is reasonable to assume that abrogation of official recognition of the nesiut dynasty paved the way for entry of new-old elements into the field of public leadership – members of the priestly caste. It, too, represented something of the old order that had been based on ancestry and descent, something that had declined in force and splendor since and due to the destruction of the Temple. But as early as the Yavneh generation and for hundreds of years afterwards, the priests had sought to maintain their special status, at times in conflict with the sages. When the nesiut no longer existed, they were,

the Christians by the Judaizing Himiyarite kingdom in southern Arabia (see below). It is difficult to assume that these Christian authors, some of whom were converts from Judaism, made faulty use of the term priests or were actually reviving a concept from the past. It is legitimate, therefore, to pose the question: Are we indeed dealing with a representative leadership, a substitute for the nesiut, and if so, what was its character?

It seems that at that time Jewish society in the Land of Israel had begun to undergo a process similar to one that had slowly developed over the second half of the fourth century in the leadership of Christian society – the increased power of the bishops and those associated with them in the ecclesiastical establishment. The bishops had become the ruling class in the empire, a class to which they belonged by virtue of their origin, culture, and autocratic authority. These men followed the concept that they

115

alone held the power to maintain and fortify the status of Christianity in the empire. They became the leaders of Christian

Dedicatory inscription from the synagogue at Susiya in honor of the donor of the mosaic

communities in the villages, towns, and big cities. It was they who molded the patterns of worship and supported the needy among their flock; it was they, too, who created a hierarchical framework parallel to that of the secular authorities, yet more powerful than the secular in its control over the public and its influence on the establishment. Above all, the great change in the rhythm of Christian public life that developed during the period under discussion took place within the churches themselves. It was there that the yearly cycle of events, as dictated by the traditional Roman calendar, was being replaced by the one created by the Church.

A somewhat similar model of leadership, albeit lacking the ideological framework, existed among the Jews of the Land of Israel, and particularly among those residing in Galilee. As the age of a centralized establishment in the form of the nesiut and the yeshivot came to an end, the stage was set for the renewed public role of the priests, whose status derived from their lineage rather than from involvement in one institution or another. Their involvement in Jewish communal affairs, both in the Land of Israel and the Diaspora, indicates their assumption of power and the provision of an effective substitute for at least some of the tasks of the nesiut. We are not able to infer from this anything about the precise nature of their administrative and political activities, nor whether their leadership was a centralized one, only that it was a collective institution that drew its strength from the entire priestly caste. However, the most important transformation by far of Jewish communal life involving the priesthood occurred in the synagogue.

With the disintegration of the traditional leadership, the synagogue remained the last factor which could still serve as a focus to attract local leadership. This, then, explains the

enhanced status of the priesthood as a central force possessing the prestige of lineage and antiquity in the life of the community and in its liturgy. It is in this period that a list of "priestly courses" was drawn up which included the names of the various watches (divisions) that had served in the past in the Temple in rotation, and their places of residence. Galilee took the the lion's share of this list. Though the accuracy and historical authenticity of the list are in fact subject to doubt, its importance lies in that it strengthened the status of the priesthood in general and in the frameworks of local communal life in particular (see below). The many early liturgical poems (*piyyutim*) dealing with the list which have survived, the references to it in synagogue inscriptions in the Land of Israel and in the Diaspora (Yemen), and the custom of proclaiming the watches, their place of residence, and the chronological order of their service every Sabbath in the synagogues, reinforced this image. This old-new leadership understood that if it wanted to sustain Jewish society and its spiritual assets in the face of a hostile world, it must mold that society's identity and foster it by forging a link to the synagogue. Only the priests, whose image had always had a ritual-liturgical connotation, could fill this role.

"The Season of Tishrei" (Fall) from the zodiac in the synagogue mosaic at Sepphoris, Byzantine period

Sages vs. Liturgical Poets and Preachers –
The House of Study vs. the Synagogue

Another outcome of the collapse of the central leadership was a shift in the focus of leadership in Jewish society to the local synagogue, the cornerstone of community organization. The

"The Seat of Moses" from the synagogue at Chorazin on the north of the Sea of Galilee, second half of 4ᵗʰ–early 5ᵗʰ cent.

words of the anonymous homilist: "A small city, that is a synagogue" (*Ecclesiastes Rabbah* 9:14), signify more than anything else the socio-cultural atmosphere of the times. Synagogue inscriptions including the terms *kehillah* (the community), *kehillah* or *karta kadishah* (the holy community or village) illustrate the homilist's statement. In these restricted contexts, the influence of the communal leaders, the congregational leaders (*archisynagogoi*), the attendants (here called *hazanim*), and the priests greatly increased, while, the status of the sages – who addressed those who came to the synagogue with their sermons – declined. The vast repertory of synagogue inscriptions in Hebrew, Greek, and Aramaic, that served equally as everyday languages (with a somewhat greater frequency of use for Aramaic), reflects this reality and reveals the social stratification of these communities, particularly the involvement of the prosperous and the influential. Thus we learn of their origin (Sevrianos Ephros, the much praised archisynagogos of Tyre who settled in Sepphoris); their trades (Menahem and Yeshua, wood merchants in Gaza, or *sacholastoi* [lawyers] in Sepphoris); and their financial means, about which we know from their contributions to the synagogues.

The significant social-communal endeavor of establishing

and caring for the communal synagogues symbolized, more than anything else, the democratization of Jewish cultural and public life in that period and the decline of the regional and national centers, whose status had depended on the centers of learning functioning within them. The florescence of the local communities, especially in Galilee and its periphery, elicited the great intellectual work befitting it – piyyutim (liturgical poems) and homilies in the synagogues. These decisively influenced the shape and contents of the liturgy. Many poems were composed to accompany sections of the services and the order of reading the Torah, thereby shaping the nature of the synagogue for generations to come. The fact that piyyutim were accepted and integrated into the established synagogue liturgy, although perhaps meeting with some opposition, obviously attests that we are dealing with works suitable for all. Modern scholarship holds the accepted view that these works were complex, embracing various hues and cultural tastes, and apparently they were also adapted to meet the general public's level of knowledge and understanding.

Among the *paytanim* (liturgical poets) who are well-known by name, there were quite a few priests, such as Yose ben Yose (perhaps the earliest of them all, though his priesthood has been contested), Shimeon ha-Kohen be-Rabi Magis, Yohanan ha-Kohen, and Pinhas ha-Kohen son of Jacob from Kifra (a suburb of Tiberias), nearly all of them Galileans. Priestly matters occupied a prominent place in their works. They lamented the low status of the priesthood because the Temple was still in ruins, and expressed profound yearning for a change and speedy Redemption. Thus, they composed long works on the order of the High Priest's worship in the Temple on *Yom Kippur* (the Day of Atonement), works that were meant to elaborate on what is described in the Mishnah and to accompany the *Mussaf* (Additonal) prayer on this holy day. Indeed, it seems that their intense preoccupation with priestly matters did not derive merely from the need to remind the public of the status and value of the priesthood. Rather, it was meant to express profound messianic expectations enhanced by the growing prevalence of calculations of the End of Days in the Land of Israel and Babylon alike from the fifth century onwards. Preoccupation with the oppressive subjugation and concern with approaching Redemption were not limited to a few individuals. They expressed the deepest, most existential aspirations of all strata in the entire community of worshippers. In this regard, too, it should be noted that the rise of liturgical poetry and the significant role of redemptionist themes within it were paralleled in time, and perhaps even in

117

content, by a similar process among Christians. From the second half of the fourth century, there were major transformations in the formation and shaping of Christian religious rites, in which the Jerusalem Church played a decisive role. During the fifth century, especially towards its end, anxious Christians aroused by millenial anxiety were also awaiting the approaching Salvation.

The lintel of the synagogue in Kazrin on the Golan Heights, Byzantine period

There are signs that both phenomena, within the Jewish and Christian camps, were connected in some way, inspiring mutual agitation. However, such a conclusion necessitates further study.

The liturgical poets had important partners in the process of transforming the synagogue into a central institution of Jewish society in the Land of Israel. These were the interpreters (from Hebrew to Aramaic) and the preachers. Both accompanied the three-year cycle of readings from the Torah (although there are some who contend that a one-year cycle existed in the Land of Israel too, and consider it to be the more ancient one which for some reason has become fixed in people's minds as a Babylonian custom). Aramaic, whose first roots are during Second Temple times, was meant to accompany the public readings from the Torah by way of explanation and clarification. The sages established the manner in which the interpreter was to carry out his task, and by these means they mainly sought to prevent his art from overshadowing the reading itself, but he became part of the regular establishment of the synagogue. The interpreter, who was a skilled professional and earned his living from this craft, became a kind of central mediating link between the biblical text and its "consumers," the synagogue worshippers who came from the broader social strata, and students in the early stages of their

studies. The interpreter's repertoire of commentary touched on various matters in the abundance of philosophical issues that preoccupied those who attended the synagogue.

The encounter between the biblical text and the public ceremonies on the various holidays (Sabbaths, festivals, days of mourning) was achieved by means of the public sermon. This custom, too, was ancient and went back to Temple times. However, we must distinguish between ordinary lectures and studies whose place was in the house of study, and the sermons in the public liturgical context, delivered in the synagogue in the presence of tanners, filigree makers, women, and infants. This distinction does not touch on the much discussed question as to whether we are dealing with different places of assembly – different spaces, or different rooms – but on the character of the assembly itself. Researchers have recently come to understand that many anecdotes scattered through the Talmuds and the Aggadic literature concerning the delivery or preaching of sermons, so to speak, to the public (i.e. "the community") were in fact expounded to students in the houses of study. These sermons bore a learned, elitist character and were generally not understood by the public at large, although there is some evidence that this public too, at times, flocked to the houses of study (Jerusalem Talmud, *Baba Mezia*, 2:13:8d). It stands to reason that precisely the exalted image of lessons taught in the house of study (that the sages fostered while inclining to disparage the synagogue preachers) is what was likely to attract a large public – and not specifically from among the students – to the lectures in the academy. In contrast, the regular, popular sermons in the synagogue were delivered as an explanation of and an elaboration upon the cycle of biblical recitations (along with their rendering into Aramaic) or as a response to the immediate issues which weighed upon the community. Here too, as in the liturgical works, the wording was adapted to suit the audience, its geographic setting, and its socio-cultural standing. When matters of Jewish law were part of the sermons, they were presented clearly enough so as not to mislead the public.

At the end of the third century there occurred a volte-face in the sages' attitude to the synagogue sermons and to those who

A basalt ornamentation in the form of a conch shell from the synagogue at Chorazin, second half of 4th or early 5th cent.

prepared and delivered them to the people. It is difficult to know what caused this turnabout and whether it was connected to the fact that creativity had come to an end in the academy; perhaps it was also linked to the early stages of this institution's decline. According to one tradition, at least, it seems that the growing stature of the sermon was an outcome of the unique, social needs of the public as it experienced increasing distress. Thus, for example, R. Isaac said: "Formerly, when a man possessed a *prutah* (small coin), he yearned to hear passages from the Mishnah and the Talmud, and now when he does not have a prutah, and especially when we are sick of the government, a man longs to hear words from the Bible and the Aggadah" (*Pesikta de-Rav Kahana*, 12:3). The public's affinity with and sympathy for the preacher were not at all assured; they depended upon his merits, the content of his sermon, and the manner in which it was delivered. His strength lay in his ability to fascinate his public and give it not only a moral lesson, but entertainment and esthetic pleasure as well. Allegories, tales, expositions, and narratives done up in a wealth of rhetorical devices imbued the sermon with beauty and helped to draw the public's attention. True, rhetorical devices of the synagogue sermon did fall short of the perfected rhetoric in classical civilization (after all, it is very doubtful whether any Aggadic scholar or preacher was exposed to the guides for rhetoric compiled by Menander of Laodicea or Quintilianus, though some scholars do claim that this was very well the case). However, it served as a factor binding and sustaining the community and as a tool of the first order for persuasion, or illustrating a point. If we are to judge by the sarcastic comments of the Church Father Jerome, the preachers did their work well, since "they succeed through theatrical means in causing their listeners to believe in the fictions that they invent" (*Commentary on Ezekiel*, 34:3).

The third element in the public liturgical framework was the work of the artists who decorated the synagogues with wall paintings or mosaics. These decorations first appeared in synagogues during the third and fourth centuries, and even enjoyed the sanction of the sages or at least their tacit approval. Especially famous are the traditions according to which, "in the days of R. Johanan they painted on the walls and he did not try to prevent them" (Jerusalem Talmud, *Avodah Zarah*, 3:42d), and more than a generation later: "In the days of R. Avon they painted on mosaic and he did not try to prevent them" (ibid.). This tacit agreement began almost with the introduction of the phenomenon, and may have been based on recognition of the importance of ornamentation in the synagogue as a liturgical tool. We should bear in mind that approximately at that time synagogue architecture underwent a thoroughgoing transformation that was especially evident in Galilean

A mosaic representation of the zodiac from the synagogue at Bet Alfa, with the sun god Helios at its center, 6th cent.

119

synagogues. Archaeologists have shown that while synagogues of the old Galilean type, such as those prevalent in Upper and Eastern Galilee, that were distinguished by their monumental structures and large basalt building stones, with impressive facades and stone carvings, were meant to impress the observer from the outside, while their interiors were notably plain. Later edifices gave way to buildings of the new type, noted for their elaborate internal decorations. These prevailed mainly in Lower Galilee, though also found in Judea , the Jordan Valley, and the

attention of the visitor-worshipper on what was happening inside the walls of the building. The synagogue was a faithful reflection of society. It is no wonder then that in an atmosphere redolent of syncretism, Jewish society did not hesitate to adopt, for instance, the symbol of Helios and even turn towards it in prayer. Thus, in *Sefer ha-Razim* (*The Book of Secrets*, a treatise on magic from the second half of the fourth century) there is a prayer to the adored Helios, the radiant leader (ed. Margalioth, p. 99). In another case, amulets containing spells for healing and

Main entrance to the synagogue at Sardis, Asia Minor

Dead Sea area. Earlier forerunners of the latter type were to be found in the Diaspora, in places such as Dura Europos.

Indeed, a great effort was made to decorate their interiors. The stunning mosaic floors with their abundance of decorations and symbols – some of them clearly Jewish (candelabrum, shovel for incense burning, the Four Species, and the ram's horn) and biblical scenes (chiefly the Binding of Isaac); others that were obviously Hellenistic symbols (the zodiac and representations of the Four Seasons); and even ritual symbols (the sun god, Helios, perceived by the artists and the worshippers as the embodiment of the sun itself) – point to the endeavor to direct and focus the

deliverance have been found lying next to the Ark of the Law in synagogues dating from the fifth and sixth centuries in the north and the south of the country. Hence, the synagogue concentrated several strands of expression of the spirit of that time.

As already noted, the synagogue's focus was on decorative art, whose intention was without a doubt to teach and to instill by visual means the biblical stories, which at times also expressed the thoughts and allusions of the preachers. The words of Church Father Gregory of Nyssa (second half of the fourth century) can well be applied to synagogue floor mosaics (even if in some places the work was primitive and naive). Referring to the Church of

The Binding of Isaac on the synagogue mosaic at Bet Alfa, 6th cent.

Theodore the Martyr, he wrote: "The hues of the ornamentation in the church are veritably like a book that speaks, because even a mute picture knows how to speak from the wall." The different biblical scenes, the complex symbols and their various interrelationships required from the observer a considerable intellectual effort, in which he may not always have been successful, although it is reasonable to assume that he – rather than the patrons who had commissioned the work – was the targeted audience for the artist's messages. Here, too, we are not dealing with an elitist work, but, like the liturgical poem and the sermon, the graphic works, too, were adapted to the taste and ability of the observer who apprehended their inner nature, either of the whole or of some part.

Combining the several strata of all the creative works connected to the synagogue in that period presents a rather complex, intricate fabric of various sorts of discourse that nurtured one another. The perceptions arising from the meeting between liturgy and the poems that accompanied it, to which are added the readings from the Torah and the sermon, created a unique emotional and intellectual harmony which imparted to the simple congregation of worshippers a spiritual experience from the world of the traditional community of scholars. In this context, the synagogue mosaic floor recently discovered at Sepphoris (Zippori) is especially notable. It includes a significant wealth of symbols and biblical scenes, some previously unknown. Analysis of the various sectors and the relationship between them, and then taking them all together as one complex, has led researchers to believe that the conceptual link unifying the sectors is the direct

link between God's promise (to grant seed to Abraham in the episode of the Binding of Isaac), and approaching Redemption. This connection was made clear to those frequenting the synagogue by means of divine worship, which depicted the consecration of Aaron the Priest and described the sacrifice of the regular daily offerings, the latter symbolizing the continuity of the ritual. We need only go on to imagine the sermons and liturgical poems that were heard in that same place on those very topics (and there were many of these). By means of perfect integration between what was heard and seen, the expectation of

An amulet against the evil eye made of clay and stone, 4th or 5th cent.

121

Fragment of a text from the New Testament on a wall painting in the Hebron area, Byzantine period

Redemption and the promise of its fulfillment were instilled in the hearts of those who entered the synagogue to pray.

These expressions had another feature with an obvious link to the aspect of salvation: undisguised hostility toward the Sons of Esau, that is, Edom, the Empire of Heresy (i.e., Christianity) that ruled over the Jews. As expressed above, in that period Jews entertained rising hopes (nurtured by sermons and piyyutim) that the time was near when Obadiah's prophecy would be fulfilled: "For liberators shall march up on Mount Zion to wreak judgment on Mount Esau" (Obadiah 1:21). In the world of the sages, the polemic with the Church was conducted on an intellectual plane in a cultured manner, whereas in the emotionally charged atmosphere of the synagogue the dispute became a quarrel exuding hostility and rancor. The poets set the tone, filling their poems with expressions of scorn and haughtiness towards the Christian Savior, as in the words of Yannai: "Those who praise the *kilai sho'a* (generous miser; also a play on the Hebrew name for Jesus and on the word for salvation, *yeshu'a*). And they made a resolute demand on God: 'Uproot the Empire of Dumah'" (*Piyyutey Yannai* 11; again a

play on words; Dumah = Edom, and perhaps also an allusion to Rome). A possibly Christian reply to those aspirations was a Byzantine melody called "On Earthquakes and Fires" written by Romanos who was living in Byzantium at that time. It mocked the ruins of Solomon's Temple in Jerusalem by contrasting them with the splendor of the Church of Hagia Sophia, which had also been damaged and punished by Heaven with fire and earthquake, but had immediately been reconstructed. The similarities between the cultural worlds of Judaism and Christendom extended even further.

Just as the socio-cultural focal point of the Jews in the Land of Israel was transferred from the scholarly elitism of the academy to the public arena of the synagogue, so did a parallel development take place, albeit in a different manner, in Christian society of the time. Not without hesitation, and despite open hostility on the part of the zealots, the churches were adorned with striking ornamentation. Mosaic floors and decorated walls quickly became the outstanding marks of recognition of the church. Already by the fourth century, the churches echo to orderly, well-executed liturgical ceremonies that were based on selected readings from Holy Scripture, and also accompanied by public sermons. Simultaneously, Christian liturgy reached a significant degree of refinement, and was shaped by the hallowed space in which the ceremonies were held both inside (within the church and in its various components) and outside (in relation to nearby churches and holy sites), in an obvious attempt to create a nexus and harmony between the two and to make the worshipper-pilgrim feel as close as possible to the event being singled out and celebrated. More than anywhere else, this concept was made tangible in the Jerusalem liturgy shaped in that period, which was to decisively influence the liturgies of other Christian centers, such as Antioch and Constantinople.

While there was considerable innovation in ritual and ornamentation in the churches, in the field of sermons church preachers had resource to the traditional world of classical rhetoric. Although they avoided admitting as much, their sermons and treatises attest that they had internalized rhetorical devices, while demonstratively avoiding rhetoric's pomposity, preferring the public good and welfare over "adoration by individuals." The public welfare mandated making the sermon suit the audience. Origen, the famous presbyter of Caesarea (a contemporary of R. Hoshaiah), saw the High Priest's service in the Temple – slaughtering the sacrificial animal, flaying it, separating its organs and sacrificing them – as a kind of paradigm of the task of the preacher who stripped the text of its attire and divided it into its several meanings (from the plain and simple to the esoteric – *Sermons on Leviticus*, 1:4). If the preachers took care to follow in his footsteps, then all worshippers in the church would be able to flavor the texts. Later preachers like Jerome and John Chrysostom (active at the end of the fourth century) repeatedly advised preachers to take account of the narrow-mindedness and shallow knowledge of their listeners, and to deliver their sermons calmly and logically, and not in a loud voice or hastily (Jerome, Epistle 52, to Nepotianus).

Internalizing the rules of rhetoric as a central component in Christian public discourse was clearly expressed in Christian art, both in choice of subject matter and in the location of works of art within the church's space. In the place where the public at large gathered, whether newly baptized or scholars, it was

Detail of a mosaic from the church floor, Ein-Sheva (Tabgha) on the shore of the Sea of Galilee, Byzantine period

especially important to combine all the components of the discourse described above into a entity. By this means did the church become a socio-religious focus of the first order in Christian society. Here, too, there was a marked trend towards democratization of public and religious life. John Chrysostom asked: "Did you know of such a burning desire to hear sermons among our Christian contemporaries?" (*On the Priesthood*, 5:8). All this points to increasing involvement of the simple masses in shaping the spiritual atmosphere. Public involvement was directed more than once towards the resort to violence in the course of dogmatic disputes or Church politics, and John himself fell victim to it. The Church was thus the central arena in which the believer absorbed the principles of the faith, and fostered and

123

Remains of a public building in Tiberias, identified by some as a house of study, Byzantine period

refined his emotional world, but was also simultaneously exposed to propaganda and to extremely venomous attacks on the enemies of the Church, whether in sermons of the preachers or from the language of prayer, whether against adversaries from within or enemies from without. The Jews occupied a special place among the enemies of the Church, and denunciations of them were often heard within its walls.

Thus the Church and the Synagogue stood facing one another, each struggling to preserve its own identity while rejecting the other, the adversary. Perhaps this was what lay behind the Church's struggle – under imperial sponsorship from the first third of the fifth century – against the synagogue as an institution. Was the florescence of this institution a real threat to the Church's profound desire to bring salvation to the Jews, in anticipation of the End of Days? As we shall see further on, the synagogue was (in the middle of the sixth century) the object of harsh intervention in its affairs, preceded, as early as the second half of the fourth century, by aggressive assaults on the part of Christians against synagogues. True, imperial legislation sought to protect the synagogues and required the attackers to pay compensation for the damage caused, but other legislation forbade the building of new synagogues. It is doubtful whether the attackers complied with the law, while at the same time there was also considerable synagogue construction in Galilee. Thus all sides disregarded the law.

Some of the processes undergone by the Jewish community in the Land of Israel towards the end of the ancient period, which we have briefly described above, seem to support the opinion already expressed by some scholars that, lacking central institutions and traditional systems of guidance, Jewish society

had lost some of its vitality. Further supporting this assumption are the endeavors to compile and redact the literary products of academies, resulting in a decline of original creativity. However, it seems that this view – that Land of Israel Judaism was in a state of decline – was influenced by the propaganda emanating from the alternative center on the rise in Babylon. The author of a pro-Babylon propagandist pamphlet from the early ninth century CE, known as "The Epistle of Pirkoi ben Baboi," provides a good description of the ongoing attitude of the Babylonian center towards what was occurring in the Land of Israel:

Thus said Mar Yehudai [one of the most important of the early *geonim*], of blessed memory: religious persecution was decreed upon the Jews of the Land of Israel – that they should not recite the *Shema* [declaration of God's Oneness] and should not pray, because the practice of renouncing religion is what evil Edom [Rome, Byzantium] decreed, religious persecution against the Land of Israel that they should not read the Torah, and they hid away all the Torah scrolls because they would burn them and when the Ishmaelites [Muslims] came they had no Torah scrolls and they had no scribes [to copy scrolls] who knew the pertinent laws for doing [this] ... and up till now they carry on like this ... But in Babylon Torah [study] has not ceased among Israel ... and the Evil Empire did not rule over Babylon ... and two *yeshivot* [academies] have not forgotten the Oral Law nor the law to be practiced from ages ago until now ... (Ginzburg, pp. 544ff.)

We cannot know which religious persecution Pirkoi was referring to. However, Emperor Justinian issued a decree in 553 which represented an obvious attempt to wreak havoc with the contents of study and ritual activity. The law forbade study of the Mishnah (Deuterosis), and obliged readers of the Bible in Greek to specifically use the Septuagint (although use of the Aquila translation was permitted too). All these were decreed in an effort to bring the Jews "for the prophecies contained in them [Holy Books] through which they announce the Great God and the Saviour of the human race, Jesus Christ" (Linder, p. 408).

If what Pirkoi wrote had any basis in reality, then even prior to his times there was no more Torah study or any halakhic decision-making in the Land of Israel, and even the prayer customs of its Jews were faulty. These categorical assertions as to the wretched spiritual status of the Land of Israel were not born in Pirkoi's time. They were the height of the process of estrangement and rejection on the part of the young, well-established, institutionalized and proud Babylonian center towards the ancient center in the Land of Israel, a process that

The blind King Zedekiah led into exile in Babylon; from a French manuscript, 14ᵗʰ cent. (Bodl. MS. Douce, fol. 213r)

had far-reaching implications. Pirkoi's blunt remarks fell on ears that had been receptive to such remarks for generations; they signify the transition from one center to another and the passage into a new age in the history of the nation.

• • • • • • • • • •

"They Shall Be Brought to Babylon and There They Shall Remain"

Everything that the Jews of the Land of Israel wished for was already the lot of their brethren in Babylon: proper treatment, on the whole, on the part of the Sassanid state; a recognized leadership, centralized and vigorous, in the form of the exilarchate; a diverse and creative world of Torah study; and economic security. All they lacked was a unique status and prestige in the network of Jewish centers in the Diaspora. The Babylonian center was the earliest of the various Diaspora centers, having existed undisrupted in a truly stable manner. But this was not

enough as long as the center in the Land of Israel still existed.

And then, precisely at the height of the golden age of Land of Israel Jewry, towards the end of the period associated with R. Judah ha-Nasi (who redacted and closed off the Mishnah, was the accepted leader of the Jews both in the Land of Israel and the Diaspora, and had close relations with the Roman authorities), Jews in the Babylonian Diaspora began their energetic attempts to make a name for themselves. It is doubtful whether this was a planned, preconceived effort. Yet, with hindsight, we can say that the seeds of change were planted in that period. The event that laid the foundation for Babylon as an independent spiritual center was identified by the important, though late (eleventh century), chronicler of Babylonian Jewry, Rav Sherira Gaon in his famous epistle: "In the days of Rabbi [Judah ha-Nasi], Rav went down to Babylon in the year 530 [=219 CE]" (*Epistle of Rav Sherira Gaon*, p. 78). The date of Rav's emigration to Babylon is the first date in the letter that is not drawn from known Talmudic sources. The emigration to Babylon of a man who was one of the

125

outstanding students of R. Judah ha-Nasi, and who brought with him the Mishnah, symbolized the new age of Babylon as a center of Torah study. This date is viewed as a watershed in the history

A stone relief with Temple candelabra and the Four Species, found in Corinth, Greece, Byzantine period

of the Babylonian center, after which the expression "since Rav came to Babylon" became common. For the Jews in Babylon, Rav's arrival signified the beginning of the end of the Land of Israel's spiritual hegemony and the outset of dependence on the growing vitality of the yeshivot in Babylon. This center started conducting a struggle to achieve autonomy in determining Jewish law in various fields. Moreover, at this time we first come across the leadership institution in Babylon that was parallel to the nesiut in the Land of Isael: the exilarchate. It is symbolic that, as is related, at the very time that a genealogical scroll was discovered in the ruins of Jerusalem pointing out that Hillel, the ancestor of Rabbi, was a scion of the House of David, in Babylon they similarly began to ascribe the exilarch, too, to the House of David.

These two elements were part of the effort to create an ideological infrastructure claiming historical seniority for Babylon. Implementation of this concept was not slow in coming. Babylonian Jews began to stress the primacy and antiquity of their synagogues, such as the one in which Daniel had worshiped, or like those in Huzel or in Shaf and Yatib, to which the Divine Presence had exiled itself when the First Temple was destroyed. Not content with this, they also soon began to identify biblical sites from the Book of Genesis with Babylonian and Persian cities of their own time. Thus, Erech, Accad and Calneh (Genesis 10:10) were identified with Edessa, Nisibis and Ctesiphon. Furthermore they pointed to palm trees allegedly planted by Adam and locales to which Israel had been banished during the exile in Assyria. Babylonian Jews continued this tendency until the time of the

geonim when they added another level of mythological coloring to the establishment of these synagogues by claiming that they had been built from the rubble and stones of the destroyed First Temple. The intent of such a transfer was to reinforce Babylonian Jewry's self-image of superiority through a mythical nexus between later Babylon and archaic Land of Israel, while disregarding an important historical period – Second Temple times – a period of time with whose history they were unacquainted.

This mythic perception of the Babylonian past was not confined to the conceptual sphere. It became a central component in Babylon's claim for Jewish social hegemony and supremacy in *halakhah*. The Babylonians believed themselves to be of purer lineage than the Jews of the Land of Israel: "All the countries are dough [compared] to the Land of Israel [which was clean flour compared to them since they were mixed like dough], and the Land of Israel is dough [compared] to Babylon" (Babylonian Talmud, *Qiddushin* 69b). Even in Babylon itself the different districts were graded, and likewise the adjacent regions of Meshan and Media were ranked in comparison to Babylon. Local patriotism reached even a higher degree when Rav Judah, founder of the Talmudical academy of Pumbeditha (second half of the third century), remonstrated with R. Zeira who wanted to immigrate to the Land of Israel: "Rav Judah said, Whoever goes up to the Land of Israel transgresses by commission, as it is said: 'They shall be brought to Babylon, and there they shall remain, until I take note of them – declares the Lord' (Jeremiah 27:22). And if [so when they are] alive, so too after death; whoever is buried in Babylon is as if he were buried in the Land of Israel" (*Avot de-Rabbi Nathan*, p. 82).

It is dubious whether the Jews of the Land of Israel could prevent these far-reaching developments, most of which took place in the period of the *amoraim*. They certainly did not agree with Babylonian Jewry's attempt to attain halakhic autonomy at that time. This conflict intensified during the Middle Ages, in the time of the geonim, when the sages of Babylon claimed for themselves the authority to decide in issues applying to the Hebrew calendar which had always been considered the exclusive prerogative of the Land of Israel Jewish religious leadership.

Some of the intensified conflict between the two centers could be ascribed to the rude, arrogant, and hurtful manner in which the Jews of the Land of Israel treated their Babylonian brethren. Even in Second Temple times Jews in the Land of Israel had exhibited aloofness, even hostility, towards Diaspora Jews, whether they were Alexandrians or Babylonians. The

Elijah the Prophet leads the Messiah to the gates of Jerusalem. The Dome of the Rock is visible in the center of the city. From a Passover Haggadah, Germany, 1753. An identical illustration is found in a Haggadah from Venice, 17th cent.

Babylonians who came to settle in the Land of Israel, like Jews from other diasporas, did not mix to any great degree with the local inhabitants and created communal frameworks that preserved their sense of common origin. This in itself was sufficient to perpetuate the Babylonian immigrants' sense of alienation, yet the Jews of the Land of Israel added to it even more. R. Shimeon ben Lakish, a colleague of R. Yohanan and one of the most important *amoraim* in the Land of Israel during the second half of the third century, rudely told a Babylonian sage, Rabbah Bar Bar Hana:

God hates you. For it is written: "If she be a wall, We will build upon it a silver battlement; If she be a door, We will panel it in cedar" (Song of Songs 8:9). If you had made yourselves as a wall and had all come up [to the Land of Israel] in the days of Ezra, you would have been compared to silver that decay cannot affect; now [at the time of R. Shimeon ben Lakish] that you have come up as doors, you may be compared to cedar wood that is overcome by decay (Babylonian Talmud, *Yoma* 9b).

When the rude remarks of Shimeon ben Lakish were repeated by people in the street, they took on an especially harsh tone. The latter not only protested the aloofness of the Babylonians, but put the blame for the destruction of the Second Temple upon them and their deeds. In fact, they blamed them for the harsh fate of the entire nation, because they had not returned to the Land of Israel as one man in the time of Ezra. Did the Jews of the Land of Israel seek in this fashion to pay back in the same coin the people of Babylon who claimed historic primacy? Or did they seek to respond in this fashion to the Babylonian amora Abbaye,

who claimed that the birth pangs of the Messiah would not be felt in Babylon? We cannot know in what manner and to what extent was this ambiance of estrangement – which did not appertain to all the inhabitants of the Land of Israel – in fact the moving force behind the historic transformation that we have described. Be that as it may, by the fifth and sixth centuries a center competing with the Land of Israel was already an accomplished fact. Nevertheless, the influence of the Land of Israel continued to be felt long afterwards in areas of Jewish settlement in the Hellenistic-Roman world: in the area between Himyar (in the southern Arabian peninsula) and Athens, as well as between Antioch and Clermont, in Gaul.

Although the splendor of the Land of Israel had faded somewhat for the Jews, the Gentiles now turned their attention to it. The sixth and early seventh centuries were a stormy period for its Jews, one imbued with apocalyptic sensations, an age when ruling empires changed position, a time of tidings of Redemption.

. . . .

An Age of Transition: Empires in Conflict

In the year when the King-Messiah is revealed,
all the kings of the nations of the world will
challenge each other (*Pesikta Rabbati, Qumi Ori,* 36)

About a hundred years after the nesiut ceased to exist, the leadership of the Jewish community in the Land of Israel found

127

The Valley of Arbel, the scene of apocalyptic events in *The Book of Zerubbabel*

itself up to its neck in a political-religious conflict that was flaring far from its borders. The focus of the conflict was Himyar in the southern Arabian peninsula, but its reverberations were felt far away, in the capitals of Persia and Byzantium. At that time, in the twenties of the sixth century, the accumulative influence of the Jewish presence around the southern shores of the Red Sea and along its important trade routes was being felt – according to Christian tradition – in the act of conversion to Judaism of the Himyarite kingdom. Contemporary Christian documents tell of a local king named Joseph Dhu Nuwas who became a Jew. These documents ascribe to emissaries of the Jewish priestly leadership in Tiberias a significant role in the affair through the aid and advice they extended. Were it not for the important geopolitical location of this kingdom – on the southern shores of the Red Sea very near the trade routes to the kingdom of Axum (Abyssinia) which had only recently been Christianized – and if Dhu Nuwas had not begun to mercilessly persecute the Christian communities in his kingdom and in the area to the north, in the city of Najran, it is doubtful whether this episode would have attracted so much attention. One Christian author even claimed that the objective of the involvement of the Tiberian priests, and

of their incitement of the king, was to alleviate the Byzantine Empire's pressure on its Jews. According to a later, somewhat legendary, tradition, at that very time a sage from Babylon, Mar Zutra, became part of the institutional leadership in the Land of Israel. This sage was the only son of the exilarch – also named Mar Zutra – who had been executed by the Persians towards the end of the fifth century after an uprising which reached its climax with the creation of an autonomous Jewish territory. Did the appearance of a new scion of the House of David infuse the events in Babylon and Himyar with a messianic tint? Did the Jews of the Land of Israel seek to restore past glory by replanting an offshoot of the stock of Jesse in the Land of Israel? This is very doubtful. In any event, the episode in Himyar ended with the defeat of Joseph, king of Himyar, by a unified Byzantine camp. This was a portent of what was to come.

The death of Justinian (565) foretold the approaching end of Byzantine imperial rule in Palestine. Domestic conflicts, increasing difficulties along its borders with barbarian Europe, and rising tension with the Sassanids brought nearer the end of the Byzantine presence in Palestine. Towards the end of the century, centers of hostility between Jews and Christians emerged,

128

both in the Land of Israel and in the Diaspora. This unrest and signs of the empire's collapse fanned messianic hopes among the Jews in the Land of Israel. In this spirit, the liturgical poet Yannai wrote the following uncompromising words:

May it be reported of Edom as it was reported of Egypt / The vision of Dumah like the vision of Egypt / Receiving retribution from Pathros [Parthians?] at the end of a tenth plague / And a tenth horn shall utterly settle accounts with Edom / (*Piyyutei Yannai*, p 90)

A converted Jew named Jacob attested to these hopes in a unique testimony some time later. While describing an encounter in Acre he witnessed in his youth during the reign of the Emperor Maurice (582–602), Jacob told of "a **priest from Tiberias**" who had a vision that the Messiah, King of Israel, would come at the end of eight years. If the Tiberian indeed saw this vision towards the end of Maurice's reign, then its "fulfillment" would have begun in 611 with the conquest of Antioch by the Sassanid army. We may assume from this story that messianic fervor had not waned among Galilean Jews and their leadership. These Jews in fact played an important role during the Persian invasion of the country. According to Christian sources, the Jews joined forces with the Persian who invaded the country through Eastern Galilee. Their line of advance passed through Lower Galilee to Caesarea and Jerusalem, where they slaughtered many Christians, apparently with the Jews' help. Jerusalem was the crowning achievement of the Persian military campaign, viewed by the Jews in redemptionist terms. The foundations of redemptionism were laid in Galilee, where such expectations were first expressed. Early in the seventh century, the author of the apocalyptic *Book of Zerubbabel* wrote:

All the children of Israel will see the Lord like a man of war with a helmet of salvation on His head... He will do battle against the forces of Armilus [an epithet for the king of Rome] and they will all fall dead in the Valley of Arbael (*Book of Zerubbabel*, p. 78)

This tradition once again illuminated the array of mythic traditions that the Galileans had formed about their region, according to which the staff of Aaron and Moses and King David had been hidden in Raqat, that is, Tiberias. It was given into the keeping of the Messiah of the House of Ephraim (the herald of the Messiah of the House of David). These traditions, which were rooted in Jerusalem, would not have been transferred to Galilee if Tiberias had not assumed for itself the status of a substitute for Jerusalem as a place of pilgrimage and prayer. Karaite traditions from the ninth and tenth centuries attest:

Because before his coming [of the king of Ishmael who had defeated the king of the South, that is, the Byzantine emperor], they could not come to Jerusalem, therefore from the four corners of the earth they came to Tiberias and to Gaza [and in another source, to Zo'ar too] to see the holy domain... (Daniel al-Qumisi, *Commentary on Daniel* 11:32).

The reconquest of the Holy Land by the Byzantine Emperor Heraclius in 630, a conquest entailing clear Christian messianic connotations (restoration of the True Cross to Jerusalem from its Persian captivity, and a campaign of persecution against the Jews), added to the sense of the approaching End of Days with the kingdoms challenging one another. And when the Muslims appeared in Palestine in 634, an anonymous liturgical poet imagined seeing in the events of the time a realization of the apocalyptic vision of Zerubbabel son of Shealtiel, most of which is played out in Central Galilee:

[The kings from the land of] Edom will be no more

And the people of Antioch will rebel and make peace

And Ma'uziya [Tiberias] and Samaria will be consolated

And Acre and the Galilee will be shown mercy

Edomites and Ishmael will fight in the Valley of Acre

(From "On That Day," a piyyut for the Ninth of Av, p. 199).

Redemption did not come for the Jews of the Land of Israel, but a new age of cultural-spiritual bloom did dawn, and once again, as in olden times, Judea and Jerusalem were the focus of this florescence.

The Middle Ages

From the Muslim to the Ottoman Conquests (634–1517)

Avraham Grossman

Five prominent trends characterized the manner in which Jews in the Middle Ages conceived of the role played by the Land of Israel in their Jewish identity.

A. The Middle Ages were the Age of Faith. Monotheism exerted a decisive influence on people's emotions and world outlook. This applies to Jews, to Christians, and to Muslims:

In the Middle Ages, man wove the fabric of his life, for good or for ill, around the axis of faith… For medieval man the unity of feelings and deeds was created by virtue of faith, of subordination to what was decreed from Heaven… the predominant concept was the Jewish one, that man has a mission on earth, a concept that was passed on to Christianity and Islam from Judaism. In this common setting in which Jews, Christians, and Muslims – who held a religious view in common – came together, was the history of the Middle Ages created… The decisive majority of people in Europe and in the Near East acted under the assumption that they were living in the sight of God. This was the climate in which Jews existed and wove their lives, and in this ambiance they entered into relations and competition with their rivals. [Ben-Sasson, p. 7]

B. The vast majority of the Jewish People – ca. 90 percent – in the seventh to the eleventh centuries lived in Muslim lands, particularly in what are today Iraq and Iran. There were other large Jewish concentrations in North Africa, Syria, Egypt, Spain, and Yemen. Due to their relative proximity to the Land of Israel they could maintain economic and cultural contact with its Jewish population. This is especially true for the period from the seventh until the ninth centuries.

Though the number of Jews in Christian Europe was gradually increasing from the eleventh to the thirteenth centuries, most of the Jewish People still lived in Islamic lands. The numbers reported by Benjamin of Tudela, who traveled through the Orient and some European cities in the second half of the twelfth century, bear this out.

C. Medieval Jewish society was marked by great migrations, especially at the beginning of the period. New centers were established, including those in North Africa and in Germany.

D. The Jews maintained close cultural, social, and economic ties with their Muslim and Christian neighbors. Though these ties declined somewhat from the thirteenth century onwards, they greatly influenced the world outlook of Jewish society.

E. Judaism, Christianity, and Islam all evinced an inclination for a connection to a sacred center, a link that included pilgrimage.

The Land of Israel was the scene of great political, economic, and social change during this period. The Muslims ruled it until 1099, when it was conquered by the Christian Crusaders who came from Europe. The land was reconquered step by step by the Muslims beginning in 1187, and especially after 1250 when the Mamluks came to power in Egypt. In 1291 they took Acre from the Crusaders who also abandoned Athlit and Tyre, their last footholds in Palestine. Mamluk rule continued until 1517. These great political transformations also had a decisive effect on the fate of the Jewish population and on the nature of Diaspora Jewry's relationship to the Land of Israel.

The discussion of the Middle Ages will be divided below into three separate chapters: The Early Muslim Period (634–1291); the Crusader Period (1099–1291); and the Mamluk Period which lasted until 1517 (the Mamluks gradually took control over all the territory of Eretz Israel from 1260 to 1291). Most of what we have to say focuses on the Jewish population. However we ought to bear in mind that throughout the whole epoch the Jews were a minority in the country. In the first period, most of the inhabitants of the country were Christians, while the weight of the Muslim population gradually increased. Scholars are still divided over the issue of whether the Muslims became a majority in the country or whether the Christians continued to be numerically dominant in the population. At the same time, the Jews comprised a sizable, influential minority. The same applies to the Samaritans and the Karaites, whose numbers were large and whose influence was great. The number of Jews in the other two periods was very small, and they lacked any real influence on the political, social, or economic life of the country.

The Gate of Mercy in the eastern wall of Jerusalem

The Early Muslim Period

Avraham Grossman

The history of the Land of Israel in the Early Muslim period can be broadly divided into three sub-periods: from the beginning of the Muslim conquest until the end of the Umayyad dynasty (634–750); Abbasid rule (750–969); Fatimid rule (969–1099, with short intermittent breaks). The first sub-period appears to have been a golden age for the Jews of the Land of Israel in medieval times in respect of their status and their relationship with the Diaspora. True, we have very few historical sources dealing with the history of Palestine from the sixth to the eighth centuries, and these do not enable a full and precise reconstruction. Nevertheless, despite the problematics involved in arriving at conclusions upon the basis of the silence of the sources, it seems that we may consider this to be the best period for the Jews of the Land of Israel, from the economic, security, social, and cultural aspects. The capital of the Umayyad Muslim caliphate was located in Damascus until 750. Thus, the center of authority was very near to the Land of Israel. Trade caravans on their way to the capital of the caliphate also passed through Palestine. Even though the Arab tribes that had penetrated the country after the conquest fought one another, this was – relatively speaking – an age of security. The Umayyad Muslim rulers restored the coastal cities and rebuilt the country's roads. They intended to glorify Jerusalem which served as a substitute of sorts for holy and distant Mecca that was located in the sphere of influence of their rivals. To this purpose they encouraged building projects in Palestine, of which the two most important were the Dome of the Rock in Jerusalem, erected ca. 692, and the adjacent al-Aqsa mosque. Likewise, between 712 and 717 they built the city of Ramlah, that served as the capital of the district of Filastin, one of the three into which Palestine was divided. Many Jews came to live there, and it became a rather wealthy community that sometimes even surpassed in importance the Jewish community of Jerusalem. Jews from Babylon too settled in Ramlah, establishing their own synagogue, and there was a large Karaite community in the city as well.

In addition to the two large communities in Jerusalem and Ramlah, many Jews lived in Galilee, especially in Tiberias which served as a district capital (of Jund al-Urdunn). The Christian traveler Wilibald, who visited the country around the year 724, mentioned the Jewish synagogue in Tiberias. Hence, it must have made an impression on visitors to the city. He also noted the many churches in Tiberias. There was also an important Jewish community in Tyre, which served as a central port for Palestine's trade throughout the entire Early Muslim period, and also Jewish settlements in the center and north of the country, including Acre, Haifa, and Lod. Additional Jewish communities were found in the southern coastal and lowland cities (such as Ascalon, Gaza, Rafiah, and el-Arish), as well as in Hebron, Eilat, the Dead Sea area, and east of the Jordan, while many Samaritans lived in Shechem.

The Jews, like the other inhabitants of the country, earned their livelihood from agriculture, crafts, and trade. We cannot determine how many Jews lived in the country at that time, but they

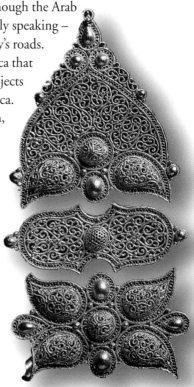

Jewelry set with diamonds, found in Ascalon, 11th cent.

135

Administrative division of Palestine 7th–11th cent., showing location of Jewish communities

The Muslims, who at first were a small conquering army and lacking in administrative experience, needed Christian and Jewish officials. The Jews were also credited with helping the Muslim conquerors in their war against the Byzantines in Palestine. Mu'awiya also settled Jews in Tripoli (Syria), for he relied on their loyalty and intended to fortify the northern coastal cities with their help. Though by the end of the Umayyad dynasty, during the reign of Caliph Umar II (717–720), the status of the Jews and Christians began to deteriorate due to various restrictions and harmful decrees, it was, on the whole, still rather favorable.

The Muslim authorities granted Jews and Christians residing in the country and throughout the caliphate fairly broad autonomy. The Jews were led by the Head of the *Yeshiva* (academy), the *gaon*, whose seat was in Jerusalem. Remnants of more creative literary works emanating from the *Yeshiva* in that period have survived than from later periods. Especially noteworthy is *Sefer ha-Ma'asim li Venei Eretz Israel* (The Book of Rulings of the People of the Land of Israel) which comprised halakhic decisions made in the center at Tiberias that were collected and edited at the beginning of the Muslim period.

Tiberias was the Jews' spiritual center at the end of the Byzantine and the beginning of the Muslim periods. However, not long after the conquest, when the Muslims had allowed the Jews to return to Jerusalem, the spiritual center too was transferred there. The masoretes (experts in the textual tradition of the Bible) were also active in Tiberias, and it was they who created the Tiberian system of vocalization that was eventually accepted wherever Jews lived. This was also the period in which many poets and *paytanim* (liturgical poets) flourished throughout the country. Particularly noteworthy are Yannai and Kalliri, many of whose *piyyutim* (liturgical poems) have survived and whose influence on the Jewish prayer book has been considerable up to our own times. Early *midrashim* (homiletic interpretations of biblical passages) were collected and redacted in the Land of Israel during that period, and new ones were composed. Even though the literary works created in the Land of Israel in the early Muslim period do not compare with those compiled in Babylon, the Umayyad period was clearly better and more fruitful than the two that followed.

* * * * * * * * * *

Jewish Immigration to the Land of Israel

Much attention has been devoted in the scholarly literature to Jewish immigration and the Jews' relationship to the Land of Israel in the Fatimid period (969–1099), while little attention

certainly numbered several tens of thousands. On the whole, the first century of Muslim rule was a period of growth and prosperity for both Jews and Christians, who accounted for the majority of the population of Palestine. Since the Caliph Mu'awiya (661–680) and his heirs were intent upon consolidating their rule, they treated Jews and Christians, the "protected peoples" (*ahl al-dhimma*), with tolerance, guaranteeing the security of their persons and property, and did not hamper their economic activity.

has been given to these aspects in the Umayyad and Abbasid periods. This is the result of the abundant sources dealing with the country in the Fatimid period that were discovered in the Cairo genizah and from the paucity of such sources for the earlier ones. Nevertheless, a comprehensive examination of the historic conditions – especially the state of security and the economic situation – that encouraged and shaped the character of waves of immigration supports the hypothesis that immigration prior to the Fatimid era was even more widespread.

The Umayyad Muslim rulers encouraged immigration to Palestine to protect the coast against Byzantine invasion. Many Muslim immigrants arrived from Iraq and Persia, which were also large centers of Jewish population. It is difficult to assume that when the Jews saw thousands of their neighbors migrating to the Land of Israel their own sense of attachment to the country was not aroused. The Arab geographer al-Yaʻqubi, (second half of the ninth century) noted a Persian population in the northern cities of Palestine. In any case, even if this wave of immigration was caused by "security considerations," it is difficult to assume that it did not leave its impression upon the Jews in those countries.

Two additional factors encouraged Jewish immigration from Babylon and Persia at this time: the rise of many messianic movements in the seventh and eighth centuries and large-scale emigration of Jews from Babylon and its environs to other centers. Of the messianic movements that emerged in that period, several were mass movements. True, the numbers noted by Arab and Karaite geographers and chroniclers were exaggerated, but they are a clear indication of the broad scope of the movements and the powerful impression that they left on their contemporaries. Messianism sometimes took on a political form when the false messiahs claimed that they would defeat the Muslims by force of arms and lead the Jews to the Land of Israel. We may assume that this messianic awakening – so widespread – and the expectation of Redemption that would return the Jews to Zion, aroused a longing for the Land of Israel, and apparently also encouraged Jewish immigration there. Messianic expectations are also reflected in several piyyutim composed in the Land of Israel at the time, including those of Kalliri. The great body of apocalyptic literature written in that era also encouraged this phenomenon.

The motives for Jewish emigration from Babylon were chiefly economic. Many Babylonian Jews abandoned their lands, becoming merchants and traders. Thus came to an end the emotional bond that tied a man to his own soil. Jews were attracted to the developing commercial centers in the West, along

the shores of the Mediterranean Sea. Though most of the migrants went to Egypt, Spain, and especially to North Africa,

Fragment from *Sefer ha-Ma'asim*, an important source for the history of Jewish law and lifestyle in the Land of Israel towards the end of the Byzantine and the beginning of the Muslim periods (NLR, MS. Ant. 35)

Page from a liturgical poem by Yannai , corresponding to Gen. 31–32 (Bod. MS. Heb. c20, fol. 3v)

some may have settled down in the Land of Israel, through which many of them passed on their westward journey.

The hypothesis that Jewish immigration from Babylon and Persia was relatively greater in that earlier epoch finds support in what Pirkoi ben Baboi, a Babylonian sage who lived at the beginning of the ninth century, wrote:

Until now they do not say kadosh and shma [part of the prayer ritual] in the Land of Israel except on the Sabbath and holidays and only in the morning, except for Jerusalem and every city where there are Babylonians, who raised a quarrel and a controversy until they [the native inhabitants] agreed to recite

137

Shechem (Nablus) between Mount Gerizim and Mount Ebal, etching by Harry Fenn, 1881

kedushah every day. However, in the rest of the cities and towns in the Land of Israel, where there are no Babylonians, they do not recite kadosh except on the Sabbath and holidays. (Ginzburg, pp. 555–556)

We cannot determine the number of cities and towns in which the Babylonian immigrants Pirkoi referred to had settled. However, his use of the plural "every city where there are Babylonians" indicates that there were at least several of them. In the Middle Ages, Jews zealously preserved the prayer customs of their forefathers, vehemently refusing to change them. The fact that the Babylonians "defeated" the residents of the Land of Israel and forced them to forego the ancestral customs which they had practiced for many generations indicates that there were many Babylonians in those cities, perhaps even a majority of their Jewish population. Jerusalem, as we have seen, was one of those cities.

We do not have much explicit information about the emotional ties of Jews in this period to the Land of Israel. However, we may assume with a high degree of probability that the intensive political developments gave rise to powerful messianic expectations. The relatively large waves of Jewish immigration to the country greatly strengthened this relationship, a matter to which we shall return.

The Abbasid Period

During the Abbasid Period (750–969), three factors contributed to a slight deterioration in the condition of the inhabitants of Palestine, especially Jews and Christians: the transfer of the capital from Damascus to Baghdad was detrimental to commercial activity in the country; a change for the worse in the attitude of the Muslim authorities towards the protected peoples – the Jews and the Christians; the outbreak of several revolts and the increased tax burden. But the Muslims did not always strictly enforce the discriminatory laws, and during most of this period the condition of the Jews in the country was rather good. After the death of Harun al-Rashid there was a state of anarchy in Palestine. During the reign of his son, Caliph al-Ma'mun (813–831), the Samaritan and Christian communities in the country suffered especially and many of their members abandoned the country, emigrating to other lands. Ahmad ibn Tulun revolted against the Abbasids, established an independent state in Egypt in 868, and some time later conquered Palestine and Syria. Unrest continued in the country even after his rule, particularly during

Samaritan Torah scroll in ancient Hebrew script. A colored photograph from the early twentieth century

the reign of Muhammad al-Ikhshid (922–946). Construction work declined, and Jerusalem no longer enjoyed the favored status it had attained during the Umayyad caliphate, though several Muslim scholars still lived there, while some of the Abbasid caliphs visited the city.

The Samaritans, until then a large and powerful community living in various locations throughout the country, especially around Mount Gerizim, suffered heavily, more than any other minority in the country during the Early Muslim period. At first they had good relations with the Muslims, even helping them in their conquests. The Samaritans participated in the bitter struggle for power by the sons of Harun al-Rashid and revolted against local Muslim rulers. The Abbasid period was disastrous for their

community. A Samaritan chronicler, Abu al-Fath, noted that the Samaritans suffered a very severe blow, and many abandoned the country, fleeing eastwards. Even a generation later, during the reign of Caliph al-Mu'tasim (833–842), attacks were mounted against the Samaritans in Shechem and their houses of prayer were set on fire. They were dealt such a lethal blow, that in the Crusader period their presence was scarcely noticed.

The sources do not contain much information about the occupations of the Jews in Jerusalem. Al-Muqaddasi, who lived in Jerusalem at the end of the tenth century, reports that most of the bankers and the moneychangers, the dyers of cloth and the tanners in the country were Jews. Weaving, too, was a Jewish craft, while many Jews engaged in trade. Many others, particularly

139

Arhuta Qadishata (The Holy Torah) – a Samaritan manuscript written in Shechem (Nablus) in 1215/16 (JNUL Sam 2° 6)

A reed mat woven in Tiberias, 10th cent. (Benaki Museum, Athens)

of the Abbasid period, early in the tenth century, a severe dispute arose over calculation of the calendar between the yeshivot (talmudical academies) in Babylon and the Yeshiva of the Land of Israel. We shall return to this episode, which dealt a harsh blow to the status of the Land of Israel.

The Fatimid Period

The fact that the seat of Fatimid rule (969–1099) was in Egypt should have been beneficial for commercial activity in the neighboring Land of Israel. However, unstable security struck very hard at the country's population, particularly its Jews. Many Jews left the country, especially for Egypt.

Bitter fighting raged for a period of sixty years, between 969 and 1029, with the Qarmatians and other Bedouin tribes that conquered Palestine for short periods of time. Such conditions enabled the Byzantines to penetrate the north of the country towards the end of the period.

What marked the great chaos prevailing in those years in Palestine were the severe blows dealt to individuals and their property. Many contemporary documents have survived in the Cairo genizah which describe the state of extreme insecurity that reigned throughout the country. From the desperate appeals for help which the leaders of the Jewish community in the Land of Israel addressed to their brethren in Egypt we learn just how severe conditions were. For example, residents of Jerusalem reported that only fifty Jewish families remained there, virtually stripped of their clothing and completely destitute. The same letter goes on to describe the harsh events that occurred in Ramlah:

And men and women died, some from the blows and some from the terror and some who threw themselves into the pits... and no sustenance was left for a man... And those who survived wept and moaned, one man to his brother, until they stopped paying [the taxes]... and the persecutor once again struck and tormented... because on account of sins our elders died and our associates perished and our young men expired and our wealthy men have become impoverished and we remain just a few, about fifty persons... and most of our sustenance came from the [Jewish community] officials of Ramlah and its merchants from whom we used to take on credit and sell and pay off the debts with interest. And because of our iniquities, the bad time has come for Ramlah, and they stopped supplying us, and the daily burden is heavy to the point where there is no peace, and no way to escape, and if it were not so, we would flee... And life throughout the Land of Israel is in a state of turmoil because of the troops... and we are plagued with many evil troubles, the like of which have not been seen in the Land of Israel [since it has been] under the dominion of Ishmael   (Gil, II, pp. 86–87)

in Galilee, continued to engage in agriculture. Jews were also occupied in copying books; from the colophons of several manuscripts we know that they were copied in the Land of Israel, especially in Jerusalem, during the eleventh century.

On the whole, the Jewish community in the Land of Israel continued to establish itself and to maintain its institutions as it did in the Umayyad period. Regular ties with Diaspora communities continued, and the status of the Land of Israel vis-à-vis the Diaspora and the relationship between them remained firm as in the past. Towards the end

The Roman street of columns in the city of Bet-Shean which collapsed in the earthquake of 749

If this difficult security situation were not enough, not to mention the hardship involved in paying the heavy taxes imposed on the Jews, the wars greatly limited the number of pilgrims who contributed to the economy and the morale of the Jewish inhabitants of Jerusalem. Under such conditions connections with the Diaspora suffered severely as well. The Fatimid Shi'ite authorities, however, considered the Jews and the Christians to be loyal elements, on whom they could rely and base their rule against the Sunni majority among the Muslims of Egypt, Palestine, and Syria. That is why they also appointed Jews to senior posts of authority in their administration, even in the army. However, this only slightly alleviated the harsh suffering of the Jewish population in the Land of Israel at that time, which had led to a dwindling of their numbers.

In addition to Jerusalem, other cities suffered as well, including Ramlah and Ascalon. Two severe earthquakes which shook the country in 1016 and 1033 added to the destruction, while several milder earthquakes are mentioned in the sources. We have reports of about twenty earthquakes in Palestine from the seventh through the eleventh centuries.

In 1012, Caliph al-Hakim issued harsh decrees against the Christians and Jews, causing a further decline in the condition of the latter. He issued a sweeping order to demolish churches, monasteries, and synagogues. Though only partially enforced, its effect was severe. In the twenties of the eleventh century, R. Joseph ibn Abitur – one of the outstanding sages of Spain in those times, who visited the Land of Israel – described the severe blows dealt the Jews, particularly women, and the atmosphere of despair:

Weep for men who see / their praiseworthy sons

Valued in gold / violated by Kushites.

Weep for blind men who wandered about / in Zion, fouled

By the blood of pregnant women ripped apart / and the blood of old men and babes.

Weep for the pure whom the polluted / beat to [make them] eat their abomination,

To make them forget the Covenant of their Lord / and their Land, the place of their desire.

Weep for purified women / careful, always pure

Who were subject to the seed of Ham / impregnated in their birth pangs...

Weep O weep for our living / and do not weep for our dead,

Because to be like them / is our desire at all times.

And therefore, my friend / do not think of me as consolation

For all those torn to pieces in Zion / and there is no one to bury them.

(Schirmann, pp. 64–66)

141

Pirkei de-Rabbi Eliezer (The Chapters of Rabbi Eliezer), a Land of Israel midrash edited in the eighth century. Right: title page of the Sabbioneta edition, 1567; left: title page of the Venice edition, 1608

Those were the most difficult times for the Jews of the Land of Israel since the Arab conquest, and their numbers dwindled greatly, especially in Jerusalem and Ramlah.

Even a temporary period of relative calm that began in 1030 did not bring succor to the Jewish population. True, as we shall see, the ties with the Diaspora were renewed, but internal confrontations within the Yeshiva of the Land of Israel, especially during the second half of the eleventh century, and a severe earthquake (1068), which were followed by the Seljuk conquest of Palestine (1070–1078), once again worsened the situation.

• • • • • • • • • •

Internal Communal Organization and the Yeshiva of the Land of Israel

The organizational pattern of the Jewish community also greatly influenced intellectual and social life in the country. The communal leader was the Head of the Yeshiva, the gaon of the Land of Israel. Formally, he was head of all Jews in the entire Fatimid caliphate. He was assisted by a group of seven men, at least some of whom were often members of his family. Essentially, this was a centralized system of government par excellence. A writ of authority granted to the gaon early in the eleventh century that has survived in the Cairo genizah, indicates that he was invested with very broad authority. In addition to his role in social and intellectual life, he was the political leader of the Jews, representing them before the authorities. Even teaching the Torah in public required his authorization. This centralization also had its drawbacks. The gaon's preoccupation with political leadership – which in the circumstances of those times was a complex, difficult role, demanding much time and thought – was detrimental to the creative work of the Yeshiva. This may provide a solution to one of the puzzling riddles concerning the nature of the Yeshiva, which enjoyed the glory of yore as the successor to the ancient Yeshiva of the Land of Israel: the almost total absence of literary works that emanated from it in the tenth and eleventh centuries.

The literary creativity of the Jews in the Land of Israel in that period encompassed most branches of rabbinic literature – midrashim, rulings on halakhah (religious law), responsa

142

(responses to questions of religious law), piyyutim, apocalyptic visions, works dealing with Hebrew, the biblical textual tradition and accents for biblical cantillation, and perhaps also translation of compositions on religious law from Aramaic into Hebrew. Though only remnants of this literature have come down to us, they clearly indicate that these creative works were overwhelmingly produced during the Umayyad and Abbasid periods, while only a small part (chiefly the continued composition of piyyutim) was accomplished in the Fatimid age.

There was relatively much activity in the genre of midrashic literature: some books were then composed, while other midrashim were collected and redacted. Among those written in the Land of Israel at that time, one should especially bear in mind *Pirkei de-Rabbi Eliezer*, apparently composed in the eighth century. It preserves allusions to historic events that occurred during the period of Muslim rule in Palestine. This was also one of the most productive periods for apocalyptic literature and piyyutim. It has been described as "the classical period of the piyyutim," ranging from about the mid-sixth century to the end of the eighth century:

It seems that composing piyyutim was a very vibrant and fruitful phenomenon in the classical age, and undoubtedly hundreds of paytanim were active then. The number of such works that have come down to us is very great. Nevertheless, it is certainly only a small part, perhaps a very small part, of what was created then... All the paytanim of the classical period lived in the Land of Israel. This fact is indisputable. For some paytanim we know exactly where they were active; in the case of others their piyyutim attest that they followed the customs of the Land of Israel. (Fleischer, pp. 117–118)

Few works of halakhic literature were produced. At the beginning of the period (the sixth and seventh centuries), the editing of the lesser tractates of the Talmud was completed, intended to complement the Mishnah on various matters. During the last years of Byzantine rule and the beginning of the Muslim age, *Sefer ha-Ma'asim* (The Book of Rulings), the most important book of halakhah reflecting the teachings of the sages of the Land of Israel in that era that has come down to us, was composed. It records short legal decisions in various fields, apparently decisions in cases brought before a court. Remnants of other compositions on halakhah have survived, but they are few. It is likely that there were additional halakhic works of

A tombstone from the city of Venosa in southern Italy, 829. The date of death is given both as the year 4589 since the Creation of the World and the year 761 since the destruction of the Temple

which no traces have been found. In all probability these too were composed at the beginning of the Muslim period, and not after the Fatimid conquest.

S.D. Goitein offered an explanation for the limited number of halakhic works emanating from the sages of the Yeshiva of the Land of Israel. He believed that the Yeshiva was essentially not a place of learning, but rather a sort of high council of the Jewish community, filling the role of Sanhedrin and high court. Thus the function of the gaon of the Land of Israel was similar to that of the Rosh Golah (exilarch) in Babylon. Whereas the gaon of the Land of Israel focused on political activity, the Babylonian gaon was mainly involved in the functions of learning and teaching the law, political activity being entrusted to the exilarch. This explains, according to Goitein, the voluminous literary activity in the Babylonian academies.

Goitein's explanation is attractive, but does not provide an explanation for the almost total literary silence in the Fatimid period. Except for several halakhic responsa and some piyyutim, we know of no other literary work produced in the Land of Israel. This is especially surprising when compared with the great flourishing of Karaite literary work in Jerusalem in the same period. Perhaps the centralized authority and the need for explicit

143

The doorpost of the Karaite synagogue in Jerusalem, bearing the Ten Commandments due to the Karaite interpretation of: "Take to heart these instructions with which I charge you this day... inscribe them on the doorposts of your house"

permission from the Head of the Yeshiva to teach Torah in public and to record teachings in writing served as a negative and repressive factor. A Hebrew saying declares that "the rivalry of scribes increases wisdom," but when there is no capacity and authorization to create, such rivalry cannot exist. Of course, additional factors were the difficult security situation prevailing in the country, as alluded to above, and the sharp competition for leadership of the Yeshiva.

Especially astonishing is the very limited number of responsa we have from the hands of the geonim of the Land of Israel. Perhaps those with questions preferred the teachings of the geonim of Babylon, for the level of the Babylonian yeshivot was much higher and they enjoyed much greater renown throughout the Diaspora. Jacob Mann's opinon is likely to be correct: he believed that most of the responsa by the geonim of the Land of Israel were not despatched to the countries around the Mediterranean Sea through Egypt, and therefore they were not preserved in the Cairo genizah and were lost. We may conjecture that the Syrian community, which was under the authority of the Land of Israel gaonate for part of the period, also forwarded its questions to the sages of the Land of Israel.

A Cairo genizah fragment from the letter of Pirkoi ben Baboi (NLR, MS. Ant. 195)

View of Jerusalem from the Mount of Olives that rises to the east of the city, where from the seventh to the eleventh centuries many ceremonies were held on Hoshana Rabba

Notice should be taken, if only briefly, of three traits characteristic of the method adopted by the sages of the Yeshiva of the Land of Israel in their halakhic decisions:

1) Priority was given to the customs and sources of the Land of Israel. The influence of the Babylonian Talmud was as yet insignificant in the Land of Israel at the beginning of the Muslim period. However, it did increase during the Abbasid period;

2) Close attachment to the Bible, not only when producing midrashim and piyyutim, but also in halakhic rulings, through interpretive deductions from biblical verses which served as an authority;

3) The sages of the Land of Israel wrote their works in Hebrew. This applies not only to *aggadot* (legends, etc.) and piyyutim but also to works of halakhah, including responsa. This they did despite the high degree of Arabization that the subject peoples in the country – Christians, Karaites, and Jews – were undergoing. However, as we pointed out, the lion's share of the creative work of the sages of the Land of Israel was carried out during the first phase of the Early Muslim period.

· · · · · · · · · · ·

The Diaspora and the Land of Israel in the Early Muslim Period

Five major factors influenced the Diaspora's relationship to the Land of Israel, and the latter's place in Jewish consciousness, during the Middle Ages:

1) The biblical and talmudic heritage concerning the status of the Land of Israel and the relations between it and the Babylonian Diaspora;

2) The changing political, security, and economic conditions of the Jewish population in the Land of Israel;

3) The changing political, security, and social conditions of the Jews in the Diaspora;

4) The relationship to the Land of Israel and particularly to Jerusalem in medieval Christianity and Islam;

5) Changes in the intellectual life and concepts of the Jews.

There is a bitter dispute recorded in the Babylonian Talmud over the status of the Land of Israel vis-à-vis Babylon. Appearing at the end of Tractate *Ketubbot* (111a & 111b), it was conducted between two major scholars of the third century, who studied together under Rav (Abba Arikha) and Mar Samuel in Babylon – R. Judah ben Ezekiel and R. Eleazar ben Pedat. R. Eleazar immigrated to the Land of Israel and became one of its outstanding standard bearers. Several of his sayings in that tractate in praise of the Land of Israel and its great virtues became basic

A carpet page from a Bible (Egypt, 1008 to 1010) with micrography in the form of a menorah (NLR, First Firkovich Collection B19a, fol. 476v)

components of Jewish thought in the Middle Ages, and even in modern times. For example: "Everyone who lives in the Land of Israel is in a sinless state"; "Those who die outside the Land of Israel will not be resurrected [at the End of Days]"; and even the statement that whoever is brought after his death for burial in the Land of Israel does not merit the same degree of virtue as someone who dies there. In opposition to this, the Talmud records the opinions of R. Judah (who in the meantime had become the head of the yeshiva of Pumbeditha) to the effect that it is forbidden to immigrate to the Land of Israel from Babylon, and whoever does so is guilty of a "sin of commission," or: "Whoever lives in Babylon it is as if he lived in the Land of Israel." Additional opinions of sages are also quoted on this issue in that same tractate.

Obviously, then, the medieval sages were aware of the various issues and the opposing opinions that were explicitly expressed on this topic. Nevertheless, there is no real, orderly, detailed discussion of this issue until the Crusader period, and this comes as no surprise. The first works dealing with Jewish thought – philosophy, beliefs, and opinions – began to be written only at the end of the Early Muslim period, but the attachment to the Land of Israel is not among the issues they discussed. Only the

145

dramatic events of the Crusader conquest of the Holy Land together with domestic troubles in European and Islamic countries, such as the decrees of 1096 and the Almohad violence (1148), were what raised the issue of the role of the Land of Israel in the anticipated process of Redemption.

However, this "silence" should not mislead us. The subject was broached in various forums, even though it left few traces in the written sources. Pirkoi ben Baboi, in his bitter polemic against the Land of Israel, to which we shall return, adopted the outlook of R. Judah, going even one step further in seeing in Babylon a "substitute" for the Land of Israel. Daniel al-Qumisi, one of the leaders of the Karaite community in Jerusalem in the tenth century, made the accusation that "the scoundrels who are among Israel say one to another: 'We do not need to ascend up to Jerusalem until [God] gathers us in, just as He cast us out,' so say those who cause us anger" (Mann, p. 283). He was referring to the three things that God made Israel and the other nations foreswear, oaths that are mentioned in the talmudic discussion in *Ketubbot*. The two oaths taken by Israel were that they would not go up [to Jerusalem] *en masse* and that they would not rebel against the nations of the world. The oath taken by the nations of the world was that they would not subjugate Israel "too much." Al-Qumisi's testimony is reliable. He would not have made up such an accusation, one that would be very easy to refute, if it were not true. Hence the question of immigration to the Land of Israel was a central issue among Jews even in the Early Muslim period.

There was a great awakening of messianic expectations among Jews in the Land of Israel and the Diaspora at the beginning of the Muslim occupation of Palestine, and it continued to a lesser extent even afterwards. Midrashic literature gave two clear omens that would signal the coming of Redemption: global catastrophes and times of great trouble for the Jewish people. In the words of the sages, "When you see empires challenging each other, expect the footfalls of the king-messiah" (*Genesis Rabbah* 42:4); "In the generation when the son of David will come… multitudes of trouble and evil decrees will be promulgated anew, each new evil coming with haste before the other has ended" (Babylonian Talmud, *Sanhedrin* 97a).

In the second decade of the seventh century, the Persians conquered Palestine and Jerusalem from the Byzantines. At first they treated the Jews of Jerusalem very well, but conditions soon deteriorated. Within a short while the Byzantines reconquered the city, after which their commander, Emperor Heraclius, issued harsh decrees against the Jews in the Land of Israel in general and those of Jerusalem in particular. A few years later, it was the turn of the Muslims to conquer the country. Within a relatively short time, then, we are witness to a combination of momentous political turnovers and severe suffering for the country's Jews – especially those in Jerusalem. Could one ask for greater or speedier events to serve as omens of Redemption?

These redemptionist expectations gave an impetus to the many messianic movements that had sprung up during the seventh and eighth centuries, especially in Persia and Iraq. If we include those that were small and local, their number totals several dozen, some of which were mass movements. Even if it is certain that the numbers cited by Arab and other geographers and chroniclers are exaggerated, there is no doubt that these figures are indicative of the broad scope of the movements and the strong impression they left upon contemporaries.

Clearly, the Muslim conquests also contributed greatly to this awakening. In any event, it is reasonable to assume that such a broad-scaled awakening and widespread expectation of Redemption that would return them to Zion aroused among Jews a longing to immigrate to the Land of Israel. This holds true even if some of the behavior of the would-be messiahs and their faithful deviated from talmudic law. In that era we are witness to a renewed flowering of apocalyptic literature which linked the Muslim conquest to the coming of Redemption. Messianic expectations are also found in several piyyutim composed then in the Land of Israel, including those of Eleazar Kalliri. These, too, prepared people for Redemption and increased expectations for the return of the exiled to Zion in their own lifetime.

Attesting to the great power of the apocalyptic visions is the fact that even two of the greatest Babylonian geonim were influenced by them. The vision of Redemption in the doctrine of R. Sa'adiah (tenth century) and R. Hai (early eleventh century) closely follows the description in *The Book of Zerubbavel* and other apocalyptic works. R. Sa'adiah Gaon's ideas on "the Last Redemption," presented in minute detail, stage after stage, were included in his book *Beliefs and Opinions*. Those of R. Hai Gaon have been preserved in one of his responsa. They both place all the events preceding Redemption in the Land of Israel – in Galilee, in Judea, and in Jerusalem. Jews would first be redeemed there, not in Babylon. The total rejection by the greatest Babylonian geonim of the teaching of Pirkoi ben Baboi that redemption would begin in Babylon, to which we shall return, is a fact of major importance. Pirkoi's doctrine was not accepted even in Babylon. The acceptance by two outstanding masters of halakhah of visions of Redemption that would be realized in the Land of Israel made a greater impression upon ordinary people than did the piyyutim of the country's sages. Their stamp of approval strengthened the attachment to the Land of Israel in the various Diasporas, for these two geonim were held to be the highest authority in every medieval Jewish community.

Hope for Redemption in the Land of Israel was part of the fabric of life and in the mind of every Jew in the Middle Ages. Faith in the prophetic mission already appears in the Bible, talmudic literature, and the midrashim. It is reiterated in the daily prayers and the piyyutim. As noted, medieval Jews were

setting aside offerings and tithes for the Temple outside the Land of Israel, so that these practices would not be forgotten when Redemption came. We will briefly discuss these several elements.

Works of Literature and Expressions of Faith

Many hundreds of piyyutim, apocalyptic books, and other works were written in the seventh to the eleventh centuries, in which their authors recounted the praises of the Land of Israel in general

Reconstruction of the pilgrimage to the Mount of Olives that was held every year on Hoshana Rabba

convinced of the pertinence of the prophecies in the Holy Scriptures. The omens of the coming of Redemption, that intensified their expectations and hopes, consolidated their deep faith in approaching Redemption even more.

The close attachment of Diaspora Jews to the Land of Israel found expression in several components: all types of religious works, particularly prayers and piyyutim; immigration to the Land of Israel; pilgrimage; burial in the Land of Israel; monetary support for the Yeshiva of the Land of Israel; practicing the customs of the Land of Israel in certain Jewish centers, even when these customs were opposed to those of Babylon; and finally,

and of Jerusalem in particular, and the profound yearning to return. Of course, praises of the Land of Israel and Jerusalem were also recited in the prayers. However, in the piyyutim, whose more animated recitation (unlike prayers recited by force of habit) accompanied joyful and sad events in communal life, the affection expressed for the Land of Israel and Jerusalem was more intense. We will make do with two examples. R. Amittai, a liturgical poet who lived in Italy in the ninth century, contemplated the beauty of Italian cities, and this evoked in him longings for Jerusalem. It was difficult for him enjoy what he saw without remembering the beauty of Jerusalem in times gone by:

147

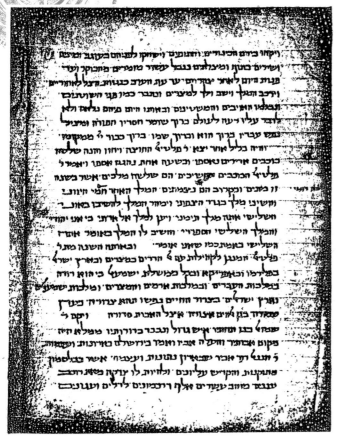

A section of *The Scroll of Ahima'az* (Italy, 1054) that tells about bringing leading members of the family for reburial in Jerusalem (CT)

I remember, O God, and I moan
When I see every city built on its hill
While the City of God is cast down to the depths of hell.
And despite all this, we belong to God and our eyes look to Him.
(*The Scroll of Ahima'az*, Appendices, p. 95)

Two generations later, R. Sa'adiah Gaon, in Babylon, composed a special prayer describing the expectation for Redemption in Zion:

May it be Your will O Lord our God that You see the misery of Your people Israel scattered throughout all the countries, and the ruins of Jerusalem that was laid waste, and Your Temple that was forsaken and forlorn like a desert, and may You be zealous for Your Holy Name desecrated among the Gentiles, and may You gather the remnant of Your flock from all places where they have been scattered, and restore Israel to its dwelling place and may the Palace [= Temple] sit upon its proper site... And for the sake of Your people and Your estate that remained few out of the many, like a staff on the mountaintop and like a standard on the hilltop, and for the sake of Jerusalem, Your Holy city, all of whose grandeur has been lost, and of our Temple and the House of our Glory that was put to the torch and that we cherished has laid waste. (*The Prayer Book of R. Sa'adiah Gaon*, pp. 62–63:79)

Many such piyyutim and prayers were then composed in all the Jewish Diasporas. It is doubtful whether there is another motif so predominant in medieval Jewish poetry as the anticipation of Redemption in Zion. Evidence of the powerful influence of this theme among the masses as well is found in letters preserved in the Cairo genizah. Many of them, written by ordinary people to their relatives far away, end with the wish that they meet soon in Jerusalem, when Redemption comes.

Immigration and Pilgrimage

We have already considered immigration during the Umayyad period that apparently was quite extensive. Due to relatively good security conditions, we may assume that this phenomenon continued into the Abbasid period, but because of the meager sources available it is difficult to determine this with certainty.

Evidence of immigration during the Fatimid period is found in the Cairo genizah, from which we may learn about the motives of the immigrants, their lands of origin, and the dangers they encountered, as well as difficulties of language and adjustment to the new society, etc. One example will suffice:

We have been obliged to notify you of a matter... that he is from the community of Rusiya and stayed with us as a guest in the community of Saloniki.... And he found his relative Rabbi So-and-So who had come from Jerusalem the Holy City... And he told him of all the magnificence of the Land of Israel and his spirit moved him to go, he too, to bow down at the place of Holiness. And he asked us for these two lines, to speak for him and be an advocate on his behalf before your honorable excellence, to give him a hand and to guide him in the best way from city to city and from island to island in the company of trustworthy people, because he does knows neither the holy tongue [= Hebrew] nor Greek, nor Arabic, for the people of the land of his birth speak the language of Canaan [= Slavonic]. (Mann, p. 192)

There were various motives for immigration. In addition to a longing to see "the magnificence of the Land of Israel," there was a profound belief that prayer there would be an act of great value for atonement. It had already been said in the name of R. Sa'adiah Gaon that "whoever wishes to make full repentance and wants his prayer to be heard, let him dwell in Jerusalem and pray" (Schechter, *Sa'adyanah*, p. 42). Those who returned from pilgrimage to Jerusalem were accorded special appellations, such as: "Man of Jerusalem," "Jerusalemite," "Prisoner of Hope," etc. Some of these were influenced by the title *Hajj* that was conferred in Islam on pilgrims to Mecca. Special tracts were written for the pilgrims in which they were given guidance on how to conduct themselves when they came to Jerusalem. For instance:

If you merit the privilege of ascending to Jerusalem, when you gaze from [Mount] Scopus, if you are mounted on a donkey, dismount, and if you are wearing shoes, take them off, and rend your clothes, and recite: "Your Holy Place has been destroyed; Zion has become a desert, Jerusalem a desolation. Our Temple and the House of our Glory where our forefathers praised You was put to the torch." (Margalioth, p. 139)

Immigrants from various Jewish centers, chiefly Babylon and North Africa, preserved in the Land of Israel a certain social cohesion and the customs practiced in their places of origin, and they served as foci of political and economic power. Nevertheless, as a rule, immigration to the Land of Israel in Fatimid times was relatively meager. We have not yet found explicit calls by the geonim of the Land of Israel to Diaspora Jews to reject life in exile and immigrate to the Land of Israel. This is deserving of special attention in view of the challenge posed by the Karaites, several of whose outstanding sages in the ninth to the eleventh centuries explicitly advocated immigration to the Land of Israel. They totally rejected dwelling in the Diaspora, viewing prayer in synagogues there to be a sacrilege. They sent letters to Karaites and Jews throughout the Diaspora, calling upon them to immigrate to Jerusalem and join the community of Karaites, who lived a life of asceticism, fasting, and prayer in the hope of speeding up Redemption.

Some have assumed that the sages' avoidance of calling for immigration lay in an ideology that rejected "hastening the End of Days" by mortals and posited waiting in the Diaspora until Redemption would come from Heaven. However, this explanation is dubious. Very few opposed immigration on this account. It is more reasonable to assume that sages refrained from encouraging immigration due to the difficult security and economic conditions then prevailing, which on the contrary led precisely to much emigration from the country. The overwhelming majority of letters in the Cairo genizah date from this era. Many of them describe hardships and request help and assistance; to add to these letters a call for immigration to the Land of Israel would have been ironical.

On the other hand, in between the lines of these letters we learn how highly their authors esteemed the Yeshiva of the Land of Israel. One such example is a very interesting letter of the Land of Israel gaon R. Solomon ben R. Judah concerning one Joshua who put aside "most of the world's pleasures... and chose a few out of many, to be saved from demon and *admon* [=Edom = Rome, Byzantium, Christendom] and from those who stray in the desert... and to live in the City of the Palace [= the Temple]." In other words, settling in the Land of Israel saves a man from the demonic forces located in the Diaspora. In what concerns

negation of the Diaspora and the virtue of the Land of Israel, this letter contains much more than mere preaching in favor of immigration. What emerges from this and similar letters is the clear implication that even though immigration to the Land of Israel and settling there involve many economic hardships, they possess great spiritual value. Descriptions of such difficulties turn up over and over again in private letters sent by Jews who immigrated to the Land of Israel in the tenth and eleventh centuries to their families in the Diaspora. They were sufficient to deter some of those who may have been considering immigration at that time.

The great enthusiasm (including vows and oaths) that accompanied the immigration of individuals are also indicative of the role of the Land of Israel and of immigration in the minds of Jews – or at least of some of them – in that period.

Pilgrimage to the Land of Israel was especially pronounced during the month of Tishri. The holiday of Sukkot (Tabernacles) was celebrated in Jerusalem by large public gatherings and with special pomp. On Hoshana Rabba the Jews customarily ascended the Mount of Olives, made a circuit around it, and conducted a splendid, impressive ceremony. That occasion was also used to proclaim the calculation of the Hebrew calendar for that year. The gaon noted and blessed the communities that had sent contributions to the Yeshiva of the Land of Israel. R. Elijah ben Menahem, one of the great sages of France in the first half of the eleventh century, excitedly recounted what he had witnessed on that occasion:

And I spent Hoshana Rabba on the Mount of Olives,
And Simhat Torah in Jerusalem, the City of our God, the mountain of His Holiness...
When we stood on the Mount of Olives on Hoshana Rabba,
Even though there were people from all the communities in the world
There seemed to be only about two hundred, yet they were twelve thousand
From Hulda's Gate to the Priest's Gate...
(Hirschmann, pp. 219–220)

Even if the number 12,000 seems to be an exaggeration, not to mention the statement that pilgrims came "from all the communities in the world," this testimony attests to the powerful impression made by the ceremony. At different periods, a ban was proclaimed against the Karaites at this gathering, resulting in harsh conflicts between them and the "Rabbanite" Jewish community. At times the Muslim rulers even prevented proclamation of the ban under the influence of the strong Karaite communities in the Land of Israel and Egypt.

The cultural atmosphere of the Middle Ages encouraged

pilgrimage to holy places. It was thus in both Islam and Christianity. From Christian and Muslim authors we learn that pilgrimage to the Holy Land, by Christians as well, was a continuing phenomenon. One of the most famous pilgrimages, from Germany in 1065, numbered 7,000 persons. On the way to Jerusalem they were attacked by Bedouin bands and many of them were killed.

Burial in the Land of Israel

It is foretold in the talmudic and midrashic literature that the messiah will come first to the Land of Israel, where the dead will arise in resurrection before those of other countries. Those buried in the Land of Israel are exempt from rolling through underground tunnels. In the Tractate *Ketubbot* (111a) it is related in the name of R. Anan that, "whoever is buried in the Land of Israel is deemed to buried under the altar." Assertions of this kind, together with the last requests of Jacob and his son Joseph to bring their remains from Egypt for burial in the Land of Israel,

as related in the Bible, led to the transfer of bodies of Jews who died outside the Land of Israel for burial within it as early as the talmudic period. This practice continued throughout the Early Muslim period as well, especially from Muslim lands. There were also deceased in Christian Europe (particularly in Italy) who had requested in their lifetime that they be laid to rest in the Land of Israel.

Important evidence of this practice, which involved great effort and the expenditure of much money, has been preserved in the remarks of al-Jahiz, an important Muslim author. He recounts that in his time (the first half of the ninth century) the sons of Aaron and the sons of David (that is, the priests and the exilarchs) used to bury their dead temporarily in Babylon, and would remove the deceased's bones from his grave one year later and send them for reburial in the Land of Israel, especially in Jerusalem. He saw this as evidence of the great love of these people for their homeland. Some North African Jews commanded before their deaths that their remains be brought for burial in the Land of Israel. *The Scroll of Ahima'az*, written in Italy in 1054, relates

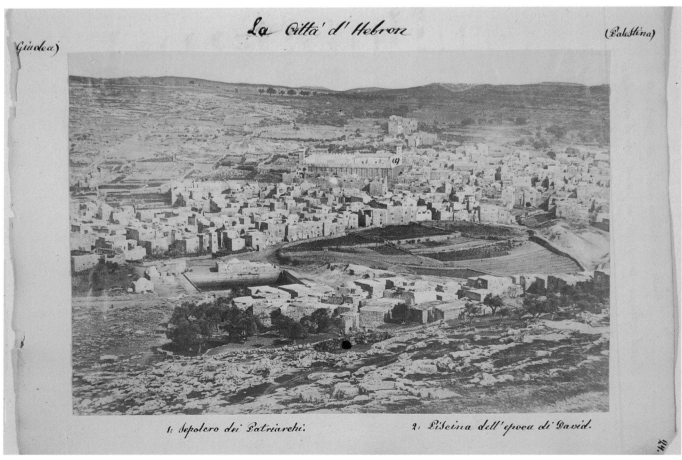

La Città d' Hebron (Palestina)

(Giudea)

1: *Sepolcro dei Patriarchi.* 2: *Piscina dell'epoca di David.*

Photograph of Hebron in the nineteenth century appended to a manuscript of Ermete Pierrotti. Medieval accounts indicate that Hebron, where the patriarchs of the Israelite nation were interred, was a preferred site for burial

150

that a member of the family of Ahima'az (Samuel ben Paltiel, who lived in Egypt at the end of the tenth century) "brought his mother and father up to Jerusalem in coffins."

R. Solomon ben ha-Yatom, an Italian sage of the eleventh century who visited the Land of Israel, described the practice of the Jews in that country of burying their dead in Hebron. R. Benjamin of Tudela, who visited the country in the 1170s, also attested to this custom: "One finds there [in the Cave of Machpelah] many casks filled with the bones of Israelites, as the members of the House of Israel were wont to bring the bones of their fathers thither and to deposit them there to this day." (*The Itinerary of Benjamin of Tudela*, p. 26)

Human beings have always been preoccupied with death. Therefore, we may assume that the custom of burial in the Land of Israel greatly influenced the role of the country in the consciousness of people, more than other factors.

Financial Support for the Yeshiva of the Land of Israel

Support for the Yeshiva of the Land of Israel and the country's needy came from all the lands of the Diaspora. Pilgrims who came to Jerusalem on Sukkot brought with them contributions that helped the city's residents pay their taxes, just as they also supported the Yeshiva and its institutions. It was customary for the geonim to publicly proclaim the names of the contributors at the assembly on the Mount of Olives on Hoshana Rabba and wrote them down in a special memorial book. All this was meant to increase the motivation of potential contributors and the size of their donations.

Egypt was a major source of support for the Jews of the Land of Israel, providing much aid in the difficult times of the Fatimid period. Contributions, however, were sent from other centers too. For example, it is told of R. Samuel ha-Nagid of Spain that he helped the Yeshiva, while in *The Scroll of Ahima'az*, a member of the family is described as having made a vow when he was called up to the Torah on Yom Kippur:

After he finished reading / he donated to the glory of his God / five thousand good dinars / sound and of full value / one thousand for the head of the Yeshiva and the sages / and one thousand for the mourners of the Temple / and one thousand for Babylon, for the yeshiva of the geonim... (*The Scroll of Ahima'az*, p. 35)

The first two donations were made to the Land of Israel: to the sages of the Yeshiva and to the Mourners of Zion who devoted most of their time to lamenting the destruction of the Temple. Even if they do not represent unambiguous historical data, it is clear that they reflect the worldview, the records, and memories

of the author, R. Ahima'az. Elsewhere in that work, another family member is reported as contributing to institutions in the Land of Israel, including "oil for the sanctuary at the Western Wall... and for the mourners of the Temple and the sanctuary, they who sorrow over Zion and grieve, and for the Yeshiva..." (ibid., p.

A relief of a vine, one of the Seven Species for which the Land of Israel was praised, from the synagogue at Capernaum, 3rd cent.

37). The donations were generally proclaimed in public in the synagogue. Sometimes special emissaries came from the Land of Israel for this purpose. Occasions of this kind made a significant impact on the life of the community.

Temple Offerings and Tithes in the Diaspora

According to Jewish law, there are commandments pertaining only to the Land of Israel that do not have to be observed in the Diaspora. Among them are setting aside offerings and tithes for the Temple. Nevertheless, some of these commandments were observed in various Diaspora communities so that they should not be forgotten when Redemption came. We have evidence to this effect from the period of the geonim and even later. For example, it is told of R. Ephraim, the disciple of R. Isaac Alfasi, who lived in Spain at the beginning of the twelfth century: "He had one trailing vine in his courtyard and he used to take an offering from its wine and give it for drinking to the minor *kohanim* [hereditary priests]. And all of this was the measure of his piety, despite that he lived outside the Land of Israel"(R. Ephraim, p. 257). In time, such practices became more infrequent, but people still continued to observe them in various places, even in Christian Europe.

The Diaspora and the Customs of the Land of Israel

Benjamin Klar, one of the leading scholars of ancient *piyyutim*, claimed that until the end of the eleventh century the world of Jewry was culturally divided in two: the Land of Israel and the center under its influence, on one hand, and Babylon and the

The earliest extant illuminated Hebrew manuscript, Cairo, 895. The colophon states that it was written by "the son of Solomon for himself"

centers which it influenced, on the other. Among the communities following the heritage of the Land of Israel, remaining under its influence, were Italy, Germany, and northern France.

It is difficult to accept Klar's opinion that this division of influence between the two centers continued for a thousand years after the destruction of the Temple, that is, until the end of the eleventh century. It holds true until the tenth century. We are witness to a gradual process of "abandoning" the practices of the Land of Israel and a transition to those of Babylon, which had already begun in the ninth century. Nevertheless, traces of the customs of the Land of Israel and its tradition of religious poetry were quite noticeable in Italy, Germany, and France throughout the Middle Ages, but this was on the whole force of habit and cannot attest to influence of the Land of Israel upon these communities in the late Middle Ages. Jews were not conscious of the Palestinian source of their customs, which they zealously

performed because they were the legacy of their forefathers and part of their own literary and religious heritage, without inquiring into their historical source. As early as the tenth century, various communities gradually came under the influence of Babylon. Nevertheless, important evidence has been preserved in these customs indicating the strong attachment of those communities to the Land of Israel in the Umayyad and Abbasid periods. R. Hai Gaon attested that the North African Jewish community too, during the first period of its development (the eighth and ninth centuries), was influenced by the customs of the Land of Israel.

The increasing influence of Babylonian customs is even more significant when viewed against the backdrop of developments in Christian Europe in the tenth and eleventh centuries. The general atmosphere in Western Europe in the tenth century, and more so in the eleventh century, could have served as fertile ground for a stronger attachment of the Jews in Christian Europe to the Land of Israel. In that period, the Christian connection to the Holy Land in general and to Jerusalem in particular was intensified. Christian institutions began to compete among themselves to gain possession of holy sites in Palestine, especially in Jerusalem, with the acquiescence of the Muslim authorities. At the beginning of the ninth century Charlemagne had supported ecclesiastical institutions in Jerusalem and aided pilgrimage to the Holy City. The belief that Jesus had created a kingdom that would last a thousand years, after which the universal Judgment Day would come, followed by the absolute rule of the Kingdom of Heaven on Earth, sparked an increase in the number of Christian pilgrims to Jerusalem towards the year 1000. Another factor adding to the interest in Jerusalem in the second half of the tenth and in the eleventh centuries was the rise of the Cluniac movement and its growing influence on the religious and spiritual world of European Christians. There came at this time relatively many Christian pilgrims from Western Europe, generally led by bishops and noblemen. This Christian attachment to the Holy Land greatly increased at the end of the eleventh century when the Crusaders conquered Jerusalem in 1099. It is reasonable to assume that all these phenomena must have also enhanced interest in the Land of Israel and Jerusalem on the part of the Christians' Jewish neighbors, and increased their expectations of Redemption. Therefore, the enhanced influence of the Babylonian tradition and the primacy it achieved were of great significance.

All this notwithstanding, the primacy of Babylon in the tenth century, and more intensely in the eleventh, did not diminish the significant linkage of those Diaspora communities to the Land of Israel tradition. This is one of the most important pieces of evidence for the great influence of the teachings of the Land of Israel and for the emotional attachment to it for hundreds of years during the Middle Ages.

Between Babylon and the Land of Israel

The conflict between Babylon and the Land of Israel for primacy in the Jewish world influenced the status of the Palestinian center more than any other factor. We have already discussed the relationship of medieval Jews to the hallowed place that God had chosen. This was an ancient tradition in Judaism, clearly expressed in the commandment to make pilgrimage to Jerusalem at festival times and by the practice of turning for decisions to the elders of the nation who sat in Jerusalem: "If a case is too baffling for you to decide... you shall promptly repair to the place that the Lord your God will have chosen, and appear before the levitical priests, or the magistrate in charge at the time... you shall carry out the verdict that is announced to you from that place that the Lord chose..." (Deuteronomy 17:8–10).

But which was that chosen place in the Middle Ages? Was it the Land of Israel with its ancient glory and sacred sites? Or was it Babylon, where the great majority of Jews lived, where the Babylonian Talmud had been created, and where there were large and prestigious yeshivot? The fact that the Babylonian community was led by the exilarch – a scion of the House of David – surely added to its claim to primacy. Tension between the two centers had already existed in the talmudic period. Documents from the Cairo genizah indicate that it continued more intensely throughout the Early Muslim period. At first, the Land of Israel was very powerful, exerting much influence over the Diaspora. However, three major factors contributed to its gradual decline:

1) Deterioration in the security of Jews and Christians in Palestine. The constant wars waged in the country in the late Abbasid period, and especially during the Fatimid period, considerably reduced the number of pilgrimages and visits by commercial caravans, which served as the main channel of intercourse between the Diaspora and the Land of Israel;

2) A drastic reduction in the number of literary works produced in the country, especially during the Fatimid period, as already noted, that undermined the status of the Land of Israel

as a center of spiritual creativity;

3) The establishment of independent communities in the Diaspora, including centers of Torah study. In the tenth and eleventh centuries there were outstanding yeshivot and scholars in North Africa, Spain, France, Germany, and Italy, whose Jews now had less resort to the institutions and sages of Babylon or the Land of Israel.

Documents from the Cairo genizah illuminate the intensity of the conflict between the Land of Israel and Babylon, the ideology that each center developed to justify its superiority, and the stages in the development of the struggle. We will now consider four crucial episodes in this polemic, to exemplify its intensity and implications.

The Polemic of Pirkoi ben Baboi. Pirkoi was one of the outstanding sages of Babylon in the early ninth century. In his letter to the Jews of North Africa, apparently also addressed to the Jews of Spain, he tried to dissuade them from forging a

A children's tablet for learning the alphabet, from the Cairo genizah, with a depiction of the Temple and its utensils, 10th or 11th cent. (CUL, T-S K5.13)

relationship with the Yeshiva of the Land of Israel. He venomously argued against the Land of Israel tradition and stressed the superiority of Babylon. According to Pirkoi, God had already chosen and shown His preference for Babylon during the exile of Jehoiachin. Unlike the Jewish population in the Land of Israel, God had ensured that the Jews of Babylon would not suffer from warfare or be taken captive. He claimed that the customs of the Land of Israel and its teachings contained some elements of apostasy – by which he meant that they had absorbed unfitting

153

practices under Roman influence. Moreover, he asserted that these customs had already influenced the teachings of the Land of Israel 500 years earlier, that is, from the beginning of the fourth century CE. The point of this argument was to undermine the authority of the Jerusalem Talmud, which had been compiled in the fifth century. Another tendentious argument was that Redemption would begin in Babylon and only afterwards reach the Land of Israel. Further, in Babylon "the birth pangs of the messiah are not felt." All this is in stark contrast to what is generally found in the talmudic and midrashic literature, perhaps with the intention of stifling the desire to immigrate to the Land of Israel.

Pirkoi also took a verse from the Book of Zechariah (2:11): "Away, escape, O Zion, you who dwell in Fair Babylon!" whose meaning, by its context, is unambiguous – a call to the Babylonian exiles to flee to Zion. Pirkoi turned the meaning around, interpreting the phrase as a call to those in the Land of Israel ("Zion") to flee to Babylon to be saved from "evil Edom" (Rome and the Christian world). True, Pirkoi could find support for some of his interpretations in the sayings of R. Judah and Abbaye in Tractate *Ketubbot* (111a), but there are many opposite sayings that he disregarded.

Pirkoi's preaching is indicative of the distress and heavy fears that were the lot of the Babylonian sages in that period due to the great influence of the Land of Israel on the Diaspora. This was more than a question of prestige and influence; it also involved an aspiration to be the recipient of contributions from various centers, and perhaps also apprehension of the spread of Karaism, hence the Babylonian sages' desire to unite the Jewish people under one recognized leadership.

The Calendar Polemic of 922. The most outstanding attribute of the primacy and holiness of the center in the Land of Israel was the authority to calculate the Hebrew calendar and to determine the festivals for the entire Jewish Diaspora, which had rested with the sages of the Land of Israel from days of yore. In 835 the exilarch in Babylon had told of a delegation comprising himself and the heads of the Babylonian yeshivot who went to the sages of the Land of Israel in order to receive the calender calculations from their hands, and thus to preserve the unity of the Jewish people. The primacy on this matter was severely challenged and then abolished in the years 921–922. This resulted from a harsh controversy which centered round Aaron ben Meir, son of the gaon of the Land of Israel, and R. Sa'adiah, even before his rise to the gaonate of the Sura Yeshiva in Babylon.

In 921, Aaron ben Meir announced to the Diaspora that in the Hebrew year 4682 the months Heshvan and Kislev would have but 29 days each, whereas Sa'adiah Gaon proclaimed that

they would be full months, having 30 days each. Arguments of principle over the primacy of the Land of Israel were to become part of this polemic. For example, Aaron ben Meir wrote:

Because they [Sa'adiah and his supporters] lack a basic understanding, all the more do they involve themselves in what Eternal God never granted them and did not permit them to announce publicly. For you know that the first prophets and the sages avoided intercalating a leap year outside the Land of Israel... And as a consequence of all these matters we deduce the authority of the body of scholars of the Land of Israel over the sages of the Diaspora and those in the Diaspora do not have authority over those in the Land of Israel... And it has never been seen and never been heard of that those living in the Diaspora should instruct or judge those living in the Land of Israel or collect taxes from them. (Bornshtein, pp. 64–65)

In 4682 (922), many Jews in the Land of Israel, together with Jews in other lands, celebrated the Passover two days earlier than did the community in Babylon. We may assume that due to some uncertainty there were some who celebrated it for nine days, and similarly with respect to other holidays as well, including Yom Kippur (the Day of Atonement). Obviously, this polemic had tremendous reverberations throughout the Jewish world, and outside it as well. Even Karaite and Muslim authors took note of this harsh dispute among the Jews, it being an intense and notorious struggle for Jewish leadership. Babylon's victory was in effect recognition of its primacy. Historically, this was an event of the first order of importance for the issue under discussion. We may assume that the defeat of the Land of Israel served as a catalyst hastening the decline of its influence even over those Diaspora centers that had until then recognized its supremacy.

The Polemic between R. Hai and R. Solomon ben R. Judah. One hundred years after the calendar controversy, a bitter conflict arose between the Babylonian gaon R. Hai and the Land of Israel gaon, R. Solomon ben R. Judah, over control of the Fustat (ancient Cairo) community in Egypt. This community served as the main source of support for the Yeshiva of the Land of Israel, providing for most of its needs. R. Hai sought to transfer its contributions to himself. In this controversy R. Solomon proved to be hesitant and compromising, as someone who had come to terms with the loss of the last stronghold of support for his yeshiva. He sought consolation in the fact that the Torah taught one to be content with the bare necessities, and he hoped that God would reward him for being so yielding.

The Polemic between R. Elijah ha-Kohen and his sons, and Daniel ben Azariah and his son. As if the Yeshiva of the Land of Israel had not suffered enough when all its "strongholds" were taken over by the Babylonian geonim, it became the chief object of conflict in the second half of the eleventh century. Two scions of the exilarchs (R. Daniel ben Azariah and his son David) claimed that the Land of Israel gaonate belonged to them by virtue of their descent from the House of David. Many Egyptian Jews and members of the Karaite community there, as well as the Muslim authorities, were involved in this struggle, which continued for almost a generation. It was one of the most difficult episodes for the Land of Israel gaonate.

Around the year 1070, R. Meshullam ben R. Moses, one of the outstanding sages of Germany, forwarded questions on halakhah to the Land of Israel gaon. However, this was the swan song of the Jerusalem Yeshiva. Three years later, in 1073, the Yeshiva was forced to move to Tyre on account of the Seljuk invasion, which dealt a harsh blow to the Jerusalem Jewish community. From there, it was transferred to Damascus and finally to Egypt. By leaving Jerusalem, it was further weakened, as were its image and authority vis-à-vis the Diaspora.

The irony of history is that precisely in the period when the concrete influence of the Land of Israel over the Diaspora was greatly diminished, Jewish sages extolled its sanctity and virtues, a concept that developed and became prominent in the twelfth to the fifteenth centuries. We will deal with this phenomenon in the chapter on the Crusader period. For instance, at the end of the eleventh century Rashi proposed the theory – for the first time in Jewish medieval thought – that the entire Torah was fundamentally the Torah of the Land of Israel, and only there could one fully observe all its commandments. Nahmanides was to carry this theory to an extreme five generations later. Rashi had included this theory in his interpretation of: "...and bind them as a sign upon your hand..." (Deut 11:18). This view turns up again in his interpretation of the Talmud. There is a talmudic saying, that when a man dreams that he is standing naked in Babylon, this is a good omen, meaning that he "is standing without sin." Rashi's interpretation was that, "since the Diaspora

has no merits, it is an iniquity to dwell there, thus this [man] stands naked without those sins." Had Rashi's understanding been that the commandments which a Jew observes outside the Land of Israel were not absolutely worthless, there would be no room for his remark that "the Diaspora has no merits." Even the

Opening page of *The Book of Worship* from the *Mishneh Torah* of Maimonides dealing with the laws of worship in the Temple, here depicted in the form of the Muslim Dome of the Rock. Italy, 15th cent.

emphasis, "it is an iniquity to dwell there," expresses with great intensity his concept that not only is there no full value in observing commandments outside the Land of Israel, but the very act of dwelling there is a sinful deed.

The effect of the Christian and Muslim attachment to Jerusalem, together with the ever-increasing suffering of Jews everywhere that began in the eleventh century, was to strengthen the Jewish bond with the Land of Israel and the hope for Redemption there. While the Land of Israel and Jerusalem were gradually distanced from the real life of the Jew, they became an ever more integral part of his emotional world.

Ceiling of the Rabbi David
ha-Levi Dra' synagogue,
near Demnate, Morocco

Jewish Communities in the Middle East during the Early Muslim Period

Menahem Ben-Sasson

It is generally accepted by scholars dealing with the geonic period that in the struggle for leadership of the world of Jewry at that time the Babylonian *geonim* intended to encroach upon the influence of the leadership in the Land of Israel. The meager historical evidence of concrete ties between the Jewish Diaspora and the Land of Israel has led to the conclusion that there was no hierarchical relationship of center and Diaspora communities in this era. Thus, a consensus has emerged that relationships were at most in the spiritual realm, not in practical matters, and that those ties found expression in literary works in the fields of philosophy, Jewish law, customs and their sources, liturgical and other poetry, and linguistic traditions.

A glazed ceramic wall tile from a Jewish building in Iran, Bearing an inscription in Hebrew letters, late 12th–early 13th cent.

A hierarchical relationship between a central authority and a subordinate community can manifest itself in three ways:

a) Formal authority of the center is established on the one hand by the law of the secular authority, and by the *halakhah*, on the other.

b) The existence of a functional link of the local community to the center – the extent to which a local community has recourse to the center for the solution of real, everyday problems.

c) The extent to which the center receives economic support from the local community for its upkeep and for recognition of its primacy. In practice, this need reverses the balance of power, emphasizing the dependence of the center upon the community. This may lead the community in any case to display deference to the center, even if it does not turn to it to solve specific problems that have arisen in the community. In this case, the relationship is merely ceremonial – one of gestures – lacking any functional content. We shall now examine the relationship of Diaspora communities to the Land of Israel using these three criteria.

The Maghreb Communities and the Land of Israel

The Muslim Maghreb – North Africa – enjoyed many economic advantages and its Jewish communities therefore existed under good economic conditions and possessed stable communal institutions. Consequently, the Maghreb attracted migration from the East. However, there was also migration from the Maghreb eastwards. There were many concentrations of Jewish migrants from the Maghreb in the Mediterranean basin, including that of the Land of Israel, who continued to maintain economic and social ties with their communities of origin. These concentrations were distinct Maghrebi bodies that often considered themselves to be subject to the leadership in the Maghreb, although from various aspects they were subordinate to the local leadership or to that in the Land of Israel. These groups were a principal channel for relations between the Land of Israel and the Maghreb.

The Ninth Century

In a letter sent by Pirkoi ben Baboi at the beginning of the ninth century from Babylon to Kairouan, in Tunisia, he severely criticized the Maghrebi Jews in general and those of Kairouan in particular for observing the customs of the Land of Israel.

Page from an early illuminated Hebrew manuscript, Cairo, 895

According to Pirkoi, scholars who had studied in, and been influenced by, the Land of Israel had tried to introduce its erroneous customs to the Maghreb, thus leading the Jewish communities there into error.

We might deduce from this letter that in the ninth century, as a result of the arrival of scholars from the Land of Israel, the Maghreb had come under the influence of the Yeshiva of the Land of Israel – influence that was expressed by the Maghrebi Jews practising the customs of the Land of Israel. Pirkoi's remark about the migration of scholars to the new houses of study established in North Africa is confirmed by other sources. However, we need to examine whether the customs that he condemned were in fact brought to the Maghreb by these scholars, or whether they were age-old customs that had taken root in North Africa. If the latter is correct, then even if their roots lay in the traditions of the Land of Israel, their observance attests to routine and force of habit rather than to an acceptance of the authority of the Land of Israel leadership.

In the ninth and tenth centuries, marked by the overt struggle for primacy between Babylon and the Land of Israel, even observing age-old customs was likely to be of significance. Moreover, Pirkoi ben Baboi's letter made Maghrebi Jews aware of the subordination implied in accepting traditions and customs from one particular center. However, in the first half of the ninth century the house of study at Kairouan followed the traditions of halakhic decision-making and study of Babylon alone, recognizing only its authority in halakhic matters. The source that served as a basis for study in Kairouan was the Babylonian Talmud. The only evidence for Land of Israel sources appearing in the Maghreb is Pirkoi's letter, which is a polemical text. Therefore, even if we accept this evidence we should not give it the wider significance of affirming the development of a special relationship between North Africa and the center in the Land of Israel. Even more so, halakhic questions and financial contributions from the Maghreb communities were directed to Babylon, and even the authority of scholars arriving from the Land of Israel stemmed from their having studied and received ordination in the Babylonian *yeshivot*.

The late eighth and early ninth centuries were a period in which the status of the Land of Israel as a political center was at an ebb. Even the unique authority of its religous leaders to set the calendar – by intercalating leap years – was in danger. Sages from Babylon came to the Land of Israel in 835 to learn how this was done, and when they

158

The ancient Ark of the Law in the Ezra Synagogue in Cairo. The Cairo genizah, extremely important for modern research, was discovered here in the late 19th cent.

returned to Babylon they were able to set the calendar themselves. The ninth century was therefore a period of decline in the status of the center in the Land of Israel. Even if Maghrebi Jews observed Land of Israel traditions received from their forefathers, there is no indication in the ninth century of Land of Israel influence on any one of the levels of contact mentioned above between a Diaspora community and the center – neither formal, functional, nor ceremonial-gestural ties.

The Tenth Century

Despite more evidence of a link between the Land of Israel leadership and the Maghreb communities during the tenth century, it is doubtful whether there was any change in the state of independence or of subordination of the region as depicted for the ninth century. The Jews of the Land of Israel were held to be the highest authority in matters concerning the Hebrew language, as evident from the status afforded the Masoretes of the Land of Israel as transcribers of books of an agreed textual tradition – but no more than that.

The Temple and its utensils, from a Bible copied in Egypt, 969 (NLR, MSII, fol. 17)

The transfer of the Fatimid court from Tunisia to Egypt in 973 led to a closer relationship between the Jews of North Africa and the leadership in the Land of Israel. In the late tenth century, Maghrebi Jews participated in fundraising efforts to alleviate the economic distress of the Yeshiva of the Land of Israel, and from the eighties of the tenth century onwards North African Jews sought to play a role in the leadership of the Yeshiva and succeeded

in attaining senior positions within it (see below). However, none of this is evidence of involvement of the Land of Israel sages in the communal affairs of the North African Jews, neither by way of a priori guidance, nor by means of responding to halakhic questions. Furthermore, there is no evidence of the involvement of the Maghrebi communities on one side or the other in the controversy between R. Sa'adiah Gaon and his Land of Israel counterpart, ben Meir, over setting the calendar.

That the Land of Israel played an especially important role in the consciousness of the Jews in North Africa is evident from surviving remnants of their religious poetry, as well as in formulations expressing a longing for Zion, for the ingathering of the exiles and for the restoration of the Kingdom of Israel. Nevertheless, the evidence is meager and we cannot assume much from it except that the conventional phraseology of religious poetry was also known in the Maghreb. It is doubtful whether Maghrebi Jews who expressed the hope for the restoration of communal life and for the lifting of the yoke of exile connected it in any way with the Jewish entity then in the Land of Israel.

The ideal of a Jewish society with excellent institutions and practices was connected in the consciousness of Kairouan's Jews with another Jewish political entity, that of the Ten Tribes, about whom rumors had reached Kairouan many years earlier through Eldad ha-Dani. This ideal image did not involve the Land of Israel leadership, which was dependent upon Muslim rulers.

The Jewish center in the Land of Israel was aware in this period that it was considered inferior by the Diaspora communities and their sages. This is evident from their overt expectations that Diaspora communities would turn to them with halakhic questions, rather than questions about Redemption and ordinances relating to the Coming of the Messiah.

The Eleventh Century

At the beginning of the eleventh century, a change occurred in the character of the relationship between the Maghreb, above all of Kairouan, and the Land of Israel, at least on the ceremonial level. Rabbinic works produced in the Land of Israel – the Jerusalem Talmud and literature dealing with the difference in customs between the Jews in the East and those in the West (the Maghreb) – first appeared in the North African communities in the second decade of that century, but they were not consulted to solve practical questions. The practical and theoretical issues raised by these Land of Israel works were

A page of the Book of Proverbs from the Aleppo Codex of the Bible copied in the Land of Israel, late 9th–early 10th cent.

circumstances in the region; new powers invested in the Jewish leadership in the Land of Israel; eastward migration from the Maghreb, particularly to Egypt but also to cities in the Land of Israel; development of the North Africans into a pressure group in Egypt; and the appointment of members of Maghrebi families to very senior positions in the Yeshiva of the Land of Israel.

This rapprochement derived, therefore, mainly from external factors, only emphasizing even more the dependence of the Yeshiva of the Land of Israel on support and personalities from the Maghreb. The new balance of power did not necessarily take the form of a relationship between the center and a subordinate community; rather it was one between two authoritative centers. The Yeshiva had no formal or functional authority over the Maghreb, whose economic condition was superior to that of the Land of Israel. Moreover, the level of study in the Yeshiva was inferior to the traditions of study and level of learning in the Maghrebi houses of study, so much so that even Jews from the Land of Israel at times resorted to the latter. North Africa also enjoyed relative political stability in contrast to the vicissitudes of warfare in Palestine, at least until the thirties of the eleventh century. The proximity of Maghrebi Jews to key officials in the Fatimid court, located in Egypt, together with the fact that this state had originated in the Maghreb and that some parts of the Muslim army were of Maghrebi origin, emphasized even more the advantage of the Maghreb over the center in the Land of Israel. Moreover, these factors led Maghrebi Jews, both inside and outside their homeland, to develop a sense of being a unique community.

All this notwithstanding, Maghrebi Jews continued in many ways to give outward expression to the primacy of the Land of Israel: many declarations of messianic expectations – Redemption of the nation and the ingathering of the exiles to the Land of Israel; pilgrimage; donations pledged to the Yeshiva of the Land of Israel when making expiation for sins; transfer of the dead for burial in the Land of Israel; large financial contributions to alleviate the distress of the Yeshiva and support its daily activities; and attempts to have North African Jews or their confidants fill leadership positions in the Yeshiva.

brought for clarification to the Babylonian sages rather than to those in the Land of Israel. Obviously, from the Maghrebi Jews' point of view, functional authority continued to rest with Babylon.

The heads of the Yeshiva of the Land of Israel did devote some of their time in this period to dealing with halakhic issues that arose and were brought before them. However, whereas in their letters to the Maghreb the Babylonian geonim requested that the communities append halakhic questions to their financial support, the geonim of the Yeshiva of the Land of Israel appealed to the North African Diaspora in this period for financial aid only. And indeed, the Maghrebis did much to organize financial support for the Yeshiva through special campaigns, and even collected small sums for the Land of Israel when raising funds for the Babylonian yeshivot.

Actually, this was a period marked by a rapprochement between the Jews of the Maghreb and those in the Land of Israel resulting from several causes: changing political

161

These outward expressions in no way represent formal authority of the center in the Land of Israel over the Maghreb.

Wedding plaque in a synagogue in Tangiers, Morocco, 20th cent. (CJA, Sc_342, 50/1)

Jews in North Africa were not subordinate to the authority of the head of the Yeshiva of the Land of Israel as were their brethren living in Egypt, Syria, and the Land of Israel, despite the fact that the Maghreb was part of the Fatimid domain. Likewise, these acknowledgments of primacy neither express a need of the Maghrebi communities for Yeshiva help in the everyday life, nor for functional intervention by the Yeshiva in the North African communities. Yet, the leadership in the Land of Israel had the power, by virtue of the authority of the head of the Yeshiva (whom the authorities recognized as chief of the Jews), to aid Maghrebis living in areas adjacent to the Land of Israel. Since there were frequent social and economic contacts between Jews in the Maghreb and those in the Land of Israel and Egypt, and since the Egyptian community was under the authority of the Yeshiva of the Land of Israel, the Yeshiva leadership also was indirectly, yet very importantly, involved in the economic affairs of the Maghrebi communities. Thus there

Jewish money changer in Tunis, ca. 1920–1924

was a functional nexus between the Maghreb and the Land of Israel leadership, not on the level of the community and its institutions, but rather that of individuals within the community. However, these contacts had no significance in regard to the communal establishment in North Africa and its independence from the centers both in the Land of Israel and Babylon. The extensive involvement of Maghrebis in appointing heads of the Yeshiva of the Land of Israel is indicative of their lack of institutional subordination to the Land of Israel on the one hand, and of the interest they displayed in influencing these appointments.

Gestures of subordination to the Land of Israel took the form of contributions to the Yeshiva, participation in the pilgrimage holiday ceremonies conducted by the heads of the Yeshiva, prayer for the welfare of the Land of Israel, and of a desire to be buried there. The gestures of subordination were therefore reduced to recognition of the unique quality of those who lived in the Land of Israel, resulting from the merits of their country of residence, and not by virtue of their Torah study traditions or their jurisdictional authority. It was commercial interest and the appointment of North African Jews to positions in Egypt and the Land of Israel, combined with recognition of the sanctity of the Land of Israel and its institutions that led to involvement by the Maghrebis in the Yeshiva's affairs. However, it did not bring about subordination of the communal institutions in North Africa to the Yeshiva, neither formally nor functionally.

The basis and content of the attachment to the Land of Israel were different from those of the Maghrebi communities' relationship with Babylon. The Yeshiva of the Land of Israel recognition demanded neither of its scholarly authority nor of its works. Moreover, it was certainly difficult for the heads of the Yeshiva to claim that they were the keepers of the original traditions for regulating daily life, when throughout the whole Jewish world – including the Land of Israel itself – the Babylonian Talmud had become the basis for religious law. Since the basis of the Jewish community's existence depended upon political leadership, Maghrebi Jews were not completely isolated from the leadership in the Land of Israel. However, their way of life, in the broadest sense of the term, derived from the laws in the Babylonian Talmud, and in this domain the Yeshiva of the Land of Israel could not pose as an alternative to the claims of the Babylonian yeshivot. It seems that the geonim of the Yeshiva were also aware of this distinction when they formulated their requests for financial and political support in the form of gestures by the Maghrebi

163

Interior of the "Kohanim Dighet" Synagogue in Djerba, Tunisia. According to a local tradition, a group of *kohanim* (hereditary priests) was exiled here, taking with them a door from the First Temple after its destruction (CJA, "Kohanim Dighet" Synagogue, photo no. 4/6)

community in favor of the center, without exhorting its members to refer halakhic issues to them.

We may conclude by saying that despite a rise in the status of the Yeshiva of the Land of Israel in the Maghreb between the ninth and eleventh centuries, no formal or functional relationship was established in this period. At most, there was an attachment expressed in ceremonial gestures in the second half of this period. This neither detracted from the strong functional relationship between the Maghreb and the center in Babylon, nor did it challenge the authority of Babylon as perceived by the Maghreb communities.

Wedding plaque in a synagogue in Tangiers, Morocco, with the passage: "If I forget thee, O Jerusalem, let my right hand forget its cunning," 20th cent. (CJA, Sc_342, 49/1)

- - - - - - - - - -

The Maghrebi Community in Egypt and Its Relationship to the Land of Israel

The Maghrebi community in Egypt was one of the most important established by migrants from North Africa in the Mediterranean region, and served to preserve North African traditions and customs in Egypt. It began to take shape following the transfer of the Fatimid court to Fustat in the seventies of the tenth century, its members maintaining close commercial ties with members of their families who had remained in the Maghreb, ties that constituted a basis for joint activity. Common economic interests both inside and outside Egypt together with familial and social ties between members of the various communities in the Maghreb were among the factors that led to the development of a separate Maghrebi community in Fustat, whose members did not become part of the local community. The regular meeting place of the Maghrebis was the Synagogue of the Jerusalemites in Fustat.

Restoration of the Synagogue of the Jerusalemites in Fustat

After the destruction of the synagogues in Egypt in 1011–1012, during the reign of Caliph al-Hakim, worshippers at the Synagogue of the Jerusalemites in Fustat were unable to restore it, and could not look to the center in the Land of Israel for financial aid due to its continuing economic distress. It seems, too, that several worshippers in the synagogue abandoned it and went over to the Synagogue of the Babylonians. In 1030, the possibility arose of restoring the Synagogue of the Jerusalemites with the help of prosperous immigrant members of the Maghrebi community which was then developing in Fustat. At this point the beadle of the synagogue appealed to the Land of Israel gaon, Solomon ben Judah Fasi:

And what we ask of you, our Master, our honored "Head," may God destroy your enemies, is that you help us advance local affairs by means of a letter from you... with the intention [of arousing people] for restoration of this synagogue and to increase [the number of those who attend] it... And mention the Maghrebis who pray in this synagogue – for a group of Maghrebis has begun to pray with us, may God reward them [Moshe Gil, *Eretz-Israel*, II, pp. 601–602].

He also hinted at a possible way of tempting these Maghrebis:

And you are not unaware, my Master, that without exception the titles of the dignitaries of this city originate in Iraq. All this is [done] to... destroy this place.

And so the North Africans took it upon themselves to restore the synagogue, being awarded titles of honor by the Yeshiva of the Land of Israel, and gaining a place of worship in Fustat, where they would be joined by more immigrants from North Africa in the coming years.

The episode of the restoration of the Synagogue of the Jerusalemites in Fustat clearly reflects the growing strength of the Maghrebi group at an advanced stage of its consolidation. It also explains the closer relationship between Maghrebi Jews in Fustat and the Yeshiva in Jerusalem, whose head was also recognized as chief of the Jews in the Fatimid state, and thus bore responsibility for many matters in the life of the Jewish communities in Egypt. The first to benefit from the restoration were members of the Land of Israel community in Fustat and the leadership institutions in the Land of Israel. A strong community of Land of Israel Jews in the Fatimid capital was beneficial to these institutions, both for their activities within the Jewish community and when they needed someone to represent them before the Fatimid authorities. Thus, attending that synagogue or absenting oneself from it could be construed as an act of support for or opposition to the Jewish leadership in

164

Manuscript of Numbers, Chap. 13–15, probably written in Persia, 1106 (JNUL 8° 2238)

foreigners from settling in the city. These factors emphasized even more the self-segregation of the Maghrebi community, and were not always compatible with the interests of members of the veteran local communities.

The strength of members of the Maghrebi community in Fustat should not be measured solely by their economic and social power. Their access to the Fatimid court, where Jews held important positions, should also be taken into account. It seems that those who had access to the Fatimid court while it was still in the Maghreb had been able to further Jewish interests in Egypt and adjacent regions by virtue of their ties with officials in both centers of Fatimid rule – the Maghreb and Egypt. Leading merchants maintained contacts with government officials in key positions. These ties were intended first and foremost to further the business affairs of the merchants and the political and economic interests of the Fatimid state. The government realized that trade routes could stabilize the economy and diffuse the state's religious and political concepts. The most outstanding among the merchants in Egypt were

the Land of Israel or it representatives in Egypt. Indeed, in times of crisis, an empty synagogue served as testimony that the worshippers lacked confidence in the leadership.

The Maghrebi "Lobby"

Independent social organization and the great involvement in public affairs of "the recent newcomers from the Maghreb" also aroused opposition. There were even some who argued:

The Maghrebis have become great! The Maghrebis have brought controversy to Israel and the Maghrebis have brought controversy to Egypt [Gil, ibid., p. 176].

The Maghrebi community initiated mutual responsibility for paying debts, and banded together to attain good commercial terms, such as in the case of the collective protest lodged by the North Africans against the tax imposed in Alexandria to deter

the Maghrebi Jews. Those with close relations to the Fatimid court and its officials became a lobby that made efforts to solve various problems which arose in the Jewish communities of Egypt and elsewhere under Fatimid rule. Much of their activity centered around the affairs of the Yeshiva of the Land of Israel, which served as the formal leadership of the Jews in the Fatimid state.

The Maghrebis in Fustat also maintained a relationship with the centers of spiritual activity in their former homes. The communal institutions, courts and houses of study of the North African communities had acquired much strength and great prestige, and their authority was recognized by Maghrebi Jews wherever they lived. We see this in the questions on religious law that were sent from Egypt to the houses of study in the Maghreb, and, when these houses of study declined in the middle of the eleventh century, in the effort made to transfer books and

Kairouan, ca. 1920

Hence, the relationship between the Maghrebis living in Egypt and the Yeshiva of the Land of Israel was one of mutual dependence, embracing economic, institutional and social interests between a regional center and one of the most active pressure groups at the center of power in Fustat. This was a group formally and functionally subordinate to the center, yet superior to it in its economic conditions and political status.

The Maghrebis in the Land of Israel

The third concentration of Maghrebi Jews was in the Land of Israel. The circumstances of their immigration to the Land of Israel were varied. Religious motives had led some to immigrate: to atone for a sin that had been committed, to fulfill a vow made at a time of duress, to seek healing for an illness, or to live in the land where prayer was considered superior to worship elsewhere. Others came for family reasons, following in the footsteps of family members who had emigrated to the Land of Israel, or women and children who accompanied the heads of their families. Some came for economic reasons, among them agents of great commercial houses which had established outposts along the arteries of international trade, or religious functionaries who hoped to find a livelihood in the communities in the Land of Israel, or paupers who preferred to live in an inexpensive country until their

traditions of study from the Maghreb to Egypt. The houses of study in the Maghreb also exerted some influence over the Yeshiva of the Land of Israel. Nathan ben Abraham, who contended for the post of head of the Yeshiva and was appointed gaon for a short period of time, had studied in Kairouan for many years under R. Hushiel, and remained in contact with him and the communal institutions in North Africa even after he returned to the Land of Israel.

The financial support provided by the Maghrebis for the Jews in the Land of Israel and the Yeshiva was an important element for the Yeshiva's activity. Any stoppage or reduction in the transfer of money would have brought it to the brink of crisis. These contributions were first sent from the Maghreb to Egypt, and from there to the Yeshiva – with additional contributions from the Jews in Egypt. The fact that the North African Jews in Egypt served as a channel for the transfer of funds from the Maghreb to the Land of Israel added another dimension to the importance of this community.

In addition to this description of the power of the Maghrebi group in Egypt, it should be pointed out that it was nominally dependent upon the Land of Israel leadership. Since the head of the Yeshiva of the Land of Israel was also chief of the Jews in the Fatimid state, he was capable of influencing – directly or through officials and communal leaders dependent upon him – affairs in the Jewish communities in regions subject to his authority. This was of immediate and practical significance in the economic and social spheres, for close formal and social ties with leadership institutions in the communities along the trade routes were a necessary condition for success in international commerce.

Jewish women in Tunisia, ca. 1920

166

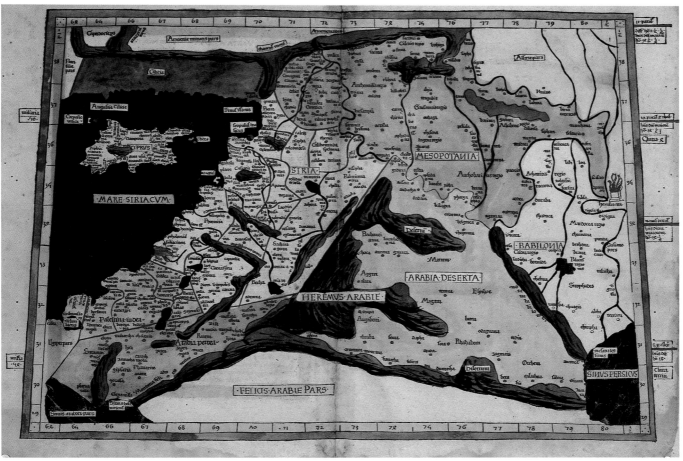

Map of the Middle East based on that of Ptolemy, Ulm, 1482, woodent (JNUL, Laor 602)

fortunes took a turn for the better. There may also have been some who came to study certain subjects such as Hebrew grammar, a field in which the primacy of the Land of Israel was recognized. Nevertheless, there is no evidence of propaganda by the Land of Israel leadership or the Maghrebis themselves to encourage Jews to emigrate to the Land of Israel.

Since they lived in communities in the Land of Israel, the Maghrebis there were formally subordinate to the leadership of the Yeshiva of the Land of Israel and its officials. However, they also served as a channel of informal information about what was happening in the leadership institutions in the Land of Israel, information that was passed on to the Maghrebis residing in Egypt and the Maghreb who on that basis decided the fate of their significant financial contributions. For example, a report was circulated about the disappearance of sixty *dinars* that had been sent from Afriqiya (North Africa) to the Land of Israel. Subsequently, the head of the Yeshiva was pressed to explain the circumstances surrounding the rumor, or the missing funds.

Some Maghrebi Jews reached powerful positions of control and leadership in the Land of Israel communities. The Maghreb

houses of study were capable of training suitable candidates to serve as teachers, cantors, and local judges. However, since the appointments were made by a central institution – the Yeshiva of the Land of Israel – there was a need for an initiative, in addition to the talents of the candidate, to have him appointed to a position entailing income, power and honor. Indeed, several factors did combine to produce such appointments: certain candidates for leadership positions were from the Maghreb; the Maghrebis living in Egypt pressed to have them appointed; and those living in the Maghreb learned of the appointment. This combination was especially efficient in appointments to offices in the Land of Israel communities.

Despite the power possessed by Maghrebi Jews, one position was closed to them: head of the Yeshiva of the Land of Israel. Until the beginning of the eleventh century this office was in the exclusive possession of members of three families: two of *kohanim* (the hereditary priesthood) and the ben Meir family. Furthermore, other key posts in the Yeshiva, positions of importance in the leadership of the communities in the country, were traditionally held by a limited number of families. There

167

were, however, cases in which persons who did not belong to these families filled such positions even before the eleventh century, but this did not apply to the head of the Yeshiva.

In the eleventh century, several persons who were not members of the prestigious Land of Israel families assumed the leadership of the Yeshiva and filled other key positions. The most

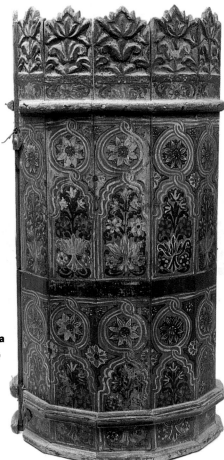

Torah scroll case, Tunisia (CJA, Sc_94, 17/3)

outstanding among them was Solomon ben Judah Fasi, gaon [=head] of the Yeshiva in the years 1025–1051. However, before and after Solomon this post was filled by men who did not belong to the three Land of Israel dynasties: before him there was Solomon ben Yehosef ha-Kohen Sijilmassi; after him came Daniel ben Azariah, a scion of the family of Baylonian exilarchs. Candidates for this position and the leadership of the Jerusalemites in Fustat were Nathan ben Abraham and Judah ha-Kohen ben Joseph, both of whom had learned in houses of study in the Maghreb.

Three groups of Maghrebi Jews were repeatedly involved in these appointments: those living in the Maghreb, in Egypt, and in the Land of Israel. Their degree of involvement was relative to the communal consolidation and strength of each

group. The object of their efforts was to achieve a common goal – appointment of persons preferred by the Maghrebis. Just as the Maghrebi community in the Land of Israel took pains to inform the Maghrebis in Egypt and North Africa of occasional financial or other problems in the Land of Israel, and responses were not long in coming – directly and indirectly – in the form of political and financial support, so did they keep their brethren informed of what was happening in the highest leadership circles, and their responses helped to select the Maghrebi candidates for leadership offices. The group that was least dependent upon the central leadership institutions was the one in the Maghreb, while the most subordinate group was that of the Land of Israel. Maghrebi Jews in Egypt had considerable room for maneuver, despite being formally subordinate to the Land of Israel leadership and functionally, socially, and ceremonially connected to that in the Maghreb.

The method used to train rabbinical scholars in the Maghreb's houses of study, and the frequent contacts between North Africa and the Land of Israel, brought not only Maghrebi merchants but also scholars to Egypt and to the Land of Israel. Some engaged in trade while others sought their livelihood according to the nature of their own unique capabilities – as judges in religious courts, cantors, or preachers in the various communities. An examination of the origin of members of the communal leadership in Egypt and the Land of Israel indicates that many of them were immigrants, and most prominent among them all were the Maghrebis. On the basis of their training in the yeshivot of North Africa and through their advancement within the hierarchies of leadership and learning in the Land of Israel, immigrants from the Maghreb contracted matrimonial ties with families of the traditional leadership in Egypt and the Land of Israel. Incidental reports of such marriages reached the Maghreb countries in letters from the newlyweds, letters of other Maghrebis, and also in marital legal documents – betrothal agreements, marriage contracts and court decisions – in which the Maghrebis appear with appellations that indicate their lands of origin.

Involvement of the Maghrebis in Leadership Conflicts in the Land of Israel

The tradition of study, economic power and access to centers of political power made it possible for Maghrebi Jews with the proper qualifications to rise to the most senior position – head of the Yeshiva of the Land of Israel. This explains how two Maghrebis, one of whom had studied in North Africa, were appointed to that prestigious office in the eleventh century.

Interior of Assayag Synagogue in Tangiers, Morocco, 20th cent. (CJA, Assyag Synagoge, no. 1)

Indeed, Maghrebis were already involved in all the episodes that preceded the appointment of geonim in the Land of Israel from the late tenth century onwards. In a controversy over the office of the gaon at the end of the tenth and the beginning of the eleventh centuries, members of a priestly Maghrebi family from Sijilmassa challenged the gaonate of Samuel ben Joseph ha-Kohen, a member of a Land of Israel family of kohanim. Despite their failure on this occasion, not long afterwards members of this Maghrebi family filled the senior leadership roles in the Yeshiva. Joseph ben Menahem ha-Kohen Sijilmassi presided as *av bet din* (president of the rabbinical court) in the first quarter of the eleventh century, and his son Solomon was appointed gaon in 1025. Solomon ha-Kohen the Maghrebite appointed Solomon ben Judah Fasi (i.e., from Fez) as gaon. The latter relates that when the previous gaon decided to appoint him president of the court, there were some who tried to challenge his promotion, arguing that he did not belong to one of the families worthy of the appointment. This argument was repeated in another context, in a description of how the Maghrebis gained control of positions and offices in Egypt and the Land of Israel. When Solomon ben Judah fell into disfavor, after nearly fifteen years in office, it was precisely Maghrebis living in Egypt and their associates who were involved in an attempt to replace him with Nathan ben Abraham. They pressed for Nathan's appointment and, according to members of Solomon's party, Nathan arrived in Egypt from the Maghreb with letters of support from the Maghrebi leadership recommending his appointment

as gaon of the Yeshiva of the Land of Israel. In this affair, both sides tried to mobilize the support of the *nagid* who resided in North Africa, asking him to make public his position on the appointment of a gaon for the Yeshiva. The appointment of Daniel ben Azariah, too, was not devoid of controversy, and in this case, too, Maghrebis living in Egypt were enlisted to help him obtain the post. In the eighties of the eleventh century, when David ben Daniel sought the office of chief of the Jews, the Maghrebis in Egypt and Jerusalem came to his aid. Those of North Africa were not involved since at that time they were busy restoring their own communities after the great sack of cities to which the Maghreb was subject in that decade.

Political intervention did not always take the same form, and not all Maghrebis were in the same camp. However, the following elements are found in all four episodes mentioned above: in each one candidates were proposed either from the Maghreb, or ones who had been educated in Maghrebi houses of study; the candidates used informants among the Maghrebis living in Jerusalem to spread information favorable to themselves and detrimental to the rival candidate; the Maghrebi group in Egypt used its connections with Muslim officials, who had to approve the appointments, even reaching the caliph himself. In several of the affairs, the group in the Maghreb decided whom to support on the basis of a decision by the nagid. The nagid's support influenced both Fatimid officials in Egypt and the decision of the Jews in North Africa.

The manner in which influence was brought to bear on the

169

appointment of this or that person as head of the Yeshiva required the involvement of the three groups and frequent, vital contact

Entrance to an old house in Tunisia

among them. However, as might be expected, most influential were the Jews living in the Maghreb, despite their being furthest away. This was because the presence of the nagid there, who held informal authority over the North African Diaspora and the authority to allocate the monetary contributions to the Land of Israel and to Babylon. Furthermore, he could also influence Muslim state officials. Precisely these frequent appeals to the nagid at times when the head of the Yeshiva was to be replaced, as well as the need to make his decision public, attest to the important role that he played in appointments of heads of the Yeshiva of the Land of Israel. Moreover, once the Maghrebis had helped a certain person to gain the appointment, North African Jews were awarded other appointments and posts by the elected gaon. Such was the case soon after the appointment of Solomon ben Judah, Daniel ben Azariah, and David ben Daniel to the office of head of the Yeshiva.

This involvement might create a sense of mundane affairs

and petty calculations, and lead to the conclusion that not only was the Land of Israel no more than a remote vision in the minds of Maghrebi Jews but, additionaly, that its leadership in the eleventh century was not appreciated, on account of the frequent intervention by Maghrebi Jews in its affairs and their capacity to exert influence on the choice of leaders in the Land of Israel. The opposite is true: the involvement in and financial support for the existing leadership institutions indicate a level of ties between a center and a Diaspora unprecedented in the Middle Ages until then. These ties included a maximum of aspects of the relationship between center and Diaspora, and were grounded in the basic assumption that what happened in the Land of Israel was of great interest to the Jews of the Maghreb. From the various ways in which this relationship was expressed, we learn the importance Maghrebi Jews attached to the center in the Land of Israel by virtue of its sanctity and on account of its direct influence on Maghrebis living in Egypt and the Land of Israel. That is why Maghrebis sought to be partner to what was being done in the Land of Israel. This partnership was expressed in ways more convenient to the leadership in the Land of Israel – such as financial support and pilgrimage – together with less convenient aspects resulting from intervention in internal controversies concerning the leadership of the communities in the Land of Israel.

Frequent contact and extensive involvement, then, should not blur the fact that the center in the Land of Israel was important for North African Jews. Conversely, this contact and involvement enhanced the importance of the North African Diaspora for the center in the Land of Israel which was engaged in efforts to ensure its physical existence, and in internal polemics.

• • • • • • • • • • •

The Jews of Syria and the Land of Israel

Until 1078, the Yeshiva of the Land of Israel, located either in Tiberias, Ramlah, or Jerusalem, was for both the authorities and the Jews themselves the formal leadership of the Rabbanite Jews in the area of its jurisdiction – the Land of Israel and Greater Syria. The Yeshiva's leadership appointed the heads of the communities under its jurisdiction, and the heads of the communities, by virtue of their authority and ordination from the head of the Yeshiva, appointed the communal officials – cantors, scribes, *parnasim* (heads of congregations), ritual slaughterers, and circumcisers.

The Jewish community in Damascus customarily marked the years on its documents as was the custom in the Land of Israel:

counting by sabbatical years back to the destruction of the Second Temple and to the Creation. This also applied to documents dating from the first third of the tenth century which were drawn up in the synagogue of the Babylonians in Damascus. The heads of the communities and the judges were appointed by Yeshiva of the Land of Israel.

Covering for a Torah scroll, Morocco, 20ᵗʰ cent.

In exercising its authority, representatives of the Yeshiva of the Land of Israel – sometimes even its head visited cities in Syria in order to hold court, to supervise the activities of the local Jewish administration, to expedite collection of Jewish communal taxes and to enlist support among local Jews for various factions in the internal struggles for leadership of the Yeshiva. This activity of the sages and representatives of the Yeshiva is highly indicative of the formal status of the Land of Israel leadership in Syria.

Formal ties between the leadership of the Yeshiva and communities under its jurisdiction also existed between Jerusalem and Egypt. Nevertheless, though Egypt and Syria were formally on the same level of subordination to the center in the Land of Israel, Egypt's status was different. The functional dependence of the heads of the Yeshiva of the Land of Israel on the dignitaries in Egypt enabled community leaders there, principally those in Fustat or Cairo, to intervene and exert great influence on how the Land of Israel leadership functioned. The communities in Syria generally had no such pretensions.

In the first decade of the eleventh century, a member of the family of the Babylonian exilarch, who bore the appellation "Shem-Tov," arrived in Tiberias. He conducted himself like the head of the Jews in the northern part of the Land of Israel and Syria, appointing heads of communities, sitting in judgment and proclaiming dates of holidays and the intercalation of leap years. This episode should not be construed as an expression of a desire on the part of communities in Syria to be independent of the Land of Israel leadership; after all, what Shem-Tov did was to apply a regional authority of the Land of Israel to communities under its jurisdiction. Moreover, he was obeyed precisely because he represented the values of the central Jewish leadership. He belonged to the family of the exilarch and exercised his authority from Tiberias, the seat of authority before it was transferred to Ramlah and to Jerusalem. It seems that this episode is connected with the transfer of the leadership to Ramlah and Jerusalem, while its social and economic hinterland was still located in Galilee and Tiberias area. Members of prestigious, established families, such as the hero of this episode, might have sensed the vacuum that had developed in the leadership of a region populated with Jews, and tried to fill the void themselves.

Until the Yeshiva of the Land of Israel left the country in 1078, Egypt and Syria were its dependencies. Egypt was the senior of the two, and although it was powerful enough to lead the Jewish communities in the region it refrained from doing so and supported the Yeshiva's leadership, helping it rule within its area of jurisdiction. The communities of Syria, the junior of the two dependencies, were subject to the authority of the Land of Israel without any pretension or ability to assume the role of central leadership. This weakness was beneficial to the Yeshiva of the Land of Israel when it fell upon hard times in 1078.

Transfer of the Leadership to Tyre

At the beginning of the seventies of the eleventh century, Turkoman forces invaded Palestine and the area around Jerusalem. These were the Seljuks. They sowed destruction among the urban population in Jerusalem and Ramlah, thereby provoking a great wave of migration from the cities of Judah. Jerusalem, too, was almost emptied of its inhabitants, and the Yeshiva of the Land of Israel left that city for Tyre.

The leaders of the Yeshiva preferred not to move to Egypt, although it was the logical land of refuge, because of the danger in being far away and cut off from the communities of Judah and Galilee, and out of fear lest the power of the Egyptian Jewish leadership overshadow the activity of the Yeshiva leadership when they were in close proximity. On the other hand, the advantages

171

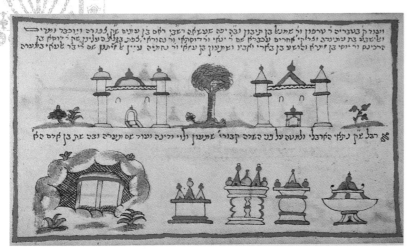

Plan of ancient tombs in the Galilee, including that of R. Samuel ben Tibbon, Italy, late 15th cent. (LUL, Roth Collection, 220, fol. 6v)

of Greater Syria were obvious: from Tyre they could maintain regular contact with the center of Jewish life in Galilee that had been left almost untouched and was one of the bases of the Land of Israel leadership's strength. Moreover, the communities of Greater Syria did not and could not overshadow the leadership of the Yeshiva at that time.

From 1078 until the beginning of the thirteenth century, the Yeshiva of the Land of Israel based its activity in Syria, at first in Tyre, and then, after less than twenty five years in that city, for about a century in Damascus. The most significant upheaval in the supra-communal organization of the Jews of the Land of Israel, Egypt, and Greater Syria took place in 1082, a few years after – and as a result of – the transfer of the Yeshiva to Tyre. It began with an open revolt by the community in Egypt against the leadership of the Yeshiva and its head, Evyatar ha-Kohen. Certain persons in Egypt chose as their leader a young man (twenty one years old), a scion of the family of the exilarch. He was David, whose father, Daniel ben Azariah, had been gaon of the Yeshiva of the Land of Israel in 1051–1062. Though David called himself exilarch, he conducted himself only as the head of the authority in the Land of Israel. He sent emissaries to the communities in that country and in Syria in an attempt to usurp the authority of the Yeshiva and its appointees, while trying to appoint communal officials loyal to himself, endeavoring thereby to establish his control over the traditional area of jurisdiction of the Yeshiva. David ben Daniel's challenge came to an end in 1094, but the victory of the Yeshiva, now in Greater Syria, was a pathetic triumph. It had been obtained with the help of Jews at the true center of power in the region – the negidim of Egypt.

In those years the conflict was also waged on the ideological level. Evyatar, head of the Yeshiva now located in Tyre,

pronounced that Egypt was not considered a land of exile, and therefore it was subject to the hegemony of the Yeshiva which bore the legitimate authority of the Sanhedrin, even though Tyre was outside the Land of Israel. It is likely that towards the end of the eleventh century the heads of the Yeshiva of the Land of Israel in Tyre still hoped to impose their authority over all the areas that had been under their jurisdiction when it had been located in Tiberias, Ramlah and Jerusalem – including Egypt.

The revolt of the Egyptian leadership, led by David ben Daniel ben Azariah, lasted for only twelve years, but it indicates a new trend that would be part of the Jewish balance of power in the region until the beginning of the sixteenth century. The relationship of the Diaspora with the communities in the Land of Israel and the latter's subordination to the Jewish leadership in Syria or Egypt were to indicate, more than anything else, the measure of success of each one of the forces competing for primacy.

Transfer of the Leadership to Damascus

After the Crusaders arrived in the Middle East, the Yeshiva moved from Tyre to Hadrak, in Damascus, and from there, in the first quarter of the twelfth century, it became the exclusive leader of the Jews in the region. We have some sparse evidence indicating that the communities of the Land of Israel turned to the Yeshiva in Syria in matters of communal administration, thus attesting to their recognition of its primacy. Yet, the very same communities turned to Egypt in matters to do with economic assistance and lobbying at the court of the rulers – evidence that Egypt preserved its status as the focal point of Jewish power in the region. The strength of the Egyptian center grew, for example, as a result of efforts to rescue the head of the Yeshiva, Masliah, who had been taken captive by pirates in Tripoli. His loyal followers appealed for help to Egypt. Masliah, who was released from captivity, completed the cycle of the Yeshiva's wanderings and transferred it to Egypt in 1127, though another "Yeshiva of the Land of Israel" continued to exist in Damascus.

However, this move did not empty Damascus of its Jewish institutions. In fact, in the century or so between the mid-twelfth century and 1260 the opposite was true. Damascus developed because the Ayyubid regime became firmly rooted there. For a period of about fifty years it even became once more the capital of a united, independent Muslim state. At that time, central Jewish leadership institutions operated from Damascus – the heads of the Yeshiva of the Land of Israel, leading members of

172

the exilarch's family, and the office of the nagid – with power that was unprecedented in Syria. The heads of the Yeshiva belonged to the family of its traditional leadership. However, from the fourth decade of the twelfth century onwards both "Land of Israel" yeshivot, the one in Damascus and its counterpart in Cairo, sought additional sacral support in the alternate center of Jewish leadership, in Babylon. The head of the yeshiva in Damascus was ordained by the yeshiva in Baghdad, while the head of the Cairo yeshiva was ordained by the exilarch in Baghdad.

It would seem that the center in Egypt in principle recognized the jurisdiction of the yeshiva in Syria over the communities in the Land of Israel, at least for a short time. This emerges from the letter of the Babylonian exilarch, Daniel ben Hisdai. He sought to sever Egypt's link to the Yeshiva of the Land of Israel, claiming that the Yeshiva had never had authority over Egypt, which was considered a land of exile, but only over the communities in the Land of Israel and in Syria. Thus, the Babylonian exilarch, too, admitted the authority of the Yeshiva over Syria, in addition to the Land of Israel.

Since only one member of the exilarch's family could preside as exilarch, those who did not attain that position sought an alternate field of activity. After Syria came under the authority of the Babylonian leadership and living conditions became difficult in Baghdad and Mosul, and as contact increased between those cities and Syria, members of the exilarch's family arrived there too. Their support for the Damascus Yeshiva of the Land of Israel was especially significant precisely because the exilarchs in Babylon supported the leadership of the parallel Yeshiva in Egypt.

Despite the fact that the *nesi'im* (princes of the exilarch's family) were supported from communal funds, they did not fill any official function in Damascus, in Syria or in adjacent areas. Nonetheless, by their very presence in Damascus its Jewish community felt it was a center in relation to other communities. To ease matters for the Damascus community, the nesi'im often traveled to other communities in Syria, the Land of Israel, and Egypt, expecting that upon their arrival they would be received with honor and obtain fitting financial support. Much activity accompanied the itinerant journeys – letters were sent to and from Damascus concerning the details of the journeys and the fine points of the honors bestowed by the host communities. Therefore the presence of the nesi'im in Damascus attracted attention, as well as finances from communities in the Land of Israel, to Damascus, funds that were gestures of informal subordination to the families of the House of David.

The third and firmest source of support for the centralized leadership of Syria was that of the negidim, Jewish communal leaders who had the backing of the Ayyubid rulers. In the last decade of the twelfth and the beginning of the thirteenth centuries, "the great prince Rabbi Obadiah" was active in Damascus. The poet Judah Alharizi described him as "the choicest of princes and trained in the company of kings... Obadiah the great nagid, prince of the Torah, nagid of the Land

Fragment of a letter from the Cairo genizah dealing with the Jews of Ramlah, 10th–11th cent. (JRUL, Gaster 1770. 19)

173

of Israel and Judah, al-Rais Bu [=Abu] al-Rida." Indeed, definition of the nagid's area of jurisdiction as "the Land of Israel and Judah" appears in more than one document, and it refers to the area of jurisdiction of the Yeshiva of the Land of Israel when

Panoramic view of Damascus, painted by Margaret Thomas, early 20th cent.

it was still located in Jerusalem, excluding Egypt, an area now subordinate to the leadership in Damascus. He was followed by Hillel ben Moses, bearing a similar title of office. Obadiah's writ of appointment as chief of the Jews, that was given to him by al-Malik al-Afdal Ali, the elder son of Salah al-Din (Saladin), in 1193, survived in the Cairo genizah. In it, al-Malik indicates that he is granting to Obadiah:

The leadership of the community of the Jews and their sects, the Rabbanites, Karaites and Samaritans in Damascus, the protected city, of all Syria, and al-Salt together with its district. We have placed you at the head of the people of your community and of the local leaders of your sect, every one, whether near or far, of low or high social status (Khan, p. 101).

We learn, therefore, that side by side with the continued existence in Damascus of the leadership of the Yeshiva, and the grand and honorable presence there of the nesi'im, there was also an official appointed by the court in that city. He was the chief of all the Jews in the Land of Israel and Syria: "nagid of the Land of Israel and Judah." The date of the writ of appointment, 1193, indicates that it was no coincidence that three central institutions which also had authority over the Land of Israel were located in Damascus in that period. In that year the Ayyubid dynasty transferred the center of its government from Cairo to Damascus, from where they endeavored to manage the state's affairs in the Land of Israel after taking it from the Crusaders, and in Egypt. It was also convenient to administer Jewish affairs from the same center.

In the twelfth and thirteenth centuries, therefore, the wheel had turned full circle. The Jewish communities in Syria, which in the tenth and the eleventh centuries had been under the authority of the leadership in the Land of Israel, were now the seat of an officially appointed leadership responsible for the Jewish communities of the Land of Israel. This, at least, was the formal aspect of the relationship.

Interestingly enough, precisely in this period when the centralized Jewish leadership in Syria had unprecedented power and was not formally subordinate to the leadership institutions located in the Land of Israel or Egypt, appreciation of Jerusalem sages was expressed in letters from Syria. Thus we find students from Syria studying in Jerusalem, while others express a desire to join the fellowship of French scholars studying in the Holy City; rabbinical works are transcribed in Jerusalem and sent to Syria; and Jerusalem scholars are considered to be authorities whose opinions should be consulted. These and other aspects do not represent mere gestures towards those who dwell in the Holy City and sanctify its ruins, but rather expressions of functional subordination to a leadership that was on a much higher level than the centralized, appointed leadership of prestigious lineage located in Damascus.

The Jewish cemetery in Mogador, Morocco, on the Atlantic coast. In the center is the mausoleum over the grave of R. Hayim Pinto (d. 1844)

174

Between the ninth and the fifteenth centuries, the relationship of the various communities in the region to the Yeshiva of the Land of Israel changed in accordance with the political changes and shifts in the location of the local foci of power and strength. In conclusion, we may say that Egypt was formally subordinate to the Yeshiva of the Land of Israel from the ninth to the eleventh centuries. However, in practice it exhibited extensive involvement in Land of Israel affairs during twelfth and thirteenth centuries, as the Ayyubid rulers consolidated themselves in Damascus, to which the Yeshiva had also moved, and the relationship between Egypt and the Yeshiva became one of functional subordination. From the middle

The Mount Hermon ridge photographed by Felix Bonfils, who was active in the Middle East between 1867 and 1885. The photograph was subsequently colored, apparently by his son, Adrien

of the thirteenth century onward, the Yeshiva's authority became once again essentially formal. From the ninth to the thirteenth centuries the attitude of Syrian Jews towards the Yeshiva of the Land of Israel was one of formal subordination, afterwards becoming essentially one of courtesy and ceremonial gestures.

Even the Maghrebi Jewish community, which had never been formally subordinate to the Yeshiva of the Land of Israel throughout the entire period, maintained ties of ceremonial subordination to the center in the Land of Israel until the eleventh century.

Copper tray with the inscription: "Zion – souvenir of Holy Jerusalem – work of Jews in Damascus," early 20th cent.

175

Kokhav ha-Yarden, at the eastern end of Lower Galilee overlooking the Jordan Valley, includes remnants of the Crusader Belvoir Castle built in 1140 and conquered by Salah al-Din in 1189

The Crusader Period

Avraham Grossman

No period in the history of the Jewish people from the destruction of the Second Temple until the beginnings of Zionism had greater influence upon the role of the Land of Israel in Jewish thought than did the Crusader period. Moreover, it also deeply influenced Muslim and Christian consciousness. To this day, the term "Crusaders" arouses very strong emotions in the world of Islam, underlying the actions and reactions of millions of Muslims. The names of admired leaders and military commanders, as well as those of battle grounds upon which the Muslims defeated the Crusaders, are commemorated in diverse ways to this very day. This is so despite the fact that it was a relatively short period in the history of Palestine, lasting for less than two centuries, not to mention the fact that Crusader rule over most of Palestine had ceased decades earlier. The intense impact of this period on the Jewish People was not only the outcome of events in Palestine. The deterioration of the political status and security conditions of the Jews in Christian Europe, the ongoing Jewish-Christian religious polemic, and the rise of various intellectual movements within the Jewish People also contributed to this phenomenon.

The sanctity of the Land of Israel to the three monotheistic faiths had an unfavorable effect on its fate, as it became a constant battlefield between Christianity and Islam. The many mighty battles waged for nearly two hundred years left the country in ruins, especially when some of the Islamic rulers adopted a "scorched earth" policy, destroying fortresses and cities in order to prevent them from serving as a refuge for Christians. On the other hand, during this period the Land of Israel enjoyed a degree of economic prosperity unparalleled in its past history for a very long time.

Before discussing these developments and their results, let us briefly survey events in Palestine. In 1099 the Crusaders conquered Jerusalem, cruelly

The battle for Jerusalem (1099), a miniature from the manuscript *Romans de Godefroi de Bouillon et Salehadin* (BN)

massacring its population, which numbered about 20,000. Many of Jerusalem's Jews were killed while others were taken captive and sold into slavery. That very year they also conquered other cities in the interior of the country, including Bet-Shean and Tiberias.

During the following decade the Crusaders took the coastal cities, with the help of the fleets of Italian city-states, and these ports became the main base of Crusader rule in the country, serving as a connecting link between the Crusader kingdom established in Palestine and Europe. Ascalon did not fall to the Crusaders until 1153. The Kingdom of Jerusalem (*Regnum Hiero-solymitanum*) was one of five Crusader states, and the most important of them due to its special status.

The great rivalry between Fatimid-Shi'ite Egypt and Sunni Damascus prevented cooperation between these two states against the invaders from Europe, enabling the Crusaders to establish themselves in Palestine and adjacent areas. Salah al-Din (known in the West as Saladin) came to power in the 1180s and successfully united Syria, Iraq, and Egypt. As a result, the Crusaders were weakened and lost several strongholds, a process that culminated in their severe defeat at the Horns of Hattin in 1187, a glorious Muslim victory celebrated to this very day. In the wake of this severe defeat most Crusader cities, including Jerusalem, surrendered to Salah al-Din.

When Salah al-Din died in 1193, the Muslim empire was again divided. Subsequent Crusades restored a large part of the territory of Palestine to the Crusaders, especially by the terms of the Treaty of Jaffa contracted in 1229 between Frederick II, Emperor of Germany, and the Egyptian ruler al-Malik al-Kamal. In 1244, however, Khwarezmian forces invaded the country with the encouragement of Egypt, taking various areas of the country from the Crusaders. In 1250, after the Mamluks came to power in Egypt, they began to gradually gain control of additional fortresses that were still in Crusader hands. Furthermore, the Crusaders failed to exploit the Mongol invasion of the country

in 1260, not taking sides during the Mongols' war with the Egyptians. The defeat of the Mongols in the battle of Ein Harod presaged the end of the Crusader kingdom. The Egyptian ruler Baybars took one castle after another from the Crusaders. In 1291, Acre fell to the Egyptians, while Athlit and Tyre were evacuated by the Crusaders, who fled to Cyprus. Thus came to an end the Crusader kingdom in Palestine and adjacent areas.

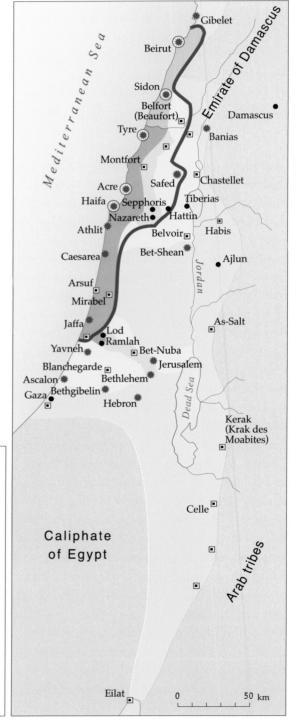

178

The Crusader Kingdom of Jerusalem and the boundaries of Crusader control in Palestine

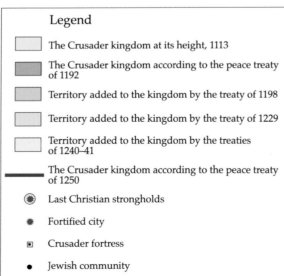

Legend

The Crusader kingdom at its height, 1113

The Crusader kingdom according to the peace treaty of 1192

Territory added to the kingdom by the treaty of 1198

Territory added to the kingdom by the treaty of 1229

Territory added to the kingdom by the treaties of 1240–41

The Crusader kingdom according to the peace treaty of 1250

Last Christian strongholds

Fortified city

Crusader fortress

Jewish community

Population and Economy

The inhabitants of Palestine during the Crusader period were overwhelmingly Muslims, Oriental Christians, Jews, and Samaritans. The Franks (Westerners), a small minority, were dependent upon the local inhabitants who worked the land. Due to the feudal system in the country, the latter were bound to the land, but not in the same manner as the serfs in contemporary Christian Europe. They provided the Crusaders with diverse services, and even helped them build the many strong castles and fortresses that were erected throughout the country.

Agriculture was the basis of the Crusader kingdom's economy. As noted, it was primarily the indigenous population that worked the soil, paying part of the crops to the rulers as taxes and living in small villages. Attempts to establish villages of European immigrants were unsuccessful. Trade, which greatly flourished in the Crusader period, was another important branch of the economy as the country once again served as a significant center of international commerce. In the thirteenth century the coastal cities of Palestine were an important channel for the import and export of goods, in which the Italian city-states played a leading role. The continuous traffic between Europe and Palestine had a major influence on the relationship between Jews in Europe and the Land of Israel. We shall return to this matter below.

The Jewish Population

During the first decade of their conquests, the Crusaders perpetrated many massacres of the local population. Since in that decade they took Jerusalem and the coastal cities, it may be assumed that the Jewish communities in these cities were destroyed. Almost all Jerusalem's Jews, who had fought furiously alongside the Muslims to defend the city, were massacred. The few survivors were taken captive and sold into slavery. There were as yet Jewish communities in Tyre, Banyas, Ascalon, and Rafiah, cities which still held out against the Crusaders. We may conjecture that the Jewish population in Galilee, which lived in villages and earned its livelihood from agriculture, continued to exist. The sources point to more than ten settlements in which Jews lived.

After 1110, when the Crusaders put a halt to the slaughter of the conquered population, deciding to allow it to remain and

The Horns of Hattin, west of Tiberias, where Salah al-Din defeated the Crusaders in 1187

exploiting it as a labor force in agriculture and other services, there was an increase in the number of Jews in the Holy Land. The constant traffic of ships between European and Palestinian ports also brought Jewish immigrants to the country and strengthened the ties between them and the Jewish communities in Europe. Nevertheless, on the whole, the Jewish community in Palestine was very small, perhaps at its lowest number since the Return to Zion from exile in Babylon.

There is no evidence of any special Crusader discrimination against the Jews in this period, and we may assume that their legal status was similar to that of the Muslims and the Syrian-Christians; i.e., they were treated with much tolerance. However, they were forbidden to reside in Jerusalem, with the exception of a few families who received special authorization from the king.

As we shall see below, Jewish immigrants arrived in the country throughout the entire period, and indeed relatively large waves of immigration came from Christian Europe, gradually effecting a significant change in the character of the Jewish communities in the Land of Israel. A population of considerable cultural influence, whose education, concepts, and spiritual world had been shaped in Europe, was now added to the local element that predominated in several of the communities, particularly Acre, carrying on the traditions of the Jews living in the Islamic countries. Such encounters engendered much tension, but they were also a blessing for both groups due to the fruitful encounter between them. R. Judah Alharizi noted the great tension between Jewish groups of diverse cultural-geographic origins in the country at the time of his visit to the Land of Israel during the Ayyubid period, in 1218. In his, *Tahkemoni*, Alharizi described

179

clearly the passage reflects the social situation during the Crusader period in other communities as well. This is abundantly clear from other sources, including the responsa of Meir of Rothenburg, who attested to what he heard from the sons of Jews who had immigrated to the Land of Israel from Europe at the beginning of the thirteenth century, as to the lack of brotherly love among the Jews there.

Acre, which had an extremely important Jewish community, was the central city – from the Jewish standpoint – in the Crusader period. Jews from Islamic countries settled there, as well as many others who came from Europe. It was the scene of significant intellectual activity, and played an important role in the controversy over the writings of Maimonides in the year 1285. One of its sages, R. Solomon Petit, even traveled to Europe to enlist support there for a ban on Maimonides' works. Most Jewish immigrants in the early thirteenth century came to Acre.

• • • • • •

Jewish Reaction to the Crusader Conquest

The Crusader conquest of Jerusalem and the mighty struggles for control of the city between Christians and Muslims in the twelfth and thirteenth centuries, as each side claimed its sacred right to rule the Holy City, left a harsh impression upon the Jews – foreigners struggle over the Jewish patrimony, each side claiming it for itself. The Christian conquest was especially difficult to bear. The polemic with Christianity had already deepened during the eleventh century, becoming more intense in the twelfth and thirteenth centuries. The classic Christian claim was that Christendom was "the true Israel" (*Verus Israel*), "the Israel of the spirit," and it considered its successes and expansion as Heavenly confirmation of this claim. And just as the success of Christianity was evidence of the truth of its faith, so humiliation of the Jews was evidence of their Divine rejection. For Christians, their conquest of the Holy Land and control of its holy places was one of their religion's greatest attainments of all time.

Jewish suffering in exile as clearest testimony of the rejection of the Jews and their replacement by the Christians as God's chosen people was the classic Christian argument in the medieval Judeo-Christian polemic, a claim that ran through the entire corpus of literature of religious disputations. More than any other argument,

Tahkemoni, a Hebrew book by R. Judah Alharizi (1170–1235), written with much humor. Title page of the Constantinople edition of 1577–1578

what he witnessed in the Jewish community in Jerusalem:

For we are afraid because of the evil deeds which are done in it / and of the violence and the wickedness that are within it / And the fire of hatred and factional strife / that in it is rife / and divides the hearts of its inhabitants like a knife. / They all want to be head / and are hard, cruel tyrants instead. / Each man seeks with malice to make his fellow man forlorn. / The father hates his son, his first-born / and the son holds his father in scorn. / The sons gather the wood / and the fathers would set them afire if they could. / All the deeds of their heart are done in duplicity / and there is none that does anything for the sake of Heaven, and in sincerity. / Every day they increase quarrels and divisions / and all the hearts are cleft by derisions / so that I nicknamed the city: "The Rock of Divisions." (Judah Alharizi, *Tahkemoni*, II, p. 148)

Though this was written in the Ayyubid period, after Salah al-Din had allowed the Jews to return to Jerusalem, it is doubtful whether the situation had changed significantly, and the Jews found it difficult to refute, especially in view of the fact that they had been in exile for more than a thousand years.

Evidence of the Jews' deep distress has been preserved not only in the *piyyutim* of the sages, but also in their commentaries on the Bible and on piyyutim. They used forced interpretations of biblical passages to deal with the specific claims of the Christians. There was already marked use of this strategem in the commentaries of Rashi (R. Shlomo Yitzhaki) on Psalms, for example, that on Psalm 39:

We had it in mind to save ourselves from all the troubles that come upon us, so we will neither question nor speak harshly about the severity of divine justice, despite the evildoers who oppress us, and we kept silent for many days and were even silent with respect to good, even concerning the words of Torah, because of the fear of them [our adversaries]; and for that reason we were pained, disturbed, and frightened, yet in our silence our heart burned within us and in the meditations of our heart [it] flames within us like fire and it causes us to beseech you …

Rashi interpreted the verse in that Psalm, "Make me not the butt of the benighted," as follows: "Do not impose upon me the shame of evil Esau, bring upon him, too, afflictions and pains, so that he will not be able to say: 'You are afflicted for me, but we are not afflicted.'" Esau is the representation par excellence of Christians and Christian power in medieval Jewish literary works, and earlier ones as well. Hence Rashi was referring to Christendom in the guise of Esau.

Emotionally stirred but powerless, the Jews watched the mighty struggle waged between Christians and Muslims for Palestine and Jerusalem. Each side

claimed its religious right over the Holy City. One of the most impressive expressions of this state of mind is the piyyut, "How Can I Come Up to You," by R. Isaac ben R. Sa'adiah:

How did the haters of all purity come to dwell in Zion?

Who would have believed, and who would have imagined?

And they are rich princes situated on high

And I poor and poverty stricken:

How did they dwell in my palaces and indeed reside in them / From on high to the lower depths and from below to the middle?/

/ From the highest to the lowest, and from the lowest to the middle? /

And they have inherited a treasure of gold and drachmas

And I am ready for calamity.

(Goldschmidt, *Seder ha-Selihot*, p. 169)

Ecclesia versus Synagoga – the Church against the Synagogue. Christianity is depicted as victorious over humbled Judaism in an illuminated French manuscript, 14th cent. (BN Cod. Th. 26, initial "T")

181

Religious disputations were part of medieval culture. In a detail from a 13ᵗʰ cent. manuscript, Ildefonso, Bishop of Toledo in the seventh century, is preaching to Jews in the synagogue (Esc. MS. "Cantigas de Santa Maria," fol. 7r)

Even harsher words were written by Nahmanides when he, too, referred to the Crusaders' victories and their conquest of the Land of Israel and Jerusalem, as well as their incapacity to hold on to the country until it passed into other hands:

I have likened you, my mother, / to a woman in birth whose child died in her lap. / The milk in her breasts causes her pain, / and so she gives suck to the pups of dogs. / And with all this, *thy lovers despise thee* [Jer. 4:30] / and enemies are desolate in you. / They remember you in distant places, / and pride themselves over the holy city, / saying, *She is given to us for an inheritance* [Ez. 33:24]. / Yet, when they come to you and find / *all that is pleasant to the eye* [Lam. 2:4], / they flee therefrom as it were / before the enemy, *when none pursueth* [Lev. 27:37]. (Nahmanides, *Writings & Discourses*, II, p. 714)

Thus it comes as no surprise that the Jews in Christian Europe rejoiced in the Crusader defeat, seeing in it a sign from Heaven that the Jews alone had a right to the country, and only to them would it respond and yield its fruit. Therefore they alone were fit to build it up in permanence. Christians and Muslims would not know how to work its land, and in their hands it would remain desolate. The very fact that various parts of the country passed from hand to hand was proof of this. Such interpretation of the events was repeated by several Jewish sages in Europe, from Spain and central Europe. One of the outstanding expressions of this outlook is Nahmanides' commentary on the verse, "Your enemies that shall dwell therein shall be desolate in it" (Lev. 26:32):

Similarly, that He stated here, *and you enemies that shall dwell therein shall be desolate in it*, constitutes a good tiding, proclaiming that during all our exiles, our Land will not accept our

enemies. This is also a great proof and assurance to us, for in the whole inhabited part of the world one cannot find such a *good and large Land* [Ex. 3:8] which was always lived in and yet is as ruined as it is [today], for since the time that we left it, it has not accepted any nation or people, and they will all try to settle it, but to no avail. (Nahmanides, *Commentary on the Torah – Leviticus*, p. 473)

As we shall see below, the Crusader defeat also served as an important cause in R. Meir of Rothenburg's attempt to immigrate to the Land of Israel, accompanied by a sizable group of Jews from Germany. From the moment that this Jewish reaction to events was combined with transformations in Jewish spiritual life – particularly the spread of philosophy and Kabbalah – a broad and comprehensive discussion developed over the unique qualities of the Land of Israel.

· · · · · · · · · · ·

The Land of Israel in Jewish Thought

The transition from the Crusader period to that of Mamluk rule in Palestine did not influence the Jews in the Diaspora. Hence, in the rest of this chapter we will deal with developments outside the Land of Israel in the two periods taken as one. The next chapter will survey developments within the country during the Mamluk period.

Since the earliest days of the Jewish nation there was no comparable comprehensive discussion in Hebrew literature of the uniqueness of the Land of Israel – as the Chosen Land, with

The personal seal of R. Moses ben Nahman (Nahmanides, 1194-1270), who immigrated to the Land of Israel from Gerona, in Spain, in 1267. This rare find was discovered near Tel Kison in the Valley of Zebulun, not far from Acre, where Nahmanides lived after settling in the Land of Israel

The Kuzari **by R. Judah ha-Levi (ca. 1075–1141). Written to uphold the truth of the Jewish religion, it also discussed at length the role of the Land of Israel in religious consciousness, and exemplifies the yearnings of the people for its country. Right: the edition published in Venice 1547; left: another edition, with commentary, Venice 1589**

its particular qualities, and its holiness – as is found in the Crusader and Mamluk periods. Though the Talmud and the various branches of midrashic literature include many expositions in praise of the Land of Israel, these do not represent a comprehensive, systematic treatment of the subject. Nor is there such a discussion in the various written sources from the Early Muslim period. Hebrew literature was not yet ripe for an elucidation of this kind. This would only come about after the extensive development of Jewish philosophical literature. Since this body of literature developed primarily in Spain, it was not by chance that almost all the systematic discussions of the unique character of the Land of Israel were produced there, and in a wide perspective: the significance of the choice of the Land of Israel, its relation to diverse spiritual phenomena such as prophecy, sanctity, etc., its status in the age of exile, the nature of the future Redemption there, and other topics.

Nevertheless, it would be a mistake to believe that these discussions were limited only to Jewish society in Spain. In France and Germany too, there are traces of such elucidations, but these are not comprehensive discussions as in Spain. In the Crusader

and Mamluk periods, the Land of Israel became one of the central topics dealt with in the various genres of Hebrew literature – philosophy and Kabbalah, *halakhah* and commentary, piyyutim and other poetry. The development of philosophical speculation was not the sole cause of this development. Several additional factors were at work as well, five of which were of major importance:

a) The enhanced role of the Holy Land in the consciousness of European Christian society as a consequence of the Crusades and of the conquest of Jerusalem and the Holy Land from the Muslims. The propaganda of leading churchmen who called upon the faithful to take part in these campaigns, the positive response of kings and knights to the call, the military achievements and failures, and the discourse about the Crusader ideal – all these led to the Holy Land becoming a part of public consciousness on a much wider scale than in the past.

b) Deterioration of the political, social, and juridical status of the Jews throughout Europe as of the thirteenth century, and especially during the following two centuries. The restrictive edicts of Pope Innocent III, climaxing in the decisions adopted at the Fourth Lateran Council (1215), were an obvious sign

183

The Crusades and the destruction they wreaked on several Jewish communities left a deep impression. Pharaoh and his army are depicted as Crusaders in the manuscript "Rylands Haggadah" (JRUL, MS. 6, fol. 186)

signaling the coming change for the worse. This was soon evident in hindrance of economic activity by Jews, aggravation of their

Burning Jews at the stake in the Middle Ages, a woodcut from the *Liber Chronicarum*, by Schedel, Nuremberg 1493. The destruction of Jewish communities in Germany by the Crusaders as they advanced towards the Holy Land was a very important factor in shaping Jewish historical memory

political and juridical status, and an increase in religious disputations, blood libels, and expulsions. True, some of these aspects had already begun to emerge in the twelfth century, but they intensified with time. The *Rindfleisch* decrees in Germany (ca. 1300), the dreadful days of the "Black Death" throughout Europe (1348), and the severe measures against the communities in Spain beginning in 1391 were some of the harshest experiences of the Jews in Europe in that era. The Land of Israel as a symbol of Redemption, and sometimes even as a place of refuge, rose in public consciousness, and was now even more predominant.

c) The defeat of the Crusaders in the Holy Land in the course of the thirteenth century constituted a weightier factor than it might seem at first glance. As mentioned above, a bitter polemic was conducted between Judaism and Christianity as to the identity of "the true Israel." One of the principal proofs provided by Christians to substantiate their own claim to be "the true Israel" was their political and military success. The Jews, on the other hand, argued – this theme was often repeated in the polemical works composed in that era – that since Islam too, had recorded successes, what assurance was there that Christianity was the chosen religion? And then came the Crusader conquest of the Holy Land from the Muslims, and in the name of Christianity! This undermined the Jewish argumentation. Hence the blows that Salah al-Din dealt the Crusaders and their final defeat in the second half of the thirteenth century were for Jews a Heavenly sign of the fallaciousness of the Christian claim. Not for nothing did the Jews describe Salah al-Din as a new Cyrus who had presented them with a proclamation that included a call to immigrate to Jerusalem and settle there. We have also seen above that two leading medieval Jewish personalities, Nahmanides and Meir of Rothenburg, integrated the virtues of the Land of Israel and its profound relationship to the Jewish people into this discourse by explicitly designating the Crusader defeat as a sign of the profound, unique bond between the People of Israel and the Land of Israel. The Land of Israel would not welcome any other nations and yield them its fruits; it awaited only the return of its Jewish children. They alone were the true children, and only they could make its wastelands bloom again.

d) The extensive preoccupation with biblical exegesis, especially in northern France, in Provence, and in Spain, particularly of passages directly and indirectly related to the special features of the Land of Israel, was another factor. The exegetes sometimes also had recourse to discussion of the virtues of the Land of Israel and its role in the processes of Exile and Redemption of the Jewish people.

e) The rise and spread of the Kabbalah – Jewish mysticism. True, in several of their discussions the Kabbalists continued to follow the path trodden by the early sages. However, they also added a new dimension to discussion of the unique features of the Land of Israel, as we shall consider below.

In religious polemical literature, in piyyutim and poetry, in chronicles and moralistic works, the Jews continued, as in the past, to give much attention to the Land of Israel. But the major innovation came in speculative literature and the Kabbalah, to which we shall dedicate our following remarks.

The Holy Scriptures shaped the consciousness of the Land of Israel among Diaspora Jews. Page from a polyglot (multilingual) Bible, Alcalà (Spain), 1522

Developments in Jewish Thought
and the Land of Israel

Medieval Jewish thought underwent a great transformation, especially beginning in the twelfth century with the rise of rationalism. The Jews were deeply influenced by Aristotelian Greek philosophy which is founded on the concept that the world is guided by the laws of nature, from which nothing could deviate. In any event, it was difficult to consider the Land of Israel as the Chosen Land without linking this affirmation to the laws of nature. Hence the need to reconsider this subject, as well as others, such as God's choice of the Jewish People, in accord with the new conceptual framework adopted by Jews educated in rationalism, particularly in Spain.

We may discern several approaches in medieval Jewish thought regarding the relationship between the Land of Israel and the People of Israel. Other transformations flowed from political changes, especially from the conquest of Palestine by

"One land has been set apart in some way from all other lands... One place is better than all other places for a particular plant... " (Judah ha-Levi, *The Kuzari*, Book 2)

the Crusaders. We shall briefly consider below eight issues related to the Land of Israel that underwent change when compared with earlier concepts which had been based on biblical texts and the expositions of the early sages.

The Land of Israel as a Chosen Land
and the "Climatic Theory"

The "climatic theory" holds that there are certain regions in the world that excel due to their superb climate, which exerts a favorable influence upon those who reside there, enabling them

to attain especially high spiritual achievements. This theory was accepted by various Christian, Muslim, and Jewish scholars in the Middle Ages.

There are two contradictory positions in the climatic theory in medieval Jewish thought. The first claimed that the Land of Israel was located in a region of ideal climate; therefore it was the ideal land according to the universal laws of nature. The second refuted this assertion, claiming that the uniqueness of the Jewish people did not stem from its connection to the Land of Israel, but rather because the Jews accepted the yoke of the Torah and the commandments, and this in turn led to the country's sanctity. The outstanding representative of the first opinion was R. Judah ha-Levi, and of the second, Maimonides. Judah ha-Levi believed that without suitable environmental conditions the Jewish people could not have realized its potential. He used the theory of climate to prove the unique and special nature of the Land of Israel. Maimonides, on the other hand, posited that the Land of Israel was located in a climatic region common to other countries as well, and therefore its status as the Chosen Land did not depend upon a unique climate but rather upon the uniqueness of the Jewish people, who took upon themselves the yoke of the Torah.

Other sages, too, dealt with this issue, basing themselves to a great extent on the conceptions that typified accepted worldviews at that time in their surroundings. R. Moses ibn Ezra, who lived in Spain early in the twelfth century, adopted an interesting and "revolutionary" position. In his opinion, the Land of Israel was not located in an optimally favorable climatic zone – on the contrary, it was far removed from it. That ideal clime was to be found in the Arab countries. Therefore, the Jews who lived in them had attained the highest level of cultural development. His remarks carried a clear apologetic connotation.

A group of exegetes emerged in the fourteenth century who had been influenced by R. Abraham ibn Ezra's commentary on the Pentateuch, which accepted the influence of climatic and astrological forces. This led to the creation of a theory of "special places," i.e., that there were certain places on earth which, by the nature of their creation and the situation of the stars that influenced them, were superior to others. Such places were suitable for the spiritual exaltation, including reception of prophecy, of the people who lived there. The Land of Israel was pre-eminent among these "special places."

186

Acre, the main gateway to the Holy Land in the Crusader period, and one of the centers of Crusader government. Towards the end of the period it became an important Jewish center

The Land of Israel and Prophecy

The Jewish sages considered prophecy to be the highest degree to which a human being could aspire. How, then, could one explain by the law of nature the fact that there were prophets only among the Jews (except for Balaam, who was considered an exceptional case)? In the opinion of Judah ha-Levi, since the Jewish people dwelt in the temperate zone, i.e., in the Land of Israel, and they came from a chosen and superior stock, they had the capacity to attain prophecy, the highest level of human perfection. Just as mental prowess distinguishes mankind from other animals, so does the prophetic faculty distinguish the Jewish people from other nations. Like the philosophers, Judah ha-Levi did not consider prophecy to be a mission, but the utmost perfection of man.

These concepts led Judah ha-Levi to believe that every Jew was capable of prophecy, provided that he lived in the Land of Israel. Maimonides was of a different opinion. He too considered prophecy to be the highest perfection of man, but it was dependent on his temperament, on his moral virtues, and on his intellectual faculties. Only someone blessed with all these attributes could prophesy. Maimonides made no mention of the opinion that the Land of Israel was specifically suited to prophecy on account of its climate and special qualities. When a person was preoccupied with worldly affairs and sunk in the depths of sadness, he could not prophesy, for these distractions harmed his intellectual perfection. It was emotional, intellectual, and social "exile" that hindered prophecy – not geographical, physical exile. In any event the Land of Israel was not an essential factor for the attainment of prophecy. The superiority of the People of Israel and the Land of Israel originate in their close bond to the Torah and its commandments, rather than in their natural qualities.

Most medieval Jewish sages followed the reasoning of Judah ha-Levi, not that of Maimonides. Even if they did not absolutely accept Judah ha-Levi's outlook, that dwelling in the Land of Israel was a sine qua non for obtaining the faculty of prophecy, they did believe it to be advantageous.

An analogy should not be drawn between Maimonides' position concerning the Land of Israel in the context of prophecy and observing the commandments, and his general attitude to that country. As Isaac Twersky has pointed out, Maimonides' profound emotional tie to the Land of Israel

Conquest of Acre (1187) in a manuscript of William of Tyre's *Outremer*, 14th cent. (BN)

187

one walks four cubits in it, one is assured of life in the world to come. So too, one who is buried will obtain atonement; it is as though the place [where one lies] were an altar which effects atonement, as it is said: *And the land doth make expiation for His people* [Deut. 32:43]. (Maimonides, *The Book of Judges*, p. 219)

The Merit of Observing the Commandments outside the Land of Israel

In our discussion of the Early Muslim period, we saw that in Rashi's opinion there was no full merit in observing commandments outside the Land of Israel, including those whose observance is not limited to the territory of the Land of Israel, such as *tefillin* and *mezuzot*. Nahmanides adopted a similar, but more extreme stance – only in the Land of Israel, which is directly influenced by the Heavens, is there a direct Godly presence. By the nature of its creation, it is suitable for the worship of God, and only there is it possible to observe all the commandments perfectly, "because the essence of all the commandments is for those who dwell in God's land." This is a great, unique virtue of the Land of Israel, but precisely due to its extreme sanctity its inhabitants are dealt with in strictness, and they are duly bound to respect its holiness – they bear much religious responsibility. Thus did Nahmanides describe this attribute in a sermon for the New Year written when he was in the Land of Israel, towards the end of his life: "Those who are privileged to dwell before the Holy One blessed be He, in His land, are those who see the face of the King, and if they are careful of His glory, it is good for them and they are happy. And if they cross Him, woe to them more than to all other people." Thus, Nahmanides' doctrine exalted the Land of Israel to the highest degree from a religious vantage point, for only there could one observe the Torah's commandments in the fullest. His doctrine greatly influenced sages in Spain and elsewhere in later generations, especially among the Kabbalists. Some of them accepted it fully; others tried to moderate it. Obviously, Nahmanides' approach was absolutely different.

There were some who adopted the approach of Rashi, Nahmanides, and their followers, bringing this *ad absurdum*. They claimed there was no need at all to observe the commandments outside the Land of Israel since, after all, there was no real merit in performing them abroad. Other sages

Opening page of Book Seven of Maimonides' *Mishneh Torah*, listing commandments relating to the Land of Israel, France 1296 (HAS, Kaufmann Collection, MS. A77)

is expressed "not only in abstract, complex religious laws, not only in traditional concepts about the Temple, the kingdom of the House of David, and the Sanhedrin, or in messianic beliefs, but also in emotional passages in his writings" (Twersky, p. 112). Thus, for example, wrote Maimonides in *Hilkhot Melakhim* (The Book of Judges) 5:10–11:

The greatest of our sages used to kiss [the rocks] on the borders of Palestine. They used to kiss the stones of the land and roll themselves in its dust... The rabbis said that the sins of him who live in Palestine are forgiven... Even if

disputed with them, such as R. Zemah ben R. Solomon Duran in Algiers who wrote:

Those who stray, who are become mad in their faith, who rebel against God, who say that all the commandments are to be practiced only in the Land [of Israel], but outside it no commandment is to be practiced at all – God forbid – and may the Merciful One save us from the opinion of these fools. (*Responsa Yakhin u-Vo'az*, I, 134)

Setting Aside Offerings and Tithes outside the Land of Israel

The setting aside of offerings and tithes is a commandment that is practiced only in the Land of Israel, and Jews in the Diaspora are exempt from it. Nevertheless, there were some abroad who continued this practice during both the talmudic period and the Middle Ages. This was in accord with the text in *Sifri* (a legalistic elaboration on Deuteronomy), chapter 43: "'Erect markers' (Jer. 31:21) ["markers" here interpreted as "command-ments"] – so that when you return they will not be new to you." There is evidence of the practice of this commandment from the geonic period to the thirteenth century. True, only a few carefully observed it abroad, but precisely because this was a deviation from accepted practice it made an impression upon the wider public, and thus was the memory of the Land of Israel exalted among the masses.

Use of Earth from the Land of Israel in Burials in the Diaspora

As early as the twelfth century, there were some Jews in Germany who placed earth from the Land of Israel under the heads of the deceased. The assumption was that this would be considered as if the deceased was buried in the Land of Israel, and would be saved from "rolling through underground tunnels" at the Resurrection of the Dead.

R. Isaac ben R. Moses of Vienna, who lived at the beginning of the thirteenth century, noted this as a custom that was already widespread in his time, and it is obvious that it began earlier: "And that they are accustomed to put earth of the Land of Israel in the grave..." (*Or Zaru'a, Hilkhot Avelut*, 419). Late in the thirteenth century, one of the sages of Germany attested that this was the custom of "many people." R. Meir of Rothenburg

Sacks of earth from the Land of Israel. Sacks of this kind were placed in the graves of Jews buried in the Diaspora

expressed astonishment at this custom, which was of no benefit, for, after all, the body of the deceased will touch the ground in the Diaspora after the shrouds and the coffin disintegrate. Nevertheless, the custom continued. One of the sages of Germany related that in his time (the early fourteenth century) "many people were accustomed to put earth from the Land of Israel in their graves." Since matters relating to death and burial gain much attention, clearly this practice substantially influenced the role of the Land of Israel in the concepts and emotions of many people.

Dwelling in the Land of Israel – A Positive Commandment of the Torah?

Maimonides and Nahmanides disagreed on this issue, which was also widely discussed by sages in later generations. In his *Sefer ha-Mitzvot* (Book of Commandments), Maimonides did not list dwelling in the Land of Israel as one of the positive commandments. Hence, he obviously did not believe this commandment to be an obligation imposed by the Torah. In his critique of *Sefer ha-Mitzvot*, Nahmanides differed with

Maimonides, claiming that according to the Torah it was a duty of every Jew to dwell in the Land of Israel, even in a period of exile. He decreed that there is a commandment to rule the Land of Israel and settle within its bounds. This is a commandment that is binding upon every single Jew "even during a period of exile," and that residence is the Land of Israel "outweighs all other commandments taken together."

Immigration to the Land of Israel in the Middle Ages – Commandment or Prohibition?

In the Babylonian Talmud, Tractate *Ketubbot*, 111a, it is written that the Holy One, blessed be He, made Israel take two oaths: not to immigrate *en masse* to the Land of Israel and not to rebel against the nations of the world; similarly, He made the heathen nations swear that they would not subjugate Israel "too much."

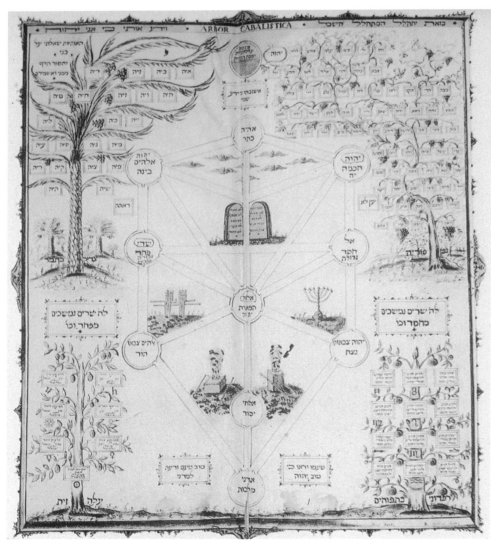

***The Tree of the Spheres**, by the Kabbalist R. Abraham Herrera (ca. 1570–ca. 1635); a copy from 1675*

Jewish sages in the Middle Ages gave much thought to whether or not these commandments applied in their time. Did the fact that the nations did not keep their oath and "subjugated Israel too much" annul the first two oaths, or not? Various opinions radically differing one from another, were expressed on this issue. Here we shall refer to only a few of them.

An especially bitter dispute arose in the Jewish communities of Germany during the thirteenth century. Sages among pietist circles opposed immigration to the Land of Israel in their time, especially immigration of groups, and expressed their opposition in very clear terms. One of them based the prohibition on the biblical passages describing the giving of the Law in Sinai: "Beware of going up the mountain" [Ex. 19:12] – [This is] a hint that He adjured Israel not to hasten the End of Days and not to ascend to the Land of Israel before the time, for it is written, "I adjure you..." [Songs 2:5]...

"Beware of going up the mountain" – the mountain is the Land of Israel and the Temple Mount... Another thing: "Or touching the border of it" – [This means] not to hasten the End of Days and not to be hurried... "Or touching the border of it," [means] the End of Days. "Whoever touches the mountain shall be put to death" [Ex. 19:12] – Whoever hurries to ascend to the Land of Israel will surely be put to death. "No hand shall touch him, but he shall be... stoned" [to death] [Ex. 19:13] – Whoever hastens will not live; [that is] whoever ascends before the End of Days. (Ta-Shma, pp. 315–316)

Only when the Messiah's *shofar* would sound would it be permissible to ascend to the Land of Israel. Conversely, one of the disciples of R. Isaac ben Abraham, one of the greatest of the Tosafists in France, proposed at the beginning of the thirteenth century a totally different point of view. He believed that it was the duty of every Jew to immigrate to the Land Israel and to settle there. Immigration was a precondition for the coming of Redemption. The Messiah would not come until many Jews had settled in the Land of Israel:

190

No one should imagine that the King-Messiah will appear in an impure country, nor should [anyone] mistakenly think that he would come even to the Land of Israel among the Gentiles [there]. He who errs on this matter has no sense of the honor of the King-Messiah. But Jews who adhere to the Torah, pious men of deeds from the four corners of the world, one from a city and two from a family, every man whose heart lifted him up and whom a pure spirit made willing and who is worthy [because of] love of the holy to come to the Land of Israel, to them will the King-Messiah be revealed... And now many are being aroused and intend to ascend to the Land of Israel. And many believe that we are near the coming of the Redeemer, because they see that the nations have made their yoke heavier upon Israel in most places, and other known signs [of the coming of Redemption] have been revealed to the righteous. (Yaari, *Masa'ot*, p.98)

However, not all the Tosafists agreed with this opinion. A generation prior to R. Isaac ben Abraham, R. Hayyim Kohen had ruled that in his days the commandment to immigrate to the Land of Israel and reside there did not apply: "And our teacher Hayyim used to say that at the present there is no commandment to live in the Land of Israel, because there are several commandments that can only be practiced in the Land of Israel and several punishments that we cannot be meticulous in their application" (*Tosaphot, Ketubbot*, 110b).

This was one of the bitterest disputes among the Jewish sages in Germany and France at that time. From the responsa literature we learn that many people were in a quandary over this issue. R. Meir of Rothenburg, the greatest of the sages of Germany in the thirteenth century, continued the tradition of his teachers in France and ruled that the duty to immigrate to the Land of Israel was in effect in his time. And as we shall see below, in his case he practiced what he preached, and tried to immigrate to the Land of Israel together with dozens of families from Germany.

Rabbi Judah ha-Levi had already advocated this outlook, but he expressed it very cautiously and moderately in his *The Kuzari*: The Rabbi said: Indeed, you have shamed me, O King of Khazaria, and this sin [= not immigrating to the Land of Israel] is what prevented us from fulfilling what God had designated for us in Second Temple [times]... Because the divine affair was destined to come about as [it had been] at the beginning [= before the exile], if they had all agreed to return with a willing soul, but [only] some of them returned and most of them – and their great men – stayed behind in Babylon, preferring exile and servitude, so that they would not be separated from their residences and their interests. (R. Judah ha-Levi, *The Kuzari*, 2:24)

His statements also contain a clear accusation against sages and courtiers of his generation who sought various pretexts for not immigrating to Eretz Israel, while their true argument was the good life that they lived in the Diaspora.

Even among the Kabbalists, opinions were divided. Many of them considered immigration to the Land of Israel and residence there to be an extremely important commandment, and dedicated detailed discussions to explaining their approach. For instance, R. Abraham Azulai wrote that a change would take place in the life of a man who is privileged to ascend to the Land of Israel. When he treads on the holy ground, he will be provided with a new soul that is not deserving of punishment, for the sins of the immigrant to the Land of Israel are forgiven. On the whole, the Kabbalists considered returning to the Land of Israel as being like the closing of a circle and removal of the shame of exile and its bad effects. In the sixteenth and seventeenth centuries they forcefully condemned the wealthy who continued to live in the Diaspora, putting the Land of Israel out of their mind.

However, there were also Kabbalists who held other opinions. For example, R. Ezra of Gerona wrote in the first half of the thirteenth century: "In this time, the Jews have already been released from the obligation of the Land of Israel, and it is an altar of atonement for them when they suffer exile for the love of the Holy One blessed be He and suffer torment and subjugation." Nevertheless, those scholars who have ascribed to him the opinion, that even in the time of the Messiah the Jews might return to the Land of Israel only if they received permission from the kings of the Gentiles, are fundamentally mistaken. When Ezra wrote that the Jewish people would return to their land "with authorization of the kings of the Gentiles," his intention was – according to the context – that the age of Redemption would be so wondrous that all the nations of the world would be under its impression and permit the Jews to return, even helping them to do so. There is no limitation here, but rather an addition intended to describe the magnitude of the miracle and its universal recognition, even on the part of Gentiles.

The Land of Israel and Kabbalah

More than any other trend in Judaism, Kabbalah stressed the central role of the Land of Israel in the universe and the relationship between the deity and the Jewish people. The Land of Israel was described as "the navel of the earth." True, some of these motifs are already found in the Bible and in early rabbinic literature; however, in the Kabbalah they take on a new dimension.

The Kabbalah developed the ancient Jewish conception of the Land of Israel as a feminine entity with sexual attributes. Within the framework of Creation, the Land of Israel was connected to the kabbalistic doctrine of "spheres." It was seen as an expression of the link existing between the sphere of splendor and the sphere

191

Sequence depicting the journey of a merchant from Spain to the Crusader port of Acre, an illustration from a 13th cent. Spanish manuscript (Esc., MS. "Cantigas de Santa Maria," fol. 229v)

of kingship. Those dwelling in the Land of Israel were directly influenced by the sphere of kingship. R. Ezra of Gerona, for example, described this nexus in the following manner:

[The] internal line from the populated [part] of the world is the Land of Israel that is called the navel of the earth, and its surroundings are the seventy nations; thus, due to the honored Name, the internal line and the heart are the strength of Israel, and it [= Israel] is like the spine in the *lulav*... and they are all dependent on and satisfied [= receive their needs] from the mean as the branches of the lulav from the spine... And this is the virtue of the Land of Israel that there is no virtue greater than it. (Shalom, p 161)

Exile had supposedly created a division in the supernal worlds too, not only in regard to the bond between the Jewish people and its God. Other Kabbalists too described a close connection between the state of the Divinity and the Land of Israel. For example, R. Abraham Azulai claimed that the Divine Presence is not perfect or complete as long as the entire Land of Israel is not in the hands of the Jewish People.

Kabbalistic literature listed additional merits of the Land of Israel. A few more examples will suffice here (following the analysis of M. Halamish, pp. 225, 227): No perfection is found but in the Holy Land; there is no holiness anywhere like that in the Land of Israel; the Land of Israel is an important means for attaining mystical merits ("the main part of the devotion for attaining the exalted life is in the Land of Israel"; "Whoever wants to see the Divine Presence will study Torah in the Land of Israel"); whoever is privileged to be connected in his lifetime to the Holy Land, will merit after his death being connected in the upper worlds with the sphere of kingship. In contrast, the countries of the Gentiles "are polluted dust and their air is unclean and whoever enters them is very near to faltering." These are only a few of the many statements in praise of the Land of Israel found in Kabbalist writings.

However, one should not speak of a uniform viewpoint of all Kabbalists. There were some who did not assign to the Land of Israel the same virtues as did their colleagues. For instance, R. Ezra of Gerona, whose statements in praise of the Land of Israel are discussed above, did not believe that the obligation to immigrate to the Holy Land applied in his days. Moreover, it was his opinion that suffering in the Diaspora served, from a spiritual standpoint, as a substitute for living in the Land of Israel. The torments involved in loving God while in exile, together with inner spiritual concentration could serve as a substitute for immigration to the Land of Israel.

Another mystic, R. Abraham Abulafia, went even further. He believed that the body of a man in which prophecy was received was equivalent in importance to the Land of Israel, and, on the whole, he assigned little importance to the Land of Israel in his detailed description of the End of Days. Yet, these were exceptions to the rule. As noted, the Kabbalah raised the bond between the People of Israel, the God of Israel, and the Land of Israel to one of its highest peaks, while adding some new elements.

The Kabbalah had indirect influence on the sages of Germany too in the fourteenth and fifteenth centuries. For example, one Jewish sage living in Prague foresaw a great disaster for the Jews of Austria, one which would occur at the end of the fourteenth century. He called for twelve rabbis, to be chosen from among the Jews in that country, to immigrate to the Land of Israel and perform various deeds there to nullify their evil fate. Many of the terms that he used were borrowed from the world of Kabbalah (Grossman, pp. 198–190). Likewise, one generation later R. Jacob of Molin, the greatest of the Jewish sages in Germany at the beginning of the fifteenth century, wrote: "The merit of the Land of Israel…: The air of the Land of Israel makes one wise and leads one's heart to do repentance, as it is written: 'Wisdom begins in the fear of the Lord' " (Peles, p. 255).

192

Immigration to the Land of Israel

Jews immigrated to the Land of Israel throughout the entire Crusader period. Information that has reached us concerns mainly famous sages from Europe, whose disciples and associates referred to their immigration, thus perpetuating its memory for many generations. At times they did so on account of the bitter polemic over immigration to the Land of Israel which was conducted at that time, a subject to which we shall return.

No records have been preserved regarding immigration of "simple folk," but it is clear that it did take place. For instance, R. Judah Alharizi related that when he visited the country in 1218 he found in Jerusalem a kind of ingathering of Jews from far-flung exiles – from Ascalon, Yemen, North Africa, and France. This is how he described the North African community: "And an important and good community of the Maghrebis [North Africans] is there, led by R. Elia ha-Ma'aravi" [= the Westerner, i.e., the Maghrebite]. We have no other evidence of immigration during the twelfth century that created "an important... community" of North African Jews in Jerusalem.

Accounts of immigration are not only important for the study of the Jewish community in the Land of Israel and the relationship of Diaspora communities to the Holy Land; they are also significant sources for studying the motives for immigration and Jewish attitudes towards it. While in the Early Muslim period most immigrants came from the countries of the East, during the Crusader period it may be that most came from Europe. Immigration from Islamic countries did continue, but it is doubtful whether its dimensions were as great as in earlier times, though no hard and fast conclusions can be drawn on the basis of the meager sources available. Political conditions and the cultural milieu in the Crusader kingdom, in addition to more convenient means of transportation, support the assumption that indeed most of the Jewish immigrants in this period came from Europe. It is likely, however, that after Salah al-Din's victories and his explicit grant of permission for Jews to return to Jerusalem, Jews from Islamic lands also responded to his call. Alharizi provides support for such an assumption when he tells of having met various Jews in Jerusalem, including some from Islamic lands.

Immigration from Spain

The written sources provide us with evidence for the immigration of a few Jews from Spain during the Crusader period. The most famous of them was R. Judah ha-Levi who in his old age, in 1140, decided to immigrate to the Land of Israel. The step he took stemmed from both religious and nationalist motives. His

Sefer ha-Trumah, by R. Baruch of Worms, devotes a special section to laws relating to the Land of Israel; a page from the Venice edition, 1523

conception of the Land of Israel and his yearning for it were romantic and imbued with powerful longings, but they were combined with rationalist elements. Judah ha-Levi hoped to encourage others to follow in his footsteps, while simultaneously expressing in his poems his deep conviction that there was no hope for Jews in their lands of exile, but only in the Land of Israel. He was delayed in Egypt for several months, but it turns out from genizah documents, discovered and published by S.D. Goitein, that at the beginning of the month of Sivan (June) 1141 he sailed for the Land of Israel and died there two months later, though we do not know the circumstances of his death (Goitein, pp. 245–250).

In one of his poems, Judah ha-Levi argued with those who opposed his immigration. His opponents asserted that the Land of Israel was in ruins and living conditions there were extremely difficult and dangerous. In Spain, the land of his birth, on the other hand, there was a lively, diverse community and colleagues with whom he could

Disputation between Jewish and Christian scholars, from a woodcut by Johann von Arnsheim, Germany 1483

193

Remains of a Crusader structure at Aqua Bella, near Jerusalem, which apparently served as an agricultural farm

considered by every generation since it was composed as the most intense expression of the bond to and love for Zion. It was introduced into the liturgy of the Ashkenazi Jews, and has been regularly recited since the thirteenth century in the lamentations for the Ninth of Av. This is how Israel Levin describes the poem:

By its means, many generations have wept at the destruction [of the Temple] and have dreamt of Redemption. Everything in it flows towards one focus, Zion... One is carried away by its cadence which has an almost magical impact, and nothing remains that has significance other than its profound relationship to the Land of Israel. The special virtues of its sanctity are detailed at length with lyrical emotion that bears the poet, on the wings of his imagination, on a journey to the places of the revelation, of prophecy, of kingship and of the tombs of the forefathers. (*Hebrew Encyclopedia*, XIX, p. 194)

Judah ha-Levi expresses his pain at the destruction of the country and his humiliation at its subjugation, with a unique poetic outcry:

How can it be pleasant to me to eat and drink, when I see
That the curs drag the young lions? Or how can the light of the day be sweet to my sight, when
I see the flesh of thine eagles in the mouths of ravens?
(*Post-biblical Hebrew Literature*, II, p. 107)

Other poets tried to imitate this wonderful poem, and though they did not meet with much success their attempts attest to the deep impression it made, not only in Spain but elsewhere as well. Perhaps it also influenced Meir of Rothenburg to attempt to immigrate to the Land of Israel. His own lamentation at the burning of the Talmud and other holy books in Paris in 1242 was patterned after "Zion, Wilt Thou Not Ask...?"

Judah ha-Levi did not live in complete isolation. He was influenced by the pursuit of a life of luxury and hedonism, common among the Jewish courtiers in Spain. In his youth, he was intimately connected with these circles. However, he finally cut himself off from them and saw in the life of pomp and ostentation led by Jews in the Diaspora an element that removed the Land of Israel from Jewish consciousness, and a factor delaying Redemption. He demanded of Jews everywhere that they suffer the pain of exile and accept their suffering with love, but never to come to terms with it rationally or emotionally. They must direct all their emotions and desires towards the future Redemption in the Land of Israel. He defined the Jews' prayers for a return to Zion as "the chirping of the starling," i.e., as fine but hackneyed rhetoric that did not flow from the depths of a man's heart. He believed that the lack of a desire to return to the Land of Israel was the major reason for the continuation of exile.

His own attempt to immigrate was not only the result of a deep emotional tie to the Land of Israel. It was also the result of

spend his time and study Torah, not to mention the graves of his ancestors. Judah ha-Levi argued against them that there was no hope for the Jews in the Diaspora ("Have we in the East or the West a place of hope where we can dwell in safety?"), and though the patriarchs of the nation had been a small minority when they came to the Land of Israel upon God's command, they nevertheless made the effort to settle there and their spirits did not fail. This and other poems were publicly circulated, and we may assume that they made a great impact. Other poems by Judah ha-Levi that express his yearnings for Zion are also full of intense longing for the Land of Israel, and we may assume that they too made a powerful impression.

194

In his eight-month stay in Egypt on his way to the Land of Israel, Judah ha-Levi propagated his belief concerning the obligation imposed on Jews to ascend to the Land of Israel, despite the difficult political and economic conditions. Expression of his longing for Zion reached a peak in his poem "Zion, Wilt Thou Not Ask How Thy Captives are Faring?" This poem has been

a comprehensive, systematic ideational concept that he expressed in his book, *The Kuzari*, as noted above. Another factor which apparently influenced Judah ha-Levi was the controversy in Muslim society between those who supported the school of *'Arabiyyah*, which claimed superiority of the Muslims who came from the Arabian Peninsula, and those who raised the banner of the *Shu'ubiyyah*, which was based on Spanish nationalist foundations.

Another Spanish Jewish sage whose immigration to the Land of Israel gained much fame was R. Moses ben Nahman (Nahmanides). Though his immigration may have stemmed from apprehension that leading Spanish churchmen might harm him because of his firm stand against them in the religious disputation conducted in Barcelona in 1263, it was also firmly based upon a cogent, unique world outlook, as we saw above. Nahmanides came to the Land of Israel in 1276 and was astonished at the extent of its ruin and desolation, especially in Jerusalem. He played an important role in the attempt to revive the Jewish community in Jerusalem, which had almost totally vanished as a consequence of the Mongol invasion of the country in 1260.

He described his great excitement upon his arrival in Jerusalem in letters to his family and friends in Spain. His missive, "Our Feet Stood inside Your Gates, O Jerusalem," expressed not only his profound excitement and intense love for Jerusalem, but also his sense of insult and helplessness as a consequence of suffering and humiliation in exile: "A city without action, without cattle and property; *an afflicted people* [II Sam 22:28], poor and impoverished, needy, wandering beggars... today I have seen its dwellers *sighing and crying* [Ez 9:4], and they are festered with wounds" (Nahmanides, *Writings & Discourses*, II, pp. 713–714). Whoever reads these lines clearly senses that the humiliation of the Jews and Christian contempt for them were a powerful motive for his immigration to the Land of Israel, his laments, and his prayers.

The teachings of Judah ha-Levi and Nahmanides about the merits and special qualities of the Land of Israel even while the Jewish people was in exile, their call to immigrate to the Holy Land as a religious and national duty, their poems and laments about Jerusalem, and above all – their personal immigration, left a deep impression on Jews in later generations. We should bear in mind that they were two of the greatest, most outstanding Jewish sages of Spain in the Middle Ages.

The written sources contain evidence of immigration to the

Land of Israel by other Spanish Jews prior to the Decrees of 1391. Apparently these immigrants were relatively few, mainly scholars and merchants. However, after the Decrees, we find a thin but steady flow of emigration from Spain to the Mediterranean region. These emigrants came from more varied social strata, their ideological motivation was undergoing change, and families too, left Spain, not only individuals or the elderly. Obviously something had changed in the attitude of Spanish Jews and forced converts to Christianity towards the land of their residence. There was much more willingness to depart for other centers, including the Land of Israel (Hacker, p. 133).

Many Spanish Jews reached the Land of Israel in 1447, settling mainly in Jerusalem. After the Ottoman conquest of Constantinople in 1453, Jewish emigration from Spain increased, for Jews believed the conquest to a heavenly omen of their forthcoming Redemption. Such hopes intensified in the sixties of the fifteenth century, due to the "juncture of the stars," i.e.,

The tombstone of R. Meir ben Baruch of Rothenburg (born ca. 1215), in the cemetery at Worms

astrological prognostications accepted among both Jews and Christians that calculated the End of Days and Redemption as particularly falling during the years 1464–1468. These astronomical reckonings also influenced leading Jewish sages in Spain, including R. Isaac Abravanel and R. Abraham Zacutto, as well as broad circles among the forced converts there. They even drew a connection between the juncture of the stars and the rise of the Ottoman Empire.

The conquest of Constantinople brought in its wake a messianic awakening among the Jews throughout all the lands of the Mediterranean basin. The ancient belief connecting warfare between empires and the coming of the Messiah re-emerged, particularly since the Christians had suffered another severe defeat. Evidence is preserved in the sources of a large movement of people – men, women, and children – who left Castile for Aragon in order to embark for the Land of Israel.

Other immigrants came from the ranks of the forced converts who returned to Judaism and immigrated to the Land of Israel, also in order to atone for their conversion to Christianity. This situation serves as fitting background for the remarks of R. Simeon ben Zemah Duran who left Majorca after the Decrees of 1391 and came to Algiers. He was asked if a man "who ascends to the Land of Israel and enters its territory, are all his sins atoned for, the minor and the major, through repentance, and likewise, someone who was immigrating to the Land of Israel and died on the way, is his intention accepted [by God] as if he had dwelt in the Land of Israel, or not?" Duran responded:

Dwelling in the Land of Israel is a great commandment and Nahmanides, of blessed memory, already counted it among the 613 commandments... And whoever is buried in the Land of Israel is as if he were buried under the altar... And the sages of Israel endangered themselves by crossing rivers in order to enter the Land of Israel... And they used to kiss the stones and grovel in its dust, as it is written: "Your servants take delight in its stones, and cherish its dust."... From this you will understand [the answer to] your question: that whoever is a penitent and regrets his sins and wants to ascend to the Land of Israel, even though repentance brings expiation, ascension to the Land of Israel brings him added merit and guards him from sin all his life. (Duran, *Tashbetz* III, 288)

Jews from Spain held respected public offices in the Jerusalem community during the sixties and seventies of the fifteenth century. All this was one generation before the expulsion from Spain (1492) which much intensified the number of Spanish expellees who immigrated to the Land of Israel.

Immigration from France and Germany

In the thirteenth century, particularly its first half, groups of sages from France immigrated to the Land of Israel, led by several of the greatest of the Tosafists. This immigration earned the name "the ascension of the 300 rabbis," in consequence of the account by R. Solomon Ibn Verga in his book *Shevet Yehudah* (Scepter of Judah), written shortly after the expulsion from Spain:

In the year 171 [= 1211 CE] the Lord aroused the rabbis of France and the rabbis of England to go to Jerusalem, and they were more than three hundred, and the king paid them great honor and they built for themselves synagogues and study houses there. Also, our teacher, the high priest, our rabbi

Yehonathan ha-Kohen, went there, and a miracle happened to them: they prayed for rain and their prayers were answered, and the Name of Heaven was sanctified by them. (Solomon Ibn Verga, *Shevet Yehudah*, p. 147)

Though it is clear that there was no convoy of 300 rabbis, it was a sizable group of immigrants in at least two waves: one in 1209, and the other in 1211. Among the immigrants were R. Yehonathan ha-Kohen of Lunel and R. Samson of Sens, two of the most outstanding Tosafists. One generation later, in 1259, R. Yehiel of Paris immigrated to the Land of Israel. He was the leading Tosafist of his generation. From the responsa literature of that time we learn that the aspiration to ascend to the Land of Israel encompassed wide circles of scholars in France. Some of the immigrants settled in Jerusalem while others left the Holy City for Acre, where there was a relatively large community of emigrants from Europe.

What motivated these outstanding scholars to take their families and some of their disciples and immigrate to the Land of Israel? And what eventually happened to them? It is clear that they were motivated by powerful faith in Redemption that was drawing near, and they believed that by immigrating they would hasten its coming. We have quoted above the words of a disciple of R. Isaac ben Abraham, who unequivocally established – apparently in the name of his teachers – that the Messiah would not come unless the Jews first immigrated to the Land of Israel. He recounted that many believed that the age of Redemption was approaching. The study of commandments that could only be practiced in the Land of Israel, in the works of several sages of that time, is certainly connected with this belief. Perhaps we should also link it to the end of the fifth millenium of the Hebrew calendar (1240 CE), which Jews believed to be the time of Redemption.

The immigrants were to meet with great disappointment. They faced many difficulties in earning a living and integrating into the local community. Apparently, they were not exactly welcomed by certain groups living in the Land of Israel. Meir of Rothenburg related that he heard of the immigrants' disappointment from their sons, some of whom even returned to Europe.

There were fewer immigrants from Germany. One tradition has it that R. Baruch of Worms immigrated to the Land of Israel in 1237. In any event, he devoted a chapter of his *Sefer ha-Trumah* to consideration of the commandments practiced only in the Land of Israel. He began his remarks there with its praises:

For the sake of Zion I will not be silent, For the sake of Jerusalem I will not be still, Till her victory emerge resplendent and a teacher of righteousness come to us... It is true that the Land of Israel is beloved and the man who dwells there is happy... And all the more since the man who dwells there observes the commandments dependent on it [the Land] and is privileged to be close to the Holy One blessed be He. (*Sefer ha-Trumah*, 213)

Meir of Rothenburg's attempt to immigrate, in 1286, was especially important. He was the greatest of the sages of Germany in the thirteenth century. Clearly, his attempt, together with dozens of families from various communities in Germany, resounded far and wide, especially since it conflicted with the opinion on this matter held by the German pietists, who opposed immigration to the Land of Israel before the coming of Redemption, as we have discussed above.

By immigrating, Meir of Rothenburg intended to materialize his intense love for Jerusalem. Every evening, before retiring and after saying the *Shma* (declaration of God's Oneness), he used to recite Psalm 122: "I rejoiced when they said to me, 'We are going to the House of the Lord.' Our feet stood inside your gates, O Jerusalem." As he uttered the name of Jerusalem in prayer, he would get down on his knees and bow to the east, that is, in the direction of the Land of Israel. He instituted recitation of the prayer "These Candles that We Kindle" as part of the blessing over the candles for Hanukkah, since he found that tradition in the treatise *Soferim* which was composed in the Land of Israel. Other examples of his great love for Jerusalem and the Holy Land have been preserved in the written sources, some still only in manuscript. His emotional link to Jerusalem, together with the defeat of the Crusaders and the deterioration in the political and

juridical status of the Jews in Germany, led him to decide to immigrate to the Land of Israel at the head of a group of immigrants from five communities in Germany, and to found an Ashkenazic community in Jerusalem that would attract additional Jews from Europe. When in Italy on the way to the Holy Land, he was seized, taken back to Germany, and put in jail until the end of his life. Two generations later, after the "Black Death" which dealt a severe blow to the population of Europe, an Ashkenazic community did indeed arise in Jerusalem, in whose yeshiva there were also scholars from Germany for a certain period of time. Their cultural encounter with Jews who had immigrated from Spain and the latter's rationalist tradition enriched their intellectual world, but this cannot be considered an important event in the history of the Land of Israel. German Jews migrated in the fifteenth century to northern Italy and Poland; the Land of Israel, far removed both geographically and culturally, did not attract them.

Examination of the ties of Jews in Europe and the Islamic countries to the Land of Israel in the Crusader and Mamluk periods reveals a wondrous phenomenon: during most of this time – and certainly in the Crusader period – the Jewish community in the Land of Israel was extremely small in size (the smallest since the return to Zion from Babylon), yet the relationship of the Jewish communities in the Diaspora to the Land of Israel gained in strength and intensity, and was grounded in a well-founded elaborate worldview.

The opening page of *Sefer ha-Tashbetz* which includes customs and teachings of R. Meir of Rothenburg, part of the Rothschild Miscellany, northern Italy, 1450–1470 (IMJ, MS. 180/51. Fol 79v)

197

Qala'at Nimrud, a medieval castle on the slopes of Mount Hermon

The Mamluk Period

Abraham David

The previous chapter discussed the relationship of the Diaspora Jewish communities to the Land of Israel and its Jewish population during both the Crusader and Mamluk periods. In the present chapter the picture will be completed by focusing on developments within the Land of Israel during the Mamluk period from 1260 until the end of 1516. Their realm, with its center of government in Cairo, was divided into several provinces. Syria and the Land of Israel formed one political unit which itself was subdivided into six or seven provinces: Aleppo, Hama, Tripoli, Damascus, Safed, and Kerak (in trans-Jordan), with Gaza, too, at times a province in its own right. Each province was ruled by a military governor called a *na'ib* (viceroy), while each of its districts was in turn administered by a lower-ranking governor, a *wali*. The largest province was that of Damascus which included the major part of Syria and the Land of Israel, from el-Arish in the south to the banks of the Euphrates. It included various districts within the Holy Land, such as Jerusalem, Ramlah, Qaqun (in the Sharon Plain), Lod, Shechem (Nablus), and others. From 1376, Jerusalem and its environs became a region governed by a na'ib with a status equal to that of the other provincial governors, who were directly subordinate to the sultan's court in Cairo.

The provincial governors were Mamluk emirs whose rank in the military hierarchy was not uniform. They served in their posts for short periods of time, frequent changes which caused much suffering to the local population. Each new governor increased the tax burden on his subjects to justify his appointment and to find greater favor with the sultan and his senior officials. The Mamluk sultans treated the Land of Israel as a distant province, parts of which – especially the cities of Jerusalem and Hebron – interested them only because of their sacred status. They saw no reason to develop the country: they did not believe that it had economic potential, nor did they see any reason to encourage trade, industry, or agriculture, or to reduce the tax burden that weighed very heavily upon the inhabitants. The Mamluk authorities and their predecessors adopted a policy of ruin and destruction, particularly of the coastal cities, due to constant fear that the European powers might renew their attempts to drive them out of the Holy Land and Syria. Nor did the central government have much success in imposing its authority over the Bedouin tribes or the bands of highway bandits who filled the local population and wayfarers with dread. As a result, the Land of Israel was left with a sparse, shrunken population, sunk in almost total decadence due to difficult living conditions.

The condition of the Jews in the Land of Israel was much worse than that of the Muslims, since they were, just as in other Islamic lands, the subject of discrimination on various levels. Although this discrimination stemmed from ancient Muslim law, under Mamluk rule the discriminatory edicts against Jews were even more severe. In 1301 they were forbidden to erect houses higher than

Model of a Mamluk cavalryman in the Tower of David Museum of the History of Jerusalem

199

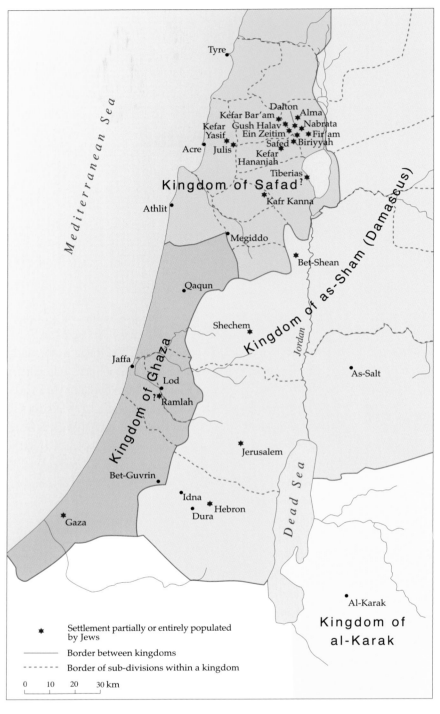

The Land of Israel in the Mamluk period, showing sites with a Jewish population

Map labels:

Tyre

Dalton
Kefar Bar'am
Alma
Kefar Yasif
Gush Halav
Nabrata
Ein Zeitim
Fir'am
Safed
Biriyyah
Acre
Julis
Kefar Hananiah
Tiberias

Kingdom of Safad?

Athlit

Kafr Kanna

Megiddo

Bet-Shean

Kingdom of as-Sham (Damascus)

Qaqun

Shechem

Kingdom of Ghaza

Jaffa

Lod
?
Ramlah

As-Salt

Jerusalem

Bet-Guvrin

Dead Sea

Idna
Hebron
Dura

Gaza

Al-Karak

Kingdom of al-Karak

Mediterranean Sea

Jordan of as-Sham (Damascus)

★   Settlement partially or entirely populated by Jews

―――   Border between kingdoms

- - - -   Border of sub-divisions within a kingdom

0   10   20   30 km

those of their Muslim neighbors, while in 1354 they were not permitted to purchase real estate. However, it seems that this prohibition did not endure, for we know that Jews did possess land in later periods. From the beginning of the fourteenth century discrimination was noticeably more severe in the social sphere as well, bringing tangible signs of disgrace and humiliation such as the edict prohibiting Jews from riding a horse on city streets, and the application of the 1301 edict concerning turbans

which decreed that members of every religious community were to wear a turban of a distinct color to identify the wearer.

● ● ● ● ● ● ● ● ● ●

Centers of Jewish Population

There is scant information on where Jews lived in the Land of Israel during the Mamluk era, or even earlier, so that the little we have is not enough to draw a complete map of Jewish settlement in the country in this era. We may assume that information about Jewish settlements in previous or later periods also reflects to a certain extent the situation under Mamluk rule. We will briefly survey the major population centers.

Hebron, as city of the Patriarchs, containing their tombs within its confines, was sacred to both Muslims and Jews. There are a few mentions in the sources of a Jewish community in Hebron in the fourteenth century, and even earlier. It seems that there was a small community there which apparently provided services for Jewish pilgrims to the Tombs of the Patriarchs. There is also additional information about Jews in Hebron in the fifteenth century. R. Meshullam of Volterra, who visited the city in 1481, noted in his itinerary that "about twenty Jewish heads of households, and no more" lived in Hebron (Meshullam of Volterra, p. 69). R. Obadiah of Bertinoro, who visited Hebron seven years later, in 1488, also counted "about twenty heads of households, all of them rabbis, and half of them descended from forced converts (*conversos*) who have recently come to find shelter under the wings of the *Shekhinah* (Divine Presence)" (Obadiah of Bertinoro, *Letters*, p. 64). R. Isaac Sholal, who officiated in Egypt as *nagid* in the years 1502–17, spent time in Hebron on business before his appointment to that post.

Gaza was the capital of a district in the Mamluk administrative system of the Land of Israel, and caravans from Egypt to the Holy Land passed through it. The earliest information about a Jewish community there in the Mamluk period is found in the remarks of the Italian Christian pilgrim Giorgio Gucci, who visited the city in 1384. Jewish and Christian sources from the second half of the fifteenth century tell of a significant, substantial Jewish community in Gaza. Meshullam of Volterra and Obadiah of Bertinoro note in the 1480s a community of about fifty to seventy Jewish heads of households there, alongside a small, more ancient, Samaritan community. Meshullam emphasizes that the Jews of Gaza excelled in cultivating vineyards and winemaking, and there is evidence that they also engaged in other branches of agriculture, as well as in crafts and trade.

There is only slight information about a Jewish community

in **Ramlah** during the fourteenth century. In **Shechem** (Nablus) there was a small Jewish community in the sixteenth century that probably dated from an earlier period. As for **Bet-Shean**, R. Eshtori ha-Parhi, the first researcher of the Land of Israel, settled there for a short period after immigrating in 1313.

We may deduce from the writings of Eshtori ha-Parhi (in his *Kaftor va-Ferah*) that there were several Jewish communities east of the Jordan River, such as **Ajlun** and **Edrei**, in his day. As for the north of the Land of Israel, we have scant information about the presence of Jews in **Kefar Hananyah**, **Biriyah**, **Kefar Almah**, **Kefar Kana**, **Ein Zeitim**, and **Peki'in**. **Tiberias** was a quite desolate city in Mamluk times, but it is not improbable that a small Jewish community resided there. With the fall of Crusader

A synagogue mosaic from Gaza dating from the Talmudic period, portraying a zebra.
A Jewish community existed in Gaza from the Middle Ages until the twentieth century

Acre in 1291, its Jewish community was wiped out. However, it is likely that Jews – perhaps only individuals – returned later to once more settle either there or in the surrounding area. To this we should add some information about a Jewish community in **Sidon** in the late fifteenth century.

Little information has survived concerning a Jewish community in **Safed** during the fourteenth century. Eshtori ha-Parhi noted that he found there "a large congregation." In 1325, the Spanish Kabbalist R. Shem Tov ibn Gaon settled in Safed. We shall see below that Jews from various ethnic communities lived in Safed at that time. In his description of that city's Jewish community at the beginning of the 1480s, R. Joseph of Montagna wrote: "Safed is a large community, and there are 300 heads of households, together the nearby villages,

Narrow street in Safed

which are within its area" (Ya'ari, *Letters*, p. 91).

Judging from Obadiah of Bertinoro's description, the Jews of Safed lived a life of poverty. It seems that after their expulsion from Spain and the Portuguese anti-Jewish decrees at the end of the fifteenth century, many Jews from the Iberian peninsula found their way to Safed, as we shall see below.

As for **Jerusalem**, a Jewish community had existed there almost continuously since the Arab conquest of the country in the seventh century with the exception of a few decades at the beginning of Crusader rule in the twelfth century. The fragmentary information about the Jewish community steadily increases during the second half of the fifteenth century. With the establishment of Mamluk dominion in the Land of Israel the Jews abandoned the city, greatly fearing what their lot might be should the Mongols invade the country – as they indeed did, entering Jerusalem in 1260. A few years later, in 1267, one of the greatest sages of Spain, R. Moses ben Nahman (Nahmanides), arrived in the Holy City, living for some time in devastated Jerusalem before taking up residence in Crusader Acre. During that short stay, he was probably the moving spirit behind the renewal of Jewish settlement in Jerusalem.

We have no data on the size of the Jewish community in Jerusalem in the fourteenth century. We may assume that it comprised no more than several dozen families. Apparently the community grew, though not greatly, during the second half of the fifteenth century in the wake of waves of Jewish immigration of individuals and groups coming from both east and west. In any event, in the second half of that century one of the immigrants who settled in the city recorded that there were "about 150 [Jewish] heads of households" in Jerusalem. By 1481, Meshullam of Volterra could note "about 250 Jewish heads of households." Nevertheless, seven years later Obadiah of Bertinoro wrote that the Jewish population of the city numbered no more than "seventy heads of households." That decline was soon reversed due to the energetic efforts of Obadiah on behalf of the community. Several years later, at the end of 1495, there were in the Holy City "about 200 Jewish heads of households."

Various Jewish and Christian sources indicate that from the middle of the thirteenth century Jerusalem's Jewish quarter was located on Mount Zion. When the Franciscan monks established themselves on Mount Zion after having received permission from the Mamluk authorities in 1333 to establish the Custody of the Holy Land (*Custodia Terrae Sanctae*) with the objective of safeguarding and supervising the Christian holy places in Jerusalem and the surrounding area, the peace and quiet of the Jews in their neighborhood on Mount Zion was disrupted. The monks, who considered the Jews to be enemies of Christianity,

The Valley of Jehoshaphat in a painting by Thomas Seddon, 19ᵗʰ cent. (Tate Picture Library)

used any means at their disposal to drive them out of the sites holy to both religions in the city. Even more, they did all in their power to reduce the Jewish presence in Jerusalem as a whole. They apparently succeeded to a great extent, for at the end of the fourteenth or the beginning of the fifteenth century the Jewish neighborhood on Mount Zion was expropriated and moved to another location – that of the modern-day Jewish Quarter. One Christian source, dating from 1344–1345, indicates that Jews lived in another neighborhood as well – in the Valley of Jehoshaphat – but this information is not corroborated by any other source.

Various sources indicate that from the fourteenth to the sixteenth centuries Jews also lived north of Jerusalem in a place called Mizpah or Ramah, identified in both Jewish and Muslim tradition as the tomb of the Prophet Samuel, hence its current name in Arabic – Nabi Samwil. According to an ancient tradition, the Jews used to visit the tomb on the anniversary of the prophet's death, the 28th of the Hebrew month of Iyyar. It emerges from the written sources that Jews lived here all year round and had even built a synagogue which, however, was expropriated by the Muslims after the mid-1560s. The small group of Jews dwelling at Ramah was evidently an integral part of the Jerusalem community.

Immigration to the Land of Israel

We have scant information about groups of Jewish immigrants to the Land of Israel in the Mamluk period. This was a direct result of the economic and geopolitical condition of the Jewish population in the country, which experienced various degrees of difficulty due to wars, natural disasters, changes of government, and the lack of interest in developing the country displayed by the various Muslim rulers from the Arab conquest until the end

Nabi Samwil north of Jerusalem, traditionally the tomb of the Prophet Samuel. Descriptions of the site and the Jewish custom of visiting it are mentioned from the Middle Ages until modern times

203

of Mamluk rule. At times the Jewish community recovered somewhat through waves of immigration from western and central European countries, from the Mediterranean countries or those of the East. However, the immigrants could not always withstand the difficulties of adapting to conditions in the country and returned to their places of origin or settled down in nearby communities in the East.

In addition to the difficult living conditions that prevailed in the Land of Israel in those days, the newcomers more than once found themselves in bitter strife with the local Jewish population, which was not always able or willing to accept them either because it feared competition or due to differences in mentality and culture. Nevertheless, in several cases immigrants did fill prestigious positions in Jewish society in the Land of Israel. Some of them, such as Nahmanides, R. Shem Tov ibn Gaon, and Obadiah of Bertinoro, successfully integrated into local society in a short time, even attaining high rank as leaders and heads of their communities.

Immigration to the Land of Israel was generally motivated by religious, national, and messianic impulses, although at times groups or individuals came in the wake of disasters or harsh decrees of persecution in their countries of residence; they were either expelled or their lives were made unbearably difficult. Since they were forced to uproot themselves in any case, some preferred to resettle in the Holy Land.

Sporadic evidence has survived from the fourteenth century concerning immigrants to the Land of Israel, chiefly from Spain and Germany. In contrast, in the fifteenth century we have increasing evidence of immigration from several Diasporas, including western Europe, Spain, Italy, the eastern lands, and North Africa. Nevertheless, this does not attest to a dramatic change, for not only did conditions in the country not improve but the Mamluk authorities treated the non-Muslim minorities with even greater severity, particularly after 1354.

After the expulsion from Spain and the decrees of persecution in Portugal in the last decade of the fifteenth century, many of those expelled from the Iberian Peninsula emigrated to countries around the Mediterranean basin, establishing new Jewish centers or adding strength to existing ones such as Constantinople, Salonica, Fez, Naples, Ferrara and Cairo. Neither did they pass over the Land of Israel. It seems that Spanish Jews began only slowly to firmly establish their status. At the beginning of the sixteenth century they formed but a small part of the Jerusalem community, but in Safed, in contrast, they were already the dominant Jewish element as early as 1504.

There is increasing evidence from the second decade of the sixteenth century concerning sages from among the Spanish expellees who lived in Jerusalem and were active side by side with scholars of other origins. Various sources testify that as early as the first half of the second decade of that century there were Jews in Jerusalem who had been sages of the first rank in Spain at the time of the expulsion. They were renowned for their earlier spiritual and public activity, or gained later fame at the beginning of the Ottoman period in Jerusalem, Safed, and elsewhere.

Extremely interesting information has survived about immigrants who arrived in the country as individuals or in groups, about their experiences during their sea voyages or overland travels, the routes they followed, and about their first activities in the country. These immigrants also provided us with important data about the Jewish communities through which they passed on their way to the Holy Land. The most detailed sources are the itinerary of Meshullam of Volterra, from 1481, and the first letter that Obadiah of Bertinoro sent from Jerusalem, written in 1488.

Pilgrims in an etching by Olbrecht Dapper, 1677

204

Civitas Iherusalem, detail from map in Bernard von Breydenbach, *Peregrinatio in Montem Syon*, Mainz, 1486 (JNUL, Jer 30)

. . . .

Character of the Jewish Population of the Land of Israel

The Jewish population of the Land of Israel was heterogeneous and diversified. Besides the *Musta'arabin* (indigenous inhabitants of the land and surrounding areas for generations who resembled their Muslim neighbors in speech and lifestyle), other Jews in the country had over the years come in groups or as individuals from various Diasporas: Ashkenazim (Jews from Germany, France, or Bohemia), Italians, Spaniards (including *conversos* who had discarded their pseudo-Christianity), Maghrebis (from North Africa), Yemenites, Sicilians, and Romaniots (Greek-speaking Jews). While it seems that the urban Jewish population was comprised of people from various origins, the lion's share of the Jewish inhabitants of the Land of Israel were still Musta'arabin, who accounted for almost all the rural Jewish population. The immigrants were drawn more to the cities than to the villages, since in their lands of origin they had generally been town dwellers.

Tension developed between the Musta'arabin and the newly arrived immigrants, mainly in matters of power, leadership, and custom, a few traces of which could still be found in a later period. The Musta'arabin could not bear the arrival of immigrants with their foreign customs and mentality. Many of the immigrants were proficient in intellectual pursuits and experienced in public life, and therefore it was only natural that they quickly gained control of various communal institutions. From the little that we know of the communities in Jerusalem and Safed, it seems

that the non-Musta'arabi population steadily gained in numbers as a result of the increasing waves of immigration to the Land of Israel, mainly in the second half of the fifteenth century and even more so in the early sixteenth century, by which time the new immigrants considerably overshadowed the Musta'arabin. Apparently, Spanish Jews already dominated the Jerusalem Jewish community by the 1460s, for a letter sent from "the Jewish court of Jerusalem" in 1467/1468, bore the signatures of four sages, two of whom were certainly Spaniards, including the chief judge, "Rabbi Joseph son of Gedaliah, Ibn Emanuel … Sefardi." Moreover, an emissary of the Jerusalem community to Candia (Crete) and Italy in 1473 was R. Joseph ha-Dayyan [the judge] ha-Sefaradi. This may indicate the enhanced status of the Spanish group in Jerusalem at this time. From the Jewish sources of the 1480s, it emerges that hegemony of the Jerusalem community had passed to members of the Ashkenazi group, both in spiritual matters and public life. It is not clear what caused the decline of the Spanish group, which is hardly mentioned in these sources. Perhaps the reason is rooted in the declining number of emigrants from Spain or in the rising status of the Ashkenazim who, although they did not make up the majority of the community, nevertheless accounted for its most important members. From the beginning of the sixteenth century, the influence of Jews expelled from Spain and Portugal apparently once again increased in Jerusalem and Safed, and perhaps elsewhere as well.

The status of the other Jewish ethnic groups is not clear. Did they preserve their uniqueness as separate communities, or were

205

they integrated into the dominant groupings? Furthermore, the nature of inter-group relations is also not clear. We may assume that there were conflicts between the Spanish and Ashkenazi groupings over dominance of the Jerusalem community, just as was the case in later periods, over the course of the sixteenth century. In any event, we know of a conflict between Maghrebis and Ashkenazim in Jerusalem from one of the rulings of R. Israel Isserlein dating from the first half of the fifteenth century.

· · · · · · · · · · · ·

The Muslim Authorities and the Jews

It seems that in normal times the Jews of the Land of Israel, like their brethren in other eastern lands, well knew how to live in

the shadow of the Crescent and to adapt to the administrative and juridical restrictions imposed upon them. Often, the local authorities (governors of provinces and districts, and their officials) treated their Jewish subjects, like other non-Muslims, with excessive tyranny. This sometimes happened upon the initiative or with the encouragement of the central authorities, while at other times it was against their express wishes. Both Jewish and Christian sources record manifestations of brutality on the part of the rulers which were far from rare. As already noted, district governors were frequently replaced and each new governor was eager, at the outset of his rule, to show the heavy fall of his hand on his subjects by imposing additional taxes and other despotic acts. Jerusalem, as a provincial town far from the Mamluk center of political, economic, and public life, served as

Trainee Mamluks performing sword exercises. An Egyptian manuscript, 14th cent. (BL Add. MS. 18866, fol. 243v)

a place of banishment for ministers who fell out of favor or were deemed dangerous to the rulers, or for those for whom no better position was found. Since the benefit and development of the city were not the major concerns of these officials, they displayed very little interest in the welfare of Jerusalem's inhabitants.

The consumption of wine by non-Muslims (*dhimmis*) in Islamic lands was an especially sensitive issue. The blame for natural disasters and other catastrophes would be cast by Muslims on the use of wine by non-believers. Its consumption, therefore, was limited to religious purposes only, and general trade in wine was forbidden. To restrict the use of wine even further, a special tax was levied on non-Muslims for its consumption; at other times it was totally forbidden.

We know of two crucial events that dealt harsh blows to the Jewish community in Jerusalem in the second half of the fifteenth century. In a letter written by the Jerusalem *dayyanim* (judges) late in 1455, an account is given of a trying event that greatly perturbed the Jews of Jerusalem in particular, and those in the Mamluk state in general. Sultan Jaqmaq, who had ascended the throne in 1453, decreed conversion on his Jewish subjects on pain of banishment from the state. These decrees were abolished after considerable lobbying and by placating the sultan with sizeable monetary payments which, however, totally bankrupted the treasury of the Jewish community in Jerusalem. The other episode involved the destruction of a synagogue. This affair began late in 1473 when the Muslims claimed that a synagogue had been built unlawfully, that is, not in conformity with the discriminatory laws prohibiting the erection of synagogues. The Jews produced a document confirming their rights to the site, claiming that it was indeed their lawful property. Furthermore, they declared that their forefathers had bought it seventy or eighty years earlier and that the deed of purchase was held by the elders of the community in Egypt. In 1474, the synagogue was destroyed, against the wishes of Sultan al-Ashraf Qayit Bey (1468–1496), who treated the religious minorities with much tolerance and did not allow anyone to deprive them of their rights. When the sultan learned of the synagogue's destruction he became very angry, ordered that those responsible be punished, and permitted the rebuilding of the synagogue. This decision gave rise to unrest in Jerusalem and exacerbated the tension between Jews and Muslims in the city.

· · · · · · · · ·

The Tax Burden

In addition to the regular taxes collected from all the inhabitants in the country, such as the land tax (*kharaj*) or that imposed on those engaging in commerce, industry, or crafts, the Jews, like the other non-Muslims, paid special fixed taxes that placed a very heavy burden upon them.

Among these we should note the notorious head tax (*jizya* in Arabic) obligatory for every male aged fourteen and over. It had already been instituted in the Pact of Omar, and was intended as an annual payment of compensation for the grace with which the Muslims treated their non-Muslim subjects by granting them protection. Another tax was the highway duty, the *gafir,* collected at special customs stations along the main roads. The sums from this tax were raised to pay for the military escorts that protected caravans along the roads. Whereas a small sum was collected from Muslims, a much larger one was levied on Christians and Jews. In addition to all of these and to the wine tax mentioned above, there was another special levy in the form of a forced gift to a high official in the Mamluk administration when he took up the duties of his office. The law of inheritance of 1354, one of the Muslim discriminatory laws against infidels, also had as its outcome an inheritance tax. By this law government ministers were obligated to deal with the legacies of non-Muslims according to Muslim law: the heirs would receive their due according to the religious law of Islam, while the rest would go to the state treasury. Moreover, all the property and funds of a person who died without heirs devolved to the state treasury. The Jews living under Mamluk rule did not reconcile themselves to this decree and tried to circumvent it by various stratagems.

In addition to the fixed taxes, based upon Islamic religious law, there was also an irregular system for collecting funds. In times of emergency and crisis, the various rulers collected from the nonbelievers – in violation of Islamic law – special one-off taxes, defined at times as fines.

Monies collected from the head tax and the inheritance tax were transferred directly to the state treasury. Each non-Muslim had to pay the head tax directly to the tax administrator of the central government. However, agreements were at times made with small and large communities for centralized payment of the tax. In such instances, the communal leaders undertook to pay the authorities a certain sum fixed in advance, irrespective of the number of persons in the community. Thus, when the community grew a reduced tax was imposed on each individual and if the population decreased, the rate of taxation increased. This, apparently, was the manner in which this tax was paid by Jerusalem's Jews, at least in the fifteenth century. However, it was detrimental to the community since, in the wake of various disasters, the Jewish population in the city had dwindled and accordingly the rate of the head tax paid by each individual increased. When the meager Jewish community in Jerusalem could no longer bear the heavy tax burden, the "elders" – the tax farmers (this matter will be elucidated below) – did not hesitate

Una delle molte fontane che trovansi in Palestina, e che datano dall' epoca del Sultan Solimano.

Drinking fountain (*sabil*) near the Sultan's Pool in Jerusalem, first erected on this site in the late Crusader period. Drawing by Ermete Pierotti, 19ᵗʰ cent.

to apply any means they thought suitable to collect the funds. Among these, as listed by Obadiah of Bertinoro, was the sale of Torah scrolls and other sacred objects belonging to the synagogue in Jerusalem, or dipping into religious trusts belonging to the community. The method adopted by the elders to pay the tax itself caused the Jewish community to diminish, increasing distress and poverty even more. Obadiah of Bertinoro, who did all in his power to restore and strengthen the Jewish population in Jerusalem, acted to change the situation. Indeed, in the second year of his stay in the Holy City there was a significant improvement in collection of the head tax, this time in accordance with an assessment that had been fixed many years earlier. According to Obadiah himself, this change subsequently led to a sizable increase in the number of Jews in Jerusalem, "and many who had wandered away now changed direction to once again settle in the Land."

208

· · · · · · · · · ·

Economic Life in the Land of Israel

We have already noted the difficult plight of the population in the Land of Israel during the Mamluk period as a result of the

Mamluk authorities' deliberate policy, for strategic motives, of preventing economic growth, unlike their Crusader predecessors and their Ottoman successors. The country was in a difficult economic situation at this time: purchasing power was very low since sources of livelihood were scarce in the country in general and in Jerusalem in particular, and basic commodities – that were in fact relatively cheap – could not be afforded by many of the inhabitants. Visitors and pilgrims who had recently arrived in the country praised the abundance of fruit in the marketplaces of Jerusalem, as well as their low prices, comparing them to those in their countries of origin. One of these, Obadiah of Bertinoro, stressed this fact:

And the foodstuffs in Jerusalem are very cheap: meat and wine, and oil – olive oil and sesame oil –... And the land is still good and broad and fertile, but there is no livelihood there. And a man will not expect, nor will he hope to make a livelihood from any skill or any craft, unless he is a cobbler, a weaver or a goldsmith; these earn their livelihood, but with difficulty (Obadiah of Bertinoro, *Letters*, p. 73).

An anonymous traveler, in a letter from late 1495, even tried to compare the situation in Jerusalem to that prevailing in Syria and Egypt:

Livelihood is more meager here in Jerusalem, the Holy City, than in all these lands. And whoever knows a craft, like a goldsmith, or a blacksmith, or a flax-weaver or a tailor, will earn his living, but scantily. However, in Damascus and in Egypt, in Alexandria and in Aleppo... in all these places they will earn as much as their hearts desire (Ya'ari, *Letters*, p. 157).

We can gather but few details about the role of the Jews in the economic life in the Land of Israel from the scant surviving sources. They engaged in petty trade and crafts. In his first letter from Jerusalem, Obadiah of Bertinoro describes the city's marketplaces writing, among other things:

Jerusalem, despite all its ruins and destruction, has four long and very beautiful marketplaces... the merchants' market, and a market where they sell perfumes, and a vegetable market, and a market where they sell all sorts of cooked foods and bread (Obadiah of Bertinoro, *Letters*, p. 72).

A Christian source contemporary to Obadiah indicates that

"the merchants are mostly pagans [i.e. Muslims], and the livelihoods left for the Jews and Christians are miserable." It seems, according to a later source, that the "market where they sell perfumes " was "of Jews." It is not improbable that the same market was owned by Jews even in the time of Obadiah of Bertinoro, and perhaps earlier. In late fifteenth-century Safed Jews engaged in various branches of commerce, as Obadiah's anonymous disciple recounts at the end of 1495:

And most of the Jews run shops of perfumes and cheese and oil and various kinds of pulses and fruits (Ya'ari, *Letters*, p. 151).

Jews earned a living in various trades. Jewish sources emphasize several such occupations in Jerusalem: ritual slaughterers, butchers, weavers, cobblers, goldsmiths, blacksmiths, tailors and carpenters. From a Christian source we

A Jewish money changer, as depicted in the book of Bernard von Breydenbach, Mainz, 1486. Woodcut by Erhard Reuwich (JNUL, Jer 30)

learn that Jews in Jerusalem also engaged in pottery making and ironwork. Fabric dyeing, which had been a Jewish monopoly in Jerusalem and elsewhere in the Holy Land in the twelfth and thirteenth centuries, is not even mentioned in sources of the fourteenth and fifteenth centuries. Another Christian source, from the first half of the fourteenth century, indicates that Jews also engaged in loaning money at interest. It is likely that Jerusalem's Jews were involved in that occupation in the sixteenth and seventeenth centuries too.

There were also Jews who tilled the soil, despite the fact that non-Muslim communities were prohibited from purchasing land in the Mamluk domain by the law of 1354. It transpires that a few decades later Jews once again purchased land, though not openly. In any event, Jews in the country engaged, in one way or another, in raising crops.

A not inconsiderable number of Jews earned a livelihood from visitors to the Holy Land. These were mainly Jews who had emigrated from Europe and, fluently speaking the languages of most of the pilgrims from western Europe, now served as guides and innkeepers. The monk Jacob of Verona who visited the Holy Land in 1335, recommended the services of Jews:

For the Jews are well acquainted with all the ancient sites to an extent that they can explain [to the visitor], since they are very expert in their Law and in the sites mentioned by their forefathers and sages. Therefore, when I came to tour places across the sea, I sought and very often obtained a good guide from among the Jews who live there(Ish-Shalom, p. 228).

Sometimes pilgrims complained that were cheated or exploited by Jews. Felix Fabri wrote in the 1480s that pilgrims were even accustomed to buying wine from the Jews of Jerusalem.

There is almost no mention of Jews holding

Mercanti Ebrei Arabi (Tiberiade)

Jewish and Arab merchants in Galilee, painting by Ermete Pierotti, 19th cent. Note the similarity of their attire

209

A 19th cent. etching of a Jewish cotton worker, by Harry Fenn

who helped the Jews living there merited great reward in the afterlife. Donations came from North Africa, Egypt, Italy, Germany, and Bohemia in the fourteenth and fifteenth centuries. Apparently, by that time centers for collecting funds had been established in the major cities of those lands.

Obviously, contributions from the Diaspora – and we have no information whether they reached their destination in a regular, orderly manner – did not meet the grave needs of those living in the Holy Land, despite their efforts to live as frugally as possible. From time to time, communal leaders found it necessary to send emissaries to various Diaspora lands to encourage donors in those communities to open their hearts and purses and increase the amount and frequency of their donations. As a rule, emissaries were sent at times of special emergency, which were quite frequent. Nevertheless, we know very little about such envoys of the Jerusalem community. At the time of R. Isaac bar Sheshet, before 1371, an emissary on behalf of the Jerusalem community went "from city to city in France and Germany," arriving in Barcelona a year and four months later. Late in 1455, an envoy known as "Abraham ha-Levi" was sent on a mission for the leaders of the Jerusalem community. He apparently traveled from city to city along the Aegean coast, and perhaps to other places as

government positions in the Land of Israel, except for rather vague information in one Muslim source concerning a Jew in Safed named Joseph ben Abi al-Biyan, whose sobriquet was al-Isra'ili. He was a government official in the financial administration of that city in 1340–1341.

Aid from the Diaspora for the Jews in the Land of Israel

Economic distress and religious and social discrimination were the lot of the Jews in the Land of Israel during the Mamluk period. On the basis of diverse information from the second half of the fourteenth century, it seems that those few who stubbornly remained in the country, whether members of old families or more recent immigrants, could not provide for their needs without material aid from Diaspora Jewry.

The relationship of Diaspora Jews to the Land of Israel was expressed in various manners, including immigration or through visits to tour and see the country. However, many Diaspora Jews were content with providing monetary aid to strengthen and consolidate the Jewish community in the Land of Israel. Donations were made by benefactors who pledged money in their lifetime or directed their executors to donate funds in favor of the Jews in the Land of Israel after their death. Sometimes community leaders in the Land of Israel appealed for donations from abroad through emissaries. At times the donor made his donation for the exaltation of his soul, or as expiation for his sins, since he was aware of the merits of the Land of Israel – anyone

Document presented as a token of esteem
for monetary assistance from the Diaspora

well. He carried with him copies of "a letter of delegation" which he had received "from the Jerusalem community," detailing the community's distress in the wake of the harsh decrees of Sultan Jaqmaq. Another mission on behalf of the Jerusalem community, at the end of 1472, has come to light in the writings of R. Michael Balbo, one of the most important sages of Candia at that time. He mentioned an emissary named "Joseph ha-Dayyan Yerushalmi" (Joseph the judge, of Jerusalem). Michael Balbo, who wished to lend his support to this emissary, appended a warm recommendation to his letter of delegation. Perhaps this letter, composed in florid language by the leaders of the Jerusalem community, provides us with an opportunity to gain some understanding of what was then happening in the Holy City. The community's coffers were totally emptied immediately after Sultan al-Ashraf Qayit Bey came to power at the beginning of February 1468. And perhaps the first stages of bitter tension and inflamed passions between Muslims and Jews in Jerusalem that marked the years 1474–1475, culminating in the destruction of the synagogue, were already evident in that year, as hinted in the letter of delegation carried by the emissary.

· · · · · · · · · · ·

Jewish-Christian Relations

Jews and Christians in the Land of Israel shared a common fate as ethnic minorities in an Islamic society. Both groups were the object of persecution, humiliation and discrimination by the Muslims. Nevertheless, despite their common fate, local Christians and visiting pilgrims could not overcome their intense hatred of the Jews, whom they universally considered to be enemies of Christianity. Despite this hatred (expressed in Western Christian sources, most notably in the writings of Franciscan monks and of pilgrims) mutual contacts between Christians and Jews were not prevented. Christian authors recounted how, as the pilgrims did not understand Arabic, they developed relationships, mainly of a business nature, with Ashkenazim and other Jews with whom they shared a common language. Jews were of great help to them as interpreters, assisting them in various matters, particularly lodging and other tourist services. Sometimes they even conducted theological disputes with them.

Tense relations between Jews and Christians at times called for intervention on the part of the authorities. The Italian pilgrim Pietro Casola related in his itinerary (1494):

A Jew who lives in Jerusalem – a doctor ... had accused the Christians to the said governor saying that certain of the pilgrims had refrained from going to the River Jordan in order to spy out and explore Jerusalem, and that he

had heard certain of the pilgrims say that within two years the Christians would be masters of Jerusalem. Upon this accusation he caused those poor men to be chained (Casola, *Pilgrimage to Jerusalem*, p. 271).

Tension between Jews and Christians in Jerusalem in the fifteenth century reached its height over the ownership of the tomb of King David on Mount Zion. In the 1420s, an Ashkenazi Jew sought to purchase David's tomb which, according to popular belief, was located underneath the Church of the Holy Spirit, believed by Christians to have been built on the site of Jesus' Last Supper (Coenaculum). Since that church was in the possession of the Franciscans, they began to take steps to prevent the transfer of the tomb to Jewish ownership. The Muslims, however, reacted by designating the site of the tomb as a mosque in 1428, not hesitating even to destroy the church above it. As a result, punitive decrees were issued against the Jews in Christian countries, such as the one issued in Venice forbidding ship captains to transport Jews to the Holy Land. The church was later rebuilt, but demolished once again in 1467/68. The Jews were once more blamed for its destruction and the reaction of Christendom was apparently identical to that of 1428.

It was due to the tension between Jews and Christians in Jerusalem, which obviously greatly increased after these events, that the Mamluk sultan al-Ashraf Qayit Bey (1468–1496) issued

Remnants of an old caravansery in Galilee for wayfarers, pilgrims, and merchants

211

The Emir Tankiz, the Mamluk governor of Damascus, carried out much construction work in the Land of Israel. The prayer niche in the *madrasa* he built on the Temple Mount in Jerusalem in 1328–29 bears his name an order forbidding the Jews from passing near the entrance to the Church of the Holy Sepulcher or through the area of the Franciscan monastery on Mount Zion.

Karaites in Jerusalem

We have but scant information about the Karaites in the Land of Israel following the Crusader period. It seems that the Karaite community, which vanished under Crusader rule, was re-established in the late thirteenth century. R. Eshtori ha-Parhi indicates in his book, *Kaftor va-Ferah* (1322):

And you will find with us today in the Land of the Hart [i.e., the Land of Israel] many Sadducee [i.e., Karaite] scribes, and many elegant books of their writings on the Torah, the Prophets, and the Hagiographa (Eshtori ha-Parhi, p. 61).

After this we have only sporadic evidence of the presence of Karaites in Jerusalem and Safed. We know of a Karaite family in Jerusalem by the name of ha-Sakhni, several of whose members were scribes copying manuscripts as early as 1373. Obadiah of Bertinoro, who took great interest in the Karaites and their practices while he was still in Egypt, emphasized in his remarks about the Gaza community: "And I did not see Karaites there." When writing about the Jews of Hebron, he indicated that there were there "about twenty heads of households, all of them Rabbanites [i.e., not Karaites]." On the other hand, he did come across Karaites in Jerusalem, and was even well acquainted with their customs.

Internal Organization of the Jewish Community

In the itinerary of his visit to the Land of Israel in 1481, Meshullam of Volterra recorded information about the leadership and composition of the Jerusalem Jewish community. He listed the names of "the Jewish dignitaries" in the city, and among them a *parnas* (communal leader), a deputy *nagid*, rabbis, and judges. The key to an understanding of the status of the persons who bore the title of nagid or deputy nagid is the political and social situation prevailing in Jerusalem at this time. The fact that the Jerusalem district governor was directly subordinate to the center of Mamluk government in Egypt from 1376 onwards, together with the direct involvement of the nagid in Egypt in affairs in Jerusalem in particular, and the Land of Israel in general, clearly indicates the connection between the Egyptian nagid and the

A Karaite manuscript, 10th cent. The language and vocalization are Hebrew, the script is Arabic

leadership of the Jerusalem community. Therefore, the Jerusalem negidim should not be considered independent communal leaders, but rather as subordinates to the heads of the overall leadership of the Jews in Egypt. It may be assumed that the Jerusalem leadership resembled that of Jewish communities in Egyptian cities that were under the supervision of the nagid.

There was a *muqaddam* (a supervisor of communal affairs) in the various communities as the local representative of the nagid, alongside the communal leader, and his office was recognized by the authorities.

R. Meshullam of Volterra also mentions judges, members of the religious court. This institution apparently comprised four judges: three who made up the regular bench of the court, and a fourth who served as a substitute. He also mentioned *maskilim*, apparently referring to sages and scholars, decisors of religious law, preachers, or those who taught lessons in the synagogue. Also appearing on his list are *shoftim* (literally "judges"), but we do not know what function they had. It is clear that he was not referring to persons with judicial authority within the community, since he mentioned the dayyanim separately. It is quite certain that Meshullam considered the five "shoftim" to be persons entrusted with the Jerusalem community's endowments, and these were also the "elders" who were made infamous by Obadiah of Bertinoro.

The most outstanding leader of Jerusalem's Jewish community in the fifteenth century was without a doubt Obadiah of Bertinoro, the renowned commentator on the Mishnah, who arrived in Jerusalem in 1488. He found there a small Jewish community, no more than seventy heads of households, overburdened by heavy taxes. The people were poor and wretched, hungry and sick, and suffered severely from the heavy hand of their "elders," who did not balk at any means to rob and impoverish the public. Upon his arrival Obadiah immediately took initiatives of great importance for the public welfare in both the social and spiritual realms, in order to improve as much as possible the difficult conditions of daily life. He tried to bring order into burial arrangements after he saw "that there are none [here] who bear the dead and escort the bier." He also recounted that he used to "preach to the congregation here twice a month in the synagogue in the Holy Tongue" (i.e., Hebrew) and was engaged in teaching the Law. His initiatives included the establishment of charitable institutions through donations, while he also brought about important changes in the area of taxation. We may conjecture that his efforts on behalf of the community were made in consultation with the nagid Nathan (Yehonathan) Sholal who lived in Egypt, and with whom he had been acquainted while staying in that land. He was even entrusted with the nagid's house in Jerusalem, and it is

A letter sent from Jerusalem to the Jewish community in Egypt, late 15th cent. The writer indicates that he was accustomed to preaching "in the presence of significant congregations at the place of our Master Prophet Samuel," i.e., Nabi Samwil, north of Jerusalem (BM Or. 56616, 7)

also likely that he filled the office of deputy nagid. At the outset of his activity in Jerusalem Obadiah was warmly accepted by the "elders." They went so far as to exempt him from paying taxes in his first year, including "the poll tax from which no one is exempt."

Shortly after his arrival, the elders changed their attitude towards the members of the community. It is not improbable that this change derived from their own weakness or from a deliberate undermining of their status, a change apparently connected to the dynamic and industrious personality of Obadiah. Apparently, the clash of interests between the elders and Obadiah of Bertinoro manifested itself in friction and conflicts, the nature of which is not clear. In the end, Obadiah was forced to flee from the elders to Hebron. However, several years later he again found his proper place in Jerusalem, as an anonymous traveler indicated at the end of 1495:

And the man is very great, and the whole does his bidding, and without him [his approval] no one will raise his hand, and from the ends of the country Gentiles will ask for his help and will abide by his decision (Ya'ari, *Letters*, p. 155).

One of the greatest halakhic decisors in the sixteenth century called him "the chief of all rabbis of Jerusalem," adding that "all the sages of France and Spain and Ashkenaz who are in Jerusalem used to sit subservient before him." It seems, therefore, that Rabbi Obadiah's efforts to rehabilitate and strengthen the Jewish community in Jerusalem bore fruit, for eight years later, as we have seen, the Jewish population had grown and already numbered about two hundred Jewish households.

A Mamluk silver coin bearing a leopard, the regal symbol of Sultan Baybars (1223–1277)

Spiritual Life

From the little we know about spiritual life in Jerusalem after the Crusader period, it seems to have become significant in the city, and perhaps elsewhere, in the last quarter of the fourteenth century. One indication is the data we have about the relative increase in the number of Hebrew manuscripts copied mainly in Jerusalem, or in the Diaspora by emigrants from Jerusalem, from 1373 onwards. Although the survival of these manuscripts may be no more than accidental,

The Mamluk tower in Ramlah and Crusader remains in a drawing by Ermete Pierotti, 19th cent.

they doubtless reflect an intellectual milieu that prevailed in Jerusalem at that time. Most of these manuscripts were copied by scribes who had emigrated from Spain, and a minority of them by emigrants from Byzantium and western Europe. Their subject matter indicates that Jews in Jerusalem took a great interest not only in matters of *halakhah*, but also in Kabbalah, biblical commentary, philosophy, and liturgy.

The first information about institutions for the study of the Law in Jerusalem relates to the second half of the fourteenth century. A *yeshivah* was founded in Jerusalem by R. Isaac ha-Levi "Asir ha-Tikvah" ("Prisoner of Hope"), also known as R. Isaac ha-Levi Bilstein, who came from Germany to the Land of Israel with his students before 1359, after the anti-Jewish decrees that came in the wake of the Black Death.

During this period there were two institutions in which *Torah* was studied on different levels and in dissimilar forums: the synagogue, which served principally as a place of prayer and occasional gatherings, but also conducted lessons in the Law intended for the entire Jewish community, with scholars and laymen regularly studing together at set hours, around the time of daily prayers; and a study house or yeshivah for sages whose profession was the study of Torah, to which they dedicated all their time. Here study was more intensive and profound.

One source of information concerning these two institutions in the mid-fifteenth century is the letter of the Jerusalem judges of October 1455, which we have already mentioned in reference to the mission of Rabbi Abraham ha-Levi. It reads in part: "… and in the synagogue of Jerusalem and in the yeshivah which is permanently in Jerusalem…. And just recently men have come, great sages, great elders, with their disciples… and they have added to the academy, and greatly increase the study of Torah" (Neubauer, p. 49).

We have already learned from the letter of delegation from the Jerusalem communal leadership (late 1472) borne by the emissary "Joseph ha-Dayyan Yerushalmi" that the community was in deep distress, the reasons for which are not sufficiently clear. The financial situation was dismal due to the greediness and rapacity of the authorities. As a consequence, "the voice of the Torah was stilled," i.e., the yeshivah had been closed. And indeed, later sources are silent about the Jerusalem yeshivah. Meshullam of Volterra did not hint at the existence of a yeshivah when he described the community in his itinerary of 1481. Obadiah of Bertinoro, too, did not refer in his letters to any involvement on his part in the studies conducted in the yeshivah, mentioning only such activity in the synagogue. In his second letter, of 1489, he reported:

I am living today in the house of our master the nagid, for he placed me in charge of his house here in Jerusalem, and I preach to the congregation here twice a month in the synagogue in the Holy Tongue… And we gather together evening and morning to study halakhah. And two Spanish students are studying with me regularly. And with us here today are two Ashkenazic rabbis (Obadiah of Bertinoro, *Letters*, p. 87).

Siddur, Italian rite, Mantova, 1480 (JNUL 8° 5492)

The fact that he does not mention another institution, where studies were more intensive, indicates that in the last quarter of the fifteenth century the Jerusalem yeshivah had ceased to exist. It is not surprising that Obadiah noted that he preached in Hebrew, for Hebrew was the language common to the Jews of all geographic origins then living in Jerusalem – Must'arabin, Ashkenazim, Jews from France, Spain, Italy, and elsewhere.

The Jerusalem yeshivah apparently began to function once again as the Jewish community in Jerusalem gradually recovered at the beginning of the sixteenth century, following the increase in the numbers of immigrants reaching the city in the wake of the Spanish expulsion in 1492 and the Portuguese anti-Jewish decrees of 1497. This also had much to do with the energetic efforts of R. Isaac Sholal, who was appointed nagid in Egypt in 1502 and invested much effort in fostering spiritual activity in the Holy City. His initiatives in this sphere took two forms: first, he founded two yeshivot in Jerusalem and raised money for their upkeep; second he instituted a series of social ordinances, the most famous of which was a regulation exempting scholars from paying taxes which was issued by the nagid's court in Egypt in 1509. The nagid's main objective in these and other endeavors was therefore to establish a spiritual center in Jerusalem to which sages and students would be attracted from all over the Jewish Diaspora.

The western stoa on the Temple Mount, a Mamluk structure from the early 14ᵗʰ cent.

There is evidence of intellectual activity in Safed from as early as the beginning of the sixteenth century. The Spanish sages there, who were already a decisive majority, enjoyed the financial support of R. Isaac Sholal, aid which was not extended to those of the Musta'arabin community. Moreover, by that time there were mutual relations and exchanges of opinion on matters of halakhah and custom between the sages of Jerusalem and those of Safed. This even led to tension between the two groups, among other things over hegemony in spiritual matters in the Land of Israel.

Besides the intensive preoccupation with the study of halakhah in Jerusalem and Safed, and certainly elsewhere in the Land of Israel as well, there were also sages in the country who engaged in studying and teaching the Kabbalah. There is interesting information about this phenomenon dating from the second half of the thirteenth century. The famous Kabbalist R. Abraham Abulafia, who reached Acre in 1260 (but left the country that very same year because of the war being waged there between the Mongols and the Mamluks) left his mark on the Land of Israel through his disciples and their students, the most famous of them being R. Isaac of Acre. They were considerably influenced by Abulafia's mystical thought, and it seems that one of them settled in Hebron at the end of the thirteenth century. Abulafia's Kabbalistic thought also influenced later Kabbalists who settled in the Land of Israel, such as R. Shem Tov ibn Gaon, the Spanish sage who took up residence in Safed in 1325. Abulafia's Kabbalistic school of thought enjoyed unprecedented development in Jerusalem and Safed in the sixteenth century. We learn of other Kabbalists in Jerusalem in the fifteenth century from the historian R. Elijah Capsali, who wrote of one of his forefathers: "Our great teacher R. Shabtai Capsali, of blessed memory, who was... nagid in Jerusalem," whose "books and commentaries written in the spirit of the Kabbalah" were found "in Jerusalem in the hands of Kabbalists." At the beginning of the sixteenth century there were in Jerusalem "recently arrived Kabbalists" who suffused the city with a mystical, Kabbalistic and apocalyptic ambience, this even before the diffusion of the Safed school of Kabbalah in the second half of the sixteenth century. The most outstanding and important of them was the renowned R. Abraham ben Eliezer ha-Levi, an expellee from Spain, who arrived in Jerusalem several years before the Ottoman conquest of the Land of Israel. He fitted in well with the messianic expectations that were widespread in Jerusalem during the second and third decades of the sixteenth century.

Philosophical activity was already evident in Jerusalem in the late fourteenth and early fifteenth centuries. It seems, however, that interest in philosophy towards the end of the Mamluk period was not at all substantial. We may deduce this from the remarks of Obadiah of Bertinoro who wrote in his first letter (1488):

There is not to be found here a Jew or an Ishmaelite whose heart turns away from God towards heresy or evil beliefs, nor is there anyone in all these places who will engage in philosophy and incline towards the opinions of Aristotle and the like, may the names of the evil rot, and someone came to Egypt from the Maghreb and began to be a root that beareth gall and wormwood and to spout philosophy, and the nagid rejected him with both hands (Obadiah of Bertinoro, *Letters*, pp. 70–71).

Our survey of the spiritual and intellectual life of the Jews in the Land of Israel during the Mamluk period would be incomplete without at least mentioning some of the outstanding sages at that time. R. Moses ben Nahman (Nahmanides), who had been forced to leave Spain, settled in Jerusalem in 1267 and a year or two later moved to Acre where he passed away. Eshtori ha-Parhi, one of the first researchers of the Land of Israel, came from Spain in the first half of the fourteenth century and settled in Beth Shean. He gained fame for his book, *Kaftor va-Ferah*, in which he discusses a whole array of topics pertaining to the Land of Israel, including its geography. His contemporaries were R. Shem Tov ben Abraham ibn Gaon, a Spanish Kabbalist and expert in halakhah, author of *Migdal Oz*, a commentary on Maimonides' *Mishneh Torah*, and of *Keter Shem Tov* , and R. Hananel ben Abraham. They both settled in Tiberias, although Shem Tov later (1325) moved to Safed. R. Jacob Sakili was a disciple of R. Asher ben Jehiel in Toledo, Spain. He compiled a midrashic anthology, *Talmud Torah*, and other works, and afterwards moved to Damascus. R. Joseph ben Eliezer Tov Elem ha-Sefardi, one of the most important interpreters of R. Abraham ibn Ezra's commentary on the Torah, settled in Jerusalem in the second half of the fourteenth century. R. Obadiah of Bertinoro, to whose testimony we have often referred to above, the famous commentator on the Mishnah, immigrated from Italy to Jerusalem in 1488 and became the leader of its community. In the first and second decades of the sixteenth century, several outstanding Spanish sages of the time of the expulsion settled in the Holy City, leaving their mark on Jerusalem and Safed both in that generation and the next. They included the Kabbalists R. Isaac Mor-Hayyim and R. Abraham ben Eliezer ha-Levi, the famous astronomer and historian R. Abraham Zacutto, and R. Levi ibn Habib, the most important sage in Jerusalem in the twenties and thirties of the sixteenth century.

The era of Mamluk rule in the Land of Israel was a dark period for the Jews of that country, one in which the hands of the rulers lay heavy upon the Jewish community, especially influencing its economic and social life. The Mamluks did nothing to encourage economic growth and development in the Holy Land, while increasing the taxes and fines levied upon the non-Muslim minorities and enacting ever more severe discriminatory edicts against them. As a result, only individual Jews immigrated to the Land of Israel during almost all of these two and one half centuries, coming from the diverse lands of the Jewish Diaspora. However, towards the end of the Mamluk period the stream of immigrants notably increased as Jews expelled from Spain arrived in the country, settling mainly in Jerusalem and Safed. A generation later, the country would fall to the Ottoman Turks, beginning a new era in the history of the Holy Land and its Jewish population.

Bridge at Lod known as Jindis Bridge or Baybars Bridge, a Mamluk structure bearing the symbols of Sultan Baybars and in use to this very day. Stones from a Crusader church in nearby Lod were used in its construction

The Modern Period

The People and the Land

Yehoshua Kaniel

With the Ottoman conquest a period of change began in the history of the Land of Israel and its Jewish population. The Land entered a period of four hundred years under the rule of a great empire, powerful and strong at its beginning, which underwent a slow and prolonged process of debilitation and disintegration till it came to an end.

At first, the Ottoman rulers invested great efforts and means to stop the process of decline that infused the Land towards the end of Mamluk times. Proper administration was instituted, order and security were imposed on the highways, and agricultural development and commerce were encouraged. The stable governmental authority brought about a building boom and a population growth, including the Jews. Prosperity did not continue for long. The internal and political strength of the central government was undermined, influencing the provinces throughout the Empire as well. The seventeenth century in Eretz Israel was characterized by governmental instability, revolts, and disorders which led to a deterioration in the security situation, in the economy, and of the population. In contrast, in the eighteenth century a certain recovery took place after the rise of strong local rulers, who instituted centralized government for several decades. These rulers invested a great deal in developing the north of the country and the coastal strip, with the port city of Acre at its center.

At the beginning of the period there was no significant European involvement in the country. European involvement focussed mainly on Christian pilgrimage and commercial ties. However, as a consequence of the weakening of the Empire and of increasing rivalry among the great powers, European states began to pay attention to their political and religious interests in the Land of Israel. They intensified their activity and involvement there, reaching a peak during the nineteenth century.

The Arab population in Eretz Israel in the sixteenth century has been estimated at 250,000 to 300,000 persons, reaching about 700,000 by the end of the Ottoman age. The basic division within this population was between the Qays and Yaman factions, which became an expression of political-regional loyalty more than a tribal-historical link. The fundamental tie was to the tribe, to the extended family or clan (the *hamulah*), and to local *shaykh*s. In the cities, the political leadership of powerful and propertied old families stood out as they competed with each other. Towards the end of the nineteenth century, signs of awakening national consciousness began to appear among the educated Arab public. They again took up use of the territorial term Filastin as defining Eretz Israel or part of it. This consciousness developed and deepened in the Mandatory period and became the central factor in the struggle between the two national groups, the Jews and the Arabs, for control over the country, and the focus of the Israeli-Arab conflict with the establishment of the State of Israel.

The Ottoman conquest of Eretz Israel reinforced the Jewish community and altered its situation in various fields. First of all, the Jews became part of a vast empire under a single government. Ties with various other Jewish communities became closer, especially with the great and prosperous Constantinople community, which was influential in the courts of power. This influence was used on behalf of the Jewish population in Eretz Israel. They obtained protection in the shadow of "the Realm of Benevolence" that displayed sympathy and tolerance towards the Jews. The immigration of the exiles from Spain and the gathering of the intellectual religious elite in Safed and Jerusalem turned the Land of Israel into a focus of spiritual effervescence. It was exhibited in the founding and development of two central bases in Judaism: Jewish law (*halakhah*) in Rabbi Joseph Karo's opus, the *Shulhan Arukh*; and the mystical doctrine, the Kabbalah, the wellsprings of which burst forth in the logic and leadership of Rabbi Isaac Luria (known as "the Ari") and his pupils. However, the time of spiritual and economic high tide did not last for long. The years of decline returned and with them the dwindling character of the Jewish community. The fate of the Jewish population was dependent first and foremost on the political and security conditions prevailing in the country. The fate of the Jewish population improved in periods of political calm, when the central authorities or the local rulers maintained order and security and displayed a decent attitude toward the minorities, not making things difficult for them religiously or economically. On the other hand, when central power was lax, and during local revolts when a strong, guiding hand was lacking, disorders and highway robbery increased, the security of persons and property in the cities was undermined, the treatment of the minorities – including the Jews – worsened, and economic and political pressure on them increased.

This situation led to a decline in the number of Jews in the country, resulting in a weaker Jewish community. These processes were also influenced by the country's economic possibilities, since proper conditions for trade, together with encouragement and development of the economy by the authorities, indirectly brought about a recovery of the Jewish population. On the other hand, economic backwardness or even natural disasters, plagues, or drought years, caused recurring crises and struck hard at the Jewish population. The situation of the Jewish population was dependent too – in large measure – on the intensity of connections between it and the Diaspora Jews who served as a vital source for the community's sustenance, and in particular as a human reservoir for its growth and development.

Palestine did not form a separate political-administrative unit, but rather was integrated as a part of the geographic-administrative system of the region, headed by governors sent from Turkey. The names "the Land of Israel" or "Holy Land," which were used by Jews and Christians to define the country, related to the biblical realities and to the profound historic and religious bond between the People and the Land. The People of Israel, which despite long years of exile had not forgotten the Land of Israel, gave it a prominent place in their prayers, and it also served as a source of hopes for future Redemption. The bond on the spiritual-religious plane was also reflected on the physical

level through immigration to Eretz Israel and settlement there. Of course, we are dealing with limited numbers; nevertheless, they were meaningful from the viewpoint of the possibility of sustaining a Jewish population in the period under discussion. This immigration sometimes flowed from messianic enthusiasm and at times formed a current in a broader spiritual-religious movement which had arisen in the Diaspora. To be sure, even personal motives were a factor in immigration, such as a vow at a time of hardship, or deep ecstatic excitation. Sometimes, the impulse to immigration derived from political, security, or economic conditions which prevailed in the countries of origin. Jews wandered from place to place and a thin trickle arrived in Eretz Israel as well. The outstanding waves of immigration were generally made up of high minded groups or individuals who, with their pupils, made a mark on the Jewish community. Sometimes there was an interval of dozens of years between one such wave of immigration and the next one. Meanwhile, the immigrants joined the existing community, added another stratum to its diversity, and also became a part of the veteran population, the Old Yishuv.

However, even between one wave of immigration to the next, the link was never broken, and we generally witness a continuing process of Jewish immigrants coming to settle in the Land of Israel. To be sure, we have little information about them, since they did not leave behind texts or evidence. This trickle of immigrants was sometimes very thin and not at all noticeable, because at the same time emigration from the Land, which was also a known phenomenon, led to a further dwindling of the Jewish population. However, sometimes immigration grew and the Jewish community recovered. The decline in the status of the Jewish community from the demographic aspect came to an end from the nineteenth century and onwards. Since then, immigration and progress have been continuous.

The bond to Eretz Israel was also reflected in Jewish pilgrimage, coming principally from the countries of the eastern basin of the Mediterranean Sea. An extensively ramified system of collecting funds in the Diaspora for the Jewish population in Eretz Israel also expressed the bond between the People and the Land. The system preserved, developed, and deepened this bond. The emissary (called a *shadar*, initials of "emissary of our rabbis"), who left the Land in order to travel among Diaspora communities, generally found readiness to contribute, for he exemplified to Diapora Jews the dimension of enhanced holiness shrouded with the glory of the site of the Temple in Jerusalem, "the mountain of God," the longing of the prayers of generations of Jews for the holy places and for the tombs of the Patriarchs. The Western Wall, the Tomb of Rachel, the Cave of Machpelah in Hebron, and the tombs of the Tannaim and Amoraim (Talmudic teachers) in Tiberias and the Galilee served as symbols of an enhanced spiritual experience that was lacking in the atmosphere of the Diaspora. This experience may not have been the focus of the existential, everyday condition of Diaspora Jews, and for that reason we sometimes witness difficulties in the process of collecting funds for the Jews of Eretz Israel. The centers operating on behalf of Eretz Israel which existed throughout the period in various regions of Jewish communities (such as Venice, Constantinople, Metz, and Amsterdam, and in the nineteenth century, more widespread throughout Eastern and Central Europe), charity boxes in the name of Rabbi Meir Ba'al ha-Ness which were placed in Jewish homes, and the large sums that continued to stream to Eretz Israel, prove that giving money was not only a context of economic activity, that is, for the purpose of helping the livelihood of the Jews of Eretz Israel, but was also meant to express the deep link of the Jew to the values of the sanctity of the Land of Israel and its holy places, of studying the Torah in the Holy Land, and of performing the commandment of settling Eretz Israel.

This bond between the People and the Land was enriched with a new dimension from the second half of the nineteenth century, with the appearance of modern Jewish nationalism. The Hibbat Zion movement and Zionism introduced a dimension of realism and the mundane into the religious link to the Holy Land. The idea that the Land of Israel was the historic, territorial homeland of the Jewish people was reinforced, and hopes were renewed that in that land the nation would revive its culture and ancient language, build a normal, modern society different from the Jewish society of the Diaspora, and establish its independent entity there.

Along with the national ideal, the Land of Israel increasingly became a refuge for persecuted Jews and a territorial concentration for world Jewry. Among them, we may mention the refugees from pogroms in Russia, the victims of the antisemitism and economic pressure which were the lot of the Jews of Poland in the 1920s and 1930s, the Jews of Germany who left that country upon the rise of Nazism, the survivors of the Holocaust who were striving for a safe harbor and longed for their Land, and entire Diaspora communities which picked themselves up from their place of exile after the establishment of the State of Israel and returned to their homeland.

The Ottoman Period – The First Centuries

Yaron Ben-Naeh

For the Ottomans, whose empire extended over three continents, the Land of Israel was no more than another peripheral territory, small and impoverished, whose importance derived merely from its religious status and its function as a land bridge between Asia and Africa. The Ottoman period, which began in the late Middle Ages and came to an end in the twentieth century, was one of great importance in the history of the Land of Israel and the Jewish people. In these four centuries the bonds and relationships that linked Diaspora Jews to the Land of Israel and its Jewish community increased and grew stronger. The rise of the Ottomans and their expansive conquests, on one hand, and the expulsions from the Iberian Peninsula on the other, brought in their wake profound changes in Jewish thought. In the sixteenth century, and even later, Jewish thinkers in Islamic lands and in Europe developed new doctrines: living in exile – in the Diaspora – was considered to be a sin. Some viewed immigration to and settling in the Land of Israel as a binding commandment and an end unto itself, while others went so far as to connect immigration with the speeding up of Redemption, thereby transforming the settlement of the Land of Israel into a means.

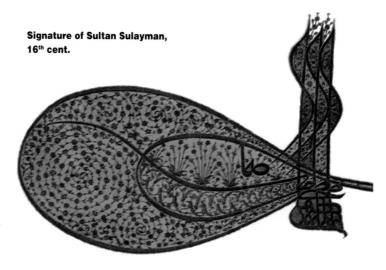

Signature of Sultan Sulayman, 16th cent.

The Ottoman period is characterized by the abundance and variety of information available to the modern scholar, making it possible to draw a full and balanced historical picture. Jewish sources include itineraries, chronicles, letters, isolated documents, and an extensive corpus of printed and manuscript religious works. Muslim sources are chiefly the records of the *shari'a* (religious) courts and documents from the Ottoman archives in Istanbul, while Christian sources take the form of itineraries, in addition to archives of European trading firms and of the churches and monasteries in the Land of Israel.

In 1453, Sultan Mehmed II conquered Constantinople, the capital of the Byzantine Empire, resettled the city and made it the capital of his empire, renaming it Istanbul. When he died in 1481 the Janissaries raised his son Beyazid to the throne. His reign was marked by cultural reactionism and religious extremism, yet this did not prevent Beyazid from permitting thousands of Jews to enter his domains. The wars he conducted with the Mamluks and the Venetians did not result in substantial border changes, and he even avoided responding to the growing power of Safavid Persia (from 1501). After the revolt of the Kizilbash (Shi'ite Turkoman tribes in eastern Anatolia) and their rapid westward advance, Selim dethroned his father Beyazid and usurped his rule. He took immediate action, massacring the supporters of the Persian Shah Isma'il and advancing eastwards. Selim defeated the Shah's forces in the battle of Chaldiran (August 1514), conquered and annexed eastern Anatolia and the state of Dhu-l-Qadr, and seized the territories of present-day Iraq and the city of Tabriz. Increasing embitterment among his

◄ Map of the holy places in the Land of Israel, Italy, 18th cent.

soldiers due to conditions in the field and the approaching winter led him to halt his advance into Persia and withdraw his forces to Anatolia.

The Mamluks, Shah Isma'il's allies who ruled Egypt and the province comprising of Syria and Palestine, were not a significant rival for the Ottoman power. Already in the late fourteenth century, corruption had become rife in the Mamluk military and governmental systems. Heavy taxes led to the ruin of agriculture and the decline of trade, while the army avoided introducing any innovations in weaponry and tactics. The Ottomans took advantage of the opportunity with which they were presented: within two and a half years they had put an end to the Mamluk state. Selim turned southwards and in August 1516 his armies vanquished the troops of the elderly Mamluk sultan, Qansuh al-Ghuri, at the battle of Marj Dabeq, near Aleppo. Qansuh and many of his commanders were killed in the battle, the caliph was taken prisoner, and the Syrian cities fell to the Ottomans. From Damascus, Selim sent his men further southwards and within a short time Druze leaders and Bedouin sheikhs appeared before him to pledge their loyalty. As the army advanced along the seacoast in the direction of Gaza, delegations of dignitaries from the central region of Palestine came to Sinan Pasha, the grand vizier, to express loyalty and submission to the sultan. Resistance in the southern cities of Ramlah and Gaza was immediately suppressed with great cruelty and it seems that all of Palestine passed into Ottoman hands in the course of that year. Chaos prevailed in Cairo, the Mamluk capital, while the attempts of Tuman Bey – the recently enthroned Mamluk sultan – to reorganize the army and the administration proved to be ineffective. Contradictory rumors concerning the Ottoman army and Selim's intentions aggravated the situation. In January 1517, over 20,000 soldiers assembled under Tuman Bey's command at Raidaniyya, near Cairo, to face Selim's forces. The Mamluks suffered a crushing defeat, their ruler was taken captive and hung publicly at the gates of Cairo, and all Egypt fell to the Ottomans. The Hejaz, with its Islamic holy places, recognized the sovereignty of the Ottoman sultan, who was now called "the Servant of the Two Holy Places," and in fact became the caliph. Khayr Bey, formerly the Mamluk governor of Aleppo, was now appointed to govern Egypt, and Janbardi al-Ghazzali, one of Tuman Bey's commanders, was appointed governor in Damascus, from where he ruled over Syria and Palestine. Selim returned to Istanbul, where he died in 1520. When his son Sulayman came to the throne, Janbardi intended to become an independent ruler and took up arms against Sulayman. He began to advance his army and even conquered several Syrian coastal cities. He was eventually defeated, decapitated, and his head sent to Istanbul. The sultan speedily set out to set up a new administrative system that would be loyal and efficient, and ensure order, security, and proper tax collection. Most of the territory of Palestine was now part of the province (*vilayet*) of Damascus, which was itself

Palestine under Ottoman rule in the 16th cent., showing places where Jews resided

Sulayman the Lawgiver (1520-1566), a miniature by Nigari, 1560 (TP)

divided into five districts (*sanjak*s): Jerusalem, Gaza, Shechem (Nablus), Ajlun, and Safed.

Until the death of Sulayman in a military campaign in 1566, the Ottomans had conquered a vast territorial expanse in North Africa, eastern Europe (the entire Balkans came under their control), and the eastern Mediterranean islands. The reign of Sulayman, known as "the Lawgiver" or "the Magnificent," is considered the height of the Ottoman Empire from all points of view – military, political, economic, and juridical, as well as cultural. The imperial capital, Istanbul, became a cultural, artistic, and scientific center, due in no small part to the patronage of senior court officials. During the reign of his successor, Selim II, the struggle intensified on the eastern front against the Persians, and even more so against the Russians. The Ottomans conquered Cyprus in 1571, but shortly afterwards suffered a severe defeat in the naval battle of Lepanto. In the course of this battle with the Spaniards almost the entire Ottoman fleet was destroyed. Despite the speedy restoration of the fleet, the empire had lost its predominance in the Mediterranean basin. Selim died in 1574, to be replaced by Murad III, a weak ruler. The need to maintain a constantly growing army and to conduct warfare on two fronts weighed extremely heavily on the imperial treasury which had to contend with rising inflation and dwindling revenues from taxes and duties due to changes in trade routes and other factors. Ottoman currency was depreciated and heavier taxes were

imposed. The harmful influence of the sultan's advisors and the women of the seraglio together with increasing strength of the Janissaries in the imperial court led to a decline in the quality and abilities of the administrative and governmental system, which was tainted by growing corruption on all levels. Several violent uprisings erupted in the capital itself. In 1595, Mehmed III came to power and was immediately forced to deal with the Jelali revolts that continued until 1610. The situation in the 1620s steadily deteriorated: Cossack raids, renewed revolts and disorder in Anatolia and the capital, the murder of Sultan Othman II in 1622 together with intrigues at court did not leave much room for hope. The empire seemed to be quickly approaching its end. However, in the seventeenth century it made a surprising recovery, and many historians nowadays see that age as one of transition which prepared the Ottoman realm for the transformations that would confront it in the coming centuries.

The second half of the reign of Ahmed III (1703–1730) is known as "the Age of the Tulips." This extended period of peace was accompanied by economic growth and flourishing culture, as well as by the penetration of European influences. The popular uprising of 1730 led to the deposal of the sultan and the end of an era. His successors adopted a more conservative policy, once again becoming involved in several wars. The peace treaty of

Ottoman warriors in the 15th cent., reconstruction by Angus McBride

227

Kuchuk Kainarji (1774) once more indicated the empire's weakness vis-à-vis Europe, and encouraged displays of independence on the part of powerful groups and local governors. Real reforms only began during the reign of Selim III (1789–1807), presaging the great change that was to occur in the nineteenth century.

• • • • • • • • • •

Under Ottoman Rule

When Ottoman rule was established in Palestine, steps were taken to incorporate that country into the imperial administrative structure, and to improve the conditions of daily life there for the benefit of its inhabitants and the state's revenues. Old highways were renovated and new ones constructed. Way stations and caravansaries were built along the roads as facilities for travelers and for collecting duties. Efforts were even made to suppress highway bandits and to move the Bedouin tribes away from the settled areas. As early as 1525, the first known detailed population census was conducted in Palestine; the entire population was recorded, real estate was surveyed and registered, and tax rates were set. Throughout the century, several additional censuses were conducted. Despite the difficulties that they pose

for the researcher, the censuses are of immense value due to the information they contain about living conditions in the Land of Israel and its population in the sixteenth century. Only sporadic censuses were conducted during the following centuries. As a result, the allocation of taxes was not based on accurate, up-to-date data. Tax farmers and their representatives tried to collect larger sums, and taxes were levied according to a compromise reached between state officials and the religious minorities, usually with the help of sizeable bribes. Obviously, in times of crisis the financial burden placed on both Muslim and non-Muslim subjects increased.

The censuses indicate the size and distribution of the population of Palestine in the sixteenth century, and enable us to discern changing demographic patterns. About 250,000 persons inhabited the country in the sixteenth century. The basic units were the city and the village, the tribe and the *hamula* (clan or extended family). Most inhabitants were peasants (*fellahin*) who lived in rather harsh physical conditions. Since the conquest there had been rapid growth in the country's population, the number of villages, and the extent of tilled land. In the second half of the century the trend was reversed, and the population diminished once again. Among the common crops were wheat and barley, various pulses, fruit trees (and their by-products, such

Jews in Istanbul: left – a physician and a merchant; right – a married woman in European dress next to a widow. Manuscript, 1574 (GL)

The mosque of Ahmed al-Jazzar (1775–1804) in Acre, his capital

provinces, stimulated local leaders to implement their aspiration for independence. The Druze emirs of the Ma'n clan – Korkmaz, the son of Fakhr al-Din I, and even more so, Fakhr al-Din II, who formed strong connections with European states such as various Italian city-states – controlled most of the territory of Lebanon and northern Palestine. In the central region the families of Turabay and Mehmed ibn Farukh (for his governorship in Jerusalem, see below) gained much strength. The vigorous efforts of Murad IV, who exploited rivalries and conflicts between the heads of the powerful families in Palestine, finally brought about the fall of Fakhr al-Din, who was executed in Istanbul in 1634 together with his sons. Stabilization at the center

as olive oil and soap), sugar, and cotton. New crops were introduced from the Americas in the eighteenth century: tobacco, corn, tomatoes, potatoes, and prickly pear (cactus fruit). In suitable areas the inhabitants raised sheep and cattle (in the swampy areas in northern Palestine, even water buffaloes) and produced dairy products. In the coastal cities, as well as Tiberias, they also engaged in fishing.

Ottoman officials in small numbers, assisted by troops, conducted the administration from the few cities. The urban population earned its livelihood from trade and crafts (leatherwork, goldsmithery, and metal work). The Jews brought with them the craft of weaving, dyeing, sewing, and embroidering woolen cloth. In sixteenth-century Safed and Tiberias the Jews also engaged in silk weaving. The Christian inhabitants were mainly employed in producing religious artifacts and souvenirs for pilgrims.

From the late sixteenth century signs of decline were quite evident in the provinces, making life more difficult for the population. One of the outstanding manifestations of the authorities' weakness was the deterioration of internal security. In practice, safety was ensured only within the walled cities. Bandits controlled the roads once again, and Bedouin tribes raided settled areas. Governors and officials permitted themselves to ill-treat the local population and oppress them without fear. The declining power of the central government, the deterioration of the central administrative framework and the difficulty it encountered in enforcing its authority and directives in the

of Ottoman rule prevented the rise of such local rulers for about a century, becoming possible again only during the reign of Ahmed III and his successors, Mahmud I and Abdul-Hamid I. In 1703, a local revolt against the central authorities broke out in Jerusalem which became known as "the Revolt of the Naqib al-Ashraf." Representatives of the central government were refused entrance to the city, and Jerusalem was actually under siege for three years. In the 1730s Daher al-'Umar, who began his career as a tax farmer in the District of Sidon, gained considerable power, exercising control over Galilee from his fortified position in Tiberias. In 1750 he conquered and fortified Acre, making it his capital. Daher forged ties with European merchants, and in the early 1770s extended his control southwards by occupying large territories in central Palestine. By this stage he had already lost favor with the Ottomans and was murdered in the summer of 1775. There is some resemblance between him and Ahmed al-Jazzar, who was appointed to replace him as governor of Acre which now became the capital of the Sanjak of Sidon. Al-Jazzar gradually gained strength, creating his own large mercenary army, and in the 1790s became governor of the Vilayet of Damascus. It was during the terms in office of Jazzar and his successor that the influence of a Jew named Hayyim Farhi reached its peak. He served as Jazzar's advisor and minister of finance.

Napoleon's forces advanced northwards after their conquest of Egypt, taking Gaza, Ramlah, and Jaffa. Ahmed al-Jazzar was actually the only man standing in Napoleon's way. From 1799,

229

he avoided cooperating with Napoleon and withdrew to Acre, until the French army retreated after failing in all its efforts to conquer the city. Jazzar died in 1804. The careers of Daher and Jazzar illustrate the ambivalent relationship between local rulers and the central government in Istanbul. On one hand, the government feared an overly strong and independent local ruler. On the other hand, a local strongman brought administrative and financial benefit to the imperial treasury. The central authorities did not follow a consistent policy in dealing with such cases. Sometimes they tried to subdue a rebel through force, while at other times they acquiesced in post factum recognition of his status by granting him an official appointment, and even additional territories.

European influence in Palestine, particularly that of the French, increased during the eighteenth century as a direct result of the development of commerce between the European powers and the Ottoman Empire through the Levant trading companies, as well as the rising interest that the European powers displayed in sites holy to Christendom and in the Christian communities living in the Holy Land.

· · · · · · · · · ·

Ottoman Constuction in Palestine

The Sixteenth Century

Large scale building activities were conducted throughout the country. During the reign of "Sulayman the Lawgiver," Jerusalem went through a building boom of major dimensions that shaped the urban landscape that we see before us today: the Dome of the Rock was thoroughly renovated, and several memorial structures built on the Temple Mount; the city walls and the citadel were rebuilt; markets were established, as were drinking fountains and public facilities. The Ottomans also restored the city's water supply system.

A large fortress was constructed between 1571 and 1573 at Rosh Ha-Ayin (Antipatris). Another fortress was erected at Jenin, and that at Bet-Guvrin was restored. In the northern part of the country commercial roads were renovated and several caravansaries built along them, including Khan al-Tujjar in Lower Galilee which was restored and enlarged at the end of the sixteenth century by the governor of Damascus (who also erected a mosque inside it), the khan known as Khirbet Job Yusuf near Ami'ad, Khan Qamun near Yokne'am, and Khan Jaljuliya in the north of the Afek Valley. Customs stations were located at some of these places.

Safed and Tiberias, which had become the two major cities in northern Palestine, quickly grew and prospered as a result of a large influx of Jews. They were both walled cities in which many houses were built. Some of the fulling mills that Jews established as part of the woolen industry can still be seen in the stream canyons in the vicinity of Safed. In the 1580s, a "Citadel of the Jews" was built inside the city, now called Khan al-Pasha.

The Seventeenth Century

In Jerusalem, building and renovation work was mainly conducted on the Temple Mount – construction of the Dome of Yusuf Agha, renovation of the Dome of Joseph in 1681 and

Khan Jaljuliya east of present-day Kefar Saba. Built in the Middle Ages, it was renovated in the early Ottoman period as part of an effort to restore trade routes in Palestine

An Ottoman fortress erected in 1571–1573 on the remains of the city of Antipatris built by King Herod Antipas

restoration of the Sabil of Sha'alan in 1628 – by the city's governor, Muhammad Pasha. In addition, a minaret was erected in the courtyard of the Citadel in 1655. The water supply system was restored, and as early as the beginning of the century the structure known as Qasr al-Buraq was built in order to defend Solomon's Pools. The structure above Rachel's Tomb was rebuilt by Jerusalem's governor in 1623 and, apparently, also that over the tomb of the Prophet Samuel (Nabi Samwil).

The Eighteenth Century

Building activity in Jerusalem was still centered on the Temple Mount, and included restoration of al-Aqsa Mosque (1702–1703); the *mihrab* (prayer niche) of the Dome of the Chain was surfaced with decorated ceramic tiles; Mustafa, the governor of

Jerusalem, constructed the Sabil al-Shaykh Badr (1740) and Ahmad Qollari paved an open space set aside for prayer (1760).

Efforts were made to fortify and develop the coastal cities upon the initiative of the central government. At Jaffa (the main port of entry for many of the pilgrims, which had become an important commercial harbor), a military garrison was stationed and a citadel built upon the orders of the grand vizier Rami Pasha in 1703, a city wall was erected by Daher al-'Umar, and a moat dug around it in the last third of the eighteenth century. At Haifa, two citadels were built to protect the entrance to the harbor, and troops and cannons stationed there to defend it against pirates (1722–1725). In the last quarter of the century, Daher encouraged permanent settlement near the citadels.

231

The Tomb of Rachel near Bethlehem – a structure that went through several stages of construction. Below – the site as painted by Luigi Mayer in 1803; above – its later appearance (on a woven carpet) after being renovated upon the initiative of Sir Moses Montefiore in the 19th cent.

During the second half of the eighteenth century, the governors of Palestine initiated various works of construction in Galilee. Members of Daher's family built fortresses at Yokne'am, Deir Hanna, Shefar'am, Yehi'am, Safed, Sepphoris, and elsewhere. At Tiberias, the sixteenth-century walls were renovated and a mosque erected. Acre, which became the capital of the Vilayet of Sidon, went through a building boom during the time of Ahmed al-Jazzar. The Great Mosque and other mosques were constructed, as well as city walls, a *hammam* (bath house), caravansaries (Khan al-'Umdan, Khan al-Afranj, Khan al-Tujjar), market-places, and even a *seraya* to house the local administration. The aqueduct built by Selim Pasha was in use up to the twentieth century.

The Jews in the Land of Israel from the Sixteenth to the Eighteenth Centuries

About 6,000 Jews lived in the Land of Israel towards the end of Mamluk rule, a diverse population both in its origins and customs. There were Arabic-speaking Musta'arabs (ancient inhabitants of the country), Maghrebis from North Africa, immigrants from the Iberian Peninsula including former crypto-Jews (whose number steadily increased, many of them having arrived after years of wandering), Italians, and Ashkenazim from Germany and Central Europe. Karaites lived in Jerusalem throughout this entire period and were formally considered to be part of the Jewish community.

The rate of growth of the Jewish population during the Mamluk period greatly increased following the expulsions from the Iberian Peninsula, and especially

232

after the conquest of Palestine by the Ottomans. It was also related to the awakening of messianic hopes at the time and in subsequent years. With the beginning of Ottoman rule, most of the Land of Israel's Jews lived in Jerusalem, Safed, and Gaza. There were also small communities in Ramlah, Hebron, Shechem (Nablus) – alongside an ancient Samaritan community – and in several coastal cities (Sidon, Caesarea, and Jaffa). Dozens of Musta'arab families lived in various villages in Galilee where they engaged in agriculture (Banyas, Ein Zeitun, Biriyah, Almah, Peki'in, Kefar Hananyah, Kefar Kanna, Kefar Yasif, Shefar'am, and Kabul). The censuses indicate a continuity of Jewish settlement throughout the fifteenth and sixteenth centuries, and then a disappearance of a considerable part of those small Jewish communities in the seventeenth century. Over the course of time, the Musta'arab community became assimilated and almost totally disappeared. From then on the Sefardi group, with its unique lifestyle, customs, and language (Ladino), became the dominant Jewish ethnic group in the country. The rapid increase in the number of Jews, 10,000 at its height, reversed itself in the third quarter of the sixteenth century from which time it steadily decreased until the mid-eighteenth century. Simultaneously, the mood of messianic expectation that had typified the Jewish people in the Land of Israel at that time waned and was replaced by a sense of "exile in the [Holy] Land," to use the phrase coined by Israel Bartal.

As a result of the rule of independent governors, such as those of the Ma'an family in northern Palestine and the Ibn Farukh family in Jerusalem, the Jewish community was in difficult straits. From the 1620s on, the total Jewish population was less than 4,000. Only towards the end of that century did a certain recovery become evident. The energetic activity of The Istanbul Committee of Officers of Jerusalem (and later of the other holy cities) established in 1724 brought about a turn for the better, and from the late 1720s the Jewish community once again steadily increased in numbers. Among the well known immigrants who arrived then were R. Hayyim Abulafia of Izmir who settled with his followers in Tiberias and in fact was the renovator of Jewish settlement there(1740), R. Hayyim ben Attar of Morocco (1741), the Italian, R. Moses Hayyim Luzatto, who resided in Acre (1743), R. Abraham Gershon of Kutow (1746), R. Menahem Mendel of Peremyshlyany, and R. Nahman of Horodenka (1764), the latter three being leading Hasidic rabbis. Most of the immigrants continued to arrive from other areas within the Ottoman Empire and North Africa, and only in the last quarter of the century did the number of Ashkenazim significantly increase. The immigration of Hasidim in 1777, led by R. Menahem Mendel of Vitebsk, R. Abraham Kohen of Kalisk,

and R. Israel of Polotsk, and the immigration of their adversaries in Eastern Europe, the Prushim who were disciples of Rabbi Elijah (the "Gaon of Vilna"), in the early nineteenth century, symbolized the beginning of a change in the map of Jewish settlement in the Land of Israel. They were the forerunners of the beginning of ideologically motivated organized groups of immigrants, and became the basis for the Ashkenazic ultra-Orthodox "Old Yishuv." Despite the increase, the number of Jews in the Land of Israel at the end of the eighteenth century did not exceed 6,000.

A Turkish pistol made of steel, ivory, silver, and gold

The two principal and most important communities during the Ottoman period were in Jerusalem and Safed. The largest Jewish community in the second half of the sixteenth century lived in Safed. However, from the seventeenth century onwards, the Jerusalem community once again predominated and retained that status in the future as well. Among the important traits of the Jewish communities in Palestine after the sixteenth century were, therefore, communal diversity and the lack of genealogical continuity. Renewal and continuity of settlement were achieved through unceasing immigration rather than by natural increase. This was inevitable given the typical demographic cross-section of the immigrants (single men and women, generally of an advanced age), the high death rate, and the increasing rate of emigration from the Land of Israel.

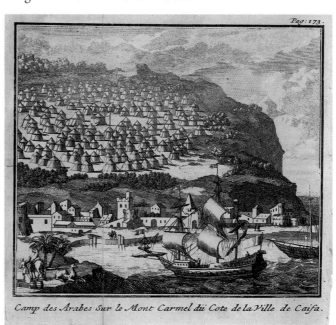

Pag: 173.

Camp des Arabes sur le Mont Carmel dü Cote de la Ville de Caifa.

An Arab encampment on Mount Carmel, above Haifa, engraving by Laurent d'Arvieux, *Voyage dans la Palestina*...Amsterdam, 1718

233

An ornamented window in the Synagogue of R. Isaac Luria Ashkenazi, Safed

Safed

Safed was set in the heart of a rich agricultural area. Due to its geographic proximity, it was closely linked to Damascus, the capital of the vilayet, and to other cities in Syria. At its peak, the Jewish population of Safed numbered 5,000 to 6,000 souls who were divided into *kehalim* (congregations) on the basis of their countries of origin, in the pattern familiar to us from other cities in the Ottoman Empire at that time. Among the congregations were those of Castile, Seville, Cordova, Ashkenaz, and others. Safed included many former crypto-Jews who had immigrated to the city, where they returned to the fold of Judaism in expectation of the oncoming Redemption.

The city's security was enhanced when a wall was built around it in 1549, and by the construction of a fortified caravansary that served for residence, trade, storage of merchandise, and safeguarding of money and valuable objects from bandits and fires. Many residents engaged in the wool weaving industry, while local merchants traded with cities in Egypt, Turkey, and Italy.

Economic prosperity and the diversified social infrastructure attracted scholars and well-known rabbis to the city, and thus Safed became a Jewish cultural center of the first order for the span of a generation. The printing shop of Eliezer Ashkenazi of Prague, who had engaged in the printing trade in Istanbul, operated in the city for about a decade (1577–1587). One of the noteworthy results of the concentration of sages in Safed was R. Jacob Berab's attempt to renew *semicha* (ordination). He intended this step to eventually lead to the establishment of a new Sanhedrin with extremely broad religious powers, and thus perhaps, to indirectly hasten the coming of Redemption. In 1538, a convocation of sages in Safed approved

the idea, authorizing Jacob Berab to ordain worthy candidates. However, the bitter opposition of the Jerusalem sages, led by R. Levi ibn Habib, eventually brought about a cessation of these efforts. Before fleeing to Damascus, Jacob Berab had ordained four of his students and subsequently these four gave ordination to several disciples of their own.

Among the famous sages of Safed were R. Joseph Caro (author of the *Shulhan Arukh*), R. Moses of Trani, R. Abraham Shalom, R. Yom Tov Zahalon, R. Ele'azar Azikri, R. Hiyya Rofeh and R. David ben Zimra, one of the greatest experts on halakhah, who for several years resided in Safed after having earlier lived in Egypt and Jerusalem; the leading Kabbalists R. Moses Cordovero, R. Isaac Luria Ashkenazi ("ha-Ari") and R. Hayyim Vital; the Bible commentator R. Moses Alshekh; and the well-known liturgical poets R. Solomon Alkabez and R. Israel Najara.

This "golden age" did not last for long. Some see as the first stage in the crisis the imperial edict by which five hundred or even a thousand Jewish families were to be banished to Cyprus, which had been conquered by the Ottomans in 1571, shortly before the edict was issued. Causing more dire consequences for Safed was the decline in profitability of the trade in woven woolen

The Ark of the Law in the Synagogue of R. Isaac Luria Ashkenazi

goods as a result of cheap European imports. In a matter of a few years this industry totally collapsed, bringing to an end the mythical and glorious age of the Safed Jewish community.

Tiberias

Doña Gracia Nasi leased Tiberias and its surroundings from the authorities in 1560–1561. A water supply system was installed,

community was even established in Acre. During all this time, and afterwards as well, Safed and Tiberias were the main destination for immigrants from eastern Europe who apparently wanted to establish a spiritual center for Hasidism in the Land of Israel. As in earlier times, their encounter with the local Jews (Sefardim from the Ottoman lands and Jews from North Africa) was no easy matter, and there is evidence of tension among the

Tiberias in a photograph by Felix Bonfils, late 19ᵗʰ cent. The photograph was subsequently colored, apparently by his son Adrien

buildings erected, a wall was built around the city, and mulberry trees were planted in order to establish a silk industry. Despite this, few Jews migrated to Tiberias. After the death of Doña Gracia in 1569, the Jews of Tiberias came under the patronage of another court Jew in Istanbul, Don Solomon ibn Ya'ish. After his death a society to aid Tiberias was established in the imperial capital. Jews also settled in nearby villages – Kefar Nahum (Capernaum), Chorazin and Bethsaida – apparently mainly engaging in fishing.

In the course of the first half of the seventeenth century the Jewish communities of Safed and Tiberias to all intents and purposes ceased to exist. A renewed and substantial increase in the Jewish population of Galilee occurred in the second third (and especially the last half) of the eighteenth century due to the efforts to the Istanbul Committee to renew settlement in Tiberias, and to immigration from eastern Europe. Several villages in the area (Shefar'am, Peki'in, Kefar Yasif) were resettled and a Jewish

various ethnic Jewish groups. The powerful earthquake of 1759 dealt a heavy blow to the Jews of Safed, thus encouraging the rise of the community in Tiberias.

Jerusalem

Most of Jerusalem's inhabitants were Muslims, and it continued to be not only a holy city but also an important Muslim theological center, as it had been during the Mamluk period. Many religious academies and Sufi monasteries were active in Jerusalem during the sixteenth century. Christians, too, lived in the Holy City, divided into various denominations: Greek Orthodox, Greek Catholic, Armenians, Roman Catholics, Copts, and others. The status of the Christian communities was unstable. It was determined to a great extent by the standing of their representatives at the Sublime Porte (these were the heads of the Eastern churches or ambassadors of European states in the capital),

235

and by their ability to meet the frequent financial demands. Side by side with the many Christian pilgrims who came to Jerusalem there was a gradually growing number of European travelers and merchants who visited the Holy City. The Jews were a minority, living in the present-day area of the Jewish Quarter.

Throughout the whole period there were tense relations between the various religious communities in the city, although not necessarily on religious grounds. Periods of political unrest, war, or natural disasters made the situation even worse. Most incidents originated in the ruler's desire to extract money from his non-Muslim subjects. Time after time, controversies and court litigation on various levels arose between the Jewish population and the city's rulers over synagogues, the ownership of cemeteries, enforcement of legal restrictions on members of non-Muslim

The Citadel of Jerusalem, rebuilt together with the city walls in the 16th cent. by Sultan Sulayman as part of his great construction enterprise in Jerusalem

communities and the tax rates imposed upon them, and so forth. When an appeal was made to the central government, it intervened and demanded fair treatment in accordance with the law. However, Istanbul was far away and its power greatly limited.

Though the Jerusalem community grew following the expulsions from the Iberian Peninsula in 1492 and 1497, it still lagged behind Safed, which became the Jewish metropolis of the Land of Israel. The Jerusalem Sefardic community included immigrants from all Islamic lands, alongside which lived a small Ashkenazic community. Among the well-known sages living in Jerusalem at the beginning of the sixteenth century were Joseph ben R. Perez Colon from Italy and several Spanish emigrants: R. Jacob Berab, R. Levi ibn Habib, and the Kabbalist R. Abraham ben R. Eliezer ha-Levi. In mid-century the Jerusalem community reached its peak, numbering nearly two thousand persons out of a total population of 15,000. They engaged in commerce, crafts, and agriculture, as well as financial services, while others lived off their savings. Like the other cities in the country, Jerusalem too experienced a certain demographic decline from the late 1560s. A notable deterioration of their situation occurred during the rule of the city governor Abu Sayfeyn, when – among other events – the Synagogue of Nahmanides was closed down in 1586. Towards the end of the century, R. Bezalel Ashkenazi arrived from Egypt, becoming the leading spiritual authority in Jerusalem.

Safed's distress was Jerusalem's gain, as its community gained in importance and from the beginning of the seventeenth century became the predominant Jewish community in the Land of Israel. In addition to those who moved to Jerusalem from Safed, there now came immigrants from Central and Eastern Europe, as well as from Italian city-states. Among the newcomers from Europe was R. Isaiah ha-Levi Horowitz, who came from Prague. At the beginning of the 1620s the Jewish community in the Holy City numbered about 2,000 persons, and perhaps even more. This felicitous condition came to an end when Mehmed ibn Farukh was appointed governor of Jerusalem in 1625. His despotism and greed totally impoverished the community (as they also did to the Christians), many of whose members fled the city while this was still possible. Those who stayed behind were compelled to do forced labor and to pay huge sums, many of them being imprisoned

The Istanbuli Synagogue in Jerusalem, drawing by W.H. Bartlett, early 19th cent.

until they paid. There were even threats that the Jews would be expelled. The community's emissaries aroused the established, well-to-do Jews of Istanbul to action. The latter protested Ibn Farukh's cruelty to the Sublime Porte. Their efforts were crowned with success, and instructions to dismiss Ibn Farukh were sent to the governor of the province at Damascus, but he did not quit Jerusalem until the end of 1626, leaving it "like a pond with no fish." At this time, one Jerusalemite sage printed his book, *Horvot Yerushalayim* (The Ruins of Jerusalem) in Venice. It described the dreadful events of Ibn Farukh's tyranny and stressed the importance of maintaining a continued Jewish presence in Jerusalem. From then on less than 1,000 Jews lived in the Holy City out of a total population of 10,000. It was only towards the end of the seventeenth century that the community slowly began to grow again.

The community was administered in this period by officers chosen by its tax-paying members. The huge debts of the community obliged it to send many envoys to Diaspora countries. The existence of an Ashkenazic congregation with semi-autonomous status within the framework of the Sefardic community gave rise to endless disputes over the distribution of the funds that were sent from Europe, and over the extent of its participation in and obligation towards the financial management of the community at large. Though there was some amelioration of the situation in the following decades, the Jewish community was in a persistent state of debt, which in fact was never wholly settled. In this period relations strengthened

between Jerusalem and the Diaspora communities. Some of the immigrants wrote works describing and praising the Holy Land, and extolling the religious obligation to tender financial support to the sages and poor of the Holy Land.

The growing Jewish population was in need of additional synagogues. Prohibition of the construction of new synagogues forced the Jews to pray in study houses and private homes. The major place of worship was the synagogue known today as "Rabban Johanan ben Zakkai." Next to it was located "*kak tat*" (the Holy Congregation "Study of the Torah") which was later known as the Synagogue of Elijah the Prophet. Apparently the Ashkenazim also had a synagogue in the city that was located within the Ashkenazic courtyard. It was here that the "House of Jacob" Synagogue was erected in the mid-nineteenth century, also know as the "Hurva" Synagogue (*hurva* = ruin, in Hebrew), in memory of the Ashkenazic synagogue that had gone up in flames 130 years earlier.

Among the special outstanding personalities who lived in the Holy City during the seventeenth century were the Kabbalist R. Jacob Zemah, and the intellectual and physician R. Rephael

Interior of the Ramban (Nahmanides) Synagogue in the Jewish Quarter, Jerusalem. Its proximity to the al-'Umari Mosque aroused the Muslim residents to demand the synagogue's closure, which they succeeded in attaining in 1586 after a lengthy conflict

237

Mordechai Malki, both of them former crypto-Jews who had immigrated to Jerusalem and produced many writings there. Another unique individual whose career was linked to Jerusalem was the false messiah Shabbetai Zevi. He arrived in Jerusalem after being expelled from Izmir and wandering through cities in the Balkans. In the early 1660s he lived in Jerusalem and was even sent to Egypt as an emissary of its community, where he made the acquaintance of the Chelebi Rephael Joseph. In Gaza, Nathan

Ashkenazi revealed to Shabbetai Zevi that he was the Messiah. Upon his return to Jerusalem the rabbis rejected his messianic pretensions, warned him, and finally caused him to leave the city. He returned to Gaza and from there traveled to Izmir. Rumors that he was the Messiah circulated throughout the world of Jewry causing great

A broadsheet printed in Amsterdam in 1665, dealing with Shabbetai Zevi

excitement and expectations of approaching Redemption. His conversion to Islam became common knowledge late in 1666, putting an end to the hopes that masses of believers had placed in him. The number of those who believed in him steadily dwindled, particularly after his death in 1676 and the death of his prophet, Nathan of Gaza, in 1680. Jerusalem was apparently one of the few cities in which a group of Sabbatean believers continued to exist even after his conversion to Islam. It is also known that certain emissaries from the Land of Israel during the last third of the seventeenth century were crypto-Sabbateans who exploited their missions to spread Sabbatean rumors among the believers in the Diaspora. Sabbateanism was one of the major factors motivating Jewish immigration to the Land of Israel at the end of the seventeenth and the beginning of the eighteenth centuries. Among such well-known immigrants were R. Judah Hasid and his entourage who came from Europe in 1700, and the wealthy R. Abraham Rovigo who immigrated from Italy with his group in 1702. From Izmir came several sages who tended towards Sabbateanism, including R. Jacob Israel Algazi and R. Hayyim Abulafia.

In the course of the seventeenth century there were various study houses and *yeshivot* active in Jerusalem. Among the most

important was the veteran local yeshivah, "Yeshivat ha-Torah," which was sustained by endowments and contributions from abroad. The "Beth Jacob" (House of Jacob) yeshivah was founded in the middle of the century by the benefactors Jacob and Israel Vega from Leghorn. It was directed by R. Jacob Hagiz (a native of Fez, in Morocco) and after him by R. Moses Galante. Another yeshiva bearing the same name was active in the city in the nineties, named after Jacob Pereira of Amsterdam and directed by R. Hizkiah da Silva.

In the last decade of the seventeenth century great efforts were made once again to raise large sums of money in central and eastern Europe to pay off the debts of the Ashkenazim in Jerusalem. The Jerusalem community was once again in a state of crisis at the beginning of the eighteenth century. The arrival of the entourage of R. Judah Hasid, a plague that broke out in the city, and the revolt of the Naqib al-Ashraf (1703–1705) caused the flight of many of the city's Jews which increased the burden of debt on the remaining members of the community. The Ashkenazim once again fell into debt when they took large loans at high interest rates. Despite the efforts of court Jews and the Austrian ambassador in Istanbul, all efforts to achieve a compromise failed, inducing the Arab creditors to set fire to the Ashkenazic courtyard and its synagogue in 1720. With the establishment in 1726 of the Istanbul Committee of Officers for Jerusalem and its energetic efforts to organize communal life in the Holy Land and to institutionalize support for it, the Jerusalem community once more mounted the path of progress. The debts were spread out over a period of years and the community's affairs were administered by an official who was

R. Joseph Hayyim David Azulai (bynamed "Hida," 1724–1806), one of the great sages of Jerusalem, an emissary, bibliographer, and famous halakhic decisor

238

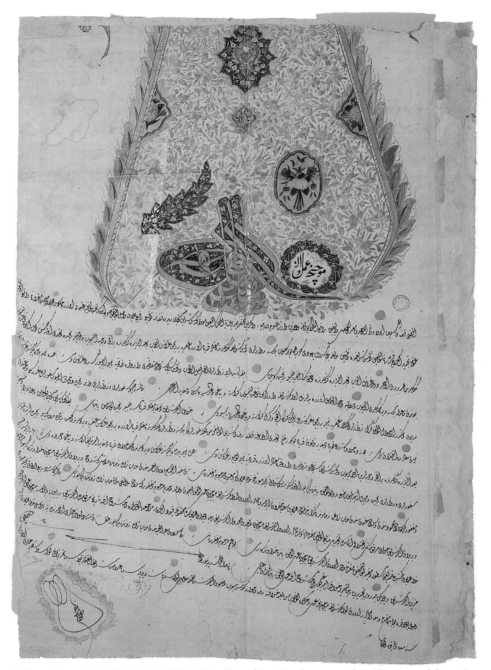

A *firman* (imperial writ) of Sultan Selim III dealing with collecting money from the Jews of Jerusalem

appointed by the committee in Istanbul. The committee did not limit itself to gathering and transferring funds; in fact it dealt with all communal affairs, instituting various regulations and even intervening in appointments and the assignment of sages to the various yeshivot. Despite the constant tension between the committee and its officials in the Land of Israel, on one hand, and the local leadership and elite on the other, the stream of immigrants (many of them poor) grew, and there was a sizeable increase in the city's Jewish population. It was only in the middle

of the eighteenth century that a well ordered, permanent communal organization began to develop, taking its final form in the nineteenth century. The number of Jews in mid-eighteenth century Jerusalem is estimated to have been about 3,000 persons, diminishing once again in the last quarter of the century.

Many important rabbis lived in Jerusalem in the eighteenth century (most of them originating from various Turkish cities), leaving behind them dozens of halakhic essays in manuscript and print. Among the famous personalities who lived or were raised

239

in Jerusalem, R. Hayyim Joseph David Azulai (1724-1806), a native of Jerusalem and fruitful author in many fields who served as an emissary and officiated for many years as the rabbi of Leghorn

Ramlah in an etching by Olbrecht Dapper of 1677 (courtesy of M. Pollak Gallery, Tel Aviv)

in Italy, is outstanding for his biography and intellectual skills.

Several yeshivot were established in the city with donations from Italy, Amsterdam, North Africa, and Turkey. These institutions were named after their founders, who provided support for their maintenance and many scholars. Specially important among them was the Kabbalists' yeshivah, "Beth El" (House of God), founded in 1737. Among those who studied there were Kabbalists who had immigrated from various countries, including some crypto-Sabbateans. Cultural life flourished in Jerusalem, and diverse religious writings were produced there.

We know that two additional synagogues were established in Jerusalem in the eighteenth century adjacent to the older ones: the first being the "Middle" synagogue, while the second, known as the "Istanbuli," was founded later.

Other Communities

The **Hebron** community was generally overshadowed by that of its neighbor, Jerusalem. This community became firmly established after purchase of the famous "courtyard" which became the center of Jewish life in Hebron until the twentieth century. It grew and diversified in the course of the seventeenth century, coming to include the descendants of Musta'arabs, Sefardim, Ashkenazim, and Maghrebis. They lived under more difficult conditions than their brethren in Jerusalem, for they were subject to the arbitrary moods and cruelties of local sheikhs, and sometimes fell victim to hostility among the rival factions in the city. The old Jewish community in **Gaza** continued to exist

until the nineteenth century, although it had dwindled considerably during the eighteenth century. There was a non-permanent Jewish community in **Ramlah** which was an important trading center and which also served as the usual refuge to which the Jews of Jerusalem fled during plagues

The Land of Israel and the Diaspora

The ties between the Diaspora and the Jewish population in the Land of Israel were closer and more widespread during the Ottoman period than in earlier times. From the seventeenth century on, the various Jewish communities in the Land of Israel were totally dependent on financial aid and the stream of immigrants from Diaspora communities. Though political upheavals and wars disrupted these ties, they were never completely severed. The inclusion of Palestine in the Ottoman empire facilitated the formation of especially close ties between communities in Anatolia, the Balkans, the Near East, and Egypt, and the Jews of the Land of Israel. Nor did the authorities prevent the passage of immigrants, emissaries, or funds into Ottoman territory from European lands, which were considered enemy countries. The tradition of extending aid, together with geographic proximity and cultural affinity, seem to have been the chief causes for the increased proportion of former residents of other parts of the Ottoman Empire in the Jewish population of the Land of Israel. Personal and family ties reinforced the special link between the communities in Turkey and the Jews of the Land of Israel beyond the ordinary relationship that always existed between immigrants and their cities of origin or former communities. This relationship was characteristic of the entire period and constituted a basic criterion for the distribution of funds from abroad and an important component in the identity and lifestyle of the immigrants.

What was the conceptual basis of this relationship? Efforts on behalf of the Land of Israel were not only the result of a unique cultural-religious atmosphere, but also a function of economic ability, and in this context, of course, there were differences within the community. The random references in the Jewish sources to immigrants and donors mainly relate to the financial and cultural elite. Middle and upper class Jews, including scholars and congregational officers, are mentioned as being involved in all affairs having to do with the Land of Israel, as office holders in the congregations, and as having the means to contribute and bequeath sizeable sums for the Torah scholars and the poor in the Land of Israel.

The absence of a clear-cut decision between the conflicting opinions of Maimonides and Nahmanides as to whether the commandment of settling in the Land of Israel was obligatory in the present, left much leeway for the halakhic decisors of the period, who adopted a rather pragmatic approach: the Land of Israel and its inhabitants have great virtue, but this is not a commandment from the Torah, and although residing there has "some aspect of fulfilling a commandment," priority is still given to those who seek the welfare of their families in the Diaspora. The practical implications of this approach were reflected in the responsa by sages living in Islamic countries to the recurrent questions posed to them concerning marital separation when one member of a married couple wanted to immigrate to the Land of Israel, or in cases in which someone reneged on a vow to immigrate there, as well as in controversies over changing the specified use of religious trust funds. There were three major opinions in this period concerning the issues of the status of, immigration to, and settlement in the Land of Israel:

A) A messianic outlook that viewed immigration to and settling in the Land of Israel, taken together with the study of Kabbalah and prayer, as a means to hasten Redemption. This view was commonly held by sages of Spanish origin who engaged in the study of Kabbalah in the sixteenth century. It almost completely disappeared during the first six decades of the next century, but was reawakened with even greater intensity in the wake of the Sabbatean movement. Although Sabbatean doctrine did not ascribe special importance to the Land of Israel, its followers considered the Land of Israel to be the arena of the future revelation of Shabbetai Zevi which would be followed by final Redemption. The immigration of such persons to the Land of Israel in the course of the first half of the eighteenth century was closely linked to various calculations of the End of Days. It was against such a background that several members of the Kabbalistic circle in Brod, which was connected to the first Hasidim, settled in the Land of Israel during the second half of that century.

B) A traditional, more neutral, approach was accepted by most Jews throughout the centuries. It was based on belief in the power of prayer and study in the Land of Israel, and on the virtue of burial in its hallowed soil. Such beliefs were widely accepted by Jews in the Islamic countries and, in conjunction with the circumstances noted above, was the reason for their being the majority of the Jewish population in Palestine until the nineteenth century. Throughout the Ottoman period, ancient concepts about the importance of living in the Land of Israel, immigration to it and burial there were reformulated, developed, and widely diffused. The Kabbalistic scholars who lived in

sixteenth-century Safed were especially instrumental in shaping such concepts, stressing motifs such as that the sins of those who reside in the Holy Land would be forgiven, or that it was advantageous to be buried in its soil. More frequent appeals by Jews in Palestine for financial aid from abroad made Jews conscious of the mutual relationship between the Land of Israel and the Diaspora and instilled a constant awareness of the importance of a continuous community there, and of the vital necessity of preserving its ancient cemeteries and holy places. The explicit demand for material support as being an obligation of Diaspora Jewry appeared only in the eighteenth century. Such support was now conceived as being active participation in this important endeavor, and no longer just an act which bestowed

Detail from the map on p. 224, Italy, 18th cent. The name "Midrash Shelomo" appears above a structure in the center, thus adopting the Crusader designation of al-Aqsa Mosque as "Solomon's Temple"

on the donors a reward from Heaven.

C) The third outlook was one of total rejection, for practical and ideological reasons, of the sanctity of the Land of Israel and the importance of residing there. This stance prevailed among certain Jewish segments, chiefly among former crypto-Jews in Western Europe. Many believed that enough Jewish capital had been forwarded from Jewish communities throughout the world to the Land of Israel, and that they must now first care for their own poor. There were even those who totally rejected the importance and significance of the Land of Israel for the Jewish

241

ספר

שפת אמת

לבקשת השואל נדפס

באמשטרדם

Title page of *Sfat Emet* by R. Moses Hagiz (Amsterdam, 1707), a book advocating the merits of the Land of Israel and of residing there

People and attributed no importance at all to residing within its borders. Some of these extreme opinions were documented in the polemical work of R. Moses Hagiz, *Sfat Emet* (Language of Truth; Amsterdam, 1707) that set out to defend the virtue of the Land of Israel. In the second half of the eighteenth century such opinions reappeared among Jewish intellectuals in Germany, from where they were adopted by European Reform Judaism.

Immigrants and Immigration

... When our eyes see this awakening among men of renown in the cities of Turkey, the Maghreb, Ashkenaz, and Poland who, even though they live at a far distance did not avoid coming along, and every year there are caravans of visitors who come, some to reside and settle down, and some at least to prostrate themselves... (R. Moses Hagiz, *Sfat Emet*, p. 25b).

In the sixteenth century Palestine was blessed with favorable political and economic conditions. In this period its Jewish population was "normal" from the demographic and economic standpoint, and even a cross-section of the immigrants shows diversification, including entire families and people of all ages and social classes.

The harsh reality that prevailed once again from the end of that century – difficulties of earning a livelihood, a heavy tax burden, and the cruelty of the local Arabs (described over and over again

in the writs that accompanied emissaries and verified by those who returned to or left the country) – produced a real image of the Land of Israel which could not have served as an incentive for mass immigration, not to speak of attracting young families. And indeed, the image of the Land of Israel had lost all its real, earthly attributes; it was now conceived as an abstract, hallowed essence. Its characterization as a place of burial was visually reinforced by portrayals of the holy places and tombs adorning synagogues in many lands. From the seventeenth century on, we find a return to the traditional pattern of immigration that was typical of earlier periods: immigration of individuals only (the elderly and scholars), who lived on allocations and grants from their communities of origin. The number of immigrants was large enough to balance out the natural decrease in population, and in the absence of genealogical continuity there was a rather speedy turnover of the Jewish population in the country. The two main groups among the immigrants were scholars and elderly widows, whose ideal was limited to study, prayer, and burial in the soil of the Holy Land. Young scholars came to study in the yeshivot of Safed and Jerusalem, later returning to their own countries in search of employment. Others came in their old age to spend their final years and die in the Land of Israel. Students of the Torah, on various levels of erudition, formed a significant element in the Jewish community of the Land of Israel, and it would seem that their proportion in the population even increased throughout the eighteenth century. The percentage of elderly widows among the immigrants was especially high, and the responsa literature contains dozens of references to women immigrants, including members of families of renowned scholars. At this stage of their lives, these women had concluded their social obligation to produce and raise offspring. Their dowries and inheritances granted them some degree of independence and the ability to finance their journey and ensure a limited sustenance, so that they could devote themselves to prayer, the performance of ritual commandments, and the acquisition of a burial plot in one of the four "holy cities."

The importance attached to burial in the soil of the Holy Land also explains the widespread phenomenon of bringing remains of deceased men for burial in the Land of Israel, usually in Jerusalem. That this was a widespread custom is attested to by both Jewish and non-Jewish sources:

The flesh consumed, they dig up the bones of those that are of their families whereof whole bark-fuls not seldome do arriva at Ioppa to be conveyed and again interred at Ierusalem imagining that it doth adde delight unto the soules that did owe them and that they shall have a quicker dispatch in the general iudgement... (George Sandys, *A Relation of a Journey begun in 1610*, London 1615).

Whoever could not finance the transfer of his bones to the Holy Land after his death made the effort to at least have earth from the Land of Israel placed in his grave. Others – few in number – came for sundry reasons. For example, some of the immigrants in the late seventeenth and the first third of the eighteenth centuries were Sabbatean believers who, relying on various calculations of the End of Days, looked to a second and final revelation of Shabbetai Zevi in the Land of Israel. Some hoped to produce, through their immigration, a certain dynamic that would hasten Redemption. A quite unusual group was comprised of indigent Jews who arrived from Amsterdam in the third and fourth decades of the seventeenth century (and perhaps later) not of their own free will. The leaders of the Portuguese Jewish community had sought to rid themselves of this element and sent them eastwards. One of the destinations was the Land of Israel, and these immigrants were provided with an annual sum after their arrival.

The immigrants made lengthy preparations for the voyage. They had to raise the money to pay for the journey, to sell or distribute their property, to purchase goods that they would need in the future, and – above all – to ensure their sustenance in the Holy Land. Bringing with them a large sum of capital was not usual nor was it recommended, and whoever was able to do so made arrangements with his heirs, legal representatives or business partners, so that he would enjoy a fixed yearly allocation after his immigration. Transfers to beneficiaries in Palestine were executed by means of promissory notes and by the use of a sophisticated credit system. The first stage in the journey was to reach a port of embarkation in Italy or the Levant from where ships sailed to the shores of the Land of Israel at regular intervals, mainly in the summer months. The port of Istanbul was one of the most important points of departure in the eastern Mediterranean basin, also serving immigrants from eastern and central Europe. There were those who availed themselves of the opportunity to have their books printed in one of the printing establishments in the area. Sailing was dangerous, since the forces of nature and pirates were a constant threat in this region. Pirates were especially pleased to take hapless Jews captive since they were sure to be ransomed. The journey, conducted under difficult conditions, was rather costly. In addition to money to pay for passage and food, one needed to fit oneself out with various items, and upon arrival in the Land of Israel it was necessary to pay taxes and duties, such as a road tax and at times even a poll tax. Every ship carried dozens, or even hundreds, of passengers in addition to merchandise, and many of the travelers were Jews. The ships anchored at Rhodes and Cyprus, where the passengers replenished their supply of fresh food and made other purchases, from where they continued to Sidon, Acre, and Jaffa. Another, perhaps more popular route, led to Egypt and then overland along the coast to Gaza, Ramlah, and Jerusalem. Dangers lurked on these roads, making an escort of Ottoman soldiers a necessity.

The immigrants were in regular contact with their cities of origin and families. This was a vital connection, for in the absence of regular support it would prove to be difficult to live in the country for an extended period of time. Such ties were also important for the immigrants' morale, and some took care to ensure that they would not be forgotten even after their death.

A ship approaching Jaffa, from *Konstantinopel und Jerusalem* by Solomon Schweigger, Nürnberg, 1608

Those who sought to take up residence turned to acquaintances (people from their hometowns or local brokers) to help them find a place to live. The Ashkenazim had an especially hard time since they spoke neither Arabic nor Ladino (the Judeo-Spanish language of the local Jews). The increasing number of Ashkenazim in the eighteenth century reinforced their inclination to break away from the Sefardi community.

Not all the travelers came with the purpose of staying; some came for relatively short periods of time (mostly around the holidays) in order to visit sacred tombs. Pilgrimage was a well-established custom throughout the Middle Ages, an expression of popular faith in the special qualities attached to tombs of holy men. In many cases, immigration was the fulfillment of a vow made at a time of duress, somewhat like a charm against death or severe disease. Pilgrimage sites were concentrated in two areas: Galilee, where many of the sites had been discovered or identified when the Safed Jewish community was at its height; and Jerusalem and its vicinity. Among the most important sites was Nabi Samwil, the tomb of the Prophet Samuel, which also attracted local residents and served as a significant source of income for the

243

Jerusalem Jewish community. On the traditionally accepted anniversaries of the death of certain holy men, popular

בדקהכת משב וקמט צדקה מאור בסןהחזבי ירושלים ד'מארבה

Charity collection boxes in the synagogue in Firenze, 17th cent. The proceeds of the two boxes on the left were intended for the Jews in the Land of Israel

celebrations were held at their supposed tombs with the participation of local residents and pilgrims. The Tomb of Rachel and the Tomb of Simon the Just were also popular destinations for pilgrims, and of course the Tomb of the Patriarchs in Hebron as well as additional, more isolated, tomb sites throughout the area. In the eighteenth century various guidebooks were written providing the pilgrim with travel routes, as well as instructions and prayers to be recited at each site.

The large number of pilgrims during the seventeenth and eighteenth centuries is reflected in contemporary sources. Pilgrimage was described in itineraries written by both Jews and Christians, and incidental testimonies have survived about overcrowding and jamming in the synagogues when the pilgrims were in town. This situation led to the composition and printing of many books and pamphlets dealing with the holy places. In the responsa literature we find several discussions as to whether pilgrims were obliged to celebrate two full, consecutive holy days on the festivals of Sukkot, Passover and Shavuot, as Diaspora Jews are required to do, whereas Jews living in the Land of Israel are obligated to celebrate only one day.

. . . .

Economic Aid and Political Support

Until the decline of Safed, the Jewish community in the Land of Israel was almost in no need of aid from abroad. Safed's severe crisis and the extensive efforts that were made on behalf of its Jewish community towards the end of the sixteenth century signify the beginning of organized support for the Jews in Palestine. More and more emissaries were sent to gather money,

and in many Diaspora cities special funds were established for that purpose. Basically, contributions for the Holy Land were made on a voluntary basis, and the donors believed that the merits of study and prayer in the Land of Israel could save them and were beneficial to their souls in both this world and the next. Women accounted for a large percentage of the donors. Prayers were recited in the synagogues of the Land of Israel for the welfare of Diaspora communities and special blessings were said for contributors and the officers of the special funds. In the seventeenth century there was as yet no universally held concept that assistance to the Land of Israel was tantamount to a duty, since the inhabitants of the Holy Land atoned for the sins of all Diaspora Jews and their prayers were beneficial to all Jewry. It seems that *Sfat Emet*, by R. Jacob Hagiz, was a landmark in this respect, and only from the eighteenth century onwards do the emissaries' writs of authority contain an explicit demand that Diaspora Jews donate funds for their brethren in the Holy Land.

We should distinguish between the voluntary contributions of individuals and the institutionalized efforts of the community. As for individuals, in the absence of means to finance immigration to the Land of Israel, or to bequeath or endow for such purposes, the contribution of the Jewish lower classes was limited to putting a small coin into the collection box for the Land of Israel in the synagogue, or to responding to this or that emergency fund appeal. Those better off could make one-off donations of relatively large sums, either as endowments or as bequests. These funds were generally contributed while specifying the beneficiary: the poor of a certain community, those studying Torah in one of the holy cities, or "the poor of the Land of Israel" in general. Funds that were sent without a specified purpose were assigned to cover debts, and sometimes disputes broke out over the manner of their allocation. Pilgrims to the Land of Israel used to give alms generously upon their arrival.

On the congregational or communal level there were diverse patterns of fundraising, depending on the organizational tradition customary in each country. For example, Ottoman Jewry dealt with matters concerning the Land of Israel in a

244

manner different from that of Italian Jewry, which at that time conducted diverse, much more meticulous efforts. In the cities of the Ottoman Empire the person responsible for organizing this aid was the congregational rabbi, and only from the eighteenth century did this responsibility pass to the general officers of the congregation. Money raising efforts by means of funds and societies, the usual form in Italy and Europe, was not customary in Turkey and the Balkans.

Formal recognition of the duty to assist the Land of Israel and of the importance of a continuous Jewish presence there took two forms: financial assistance, and reduced communal taxes for those who intended to immigrate to the Land of Israel. In contrast to the big and irregular fundraising efforts of the late sixteenth century, in which money, cloth, and food were collected and sent, the major component in seventeenth-century aid was financial. In the budgets of the Jewish communities of Istanbul and other cities in the second half of the seventeenth century one could find a sum of money that was annually transferred to Jerusalem, Safed, Tiberias, and Hebron, the "four holy cities," and distributed among them by a pre-set formula of allocation. This sum was funded by regular taxes that each community collected from its members. Some of the income from fines imposed by individuals on themselves or by the public were also designated for the poor of the Holy Land. Many communities enacted ordinances that reduced taxes to be paid by immigrants to the Land of Israel. Whereas any person who left the city was obliged to pay taxes for two or three years, and if he left property behind he was still considered a resident, the immigrant was released from this obligation and sometimes he was exempted from paying taxes on the property that he left behind, so that he would be able to provide for himself during his residence in the Land of Israel.

The monies collected were apparently coordinated in each congregation by a "treasurer of [the poor] of the Land of Israel," and when emissaries from the Holy Land arrived, the treasurers examined their trustworthiness, read the writs of delegation that they carried, and gave them some of the funds. Not all the money was transmitted through the emissaries. Many communities preferred to dispatch the funds directly to the holy cities. Since it was not customary to make transfers of funds in cash, on account of the danger involved, they used promissory notes that were an accepted means of payment in interurban and international trade, and were also accepted by Muslim creditors in Jerusalem. The responsa literature of the period is replete with questions dealing with donated funds and their transfer, and with controversies over who should take priority – the local poor, or the indigent and the sages of the Holy Land.

The Emissaries and the Centers for Fundraising on Behalf of the the Land of Israel

They however send from Saphet some of their Rabbins of the greatest learning and integrity to Constantinople, Smyrna and other trading cities of the Ottoman empire where wealthy Jews reside, and some of them even visit Germany, Holland, England and other places not subject to the Inquisition collecting by this means considerable sums to be distributed among the Jews at Jerusalem, Hebron, and Saphet though the greatest part always falls to the latter... (Van Egmont and Heyman, *Travels*, II, p. 42).

As already noted, there were no fixed patterns in the sixteenth century by which support was tendered to the Jewish population of the Land of Israel. As we have seen, it was the difficult conditions resulting from the collapse of the Safed community that led to an increasing number of emissaries being sent to the Diaspora countries to collect funds. It was during that century that the dispatch of envoys became standard practice. From the second quarter of the seventeenth century onwards, emissaries from the "holy cities" began to set out regularly for the Diaspora, bearing

R. Isaac Carigal of Hebron, the first emissary to arrive on a fundraising mission in America in 1773

245

"general" and "particular" writs of delegation. The texts of these writs were quite similar, with only the relevant details being changed from time to time. The authors described the size of the Jewish population, recounted its difficult condition at length and with exaggeration, detailed the burden of debts from loans taken at high interest, and stressed the immediate destructive results that would ensue should these debts not be paid: an end to Jewish presence in the cities of the Holy Land and the destruction of synagogues and cemeteries. Four geographic regions for such missions evolved in time: the "mission of Turkey," the most important and prestigious, which included the communities of Anatolia and the Balkans; "the mission of Francia" was the most promising from the financial standpoint and included the communities of Italy and Western Europe; "the mission of the Maghreb," that is, the North African countries; and "the mission of Arabistan," which included communities in Syria, Iraq, and Persia. The itinerant emissary traveled to cities large and small, collected money for the Land of Israel from special funds designated for this purpose, and mounted additional fundraising campaigns. Procedures were also established in the communities for the further collection of funds. In many places the emissary, who was a rabbi, would deliver sermons that were intended to encourage the public to open its purse-strings. When the envoy returned, the funds were distributed (after deducting his expenses and salary) among the holy cities according to a formula that reflected their relative size and importance. Only in exceptional cases did emissaries set out on behalf of a particular group, such as the Italians, and from the mid-seventeenth century for the Ashkenazim as well. This was the cause of constant tension and conflict between the Sefardi majority and the Ashkenazim over entitlement to funds for the Land of Israel collected in European countries. The Sefardic community, whom the Ottoman authorities held responsible for all the Jews in Palestine, demanded to receive the funds, while the Ashkenazim, seeking to keep them for themselves, complained about this situation in Europe. In the final analysis these struggles dealt a blow to donations in general.

The Sefardim divided the revenues collected by the emissaries into three parts – payment of taxes and maintenance of institutions; sustenance for some designated individuals and scholars, according to their degree of importance (on the basis of a *lista*, a fixed list); support for the poor, the sick, and the needy. The Ashkenazim, in contrast, considered these funds to be a kind of salary, an obligatory payment by the Jews of the Diaspora to their brethren living in Zion, and for that reason they distributed the money to all – in accordance with the number of members of each family without taking into account class, occupation, or

The writ of an emissary sent to the Maghreb

income. In reality, the funds were not equally distributed because some received grants from two or three sources, even if they were not in need of them.

The emissaries were part of a widespread framework that was engaged in the collection, concentration, and transfer of funds for the Land of Israel from the Diaspora. In the various countries, certain cities (centers of trade or ports) served as focal points for these efforts. These centers changed from time to time as a result of demographic, economic, and political changes. The close connection between Egypt and Palestine since the Mamluk period was weakened after the sixteenth century, and the decline of the Salonica community also led to a reduction of its involvement in the affairs of the Holy Land. In the seventeenth century there were several regional centers for gathering funds, such as Algiers which served as a transfer point for monies raised in North Africa, and Lvov (Lemberg) where funds from eastern Europe were concentrated. In the middle of the seventeenth century this latter center shifted to Frankfurt am Main, Leghorn replaced Venice as the center in Italy, and in western Europe the wealthy community of Amsterdam was an especially prominent focus of activity on behalf of the Jews of the Land of Israel, while

Vienna, Prague, and Frankfurt also served to transfer contributions from central Europe. Venice, which had channeled funds from all over to the Land of Israel as early as the beginning of the seventeenth century, was replaced in this function by the Istanbul community that from now became the leading factor in transferring financial aid to the Jewish communities in the Holy Land. In the absence of restrictions on the transfer of funds (which did exist in several European states), Istanbul served as a world crossroads for aid, even at times of financial distress for the Ottoman empire, such as in the late seventeenth century.

By the beginning of the eighteenth century it was clear to all – including the Jerusalem community's Muslim creditors – that the source of that community's livelihood and leadership lay in Istanbul. After lengthy negotiations among Jews in the Diaspora in the wake of the crisis that reached its peak in the setting afire of the courtyard of the Ashkenazim in Jerusalem, a committee of officials was established in Istanbul in 1726 to help the Jews of Jerusalem. Within a few years there were other committees to aid the other holy cities – Hebron (1733), Tiberias (1740), and Safed (1742). The committees took it upon themselves to maintain contacts with the authorities, to organize the collection of funds in the various communities and the proper use of these funds, to supervise and organize the emissary system, and to make arrangements for immigration to the Land of Israel. The initiative known as "the collection of the *para*" (1728) is worthy of special mention. Each and every individual was supposed to contribute a para (a small coin, the fortieth part of a *grush*) each week. However, the public response did not meet expectations, and the officials subsequently imposed in its place a kind of annual tax on every community in the Ottoman Empire. In practice, the Istanbul officials also administered the Jerusalem community and, to a lesser extent, those in the other three cities as well. They enacted various ordinances, shaped the communal leadership, and intervened in choosing communal officers and sages of the yeshivot.

Such centers of aid on behalf of the Jews in the Land of Israel also arose in eastern Europe in the second half of the eighteenth century: funds to aid the Hasidim were collected in Reisen (Rydzyna), while donations for non-Hasidic Ashkenazi Jews were concentrated in Shklov. A "Committee of Officers and Clerks" was established in Amsterdam in 1809 to collect funds throughout western Europe (mainly for the Prushim), to administer their transfer to the Holy Land and their fair allocation, while also making collection more efficient and increasing the sums donated. Like their forerunners, the members of the Lehren family, who led this committee for decades, demanded the exclusive right to conduct fundraising and to

determine how the monies be allocated through their appointed representatives. Their influence steadily increased, and in practice they administered the affairs of most of the Jewish population in the Land of Israel until the end of the nineteenth century.

Political Assistance

The status of the Jews in the Land of Israel was dependent to a great extent on the state of their relationship with those who wielded power on the local level – the governor of Damascus, the district governors of Jerusalem and Safed, the *qadi* (Muslim judge) of Jerusalem, and the like. Hence, the existence of a wealthy, well-connected Jewish community in Istanbul, capital of the Empire, was most important. The presence of influential Jews at the Sultan's court enabled the Jerusalem community to intervene through them in the choice of officials who would be amenable to the Jews before they left the capital to serve in the vilayet of Damascus or in Jerusalem itself, or at least to foster connections with them. It seems that in the last quarter of the sixteenth century a rather routine pattern emerged. When problems arose whose solution were beyond the capacity of the local leaders they appealed to their contacts in Istanbul, the heads of congregations and leading scholars, who, by virtue of their status in the community, appealed to Jews who had connections at court, requesting that they do whatever was necessary. These communal lobbyists were wealthy financiers, court provisioners, physicians, and those whose professions brought them into daily and close contact with the powerful men of the state. When the lobbyists were successful, edicts, orders, and warnings were sent to the governor of Jerusalem and to the qadi to treat the local Jews in accordance with the *shari'a* (Islamic religious law), that is, in accordance with accepted canons and norms. The continuing willingness of wealthy Jews with relations at the imperial court and acquainted with the powerful statesmen to use their knowledge, connections, and influence to help the Jewish community in the Land of Israel in various ways (usually without tangible compensation and at certain personal sacrifice) was a noteworthy phenomenon, although we know nothing of their motives or attitudes towards the Jews of the Holy Land. In any case, it was no accident that the Committee of Officers of Jerusalem was established in Istanbul.

Monopolization by the Istanbul community of political assistance to the communities in the Land of Israel came to an end in the eighteenth century, when we find active intervention by court Jews in European capitals. One such case is that of Samson Wertheimer who utilized his connections at the court of the Habsburg emperor to have the Austrian ambassador to

247

The blessing "Me'eyn Shalosh" which is recited after eating various kinds of grains and fruits for which the Land of Israel is renowned. An illustrated folio by Samuel Dreznitz of Moravia, 1755. (IMJ 177\65)

the Sublime Porte help in coming to an arrangement for settling the debts of the Ashkenazic Jews in Jerusalem.

Spiritual and Cultural Ties

In the spiritual and cultural sphere, it was the Land of Israel that contributed to the Diaspora, particularly to cities in Turkey and Italy with which extremely close relationships had been formed. Constant mobility back and forth by sages on all levels enhanced the network of cultural ties between the Land of Israel and the Diaspora communities.

The concentration of so many sages of Spanish descent in Safed, in unique historical circumstances, produced rich and diverse works in the fields of secular and religious poetry, Kabbalah, biblical commentary, ethics, and religious law. From the last quarter of the sixteenth century many of these works began to find their way abroad to the Jewish communities in the Diaspora, sent by their authors to be printed there, borne by sages who emigrated from the Land of Israel, by emissaries of the holy cities or others who were emissaries on their own behalf, and by pilgrims returning to their countries of origin. They took with them original manuscripts and copies, and during their wanderings spread oral traditions, religious legal rulings, traditions, and customs. The behavior of those coming from the

Holy Land served as living testimony to the Land of Israel customs, and they were sometimes asked what was customary in the Land of Israel in regard to a certain aspect of religious life. Traditions of the Kabbalah of Safed, which played an important role in this cultural interchange, were disseminated in this manner, especially pious usages and customs in the spirit of the Kabbalah that were customary among the Kabbalistic fellowships in Safed (such as customs and usages in welcoming the Sabbath, readings for the night of Shavuot [Pentecost] and Shmini Azeret, the recital of penitential prayers at night in study groups and prayer fellowships, etc.). Many of the works of the Safed sages were published in printing shops in Turkey and Italy, a fact that aided in their dissemination. It was in this very period that the *Shulhan Arukh* ("A Set Table"), the renowned compendium of Jewish law by R. Joseph Caro, was spreading throughout the world of Jewry. Together with *Ha-Mappah* ("The Tablecloth") of R. Moses Isserles, it was fast becoming the fundamental work guiding the general public and the halakhic decisors everywhere.

The prestige of the Land of Israel continued to be a weighty factor in the seventeenth and eighteenth centuries. Even when it was clear to all that the true centers of Torah study were far removed from the Holy Land, people continued to treat the Land of Israel and its sages as being of the first order. However, the abundance of expressions referring to the prestige and merits of the yeshivot in the holy cities and their sages was no more than lip service. Many of the sages of the Land of Israel had come from cities in the Ottoman Empire and were well aware of their own standing when compared with that of the great scholars in the yeshivot in which they had studied. That many halakhic questions were referred from the Land of Israel to the most esteemed rabbis of Istanbul clearly demonstrates acceptance of the latter's spiritual hegemony. In the same manner, the Ashkenazim in the Holy Land continued to have recourse to the decisions and opinions of rabbis in eastern Europe.

From the middle of the seventeenth century, the presence of the Holy Land emissaries was a regular feature in Diaspora communities. They played an especially important role in the lives of the small communities, responding to halakhic questions, initiated communal ordinances, arbitrated disputes, and gave court decisions as well as certificates and appointments. In all these activities their informal authority stemmed from the sanctity of the Land of Israel. The dissemination of the teachings of the Land of Israel by the emissaries was not limited to one field, and they also communicated halakhic practices, as well as innovations in Torah, Kabbalah, and liturgical poetry. Among the well-known emissaries in the seventeenth century were the Kabbalists R.

Benjamin ha-Levi and R. David Habilio. Several envoys played an important role in spreading the Sabbatean faith, and later in disseminating Sabbatean teachings among the "crypto-believers." In the eighteenth century, many emissaries were involved in several bitter controversies that raged in Jewish communities in Europe, particularly concerning after-growths of Sabbateanism (the struggle against Nehemiah Hiyya Hayun and the great controversies regarding R. Moses Hayyim Luzzatto and R. Jonathan Eybeschutz). In this period the number of emissaries from the Land of Israel increased significantly, and many brought with them their own works or those of their associates to be printed during their travels, and later distributed or sold the books.

The composition, printing, and influence of the volume *Hemdat Yamim* ("The Delight of Days") well illustrate this point. The book was first published anonymously in Izmir in 1733 without rabbinical endorsements, contrary to conventional practice at that time. The man who had it published, R. Jacob Algazi, ascribed it to an anonymous author in the Land of Israel, claiming to have brought the manuscript "from the holy mountain of the Upper Galilee." We now know that the book was in fact an anthology of various works written and edited by a group of several Izmir sages who were crypto-Sabbateans. Algazi himself, a native of Izmir, visited the Land of Israel in the 1720s. After the book was printed he immigrated to Jerusalem where

he joined the Kabbalist yeshivah "Beth El" and became one of the leading rabbis in the city. The book was widely circulated and went through a number of editions in Turkey, Italy, and elsewhere in Europe, even though it was suspect of Sabbateanism. It was greatly influential in spreading customs of piety in the spirit of Sabbatean Kabbalah, and contributed considerably to shaping Judaism in the eighteenth century.

The period from the sixteenth to the eighteenth centuries was one in which the Jewish population in the Land of Israel was placed on a firm demographic footing. The importance of the Jewish community in the Holy Land was not dependent upon its ethnic composition or its size, which knew many ups and downs. Its major importance lay in that it maintained – at a high cost – a continuum of Jewish presence in the country. During this period of continuous presence, the patterns of the relationship between the Land of Israel and the Jewish communities in the Diaspora that would be characteristic of the modern era were shaped and developed. Above all, recognition of the merits of study and prayer in the Holy Land, and of extending financial and political support to its Jewish residents became widespread. These are values that from now on would play a central role in Jewish national consciousness, and especially in making the Land of Israel dear to every Jew.

A page from *Limud shel Tu bi-Shevat* – a special order of study for the Fifteenth of Shevat (New Year of the Trees) influenced by the book *Hemdat Yamim*. Illuminated manuscript written in Sohar (Oman), 1805 (JNUL MS. Yah. Heb. 145\2)

Windmill in the Yemin Moshe neighborhood in Jerusalem

The Late Ottoman Period (1775–1917)

Yehoshua Kaniel

Government and Administration

The late eighteenth century did not presage any dramatic changes, although several events may have signaled future developments in certain aspects of nineteenth-century Palestine. Napoleon's campaign, that ended in failure before the walls of Acre (1799), was not the beginning of a new era. Yet, it did attest to the role of the country within the context of the policy of the European great powers as they pushed eastwards extending and defending their strategic and economic interests. In the framework of this policy the Holy Land, too, became a focus of interest and competition. As for the Jewish population, this was a period of renewed group immigration from Europe – first of Hasidim (1764, 1777) and, at the beginning of the nineteenth century (1809), of their adversaries, the Prushim, disciples of Rabbi Elijah, the "Gaon of Vilna." These groups laid the foundation for renewed communal organization in the four holy cities – Jerusalem, Hebron, Safed, and Tiberias – communities that constantly attracted newcomers throughout the nineteenth century. Thus a rather solid foundation was laid for the continuous rise in immigration that characterized the Jewish population of the Land of Israel in that century.

The period of Ahmed al-Jazzar Pasha (1775–1804), a cruel and powerful ruler, was to a great extent a continuation in its nature of that of Daher al-'Umar, who was killed in 1775. The weak central government did not exhibit a close interest in remote, out-of-the-way districts, thus enabling the rise of semi-independent local rulers who continued to demonstrate formal ties to the imperial court, mainly through payment of taxes. Jazzar, who was *wali* of Sidon, exerted his control chiefly over the north of the country, but it also extended southwards to Jaffa. He won glory in his campaign against Napoleon's invading army, but was also the subject of reserve and suspicion due to his increased power. Under his rule the country enjoyed a period of prosperity. He established an effective and

A Turkish gold coin, 1840

251

centralized administration, enforced order and security, and invested efforts in developing economic ties with European merchants, encouraging them to have their ships call at Acre which he fortified (his construction efforts there are evident to this very day). Jazzar treated the population cruelly and harshly, yet he also knew how to attract elements that suited his interests. His advisors included Jews and Christians, among them Hayyim Farhi who served him in the capacity of financial advisor and minister in charge of finances. This did not prevent Jazzar in a fit of anger from gouging out one of Farhi's eyes and cutting off his nose. His successors,

Sulayman (1804–1818) and 'Abdallah (1818–1831), continued the tradition of local strongmen, but did not leave their mark on the country.

An outstanding, significant change occurred during the short reign of Muhammad 'Ali and his son Ibrahim Pasha in Syria-

serve as the basis for a local bureaucracy subject to supervision by the central administration. One can also discern the first signs of a transfer of jurisdiction from religious courts to members of the district councils that were established at that time. A gradual reform of tax collection was initiated, with the intention of

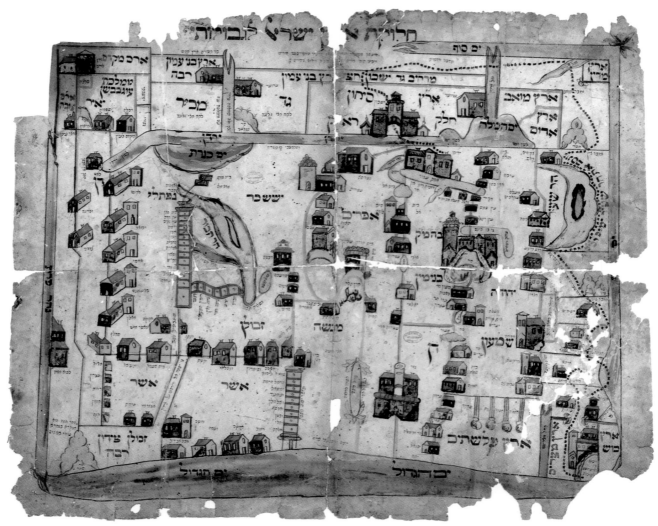

Map of the Land of Israel, hand-drawn after R. Eliahu b. Shlomo Zalman ("the Gaon of Vilna"), early 19ᵗʰ cent. (JNUL Pal. 1001)

Palestine (1831–1841). The country was thrown into turmoil when Muhammad 'Ali, the Ottoman governor of Egypt, decided to embark on a campaign of conquest. Ibrahim Pasha commanded a large, powerful, and well-organized Egyptian army in the conquest of Syria and Palestine, and then imposed a centralized regime with a well-ordered, firm administration. His seat of government was in Damascus, while Palestine was part of the Province of Sidon. Egyptian military governors were set over the various districts, but Jazzar also appointed local members of notable families to fill senior positions. Influenced by European conceptions, he began to set up an administrative hierarchy to

weakening the old feudal structure and shifting the focus of power to the central government, and compulsory military conscription was proclaimed. A poll tax was imposed on the entire population and firm measures were adopted to abolish the road tax heretofore generally collected by vicious sheikhs. There was significant improvement in security conditions: the Bedouin tribes were forcefully restrained and attempts were even made to settle them in permanent locations in the Jordan Valley and the southern part of the land, while fortified guard posts were set up along the roads and the number of soldiers patrolling them was increased. Improved conditions encouraged the development of trade and agriculture. New crops were introduced and the export of oil, wines, soap, and other goods was encouraged. The government even planned to bring Egyptian peasant farmers to the region, a scheme that was implemented only to a limited extent. The Egyptian authorities' open policy towards the European powers,

them of economic, political, and military power. Wide segments of the population, especially in the villages, rose up in opposition to the mercilessly enforced military draft, and against the harsh and effective collection of taxes. And, indeed, in 1834 a peasant revolt broke out encompassing all of the country's mountainous

Ahmed al-Jazzar sitting in judgment; his advisor, Hayyim Farhi, whose eye the ruler had commanded to be gouged out, is standing above the accused. Painting by Francis Brookhill Spilsbury, a physician with the British fleet, first printed in 1823

whose support they wished to gain, was also manifested in the tolerant treatment of the Christian and Jewish minorities. They were granted representation on district councils, age-old religious restrictions imposed upon them were abolished, and they were allowed to renew and renovate educational and religious institutions. The Jewish community of Jerusalem, for example, was permitted to renovate the ancient Sefardic synagogues, while the 'Menahem Zion' Synagogue of the Ashkenazic congregation was built on the site of the ruins of the synagogue of R. Judah he-Hasid in the Jewish Quarter.

This new administrative and social policy of the rulers struck hard at the former holders of power, arousing much apprehension among them. The status of Muslim religious circles was impaired by the limitation of their powers of jurisdiction, while they looked with great disfavor upon the granting of status and rights to the non-Muslim minorities. Some went so far as to declare Ibrahim Pasha an unbeliever. The feudal class was weakened by the establishment of a new bureaucratic administration that deprived

areas. The peasants had some success in driving the Egyptian army out of its strongholds while also conquering and looting cities. Muhammad 'Ali arrived with military reinforcements, but the rebellion was suppressed only after much effort and thanks to his technical and artillery superiority. Another uprising broke out in 1838, this time in the Hauran (in Syria), whose protagonists were the Druze. They invaded Galilee, Safed suffering their depredations more than any other place. Safed's Jews, an unprotected religious minority, suffered greatly both in loss of life and property. Egyptian rule came to an end in February 1841 after the European powers decided that Muhammad 'Ali constituted a threat to their interests in the Orient. In a combined campaign of British, Austrian, and Ottoman forces, the coastal cities were captured. Acre, its walls, and citadel were the target of a heavy artillery barrage from the sea. Muhammad 'Ali, forced to retreat from Syria-Palestine (which then reverted to the sultan's control), was finally given control of Egypt as a territory independent of the Ottoman Empire.

253

Internal Reforms and the Influence of the Great Powers

Palestine was once again formally under Ottoman rule, now an enfeebled and shrunken empire whose strength was constantly ebbing as it faced the rising force of the European powers who were undermining its authority in favor of their own strategic and economic interests. As part of their policy of colonial expansion, they sought to gain a foothold that would strengthen their hold on areas within the empire. As short-lived as the period of Egyptian rule may have been, it left its mark and signifies the beginning of the country's modern age. The rather comprehensive reforms that were initiated in this period seeped down to various segments of the leadership and the population,

and their influence was continuous. The Holy Land's strategic location and sanctity made it a focus of intensive interest and intervention on the part of the European powers. In 1838 the British opened a hospital in Jerusalem as a base for missionary activity that would later be enhanced. Permanent European representation in Jerusalem was first established in 1839 with the appointment of a British vice-consul. Thus began an age of widespread consular activity on the part of other powers in the Holy City, some of whom also maintained diplomatic representations in Acre and Jaffa which were the most important commercial cities. The rights of foreign subjects, including Jews, were regulated by law. The growing number of European Jews who emigrated in this period came under consular protection, thus securing an advantageous legal status.

View of Jerusalem from the Mount of Olives in a photograph by Felix Bonfils (active in the Middle East, 1867–1885) and subsequently colored, apparently by his son, Adrien

The strategic importance attributed by the European powers to Palestine was due both to its proximity to the Suez Canal (opened in 1869), and to its position as a corridor and buffer zone between Ottoman Syria and rebellious Egypt which had already come under British influence. However, the chief reason for their interest (especially Jerusalem with its holy sites) was its historical-religious status, which took on greater consequence for the Europeans during the nineteenth century. Under the pressure of the Capitulation Agreements and in accord with a tradition set in earlier centuries, France saw itself as the defender of the Catholics in the East while Russia considered itself to be the protector of the Greek Orthodox. England and Germany were only at the start of establishing a religious basis in Jerusalem and therefore relied primarily on their military and economic potential for influence on Ottoman policy. Conflicts of interest between the great powers led to the exploitation of an internal Christian dispute over rights in the Church of the Nativity in Bethlehem and the Church of the Holy Sepulcher in Jerusalem as a pretext to set off the Crimean War (1853–1856), a conflict that claimed half a million lives. The various Christian communities began intensive acquisition of property and the construction of churches, monasteries, and hospices for pilgrims, while the Europeans conducted intensive missionary efforts throughout the Ottoman empire which met with greater success among the Arabs. This activity was viewed as a means of increasing European influence. The Capitulation Agreements granted broad civil and economic rights to foreign subjects, including unlimited movement and reduced customs duties. The right of jurisdiction over foreign citizens was removed from the local judicial authorities and transferred to the consuls. No wonder, then, that members of religious minorities, including Jewish immigrants from Europe, were careful to retain their foreign citizenship, and that those lacking it tried to acquire it in various manners.

Increased European influence was only one distinguishing facet of the new era in the second half of the nineteenth century. Another was internal change within the empire. Sultan Mahmud II (1808–1839) abolished the Janissary corps, created a modern army, and took steps to undermine the power of the religious establishment. His successor 'Abdul-Mejid (1839–1861) continued this policy. Upon assuming the throne, he initiated a series of constitutional reforms which were carried out over decades and are known by the general term of "Tanzimat." Besides the reforms in the army and the administration, major edicts and decrees issued in 1839, 1856, and 1876 had important consequences for the civil status of Ottoman subjects: equality

before the law was proclaimed and discrimination in favor of Muslims over other religious groups was abolished; new courts were established while the authority of religious courts was circumscribed; non-Muslims were allowed to serve on the administrative councils (*mejlis idara*) and the general councils (*majlis 'umumi*). Such councils operated in Jerusalem too, including representatives of the Christians and the Jews.

A guard (*kawass*) of a consul in Jerusalem, from a manuscript by Ermete Pierrotti, 19th cent.

There were also very significant administrative changes, including a new administrative division of Palestine: the district of Acre, the importance of which had diminished, and that of Shechem (Nablus), were annexed to the Province (*vilayet*) of Beirut; the district of Jerusalem, due to its religious and international importance, acquired independent status, with Jaffa and Gaza being annexed to it. It was no longer under the authority of the Province of Damascus and from 1872 onwards was directly subordinate to the center of government in Istanbul, a fact that stressed the importance that the Turks attached to preserving their status in the city.

Local governors rose from the ranks of Ottoman bureaucrats. They were appointed for limited terms in office and were replaced at regular intervals so as to prevent concentration of power by local rulers, as had been the case in previous centuries. From the late 1870s municipalities were established in the cities. The Jerusalem municipality was the second to be established in the empire after Istanbul (which began to operate in the second half of the 1860s), and it contained representatives of all the communities. Since the right of franchise belonged to Ottoman subjects alone, the composition of the council did not reflect the Jewish majority in the city.

Responsibility for security lay with garrisons stationed mainly in the larger cities. They numbered 2,000 to 3,000 troops, comprising of both regular and reserve infantry and artillery units. In contrast to the past, the military was now completely separated from the civil administration. Internal security, such as protecting

255

travelers along the country's roads and dealing with crime and violence, was entrusted to the police. The police force, however, was unable to cope with this task by itself and was aided by military forces, particularly during periods of rioting and outbursts of inter-communal violence, raids by Bedouin nomads on settled territory, or clashes between sheikhs that were a frequent occurrence in the

Bedouin women with their children in the Jordan Valley, photograph by Felix Bonfils

first half of the nineteenth century in Samaria and Judea. In the latter half of that century, tranquillity and stability increasingly prevailed due to a more stringent enforcement of the law by the security forces, and the wish of the authorities to prevent any pretext for foreign diplomatic intervention on the ground that the security, livelihood, or freedom of religion of the minorities or foreign nationals were endangered.

· · · · · · · · · ·

Landscape and Population

The image of Palestine as a sparsely populated wasteland with many ruins was only partially justified. An extensive and diverse agricultural economy had developed in the country, supplying the needs of the inhabitants and even exporting some of its produce. Most of the population earned a livelihood from agriculture, albeit as tenant farmers or on the basis of the division of a village's cultivated area into family units. The agricultural regions were mainly in Galilee and Samaria, as well as in the lowlands of Judea. In the eighteenth century, cotton had been the main crop in Galilee, and most of the cotton produced was

exported. Wheat was sown in extensive areas and it, too, was exported in large quantities, chiefly during the first half of the century. Cereal grains and pulses were principally winter crops, while in the summer millet, melons, watermelons, and vegetables (tomatoes, eggplant, etc.) were grown. Typical plantations were of vineyards and olive groves. Olive oil was exported and also served as raw material for the soap industry for which Nablus was famous. Citriculture developed greatly in the nineteenth century in the Jaffa area and citrus fruit became an important agricultural export.

Agricultural implements and work procedures were traditional and rather primitive. The Templars, a Christian sect that had arrived from Germany, introduced modernization both in agricultural methods and in modern equipment such as plows, harvesting and threshing implements, and the use of wind-powered pumps instead of those driven by animals to draw water. With the development of citrus plantations, motor-powered pumps were introduced. The Templars also developed dairy farming and livestock husbandry. Furthermore, they introduced a new building style and construction methods in their urban neighborhoods and rural colonies.

The communication infrastructure between the central cities also began to change its appearance. In 1867, the Jaffa–Jerusalem road was paved, while a network of roads also connected Jerusalem with Jericho, Hebron, Bethlehem, Nablus, and Haifa. A highway stretched from Haifa to Nazareth and Tiberias. In 1892 a railroad line was laid between Jaffa and Jerusalem, and in 1905 the Haifa–Damascus line was inaugurated as a branch line of the Hejaz railway connecting Syria with the Muslim holy cities in the Arabian Peninsula.

Means of transportation and communication with the outside world were also improved and enhanced. From the 1830s, steamships began to drop anchor in the country's ports. In the late 1860s postal services were initiated, operated by the foreign consulates, and in 1865 Jerusalem was connected to the international telegraph network. These changes contributed greatly to the development of the economy, to the growth in export volume, and to the increasing flow of pilgrims, tourists, and Jewish immigrants.

Israel Bak operated his Hebrew printing press (the first in the country for several centuries) in Safed in the 1830s and then moved to Jerusalem where he began operations anew in 1841. In the following years the Christian communities also established print shops in the Holy City. The first modern schools were founded in the 1840s on the initiative of religious minorities (including the Jews) and under the protection of the various

Plowing with a wooden plow, photograph by Felix Bonfils

consulates and churches. These schools enjoyed full autonomy, offering a curriculum in accordance with the cultural and religious spirit of the country or church under whose patronage they operated. A parallel network of state and private Muslim educational institutions slowly developed towards the end of the century.

The area west of the Jordan River was quite sparsely populated at the beginning of the nineteenth century. There was no significant demographic development in comparison with the previous centuries, and it is estimated that the inhabitants of the country numbered no more than 300,000 at that time. About half of them lived in villages, another 50,000 or so in cities, and the rest were nomads. Accelerated demographic growth began

towards the end of the nineteenth century. In the 1870s the population had risen to about 400,000, and by the eve of the First World War had reached as many as 700,000. More than 60% lived in villages, 20%–25% in cities, and the rest were nomads. The growth in population is attributed to a high rate of natural increase due to improved living conditions, security, and sanitation. The process of urbanization in Palestine led to a change in the urban landscape, first and foremost in Jerusalem and Jaffa. Construction burst out beyond the walls of the densely-populated cities as Jews and Muslims established new neighborhoods. In these new residential quarters and neighborhoods the traditional arrangement by which religious communities and sub-communities kept together was preserved.

257

Mail carriage in front of the Austrian post office building just inside the Jaffa Gate in Jerusalem

Jaffa and Haifa – especially the former – became busy ports towards the end of the century, attracting new settlers. The Christian holy cities of Bethlehem and Nazareth were also seized by a momentum of construction and expansion towards the end of the century.

In Jerusalem, and to a lesser extent in other cities as well, monumental public institutions were built, principally on the initiative of Christians. Their construction utilized techniques that had been previously unknown in Palestine. Architectural fashion combined diverse European elements with what the builders believed to be a local Oriental style, imparting a new character to the cities. There was a noticeable measure of European influence in the big cities, as Western elements imbued with a unique style the living conditions and lifestyle of the economic and cultural elite that was beginning to emerge. The change was however purely external, for even among the members of that elite the conservative system of values which had long characterized society was not transformed.

The Jewish Population – Immigration and Renewal

The major trends that characterized the Jewish community of the Land of Israel in the nineteenth century were the continuity and growth of immigration representing more diverse Jewish Diasporas, the fact that the Ashkenazim gradually became the majority, and settlement outside the four "holy cities" – Jerusalem, Safed, Hebron, and Tiberias.

Whereas at the beginning of the period there were more than 5,000 Jews living in the country, mostly in the four holy cities, their number had already doubled by mid-century. At the beginning of the twentieth century the Jewish population numbered about 55,000, and on the eve of the First World War there were about 85,000 of them in the country. The growth of the Jewish population and its spread beyond the four holy cities was given a great momentum in the second half of the century.

Bridge over the Jordan on one of the roads to Damascus

Jaffa replaced Acre as the major port with Jewish immigrants from North Africa settling in that fast-developing city, establishing a Jewish community whose members engaged in commerce and crafts. There was a similar development in Haifa where, at the beginning of the 1880s, the Jews accounted for one-tenth of the population. Small Jewish communities continued to exist in Gaza and Shechem (Nablus), and there were remnants of Jewish settlement in the villages of Peki'in and Shefar'am.

New Jaffa was open to western influence and became the symbol of the New Yishuv, serving as an antithesis to ancient Jerusalem which was surrounded by walls and whose devout inhabitants lived on donations from abroad.

Although the Sefardic community's hegemony was declining, it continued to be the dominant one in the Jewish population until the middle of the nineteenth century. In the course of that century, the Sefardic community, too, was undergoing constant social transformation and its composition, on the basis of lands of origin, was changing as well.

The power and influence of the Jews of the Ottoman Empire was also undergoing a certain decline. Among other factors, this can be attributed to the gradual impoverishment of the Jews of Istanbul and the fact that the role filled by the "Istanbul

Committee of Officers of Jerusalem" as the central institution assisting the Jewish population in the Land of Israel was taken over by "the Committee of Officers and Clerks" headed by the Lehren family in Amsterdam.

The immigration of many Jews from Morocco and Algeria is especially note-worthy. A substantial upsurge in immigration from North Africa was noticeable from the 1860s onwards. These Jews (known as Maghrebis) mainly took up residence in the north (Tiberias and Safed) and in

Sefardic and Ashkenazic rabbis, from a manuscript by Ermete Pierrotti, 19ᵗʰ cent.

259

the developing coastal cities (Jaffa, Haifa, and Acre). From mid-century Jews also came from Georgia, Kurdistan, the Caucasus, Persia, and Bukhara, the latter being renowned for their wealth. Since 1881 Jews began to come from Yemen in substantial

Letter of delegation for an emissary sent to collect funds in Bukhara and the surrounding region

numbers. Upon their arrival in Jerusalem they aroused wonder due to their unique appearance. Many of them settled in the village of Siloam, to the south of the Old City of Jerusalem.

Among the immigrants from Islamic lands were sages and wealthy families, several of whose members served as consular representatives, such as the 'Abu family in Safed, those of the Chelouche and Amzaleg families in Jaffa, and of Picciotto in Tiberias. In Jerusalem this role was filled by members of the Valero family, founders of the first bank there, and other families such as Navon and Eliachar.

Members of the Sefardic community generally worked for their living. The funds that arrived from abroad principally served to pay for communal administration and services, for support of Torah scholars and houses of study, and for aid to the needy whose numbers were considerable. Despite continuous financial hardships, the Sefardic community developed and maintained educational, charitable, and benevolent institutions, and continued to present an aura of unity.

From the middle of the nineteenth century closer connections developed between the Jews of the four holy cities and Jewish centers in Islamic countries. The reasons for this were varied: the rise in the number of emissaries from the Holy Land who, in addition to fundraising, engaged in spiritual matters; the increase in immigration; and recognition of the eminence of the sages in Jerusalem, first and foremost the *Hakham Bashi*, the Chief Rabbi. Among the renowned Sefardic rabbis in the Land of Israel at this time, in addition to Chief Rabbi Hayyim Abraham Gagin, were

Rahamim Franco and Jacob Saul Eliachar, to whom questions on halakhic issues were sent from throughout the Jewish world.

As noted above, since the last quarter of the eighteenth century the small Ashkenazic population in the Land of Israel went through a period of great growth. Two spiritual movements that had emerged in eastern European Orthodox Jewish society in the second half of the eighteenth century – Hasidim, followers of R. Israel Ba'al Shem Tov and his disciples, and the Prushim, their adversaries (led by the Gaon, R. Elijah of Vilna) – established offshoots in the Land of Israel. Leading members of these movements and disciples of their founders immigrated in organized groups. Together with them, and later on, came hundreds of followers.

The brother-in-law of Israel Ba'al Shem Tov, R. Abraham Gershon of Kutow, had already arrived in 1746, settling first in Hebron and later moving to Jerusalem, but it does not seem that he was successful in organizing a Hasidic community in the country. A group belonging to the first generation of Hasidim led by R. Nahman of Horodenka, R. Menahem Mendel of Peremyshlyany, and R. Simha of Zalozhtsy banded together in order to immigrate to the Land of Israel. This group, numbering thirty persons, arrived after the Jewish New Year in the fall of 1763 and settled in Safed and Tiberias, laying the foundation for the Hasidic communities there. A convoy numbering hundreds of persons arrived, by way of Istanbul, in 1777, led by R. Menahem Mendel of Vitebsk. They, too, settled in Galilee where they were joined by additional Hasidim who further broadened the community's foundation.

Seal of the Ashkenazic community in Hebron

A community of Habad (Lubavitcher) Hasidim was establshed in 1819 in Hebron, where it existed until the massacre of 1929.

The Prushim reached the Land Israel in 1808 in a convoy led by a disciple of Elijah, R. Menahem Mendel of Shklov. A year later R. Israel of Shklov joined them. He served as leader of the Prushim community until his death in 1839. At first the center of the Prushim community was in Tiberias from where it subsequently shifted to Safed. The Prushim can also be credited with renewing the Ashkenazic community in Jerusalem in 1816, after nearly one hundred years during which Ashkenazim had avoided settling in the Holy City due to a large monetary debt.

Fairly similar intellectual and religious concepts shared by both movements provide the ideological background to their immigration. Exile, they argued, was not only the physical exile of the Jewish people, but was also the exile of the Divine Presence which sought to be redeemed together with the nation. Through penitential correction of the soul, devotion to the Lord, and prayers for mercy, full Redemption could be attained. Yearnings for Redemption and love of the Land of Israel were also manifested in the desire of the founders of the two movements to immigrate to the Land of Israel. Both, indeed, set out on the journey but were unable to complete it. The outstanding expression of the spiritual relationship to the Land of Israel in the context of the ideological principles of these movements was how those who did settle in the country explained the purpose of their immigration. They saw themselves as emissaries on behalf of the nation "standing in God's courtyards" in order to fulfill the commandments of the Torah. What attracted them to the Land of Israel was its sanctity and their belief that it was situated before the "gate of heaven," hence their principal purpose was to assiduously study the Torah and worship the Creator.

Factors rooted in historical circumstances have also been used to explain immigration from eastern Europe at this time: unstable security conditions and the tribulations suffered by the Jewish communities there; the bitter controversy between the Hasidim and their adversaries encouraged many to distance themselves from it in the direction of the Land of Israel; likewise, a desire to establish a center for the Hasidic movement in the Land of Israel from which their ideas would be disseminated (an aspiration that was not to be fulfilled). However, there is no doubt that the spiritual-religious factor was predominant. It also constituted the ideological basis that guided the Ashkenazic Orthodox population, or as it was later called, "the Old Yishuv",

throughout the nineteenth century and afterwards.

The Hasidic and Prushic groups of immigrants may be seen as the central factor in initiating organized emigration to the Holy Land from Europe, one that laid the foundations for the modern

Hebron in a photograph by Ludwig Preis, 1925

Ashkenazic Jewish communities in the Land of Israel. They strengthened the bond between the Jews of the Land of Israel and those of the Diaspora, a bond that was manifested in the continuity of immigration as a permanent phenomenon. These immigrants proved that the Land of Israel was not merely an abstract concept but a true and tangible reality. This was an immigration movement comprised of ideologically motivated people whose founding fathers set a spiritual framework for the coming generations, and on its foundations they molded the patterns of leadership of their communities.

Thus was created a variegated mosaic of Jewish communities in the cities, with each group speaking the language of its country of origin in its own unique dialect. Immigrants from Europe generally conversed in Yiddish, whereas the members of the Oriental communities generally spoke in various dialects of Arabic, Judeo-Arabic or Ladino (Judeo-Spanish, the language of immigrants from Turkey and the Balkans). The common tongue was Hebrew. This language, that had long served only for prayer and study of the Torah, was now revived as a living and vital spoken tongue.

. . . .

Organization and Leadership of the "Old Yishuv"

Even though there was only one Jewish community in Palestine as far as the Ottoman authorities were concerned, the Jews who

261

comprised the "Old Yishuv" were divided into two general frameworks: the Sefardic community and the Ashkenazic community. The existence of the Ashkenazim as a separate entity was not something new, but now it took on political significance: whereas the Sefardim were mainly Ottoman subjects (with all that this implied), the Ashkenazim, who had come from Europe, were foreign subjects. This led to a situation in which immigrants from different European countries came under the protection of diverse European consuls. Thus, there was no factor that obliged the members of the Ashkenazic communities to accept the authority of a unified leadership.

The Ashkenazim, therefore, were organized in *kolelim*, groups of Jews having a common geographic origin – people from a particular country, district, or city who, having immigrated to the Land of Israel founded there a separate communal framework for themselves. The main functions of the kolel were in the social and economic spheres. Its officials received funds that had been collected on their behalf in their place of origin. They then distributed the funds among the heads of households and concerned themselves with supplying religious, educational, and social services. The members of each kolel prayed in their own synagogues according to their native rites.

At first there were only two main kolelim, those of the Hasidim and the Prushim. In time, splits and factions developed, usually over financial issues, out of a desire to control the funds arriving from abroad. Eventually there were more than thirty kolelim. Of course, this led to their decline since they could not fulfill their objectives. In 1866 the Ashkenazim founded the "Committee of All the Kolelim" as an overall organizational framework that would represent them before other bodies, extend financial aid to those who were not members of any kolel, and provide communal services. This committee, organized on a voluntary basis, was weakened by conflicts of interest

Seal of the Hungarian, Moravian, Bohemian, and Austrian *kolel* in Jerusalem. The Hebrew text also includes Hebron, Safed, and Tiberias

among its component elements. That was also the reason for the lack of a single spiritual leadership or a central rabbinate, which was generally a rather important focus of power in Jewish communities. R. Samuel Salant, for example, who died in 1909, had served as a judge and rabbi for dozens of years. Although he enjoyed high esteem, his authority was not accepted by all members of the Ashkenazic community.

The Ottoman authorities permitted a large measure of autonomy in communal organization, as long as it did not violate the law. There was no overall organizational framework to which the entire Jewish population was directly subordinate. There was a long-standing Sefardic leadership which the Ottoman authorities held responsible, as representatives of the entire Jewish community. Nevertheless, every group based on geographic origin set up its own leadership institutions that were formally subject to the Sefardic leadership. The organizational disunity within the Yishuv derived from the absence of any external factor that would enforce organizational unity upon them, and the lack of any internal motivation to achieve this objective. On the contrary, political, economic, social, and cultural factors impelled them to jealously guard the distinctive organizational framework of each kolel.

Although the Sefardic community had become more diversified and had changed its character, it still preserved an outward appearance of great unity in contrast to the increasing factionalism among the Ashkenazim. Its internal authority was even enhanced after the Ottoman appointment of a chief rabbi of the Ottoman empire with authority delegated by the state. In 1842 a chief rabbi was also appointed in Jerusalem as part of the general reforms in the status of minorities throughout the empire. R. Abraham Hayyim Gagin and his successors were from now on the formal leaders of Ottoman Jewry in Palestine, and their representatives served on local governmental institutions.

The years of stability and prosperity following the expulsion of the Egyptian forces were good years for the Sefardic leadership. It was during this period that patterns of leadership and action were first created, and the ordinances of the Jerusalem community collected and set in print (1840–41).

Intra-communal diversity together with a significant rise in the strength of the Ashkenazim produced a new reality, one that in fact forced the Sefardic leadership to relinquish the absolute hegemony that it had exercised until then over the affairs of the Jews in Palestine. The Ashkenazim were followed in the second half of the century by the North African immigrants who also created an independent organizational framework and leadership, as did the Yemenites after them.

Changing Conceptions

Until the First World War the traditional pattern of immigration continued, and although it was undergoing gradual change as was also the case outside Palestine, the traditional pattern of society persisted. The Sefardic economic elite quickly became a part of and deeply involved in the process of modernization, including such well-known families as the Moyals, the Amzalegs, the Chelouches, the Valeros, the Navons, and the Eliachars. Several of them are part of the Sefardic elite until this very day.

The fact that ultra-Orthodoxy did not take root among the Sefardic communities in the Land of Israel and the Diaspora led to them reacting totally differently compared to the Ashkenazim. The Sefardic community and its leadership generally adopted a moderate – even a sympathetic – attitude towards modern concepts, particularly in education.

What shaped the image of the Ashkenazic Old Yishuv more than anything else, both externally and internally, was the institution of *halukkah* (literally, "distribution"), that is, the funds that were sent from abroad and distributed among all members of the Ashkenazic community without exception, on the basis of fixed criteria. Those who received halukkah money did not see this condition as impinging upon their dignity, for they did not consider it to be charity. They believed that they rightfully deserved the funds contributed by Diaspora Jews as assistance to their brethren residing in the Land of Israel. They believed that they were performing a function on behalf of the entire nation by studying Torah in the Holy Land, by praying at the holy places, and by maintaining Jewish presence in the Land of Israel. Hence, there was a division of labor between that part of the nation living in the Holy Land and carrying out its mission, and those residing in the Diaspora, whose task it was to figuratively supply bricks and mortar to reinforce the foundations of the Temple and rebuild it. The traditional Orthodox Jewish leadership in the Diaspora also accepted this approach which was grounded in a broad ideology whose bottom line was mutual responsibility and an obligatory relationship between the People of Israel and the Land of Israel.

Not all Jews saw things that way. There were in Europe "enlightened" Jews who had abandoned the traditional lifestyle for a more modern one. They had begun to take an interest and to consciously become involved in the social and economic processes that characterized the Jewish communities in countries where Jews did not enjoy tolerance or emancipation. When they turned their gaze towards the Jews of Palestine, they found a backward, unproductive society dependent on the mercies of others. Hence, they were sharply critical of this stagnating society which opposed all modernity and seemed to have no future.

A close examination of the economic scope of halukkah shows that although these sums were vast, they could not in fact provide economic sustenance for a family. This money, like the funds sent to members of Christian communities, served as a sort of

THE ILLUSTRATED LONDON NEWS

The windmill in Yemin Moshe

initial economic base that the population complemented as much as possible through various occupations. Poverty was profound and very striking. This condition roused to action the second and third generations of the Old Yishuv, as well as immigrants who had arrived in the Land of Israel out of ideological motivation that differed somewhat from that of the founding fathers. Though these groups were part of the social structure of the Old Yishuv or had joined it, it was not their intention to undermine it or destroy it from within. Rather, they began to broach ideas and seek possibilities to reform their economically backward society and transform it into a productive one.

The key term used by all was "productivization," which, they believed, would provide a cure for the ills of the Jews in the Land of Israel. However, at this stage the country lacked the economic infrastructure for productivization. It was a neglected region in an empire lacking natural resources and the investments necessary for economic development and – at least up to mid-century – missing the attributes for modernization. As Jewish immigration increased side by side with the German Templar settlement and developments in transportation and other fields, a consumer economy emerged to a certain extent. Wide-scale building engendered a demand for craftsmen in the construction trades, in which some Ashkenazic Jews, too, found employment. Individuals and philanthropic societies made efforts to provide training in crafts and to establish light industry, such Sir Moses Montefiore's attempts to set up his famous windmill (which operated for only a short time), or a weaving factory that failed. Trades and crafts new to the Old Yishuv were introduced, such as metalworking, stonecutting, cart driving, printing, and the manufacture of sacred objects from olive wood. Even some people who received halukkah funds entered these fields.

Opposition to productivization arose within the traditional and conservative establishment in the country and abroad, and among various groups within the Old Yishuv which over the years became more fanatical and militant. Their major argument was that there should be no deviation from the original objective set by the founding fathers of the Old Yishuv: Jews residing in the Holy Land must devote themselves solely to studying the Torah, and only for this purpose were the funds raised in the Diaspora. Nor should one try to undermine the unique character of the Yishuv as one complete entity that observed the Torah and its commandments, and it is in that spirit that public life was to be conducted. The heads of the Committee of Officers and Clerks in Amsterdam were among those who held such views. For example, there was even opposition to bringing in a Jewish physician, lest he, a product of modern education, spread his concepts among the Jewish population. As we shall see below, the struggle of the fanatical groups in Jerusalem became sharper as the first signs of secularism and its outgrowths appeared in the city.

Education was one central arena in which attempts were made to introduce changes. The traditional educational framework was to teach in small classes by private tutor. These classes were known as the *heder* among the Ashkenazim and the *kutab* among the Sefardim. From the 1840s communal public schools were founded in which the children were taught Torah. The Damascus blood libel of 1840 was an important landmark in many respects. After the disappearance of a French monk, a few Damascene Jews were caught and tortured. Only after the intervention and protests of European Jewry, primarily that of Sir Moses Montefiore, Adolphe Cremieux, and the Rothschilds, were the Jews officially exonerated of this false accusation. This blood libel

signifies the growing interest shown by central and western European Jewry in the fate of Jews in Islamic lands, including Palestine, expressed principally in philanthropic and educational endeavors by societies and individuals. And indeed, from the 1850s on we see the beginnings of educational institutions of a new kind. In 1854 the Rothschild family lent its patronage and provided funding for a school for young boys in which secular subjects and crafts were also taught. One year later a similar school for girls was established upon the initiative of Sir Moses Montefiore. In 1856 the Laemel School was founded upon the philanthropic initiative of a Viennese Jew with the objective of providing children with a general education. This institution and its curriculum were the focus of a public row between reformers and conservative elements. Despite opposition, additional schools were founded. Some years later Jewish philanthropic societies such as the French Alliance Israélite Universelle and the German Ezra Society (Hilfsverein) also entered the field of educational activity. A special initiative to encourage "productivization" among the young was the establishment of the Alliance Israélite Universelle Agricultural School in 1870 in Mikveh Israel, just outside Jaffa.

The main objective of this philanthropic educational system was to provide children with basic knowledge in addition to religious studies, such as writing, reading, arithmetic, geography, and even a foreign language – usually that of the home country of the individual or society providing the funding for the school. The idea was not to revolutionize education and society, but rather to make possible the preservation of the traditional system of spiritual values. Religious studies continued to be taught and prayers conducted at the schools. The goal was to enable a boy or girl to acquire a basic education so as to be able to become part of the prevailing economy as apprentices in the crafts or commerce.

The prime supporters of the modern educational frameworks were members of the Sefardic community. They were free of the ideological inhibition that the exclusive goal of Jews residing in the Holy Land was to study Torah. They had been in the country for many generations, living a normal life that included observing the commandments and worshipping the Creator, but also earning a livelihood through labor. They saw no wrong in modern education, especially since "European" education and acquiring proficiency in languages were considered to be prestigious in the East. Above all, they believed that this type of education was likely to open new possibilities for their children to earn a livelihood. Nor were the Sefardim party to a struggle against modern education and enlightenment, as was the case in Europe where such developments had been resisted due to apprehension that they would lead to secularization and the ruin of the fabric of religious society.

The active, outspoken opponents were the leaders of the Ashkenazic community who followed in the footsteps of the founding fathers, believing that in the Land of Israel one should engage only in religious pursuits. Nor did they see any benefit in learning languages and acquiring a modern education in a backward empire bereft of enlightenment and science. Most of all, they feared that secularization would begin in the Land of Israel too. They were apprehensive of any change in the character of society in the Holy Land, where they had sought to create a refuge from the secularization process that European Jewish society was undergoing. The campaign against modern education was conducted through bans of excommunication which were still highly effective in a religious society. Those who sent their children to the schools were subject to sanctions, and warnings that they would not receive halukkah funds. And so, at first the schools were attended mainly by Sefardic children. However, as time went on the effectiveness of the bans decreased as did the threat to withhold halukkah monies. From their very beginning, through the support of consuls who wished to promote their own cultures through schools under the patronage of philanthropists from their countries, and by the financial influence of the philanthropists themselves, the schools became an integral part of the educational and social system of the Jewish communities in all four holy cities.

An informal group of educated people with moderate views began to emerge in Jerusalem in the second half of the nineteenth century. Though observant Jews, they also displayed an interest in Haskalah and secular literature. They aspired to reform their society and broached ideas and plans that reflected European influences. The first libraries were established at this time, much to the displeasure of the Ashkenazi zealots, since in addition to religious books their collections included newspapers and Jewish literature dealing with wide areas of interest. One prominent manifestation of the new spirit was the founding of two Hebrew newspapers in Jerusalem in 1862, *Havazzelet* and *Ha-Levanon*. Alongside general information about events in Palestine and the world, these papers described the condition of the Jewish population and discussed its problems in the Hebrew spoken by the enlightened class. They provided a medium for publicists who called for social change and transformation of the economic basis of the Jewish community, and were a source of information for those who aspired to escape from the primitive reality of life in the Land of Israel.

Insufficient housing in Jerusalem accompanied by rising rental prices, high density of population, and poor sanitary conditions impelled men of enterprise to seek solutions outside the Old City walls. The first to do so were Christians, although they were mainly concerned with building educational and religious institutions. Increased immigration of Jews and their intense desire to settle

Learning a trade in the school of the Alliance Israélite Universelle, Jerusalem 1913, in which primarily Sefardic children were enrolled

Children in the Etz Hayyim Talmud Torah (religious school), early 20th cent., one of the conservative Ashkenazic educational institutions still operating today

in the Holy City forced them to seek solutions to the housing problem. Settling beyond the city walls involved several problems: the lack of security which the old walls afforded to those living within them, and the fact that all the services and institutions were concentrated inside the Old City. Residing on the outside was considered a dangerous adventure. Though the impulse to build new neighborhoods outside the walls derived from a real, difficult situation, the plans and initiatives by members of the Old Yishuv, together with the daring that was an integral element of dwelling in the first new neighborhoods, gave them the aspect of trying to shake off stagnation and of progress towards a new creativity and accomplishment.

The first Jewish neighborhood outside the walls, Mishkenot Sha'ananim (1860), was built by Sir Moses Montefiore with funds from the bequest of Judah Touro, a wealthy American Jew. The housing units were intended for Torah scholars and a windmill was also built there to provide a source of income. At first not enough families agreed to live there, but once financial support

Havazzelet (here transliterated as *Habazeleth*), one of the first newspapers in Jerusalem. Under the masthead: "On the printing press donated by Sir Moses Montefiore and his gracious lady Judith"

was promised, the neighborhood was settled. The leader of the Maghrebi community in Jerusalem, R. David ben Shim'on, purchased a plot of land near the Mamilla pool, where in 1867 he began to build Mahaneh Israel, the first neighborhood erected upon the selfinitiative of inhabitants of Jerusalem. Prominent Jerusalem personalities participated in establishing the Nahalat Shiv'ah Quarter (1869) which bordered on the main road to Jaffa. Its founders were also involved in setting up many other neighborhoods, in proposing ideas and initiatives for reform of the Old Yishuv, and in transforming its image. After the Turks succumbed to pressure from the great powers and permitted foreign citizens to purchase real estate, the way was open for the establishment of additional neighborhoods, such as Me'ah She'arim, Mazkeret Moshe, and more. Some of these neighborhoods were populated by a variegated mosaic of

Jerusalem Jews of different geographic origins, while others were intended for Jews from one particular geographic origin alone. Together these constituted the basis for expanding the Jewish population of Jerusalem, creating the unique atmosphere and lifestyle of the new neighborhoods.

It would seem that the most important aspect of the initiatives for productivization, for enhancement of the bond between the people and the land, and for the significance of residence in the Land of Israel was the double concept of tilling the soil and settlement on the land. The Prushim related to the soil of the Land of Israel as a means for observing Torah commandments. They bought agricultural land with the objective of being able to perform those commandments that applied only in the Land of Israel, such as making offerings and tithing to the priests in the Temple. When such ideas first arose in the Old Yishuv in the 1830s, the intention was not that its members would till the soil themselves, but would employ tenant farmers in conformity with the widespread practice at that time. There was some change in the next two decades as various groups expressed the desire to engage in agriculture. They issued a public appeal: "Give us a field and a vineyard," intimating that they were prepared to till the soil by the sweat of their brows. Nothing came of this initiative.

From the 1860s, when Jewish circles began to promote the concept of *Yishuv Eretz Israel* ("settling the Land of Israel"), a new ideological dimension was added to the aspiration of working the land. Persons such as Rabbis Judah Alkalai and Zvi Hirsch Kalischer, the socialist Moses Hess, and David Gordon, the editor of the Hebrew newspaper *Ha-Maggid* saw – each from a different vantage point – the settlement of the Land of Israel as a concept that Jewish society must strive to turn into a reality.

There is no doubt that the advocates of "settling the Land of Israel" and working the soil were also influenced by the awakening nationalism of the nineteenth century. These are the first signs of Jewish proto-nationalism that foreshadowed the creation of the *Hibbat Zion* ("Love of Zion") and the Zionist movements. The bond between the People of Israel and the Land of Israel took on a significance that did not necessarily have religious connotations, though they were not altogether absent.

Seal of the Jaffa community, late 19ᵗʰ cent.

A new, secular dimension was added to the worldview that saw the Land of Israel only as the Holy Land.

In the Land of Israel, too, there were persons and circles connected to and influenced by this concept. Old Yishuv figures and publicists, such as Yosef Rivlin, Yoel Moshe Salomon, and Israel Dov Frumkin, (the editor of *Havazzelet*), repeatedly returned to the theme of reviving the country's wastelands and rebuilding its ruins. They were not thinking or speaking in terms of future hopes, anticipations, or wishes. Rather, their plans were of a practical nature. They sought suitable land for settlement and founded societies to that end. The crowning achievement of these innovative efforts was the establishment of two agricultural settlements: Gey Oni (which later became Rosh Pinnah) and Petah Tikvah. Despite their failure, these settlements, which were latter settled anew by immigrants of the First Aliyah (the first wave of Zionist-oriented immigration), heralded the beginning of a new age in the Land of Israel.

Only a few persons in the Old Yishuv – men of initiative, boldness, and inspiration – were party to the new spirit that imbued this concept. The traditional, conservative establishment opposed the efforts of the modernizers, exhibiting flexibility only in certain matters, when such a stance was compatible with their conceptions. Fanatic circles prevented the penetration of any winds of change into their society.

The First Aliyah (1882–1904) and the Second Aliyah (1904–1914)

Why do the waves of immigration between 1882 and 1914 bear these names? After all, we know that they were preceded by the immigration of many organized groups and individuals. Obviously, the term unjustly disregards the fact that the Sefardim and the Ashkenazim of the Old Yishuv preceded them. However, these definitions are not of chronological consequence. Their significance lies in the realm of ideas, and is defined by the purposes

and goals of these two waves of immigration which were essentially different from those that preceded them. They are defined as "First" and "Second" because a new group of founding fathers had emerged to create a "New Yishuv" which differed in its conceptions, its ideas, and the factors motivating its immigration from those of the founding fathers of the Old Yishuv (the Hasidim and Prushim) who believed that the Lord should be worshipped in the Holy Land. The New Yishuv's leaders, on the other hand, adopted the ideal of national revival in the ancestral land of their forefathers. They clearly represented a new conception of the purpose of settlement in the Land of Israel, as manifested in the vision of the early pioneers of modern Jewish nationalism and in the Hibbat Zion and Zionist movements. Religion as a direct factor influencing their immigration to the Land of Israel is almost completely lacking from their writings. On the other hand, biblical landscape, events, and personages fired the imagination of many of them, binding them tightly to the roots of their ancient homeland. It was in these terms that they would from now on conceive the relationship between the People of Israel and the Land of Israel – as a homeland.

To avoid any misunderstanding, it should be emphasized that there were religious elements among the immigrants of the New Yishuv. Many settlers in the First Aliyah colonies were religiously observant in the conventional eastern European sense. The secular "enlightened" element at first accounted for only an insignificant minority, some of them living in the colonies, and others as a small nucleus in Jaffa.

The new groups of settlers were characterized by a different world of values that drew its concepts from modern nationalism.

Colony of Rosh Pinnah, one of those established during the First Aliyah period, photograph by Ludwig Preis, 1925

The "Bilu" group of young people which held enlightened views and became the symbol of the national avante-garde (although they established only one colony, Gederah, and many subsequently left the country), expressed the ideal forcefully and very clearly. The first article in their Regulations defined their goal as "the political, economic, and national-spiritual revival of the Hebrew people." Moshe Smilansky, a farmer and author in

and the disappointment when their hopes that European Enlightenment would solve the problems of the Jews were not realized; the rise of modern antisemitism, and – above all –the pogroms of the 1880s in the Jewish Pale of Settlement in southern European Russia which had totally undermined the confidence of the Jews. The young people of the Second Aliyah, who began to arrive towards the end of 1903, were filled with socialist Zionist

An early photograph of Deganiah, situated where the Sea of Galilee flows into the Jordan River, founded as a farm in 1909 and soon to become the first collective settlement

the colony of Rehovot, stated straighforwardly that the revival of Israel would occur when it "would live in the shadow of its own self-government like every free people that lives on its own soil." The New Yishuv does not labor for itself alone, but is an emissary of the people. It is the foundation for the building up of the nation and "the revival of the People of Israel in the Land of Israel." During the period of the First Aliyah and the Second Aliyah the foundations were laid for shaping a new, nationalist and modern Jewish society in the Land of Israel.

Only a few of the masses of eastern European Jews who emigrated at this time came to the Land of Israel out of Jewish nationalist sentiment. There were also forces at work that pushed them out of their places in Europe: the failure of Emancipation

fervor. They had become disappointed with political Zionism after the Uganda crisis (in which some Zionists supported a plan to establish a Jewish state in Uganda rather than in Palestine) and the death of Theodor Herzl, the founder of political Zionism. They believed that by immigrating to the Land of Israel they would build a just society with lofty social ideals. The failure of the 1905 revolution in Russia, upon which many of the Jewish youth had placed their hopes, and the Russo-Japanese war in which they evaded enlistment, were also among the factors that impelled them to leave Russia. Additional factors that encouraged them to emigrate were the reactions to the Kishinev pogroms of 1903 and their atrocities, with the organization of Jewish youth for self-defense against the murderers and pogromists, as in

Homel and other cities. The nuclei of youthful emigrants sprang from these young people.

Post-Zionist and anti-Zionist historians have lately made claims as to the character and objectives of the beginnings of Jewish nationalist and rural settlement in the period under consideration. They present a different interpretation of the historical narrative of settlement, suggesting that the process of modern settlement should be seen as a part of nineteenth-century colonialism, when Europeans settled in lands conquered by their mother country. The colonialists gained control of land, established large agricultural farms, and dispossessed the indigenous population. The "new historians" claim that a similar process occurred in the Holy Land when European Jews migrated to the country, established agricultural colonies, and dispossessed the native Arabs of their lands.

This comparison is absolutely groundless. It derives, on one hand, from a disregard or unwillingess to understand the historical and spiritual-religious bond between the People of Israel and the Land of Israel since the Exile, and on the other hand, from ideological conceptions which tend to push aside considerations of objective research and scrupulous analysis of historical processes. Jewish settlement in Palestine can in no way be compared with colonialism. In general, colonialism was practiced by a European power in whose interest it was to settle its citizens in the conquered country for strategic, economic, or demographic reasons. The settlement of Jews in Palestine was not the outcome of the initiative of any European state, nor did any power seek to exploit the Jews for its own interests by settling them in the region. There were internal, strictly Jewish, reasons for immigration and settlement. Furthermore, European settlers were drawn to colonial territories because they abounded in natural resources such as minerals, forests, or an abundance of water and fertile soil that could be profitably exploited. Jews who sought a solution for their economic condition immigrated to the United States. Moreover, Jewish settlers in Palestine, unlike European colonialists elsewhere, made full remuneration for the land they purchased from Arab owners, at times even paying exorbitantly inflated prices. They also formally recorded the land purchases at the government land registry office. But the principal difference lies in the realm of concepts. European colonialists settled in foreign lands, far from home, maintaining at most only slight connections with the mother country. The new land was not a territory to which they held a historical attachment, even if they sought to build there a new, just society, whether on grounds of political liberalism or of religious freedom. Conversely, the bond between the People of Israel and the Land of Israel was

deeply imprinted in the very essence of the nation's historical and religious experience, a bond that had never been severed. It was a hope and anticipation of redemption both in spiritual and real terms that drew Jewish settlers to the Land of Israel.

Despite its name, the "Period of the First Aliyah and the

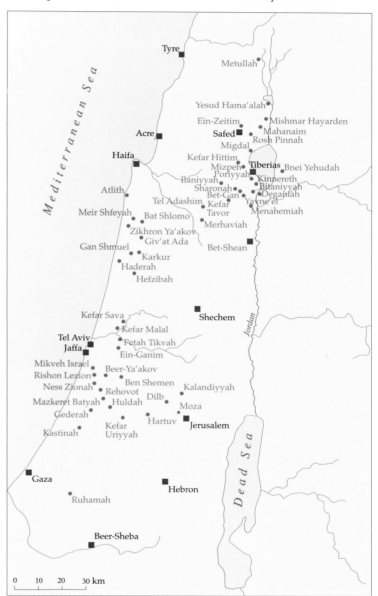

Diffusion of Jewish settlements on the Eve of the First World War

Second Aliyah" defines a timespan in the history of the Yishuv in which veteran sectors of the Jewish population – the Sefardic community and the Ashkenazic Old Yishuv – were very much on the scene. Yet, since the recently arrived settlers were social groups inspired by a unique ideology and an original mode of action, this period is named after them.

What characterized the members of the First Aliyah was that

269

most of them settled in colonies which they themselves had founded, while others resided in the cities, particularly Jaffa. Among them were teachers, nationalist activists, intellectuals, publicists, and a handful of merchants. Most were middle class persons who had purchased their homesteads while still in the Diaspora. They were generally in their thirties with families. There were many among them who observed the religious

The colony of Ilaniyyah (Sejera), founded at the end of the nineteenth century, served as a center for laborers in Galilee during the Second Aliyah

commandments and traditions, especially in certain of the colonies. Their spiritual and ideological outlook was shaped by the concepts of moderate elements in the haskalah movement and by modern Jewish nationalism of the type embodied in the Hibbat Zion movement.

The ideology of the young people who comprised the Second Aliyah, on the other hand, was a combination of ideas adopted from revo-lutionary movements in Russia and from socialist thought, together with activist Zionism – immigration to Palestine, living by one's own labor, advocating an egalitarian society, and so on. Two labor parties were founded in 1905–1906, namely Ha-Po'el Ha-Za'ir which was realistic and moderate in its approach, and the more radical Po'alei Zion. However, Po'alei Zion's leaders soon realized that the Marxist class war theory was not applicable in the Land of Israel due to unsuitable economic conditions. Hence, they began to focus more on practical activity to strengthen society and the nation.

Most members of the Second Aliyah immigrated to Palestine in their twenties, and without families. They moved around a

lot, seeking employment and new challenges. While many of them had been raised in traditionalist, religious homes, most had gone through a process of secularization and did not observe the religious commandments. This trait, together with their avant-gardist nature, was the backdrop for the tensions that developed between them and the settlers in the First Aliyah colonies. The latter were the target of much criticism by the youngsters of the Second Aliyah who accused them of alienating themselves from nationalist ideas and of preferring to employ Arab laborers rather than Jewish laborers. These young people also offered to guard the fields and property of the colonists, with the intention of replacing the Arab watchmen who were not deemed sufficiently reliable. To this end, they founded the Bar Giora organization in 1907 followed by Ha-Shomer in 1909, which were in fact the first Jewish selfdefense forces organized in Palestine.

It is difficult to determine the number of immigrants that arrived in these two waves. The Jewish population of Palestine, numbering about 25,000 persons in the early 1880s, increased to about 85,000 on the eve of the First World War. There are those who estimate that a third of the growth came from natural increase and the rest was due to immigration. However, it should be pointed out that as many as 40% of the immigrants subsequently left the country again. Most of the immigrants in that period joined the Ashkenazic Old Yishuv or became part of the Sefardic community. Those belonging to what was to be known as the New Yishuv were in the minority. The forty Jewish agricultural settlements established up to the First World War were inhabited by 12,000 persons. The number of workers in the country who were connected to the organizational framework of the Second Aliyah and its value system was no more that 1,000 to 1,500. Yet, creative endeavors and the initiatives to shape anew the Jewish population in the country developed out of this small group of the New Yishuv. Furthermore, the leadership of the Yishuv during the British Mandate period and of the State of Israel arose out of the cadres of the Second Aliyah: the first three prime ministers – David Ben-Gurion, Moshe Sharett, and Levi

Eshkol; and the second and third presidents of Israel – Izhak Ben-Zvi and Zalman Shazar.

The Turkish authorities were suspicious of the Jews' political and nationalist activity and of their plans for the Land of Israel. As early as the 1880s, they imposed restrictions on Jewish immigration and acquisition of land. These were renewed at the beginning of the 1890s when immigration increased after the expulsion of the Jews from Moscow, and once more after the First Zionist Congress in 1897. However, due to intervention of the European powers, and with the help of bribes, these edicts were not strictly enforced. During the Second Aliyah period the Turks introduced another restrictive measure, named the "red ticket" after its color. This was a kind of visa or residence permit entitling the bearer to spend up to three months in the country, during which his passport was confiscated only to be returned at the end of that period. This did not however prevent immigrants from remaining in the country, as bribes, inefficient administration, and, of course, the difficulties involved in keeping track of the "visitors" all helped to render the restriction ineffective.

The Arabs in Palestine treated the Jews of the New Yishuv (whom they called *muskubi*, Muscovites), as strange neighbors who should be kept under surveillance. They were not part of the Sefardic community, nor did they resemble the Old Yishuv type of Jew. They bought land from rich Arab landowners to establish settlements of their own, but sometimes Arab tenant farmers were living on part of those lands. At times there were disputes with the new settlers over grazing rights and land ownership. Contacts between the Arab population and the New Yishuv were generally a mixture of neighborly relations ranging from observance of the law and mutual respect to violence and the use of force. The first signs of a Palestinian Arab national consciousness appeared at the beginning of the twentieth century when educated Arab circles, chiefly among the Christians, expressed suspicion of and opposition to Zionist activity. This took the form of debates in the Turkish parliament, attacks in the Arab local press, the organized prevention of land sales to Jews, and calls for an economic boycott. At times there were also outbursts of hostile actions and physical assaults. Although the First World War prevented attempts at rapprochement with the Arabs on the part of the Zionist movement, it also hindered the escalation of hostility until the early years of the British Mandate period.

Settlement and Organizational Patterns

The crowning achievement of those who came with the first two waves of Zionist immigration was the change they introduced into the country's landscape through the establishment of dozens of agricultural colonies. With this visible change the vision of the national movement began to be transformed into reality. It was during this period that the image of a Jewish farmer firmly rooted in his ancestral soil and earning a livelihood by the sweat of his brow was created. This contrasted with the image of the weak Diaspora Jew, alienated from the soil. In this manner the soil of the Land of Israel also became the property of the nation. Unlike settlers in the First Aliyah colonies, who employed Arabs or other Jews on their lands, the young people of the Second Aliyah placed great emphasis on the value of self-help and their own labor, adhering to the dictum of their ideological mentor Aharon David Gordon: "We were afflicted in labor, and through labor we will be healed." Hence, their manner of settlement was also shaped to be in accordance with this ideology.

The colonies of the First Aliyah were typically established by

School in the colony of Yavne'el, early 20th cent., in which the curriculum reflected the modern Jewish nationalism of its settlers

members of Hovevei Zion societies who had organized to buy land for settlement in the Land of Israel. Once that mission had been accomplished by an emissary on their behalf, they immigrated to the country and settled on their land. The first four settlements of the First Aliyah were founded in this manner in 1882–1883: Rishon le-Zion, Rosh Pinnah, Zikhron Ya'akov, and Yesud Ha-Ma'alah. These also served as the model for the organization, structure, and social and agricultural lifestyle of the colonies that followed. The shortage of capital and their lack

271

of agricultural knowledge and professional expertise compelled the first settlers to appeal for help. Baron Edmond de Rothschild of Paris, "the well-known benefactor" as he was called, came to their aid, taking the colonies under his patronage. He established a ramified, bureaucratic, and professional apparatus comprising expert officials who administered all aspects of the settlers' lives. The dependence of the settlers on these officials and the social atmosphere created in the colonies elicited sharp criticism within the nationalist movement. In 1900, the Baron, who had invested millions of francs in maintaining the colonies, decided to transfer them to the Jewish Colonisation Association to ensure their economic recovery. And indeed, after a severe crisis the Baron's settlements were placed on a firmer economic basis.

The young immigrants of the Second Aliyah created new forms of settlement, mainly based on collective labor. They chose to live as a commune, sharing labor, income, housing, and social life. The foundations of different variants of communal agricultural settlement were laid in this period: the kibbutz – Kinneret (1908) and Deganiah (1909); the cooperative – Merhaviah (1911); and the workers' settlement – Ein Gannim (1908). Agricultural training farms were established, most noteworthy being that for young women founded by Hannah Meisel-Shohat at Kinneret. Just as the Executive Committee of Hovevei Zion in Jaffa was the operational arm in Palestine of that movement, so the Palestine Office, opened in Jaffa in 1907 and directed by Dr. Arthur Ruppin, became the operational arm of the World Zionist Organization. It was primarily engaged in purchasing land to become national property on which new settlements were established and existing ones expanded. In addition to national land acquisition organizations such as the Jewish National Fund or the Palestine Land Development Company, there were also private companies such as Geulah, Agudat Neta'im, Ahuzah, and others which played a considerable role in the process of acquiring land for settlement.

. . . .

Cultural and Spiritual Attributes of the New Yishuv

It was not the physical landscape alone which was transformed by the First Aliyah and the Second Aliyah. This was a period in which a new Jewish national culture was being created. As already noted, one of its features was a process of secularization centered round the New Yishuv. Some of the agents and disseminators of this new national culture were core groups of enlightened Jews

A photo postcard sent from the Land of Israel to Berlin in 1910 using the Austrian postal service. The writer, Baruch Katinka, is fourth from the right; second from the right – Izhak Ben-Zvi, who many years later would become the second president of the State of Israel

concentrated in certain colonies. Some of them had brought with them from abroad a self-acquired familiarity with the literature of modern Hebrew nationalism. They gathered in colonies known to be amenable to the spirit of haskalah, such as Rishon le-Zion, Rehovot, and Gederah.

Others were teachers in educational institutions in the colonies. A third nucleus lived in cities like Jaffa (which had become the center of the New Yishuv) and even in Jerusalem where certain circles evolved around the idea of reviving the Hebrew language, various cultural events, or first efforts to establish libraries that would in time become the national library. The workers' organizations also took an active and intensive part in cultural life in Jaffa and Jerusalem.

The educational system played a great role in fostering national culture. Of course, this does not refer to educational institutions of the Old Yishuv nor to the efforts of the various philanthropists discussed above, nor to the ultra-Orthodox educational system in some of the colonies, but rather to an educational network supported by Baron Rothschild which was transferred to the Jewish Colonisation Association together with the Rothschild-supported colonies. True, at certain times criticism was voiced of the overbearing influence of French culture in these schools. In practice, however, the teachers became increasingly independent, free to shape education in the spirit of modern Jewish nationalism. The Executive Committee of Hovevei Zion in Jaffa and the Zionist Organization were also actively involved in education, chiefly in Jaffa and Jerusalem. The Hebrew secondary schools in these two cities avowedly educated in the national spirit. All this produced a young generation, children of farmers in the colonies and graduates of the secondary schools and teachers' colleges in the cities, whose intellectual and cultural world was shaped by Hebrew national education. An important contribution to the creation of a national culture was made by Rabbi Abraham Isaac ha-Kohen Kook, then Rabbi of Jaffa, who in his own special way bestowed an aura of sanctity to the undertakings of the New Yishuv.

The modern Hebrew press that developed in this period (above all the newspapers published by Eliezer Ben-Yehuda under different names since 1885) played an important role in fostering the emerging national culture in the Land of Israel. These papers carried reports about the country and events in the colonies and the cities, with the explicit purpose of fostering a local, Land of Israel-centered spirit. At first these newspapers were the vanguard of the New Yishuv's struggle against the Old Yishuv and a platform for sharp exchanges of opinion within the Jewish community. *Ha-Po'el Ha-Za'ir* (1907) and *He-Ahdut* (1910), journals published by the workers' parties, were avowedly ideological. They advocated the realization of socialist-Zionist ideals, were highly critical of the Zionist and Yishuv establishments, and gave much attention to the new settlements. They passed their Land of Israel orientation on to their readers. *Ha-Herut* was the newspaper of Sefardic educated circles who were also inclined to support and adopt the new Hebrew culture.

The first fruits of a budding corpus of Hebrew literature produced in the Land of Israel were already evident during the period of the First Aliyah. It expressed and described life in the Land of Israel at this time and its landscapes. Towering above all the writers of the period of the First Aliyah and the Second Aliyah were two of the greatest authors of modern Hebrew literature, Yosef Hayyim Brenner and S.Y. Agnon, both of whom gave powerful expression to the Land of Israel in their works.

The revival of Hebrew as a spoken language for everyday use was the most outstanding expression of the emerging national culture. Intellectuals and educators labored unceasingly and tenaciously to make it precisely that. Such efforts began with the founding of the Tehiyat Yisrael Society by Yehiel Michal Pines and Eliezer Ben-Yehuda in 1882, and continued a few years later when moderate progressive intellectuals, including members of the Sefardic community, banded together to found Safah Berurah, a Hebrew-speaking society in Jerusalem in 1889. The highpoint came with the efforts to revive Hebrew in the colonies. One milestone in this process was the "Language War" (1913) when pupils of the Ezra Society's network of schools, in which classes were conducted in German, rebelled against the administration and the teachers, demanding that the lessons be in Hebrew. Their victory expressed the new national culture that imbued Jewish youth in the Land of Israel.

A group of workers of the Second Aliyah breaking ground for the future city of Tel Aviv, 1908

273

VISIT
PALESTINE

ISSUED BY THE TOURIST DEVELOPMENT ASS! OF PALESTINE

ARON ADVERTISING, PRINTED IN PALESTINE

Poster

The Mandatory Period

Michael J. Cohen

World War I

World War One was fraught with dangers for the *Yishuv*. In 1914, the World Zionist Organization proclaimed its neutrality and transferred its headquarters from Berlin to neutral Copenhagen. This was done to avoid the danger of taking sides and to reduce the risk of reprisals by the Turks against the Yishuv in Palestine. However, large numbers of the Yishuv were still citizens of countries with whom Turkey was now at war (Russia particularly), living in Palestine under the protection of the capitulations (rights and privileges acquired by foreign residents, originating from trade agreements between the Ottoman Empire and the Western Powers). As such, many were deported, and, in addition, all immigration was halted for the duration of the war, during which the Yishuv was reduced in numbers from 85,000 in 1914, to 56,000 in 1918.

On 2 November 1917, the British government of Prime Minister David Lloyd George issued the Balfour Declaration, undertaking to "facilitate" the establishment in Palestine of a Jewish National Home. The Declaration was initiated by the British to serve their own wartime interests; to extricate them from the Sykes-Picot Agreement (May, 1916), under which they had agreed to share control of Palestine with the French and the Russians; to secure the support (and their alleged influence on their governments) of world Jewry for the British war effort; and to persuade US President Wilson (whose Fourteen Points spoke of self-rule for subjugated peoples) to acquiesce in British control of Palestine, a vital strategic barrier to the east of the Suez Canal.

The British conquest of Ottoman Syria (which included what would become the Palestine Mandate) began in the spring of 1917: Gaza was conquered in April, Beer-Sheba in July, and Jerusalem in December of that year. Northern Palestine was conquered during the summer of 1918, and the war in the Middle East ended with the British conquest of Damascus in October.

275

Jewish laborers in a citrus grove in Rehovot, 1921

Hebrew greeting card bearing a portrait of Lord Balfour and quoting the opening sentence of the Balfour Declaration

The Establishment of the Mandate

In 1918, the Arab population of Palestine numbered some 573,000, of whom 512,000 were Muslims and 61,000 Christians. As noted already, in 1918 the Yishuv numbered some 56,000 persons. Of these, 12,000 were Zionists, and the rest ultra-Orthodox Religious Jews, known as the Old Yishuv; of the latter, 26,000 lived in Jerusalem and the rest in the other holy cities of Hebron, Safed and Tiberias. During the course of the Mandate period, the Arab population would slightly more than double to 1,200,000, while the Yishuv would multiply itself by over ten times, to reach some 650,000 by 1948.

Most of Palestine had by March 1918 fallen to the British forces under the command of General Sir Edmund Allenby, and civilian matters were administered by members of his staff. Late in 1918, after the taking of Damascus in October, former Ottoman Syria was divided into "Occupied Enemy Territory Administrations" (OETA), and Palestine was designated as OETA South, with headquarters in Cairo. It was the task of this administration to preserve the status quo in Palestine until that country's permanent disposition was decided upon at the Peace Conference. The military's prime concern was to avoid any action likely to provoke a disturbance of the peace. For this reason, they prohibited the publication of the Balfour Declaration in Palestine until February 1920. Its publication, on the eve of the first meeting of the Syrian Congress in Damascus and the Anglo-French conference at San Remo, provoked a round of protest demonstrations by Arabs in Jerusalem, Jaffa, and Haifa. Bedouin bands attacked British outposts at Tzemah, on the Sea of Galilee,

and overran the Jewish settlements of Tel Hai and Kefar Giladi in the extreme northern region of Upper Galilee. Yosef Trumpeldor, initiator of the Zion Mule Corps (which had taken part in the Gallipoli operations in 1915), was killed in the defense of Tel Hai.

The most serious disturbances occurred in April 1920, in Jerusalem, where during four days of rioting five Jews were killed and 211 wounded. The majority of the victims were from the Old Yishuv. The Jews likened the disturbances to a pogrom. The military administration was held largely responsible, especially since it had withdrawn most of its own forces from Jerusalem just days before the riots, notwithstanding Zionist warnings of impending violence.

In the meantime, in April 1920, at the Italian town of San Remo, the British and French divided up between themselves their Middle Eastern conquests: Britain received the Mandates for Palestine and Transjordan, and Iraq while the French received that for Syria. The League of Nations confirmed their decisions in September 1922.

יוסף טרומפלדור

נפל לקרבן בהגנת תל־חי

אדר תר"פ

Yosef Trumpeldor, who fell in the defense of Tel Hai in 1920

276

The "roaring lion" statue by Abraham Melnikoff, commemorating those who fell in the defense of Tel Hai

Following the April disturbances, the British Government replaced the military with a civilian administration, even though the Mandate had yet to be confirmed by the League of Nations. The first British High Commissioner to Palestine was a Jew and Zionist, Sir Herbert Samuel. He took office in Jerusalem on 1 July 1920. Samuel opened the gates of Palestine to virtually unlimited Jewish immigration, with a generous quota of 16,500 certificates for heads of families. But the Zionist movement lacked for funds. A rift between the European Zionists, headed by Dr. Chaim Weizmann, and the American Zionists led by Supreme Court Justice Louis D. Brandeis led to the secession of the latter's followers from the World Zionist Organization. The financial resources of American Jewry were thus largely lost to the Yishuv, and in the period between the two World Wars they gave for the relief of European Jews fifteen times the amount they donated to the Yishuv. In addition, Russia, the largest reservoir of Jewish immigration, was soon closed off by the new Soviet regime. Only 8,000 Jewish immigrants arrived up to May 1921, when a further wave of Arab riots swept the country.

This time the rioting was directed against Zionist immigration (43 of the total 47 Jewish fatalities occurred at the immigrants' reception hostel in Jaffa). The British, many of whom had blamed the first wave of rioting on the military regime, were now finally convinced of the gravity of local Arab opposition. Samuel also knew of the Zionists' difficulties in absorbing the new immigrants, many of whom were employed on temporary government projects such as the construction of strategic roads. He was also aware that Zionist representatives in London had in fact lobbied the Foreign Office to reduce the number of immigrant visas issued to would-be immigrants. In the middle of the week-long rioting, Samuel chose to appease the Arabs by suspending Jewish immigration, on the grounds that it could not have been absorbed by the Yishuv in any case. This act provoked an enduring rupture between Samuel and the Zionists, who feared that the Arabs would conclude that the British could be coerced with acts of violence.

The 1921 riots led to a redefinition of British policy in Palestine, written largely by Samuel, and incorporated in the 1922 White Paper named after Winston Churchill, the Colonial Secretary. The new policy reassured the Jews that they might live in Palestine as of right, and the Arabs that the government had no intention of imposing a Jewish state or culture on Palestine. It also limited future Jewish immigration to the "economic absorptive capacity" of the country, and proposed the establishment of a Legislative Council as a first step towards the grant of self-government. Finally, it excluded Transjordan from the area to which the Balfour Declaration would apply.

The 5th Palestinian Arab Congress, meeting in August 1922, decided to boycott the Legislative Council, since the Arabs sitting on it would be prevented by the British from questioning the Jewish National Home policy (the High Commissioner would have had the power of veto). The Arabs boycotted the elections to the Legislative Council, and it was never established.

Arabs near the Old City walls of Jerusalem, 1924 or 1925

277

The Palestinian Arabs

The two leading Palestinian Arab clans, the Husseinis and the Nashashibis, were appeased by the British. Haj Amin al-Husseini was appointed Mufti of Jerusalem in May 1921, and soon took on the title "Grand Mufti" of Palestine. In January 1922 he was also appointed by the British as President of the Supreme Muslim Council, a new body which received control of all Muslim religious institutions and endowments in Palestine, previously controlled by the Turks from Istanbul. These two positions provided Haj Amin with large sums of money and patronage, which he used to promote the interests of his own family and followers (the *Majlisin*, or "councillors"). Ragheb Nashashibi, head of the rival clan, was "compensated" with the mayoralty of Jerusalem, which also carried a large amount of patronage, duly dispensed to his own followers (the *Mu'aradin*, or the "opposition").

Political friction between the two camps increased during the 1920s, as the Mufti tightened his hold on the Supreme Muslim Council. However, his supporters suffered a number of defeats in the municipal elections of 1927. The Mufti's declining political control was one of the key factors that would lead him to incite the Arabs to riot again in 1929, ostensibly in order to safeguard the Muslim shrines on the Temple Mount in Jerusalem from a Zionist takeover.

The Yishuv

A Zionist Commission arrived in Palestine in March 1918. The commission, with semi-official status, was sent by the British government to establish a link between the Yishuv and the British authorities, to coordinate relief and repatriation work, to begin to give effect to the Balfour Declaration, and to establish friendly relations with the Arabs and other non-Jewish communities – all subject to the authority of Gen. Allenby's military administration. The commission, headed by Dr. Weizmann, soon came into conflict both with the Yishuv and the military administration. The Yishuv regarded the commission's members as haughty and patronizing, resenting the fact that it had no representative of its own on the commission, and protested that no immigration was permitted. The military administration, for

its part, claimed that it was bound by international law to preserve the status quo. Yishuv leaders thought that the commission was not forceful enough in its dealings with the British and did not promote enough new projects. The military suspected that the commission was in fact an embryonic Jewish government, trying to usurp their own authority.

The Yishuv, in fact, had begun to organize its own

"Hamashbir" cooperative store, 1920s

representative institutions even before the British had completed the conquest of Palestine. In January 1918, the first meeting of the Constituent Assembly (*Asefa Mechonenet*) was held, attended by political and communal leaders of those Yishuv organizations within the areas already conquered. The leader and dominating figure of the Assembly for the next decade was Dr Jacob Thon, Director of the Palestine Office of the World Zionist Organization.

The assembly elected a temporary committee of 36 members, whose task it was to organize Yishuv elections within three months. But elections were postponed repeatedly, due to Orthodox opposition to granting women the franchise. In 1920 women were granted the vote, but still **not** allowed to stand for election. The women's vote was an issue that was to dominate the internal politics of the Yishuv for the next eight years.

The first democratic elections were held finally in April 1920, electing what became known as the Representative Assembly (*Asefat Ha-nivharim*), which became the parliament of the Yishuv. Some 35% of the votes were won by the workers' parties, Ahdut Ha-avoda and Ha-poel Ha-tzair; 25% by the Sefardim (oriental Jews); and some 20% by the Civil List, an amorphous coalition of liberal middle class urban and agricultural interests. The first Representative Assembly convened in October 1920, with the authorization of High Commissioner Samuel. It appointed an executive body, the National Committee (*Va'ad Leumi*), whose executive secretariat became its cabinet. The religious groups soon left the National Committee due to the continuing dispute over the right of women to vote. The main struggle of the National Committee during the 1920's was to try to secure legal recognition from the British administration. But it was a small, ineffective body, whose main activity was sending memoranda and petitions to the administration. The High Commissioner preferred to deal with the Palestine Zionist Executive, which later became known as the Jewish Agency Executive. Once the Jewish Agency was recognized as the leading representative body of the Yishuv in the 1930s, the National Committee concentrated mainly on providing social services to the Jewish community, such as education and health. However, during the first years of the Mandate, these institutions were overshadowed by the World Zionist Organization, now established in London under the chairmanship of Dr. Weizmann, who was given the credit for having secured the Balfour Declaration. Above all, the Yishuv,

Poster advertising oranges grown in Palestine

not yet recovered from the deprivations of the war, was dependent for its very existence and future development upon Zionist donations from abroad.

For the Yishuv, the first decade of the Mandate was dominated by economic and social developments. Zionist historiography lists the waves of immigration from the first one, beginning in 1882. The third and the fourth waves of immigration, in the first decade after World War I, each went through periods of initial prosperity that ended with severe economic depression, leading to wide-scale unemployment and emigration. But by 1929, the Yishuv had grown to some 170,000. New urban centers in Tel Aviv and Haifa flourished. Tel Aviv became the commercial center of the Yishuv, its population having more than tripled in less than a decade, from some 15,000 in 1922 to over 45,000 in 1931. By 1939, Tel Aviv had grown again by nearly 400%, and now had more than twice the population of Jerusalem, with over 177,000 Jews, as against 82,000 in the latter city. The New Yishuv (identified with the Zionist enterprise) had become the dominant factor in the Jewish community.

During this first decade, many of the major economic and political institutions of the future State of Israel were set up. As early as in 1911, the Zionists' first labor union, of agricultural laborers, had been formed, with 200 members. This body was the precursor of the General Federation of Labor (Histadrut), founded in 1920, with David Ben-Gurion as its first Secretary-General. The Histadrut set up its own employment agency, sick fund (*Kupat Holim*), construction cooperative (*Solel Boneh*), marketing organizations (*Tnuva, Hamashbir*), bank (*Bank Hapoalim*), and a vast network of economic institutions dealing with housing, insurance, credit, health, education, and

Broadsheet (1928) repeating a decision adopted in 1920 at a meeting of "all the rabbis in the Land of Israel" which stated that granting the franchise to women was in violation of Jewish religious principles

279

**Kindergarten
in Kvutzat
Degania, 1920.
First on the left:
Moshe Dayan**

publishing. By 1930, the Histadrut had 20,200 members, 74% of all the Jewish workers in Palestine.

During the first years of the Mandate the Jewish industrial sector did not flourish. It was subordinated to the early settlers' ideological determination to return to work the land, and impeded by the Mandatory government's refusal to encourage local industry. The Fourth Aliya (wave of immigration),

numbering over 62,000 Jews, which began in 1924 brought middle class Jews from Poland who were not averse to industry and commerce, and had capital to invest. A Manufacturers' Association was established in Tel Aviv. Much of the initial prosperity was based on the construction and associated trades, which engaged feverishly in house-building for the new immigrants. However, due to the huge demand, house prices spiraled, and when the flow of capital stopped in 1926 (due to fiscal measures taken by the Polish government) the construction boom collapsed and the Jewish economy entered a serious recession. In 1928, more Jews left than entered Palestine.

During this decade, the Histadrut also led a struggle against Jewish farmers, insisting that they employ only Jewish labor. Coming from a higher standard of living in Europe, the Jewish worker demanded higher wages than his Arab counterpart, but at the same time was less productive. The Histadrut, supported by the Zionist Executive, argued that the employment of Jewish workers was also a patriotic duty upon which depended the issue of further immigration quotas, and the very growth and future of the Yishuv and the state-in-the-making. Perhaps the

"Train Passing through Herzl Street", oil painting by Sionah Tagger, ca. 1928

280

gravest crisis over Jewish labor occurred in 1927, when Jewish citrus growers near Petah Tikvah sold over 80% of their crop to Arab contractors (usually, a Histadrut company, employing Jewish labor, contracted to pick, pack and ship the oranges). When the Arabs refused to employ higher-paid Jewish workers, the Zionist Executive intervened, insisting that during a time of severe economic crisis Jewish farmers had to demand that the Arab contractor employ Jewish labor. After violent clashes of Jewish workers with British and Arab police, an agreement was reached whereby the grove owners promised to employ a certain percentage of Jewish workers in the future.

During this period also, the *kibbutz* (or *kvutza* = group) movement of communal settlements expanded rapidly. The first *kvutza*, Deganiah, on the southern shore of the Sea of Galilee, had been founded in 1909. The kibbutz practiced collective socialism and initially based its economy on agriculture. By the 1920s, the kibbutz movement began to establish industrial enterprises and grouped itself into alignments with the main political parties (including the Religious Kibbutz Movement, which aligned itself to the religious Zionist Mizrahi movement). The kibbutz movement played a vital role during the Mandate period, especially in providing officers for the Haganah (the Yishuv's underground security force, founded in 1920), and Palmach forces (a Jewish commando unit established with British help in 1941), and in the defense of Israel against Arab invasion in 1948.

The Arts

During the British Mandate period, Jewish art and culture flourished in Palestine, inspired by the conviction that the Jews' national renaissance required new literary and art forms appropriate to the change from minority status in the Diaspora to Jewish sovereignty in the ancient biblical homeland.

A small community of Hebrew novelists had existed in Palestine since the beginning of the century. But from the mid-1920s, Palestine became the universal center of Hebrew literature. Within a few years, the major Jewish literary figures of the age settled in Palestine. The older generation was headed by Hayyim Nahman Bialik and M.Y. Berdichevsky; these were soon challenged by the younger generation of Yishuv authors, led by Avraham Shlonsky and Uri Zvi Greenberg, who insisted on a clean break from Yiddish, (the language of the Diaspora), which was to be replaced by Hebrew, the ancient language of Jewish sovereignty. Another young, gifted writer was Shmuel Yosef Agnon, who would go on to win the Nobel Prize for Literature in 1966. In 1931, Nathan Alterman, who would become the Yishuv's "poet laureate" during Israel's War of Independence, published his first work. In general, the works of these authors reflected the change from Diaspora to Palestine, and described, often in a romantic fashion, various aspects of the Yishuv's life and struggle in the new homeland.

The theatrical center of the Yishuv was soon established in Tel Aviv. During the early 1920s, no less than five Jewish repertory groups were set up, although they all soon collapsed. Habimah was the first professional Hebrew theater in the world, established in Moscow in 1917. It toured Palestine during 1928–29, and established itself permanently in Tel Aviv in 1931.

In the field of music, the first conservatoria were established prior to the Mandate – in Tel Aviv in 1910, and in Jerusalem in 1918. In 1923, the Palestine Opera Company was founded, followed in 1927 by the Palestine Symphony Orchestra. In December 1936, the Palestine Philharmonic Orchestra (to become the Israel Philharmonic) gave its

Hebrew authors in Tel Aviv, 1924. Seated (left to right): Shin Ben-Zion, Mordechai Ben-Ami; standing: Hayyim Nahman Bialik, Shaul Tchernihovsky, Zalman Shneiur

281

Painting of Tel Aviv by Reuven Rubin

inaugural concert in Tel Aviv, under the baton of Arturo Toscanini. Folk music also flourished from the earliest days of the Yishuv. Many local choirs were established across the country, based on the rural settlements, and annual choir festivals were instituted. From 1944, an annual Folk Dancing Festival was instituted at Kibbutz Dalia, where it was held for many years.

The Bezalel Academy of Art was founded in 1906. As with literature and drama, art was used not only to advance the Zionist political agenda, but also as a vehicle for the promotion of the revived Jewish national consciousness and for the creation of a mythical national homeland in the imagination of European Jewry. Repeatedly, the image of the new Jewish pioneer was contrasted with the old Diaspora Jew praying for Redemption. Generalized "oriental" motifs such as the Dome of the Rock conveyed the ancient quality of the landscape. In "scientific" topographical studies, photographs or movies, the Arab, as a contemporary individual was marginalized – notwithstanding the fact that the new homeland was being built largely with Arab labor, and that the Arabs were a majority of the population, who

regularly demonstrated their violent opposition to the Jewish National Home.

The Hebrew press first appeared in the nineteenth century in the Diaspora, published mainly for Jewish intellectuals. Early attempts at publishing Hebrew weeklies in Palestine by Eliezer

Billboard advertisement for the play *Shabbetai Zvi* produced by The Artistic Theater, December 1926

282

Ben-Yehuda were made in the mid-1880s. All the articles were devoted to the New Yishuv and most urged the revival of Hebrew as a spoken language. In 1910, the first daily Hebrew newspaper, *Ha-or* (the Light), was published by Ben-Yehuda, and edited by his son, Itamar Ben-Avi. With the establishment of the Mandate, a daily Hebrew press emerged. The first daily to appear was *Ha-aretz* (the Land), the only one with no direct party affiliation, which was published by Russian Jews holding liberal-democratic opinions. During the following years, each of the political parties established its own daily: in 1925, *Davar* was published by Ahdut Ha-avoda (and later by Mapai); from 1931, the year that his party seceded from the World Zionist Organization, Ze'ev Jabotinsky's Revisionists published a series of dailies (*Ha-am*, and *Hazit Ha-am* –

A Jewish home in Hebron after the massacre of August 1929

the People, and the People's Front). Both were closed down by the British authorities; in 1948, the new *Herut* (Freedom) party, led by Menachem Begin, founded a daily paper of the same name. In 1936, the right-wing General Zionists founded their own paper, *Ha-boker* (the Morning), and the religious Mizrahi party founded the daily *Ha-tzofeh* (the Observer).

• • • • • • • • • •

The Wailing Wall Riots, 1929

In 1929, as the Yishuv was emerging from a grave economic crisis, a further wave of riots swept Palestine. The conflict began as a violent protest over the Jews' right of access to pray at the Western, or Wailing Wall. A remnant of the wall surrounding the ancient Jewish Temple, it was called *al-Buraq* by the Arabs, because the Prophet Muhammad had allegedly tied his holy steed (*Buraq*) to it, prior to ascending to heaven. The Arabs were also alarmed by the establishment, at the Zionist Congress in August 1929, of the enlarged Jewish Agency (that now included non-Zionist Jewish philanthropists). The riots began on 23 August 1929 and soon spread to the whole of the country. The British had to rush in reinforcements by rail, air, and sea, having depleted their forces during the previous years. The worst single incident occurred at Hebron, where over 60 of the Orthodox community were slaughtered in a pogrom reminiscent of Eastern Europe. Many Jewish settlements, including Hebron itself, were abandoned by the Jews. The Haganah learned the bitter lesson that the Yishuv's defense had to be coordinated nationally, rather than locally, as hitherto.

A government inquiry conducted by a British land expert, Sir John Hope-Simpson, reported that there remained no more reserves of arable land in Palestine, and recommended that all further land sales to Jews should be prohibited. In 1930 his recommendations were incorporated in a new government Statement of Policy (White Paper), which announced that no further Jewish immigration would be permitted if there was any unemployment in Palestine. However, the minority Labour Party government of Ramsay MacDonald bowed to Zionist pressure, and in February 1931, in a letter read out by the Prime Minister to Parliament (which the Arabs called the "Black Letter"), the restrictions of the 1930 White Paper were in effect cancelled.

• • • • • • •

Yishuv Developments in 1930's

Following the economic crises of the 1920s and the Arab disturbances in 1929, the two major workers' parties in Palestine, Ha-poel Ha-tzair and Ahdut Ha-avoda combined in 1930 to form Mapai (acronym for The Worker's Party of the Land of Israel). The new party challenged the dominance which the General Zionists had enjoyed during the 1920s. At the Zionist Congress in

Poster of the Revisionist Movement showing the Land of Israel as extending east of the Jordan River. Legend reads: "To your offspring I assign this land, from the river of Egypt to the great river, the river of Euphrates" (Gen. 15:19)

283

1931, Mapai won 29.5% of the seats, as against the General Zionists' 33%. That congress marked the beginning of the transfer of the seat of Zionist power from London to Jerusalem.

The elections to the Zionist Congress in 1933 took place under the shadow of the murder of Chaim Arlosoroff, a Mapai leader who had served as Political Secretary of the Jewish Agency. The murder suspect was a member of Brit Ha-birionim, a fanatical, right-wing group with links to the Revisionist Party (founded by Ze'ev Jabotinsky in 1924). The Revisionists, who had received 20.5% of the vote (52 of 254 delegates) to the 17th Zionist Congress in 1931, now plummeted in 1933 to 14% (45 of 318 delegates), and a few months before the next Zionist Congress was to be convened in 1935 they seceded from the World Zionist Organization.

In contrast, Mapai's share of the vote rose from 29.5% in 1931 to 43.5% (138 delegates) in 1933. (The "General Zionists" received 23% of the votes that year, enough to elect 74 delegates). At the 19th Zionist Congress in 1935, Mapai received 45% of the votes (209 of 463 delegates), as compared to only 28% (128 delegates) for the General Zionists.

In 1933, Mapai members assumed the three central executive posts on the Jewish Agency Executive: Ben-Gurion left his post as Secretary General of the Histadrut to become Chairman, Moshe Shertok (later Sharett) became Political Secretary, and Eliezer Kaplan Treasurer. These three would respectively become the first Prime Minister, Foreign Secretary, and Finance Minister of the State of Israel.

December 1936, about one-third of the total population.

From the inception of the Mandate, many individual Jewish immigrants by-passed the British authorities and entered Palestine without an official immigration certificate. Some came on tourist visas and simply stayed on; others gained citizenship through fictitious marriages; still others infiltrated illegally across Palestine's land borders. The first organized illegal immigration took place by sea in 1934, when the He-halutz (Pioneer) organization in Poland despatched the ship *Velos* to Palestine. Initially, the main force behind the illegal immigration were the Revisionists because the Jewish Agency, which controlled the distribution of the immigration visas issued by the British, did not allocate a generous share of the official quota to them. Since the British High Commissioner deducted the illegal entries from the official immigration quota, the Jewish Agency initially opposed this illegal traffic. However, as war clouds gathered in Europe during the late 1930s, and with the anti-Zionist turn in British policy, the Jewish Agency now adopted a dualist policy: in addition to distributing the official immigration quotas, it also began to organize clandestine, illegal immigration, both to rescue besieged European Jewry and to protest against British immigration restrictions.

It has been estimated that between 1920 and 1937 some 50,000 Jews entered Palestine illegally. During the same period, over 100,000 Arabs immigrated from neighboring Arab countries, with the full acquiescence of the British.

· · · · · · · ·

Immigration

The early 1930s witnessed mass waves of Jewish immigration from Europe, with a great increase in the number of immigrants arriving each year, from 4,000 in 1932 to 37,000 in 1933, the year Hitler came to power, reaching a peak of 62,000 in 1935. The Fifth Aliya, comprising refugees from antisemitism in Germany and Eastern Europe, brought some 185,000 Jews to Palestine during the first half of the 1930s. This, together with the Yishuv's natural growth, more than doubled the Jewish population, which reached some 404,000 by

284

Jewish National Fund poster by Iza Hershkovitz expressing the Zionist ethos of the return to the land

Jewish immigrant from Germany during the early days
of Kibbutz Hazorea

Poster calling
for Jewish
settlement
in Galilee, 1938

. . . .

The Arab Community during the 1930's

During the 1930s, local Arab landowners, finding themselves in debt, began to sell off their lands to the Zionists (during the 1920s, most of the sales had been by absentee Palestinian landlords). Whereas all Arab leaders inveighed in public against the sale of lands to Jews, in private, via agents, most of them in fact covertly engaged in this commerce.

In December 1931, the Mufti convened in Jerusalem a World Islamic Congress to stress the Islamic character of the city. It was attended by 145 unofficial delegates from 22 states, but no practical steps were taken. By now a new generation of middle class Arab leaders was emerging, based in the coastal towns of Jaffa and Haifa. They were dissatisfied with the traditional leadership (based in Jerusalem), aligned more on family than on ideological lines, whose lobbying of the British had failed to halt the Zionist enterprise.

In August 1932, the pan-Arab Istiqlal party was founded by young, educated Arab radicals who, alienated by the Husseini–Nashashibi split, favored a return to a Greater Syria. In November, 1932, a group of unemployed middle class Arabs formed the Congress of Arab Muslim Intellectuals. In October 1933, an Arab General Strike was mounted, and demonstrations held against Zionist growth.

In response to these developments, both the Husseinis and the Nashashibis formed their own political parties, the Palestine Arab Party (March 1935), and the Defense Party (December 1934) respectively.

Arab and Jewish laborers working together in the Palestine Potash
Works at the Dead Sea

285

The Arab Rebellion, (1936–1939) and the 1939 White Paper

It was against the backdrop of mass immigration, political and social developments inside the Arab community, and the rejection by the British Parliament in March 1936 of a further proposal to establish a Legislative Council, that the Arab Rebellion erupted in April 1936 (it should also be noted that the Italian conquest of Abyssinia during 1935–36 had significantly eroded Britain's position in the Middle East). Within a few days, a loose coalition of the recently-formed Arab political parties set up a Higher Arab Committee, and declared a national strike for three basic demands: cessation of Jewish immigration, prohibition of all

Arab fishermen on the Sea of Galilee

Scottish soldiers on guard in Jerusalem during the Arab Rebellion

286

further land sales to Jews, and the establishment of a national (i.e. Arab) government.

The rebellion lasted intermittently for three years, with a "cease-fire" from October 1936 until the summer of 1937. It flared up again in 1937 after the British government's endorsement of the Royal (Peel) Commission's proposal to partition Palestine into an Arab and a Jewish state. The rebellion was subdued finally during the winter of 1938–39, largely by the commando operations of the newly-formed Special Night Squads (which included Moshe Dayan and Yigal Allon), commanded by a British Captain, Orde Wingate.

The Arab Rebellion was not a military success, nor did it achieve the political concessions for which the Arabs fought. The Zionists even made some economic gains: the strike of Arab dockworkers at Jaffa led to the replacement of that port by Haifa as the main entrepot of Palestine and to the establishment of a Jewish port in Tel Aviv, while the Arabs' agricultural boycott of the Yishuv forced the Jewish economy to greater self-sufficiency. The Haganah took further steps to organizing itself on a countrywide level, and also set up its first assault units. And finally, the partition borders outlined by the Peel Commission, drawn along current demographic patterns, taught the Yishuv leaders to establish future settlements not merely according to economic criteria, but in areas required for the future Jewish state (from 1936 to 1939, some 36 "Tower and Stockade" settlements were established overnight, many beyond the borders outlined by the Peel Commission. The first one, Tel Amal, later renamed Nir David, was set up in December, 1936).

However, the Palestinian Arabs did secure a major strategic goal – the involvement of the Arab states as their advocates at a critical juncture, when Britain was faced with a second global conflict. In consequence, the British government decided to appease the Palestinian Arabs, even if they had been vanquished on the field of battle. The result was the 1939 White Paper, which in effect marked the end of Britain's commitment under the Balfour Declaration. The new policy provided for the establishment within ten years of a Palestinian (Arab) state; in order to guarantee the current majority of the Arabs over the Jews (two to one), only a further 75,000 Jews would be allowed to enter Palestine over the coming five years, after which all further immigration would be contingent upon Arab consent; and finally, all further land sales to Jews would be severely restricted, primarily in consolidation of blocs where Jewish settlement already predominated, mainly along the coastal plain.

In 1939, the British lost the allegiance of the Yishuv. The League of Nations never endorsed the new White Paper (World

War Two broke out on 1 September, before its General Assembly could meet), and the Zionists never accepted its terms. But neither did the British secure the support of the Arabs (until the nascent Arab League endorsed the White Paper, in 1944). In issuing the 1939 White Paper, the British government calculated that the Yishuv, unlike the Arabs, would have no choice but to continue supporting them, as the leading protagonists against Nazism. But the British now threatened to confine the Yishuv to minority status within a ghetto, limiting, and at times suspending, immigration at the time of the Jews' greatest need. It radicalized the Yishuv, which would rebel against the British soon after the war.

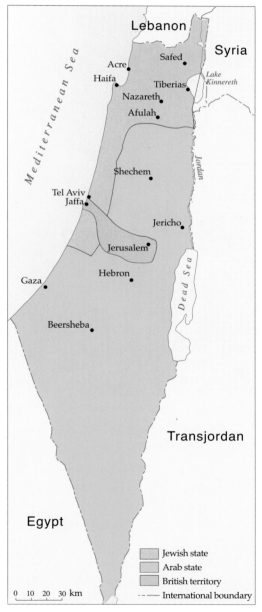

The Peel Commission's proposal for the partition of Palestine, 1937

World War Two

During the first year of the war, some 10,500 Jewish immigrants came to Palestine under the official White Paper quota, while about another 15,500 arrived illegally. This "success" led twice to the suspension of the official six-monthly quota: from September 1939 – March 1940, and again, from October 1940 – March 1941.

Italy's entry into the war in June 1940 effectively closed the Mediterranean Sea to civilian shipping and the Nazi conquest

1942, the *Struma*, a ship carrying 769 Jewish refugees, was detained in Istanbul pending British agreement to grant the passengers immigration certificates for Palestine. When the request was denied, the ship sailed into the Black Sea and was soon sunk (probably by a Soviet torpedo), with only a single survivor. By March 1944, the end of the five-year period stipulated by the 1939 White Paper, the British still had 20,000 immigration certificates in reserve.

The Zionists' rupture with the British came not with the 1939 White Paper, but after October 1941, when the Churchill

Posters urging Jewish men and women to volunteer for service in British military units

of the Balkans during the spring of 1941 shut off all exits from Europe, with the exception of Istanbul. Henceforth, illegal traffic through the Mediterranean slowed to a trickle during the war.

Two tragic episodes should be mentioned. In November 1940, the *Patria*, a ship on to which the British had crowded nearly 1,800 illegal immigrants for deportation from Palestine to the island of Mauritius, was blown up by the Haganah in Haifa harbor, the intention being merely to disable the ship. Nearly 200 Jews and a dozen British police were drowned when the ship sank instantly. At the time, it was thought to have been a desperate act of suicide by the passengers themselves. And in February

government finally shelved a Zionist proposal to mobilize a Jewish Division to fight for the allied cause. In September 1939, with the outbreak of the war, the Yishuv had called for a general mobilization for the British war effort. Some 136,000 Jews answered the call (of these, some 50,000 were women). Of this total, 36,000 volunteered for service in the British Army, the rest for service in the Haganah, or to work for the national economy. In June 1940, the British announced the formation of six companies of Palestine Buffs – three Jewish and three Arab, on a basis of parity (a total of 1,000 from each community). In September 1940, the same month in which Italian planes bombed

Haifa, only two companies of Palestine Buffs were formed, since the number of Palestinian Arab volunteers did not match that of the Jews). In the same month, Chaim Weizmann proposed to the British government that a Jewish Division be formed. The scheme was approved by Churchill's government in October 1940, but postponed in March 1941 (on the eve of German General Rommel's first offensive across the Western Desert), and finally abandoned in October 1941. This was done for political reasons – the continuing need to appease the Arabs. At the same time, thousands of Jews from Palestine served in regular British units, and were among the forces defeated by the Germans in the conquest of Crete in April 1941, when some 200 Palestinian Jews were killed in action and many taken into captivity.

In September 1944, the British finally allowed the formation of a Jewish Brigade (it has been suggested that this gesture was in partial "compensation" for the fact that the British had done virtually nothing to rescue Jews trapped and murdered in Nazi-occupied Europe). The Brigade saw active military service in Italy during the final battles of the war. After the war, it gave significant aid in organizing the movement of Jewish refugees from post-war Europe to Palestine. Many of the Brigade's officers went on to serve as senior officers in the Israel Defense Forces (one of them, Chaim Laskov, was to become its Chief of Staff).

In 1942, the Zionist movement turned to the United States, the Great Power of the future, which itself had only recently entered the war, in December 1941. In May 1942, a conference of the Zionist Organization of America attended by David Ben-Gurion and Chaim Weizmann, passed the Biltmore Resolution (named after the New York hotel where the conference was held). The resolution called for the establishment of a Jewish commonwealth in all of Western Palestine, as part of the new world order after the war. In the meantime, it demanded Jewish Agency control over Jewish immigration into Palestine.

It should be stressed that these events took place before the true nature of Hitler's "Final Solution" to the Jewish Problem was known. News of Hitler's plans was leaked to the West during the summer of 1942, and was brought home vividly to the Yishuv in October of the same year, when a group of Palestinian Jewish prisoners was repatriated from Germany to Palestine in exchange for a group of German prisoners. In December 1942, the Allies issued public warnings that anyone associated with the "Final Solution" would be apprehended and punished with all the severity of the law.

Partly in an effort to strengthen moderates such as Weizmann, a British Cabinet Committee was appointed in July 1943 and instructed to prepare a new, secret partition plan for Palestine.

Menahem Ron Wexler, *The Solution...*,
woodcut depicting concentration camp inmate committing suicide
on the electric fence, 1966

289

Holocaust survivors as new immigrants, on the eve of the War of Independence

But some elements in the Yishuv had lost their patience with the British. In January 1944, in view of the pending expiry of the 1939 White Paper's five-year time limit for Jewish immigration, Menachem Begin's Irgun Zevai Leumi (National Military Organization) units began sabotage operations against British installations and military forces in Palestine. A smaller terrorist organization, the Lehi (Freedom Fighters of Israel), commanded by Yitzhak Shamir, embarked on a path of political assassination. After a failed assassination attempt on the British High Commissioner in Palestine, Sir Harold MacMichael in August 1944, the Lehi killed Lord Moyne, British Minister-Resident in the Middle East, in Cairo in November of that year.

The Yishuv leaders, fearing that the actions of the two dissident organizations would turn the British against them and cause them to withdraw the new plan for a Jewish state, as well as the establishment of the Jewish Brigade, took preventive actions against the Irgun and Lehi in a campaign that became known as the *Saison* (i.e. hunting season). Lehi agreed to cease all action against the British, so the Haganah acted only against the Irgun, arresting and detaining hundreds of its members, turning many of them over to the British. A civil war was averted, since Begin restrained his men (the Haganah in fact greatly outnumbered the Irgun). The "Saison" was called off in June 1945 when, after the end of the war in Europe, the British government continued with the White Paper policy.

The war gave a great impetus to Jewish industry in Palestine, which mobilized and expanded to meet the needs of the huge allied armies deployed in the Middle East. The number of Jewish industrial enterprises in Palestine increased from 1,550 in 1937 to 2,500 in 1946; the number of their employees rose from 21,000 in 1937 to 47,000 in 1946; and the total value of their output during this period rose from £P8,000,000 to £P44,000,000. After the war, the Arab boycott affected the export of Jewish products to neighboring countries.

· · · · · · · · · · ·

The Palestinian Arabs during the War

In 1937, the Palestinian Arab leadership had split over the Peel Commission's proposal to partition Palestine. The second stage of the Arab Rebellion, that began in September 1937, was marked by internecine warfare between the Husseinis and the Nashashibis – with the former opposing partition, and the latter favoring the annexation of the Arab part of Palestine to Transjordan. In 1939, Haj Amin al-Husseini had engineered the Arab rejection of the White Paper policy, partly since he himself was barred from returning to Palestine. During the war, Haj Amin supported the pro-Axis revolt against the British in Iraq led by Rashid Ali. When the revolt collapsed, Haj Amin fled to Berlin, whence he collaborated with the Nazi regime, broadcasting pro-Nazi propaganda to the Balkan Muslims. In Palestine itself, the Arabs displayed increasing support for the White Paper policy.

The internal dissension and weakness of the Palestinians left a vacuum into which the Arab States entered. In March 1945, the latter established the Arab League. The new body at last

290

Hajj Amin al-Husseini, the Mufti of Jerusalem, meets Adolf Hitler

THE PALESTINE POLICE FORCE

WANTED!

The Palestine Police Force offers a reward for information concerning 29 members of the Irgun and Lehi undergrounds who escaped from Acre Prison, May 1947

recognized the 1939 White Paper as establishing the rights of the Palestinian Arabs. This led the British Foreign Office to warn that any retreat from that policy would now surely earn the enmity of the entire Arab world for Britain.

• • • • • • • • • •

The Diplomatic and Military Struggle for the State of Israel

At the end of World War Two, the British were in fact faced with an insoluble dilemma in Palestine. On the one hand, there was a traumatized Yishuv, which insisted on the mass immigration into Palestine of the Jewish survivors of the European Holocaust. But on the other hand, the Arab world was ostensibly united on the cessation of all further Jewish immigration, and the early establishment of an independent Palestinian State with a guaranteed Arab majority. The Arabs controlled huge oil reserves, needed for the economic recovery of Europe, and vital strategic bases that would be needed in the event of a new global conflict, this time against the Soviets. But it was morally impossible to deny restitution and rehabilitation to the remnants of a people who had suffered so terribly during the war – especially when their moral claims were now supported by the newly-incumbent American President, Harry S. Truman.

The British tried to involve the Americans in the Palestine problem, persuading them in November 1945 to join an Anglo-American Committee of Inquiry. In April 1946, the committee delivered its report. While recommending the immediate immigration of 100,000 Jews into Palestine, it also denied statehood to either Jews or Arabs, and recommended an international trusteeship – in effect the continuation of British rule. Future immigration and the economic development of the country would be left to the international trustee. Lastly, the report predicated its recommendations on a condition that was impossible for the Yishuv to comply with – the disarming of all armed underground forces. Further Anglo-American consultations failed to bring an agreed solution.

In the meantime, a joint revolt by all the Yishuv's underground armed forces (Haganah, Irgun, and Lehi) demonstrated effectively that the Jews could disrupt the British administration and their military communications in Palestine. The Yishuv leaders also stepped up illegal immigration, to include *"aliya gimmel"*, immigration by force. Each immigrant ship was to have a Haganah unit aboard and to resist interception by British warships. Haganah units also sabotaged British radar stations that tracked the illegal ships. The Mossad Le-Aliya Bet (Organization for Illegal Immigration) set up after the war under the command of Shaul Avigur, brought in all but one of the 65 refugee ships

British soldier guarding a train, 1930s

291

that tried to land their passengers on Palestine's beaches. From 1945 to 1948, some 70,000 illegal immigrants tried to reach Palestine, but 51,000 were intercepted by the British. Initially, the illegal entrants were interned in a special camp at Athlit, and released very slowly against the official immigration quotas, set at 1500 per month after the war. But from August 1946, once the Athlit camp overflowed, the refugees were deported to special camps in Cyprus (these internees were released after the State of Israel was established).

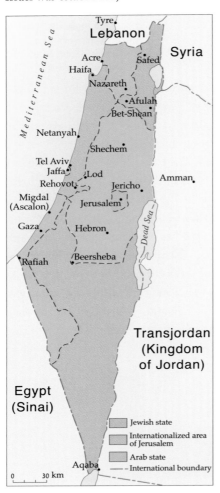

Palestine according to the partition plan adopted by the UN, 1947

The joint revolt had **not** brought the sought-after change in British policy – to the contrary, in June 1946, the British carried out a well-planned operation, code-named Agatha, against the Yishuv. On what became known as "Black Saturday," the British army impounded huge quantities of clandestine Haganah arms, and arrested and imprisoned members of the Jewish Agency Executive, as well as most of the Haganah's officer corps. The joint revolt was called off, and the Haganah never again acted against the British. In retaliation for Operation Agatha, the Irgun blew up a wing of the King David Hotel in Jerusalem which

served as the Mandatory government's administrative and military headquarters. Over 90 men, women and children were killed – British, Jews and Arabs. The Yishuv was outraged by the unprecedented loss of life, and the Jewish Agency, giving up the Biltmore Program, reverted to partition – the quest for a Jewish state in a part of Mandatory Palestine.

In Washington, Dr. Nahum Goldmann tried to induce the Americans to exert pressure on the British to return to their support for partition, abandoned by the Churchill government in November 1944 after the assassination of Lord Moyne. On 4 October 1946, one month before the elections to the United States Congress, Truman issued what became known as the "Yom Kippur statement." At the time, it was generally believed to reflect Truman's support for partition in Palestine. Indeed, this belief led the British to give up all hope of reaching a consensus with the Americans on Palestine. In effect, Truman suggested a compromise between partition and the British plan for provincial autonomy. In February 1947, following another round of fruitless negotiations with Arabs and Zionists in London, the British referred the question to the United Nations.

In March 1947, the United Nations set up a Special Committee on Palestine (UNSCOP), composed of eleven neutral members, to investigate the problem and recommend a solution. After visiting the Jewish refugee (Displaced Persons) camps in Europe, the Committee collected evidence in Palestine. While they were there, in July 1947, the Irgun executed two kidnapped British sergeants in retaliation for the execution of some Irgun members (the execution of the sergeants provoked widespread antisemitic rioting in England and a demand to "bring the boys home"). In the same month, the *Exodus 1947*, an old ferry carrying over 5,000 Jewish refugees, was boarded by British marines off the coast of Palestine and brought into Haifa harbor, whence it was sent back to Europe. The entire episode was transmitted live to the world by Haganah transmitters, and the UNSCOP members were brought to Haifa to witness the scenes of mass hysteria that accompanied the refugees' forced deportation.

These events left a deep impression on UNSCOP, which unanimously recommended that the British terminate their mandate in Palestine and evacuate the country. A majority of UNSCOP recommended the partition of Palestine; a minority recommended that Palestine become a unitary, federal state. The United Nations discussed the issue at its annual General Assembly that convened in September 1947. Following the support of both the United States and the Soviet Union, the General Assembly finally approved the partition plan by the required two-thirds majority (33 in favor, 13 against, with 10 abstentions) on 29 November 1947. The United Nations resolution gave rise to widespread rejoicing in the Yishuv. But the Arab world refused to accept it, and the Palestinians began a civil war in Palestine on the morrow of the decision. It would now be up to the Yishuv to prove to the world that it could establish its own state and successfully defend it.

The American State Department initiated a campaign to reverse the UN partition resolution. It warned about the deterioration in East–West relations in Eastern Europe, and against the possibility of the Soviets exploiting hostilities in Palestine in order to extend the Cold War to the Middle East. It argued that the partition resolution had been a **recommendation**, dependent on a peaceful transition process and upon an economic union between the Jewish and Arab states. In December 1947, the United States announced an embargo on the sale of all arms to the Middle East.

In Palestine itself, the Yishuv was besieged by Palestinian forces (and Arab militias that infiltrated from Syria), in what became known as the "war of the roads." Communications between Jewish settlements became precarious, and many of them were cut off. By the spring of 1948, Jerusalem, as well as many outlying settlements in Galilee and the Negev, were besieged. Military experts advised Jewish Agency leaders to concentrate their defenses in the coastal plain, instead of dispersing them thinly across the country.

On 19 March 1948, the American delegate to the United Nations laid a trusteeship plan before the Security Council, which would have shelved the partition plan and deferred the establishment of a Jewish state indefinitely. Many of the Yishuv's supporters advised the Jews to accept the plan. However, neither the British, the Arabs, nor the Jews were prepared to endorse the latest American proposal. Thus, by the end of March 1948 the Yishuv's fortunes, both militarily and politically, had sunk to their nadir. At this juncture, David Ben-Gurion determined to take the initiative and to establish the Jewish state at all costs on 14 May 1948.

At the end of March, the Yishuv began to receive secret shipments of heavy and small arms, mainly from Czechoslovakia, flown into Palestine under the guise of agricultural equipment. At the beginning of April 1948, the Haganah launched "Plan D," a strategic offensive which by mid-May had secured the territorial integrity of all those areas that had been allotted to the future Jewish state by the United Nations resolution. The siege of Jerusalem was also lifted, albeit temporarily. For the first time the Haganah conquered and occupied Arab settlements.

The Yishuv had proved its ability on the field of battle to establish and defend its own state. On 14 May 1948, at 4.00 p.m., David Ben-Gurion, Prime Minister of the Provisional Government of Israel, proclaimed the new state's independence at the Municipal Museum in Tel Aviv (Jerusalem was a war zone). Just eleven minutes later (at 09:11 Eastern Standard Time), President Truman declared the United States' de facto recognition of Israel. The American step, as indeed the powerful Zionist lobby in Washington, were vital in the struggle to secure recognition for the Yishuv's right to statehood.

Since 1918, some 483,000 Jews had immigrated into Palestine legally; a further 100,000 had tried to enter illegally. By the end of the British Mandate in May 1948, there were about 650,000 Jews living inside the borders of Mandatory Palestine, about 100,000 of them in Jerusalem. But the main battles were still ahead. At midnight on 14 May 1948, the armies of five Arab States invaded Mandatory Palestine. Israel's War of Independence had begun.

**Jews celebrate in the streets after the adoption
of the UN General Assembly resolution, 29 November 1947**

Immigrants from
Morocco aboard an
Israel-bound ship, 1950

The State of Israel – the First Decades

Moshe Lissak

The rebirth of the State of Israel in 1948 is a turning point in at least three historical contexts: in that of Jewish history, of the history of the Land of Israel as a territorial entity, and in the more limited context of the encounter between the two, embodied in the history of the *Yishuv*, the Jewish population of the Land of Israel.

The problem faced by a nation without a territorial-political center, a people that was the object of discrimination and persecution as a religious and national minority, prompted the pursuit of a solution to what both Europeans and Jews termed "the Jewish Problem." Jewish immigration to the Land of Israel reflected the ideological choice of one of the solutions to this problem – that of the Zionists. Other proposed solutions – assimilation, cultural autonomy in their lands of residence, or territorialism – had lost their attraction and, to a great extent, even their relevance, principally due to the Holocaust and the destruction of European Jewry during the Second World War.

The rise of the State of Israel was significant not only for Jewish history, but of course for the history of the Land of Israel as a territorial entity with a long history of political, demographic, and cultural transformations that had left their mark on the great monotheistic religions and on the civilizations that had arisen against the backdrop of the traditions to which these religions gave birth. The establishment of Israel also involved geographic and demographic changes that determined the borders of Israeli collectivity, both territorially and in terms of the composition of its population.

Postage stamp commemorating Independence Day, 1955

The Yishuv had emerged as a political community at the renewed meeting point of Jewish history with the history of the Land of Israel. Attributes which had earned the pre-state Yishuv the connotation of "a state-in-the-making" were manifested throughout the months of Jewish-Arab military conflict that preceded establishment of the state and continued afterwards. Traces of the pre-statehood traditions of the Yishuv continued to influence Israeli society and its political institutions even after the transition from Yishuv to state.

Israel's first two decades were marked by wars and waves of immigration that were central landmarks in the development of Israeli society. The most notable of the wars, from the viewpoint of historical significance, after the conclusion of the War of Independence was the Six Day War in 1967. It resulted in additional changes in the territorial demarcation lines between Israel and its neighbors, and in the composition of the population subject to Israeli rule. As a result of this war a discrepancy

Signing the Declaration of Independence. Eliezer Kaplan, the first minister of finance, flanked by Moshe Sharett (right) and David Ben-Gurion, the first foreign minister and prime minister respectively, affixes his signature, May 1948

aspects. The first is grounded in the strategic challenge, the response to which entailed military preparedness to meet the threat embodied in an ongoing conflict, whether this meant a military threat of general war (defined in terms of Israel's security doctrine as "certain" or "basic" security), or terrorist activity and limited border clashes (defined as day-to-day, "ongoing" security). To meet this challenge, Israel developed various mechanisms and arrangements that implied considerable mobilization of resources for national security. To bear the economic burden of the conflict, Israel needed a defense budget that, in time, became one of the largest in the world per capita, a budget partly covered by internal sources and in part by American aid.

The origin of the other aspect is the ideological-political challenge which sets before Israeli society the clashing interests of the Jewish national movement as exemplified in the Zionist enterprise in the Land of Israel, and the Palestinian Arab national movement which is supported by the entire Arab world. Deriving from this challenge are the issues of setting the territorial boundaries within which the Zionist enterprise is to be realized, international legitimacy, and Jewish-Arab relations.

was created between Israel's sovereign borders and those of the territory under Israeli control, leaving open the possibility of additional geographic and demographic changes in the future.

Ever since its establishment, the State of Israel existed in circumstances of a continuous external conflict that has two

Concerning involvement in a continuous external conflict, there was a broad consensus of opinion – at least among the Jewish population – that it represented an existential threat. Hence, the so very widespread agreement to mobilize resources for national defense and the readiness to pay the price in dead and wounded in recurring wars. As for the issue of how Israel should respond to the challenge embodied in the political aspect of the Israeli-Arab conflict, this was accompanied by much controversy which centered on several issues in pre-1967 Israel. First came the question of recognizing Palestinian nationalism and the need to compromise with it. The second issue asked what was more important from the viewpoint of the fulfillment of Zionist aspirations – the territorial dimension of control over the entire Land of Israel, or the demographic dimension of the national homogeneity of Israel's population.

Defense and the absorption of immigration required the allocation of great resources for collective objectives. This subjected Israel's democratic system to cross pressures: on one hand, the necessity to allocate resources for those purposes; on the other hand, the pressure originating in the need to respond to particularist demands by various social groups, which is one of the characteristics of a democratic regime. Thus, defense,

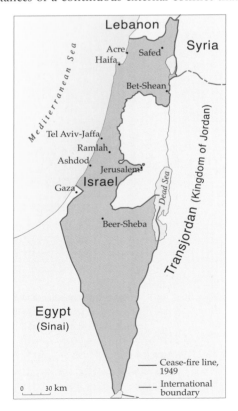

absorbing immigration, and social welfare competed for the same limited resources.

The ability of a democratic political regime to withstand pressures originating in demographic expansion, economic growth, and involvement in a protracted external conflict is conditioned to a great extent on the existence of social cohesion and broad political consensus. Achieving these conditions is especially difficult in societies characterized by a multiplicity of salient social and political schisms. The tensions originating in social, economic, and cultural rifts are made more acute by the unequal status of the sides to the conflict, for at least some of these conflicts are conducted between strong, central groups in society and weak, peripheral ones.

Israeli democracy has not been the only one to find it difficult to function in the face of social pressures stemming from an external conflict or internal divisions. However, it was (and still is today) exceptional both on account of the multiplicity of pressures which its democratic system has withstood, as well as in the diversity of patterns of how to contend with them. In any event, despite the cross pressures Israel's democratic system has withstood the tests of wars, demographic expansion, and

economic crises without its basic stability being undermined.

The state that was born at the height of the War of Independence was not identical in its territorial borders or the composition of its population with the "organized Yishuv" (the pre-state Jewish community), whose institutions operated under circumstances of "authority without sovereignty." Israel's territorial borders were identical with deployment of its military forces at war's end. These forces had stood up to the armies of the neighboring Arab states that invaded the country on the day that Israel became a sovereign state, as the inter-communal conflict was transformed into one between states.

In the young State of Israel there was a great deal of congruity between territorial borders, citizenship, and national-ethnic identity. True, the existence of an Arab minority did leave some lack of clarity as to the definition of Israeli identity and led to discrimination on a particularist-national-ethnic basis between Jews and Arabs, manifested in continued isolation of the Arab population through military rule. The Arabs, however, were granted political rights, reflecting the universal basis of Israeli citizenship. This became more prominent when military rule was abolished, a step that reflected a tendency to place the relationship

After the War of Independence Israel's borders were set by the deployment of military forces and international pressure. IDF officers in northern Sinai, from which Israel withdrew in 1949; second on the right is Yitzhak Rabin

to the state of Israel's Arab citizens on a foundation of consensus, not on control by force.

The ostensible acceptance by a majority of the Jewish population of a divided Palestine as the borders within which Zionist aspirations would be fulfilled may also attest to a tendency to prefer Israel's national homogeneity to extension of its territory. A striking change occurred in these tendencies after the Six Day War. It created a distinction between the two territorial borders – the bounds of sovereignty and the bounds of control, and between two populations – one comprising Israeli citizens, both Jews and Arabs, and the other of Arabs holding some other citizenship or none at all.

Not all changes in the State of Israel were the outcome of dramatic turning points such as wars. The extent of its citizens' sense of unity was also influenced, as noted above, by the need to strike a balance between the needs of defense, immigration absorption, and economic development, on one hand, and the available resources and the capacity to exploit them for the common good, on the other.

The government of the newly-established State of Israel accepted responsibility for the welfare of the entire population, that also included the Arab minority, marginal groups that had been outside the organized Jewish community or on its periphery, and new immigrants who had arrived in the non-selective mass immigration of the 1950s. These immigrants were foreign to the political culture of the veteran establishment, and in any case were less susceptible than the old-timers to mobilization by means of voluntary frameworks and the common symbols of identification of the pre-state period. Nevertheless, the political stability of the system was not shaken. It was considerably

Immigration was considered a means to fulfill objectives, above all settlement and conquest of the desert, depicted here in a United Israel Appeal poster

reinforced by the import of capital from abroad which made it possible at one and the same time to absorb immigration, make economic commitments, and raise the standard of living. Another stabilizing factor was that the system adapted itself to the new conditions through development, mobilization, and allocation that were based on the bureaucratic dependency of the new marginal groups on the center, and the center's paternalistic treatment of these groups.

The dependency of the new immigrants on the immigration absorption establishment became the major means of political mobilization. Moreover, the co-optation of the immigrants for the fulfillment of national goals, such as settlement in the border areas, was generally the result of exploiting a set of circumstances in which the newcomers lacked other alternatives. The "Second Israel" was caught up in a clearly peripheral situation – little was expected of them and relatively few resources went their way, as compared to the "First Israel." There was a partial matching of the class rift and ethnic-communal cleavage, and also of the gap between veterans and newcomers. This partial overlapping caused a heightening of the tensions inherent in the process of immigration absorption, tensions that had various social as well as political manifestations. Social manifestations of tensions were sporadic in character. Sometimes they lay dormant, while at other times they were expressed in outbursts of social protest – such as the Wadi Salib riot in Haifa in 1959 and of the "Black Panther" movement of the early

Hayyim Levi, an immigrant from Iraq, arrives at the transit camp in Kefar Ono, 1951

The Rosh Ha-Ayin transit camp, 1950

1970s – both the outcome of a deep sense of discrimination on an ethnic-communal basis.

The electoral expression of the ethnic-communal rift between Sefardic and Ashkenazic Jews was more long-lasting than extra-parliamentary acts of protest, in the long run leading to communal-political polarization that was not only reflected in voting for ethnic-communal parties, but also in the inclination of the Oriental Jewish communities to support the Likud and similar parties. This voting pattern implies that the correlation between ethnic-communal origin and political affiliation did not generally reflect an inclination toward self-segregation on an ethnic-communal basis, but rather disappointment that the desire for integration was not materializing at the anticipated pace.

Israeli society is the end product of a movement of migration from a scattered Diaspora to a national center in the making. There were various aspects to the relationship between Israel and the Diaspora – immigration, inward transfer of capital, and a mutual commitment to values and policies. From the viewpoint of Israel, the Jewish Diaspora was seen primarily as its supportive hinterland and as such, as a source of resources – manpower, material resources, and political and ideological support. The

least problematic connection was generally the one to do with the flow of economic resources from the Diaspora to Israel. In return the Diaspora was afforded symbolic compensation, political at best, but certainly not of a material nature. This instrumental link of Israel with the Diaspora as a source of material and human resources made possible absorption of immigration, financing of defense expenses, and economic development.

The flow of manpower to Israel is not limited to immigrants alone. Already in the War of Independence, especially its later stages, foreign recruits (from among Holocaust survivors in Europe) and volunteers from abroad were extremely vital for the Israel Defense Forces (IDF). Towards the end of the war, foreign recruits accounted for about 25% of the IDF's manpower, to which should be added approximately 1,500 volunteers from abroad. About one-fifth of these recruits fell in battle.

The unilateral transfer of capital made it possible to invest in expansion of the economy without lowering the standard of living, and at the same time to respond to demands of several groups. The unilateral transfer of funds also influenced the political regime. The possibility to simultaneously invest capital

299

(that was not raised from internal sources) and also allocate resources to raise the standard of living of various groups in the population, reduced the pressures on the system. Without the import of capital these pressures might have endangered Israel's pluralistic-democratic system of government.

The years preceding the Six Day War were a time of economic recession and stagnant growth marked by a large decline in immigration. In a cartoon by Zeev, published in the *Ha'aretz* daily, a lookout on the ship *Jewish Agency: Immigration Department* calls out: "An immigrant! I see an immigrant!"

On the ideological level, Israel had to deal with the status of the Jewish Diaspora in regard to Israel, and vice versa. Zionist ideology embodies the concept of "negation of the Diaspora," or at least an assumption of the centrality of the Land of Israel as the spiritual center of the Jewish people. "Negation of the Diaspora" (which claimed that Jews could not live a full, Jewish

life in the Diaspora) lost much of its force over the years. One reason was the Holocaust which created a tendency to look towards the Diaspora in Eastern Europe with nostalgia and to recognize that Israel and World Jewry share a partnership of fate. Furthermore, both the Holocaust and the establishment of the State of Israel broadened the network of cultural and political contacts between Israel and those Diaspora countries that had not suffered during the war. Instead of organized Zionism as the sole channel for Israel-Diaspora relations, contacts now branched out extensively, even encompassing those linking Israel with non-Zionist organized Jewry. In addition, the "normalization" of Israeli society, which had to give up the pretension of creating an exemplary society that would be "a light unto the nations," undermined its capability to serve as a spiritual center for Western Jewry which was blessed with intellectual forces of its own.

When discussing Israel-Diaspora relations, the influence of court trials focusing on the Holocaust and the behavior of Jews during the Second World War should not be overlooked. The first was "the Kasztner case" which began in January 1954 and ended in January 1958. Israel Kasztner was not in fact a defendant on trial, but a witness in a libel suit initiated by the attorney general of Israel against a person who had accused Kasztner of collaboratng with the Nazis. Kasztner was murdered in March 1957 as a direct outcome of the tension this trial engendered.

The second trial was that of Adolf Eichmann who was seized by agents of the Mossad (Israel's Secret Service) in Argentina in May 1960 and brought to trial in Israel. Eichmann was one of the central figures responsible for transporting Jews to the death camps in Poland. His trial began in the Jerusalem District Court in April 1961 and ended after his appeal to the Supreme Court was turned down in May 1962. Immediately afterwards, he was executed.

Despite the great differences in the nature of the two trials, they both led to a rather widespread change in the stereotypical attitudes of veteran Israelis towards the Holocaust survivors. In this respect the Eichmann trial was much more influential than the Kasztner case. Until these trials Israelis held a very simplistic view, manifested in two opposing images: that of European Jewry who went "as sheep led to the slaughter," in contrast to Israeli heroism.

The public traumatic experience of listening to the testimonies at these trials was

Adolf Eichmann, one of those responsible for implementing the "Final Solution," during his trial in Jerusalem, 1961

the cause of greater willingness to understand the diverse responses of Jews when they came face to face with Nazi Germany's machinery of destruction. Clear evidence of this is the fact that only after the Eichmann trial were literary works first published in Israel that tried to deal with the Holocaust. Among the these are Yehuda Amihai's book of poems *Not from Now and Not from Here*, Ben-Zion Tomer's play, *Children of the Shadow*, and *Smoke*, Aharon Appelfeld's first collection of stories.

The ideological perspective of Israel-Diaspora relations was also influenced by the demographic aspect. One of the factors that detracted from Israel's becoming a spiritual center was that it did not succeed in attracting immigrants from the West. Jews from prosperous countries, who could freely choose whether to immigrate to Israel or stay put, did not throng to Israel. The very opposite happened – a tendency developed to leave Israel for the West, above all the United States. Emigration from Israel (termed *yeridah* – literally "going down" as opposed to *aliyah* – "going up") seemed to point to the failure of Zionism. Dwindling sources for aliyah, on the one hand, and increased yeridah on the other, cause the "negation of the Diaspora" to lose its practical content.

- - - - - - - - - - -
Israel as a Society of Many Cleavages

The establishment of the State of Israel did not reduce the social cleavages which had accompanied the modern Return to Zion from its very beginning. To the contrary, the transition from a Mandate territory to an independent state added one more internal fissure that had been an external one in the pre-state period: the Jewish-Arab schism. Moreover, several of the existing rifts were widened or became more prominent. For example, that between religious and secular persons became prominent because of the need to settle the status of religion in the state. Further, the significance of the ethnic-communal rift increased due to the change in the demographic composition of the population as a consequence of mass immigration in the 1950s. However, this was also due to the high correlation created between the religious-secular rift and the fourth division in Israeli society, that between social classes. The fifth rift too – the ideological one – had not disappeared, continuing to be a point of departure for Israel's multi-party system, although some of its manifestations had been somewhat moderated.

Nevertheless, the problems inherent in transition from a community to a state significantly changed the map of social rifts. These included extending authority over new population groups that had not been partners in the political arrangements of the pre-state organized Yishuv, expanding the functions of the government, a new division of roles between state agencies and those of ideological movements (such as the Histadrut General Federation of the great Labor and the kibbutz movements), and the absorption of the great wave of immigration in the 1950s. The most striking change was, as already noted, the inclusion of an Arab population within the sovereign territory of Israel. The number of Arabs concerned, however, had been reduced due to the flight and expulsion of most of the Arab population in the territory under Israeli control.

The Arab-Jewish Cleavages

Abandonment by the Arabs of their homes during the War of Independence and afterwards, whether in flight or as a result of expulsion, brought Israel nearer to the status of a Jewish national state. However, the conquest of certain territory in the final stages of the war and the addition of additional territory following the signing of the armistice agreement with Jordan expanded the

Although the Declaration of Independence promised equal rights to all citizens of Israel without discrimination on the basis of religion, race, or sex, military rule was imposed in the Arab areas until 1966. An Arab citizen votes in elections to the Knesset

301

territorial borders, but also increased the Arab population living within them. On the other hand, the mass immigration of the 1950s reduced the proportion of Arabs in Israel's population, but it rose again when the rate of immigration declined and as a result of a higher birth rate among the Arabs.

Even though Israel had from the outset granted its Arab citizens full political rights, including the right to vote and to

Prime Minister Levi Eshkol meets with Beduin sheikhs, 1965

stand for election, the pattern of coexistence between Jews and Arabs in the first eighteen years of Israel's existence was totally asymmetrical. This was due primarily to the imposition of military rule in areas in which the large majority of Israeli Arabs were concentrated. This was done purportedly for security reasons. The movement of residents in such zones was restricted, and they needed special permits to leave them. Military rule made most of the Arab population politically and economically dependent on government and military officials. This created a paradoxical situation: citizens having the right to vote and to stand for election to the Knesset were denied the elementary right of unrestricted movement, a condition that prevented them from access to employment, the centers of government, and commerce.

Though justification of military rule on the basis of security considerations became increasingly irrelevant as the situation stabilized along Israel's borders, it continued to be in effect until 1966. Military rule created a kind of Arab ghetto. One result was the creation of a split labor market, thus preventing the influx of cheap Arab labor into the Jewish economy. In the 1950s, the years of mass immigration, there was much unemployment in the Jewish labor market, and most of the rapid development undertaken was intended to create jobs for the immigrants. Military rule prevented competition between new immigrants and Arab workers for the limited supply of jobs. This had a double

impact: on one hand, it forced the Arabs in these areas to base their livelihood on a rural economy, thus slowing down the pace at which their standard of living could rise; on the other hand, it prevented pressure to lower wages in the Jewish sector which would have been exerted should there have been unchecked competition between new immigrants and Arab workers over the limited number of jobs. Of course, military rule also enabled the Israeli political establishment to maintain supervision over public activity among the Arab population.

Freedom of movement was not the only right denied to Israeli Arabs. For example, lands were confiscated from many of them, such as those who had left their homes during the War of Independence in 1948/49. Their lands were transferred to the state's Custodian of Absentee Property. Above all, the fact that Israeli Arabs do not as a rule serve in the IDF (unlike the Druze), is the most striking expression of the fact that they had only become a part of Israeli society to a limited extent.

Israeli Arabs' sense of being second-class citizens reached a tragic peak in an episode at Kafr Kassem on 29 October 1956. As a precautionary measure on the first day of the Sinai Campaign, a curfew was imposed on the Arab villages along the frontier with Jordan. Residents of Kafr Kassem who returned from their fields were unaware of the curfew. They were shot by members of a Border Police unit. The bitter result was 47 dead and dozens more wounded, for which the policemen were put on trial. This episode left its imprint on Israeli Arabs for a lengthy period, while for the Jewish public this was the first, painful exposure to the distress of the Arab minority. As a consequence, there was a growing public demand for abolition of military rule.

Until its abolition in 1966, there was no significant change in the status of the Arab population. The vast majority continued to live in villages, poorly educated and employed chiefly in "blue collar" occupations. Nevertheless, even in this period a nucleus of Arab intellectuals emerged among the few who studied at Israeli or East European universities.

The path to abolition of military rule was paved by internal political changes in the alignment of Israeli parties. The appointment of Levi Eshkol as prime minister instead of David Ben-Gurion, and the secession of Ben-Gurion's new Rafi Party from Mapai led to change in Mapai's position vis-à-vis Israeli Arabs. The immediate result of the end of military rule was the absorption of thousands of Arab workers into the Jewish labor market, principally in seasonal employment in agriculture as well as in construction and services, such as restaurants and hotels. This led to a more diverse Arab-Jewish encounter. The number of Arab university students increased considerably, and knowledge

302

of Hebrew gradually became more common among young Arabs.

Until 1967, the problem faced by Israeli Arabs was principally one of the integration of a small national minority into the economy, politics, and society. Even though after the armistice agreements Israel was not demographically a purely national state, it was very close to being one in its lifestyle. The Arab minority could exert only very limited influence on political and social developments. This was due to its being cut off from the Arabs living beyond the frontiers of Israel and from its natural leaders, who had fled. It was also due to the de facto ghettoization of the Israeli Arabs, the overwhelming majority of whom lived in areas under military rule. The Six Day War, about a year after the abolition of military rule, once again placed the issue of Jewish-Arab relations at the center of Israeli society's public agenda.

The Rift between Religious and Secular Jews

Religion, like national identity, constitutes a divisive factor in Israeli society. Side by side with the distinction between different religions – Jews, Muslims, Christians, and Druze – there is a rift within each group between the religious and the secular. However, until 1967 the religious-secular rift among the Jews was different from those within the various minorities. This was so not only because it split the dominant majority group in

Israeli society, but also because to an even greater extent it constituted a basis for political mobilization and social and cultural segregation. Moreover, the issue of "religion and state," although it concerned all religions in Israel, was generally debated in relation to the status of the Jewish religion in Israeli society. For that reason,

Israeli identity has remained a controversial issue. In a cartoon by Yosef Bass, published in *Ha'aretz*, the three figures (from right to left) bear the legends: "I am a Zionist," "I am an Israeli," and "I am a Jew"

despite the fact that Judaism is not constitutionally the state religion, its status determines the pattern of relations between state and religion in Israel.

The religious-secular rift can be examined in various contexts: the social and political context which involves separating religious from secular persons; the juridical context which determines the formal status of religious institutions and the extent of influence of various aspects of Jewish religious law on individual and public life in Israel; and the ideological context which focuses on the significance of the State of Israel as a Jewish state.

Ultra-Orthodox Society

Any discussion of the social-political aspect should distinguish between the self-imposed segregation of the ultra-Orthodox non-Zionists (*Haredim* in Hebrew) and the relationship between the religious-Zionist group and the diverse camp made up of "traditionalist" and secular Jews (Jews who observe some of the ceremonial traditions relating to the Sabbath, religious holidays, and certain other occasions – though not out of religious conviction – are termed "traditionalist" Jews). The Haredi camp is further split by internal divisions. On one hand, there are Ashkenazic Jews and Sefardic Jews, a division that is also expressed in different prayer texts recited in separate synagogues and the appointment of two chief rabbis for the

Masthead of *Ha-Homah*, an organ of the extreme anti-Zionist Neturei Karta group, reads in part: "We do not recognize the rule of heretics and unbelievers / We do not surrender to their hegemony or to their government..."

303

country as a whole and for each city. On the other hand, among the Ashkenazic Haredim there is a distinction between Hasidim and Mitnagdim (opponents of the Hasidim) which originated in a historical controversy which has split East European Jewry over the past three centuries. The various Hasidic courts also differ one from the other in lifestyle, outward appearance, and the degree to which they wish to be segregated from the non-Haredi population. The greatest extent of self-segregation is found among those Haredi circles – such as Neturei Karta – that seek to cut themselves off totally from any connection to something expressing acceptance of the Jewish state, including any dealings with government institutions or welfare agencies. Their inclination towards ghettoization is also reflected in the considerable extent of their autarky, which is almost absolute in the social and cultural sphere, and rather extensive in the economic field.

The extreme wing of the Haredi population, identified with Neturei Karta and the so-called *Edah Haredit* ("Haredi Community"), comprises a minority even among the Haredim themselves. Nevertheless, this fringe group stands out as an extreme model of segregation from Israeli society and of an almost total severance of any connection to the political and social center. In fact, this group is even more marginal in Israeli society than the Arabs.

Demonstration against religious coercion near Heichal Shlomo in Jerusalem, seat of the Chief Rabbinate, March 1962

Most Haredim do not belong to this extreme group and are less cut off from Israeli society. However, the central Haredi social trait – an inclination towards spatial segregation – is quite obvious among them too. Moreover, they have much in common with Neturei Karta and the Edah Haredit, both as regards meticulous observance of the commandments of Jewish religious law, and their distinctive form of dress and appearance. Most of the Haredim need state budgets to maintain their network of independent educational institutions. This network is linked to the Agudat Israel movement, and serves the overwhelming majority of the Haredi population. Although it is not subject to supervision by the Ministry of Education, the state budget covers its expenses.

The second striking distinction between those Haredim that accept Israel's state institutions and those who refuse to recognize them lies in the field of political affiliation. Most of the Haredi population votes in elections to the Knesset (the Israeli parliament) and its outstanding political representative is the Agudat Israel movement (although in a later period outside the chronological scope of this chapter, a new Haredi political factor appeared on the scene in the form of *Sefardim Shomrei Torah* – Sefardi Guardians of the Torah – known as *Shas*). As a non-Zionist party that recognized the Jewish state, Agudat Israel was subject to ideological cross pressures. On one hand, it had to contend with the challenge posed by the Edah Haredit and Neturei Karta, who were critical of its relations with the Zionist establishment and acceptance of state funds, i.e. Zionist resources. On the other

Wall poster in the ultra-Orthodox Batei Ungarn neighborhood in Jerusalem reads in part: "... enlistment in the army is a grave sin..."

304

hand, it was subject to constant disputes with religious-Zionist circles due to Agudat Israel's opposition to Zionist ideology and its refusal to attach religious significance to the State of Israel as "the beginning of Redemption." Recourse to state resources on the one hand, and political involvement on the other, placed Agudat Israel in a dilemma – whether to strive to provide the Haredi community with maximal resources and services or whether to exploit their political bargaining power to try impose a religious character on public life in Israel.

The social segregation of Agudat Israel caused it to incline, much more than religious Zionism, towards focusing on providing financial resources, social services, and political benefits for the group that it represented. For example, it achieved an exemption from or deferral of military service for *yeshiva* students – which in practice was a full exemption, this in addition to having religious girls completely exempted from the military draft. It also exploited its political bargaining power to increase the percentage of state funding of its institutional network, above all its educational system. The party played a leading role in efforts by religious circles to change the Law of Return so that the validity of conversions to Judaism performed by Reform rabbis outside of Israel would not be recognized.

The Religious-Zionists

Compared with the Haredim, the non-Haredi religious camp was not clearly defined in the pre-1967 period, since it could include many of those who are called "traditionalist Jews." In any event, this group maintained and still maintains a tight link with the cultural and political center of Israeli society, and its decisive majority of religious Zionists adhered to a clearly Zionist ideology that also attached religious significance to the State of Israel.

From the very outset, this group was much less prone to social segregation than the Haredi community, but we may discern among it, even in the period under discussion, manifestations of cultural self-segregation. Moreover, its spatial self-segregation was only partial. It did exist in the religious agricultural settlements as well as in a number of urban housing projects inhabited by

concentrations of religious-Zionist residents. However, the great majority of the non-Haredi religious community lived in mixed neighborhoods of religious and secular inhabitants and was not inclined to reside in Haredi residential areas.

Demonstration by the ultra-Orthodox in Jerusalem protesting the opening of a mixed swimming pool, June 1958

Segregation of the religious non-Haredi community is most striking in the field of education. The state religious educational system is of course part of the state educational framework, administratively and pedagogically subordinate to the Ministry of Education and Culture but enjoying a large measure of autonomy, especially concerning educational content and curriculum.

The multiplicity and variety of encounters between the religious non-Haredi community and the secular public made it only natural for the National Religious Party to be greatly involved in national politics. Its involvement was reflected in the adoption of an approach different from that of Agudat Israel towards the dilemma – whether to provide religious services only to religiously observant Jews, or whether to have laws and arrangements according to religious law apply to the entire Jewish population in Israel. The national-religious movement inclined to the universal application of laws based on halakhah. This led to the enactment a series of laws, the most prominent of which was the Law of Jurisdiction of Rabbinical Courts: Marriage and Divorce (1956).

305

The Religious-Secular Rift: the Constitutional Aspect

Public controversies originating in the religious-secular rift focused to a great extent on constitutional and judicial issues, as they still do today. This derived from the fact that halakhah is an autonomous judicial method and system of laws, which in fact presents an alternative to the legal system of the state. Due to the nature of halakhah as an all-embracing juridical system, the issue of an arrangement, or of relations, between religion and state is not merely a problem of constitutional principle, solved in other states by means of many and sundry concordats and constitutional documents. In other words, the issue is not whether a certain religion should be declared a state religion. Rather, it is first of all a problem of the nexus between the laws of the state and the laws of halakhah. From this point of view Israel is exceptional. Even though there is no declared state religion, neither is there separation between religion and state.

Election poster of the Ha-Mizrahi–Ha-Poel Ha-Mizrahi Party that later became the National Religious Party. The religious-Zionist public participated in all areas of life in Israeli society, but maintained its independence in the field of education

Constitutional issues were evaded by not enacting a constitution – or even a statement of principles to serve as the preamble to a future constitution – which could determine unambiguously the relationship between state and religion. On the other hand, Israeli law granted halakhah a binding juridical status in regard to Jews in all matters having to do with marriage and divorce.

Obligation of the state's Jewish inhabitants to apply Jewish religious law in all matters of personal status had transformed them, at least in this context, from citizens of a state to members of a religious community. In other words, there is no civil marriage in Israel. Israelis can marry or be divorced in Israel only as Jews,

Muslims, or Christians, and so forth. Furthermore, marriage between members of different religious communities is impossible, unless the religious law of one of them permits it.

Making Jewish religious law binding in matters of marriage and divorce has created inconsistencies in the definition of "Who is a Jew." While for purposes of the Law of Marriage and Divorce the halakhic definition applies (by which a Jews is a person born of a Jewish mother), a binding definition was not determined in advance in regard to the Law of Return (that gives every Jew the right to immigrate to Israel) and the population register. As a result, various ministers of the interior have issued different instructions. Religious ministers, such as Hayyim Moshe Shapira and Joseph Burg, issued regulations allowing only halakhically-defined Jews to be registered as such, whereas ministers such as Israel Bar-Yehuda instructed the Registrar of Population to register as a Jew anyone who claimed to be one. This state of affairs led to a coalition crisis in 1958 and the resignation of the religious members of the government. In 1970, it was determined by law that a Jew for the purpose of the Law of Return and the Registrar of Population is someone who was born to a Jewish mother, or had converted to Judaism and did not belong to another religion. Nevertheless, even the amended definition was not acceptable to the Orthodox community, since it left open the question of recognizing Reform and Conservative Jewish conversions performed outside of Israel. Furthermore, it should be noted that the controversy over defining "who is a Jew" led in a later period, outside the scope of this chapter, to an additional amendment of the Law of Return granting rights under the Law even to non-Jewish relatives of Jews. What motivated this amendment was the aspiration to encourage immigration to Israel of Jews from countries where there was a high rate of mixed marriages.

The amendments of the Law of Return were preceded by Supreme Court decisions which reflected the ideological positions on the national and religious definitions of "who is a Jew." The decision not to recognize as Jews persons who were born of a Jewish mother but had converted to another religion was taken after the Supreme Court rejected the appeal of a Jew who had converted to Christianity (Father Daniel Rufeisen) who had petitioned for Israeli citizenship under the Law of Return, since he had been born a Jew, considered himself a Jew, and lived in Israel. Another case that preceded changes in the Law of Return and constituted a direct factor in amendment was the Supreme Court decision to register as Jews children of an IDF officer (Major Benjamin Shalit) whose wife was not Jewish. The court determined that for the purposes of the population register, the halakhic definition of "who is a Jew" was not fixed in the law. As the result of an agreement between the parties that formed the coalition government after the 1969 elections, this definition was amended in the Law of Return.

Tension between religious and secular persons concerning religious legislation was often aroused, especially in regard to laws whose passing was tantamount to enforcing a religious lifestyle upon the entire Israeli public. In order to reduce differences of opinion between the religious and the secular on legislative issues, government coalitions adopted a guiding principle that was defined post factum as "preserving the status quo." This principle, which was established in a letter sent by David Ben-Gurion, Rabbi Judah Leib Fishman-Maimon, and Yizhak Gruenbaum to the World Agudat Israel organization in 1947 (before the establishment of the state), determined that the de facto situation determining the personal status of Jews, observance of the Sabbath, the provision and sale of kosher food, etc., would remain unchanged. Thus, later disputes and controversies were primarily concerned with interpreting the nature of the status quo, and with new issues that arose after the letter was written.

Election poster of the Sefardic List, an ethnic-communal party

. . . .

The Ethnic-Communal Cleavage in the Jewish Population

The rift based on Jewish ethnic origins is unique to Israeli society, since it originated in the unique historical development of the Jewish people in the Diaspora. Though commonly defined as a division along ethnic-communal lines, it lacks the specifically nationalist connotation characteristic of ethnic rifts. Nor is it a religious schism, since it does not distinguish between members of different religions, though it does have some ceremonial-religious manifestations, the most striking of which is the difference in texts of prayers. Neither is language a dividing factor (as far as Israeli society is concerned), although the languages spoken in the Jewish Diaspora differed one from the other. Historically, ethnic-communal pluralism in Israel is primarily expressed in cultural pluralism. Nevertheless, it sometimes involves aspects of social pluralism. The ethnic-communal rift has always had its spatial manifestations in the form of neighborhoods or towns with a high concentration of Oriental communities or even members of certain communities. Extreme

examples of this are the concentration of Yemenites in Rosh ha-Ayin, of emigrants from Iraq in Or Yehudah, and the concentration of Moroccan emigrants in several development towns in the south of the Israel.

Communal concentrations in residential areas were the result of two different factors. The first was a voluntary preference for living together, while the second was the outcome of an external authority directing members of certain groups, who had arrived in the country in a specific wave of immigration, to a defined area of residence or settlement. The outstanding example of voluntary communal concentrations are the Yemenite neighborhoods of Kerem ha-Teymanim in Tel Aviv, Sha'arayim in Rehovot, and Mahaneh Yehudah in Petah Tikvah, as well as the Kurdish and Bukharan neighborhoods in Jerusalem. The outstanding example of communal concentrations resulting from administrative decisions are the development towns and urban neighborhoods that sprang up in the 1950s, replacing the transit camps set up during the great wave of immigration which were gradually eliminated.

Ethnic-communal segregation fed, and still feeds, ethnic-communal consciousness and identification. Nevertheless, in general, there is no direct connection between the extent of segregation and the strength of ethnic-communal identification. Moreover, ethnic-communal consciousness, even more than segregation, leads to cohesion around common symbols of communal identity, and makes it possible to harness ethnic-communal feeling for political advantage. In other words, the extent of social, cultural, and political mobilization on an ethnic-communal basis to a great degree enhanced the power of

307

A family in the Yokne'am transit camp, 1951

communal consciousness. This awareness is especially acute among members of the Oriental communities, since it is linked with a sense of social and class discrimination.

There were two aspects to the use of ethnic-communal identification as a lever for political mobilization in Israeli society, each more prominent in different periods. The first took the form of political organization on an ethnic-communal basis, whether avowed or implied. Such were the Sefardic and Yemenite parties of the early 1950s which vanished, paradoxically, precisely at the time of mass immigration from Oriental countries. Several ethnic-communal parties failed in the Knesset elections in the 1960s and 1970s, though they did have limited success in municipal elections. The other, more striking, aspect of the utilization of ethnic-communal consciousness for political mobilization was the attempt to create a link between such consciousness and political support for parties, such as Herut, which were not in themselves of an ethnic-communal composition. Promoting such a link was assisted by a sense of discimination, as the party in question presented itself as one that aspired to improve the social-economic, cultural, and political status of

those social groups with ethnic-communal consciousness that were customarily called the "Second Israel." The common point of departure for both these strategies for exploitation of ethnic-communal consciousness for political mobilization was the overlapping between the ethnic-communal rift and the social class rift. However, the orientation of both strategies was totally different: The first may be defined as separationist, whereas the other might be termed integrative. The use of ethnic-communal symbols and sentiments for political mobilization led to a high correlation between ethnic-communal identity and voting for a specific political party. This was first evident among the Oriental Jewish communities and subsequently, at a later stage, also among emigrants from Europe. Thus, to a great extent, especially after 1967, ethnic-communal polarization also took on the form of political polarization.

The wave of mass immigration left its mark on both the ethnic-communal rift and the social class rift. Above all, it influenced the emergence of a high correlation between the two. Due to its size, pace, and the diversity of the population that arrived, this wave of immigration was a turning point in the development of Israeli society. In Israel's first decade, nearly one million immigrants arrived in the country, as compared with a population of 650,000 in Israel on the day the state was proclaimed. The peak occurred in 1949-51, as a result of which Israel's population had already doubled by the end of 1952. True, the rate of growth of the Jewish population in Palestine in the years 1932-36 was faster than that of the first years of Israel's existence. However, we must not forget that in the 1930s the

From transit camp to development town – transit camp residents carry their possessions as they move to permanent housing

Jews accounted for a minority of the population, so that the pace of growth of the total population – Jews and Arabs combined – was lower than that of the population of Israel in its early years.

Moreover, the immigration of the 1950s also differed from that of the 1930s and 1940s from the standpoint of lands of origin. While in the pre-state period emigrants from East and Central Europe were overwhelmingly preponderant, immigration in the 1950s was more heterogeneous. About half came from Europe and the other half from Islamic lands. During the first decade – more exactly from May 1948 until the end of 1959 – about one million immigrants reached Israel, arriving in two waves. The first, from May 1948 to 1951, numbered about 700,000 persons, thus more than doubling the Jewish population. Its peak was in 1949 when about 240,000 persons arrived, half of them from East Europe. These included Holocaust survivors who had tried to enter Palestine despite British prohibition and were deported to prison camps on Cyprus and inmates of the Displaced Persons camps in Europe, as well as Jews from Bulgaria and Yugoslavia. The other half came from various countries in Asia and Africa, mainly Iraq, Yemen, and Morocco. Between 1952 and 1954 the flow of immigrants dwindled considerably, the low point being in the first half of 1953. In fact during this period more persons emigrated from the country than came as immigrants. Prominent among the emigrants were Jews of Moroccan origin, as well as new immigrants from East and Central Europe. The second wave of immigration, beginning in 1955 and ebbing in 1957, was of much smaller dimensions. In this period about 165,000 immigrants came, most of them from North Africa, chiefly Morocco. Others arrived from Rumania and Hungary, as well as Polish Jews who had found refuge in the Soviet Union during the Second World War and were now being allowed to repatriate to Poland, from where they made their way to Israel. In the final two years of the first decade immigration diminished again as nearly 40,000 emigrants from Europe and about 70,000 from Asia and Africa arrived in the country.

1951 was a turning point. For the first time since Jewish immigration to the Land of Israel was renewed in the nineteenth century, Jews of European origin became a minority among the immigrants. After only a one-year period of transition in which immigrants from Asia formed the largest group, they were replaced by those from North Africa, who were the largest group of immigrants during the 1950s as a whole. Changes in the breakdown of the immigrants' lands of origin were important factors influencing the momentous demographic transition of those years. This had many results, of which we shall list the most

important. The first was a considerable growth in the average size of families since there was an especially remarkable increase in the percentage of large families. As a consequence there was also a change in the age composition of the immigrants – many more babies and young children on the one hand, and elderly on the other. This, of course, had significant implications upon the labor force – the percentage of breadwinners among the population declined while the rate of those dependent upon them rose.

The extent and rate of immigration caused a gap of several years between the arrival of the immigrants and their integration into society as reflected in employment, housing, and the provision of services. This gap required the absorbing institutions

The Wadi Salib riots in Haifa on the cover of the journal *Ha-Olam Ha-Zeh*

to supply the basic needs of hundreds of thousands of people who were subject to insecurity concerning housing and employment, and who were not part of established Israeli culture and society. This population lived in a sort of spatial and social-cultural enclave whose points of contact with the veteran population were limited and mediated for the most part by the absorption agencies.

309

The first encounter of immigrant pupils in Kiryat Shemonah with the Israeli educational system

labor force were established to provide the new immigrants with jobs in industry. These plants paid minimal wages for non-professional work, and left no room for professional advancement. A striking example of this tendency were textile plants established in development towns in the second half of the 1950s. In the field of education, too, maximal efforts were invested to put into practice the compulsory education law which assured all children in Israel a minimum number of years of schooling. Less attention was devoted to secondary education, and even in primary education there were striking gaps between the quality of instruction in areas populated by the veteran population and that of development areas and those suburbs of the big cities where new immigrants were concentrated. In this way, absorption of the immigrants in housing, employment, and education was indeed ensured, but they were pushed to the bottom of the social ladder.

The time gap between immigration and permanent integration in housing and employment made things more difficult for the agencies that dealt with the new immigrants. They had to provide a livelihood and services for the immigrants, this at a time when Israel suffered a severe shortage of capital. As a result, in the process of permanent absorption priority was given to the pace of absorption over its quality. Elimination of the transit camps was achieved by building small standardized housing units of low quality. Factories utilizing a sizable manual

Ethnic-Communal Rift:
The Dilemmas of the Israeli Establishment

Integration into Israeli society of the immigrants who arrived in the 1950s, especially those belonging to the Oriental communities, was not solely the problem of the immigrants themselves, but also of the establishment. As a result of the wave of immigration, governmental and other agencies faced several dilemmas, particularly the need to choose between a policy of speedy integration and one than admitted and accepted the need for cultural pluralism. This dilemma was particularly salient in two spheres – the political and the educational.

The political sphere was the first in which the melting pot approach, in its extreme form, was abandoned. Though the political elites of both the coalition and opposition parties continued to oppose the ethnic-communal parties, they did not refrain from exploiting connections with traditional ethnic-

Poster, by Shmuel Katz, issued by the Government Information Office on Israel's tenth anniversay, presents an idyllic view of immigration, the reality was actually much more complex, 1958

310

Poster issued by Herut, a militant Right-wing party, on the fifth anniversary of the fall of the Jewish Quarter in Jerusalem's Old City during the War of Independence promises "We shall redeem you Jerusalem!" 1953

communal frameworks to further political mobilization. On the local plane the parties used family networks and social networks in the field of an ethnic-communal character to have the immigrants join their ranks or at least vote for them on election day. At a later stage, members of ethnic communities who were active in political parties could advance to positions beyond the local level, such as those in the Knesset or in the central institutions of the Histadrut, the General Federation of Labor. The traditional leadership of the immigrants from Islamic lands generally cooperated with the parties in power. Younger people who wanted to become part of the political system found that these leadership positions were occupied. They, therefore, often turned to the opposition parties, first of all to the largest one – Herut. This party's attraction was enhanced by the immigrants' sense of social discrimination that had emerged out of the process of absorption in the 1950s, and because they were critical of the opportunism displayed by the traditional ethnic-communal leadership.

Side by side with growing support for opposition parties, ethnic-communal social protest was also manifested by sometimes violent displays of extra-parliamentary politics. The most striking of these were the Wadi Salib riots in Haifa in 1959 and the appearance on the scene of the "Black Panthers" movement in the early 1970s. Fear of the electoral influence of these manifestations, especially of the "Black Panthers" who were active for three years, led to a considerable increase in budget allocations for housing, welfare, and education.

Education was the field in which the basic dilemma – whether to strive for integration, that would put an end to ethnic-communal social separatism, or whether to come to terms with cultural pluralism – was most noticeable. In the early stage of educational absorption of immigrant children, the educational system consciously adopted a policy of uniformity. This was a policy that ignored the differences in culture and social background that influenced the pupils' capacity to adapt to the school setting and to absorb the values that the school curriculum intended to impart to them. It strove to equalize the level of resources invested in education, but met with difficulty in attaining this goal due to the shortage of suitably trained teachers in the peripheral areas of the country. Furthermore, the shapers of educational policy at that time overlooked the fact that a technical equalization of resources invested did not mean equalization of the end product. In fact, when equal resources were applied to pupils with different cultural backgrounds, this was in practice likely to widen the differentiation of the results achieved.

Recognition of this failure of educational policy to achieve its goals led to a change expressed in "positive discrimination" – over-allocation of resources to schools in which disadvantaged pupils were enrolled – on the assumption that preferential allocation of resources would lead to more equal results. At a later stage, the shapers of Israel's educational policy admitted that there were difficulties in implementing the goal of equality in educational results. Nevertheless, they sought to transform the school into an instrument of social integration that would reduce the social segregation of immigrants from different lands of origin. Hence, a policy of integration was adopted by which pupils from different ethnic-communal backgrounds were educated in the same school.

Obscuring the differences between the Oriental and Ashkenazic communities was not possible, and is not possible even today, as long as there was and is a strong correlation between education, employment, and income, on the one hand, and country of origin, on the other. The term "ethnic-communal gap," commonplace in social and political discussions, has generally been applied to this correlation. The existence of this gap in the primary period of absorption of the wave of mass immigration was the outcome of unavoidable differences in human capital (such as education, vocational skills, and family size) on one hand, and the priority given to the pace of absorption and integration over the quality of the process, on the other.

311

The Political System

Israeli society inherited from the Yishuv, the pre-state Jewish community, a tradition of intense political activity that was inclined to intervene in areas that were not political per se. The major protagonists of this overall, comprehensive, and intensive political activity were political parties and movements. As a result, politicalization of diverse spheres of life in the Yishuv was far-reaching. Not only were public institutions and bodies staffed on the basis of the political balance of power, but efforts to provide employment, education, housing, health and medical services, culture, and sport were conducted to a great extent at the instigation and under the guidance of political movements. Although these efforts were not centralized, with many of them being conducted in enclaves representing ideological sub-cultures, the Yishuv did not lack a political-communal center. Preserving the effectiveness of this center earned the Yishuv the sobriquet of "the state-in-the-making."

Establishment of the state strengthened the center of political power, but also imposed on it additional responsibilities. On one hand there was an increase in the needs and roles required of government, placing a greater burden on the state. On the other hand, the political center could now avail itself of the coercive powers of a centralized government, enabling it not only to allocate resources but also to mobilize them, and above all to

Selling fuel in Moshav Eitan, a village of new immigrants, January 1958

enforce its authority over the various groups and sectors in Israeli society.

During the War of Independence, the government coalition included all the political components of the organized Yishuv, in addition to the Agudat Israel movement that had not participated in its institutions. However, after the first Knesset elections a very narrow coalition government was formed. It included only Mapai, the religious parties, and the Progressive Party, leaving out the main parties that were manifestly Left-wing (Mapam) or Right-wing (General Zionists and Herut). Mapam did not join the coalition until 1955. Thus was the Israeli parliamentary system characterized by a narrower coalition of political movements than had been the case during the Yishuv period. Up until 1967, even parties that were considered potential candidates for participation in the government were often left out, such as Mapam, or the General Zionists, who were in opposition during the First Knesset and again from 1955 on. Only in the wake of the Six Day War did a broad coalition emerge once again. This time it comprised not only parties that had been partners in previous government coalitions but also Herut, a party that had always been unacceptable to Mapai, in the spirit of Ben-Gurion's dictum: "Without Herut and Maki" [the Israel Communist Party].

The initial period after establishment of the state was marked by a strong tendency towards "statism," that emphasized the interests of the state over particularistic, sectoral interests. There were several reasons for the over-inclination towards political centralization. First of all, Israel had been born in war, one that it could only withstand by almost total mobilization of material and human resources. Second, the adoption of a universal legal system, under the influence of the British mandate, significantly restricted the possibility of allowing for particularist arrangements between the political center

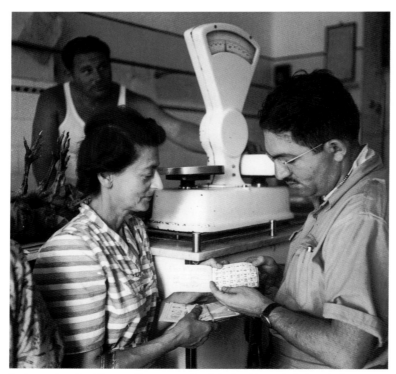

An inspector checking a ration coupon book during the period of austerity

and groups or individuals, such as those that were common under the unclear rules of the game during the Yishuv period. Third, the ritualization of sovereignty and its symbols, including fostering the charismatic influence of the national leader, David Ben-Gurion, helped to strengthen the identification of broad segments of the population with the government. Fourth, the emerging consensus that accepted the authority of Israel's democratic regime ruled out a threat to the central authority from dissident groups, or those with a tendency to break away, which had posed a challenge to the authority of the organized Yishuv during the Mandate period. Fifth, the resort by new immigrants who had arrived after the establishment of Israel to state or quasi-state bureaucratic agencies (such as the Jewish Agency) for the supply of their basic needs created direct dependence on the state establishment. Dependency of another sort was forced upon the Arab population through the introduction of military rule in Arab-populated regions. Such dependency relationships and intervention by government and state agencies in the daily life of a large percentage of the population greatly increased the power of the state's institutions.

The tendency towards centralization reached its peak in the early 1950s. Its subsequent weakening derived to a great extent from the fact that the factors that had fed it had lost their force. The War of Independence came to an end with the signing of the armistice agreements, after which mobilized manpower was considerably reduced; the universal legal system had become an accepted fact; ritualization of the symbols of sovereignty had also become routine and, in any case, they no longer possessed the ability to mobilize the population, while the attitude towards the national leadership, including Ben-Gurion, became more critical. Finally, integration of the immigrants, especially an improvement in the employment situation in the late 1950s and early 1960s, considerably reduced their dependence on public agencies. To these were added factors connected to developments in the early 1950s. The results of the 1951 elections, in which Mapai lost several of its seats, were interpreted as criticism of the government's over-involvement in the economy and also led to the gradual abolition of the austerity regime that had involved rationing essential commodities and administrative control of prices. The shortage of investment capital led to the adoption of a policy to encourage private capital investments and to broaden the private sector of Israel's economy.

In the transition from Yishuv to a state, several pre-state attributes were preserved, especially politicalization and the overly great influence of political parties. However, new patterns of non-partisan interaction between the government and the public were

Herut appealed to the new immigrants' sense of discrimination in its election propaganda. Right – in between elections Moshe Dayan calls for priority for development over tackling unemployment; left – Dayan, in a slum area on the eve of elections, urges the unemployed to demonstrate

Final preparations for elections to the Knesset

also emerging. This resulted primarily from the necessity to adapt political processes to the conditions of a government operating within a binding constitutional framework. This framework was not passed on to the State of Israel by the Yishuv; on the contrary,

313

it was a legacy from the British Mandatory administration. Since there was no orderly transfer of power, the State of Israel had no choice but to cast the political content representing the continuity of transition from Yishuv to state into the only available legal mold – the law in effect in Mandatory Palestine in May 1948. However, this did not provide a solution for establishing authority

However, when the Constituent Assembly was elected early in 1949, by a decision adopted at its very first session it transformed itself into a parliament in every respect, taking the title: The First Knesset. Moreover, somewhat more than a year later (June 1950) the Knesset decided to forego drafting an overall constitution, and instead to enact from time to time basic laws that would, in

Not until 1992 was the splendid new edifice of the Supreme Court in Jerusalem dedicated. In recent years, the Court has increasingly intervened in the legislative process in Israel

in the newly-sovereign state. To that end, the Declaration of Independence provided that the National Council – a body established before the proclamation of independence – would become the Provisional State Council and serve as the legislative branch of government until a Constituent Assembly could be elected. As to the executive branch, the Declaration of Independence provided that the National Committee, the executive arm of the National Council, would constitute the Provisional Government. These two bodies were not identical to the national institutions of the pre-state Yishuv, for they also included representatives of groups that had not been part of the organized Yishuv.

Already at this early stage, before Israel had conducted elections, its political character as a parliamentary democracy had been determined. The Law and Administration Ordinance stipulated that the Provisional Government would act in accordance with the policy determined by the Provisional State Council. The original intention was that these provisional institutions would immediately take steps to hold elections for a Constituent Assembly that would in turn enact a constitution.

the course of time, be joined together to form a constitution. Thus, the governmental and administrative framework of Israel was in fact determined by basic laws that by 1967 had dealt with the Knesset (1958), state-owned lands (1960), and the President of the State (1964). According to the spirit of these and other basic laws which were later enacted (such as Basic Law: the Government, 1968; Basic Law: the Economy, 1975; Basic Law: the Army, 1971; Basic Law: Jerusalem, Capital of Israel, 1980; Basic Law: the Judiciary, 1984; Basic Law: Dignity and Freedom of Man, 1992; Basic Law: Freedom of Occupation, 1992), the Israeli political system is a parliamentary democracy, in which the government is responsible to the Knesset.

The authority granted by law to the Knesset is extremely broad when compared with parliaments in other democratic societies. This is reflected in the fact that there is no firm constitution in Israel that the Knesset is not able to change by a simple majority. Exceptions to this rule are isolated articles in the basic laws for whose amendment a special majority is necessary. One example is the article in "Basic Law: the Knesset" which provides that Israel's parliament will be elected by proportional representation.

It may be amended only by an absolute majority of all members of the Knesset. Moreover, until changes in the election law in 1992, no body was empowered to dissolve the Knesset, except the Knesset itself. Above all, the government is responsible to the Knesset and must resign if the Knesset passes a vote of no confidence in the government. Knesset members also enjoy full immunity from any judicial action against them in regard to their voting, oral or written expression of an opinion, and any of their acts within or without the Knesset in the context of fulfilling their function as members of the Knesset.

The status of the political parties derived from the proportional representation system of elections to the Knesset. The entire country is one electoral district, and every party that receives more than one percent (later amended to one-and-one-half percent) of the votes is entitled to representation in the Knesset according to the proportional support it enjoys among the voters. This system represents the political tradition that developed within the Zionist movement and the pre-state Yishuv. Since acceptance of the authority of the central institutions was voluntary, there was always a potential threat that parties and movements that felt they did not receive due representation might break away. Only a system of elections that provided an opportunity for every political opinion to be represented could mitigate the threat of such a secession. This system, however, also represents a tradition of ideological factionalism par excellence that leaves little room for the representation of local interests.

The proportional representation system makes multiplicity of parties possible. And indeed, Israel has been a multi-party democracy, unlike the Anglo-Saxon democracies that generally have two major parties. As a result, in no Knesset elected to this day has any party had an absolute majority, and all governments have been coalitions.

Whereas relations between the legislative and executive branches of government have been influenced primarily by the political legacy of the pre-state Yishuv and the Zionist movement, those between the executive and the judiciary were molded first and foremost by the influence of British judicial tradition. Hence, the judiciary – more than any other body, at least in the period under consideration – has remained immune to the influence of party politics. This is in no small degree due to the efforts of the first minister of justice, Pinhas Rosen. Thus have the courts – above all the Supreme Court sitting as the High Court of Justice – become the "watchdog" of the rule of law in Israel.

The court system was not the only institutional

framework that played a role in ensuring the rule of law in the State of Israel. To a great extent, the attorney general, too, represented the legal-professional approach in relation to government decisions – purely administrative ones as well as those of a political nature. Paradoxically, although some of the decisions of the attorney general have been thorns in the flesh of leading political personalities, Israeli governments have been more and more inclined to have him decide in cases that are sensitive issues, whether because they touch personally upon the standing of important individuals or due to their political implications.

While a tradition of binding universal and egalitarian judicial norms has been created in Israel in all fields subject to review by the state courts, a significant area has remained outside their jurisdiction. The regular courts are not authorized to intervene in all matters of personal status (marriage, divorce, etc.). These cases are to be tried only in courts of the various religious communities – Jews, Muslims, Christians, Druzes, and so forth.

The Pattern of Political Parties

The pattern of Israel's political parties was marked by several characteristics during the 1950s and 1960s, which continued at least until the political watershed of 1977. First, a multiplicity of parties and lists have represented in the Knesset large, medium, small, and tiny movements of every conceivable ideological hue. To these we should add new lists that from time to time almost crossed the the minimum one-percentage barrier of representation. Second, the absence of any party with an absolute majority. Third, despite the lack of a majority party, one of the parties – Mapai and its successor, the Labor Party – enjoyed much greater electoral support than any other single party.

Obviously, then, despite the multiplicity of parties and their

Ben-Gurion speaking at a Rafi election rally

ideological diversity, Israel's political map was characterized by the existence of one dominant party. Only after the watershed of 1977 did the pattern of political parties become polarized. Until 1977, Mapai was not only the biggest party; it was also the core party without which a coalition government could not be formed. Hence, Mapai had a strong bargaining position, giving it room for maneuver in choosing its coalition partners. Mapai's status as the core party was threatened more from the Right than from the Left, for though it was capable of forming

Ahdut Ha-Avodah, and Rafi reunited to form the Labor Party.

Until 1967, actually until 1977, there was no transfer of power in Israel, only changes in Mapai's coalition partners. Mapai's status as a core party enabled it to choose its coalition partners from among all the parties, with the exception of Herut and Maki (Communists). Moreover, Mapai could in practice choose as it wished from among its potential partners, thus avoiding an overly wide coalition that would obligate concessions to too many partners. In this way Mapai (and the Labor Party subsequently)

Hostility between Mapai, the long-standing government party, and Herut, the major opposition party, as expressed in election posters from the 1950s. Right – Herut calls upon the voters to oust Mapai leaders from the government; left – the Mapai poster declares that the state will be built by hard work, not empty phrases

a majority together with more Leftist parties to prevent a Rightist coalition, this was much smaller than the majority it could form with Right-wing parties against the Left. In this state of affairs, the mobility of votes from Mapai to the Right, or the secession of a faction in Mapai's own right wing in order to join a Rightist coalition without Mapai might have denied it the status as a core party. Indeed, in 1964 a faction led by David Ben-Gurion, Shimon Peres, Moshe Dayan, and Yosef Almogi broke away from Mapai, seeking to exploit this weak point and enable the party they established – Rafi – to tip the balance. What Rafi's founders hoped was that a situation would emerge which would theoretically enable formation of a coalition government without Mapai. This would force Mapai to accept the political dictates of Rafi. However, in the 1965 elections Mapai successfully retained its status as the core party, while Rafi became part of the Right-wing opposition to Mapai. In the end, most of the Rafi leadership – although without Ben-Gurion himself – returned to the fold of the dominant party. In 1968, Mapai,

ensured for itself a majority within the government coalition. Only one attempt was made – in 1961 – by potential coalition partners to force Mapai to form a broad coalition that would include all potential parties, but this failed.

Correlation between Social Class and Political Voting

In the period under consideration the Israeli parties played a central role in political life in two different contexts. First, by choosing men and women for political positions and placing them in office. Although this refers above all to elected offices, senior administrative appointments also involved partisan considerations. Secondly, the parties constituted frameworks for political mobilization, particularly at election time. Voting in elections, as the broadest form of participation in political life, serves as a channel by which society influences the political system. From this viewpoint we may say that it formed a bridge between Israel's social stratification and its political and party patters.

Panoramic view of the Tiberias transit camp with Lake Kinneret in the background, 1950

In the pre-state period, there was a close relationship between social rifts, such as the economic and class gaps, and political voting. To a great extent, the correlation between division by class and the division of political power among parties fitted the model predominant in most European countries: salaried or waged employees, above all "blue collar" workers, tended to vote for Leftist parties, while the middle class was inclined to give its support to Rightist and Centrist parties. Nevertheless, even in the Yishuv period there were several instances that deviated from

this model. Several changes occurred in voting patterns after establishment of the state. The first was the outcome of political mobilization in the course of absorbing and integrating the new immigrants. Those who came from Asian and African countries in the 1950s did not follow in the footsteps of the veteran Oriental ethnic communities in the country, and did not vote for ethnic-communal parties or secular middle class ones. Rather, they gave their votes to Mapai and the Zionist-oriented National Religious Party. Thus, paradoxically, it was precisely at the time of the waves

317

of mass immigration from Oriental countries that the ethnic-communal parties of Sefardim and Yemenites vanished from the political scene. In the elections to the First Knesset, conducted in 1949, these parties together gained five seats, in the elections to the Second Knesset in 1951 they received only three, and in those to the Third Knesset in 1955 none of them managed to achieve the one-percent minimum. Since most of the new immigrants were salaried or waged employees, mainly manual laborers, their voting fit the conventional model of proletarian support for Leftist parties and middle-class voting for bourgeois parties.

To all appearances, this correlation continued to hold true in Israel throughout the 1950s, but changes that were already noticeable towards the end of that decade indicated that this was a deceptive picture. When voting for Mapai, the new immigrants had not been motivated by class incentives. Rather, they expressed support for the ruling party, whether for the instrumental reason that they were dependent upon the absorption and integration agencies, or because of Mapai's identification with the state leadership. When dependence on the absorption apparatus diminished due to improved employment opportunities and depoliticalization of state institutions, together with a dimming of the charismatic image of the Mapai leadership and David Ben-Gurion, a new voting pattern emerged. A trend towards Herut gradually developed among Oriental Jews who had immigrated to Israel in the early years of the state. It was especially prominent among the younger generation which first voted in Knesset elections in the 1960s and 1970s, but its early signs were already evident in the 1959 elections. Those same elections also pointed to signs of another change in voting patterns: an increasing

inclination among the middle class and professionals of European extraction to vote for Mapai. As a result, Mapai became a more heterogeneous party from the point of view of its class composition. Nevertheless, the correlation between ethnic-communal origin and voting patterns did not indicate – at least not in the period under discussion – a trend towards ethnic-communal separatism, at least not in politics. This is attested by the repeated failure of ethnic-communal parties.

Attributing the overlapping between ethnic-communal origin and socioeconomic status to the absorption policy of the 1950s reflects a tendency to overlook objective factors which influenced this policy: the necessity (discussed above) to choose between the quality and the pace of absorption when allocating resources for education, housing, and employment; and the cultural and educational background of a significant part of the immigrants who came from societies which had not gone through a process of modernization. Moreover, one may ascribe the search for guilty parties in the failure of the absorption process to a tendency to social extroversion – an inclination to place the blame not on oneself but on external factors. However, none of this can detract from the powerful sense of inequality among members of the Oriental communities and their families in the late 1950s, at least as far as the political dimension is concerned.

This sense of inequality and discrimination was formulated more in political than in class terms. We may attribute this to the conceptual framework the immigrants brought with them from Islamic countries. Those raised in an Oriental cultural milieu tended to view society as divided first of all into ascriptive groupings – family, clan, religious community, and nationality – while the division into social classes was of secondary importance. Hence, images of social order that stressed class division – salaried and waged employees contrasted with the self-employed, manual laborers with white collar workers, and low-income families with the well off – were alien to them. However, the tendency to formulate their sense of inequality in ethnic-communal rather than class terms was influenced not only by the immigrants' cultural background but also by the socio-economic structure that they found upon arriving in Israel. In the 1950s, most of the new immigrants were employed by the government and other public sectors of the Israeli economy. Only a minority were

318

A monument in memory of the victims of the Holocaust at Yad Vashem, the Holocaust and Martyrs' Memorial in Jerusalem

The "pre-emptive attack" strategy led political and military leaders to embark on the Sinai Campaign. IDF forces in Sinai, October-November 1956

absorbed into the private sector, to which the class struggle concepts could be applied. In conflicts over working conditions and wages, the immigrant workers usually confronted the veteran political establishment, not private employers. Thus, the conditions that had led to the development of class consciousness in Europe , or even in the pre-state Yishuv, were not present in Israel in the 1950s. Furthermore, those in Israeli society who adhered to a concept of a social order in terms of class conflict were identified with the very same bureaucratic political elite – Ashkenazic in its decisive majority – that controlled the Oriental immigrants' source of livelihood.

The Salience of Security in Israeli Society

The State of Israel has undergone more wars than any other state since the end of the Second World War. Even in between full-fledged wars there was limited military activity – border clashes, terrorist infiltrations, and reprisal raids. As a result of continuing conflict, the issue of national security became a central one in Israeli society, exerting considerable influence on values and institutions and on the everyday life of Israeli citizens. From war

to war, security expenditures accounted for a greater percentage of the Gross National Product, reaching a peak in the wake of the Yom Kippur War (about 25% of the GNP).

The State of Israel was born during a war which ended in armistice agreements that did not represent a state of peace. Thus, from the very beginning of its existence as an independent state it had to be conceptually and institutionally prepared to withstand an ongoing violent conflict. This condition – which may be termed "national security preparedness" – has both military-strategic and social-institutional aspects. The military-strategic aspect includes military doctrine and planning, the structure of the armed forces, their equipment, modes of operation, and combat techniques. The social aspect includes arrangements for the mobilization of manpower and resources for security needs, and patterns of interaction between the military and the civilian frameworks.

The threat to Israel's basic security was manifested in three strategic weak points for which its defense doctrine had difficulty in supplying a remedy: a demographic balance of power heavily in favor of the Arabs; vulnerable borders due to an absence of strategic depth; the necessity to engage in a continuous violent conflict that involved a major allocation of resources for national security.

319

The response to the first deficiency was a system of mobilization based on high exploitation of available manpower. The foundation of this system is the concept of "a nation in arms" that assumes that the total manpower potential is exploited in wartime under the heading of "emergency military service." To this end, military manpower was based on three components: a

Briefing commanders before going into battle during the Sinai Campaign, October 1956

cadre of professional soldiers; other soldiers conscripted for three years of compulsory service; and army reserves that could be mobilized immediately, in which Israeli men served until the age of 53. This framework had far-reaching strategic and social implications. For example, Israel could not embark on an all-out war without first mobilizing its reserves, thus limiting its ability to use surprise as a strategy. Furthermore, Israel was incapable of mobilizing reserves for a prolonged period of time without going to war, since its economy would be paralyzed.

Israel's response to the lack of strategic depth was the doctrine of a "pre-emptive strike." This doctrine raises the question of when does Israel conclude that its deterrent capability has been undermined, and that it must pre-empt an expected enemy attack by a military initiative of its own. A partial answer was given by determining a series of vital Israeli interests which, if they be threatened, would constitute a casus belli, such as closure of the Straits of Tiran, threatening concentrations of forces along its borders, violation of the status quo in Jordan, and so forth. The assumption was that a blow at these vital interests would serve as a warning that Israel was losing its deterrent capacity. Thus, any such act would constitute a possible motive for a pre-emptive strike.

The third challenge to Israel as a democratic nation was to

find a modus vivendi for the relations between the army and the civil administration that would enable it to withstand a continuous violent conflict. This problem had two aspects: firstly, ensuring optimal mobilization of manpower and material resources for national security under the conditions of a democratic regime; secondly, creating a system of checks and controls suitable for a state of continuous emergency that was typified by limited violent actions in periods of dormant war, and repeated deterioration every few years to an all-out war conducted in a setting of international political constraints. These two aspects of national security were interwoven. The unique characteristics of the military-state relationship that emerged determined in great measure both the extent of national consensus as to allocation of resources for defense purposes and the patterns of civilian supervision over the military establishment. These traits – broad participation of citizens in national security efforts, obscure boundaries between the two systems, and social networks and channels of communication between the military and civilian elites – are what led to the development of diverse interrelationships between the civilian and the military sectors.

The rules of the game of military-civilian relations recognized the right of military involvement in certain aspects of the civilian system, while in all other areas such intervention would be objectionable. Military involvement was considered legitimate in all matters having to do with national security in the broadest sense of the term, i.e., including foreign policy. In contrast, internal affairs, welfare policy, and democratic governmental arrangements were considered civilian in their very essence. This distinction left open the question as to what should be included in national security and what should be out of its bounds. From time to time issues arose which could be considered political from one point of view, or as security-related from another (for instance newspaper censorship). In any event, generally it was not the military establishment that was inclined to widen the limits of what was included under the term "national security." The controversy over this issue was usually conducted within the civilian sector.

The absence of a significant discrepancy between the positions

320

of the military and the civilian sectors concerning the rules of the game originated in a broad consensus as to the fact that Israeli state and society were in constant danger from an acute military threat. This implied subordinating foreign relations to national defense interests. The continuous Arab-Israeli conflict also influenced internal policy, at least in the field of inter-communal relations between Jews and Arabs. One example is the military rule that was imposed on Arab-populated areas within sovereign Israeli territory for about eighteen years, until it was abolished in 1966. In contrast, the military elite did not challenge the application of democratic values (as distinguished from the values of hierarchical military authority and force) in all matters relating to governmental and administrative procedures, freedom of speech, cultural creativity, human rights, freedom to organize, and labor relations. Thus it is evident that there was no symmetry in the mutual influence of the military and the civilian sectors.

an IDF regulation, soldiers were obligated to take an oath of loyalty "to the State of Israel, to its constitution, and to its authorized government agencies." The explicit mention of "authorized government agencies" was intended to prevent intervention by political parties in the military system, because army personnel had overt connections with political movements and parties, connections whose roots went back to the legacy of the pre-state period. Application of this principle was bound up with two acute political crises in the first months of the state's existence – the *Altalena* crisis and the crisis over dismantling the Palmah High Command. The *Altalena* was a ship commanded by the Irgun Zvai Leumi (National Military Organization), one of the two Jewish underground movements that did not accept the full authority of the "national institutions" in the pre-state period. The *Altalena* carried a shipment of arms and ammunition from Europe to Israel during a UN-imposed truce in the fighting,

The wreckage of the *Altalena* just off the Tel Aviv beach, 1948

In what pertained to national security the military greatly influenced the government's actions, whereas in the areas of internal affairs and welfare policy, there was only partial "civilianization" of the military establishment.

The most troubling issue in this respect was the danger that the armed forces would come under political influence. Under

and tried to unload its cargo on the Tel Aviv waterfront contrary to instructions from the government. Ben-Gurion ordered the IDF to open fire on the ship, which sank just off the shore. Ben-Gurion's order signified his determination to prevent displays of political-organizational autonomy in the ranks of the IDF. After the assassination of UN mediator Count Folke Bernadotte by

The Palmah fighters were not happy about losing their independence. Slogans on a wall in the village of Qastina, after the failure of the first attack on the Iraq al-Manshiyah police fort, read: "The Seventh Brigade shall arise again" and "Irregardless, and despite everything – Palmah"

members of the Lehi (Lohamei Herut Israel – Fighters for the Freedom of Israel) in Jerusalem, the IDF also disarmed units of the Irgun and Lehi in that city. The *Altalena* affair reflected the fear of Ben-Gurion and the Israeli government of the introduction of politics into the IDF through the integration of external fighting units into its ranks. This was also considered a grave danger due to the fact that these two movements represented a long tradition of rejecting the hegemony of the institutions of the organized pre-state Yishuv.

The second crisis over political influence in the armed forces – the dismantling of the Palmah Command – was in essence different from the *Altalena* issue, since it revolved around a military unit that had been an inseparable part of the Haganah (Defense) organization from which the IDF had emerged. As such, the Palmah was subject to the control of the national institutions and continued to be fully subordinate to the IDF General Staff and the Israeli government. Nevertheless, the Palmah did have some organizational autonomy within the IDF framework through a separate command that dealt with training, logistics, and manpower. Furthermore, the Palmah was considerably influenced by its informal ties with the kibbutz movements, above all Ha-Kibbutz Ha-Me'uhad, in which Mapam members of the Ahdut

Ha-Avodah (Unity of Labor) faction were a majority.

A combination of partisan interests with the ideological concept of the primacy of the state led Ben-Gurion to dismantle the Palmah Command, and later – when mass demobilization of IDF troops began at the end of 1949 – its brigades as well. Ben-Gurion's justification of the dismantling of the Palmah Command was based on the principle of depoliticalization of the army. His adversaries on the Left, who wanted to prevent or at least to delay the dissolution, stressed that the Palmah was a voluntary force that continued the tradition of the Israeli labor movement. Hence, disbanding the Palmah embodied – at least from the standpoint of its ideological justification – a victory in favor of a uniform army without particularist, political ties.

Political involvement in the army's ranks was also reflected in participation by officers on active service in party affairs by standing as candidates for election to the First Knesset. Yigal Allon, Moshe Carmel, and Shimon Avidan, for instance, were included in the Mapam list of candidates, while Moshe Dayan was on the Mapai list. This was justified, since the elections were conducted before demobilization began at war's end, and even senior commanders were considered to be conscripts rather than professional army officers. This was not repeated in later elections;

it was explicitly forbidden by the "Basic Law: the Knesset." General Staff regulations, however, recognized the right of officers to be passive party members. Political parties, primarily those of the labor and settlement movements, acted to foster affinity with their movements of regular army officers who belonged to their ranks. Hence, politicalization of the IDF took two different forms: the introduction of political considerations into the promotion of officers, and maintaining channels of communication of a partisan nature between professional officers and politicians. Another manifestation of the link between senior officers and the political establishment was the mobilization of officers, upon their retirement from the army, to represent parties or join the ranks of their leaderships. This was especially prominent in the two big parties, Mapai and Herut. Thus, the military's involvement in political decisions, on the one hand, and ties between political parties and army personnel, on the other, reflected the two facets of the porous borderline between the political and military systems. Sometimes the same case worked in both directions. The involvement of

Ben-Gurion and Moshe Dayan on his appointment as Chief of Staff, 1953. Immediately upon retiring from the army in 1958, Dayan joined the political ranks

former senior officers in political decisions served, on one hand, as a channel to influence policy, utilizing the professional knowledge and doctrines that the officers had brought with them from the IDF; on other hand, it was a means by which the political establishment could diminish its dependence on the professional advice of military personnel on active service. The influence of political personalities with a military past on the shaping of policy was very evident during the two periods in which Yitzhak Rabin, the former chief of staff, served as prime minister.

These and other phenomena afforded the military elite in Israel a more central status in society and more extensive political involvement than in other democratic states. The civilian elites, for their part, simultaneously displayed involvement in the sphere of national security, both through service in the reserves and through contact with senior military officers in the setting of common social networks. This partnership between the military and civilian elites does not represent a total blurring of the borderline between them. It was based on rules of the game that mutually defined the areas of legitimate intervention by the army in policy of a civilian character, and the dimensions of the army's professional autonomy, that restricted over-involvement of the political sector in army affairs.

Israel, though involved in a continuous violent conflict, did not behave as a society under siege. Israel did not become a garrison state ruled by experts in violence, in which all areas of life are subordinated to meeting the challenges of the external threat. It was nearer to the model of Athens which, despite no lesser involvement in wars than Sparta, maintained a democratic regime and fostered a civilian way of life in times of calm.

323

Poster calling for volunteers to join the paratroops, late 1950s

Divided Jerusalem. Children in the Mamilla neighborhood look through a hole in the protective wall towards Jordanian Jerusalem, 1961

. . . .

Conclusion

324

Development of Israeli society was accompanied by wide-ranging expectations for the fulfillment of collective goals inspired by an ideology accepted by the large majority of the population and by the dominant elites. However, several of these collective objectives were imbued from the very outset with a large proportion of utopianism, whereas the achievement of others could be attained only by mobilizing considerable resources and a great degree of willingness on the part of the population to put off satisfying collective and individual claims. In the situation created under these circumstances, there was an excess of competing collective goals and contradictory sectoral demands. The necessity to contend with them influenced the shaping of Israel's institutional structure and the ground rules of its democratic system. Most patterns of this institutional structure and the bulk of the political rules were already determined during the first decade of Israel's existence.

The only way the political system could adapt to the new conditions was by developing patterns of mobilization and allocation of resources based on bureaucratic dependence of the new peripheral groups, especially the new immigrants, and their paternalistic treatment by the authorities. Actually, during Israel's first years there were two sets of ground rules. The first applied to the veteran population which came to be known as "First Israel," where the old norms of voluntary involvement were still at work (although the administration was forced to allocate more remuneration and rewards to preserve the old level of involvement). Conversely, in respect of "Second Israel" new principles of mobilization and allocation of resources were created. In this case the dependence of the immigrants upon the absorption agencies became the main lever for political mobilization, instead of primarily voluntary involvement. In this case there was no need of great commitment, nor of a high level of reward and remuneration.

Until 1967, Israeli society was not aware of the high social cost of changing the rules of the political game, particularly alienation of new immigrants from the ruling establishment. Moreover, it was still not obligated to decide several moral-political dilemmas, as it was forced to do after the Six Day War. For instance, it did not yet have to deal with the issue of Jews and Arabs in the "Greater Land of Israel," i.e. the entire area west of the Jordan River, including those areas conquered during the Six Day War. It did not have to adopt or choose a specific political pattern, such as a democratic Jewish national state, a democratic bi-national state, a non-democratic Jewish state, or transforming Israel into a country without Arabs, but lacking both internal and international moral legitimacy. It was also unnecessary for pre-1967 Israeli society to deal intensively with the issue of religion and state. It was enough to preserve the status quo. Nor were there, before 1967, sharp differences of opinion concerning expansion of the welfare state. Taking into account that the government was over-burdened in any case, whatever disputes there were over this issue applied only to the pace of application of existing arrangements, to the grave defense issues, and to the need to hasten the integration of immigrants.

The overload of collective objectives that limited Israeli society's capacity to fulfill them and curtailed the ability of the central political authorities to respond to the just demands of the periphery did not fundamentally undermine the stability of the regime in Israel. Stability was preserved due to a series of arrangements that mitigated the influence of the overload, the most prominent being the import of capital, a considerable part of which was tantamount to a grant. Unilateral transfer of capital – contributions from world Jewry, German reparations payments, and foreign aid from the United States government – enabled Israel to achieve many of its collective objectives while even raising the standard of living.

In addition to efforts to mobilize resources that helped reduce pressures, the government also had recourse to political arrangements in its efforts to cope with the problems created by an overload of social objectives. For example, pressure generated by expectations for a solution of fundamental problems was checked by an approach that favored cloudy definitions, lack of consistency, and delaying decisions that involved radical solutions. An extremely striking example was the avoidance of enacting a constitution in order to prevent a confrontation over the issue of the status of halakhah (Jewish religious law) in such a fundamental document. As a result of this flexibility, ideological confrontations that might have occurred in the course of trying to shape a long-term policy were avoided.

The Six Day War of 1967 constituted a turning point from almost every point of view. In addition to the change in Israel's strategic situation, it soon became clear that all the controversies that had lain dormant until 1967 were becoming more intense, particularly the dispute over the physical borders within which Zionist aspirations were to be fulfilled, and the controversy over the identity of Israeli society, chiefly in matters relating to the status of halakhah and its political implications for Israeli culture in general, and Israeli political culture in particular.

. . . .

Epilogue

Eliezer Schweid

The people called "Israel" has borne several other names throughout its lengthy history. Its ancient patriarchs originated from the Hebrews. To this day, its national language is called Hebrew, and in our times, too, there are some of this nation who prefer to be known as "Hebrews", a name they esteem more highly than the designation "Jews" (*Yehudim*, literally, "Judahites"), which has been in common use since the early Second Temple period. The source of all these names is the ancient family from which the People of Israel is descended. They signify episodes in the lengthy, turbulent annals of a people which has preserved an unbroken historic memory, and whose origins are older than those of the peoples among whom they have lived in every epoch of its history. But it is also a people that has on several occasions re-established its identity, in a renewed form, after catastrophes which had threatened to destroy it, thus becoming in every epoch of its history a people younger than those among whom it lived.

According to the biblical account, the name "Hebrew" was replaced by "Israel" during the period of bondage in Egypt. The seventy souls of the House of Jacob who went down to Egypt over time increased in number becoming the twelve tribes of Israel, and later combined at the time of the Exodus to return to their homeland. The name "Israel" was replaced by "Yehudim" after the destruction of the two kingdoms of Israel and Judah that the tribes of Israel had established in Canaan. It then became clear that the ten tribes of the Kingdom of Israel had been lost in exile and only the people of the Kingdom of Judah, who had been exiled to Babylon, continued to preserve a national existence there. Part of the nation returned to its ancestral homeland,

erected there its temple under Persian rule, and was subsequently able to establish a kingdom which, however, was soon subjugated by the Romans.

However, the name Israel was not completely pushed aside by "Yehudi – Jew." It is difficult to determine a hard and fast rule governing how these two were used interchangeably. Sometimes it seems that they were employed as synonyms, but when one wanted to be precise, "Jews" signified the individuals belonging to the people in its concrete, contemporary historical reality as a people in Exile, dispersed among the nations. "Israel," on the other hand, signified its united identity as an ideal collective entity based on the memory of the Exodus from Egypt, of its founding covenant with God, of its destiny as "a chosen people" – "the people of the Torah" (the book that testified to its covenant with its God) – on the memory of its entire history since the Covenant, and on the vision of the future promised by God in which the Covenant and Israel's destiny would be fulfilled at the End of Days. The land designated for the people of Israel in the Covenant, where the messianic kingdom was destined to rise once again as in the days of David and Solomon (the Hasmonean kingdom did not enjoy this status even at its peak), has since been known as the Land of Israel, bearing the name of the people for whom it was destined.

A momentous change has occurred once again in our own times. After a holocaust unprecedented in Jewish history that threatened total destruction of the People of Israel, a Jewish state was established in part of the Land of Israel and given the name Israel. Since it is now the name of a state in which only part of

327

the surviving remnant of the Jewish People has gathered together, and due to the short historical memory represented by Israel since its establishment as a modern, secular nation-state, the original meaning of the name Israel as a collective, historic, and specific appellation for the people has been pushed into the background. In any event, "Israel" is almost never used to refer to the Jewish people's collective identity. Israelis are citizens of the State of Israel, and we must bear in mind that members of other peoples are also citizens of Israel. From now on, only the term "Jews" denotes the entire people as a collective entity, and the issue of whether the State of Israel should be a Jewish state, or in which aspects it should be a Jewish state, is the source of harsh controversy among Israeli citizens, Jews and non-Jews alike. Even the definition of Jewish identity is the subject of much debate. As a result of these two overlapping controversies, there is a tension-ridden discrepancy between the application of the terms "Israelis" and "Jews," and between the definitions of the collective entities denoted by these names, for Israelis comprise a different kind of collective entity than the totality of those known as Jews.

Only naturally, this change has also left its mark on the definition of the relationship between the nation known as the Jewish People and the land named Israel. Is this still the land that was designated for the People of Israel in the covenant that God made with its forefathers, and where its messianic kingdom was destined to arise? Or is this only a certain piece of territory, a geographic entity on which the tangible State of Israel is located, a state that is not messianic but national-secular? This question, too, has become the focus of bitter controversy between those Israeli Jews who aspire to absolute identity between these two inferred meanings of the Land of Israel – the ethnic-religious and the political – and those Israeli Jews who want the State of Israel in its present form (both in relation to the extent of its territory and to its secular constitutional character), defining the nature of its land and determining a solely national-political relationship towards it.

According to Israel's Declaration of Independence, the original intention that underlay calling the new state "Israel" was to present it as the state of the entire Jewish People on the basis of "the eternal Book of Books," i.e., on the basis of the nation's full historic memory. The goal was to gather in the Jews from their various lands of exile and to redeem the nation in the sense of "restoring our days as of old," when it had lived on its own soil as an independent nation, thereby redeeming not only itself and its history ("after two thousand years of exile"), but its land as well. But it turns out that the fact of naming the new state Israel (which has not yet fulfilled the vision of its founders) signified a far-going change, touching on the perception of the people's identity, the historical memory unifying it, and the nature of the bond between it and its land.

For the sake of historical accuracy we should note that the processes leading to this change began long before the establishment of the State of Israel. They were inherent in the crisis that accompanied the transition from the Middle Ages to modern times. Its chief traits were: secularization of Western culture, deposition of religion from its status as the hegemonic factor in shaping that culture, and the emergence of centralized nation-states. From the Jewish perspective, the crisis was intensified when Jews attained citizenship of the nation-states in which they resided and were integrated into their societies and secular cultures. Thus did the Jews leave the framework of their own self-identity.

The Jewish Enlightenment movement (*Haskalah*), whose objective was to hasten the processes of integration into Western culture, and the movements that developed within or in opposition to it, gave rise to bitter controversies that divided the people around several definitions of collective identity, most of them modern (i.e. not traditional), yet opposed to each other. These definitions influenced the way Jews related to their historical memory, their cultural tradition, the Torah and Jewish law (i.e. religion), and to the Land of Israel, so much so that the very definition of the collective entity that united the Jews as a people on the basis of its origin and continuous existence throughout the ages became a subject of controversy.

Citizenship of the nation-states of the other peoples required those who wanted to obtain it to forgo defining their own collective entity as a nation or a people (in the modern political concept). There were some Jews who went even further. In their aspiration for emancipation they were also prepared to forgo their identification with a people united by its familial-tribal origins, its age-long existence, and its unique popular culture and language. For them it was enough to be identified merely as a collective religious entity, ecclesiastical in nature, similar to Christianity. It goes without saying that they gave up their bond with the Land of Israel and the vision of a messianic kingdom. They redefined the mission of Israel as a universal religious one – to spread the belief in pure absolute monotheism among mankind. As for being part of a nation, they individually ascribed themselves to the nations among whom they resided. To this end they replaced Hebrew or Yiddish with the languages of the nations with whom they allied themselves while adopting their cultural heritage, and considered the countries of their residence to be their national homelands.

However, there were other Jews who relinquished their distinct national-political identity without forgoing their connection to the people, one they believed to be an essential component of their unique religion. They refused to give up the very things that made Judaism as an ethnic religion different from Christianity as an ecclesiastical religion. They saw loyalty to Hebrew, as the holy tongue, and to the full corpus of ancient, medieval, and modern Jewish sources, (including the popular cultural heritage produced in Exile), as the basis upon which full, national identity could be retained by a people who expressed it within its own communities, even though lacking a distinct national framework.

Opposed to these two groups were Jews who relinquished the traditional bond to religion and wanted to define their connection to the Jewish People within a modern national framework that would make possible integration into Western secular culture without assimilation. To achieve this it was necessary to return to the Land of Israel, founding there not the Holy Land of prophecy and vision, but the homeland of a sovereign nation established on its own soil, like all modern nations.

Unlike them, there were other Jews who aspired to unite all the distinguishing elements of the people, the nation, the Torah, Jewish religious law, and the Land of Israel, as conceived in the Jewish tradition, by induced fulfillment of the traditional messianic destiny. And in contrast to all the foregoing groups taken together, there were those who set themselves completely apart, who consciously rejected modern civilization and upheld the view that had been shaped within the rabbinical leadership since the failure of the Bar Kokhba Revolt: to remain as exiles wherever they lived. This meant avoiding social-cultural or political integration into their surroundings on one hand, while forgoing any independent political initiative to return to their homeland. Rather they were required only to await their messianic redemption by Providence at the End of Days.

However, despite this polarized clash of outlooks, as long as it was conducted in relation to goals none of which had been achieved, and as long as their absolute achievement encountered obstacles that gave them a messianic, utopian nature, all Jews who wanted to remain such maintained the foundations of the historical, traditional Jewish identification which were the points of departure for themselves and their parents – foundations that in practice made them all members of one people. We should add that on that very same basis Western nations continued to see all Jews as one people, totally different from themselves. And thus were the Jews united, by force of circumstances, as they

contended with issues bearing on their connection to the past and their struggle for the future.

The momentous change whose early stages – as already noted – go back to the beginning of modern times was only completed and institutionalized with the establishment of the State of Israel. Moreover, it should be emphasized that the institutionalization of secular Jewish nationalism in a sovereign state on its own soil also led to the institutionalization of the other forms of Jewish identification that were distinct from it: the unique identity of religious Zionism in the State of Israel; the variety of identities found among Diaspora Jews, following the diversity of modern movements that influenced them (modern Orthodox, Conservatives, Reformed); and the most self-segregating identity of them all – that of the Ultra-Orthodox communities that consider themselves to be in Exile both in Israel and in the Diaspora. Hence, a spectrum of identities emerged creating a new historical reality. The immediate problem was whether there was still a sufficient foundation of common memories of the past, joint activity in the present, and aspirations for the future to unite all those varieties of Jewish identification into one collective entity. And if so, what kind of collective entity would it be? Would the State of Israel, as a national-political framework, be able to provide this foundation? If so – how must it define its identity as a Jewish state in a manner that would bridge the divisions within the state itself and between it and Diaspora Jewry?

Dealing with these questions calls for an in-depth examination of the significance of the break created between the traditional pattern of identity of the Jewish People and the new ones (including the "Ultra-Orthodox" pattern, which is new in relation both to its general environment in which it operates and to the Jewish People as one whole entity). What marked the new patterns of Jewish identity was the transfer of the name "Israel" from the people to the state. This was evident both in relation to Jewish consciousness of their collective identity, and in the Jews' attitude to their land. What were the main characteristics of the traditional pattern? What, in contrast, are the traits of the collective entity emerging – if one is indeed emerging – from the new patterns of identity?

Most of the chapters in this anthology consider the relationship of the People of Israel to the Land of Israel in the period of its Exile, on which the volume has focused. Nevertheless, we should briefly consider the historical memory of those periods in which the Jewish people lived in its own land where it established its kingdom, for it is this memory that underlies the traditional historic image that took shape, as noted above, after the failure of the Bar Kokhba Revolt. In the Bible the name Israel is applied to the people as a union of all its tribes – the sons of Jacob, whose name was changed to Israel after he had wrestled with the angel of God. Accordingly, the name Israel was also applied to the kingdom in which most of the tribes of Israel had united. But it is instructive that in the Bible the country is usually called Canaan, and in the few instances where the name Land of Israel appears it refers to the tribal allocations on which the Kingdom of Israel arose, just as those which comprised the Kingdom of Judah are called the Land of Judah. If we compare this form of indicating the name of the country with how the Bible designates the lands of other peoples, we perceive that we have before us a principle that has been consistently followed. A country is named after the people whose property it is deemed to be, and a country does not become the property of a people until it establishes its kingdom there. In the same manner, a country's borders reflect the limits of the authority of its kingdom.

However, an examination of the biblical descriptions of the borders of the land promised to the People of Israel as its patrimony shows that they do not coincide with the borders of the kingdoms that it established. The Promised Land, whether it is called Canaan or indicated simply as "your land," is not defined by political possession, and the ways in which the people relates to it are not determined only by a right of possession to be realized in the future. They are determined by God's possession of a territory of unique qualities, a territory that He assigned to His people under a certain condition. Only when the people will have proven, by fulfilling this stipulation, that it is worthy of this territory will it merit holding it in its entirety, and for eternity.

According to the outlook of the biblical prophets, then, it is not the kingdom that defines the ideal identity of the people called Israel, nor does the kingdom define its patrimony. True, dominion defines the territory of all other peoples, but in regard to the People of Israel only the covenant between it and its God defines its identity in relation to the Land of Israel and the identity of the land in relation to the People of Israel. This unique conception indeed imparts to the people and its land unique spiritual qualities originating in direct divine presence, qualities of a holy nation and a sanctified land.

Was the view of the prophets, as documented in the Bible, what molded the consciousness of belonging to a collective entity and the bond between the tribes of Israel and their country in First Temple times? If we accept the opinion of biblical scholars, that the Bible reflects mainly opinions that took shape after the Babylonian exile, then it would be very reasonable to assume that the answer to this question is negative. It could be that the Israelites, especially those living in the Kingdom of Israel,

considered themselves – just as do present-day Israelis – to be members of a political nation, and like the Israelis they may have related to their country as to a material national asset. We can state with certainty, however, that consciousness of such a political identity did not become part of the historical memory that molded the self-identity of the people in the following generations. What was absorbed into its historical memory, shaping self-consciousness as to the definition of its identity and its bond to the Land of Israel, was the prophetic myth of the Chosen People that had to contend with great internal trials and with the neighboring peoples in order to be worthy of living on its land, which is God's sacred ground, and of fulfilling there its earthly, spiritual missions. This is a people that even when part of it resides in its land, it is always only on the way there.

Once more, these remarks should be qualified in view of historical observation. It could very well be that the Hasmonean kingdom, that arose out of a revolt of pious God-fearing people but at its height took on a form similar to that of any of the neighboring Hellenistic kingdoms, aspired to define within its borders a national, territorial identity, viewing Judaism as a state cult that would mold such an identity, and even aspired to force it on other peoples whom it had conquered. However, the open rift between the Hasmonean kings and the religious leadership which dissociated itself from the Hasmonean kingdom and did not grant it the religious-messianic legitimacy of the kingdom of the House of David, attests that in the final analysis the Hasmonean kings did not succeed in gaining the support of the majority of the people. The outlook that prevailed was the one shaped during the Babylonian Exile and placed on a firm foundation during the Return to Zion by Ezra the Scribe. The historic myth whose foundations were laid in the Covenant of the Written Law – the Torah – and was renewed by means of the Oral Law transmitted from generation to generation, is what shaped the consciousness of the people's unity even when only part of the people lived in its land, and without an independent state, while the majority lived in a broadly-dispersed Diaspora around it. The struggle to renew Jewish statehood did continue for several more generations, but when the last attempt failed in the Bar Kokhba Revolt, the tradition that had striven to mold the people as a collective political entity was severed. Only a few indirect references to it have been preserved in the canonical literature that continued to shape the people's self-consciousness. The vision of a kingdom that would gather the people to it took on prophetic, metaphysical dimensions. Its fulfillment was put off until the mystical, meta-historical End of Days. The people was taught to identify itself and its land on the basis of the myth whose foundations had been laid by the prophets and which had been shaped by the sages and handed down from generation to generation.

How, then, shall we describe the relationship of the People of Israel to the Land of Israel as part of its collective identity from the failure of the Bar Kokhba Revolt until the beginning of modern times? A reading of the contributions to this volume shows that there were diverse positons on this question which led to ideological and halakhic controversies. It is obvious that for lengthy periods of time, in countries where Jews lived peacefully and comfortably, they were reconciled with an existence in Exile, and were even satisfied by this condition. Moreover, there were periods in which the rabbinical leadership preferred living in Gentile countries to residing in the Land of Israel, not only on material grounds but also for spiritual, Torah-based reasons.

And so, even in periods of distress, it is clear that most Jews and most of their leaders during most periods preferred to be exiled, moving from country to country, rather than adopt a political initiative for a mass return to their land. Messianic movements did emerge from time to time, but they were grounded in the belief that the hour for realization of the meta-historical prophetic vision had already arrived, since the hardships of Exile had surpassed the limits of the Jews' capacity for suffering. However, the halakhic norm that took shape, in view of the disastrous failure of such movements, was that it was forbidden to adopt an independent initiative to return to the Land of Israel as a people.

When settlement of Jews in the Land of Israel became possible, they came as individuals. The immigrants attached great importance to a Jewish presence in the Land of Israel, especially in Jerusalem, but their intention was solely to pray in the holy places, prostrate themselves on the graves of the forefathers, and be buried in the soil of the Holy Land. They felt that as long as the Temple was in ruins, the people in Exile, the Land of Israel lay desolate, and churches or mosques built in most of the Jewish holy places, the Land of Israel was itself a land of exile bleaker and more depressing than any other. It thereby reflected the fate of the People of Israel from the perspective of its standing among the nations and before God. Hence it is clear that the Jewish community in the Land of Israel could not be perceived as a center of leadership, and certainly did not have political significance. Its only importance was as a means of preserving the religious-spiritual bond between the People of Israel and its land as a symbol of mourning and of hope.

Therefore, we may conclude that after the Bar Kokhba Revolt

what shaped the identity of the Jewish People and determined its connection to its homeland as one of a purely spiritual character, was the halakhic norm that posited living in Exile while aspiring to speedy Redemption by divine intervention, as opposed to settling in the homeland by one's own initiative, in the manner of other peoples.

All this not withstanding, it was universally argued that living in foreign lands was a state of Exile. Even in countries where Jews enjoyed material well being and flourished spiritually, and even when they felt themselves at home and saw their present condition as obviously advantageous to living in the Land of Israel, they never stopped referring to their places of residence as Exile. Even wealthy, well-established Babylonian Jewry, most of whose members did not return to the Land of Israel with Ezra and Nehemiah and which strove to establish its status as the hegemonic spiritual center of the entire people, defined itself as living in Exile.

What then is Exile from this vantage point? It is a sort of punishment for a sin committed by the people, for which it had been driven from its country. Exile is marked by an essential flaw in the relationship between God and His people and, for this reason, the people's way of life is also marred in its perfection, as is its mission as a people singled out for the worship of its God. Only in the Land of Israel, when the Temple is standing, can the people fully carry out the commandment to worship God. And only in its own Torah-based state would it be able to live a full and free national life directed towards fulfilling its mission. From all these aspects even the best land of exile is still Exile, and only because – in the absence of a Temple and a kingdom – the Land of Israel was the bitterest of exiles was it possible to justify, from the spiritual and national perspectives, a preference for residing in foreign lands. It follows from this that the aspiration and hope of returning to the Land of Israel and re-establishing the Temple and a kingdom based on the Torah, were absolute conditions without which halakhic legitimacy for continued existence in Exile could not be conferred. Even when Exile is increasingly prolonged and there is no indication when it will come to an end, living there is justified only if it is viewed as a temporary condition that one is ready to abandon and immigrate to the Land of Israel when the time comes.

Underlying these perspectives on Exile and on the relationship of the people to its land is, of course, the conception of Jewish identity on the basis of the prophetic myth of the Chosen People. However, we must first examine the norm that shaped the consciousness of Jewish collective identity in the real historical circumstances of dispersion among the nations or under their

331

domination, especially after the Persian, Greek, and Roman pagan rulers had been replaced by Christian and Muslim ones.

The two monotheistic religions that spread throughout the regions that comprised the Jewish Diaspora claimed to be the inheritors of the canonical sources of the Torah of Israel and competed with the People of Israel to fulfill its mission. Their objective was to reject and oppress Judaism, to coerce the Jews into accepting the new faith and then to replace them. To this purpose, they exploited their political power and made the condition of Exile more severe for the Jews through social restrictions, economic discrimination, and persecution. However, in the process they also encouraged the creation of the typical Jewish communal framework that emerged in an almost identical organizational-juridical-sacral pattern in most Diaspora lands and imparted to the collective segregation of the Jews from their non-Jewish surroundings a national, quasi-political dimension.

Unlike the Jews under pagan rule, those in Christian and Muslim countries could not relate to reigning imperial political systems in the same manner as could members of other peoples who submitted to domination by them. Inclusion of the Jews in these systems was conditioned from the very beginning on the establishment of a separate juridical status distinguishing them from every other collective entity, both in the rights they received for the benefit of the secular authorities, and in the restrictions imposed upon them that followed from religious requirements. The end result was the creation of an organizational framework, directly approved and authorized by the authorities, that distinguished the Jews from surrounding society not only in their places of residence but also in dress and occupations, in the law under which they conducted themselves and were judged in all internal matters, in the form of their representation before the authorities, and in most aspects of daily life. In later times, when sovereign nation-states emerged in the West, this kind of quasi-national identification was the reason why Jews were deemed to be a nation within a nation or a state within a state. But by that time the rulers had changed their mind, and demanded that the Jews forgo outward signs of separate nationality as a condition for attaining citizenship.

Nevertheless, it is clear that the communal frameworks could not shape an all-embracing collective identity for all Jews living in the Diaspora. There were several reasons for this state of affairs: there was no all-Jewish supra-national framework; local communal frameworks, lacking the authority inherent in an independent status, were weak and did not govern all facets of life; and the fact that despite their religious segregation the Jews did all they could to integrate into their surroundings – socially,

economically, linguistically, and culturally.

This was an absolute necessity. Without it, they could not receive the protection of the authorities or a legal status, that were conditioned on the provision of various economic and professional services to the secular authorities. These required deep involvement in certain occupations in which Jews specialized and excelled, such as science, commerce, and sometimes political matters as well. Thus, voluntary cultural assimilation typified all Jewish communities, each one in its own specific environment. Obviously this produced great cultural distinctions between Jews in different countries, even leading to alienation and estrangement.

This could not be overcome by means of communal frameworks. Only organic, internalized social structures, maintained as educating processes through direct interpersonal relations, grounded in the canonical sources and their language, could assure internal unity despite the geographical dispersion of the people, and the outward assimilation that dispersion involved. In other words, the forces of internal cohesion found in the nuclear family and the community were necessary to balance out the influences of assimilation and to mold a consciousness of internalized spiritual identification with the ideal of *Klal Israel* – the Jewish People as one whole – that was symbolically perceived as a metaphysical entity.

If we consider the halakhic norm that determined the all-embracing identity of the Jewish People in its places of dispersion, we note, then, that from the outset it was no different from the norm that determined the identity of other peoples in antiquity. A people, as distinct from a nation, unites its individual members and its subdivisions into a collective entity on the basis of a narrative consciousness of common origin and on the basis of a traditional commitment to be faithful to that primeval origin. The primary cell that creates the pattern of the people is the family. It expands to many families, combines into households, then into tribes, until they form a unit of the people that is capable of bearing itself. This is a bond of kinship, but it should be pointed out that the consciousness of collective belonging is sustained by a narrative memory of a link between generations, rather than by biological continuity. The familial bond between parents and offspring is the determining factor, and this bond, even when it is grounded in kinship, is fundamentally of an educational nature and rests on spiritual messages which distinguish the personality of all the members and shapes their social relationships.

The halakhic norm that fixed the identity of the Jews as a people was their being of the seed of Abraham, Isaac, and Jacob. A Jew is *a priori* someone who was born to Jewish parents and brought up by them (in the case of mixed marriages, the mother's identity is the determining factor). We should comment in this context that even joining the people through conversion is considered a process by which the outsider is adopted as a child of the nation's patriarchs. The convert becomes a child of Abraham, Isaac, and Jacob so that he will be able to worship the God of Israel, and the practical fulfillment of his becoming part of the people is accomplished by ties of marriage and birth. Thus does he become part of the continuum of Jewish existence.

Let us emphasize once again that this was the pattern of identification of all peoples of antiquity. Therefore, the difference between the Jews and the peoples among whom they lived in Exile is striking in that the Jews continued to maintain the original tribal-familial pattern on the basis of origin and continuity from generation to generation when the host peoples had already abandoned that pattern and in its stead had developed universal collective identities – ecclesiastic-religious identities on one hand, and imperial-state identities on the other. How, then, did the Jews succeed in preserving the inner strength and cohesion of the tribal-familial structure while integrating into the surrounding civilization?

The community as a protective shell indeed made its contribution. However, the principal answer to that question is the institutionalized educational process, grounded in the religious authoritative commandments of the Torah. To comprehend the significance of this explanation we should examine the nature of Jewish traditional education, through ritual and intellectual study, that became an integral part of everyday life in the family and the community. It is what shaped the processes of socialization and also developed the individual personality from infancy until old age through the year-long cycles of Sabbaths and holidays and through the stations of an individual's course of life: birth, maturity, marriage, and death.

This ritual and didactic system is what sustained family and communal life. It is what shaped them around itself and bestowed upon them religious metaphysical significance. Worshippers in the synagogue and the society of scholars in the house of study functioned as a holy congregation within the community, which was a quasi-political organizational and judicial framework, and within the family which served as a socio-economic framework. When this holy congregation gathered together, it symbolized *Knesset Israel* (the Assembly of Israel) as an ideal collective entity. Praying together, reciting portions of the Torah on every Sabbath and festival, studying Torah for its own sake in the house of study in the society of scholars – these social acts reconstituted the community anew, each and every day.

The second focus was the sacral family, reconstituted on every Sabbath and each holiday and festival around the table in every Jewish home. The festive dinner took on sacral-ritual significance: the table symbolized the altar, and the meal was a reminder of the sacrifices that were eaten, accompanied by a ritual of blessings, religious poetry, and songs. It shaped family togetherness as a process in which the parents transmitted to their offspring the legacy of generations of Jews, by practicing it and explaining its significance. In this manner, the sacral family functioned as a cell from which, and by means of which, the nation renewed itself both physically and spiritually. It built the "House of Israel" in the double meaning of both the Jewish home and the Jewish people.

These ritual gatherings in the synagogue, the house of study, and the family home were also the means by which the narrative of the historical memory of the People of Israel was transmitted. It would have been reasonable to assume that historiographic works continuing the historical books and chronicles of the Bible would be the major means of shaping this memory. However, from the destruction of the Second Temple until the beginning of modern times there were no written Jewish works that documented the continuum of the exiled people's history. In its stead an exegetical corpus of literature was produced which interpreted the biblical narrative until the period of the Return to Zion as an overall understanding of Jewish history, and was used to contend with the period of Exile by means of all-embracing contemplation on its meaning in the context of the relationship between God and His Chosen People. The ongoing state of Exile under the yoke of the pagan empires was perceived as almost being a stable condition. The only change was for the worse, as the malicious insolence of paganism increased, as did the distress of the People of Israel who awaited the End of Days that was always near – even though it was slow in coming.

The subject of this interpretation, of course, is the religious significance of the fate of Israel among the nations. Several systems of thought – theological, philosophical, and mystical – were created. Though there were great conceptual differences among them, what catches the eye is their parallel narrative structure and the similarity in their perception of the overall significance of the history of the people. The foundation, as noted above, was the biblical account: from the creation of Adam to the Patriarchs, from bondage in Egypt until the Revelation on Mount Sinai and the settlement of the Land of Israel, from the kingdom of David and Solomon to the destruction of the First Temple and the Babylonian Exile, and from the Return to Zion to the destruction of the Second Temple. This is a continuum of ascents

333

to the summits of Redemption and nearness to God contrasted with descents to the deepest depths of sin and punishment. Finally, there is the steepest, most long-lasting fall. We should stress that the ritual memory of the destruction of the Second Temple was combined with that of the destruction of the First Temple, most likely because the events of Second Temple times and its destruction were not the subject of canonical documentation. Hence, a depiction was in fact created of a lengthy Exile beginning with the destruction of the First Temple and not ending despite the Return to Zion and construction of the Second Temple in the days of Ezra and Nehemiah.

The depiction of the second Exile – after the destruction of the Second Temple – that was drawn in the thought literature did not rely, therefore, on historiography but on first-hand experience of the thinkers and on their observance of how the Gentile empires and foreign religions treated the People of Israel. For the canonical work to which traditional thought must resort, they again turned to a biblical composition from the beginning of Second Temple times: the Book of Daniel. This work continued the prophetic historiography of the Bible through visionary contemplation of the great Gentile empires that contended for world domination, fighting and replacing one another, and – from the vantage point of the author of this Jewish visionary work – each one seeming to be baser than its predecessor and more fearsome for Israel than its forerunner. Nevertheless, he looked forward – beyond their illusory, transitory dominion – to the approach of Judgment Day after which the everlasting Kingdom of Heaven on earth would be revealed.

Every account of the history of the People of Israel among the nations, that in effect begins with the creation of Man and continues until the awaited End of Days, was fashioned on the basis of the Book of Daniel as the narrative of the struggle between the people destined to be the bearer of God's word and commandments in the world and the pagan Gentile empires. In other words, it is a description of God's war against idolatry that represents the forces of evil and impurity. There is a dramatic recurring pattern in this account that reveals the inner logic of a forceful Divine Providence that directs the history of all humankind, including the fate of Israel as the hidden axis upon which it turns. The state of Exile becomes ever more somber and the forces of evil and impurity that are charging forward to conquer the world and suppress Israel constantly grow stronger. The suffering of Exile continually increases, but this condition also emphasizes the miraculous survival of Israel, the people that was chosen to sanctify God's name and, through its firm faith which sustained it despite all persecutions, to attest to the existence

of the eternal kingdom of God and that its final victory is assured.

The question remains, why is this entire episode of suffering necessary before the revelation of the Kingdom of Heaven on earth? The principal answer is that material Creation, by its very essence, must be reformed, for by its nature it has deficiencies and limitations from which evil and demonic impurity sprout. Idolatry represents man's desire to be the master of his own fate in the universe, to replace God, and to deny His dominion. Idolatry must be reformed to perfect Creation, and it is fitting that for this purpose it be revealed, layer by layer, to its very utmost depths. This is the logic and the cause behind the shape of the course of historic time.

Every time that a pagan world empire is replaced by one baser than itself, another depth of evil and demonic impurity is revealed. The clash between these empires expresses both their evil and the punishment that they justly bring upon themselves. Thus the aim of Providence is to do justice in order to cleanse the earthly world of its pollution, while the positive element in this process of reform is the role played by the People of Israel through faithful worship of God by adherence to His commandments. Reform is progressing constantly although it cannot be discerned in the growing darkness. Israel's influence increases even in the hearts of the idol-worshippers, whether consciously or unconsciously. Threatened idolatry intensifies its efforts to stabilize its sway. It storms Israel with blind hatred, but despite Israel's weakness, and notwithstanding the physical, material might of idol-worshippers, they cannot suppress Israel's spirit and annihilate it. In its desperate anger, idolatry finally tries to break Israel's spirit and tempt it to betray its mission, neglect its Torah, and become idol-worshippers like all the nations. Idolatry's increasing sophistication in recent generations is reflected in attempts by Christianity and Islam to present pagan counterfeits of the true Torah of Israel in order to expropriate the Torah and thereby to set up an idol in the holy of holies. This is the harshest, most terrifying trial of all. Yet, it also manifests the effective influence of the true Torah over all of humanity, for the pagan endeavor to resemble the true faith signifies the latter's very close victory, when the Kingdom of God will be revealed in the world.

According to this account, only in the physical manifestation of earthly existence is the Jewish People a collective entity comprised of many individuals. The secret of its eternity is its supernatural spiritual existence. It is firmly connected to the Torah that represents a sublime spiritual sphere and, according to the Kabbalistic version, this sphere owes its sanctity to God Himself. Its light illuminates the soul of every individual in Israel.

This, therefore, is the mystery of the unity of the people, despite its dispersion, and it also explains Israel's wondrous survival despite ever harsher persecutions.

We have summed up the Kabbalistic version which has most strongly influenced the People of Israel. However, we stress that this line of thought also appears in the works of theologians such as R. Saʿadiah Gaon and R. Judah ha-Levi, who had recourse to rationalist philosophical tools, and even in compositions by Maimonides intended for the general public. This line of reasoning shaped the self-consciousness of the People of Israel, and we emphasize that this applies to all Jewish communities in all countries of the Diaspora, whether under Christian or Islamic dominion. Despite dispersion and outward cultural assimilation, the uniformity of the Jewish communal framework, the common pattern of prayer that was the basis of the holy congregation in the synagogue, the uniformity of the sources learnt in the house of study, of the sacral way of life in the family home, of the nature of the collective entity of the People of Israel and the Jewish personality that internalized its bond to Klal Israel, all these succeeded in preserving an impressive measure of unity and collective cohesion.

We may easily comprehend that the relationship to the Land of Israel and the conception of its nature were an inseparable part of the internalized spiritual, metaphysical conception of the character of the people. The Land of Israel as described in the Bible became the basis for theological, philosophical, and mystical commentary. We must once again indicate that, despite the rich diversity of the commentaries and the great differences in conceptual interpretation between them, there is an astonishing degree of parallelism and similarity in the principal concepts. Already in the Bible, the Land of Israel is described as not only having outstanding traits of beauty and possessing the material resources needed for national strength, but especially as commanding special qualities possessing religious, metaphysical meaning. It is a land imbued with a unique Divine Providence, a land that God hallowed for His own sake – hence, settlement in the land is conditional upon true worship of God, free of any idolatry. Especially applicable in relation to its settlement are commandments concerning the possession of the land from the social-moral aspect and relating to the integration of its people among the surrounding nations. Law and justice in relations between men, between tribes, and between families are a condition for a lengthy existence in the land. Thus the people must avoid involvement in the evil struggles conducted merely for the sake of power by the pagan nations that surround it, because the People of Israel was not created for that purpose. If it violates these conditions, the Holy Land will eject it and send it into exile.

The commentary of the Jewish sages developed these motifs in their efforts to preserve the status of Land of Israel as the center of leadership for the entire people, and in their endeavors to curb emigration from the land, which constantly increased due to the hardships of life there and the material attractions of the Diaspora. The tendency to metaphysical idealization of the Land of Israel as a means of preserving the spiritual bond from afar increased in the thought literature of the period of Exile. What was needed now was a way to maintain the bond with the land without actually living there. The solution was to give a symbolic and spiritual nature to the image of the Land of Israel. It, too, was construed as a living entity, with spirit and breath pulsating in its material body, a wondrous spouse of the Jewish People in its earthly existence.

Just as the Jewish People is the heart of the nations and their talisman, so does the thought literature describe the Land of Israel as the navel of the world, Jerusalem as the navel of the country, and Mount Moriah – the site of the Temple – as the navel of Jerusalem. Creation of the world began from the site of the Temple. There was the link forged between heaven and earth, between the universe's spiritual and physical spheres. Therefore, only in the Land of Israel and only by means of the Temple is direct communion possible between God and man (prophecy), and man and God (prayer). Hence the exclusiveness of the Land of Israel, of Jerusalem, and of Mount Moriah; hence the continuum of the land's degrees of holiness hence its unique status as a necessary condition for prophecy and hence the special commandments that relate only to it.

There is, therefore, an inner correspondence between the unique quality of the people called Israel and the special quality of the land called Israel, and they need each other. The unique spiritual character of the people, by which it becomes united with its God, can only be manifested and fulfilled in the Land of Israel. When the people is outside its land, its unique spiritual nature is hindered and concealed; the land, too, when it is empty of its people, cannot manifest its unique nature. Exile of the people is also a state of Exile for the land; it is no longer a land of delight but a wasteland. No other people will be able to uncover its unique delightful qualities, and it will remain in its desolation, awaiting redemption at the hands of its children.

This conception located the Land of Israel not only at the crossroads from which the universe expanded in all directions, but also at the crossroads of the course of history. The People of Israel, with its unique fate, embodies God's Providence and His leadership in the world. These are reflected in the character and

335

fate of the Land of Israel: constant warfare between religions and the empires surrounding it. All nations and all religions aspire to leave their mark on the Land of Israel. It is a mirror that reflects the history of the People of Israel in its struggle with all the nations and religions, as it travels the road from Exile to Redemption. It is also destined to be the final battleground between all the pagan empires that aspire to world dominion. They will destroy each other in their efforts to conquer the Land of Israel to prove their supremacy, and will collapse on its soil. Then will the messianic Kingdom of God be revealed in all its splendor.

According to R. Judah ha-Levi, one senses in the Land of Israel a unique feeling of spirituality that distinguishes it from all other – merely material – countries. For the Kabbalists, the symbolism of the Land of Israel is identified with *Knesset Israel*, which represents the People of Israel before Heaven as a special sphere in the divine emanation. In this manner the People of Israel, the Land of Israel, the Torah of Israel, and the God of Israel, too, come together in the lower sphere of the divine emanation – that is, the *Shekhinah*. Therefore, it was possible even without immigrating to the Land of Israel and settling on its soil to become a part of the land, even to become one with it through directing one's thoughts and spiritual communion.

There were of course systems of thought that did not go to such extremes to convert the Land of Israel into a spiritual symbol. However, even in the rationalistic formulation of Maimonides, Mount Moriah – the site of the Temple – is singled out for the degree of its unique spiritual sanctity, a kind of constant divine presence, and this holiness devolves upon the entire country. Maimonides did not provide a rational explanation for the sanctity of Mount Moriah, but it is clear that he was adopting a conceptual norm which he considered to be binding from the perspective of Jewish law. It would seem that just as Maimonides accepted the miraculous, supernatural event when the Torah was given to the People of Israel on Mount Sinai, so also did he accept the miraculous, supernatural status of Mount Moriah as the site of the Temple. Thus, in his own philosophical system, he combined the supernatural status of the People of Israel as the people of the Torah with the supernatural nature of its country, the Land of Israel.

336

. . . .

CONCLUSION

According to all the systems of thought that shaped the relationship of the People of Israel to its land in the period of Exile, the Land of Israel was perceived as an idealized, corporeal-

spiritual entity that complemented the idealized spiritual entity of the people and merged with it. It was not a homeland in the political sense, but rather a holy land destined for a utopian, messianic kingdom.

Bearing in mind these conceptions of the people and the land, we can set out to interpret the transformation that occurred at the beginning of the modern period, the change that was institutionalized when a secular Jewish state arose in part of the Land of Israel, through efforts of part of the Jewish People, and was named Israel. The multiplicity of movements that proposed contradictory solutions to "the Jewish Problem" and to "the problem of Judaism" in modern times was indicative of a process of disintegration of the elements which formed the pattern of traditional identification that had been created in Exile. First of all came the collapse of the community as a quasi-national framework recognized by the Gentile authorities, and its replacement by a voluntary communal framework which one could easily quit, whose jurisdiction applied only in the areas of worship and religious practices. Second was the growing opposition from both Gentile and Jewish society to the Jewish inclination to be a community isolated from its surroundings. Both sides called for encouragement of social-cultural assimilation and citizenship on an individual basis. Third was the dissolution by secularization of the internal structure of the sacral community which led to changes in the status of the synagogue, in the order of religious services and the content of the prayers, and in the manner in which Torah was studied. In addition, the educational role of the family declined as its structure changed and it went through a process of secularization. Finally, the process can also be attributed to refutation of the narrative-historical ritual image of the Jewish People by modern historiographic research, and to undermining of the foundations of the theological, mystical, philosophical-traditional interpretation by systematic, rationalist philosophies.

As indicated, these transformations did not take place all at once. The processes that brought them about encountered internal and external opposition, resulting in the rise of a variety of movements and counter-movements that clashed with and provoked each other. Furthermore, all the movements needed a common source from which to begin their own ideas; hence, they tried to preserve elements of the compound traditional collective identity while supplying a new interpretation and new contexts. Nevertheless, the overall syndrome was changed beyond recognition, leading us to ask whether there still exists a collective Jewish entity comprising all the dispersed individuals who identified themselves as Jews. Does a framework exist that unites within it all the factions, enabling them to express themselves in common, despite the differences between them? Is there a sufficient internal foundation of consensus about the heritage and on the nature of a collective Jewish identity to enable Jews who hold such differing conceptions of their own identity to accept one another as Jews? Does a consensus exist that can unite them with the mission-oriented history of their people, that is called Israel?

A hint that an affirmative answer is possible may be supplied by the fact that all those who identify themselves as Jews are still disturbed by these questions, which they deem to be existential issues. There is a crisis over a common identity that is falling to pieces in the unabated controversy, yet still has not led to an absolute break. It would seem, therefore, that the acuteness of this controversy indicates a will to persuade or defeat the opponent, but not to give up on him. Close observation will show that all movements that offer frameworks and content for Jewish identity also strive to impose them on their opponents, whether by persuasion or by coercion. Thus, to all appearances it would seem that an all-embracing collective Jewish entity still exists in our own times, a strange mode of existence in an arena where four general conceptions of Jewish identity, whose exponents claim to be exclusive, clash with one another. Their joint appearance, albeit as disputants, in a common forum (provided mainly by institutions of the State of Israel and the World Zionist Organization, which has positioned itself between the state and Diaspora Jewry) is what constitutes – *ex post factum* – a Jewish collectivity that has no uniform definition but is moving at one and the same time towards four opposed poles of definition, which we shall now discuss.

A. The secular Zionist conception. This view claims that the State of Israel is the framework that unites all Jews living within and without it. As such, it is also the common symbol that brings together and represents a collective entity, as well as being the basis for the development of a cycle of creative dialogue that is concerned mainly with meeting contemporary challenges to that collective entity, and this on the basis of a common linguistic culture. These are the components that comprise the elements of secular national identity whose sources lie, among others, both in the canonical works of the Jewish People and in modern Hebrew and Jewish literature. However, the secular, national view does not consider its reliance upon any source to be a binding norm, but only as an inspiration and a challenge for creative thought.

It goes without saying that this is a basis for multiplicity of *Weltanschauungen* and ways of life of all kinds, not necessarily of

a Jewish character. Yet, these should be construed as representing the rich variety of Israeli culture, and not as its defining norm. That norm is grounded solely in the state as a framework for democratic government and as a set of values governing legislation, justice, and social life, on the basis of the material, scientific, and technological civilization that was created by the state to serve its national interests, though as part of Western civilization in general, and on the basis of a common language and what it has created in all areas of inter-human communication.

The attitude towards the Land of Israel is accordingly a functional one. The Land of Israel is that stretch of territory upon which the state exists. As such, it is a source of diverse material resources serving various needs – those related to settlement, the economy, and defense. Of course, a functional attitude towards the country does not exclude an esthetic and artistic relationship to its landscapes, or a link to its history through archaeology, and thus to the spiritual significance that the canonical sources and other literary works ascribed to the Land of Israel. These, too, are resources for meeting the emotional and spiritual needs of the national culture. Nevertheless, we may categorically state that the functions related to politics, settlement, defense, and the economy take first priority, and in the final analysis it is they that define the relationship to the Land of Israel as a national asset.

B. The conception held by most movements among Diaspora Jewry in the free world. The conceptual starting point of these movements is full integration into the state, society, and culture of their lands of residence. Though they look with favor upon the State of Israel as a focus of Jewish identification, this is not a political relationship. Generally, Diaspora Jews do not belong to an all-Jewish framework having political, representative significance in order to prevent having any accusation of "dual loyalty" leveled against them. As far as nationality is concerned, Diaspora Jews identify themselves as American, Canadian, Argentine, English, French, and so on.

It should be emphasized that the intensity of national identification in modern civil society is so strong that it even overcomes the sense of belonging to a people on the basis of familial continuity of generations. If persons do, nevertheless, continue to preserve distinctive ethnic features, this is at most only to diversify or folkloristically enrich the basic national identity that is determined by the state, its language, general society, and culture.

This characteristic is also reflected in the roles of the family and the community as didactic influences and as factors that

337

transmit a heritage and by its means shape the personalities of its individual members. Their influence is felt to a certain extent in the childhood years; however, it is gradually weakened by the processes of cultural socialization in the open, general society to which one belongs as an individual, as a member of a profession, occupation, or social class. In adult life, family and community culture does influence the individual to a certain extent as people spend time together and engage in leisure-time activities, but clearly these are usually marginal influences much weaker than those of the cultural messages conveyed by the general environment in which a person works and creates.

Hence, it is the general cultural environment that determines the elements of the *Weltanschauung* and way of life on an individual, professional-occupational, and class basis. Furthermore, it is in the general environment that Diaspora Jews invest their greatest efforts, and the best of their intellectual creativity is spent in the areas most important for shaping a sense of belonging and of group identity. The Jewish community also profits from this creativity, but not from the perspective of its unique identity, for specifically Jewish creativity necessarily becomes marginal both in scope and quality.

These remarks apply of course to the wider Jewish community. Its educational leadership, devoted to its role, is more intensely conscious of its Jewish identity, and acts on a higher creative level. This, however, creates a typical gap between the *Weltanschauung* and way of life of these leaders for whom Judaism is their profession, and that of most of the community. In other words, the leadership is not representative of the Jewish identity of the community but rather serves it with a dubious measure of effectiveness, for the majority of the community does not have recourse to a high level of Jewish education, Jewish artistic creation, Jewish philosophy, and the like. The increasing rate of mixed marriages in the Diaspora attests to the declining importance attached to the collective Jewish identity. On the whole, it seems like a superficial identity of a religious or ethnic sub-group within a wider society that relates to the existence of many sub-groups like these as an enrichment and diversification of its own identity.

Of course, one's attitude towards the collective identity of one's own Jewish community also determines how a person relates to Jewish communities in the other Diaspora lands and in Israel. Can this be construed as the relationship by free-world Jewry to an overall collective entity? A reply in the positive is conditioned by the level of intensity and inclusiveness one ascribes to this relationship. For most Diaspora Jews this is not full identification with an all-embracing collective entity, but rather partial identification with common traits of Jewishness. It means that a frail sense of belonging is dependent on some traits that happen to be common to all other Jewish communities, and is limited by recognition of the fact that each of the other communities belongs to a different overall framework. This can no longer refer to a Jewish nation or a Jewish people, but only to partial aspects of culture, heritage, historical memory, religion, and a vague consciousness that still exists of a covenant of fate, a consciousness that was strengthened by the events of the Holocaust.

What kind of relationship to the Land of Israel can emerge from such an attitude? There is no uniform answer. For the different varieties of non-Zionist Orthodoxy, the Land of Israel is the Holy Land. As such, it is more meaningful than the state, but only as a lofty ideal that is expressed in prayer and worship. As for the other movements among free-world Jewry, the State of Israel holds more importance than the Land of Israel, and one relates to it only as one of the components of the political entity where other Jews live and give expression to their religious or cultural-historical identity.

C. The Religious-Zionist conception. According to this conception, the State of Israel represents "the first bud of Redemption." This definition is an effort to bridge the gap between a national-secular outlook by which the fulfillment of Zionist aspirations is a historic national task achieved through the initiative of the Jewish People itself, and the traditional religious outlook that considers Zionism to be a part of a Divine scheme envisioned by the prophets. Since its fulfillment is the work of Providence, it will be accompanied by additional supernatural, spiritual dimensions yet to be revealed. The secular collective entity of the state is only a first stage in which, indeed, the people must respond to the call of its God and act on its own behalf, but Redemption in all its supernatural, messianic dimensions shall yet "sprout" from the state. True, this is a prolonged historical process that is expected to develop gradually, but even now its signs are evident. Now that the state has arisen, everyone must once again live by the precepts of the Torah, and it is necessary to increase the Torah's influence on the way of life in the state, on its laws and on its judicial system. Religious Zionism devotes maximal political and educational efforts to achieve this end.

It follows from this outlook that the State of Israel must gather all Diaspora Jewry within its borders and simultaneously extend its sovereignty over "the Entire Land of Israel," i.e. those areas west of the Jordan River conquered in 1967. Those adhering to this view hope that in this way all the components of the traditional historical identity of the Jewish People will once again merge and be reunited, after having come apart – first under the conditions of Exile and later through secularization: the People of Israel, the Land of Israel, the nationalism of Israel, and the Torah of Israel, which is the unifying and sanctifying element.

The Religious-Zionist conception applies itself to all segments of the people, but it is aware of the fact that the others still do not identify themselves with it and through it. To the contrary, they reject it. The absolute inclusiveness of Religious Zionism, which purports to be amiable and tries to persuade other Jews amicably, seems nevertheless coercive to others. It gives rise to acute confrontation both on the political plane and on the public-educational level. Obviously this continuing contradiction between its self-image and how it is conceived by others creates an inner confusion of identity.

D. The *Haredi* (Ultra-Orthodox) conception. It too, like the Religious-Zionist conception, is grounded in a meta-historical vision that combines the People of Israel, the Land of Israel, and Jewish statehood as envisioned in the Torah, while totally negating the modern secular stage in the Religious-Zionist conception of the fulfillment of Redemption. It clings tenaciously to the mystical vision of Redemption through Divine, supernatural initiative. The State of Israel is, therefore, not "the first bud of Redemption" but the very opposite: the height of the apocalyptic "birthpangs of the Messiah" that are the final stage before Redemption. The state was conceived and born in rebellion and revolt against Heaven. It is an attempt by part of the people, even though the majority, to throw off the yoke of Divine Providence and be the master of its own fate. Continuing the traditional train of thought about the struggle of paganism against the God of Israel, His people and His Torah, Ultra-Orthodoxy sees Zionism and the other modern Jewish movements as having brought the clash to its apocalyptic climax: paganism has finally broken into the fortress of the People of Israel. The majority have succumbed, and only a loyal garrison has remained which has been forced to seal itself off from the rest of the people and secure itself against it in order to be true to its original mission.

According to this outlook, the secular State of Israel that arose in the Land of Israel was from the very outset perceived to be a condition of Exile. The most consistent Ultra-Orthodox version delegitimizes Israel altogether as the gravest, most malicious of exiles, truly the work of Satan. The more moderate version has found a way to reconcile itself to Israel's existence, particularly against the background of the Holocaust and the conditions created in the post-Holocaust era. It recognizes that there are certain advantages in the existence of Israel that justify its establishment as a means of physical salvation of the people, on condition that it does not ascribe to itself any religious significance.

However, even according to this moderate version, Israel is Exile in any event. Although providing material comfort, it embodies a great spiritual danger against which the Ultra-Orthodox "garrison," which remains true to the original identity of Israel, must strongly fortify itself, just as the Jewish People has defended itself throughout its history in Exile: resolutely dissociating itself from the spiritual culture of the surrounding society, from its learning, creative works, and way of life. This took the form of encouragement of self-segregated communities; a distinct manner of dress; the formation of a "holy congregation" in the synagogue, the house of study, and the family home; shaping the ritual that would perpetuate the historical memory of the people of Israel; and molding an outlook that relates to the Land of Israel as the Holy Land that one may identify with on the spiritual-religious level, but there is no duty to live there, and certainly not to hold dominion over its entire territory.

It should be emphasized that self-segregation and entrenchment are not meant to contend with the challenge posed by the Gentiles, but rather with the challenge coming from other Jews among whom the Ultra-Orthodox communities live, both in Israel and the Diaspora. As things have turned out, they must rely on the material and political achievements of the rebels against Heaven and the non-believers, for without them the Ultra-Orthodox would not be able to cope with the realities of daily life and could not devote themselves to worshipping God in their own manner. Moreover, in the final analysis, one cannot deny that the rebels and non-believers are Jews according to Jewish law. Indeed, this is what causes pain and anger to the Ultra-Orthodox. Despite their claim that it is they who preserve the traditional collective identity of the Jewish People, they cannot evade the fact that the great revolution that accompanied the establishment of the State of Israel molded not only the character of the majority that "betrayed" its original identity, but also that of those who remained true to it. From a people, the latter were forced to become no more than a sect that shut itself off from the rest of its own people, which had changed irrecognizably.

The four forms of identity that we have described above have certain points at which they meet, or areas in which they overlap, while diverging from each other on everything else. The points where they converge or overlap, it should be emphasized, are not external, nor are they merely organizational. They do involve basic

339

values, themes that arise from a common heritage, and a common historic fate. Each of the movements that created these forms of identity chose the contents that suited itself. But the link to the full context could not be severed, first of all because those parts of the overall collective identity abandoned by each one of the movements are reflected in the lifestyle of the others; and secondly, because without the original context, it would not be possible to develop a significant and satisfying culture that would be able to sustain an identify capable of withstanding the pressures of an assimilating environment. Paradoxically, we find that each of the rival movements in the final tally constitutes both a center for itself and a periphery for all the rest, albeit in different degrees of intensity and with concepts that contradict each other.

From the perspective of assuring the continued existence of the Jewish People while preserving its historical continuity, which is the essence of the stubborn struggle for survival throughout the ages, this is a situation fraught with danger. It is obvious that should the intention of each one of these movements to impose its own form of collective identity on all the others continue to dictate the relationships among them, the stresses of polarization would cross the boundaries within which there is still readiness for mutual toleration, leading to dissolution of the partnership and severance of contact. Since none of these movements is capable of surviving by itself, the inevitable result would be complete assimilation into the surrounding environment of receptive Western civilization, or survival as a closed-off sect, which is in fact a condition of cultural degeneration.

Finding a solution that would make Jews conscious once again of being members of one people and that would reconnect them to the continuum of their historic memory calls for a reorientation of the movements towards each other, as a first step towards acceptance of pluralism and of the need to come to terms with one another. A pre-condition for such a solution is the drafting of a covenant that would obligate all of them to accept and rely on the others just as they are, while forgoing a unitary, all-inclusive definition of Jewish identity from the point of view of its content and organizational pattern, at least for the present. It would be enough that the historical point of departure – the age-long continuity of the Jewish People – be accepted by all and that all want to perpetuate their Jewish identity and develop a common national language rich enough to serve cultural communication and deep mutual understanding, free of reciprocal coercion.

Obviously, the realization of such a solution is dependent first and foremost on the State of Israel, which is the largest, most extensive organizational framework in which almost a majority of the Jewish People exists in a national setting in our times. The state is capable of initiating efforts in all spheres of collective togetherness: political-national, civilizational, social-cultural, legislative, and educational. Israel is the major arena in which all the rival movements encounter each other. Hence, the responsibility lies with the State of Israel to determine the rules of collective togetherness, of course in cooperation with Jewish movements and organizations within the state and in the Diaspora. However, such a covenant is possible and will endure only if the following four conditions are fulfilled.

A. Preserving the Jewish character of the State of Israel. This is conditional, first of all, upon its Zionist definition as the state of the entire Jewish People, which entails the adoption of a policy that recognizes Israel's responsibility towards Diaspora Jewry. Second, upon assuring the basic constitutional conditions for the existence of a commonly-shared Jewish environment in the public domain. Third, upon an educational system devoted to transmitting to the younger generation an authentic Jewish cultural heritage, that will take cognizance of different conceptions while developing common cultural values and terms. Fourth, upon sustaining the national symbols that identify the state, especially its language, religious holidays, and national public ceremonies.

B. Forging a pluralistic consensus regarding the shaping of the Jewish public domain in such a manner that all the existing movements and currents within the Jewish People are considered legitimate by the state and able to contribute freely to shared social and cultural creativity. Another condition, of course, is that Israel's national and religious minorities be granted similar cultural and religious autonomy of expression in the pubic domains of their own societies.

C. Preserving the democratic character of the State of Israel in its attitude towards all forms of Jewish identity that have developed within the Jewish People. This means that Israel must accept responsibility for the Jewish collective identity, but precisely on account of this responsibility it must restrict to the necessary minimum its direct involvement in determining patterns of social life. Furthermore, it must function as a political and constitutional instrument that encourages development of a pluralistic collective Jewish identity without favoring one of the existing forms of identity over another.

D. Distinguishing between the profound spiritual, cultural-historical and religious bond of the Jewish People to "the Entire

340

Land of Israel" in its historic boundaries, and the area that is today under the domination of the State of Israel. This entails recognition of the fact that the Land of Israel has come to be the homeland of two peoples who are fated to live side by side. Such a distinction is vital for politically-just peace with the Palestinians and the neighboring Arab states. However, it is also vital from the aspect of peace within the Jewish ranks between the opposing camps that are divided over this issue in Israel and in the Diaspora. The two bonds to the Land of Israel – the spiritual-religious and the national political ones – can co-exist and even complement each other by accepting the verdict of historical realism and coming to terms with the fact that the State of Israel is not – nor can it be in the foreseeable historical future – the messianic Kingdom of Israel. We have seen that the traditional religious norm of the Jewish People can be reconciled with this distinction and is capable of coming to terms with it.

If a consensus does emerge on the basis of these foundations, there are prospects that the controversy over Jewish identity will shift from the political arena to the intellectual sphere and will fructify vital cultural creativity which will shape anew the identity of the Jewish People as it faces the future, just as has occurred several times in the past. The momentous question is whether the movements active within the Jewish People are capable of admitting the necessity of a pluralistic consensus and of putting aside the element of coercive exclusivity that marks their ideologies. Time will tell.

Bibliography of Research Studies

This Epilogue is a summation based on many studies by myself and others, including those in this anthology. The following is a listing of central studies that support my exposition and deal with the various topics in greater detail. They are listed in the order of the topics discussed in the Epilogue.

1. Y. Kaufmann, *Exile and Alienation*, I–II Tel Aviv 1961 (Hebrew).
2. Eliezer Schweid, *The Land of Israel – National Home or Land of Destiny*, New York 1985.
3. Efraim Shmueli, *Seven Jewish Cultures: A Reinterpretation of Jewish History and Thought*, Cambridge 1990.
4. Y.H. Yerushalmi, *Zakhor*, Washington DC 1986.
5. Simha Goldin, *Uniqueness and Togetherness*, Tel Aviv 1997 (Hebrew).
6. Max Wiener, *Jüdische Religion in Zeitalter der Emanzipation*, Berlin 1933.
7. Eliezer Schweid, *The Idea of Judaism as a Culture*, Tel Aviv 1996 (Hebrew).
8. Mordecai M. Kaplan, *Judaism as a Civlization*, New York 1936.
9. A. Eisen, *Galut: Modern Jewish Reflection on Homelessness and Homecoming*, Bloomington 1986.
10. C.S. Lieberman and E. Katz (eds.), *The Jewishness of Israelis*, New York 1997.
11. Robert S. Wistrich, *Terms of Survival: The Jewish World since 1945*, London and New York 1995.
12. Laurence A. Hoffman (ed.), *The Land of Israel: Jewish Perspectives*, Notre Dame, Indiana 1980.
13. Malcolm Lowe (ed.), *People, Land and State of Israel: Jewish and Christian Perspectives*, Jerusalem 1989
14. J. Webber (ed.), *Jewish Identities in the New Europe*, London 1994.
15. D.T. Goldberg and M. Krausz (ed.), *Jewish Identity*, Philadelphia 1993.
16. Abraham S. Halkin, *Zion in Jewish Literature*, Lanham, MD 1988.
17. Yeshayahu Leibowitz, *Judaism, Human Values and the Jewish State*, Cambridge, MA 1992.

Glossary

aggadah, pl. *aggadot*, or *midreshei aggadah* = homiletical interpretations of the Bible incorporating folkloristic material.

aliyah, pl. *aliyot* = lit. "ascent" or "going up" (i.e., immigrating) to the Land of Israel.

amora, pl. *amoraim* = sages of the post-mishnaic period (ca. 200–500 CE), whose activities centered on the interpretation of the Mishnah.

Ashkenaz = N.W. Europe, primarily northern France and Germany, in the Middle Ages.

Ashkenazim, adj. Ashkenazic = in Middle Ages, Jews who lived or originated in Ashkenaz; in modern period, non-Sefardic Jews.

baraita = a historic, halakhic, or aggadic tradition not included in the Mishnah.

bet midrash, pl. *batei midrash* = lit. "houses of study" in which people assembled to listen to words of wisdom and exposition of the Law from the Second Temple period onwards.

First Aliyah = a period in Zionist historiography, 1882–1903; the first wave of Zionist immigration to the Land of Israel (see *aliyah*).

gaon, pl. *geonim* = formal title of heads of *yeshivot* in Sura and Pumbedita in Babylon from the late sixth to the mid-eleventh centuries. In the tenth and eleventh centuries it was also used by heads of *yeshivot* in the Land of Israel.

halakhah = Jewish religious law embracing all the practices and observances of Judaism.

halukkah = lit. "allocation" or "distribution"; funds raised by Jews in the Diaspora and distributed among their co-religionists in the Land of Israel, generally among those who came from the city, country, or region in which the funds were raised.

Hasidism = a popular religious movement that emerged among Jews in eastern Europe in the second half of the eighteenth century, whose adherents are called *hasidim*. Ectacy, mass enthusiasm, closely-knit cohesion, and charismatic leadership are its major characteristics.

haskalah = Hebrew term for the Enlightenment movement in Jewish society that began in the 1770s. Its adherents, known as *maskilim*, advocated secular studies, adoption of modern dress and manners, and productivization of Jewish society by engaging in professions, crafts, agriculture, and more.

Hibbat Zion = lit. "love of Zion"; a movement for Jewish settlement in the Land of Israel that constituted the intermediate link between the forerunners of Zionism in the mid-nineteenth century and political Zionism, that began with Theodor Herzl and the First Zionist Congress in 1897. Its adherent were known as Hovevei Zion (Lovers of Zion).

kibbutz, pl. *kibbutzim* = a voluntary collective, primarily agricultural, community throughout most of its existence. During most periods it had no private wealth and the collective was responsible for the welfare of its members.

kohen, pl. *kohanim* = priests who served in the Temple; after its destruction, hereditary members of the priestly families.

kolel, pl. *kolelim* = societies of Ashkenazic Jews in the Holy Land organized on the basis of their cities, countries, or regions of origin for the allocation of funds raised in the Diaspora (see *halukkah*).

lulav, pl. *lulavim* = palm fronds waved during the Sukkot Festival in the Temple, and since its destruction in synagogues.

menorah, pl. *menorot* = seven-branched candelabrum, one of the implements of the Temple.

mezuzah, pl. *mezuzot* = small parchment scrolls containing passages from Deuteronomy, affixed to the doorposts of Jewish homes.

midrash, pl. *midrashim* = anthologies and compilations of homilies consisting of biblical exegesis, sermons, and *aggadot*, forming an aggadic commentary on specific books of the Bible.

mishmarot ha-kehunah = the "priestly courses"; division of priests and Levites who served in the Temple in rotation.

Musta'arabin, adj. Musta'arabi = Arabic-speaking, old, established Jewish community in the Land of Israel. The term was first used in the fifteenth century.

nagid, pl. *negidim* = heads of Jewish communities in Islamic countries.

nasi, pl. *nesi'im* = lit. "president"; patriarchs, leaders of the Jewish communities in the Land of Israel, Babylon, Syria, and Egypt who claimed descent from Hillel the Elder.

New Yishuv = the Zionist-oriented sector of the Jewish community in the Land of Israel, in contrast to the Old Yishuv (see *yishuv*).

Old Yishuv = the traditional, ultra-Orthodox sector of the Jewish community in the Land of Israel, opposed to Zionism on religious grounds.

paytan, pl. *paytanim* = composers of Hebrew religious poetry (*piyyut*).

piyyut, pl. *piyyutim* = Hebrew religious poetry.

Prushim = disciples of Rabbi Elijah, the "Gaon of Vilna," who were opponents of the Hasidim; not to be confused with the Pharisees of the Second Temple period.

Rosh Golah = exilarch, the head of the Jewish community in Babylon.

Sanhedrin = supreme Jewish political, religious, and judicial body in the Land of Israel, from Second Temple times until the early fifth century CE.

Second Aliyah = a period in Zionist historiography, 1904–1914; the second wave of Zionist immigration to the Land of Israel (see *aliyah*).

Sefardim, adj. Sefardic = descendants of Jews who lived in Spain or Portugal before the expulsion of 1492; in modern usage, often indicates Jews of non-Ashkenazic origin.

Shephelah = area in the Land of Israel that separates the interior highlands from the coastal plain.

shofar = ram's horn, sounded on certain holy days.

tanna, pl. *tannaim* = sages of the first two centuries CE, until the redaction of the Mishnah.

tefillin = phylacteries; two small cases worn by male Jews on their head and left arm during morning prayers on weekdays, containing passages from Deuteronomy.

Torah = lit. "teaching" or "doctrine"; in narrow usage – the Pentateuch; in wider usage – the entire body of Jewish religious written and oral law.

Tosafists = those who wrote *tosafot*, additions to Rashi's commentary on the Talmud, in Ashkenaz in the twelfth to fourteenth centuries.

tzitzit, pl. *tzitziyot* = lit. "fringes"; tassels attached to the four corners of a special garment worn by observant Jewish men.

yeshivah, pl. *yeshivot* = Talmudic academy.

yishuv = a general term for the Jewish community in the Land of Israel, particularly during the pre-State period (see also New Yishuv; Old Yishuv).

Sources Quoted in the Volume (by chapter)

From the Return to Zion until the Hasmonean Revolt

Ben Sira, in *The Apocrypha*, tr. E.J. Goodspeed, New York 1959

Book of Maccabees, in *The Apocrypha*, tr. E.J. Goodspeed, New York 1959

Josephus, *Against Apion*, tr. H. St.-John Thackeray, London 1926

From the Hasmonean Revolt to the Destruction of the Second Temple

Josephus, *Antiquities*, Books XII–XVII, tr. Ralph Marcus, Cambridge, MA and London 1976–1980

Josephus, *Antiquities*, tr. A. Schalit, vol. II, Jerusalem & Tel Aviv 1955 (Hebrew)

Philo, [*Works*], tr. F.H. Colson and G.H. Whitaker, 10 vols., Cambridge, MA and London 1929–1972

Tosefta, *Shekalim*, ed. S. Lieberman, New York 1962 (Hebrew)

From the Destruction of the Second Temple to the Christianization of the Empire

Genesis Rabbah, ed. H. Albeck and Y. Theodor, Jerusalem 1965 (Hebrew)

Midrash Rabbah, Song of Songs, tr. M. Simon, London 1939

Midrash Tehillim, ed. S. Buber, Vilna 1891 (Hebrew)

Tosefta, *Bava Qamma*, ed. S. Lieberman, New York 1955 (Hebrew)

The Byzantine Period

Avot de-Rabbi Nathan, ed. S. Schechter, Vienna 1887 (Hebrew)

Epistle of Rav Sherira Gaon, ed. B.M. Lewin, Jerusalem 1944 (Hebrew)

Genesis Rabbah, ed. H. Albeck and Y. Theodor, Jerusalem 1965 (Hebrew)

Ginzberg, L., *Ginzei Schechter*, vol. II, New York 1929 (Hebrew)

Midrash Tehillim = *The Midrash on Psalms*, tr. W.G. Braude, New Haven 1959

Piyyutei Yannai, ed. M. Zulay, Berlin 1938 (Hebrew)

Sifre: A Tannaitic Commentary on the Book of Deuteronomy, tr. R. Hammer, New haven 1956

Tosefta, *Avodah Zarah* = *The Tosefta*, tr. J. Neusner, vol. IV, New York 1981

The Early Muslim Period

Benjamin of Tudela, *The Itinerary of Benjamin of Tudela*, critical text, translation, and commentary by M.N. Adler, London 1907

Bornshtein, H.Y., "The Polemic between R. Sa'adiah Gaon and R. Meir," in *N. Sokolow Jubilee Volume*, Warsaw 1904 (Hebrew)

Fleischer, E., *Hebrew Medieval Religious Poetry*, Jerusalem 1975 (Hebrew)

Gil, M., *Palestine during the First Muslim Period (634–1099)*, vol. II, Tel Aviv 1983 (Hebrew)

Ginzberg, L., *Ginzei Schechter*, vol. II, New York 1929 (Hebrew)

Hirshman, M., "The Priest's Gate and Elijah ben Menahem's Pilgrimage," *Tarbiz*, 55 (1985–1986) (Hebrew)

Maimonides, *The Code of Maimonides, Book Fourteen: The Book of Judges*, tr. A.M. Hershman, New Haven 1949

Post-Biblical Hebrew Literature, tr. B. Halper, 2 vols., Philadephia 1921

The Prayer Book of R. Sa'adiah Gaon, Jerusalem 1979 (Hebrew)

Schirmann, J., *History of Hebrew Poetry in Spain and Provence*, vol. 1, Jerusalem & Tel Aviv 1961 (Hebrew)

The Scroll of Ahima'az, ed. B. Klar, Jerusalem 1974 (Hebrew)

Jewish Communities in the East during the Early Muslim Period

Gil, M., *Palestine during the First Muslim Period (634–1099)*, vol. II, Tel Aviv 1983 (Hebrew)

Khan, G., "A Document of Appointment of a Jewish Leader in Syria Issued by al-Malik al-afdal Ali in 589 A.H./1193," in Y. Ragib (ed.), *Documents de l'Islam medieval*, Cairo 1999.

The Crusader Period

Baruch of Worms, *Sefer ha-Terumah*, Warsaw 1897 (Hebrew)

Duran, Shlomo ben Zemah, *Tashbetz*, Lemberg 1891 (Hebrew)

Duran, Zemah ben Shlomo, *Responsa Yakhin u-Vo'az*, Livorno 1782 (Hebrew)

Goldschmidt, D., *Seder ha-Selihot*, Jerusalem 1965 (Hebrew)

Hacker, J., "Links between Spanish Jewry and Palestine, 1391–1492," *Cathedra*, 36 (June 1985) (Hebrew)

Isaac ben Moses, *Or Zaru'a*, Zhitomir 1862 (Hebrew)

Judah Alharizi, *Tahkemoni*, ed. A. Kaminka, Warsaw 1899 (Hebrew)

Judah Halevi, *The Kuzari*, ed. Y. Even-Shmuel, Tel Aviv 1973 (Hebrew)

Levin, Y., "Judah Halevi," *Hebrew Encyclopaedia*, XIX (Hebrew)

Nahmanides, *Commentary on the Torah*, ed. H.D. Chavel, Jerusalem 1962 (Hebrew)

Nahmanides, *Writings and Discourses*, vol. II, ed. H.D. Chavel, Jerusalem 1968 (Hebrew)

Peles, Y.M., "Decisions and Commentaries by Maharil and Members of His Generation," in *The Rabbi Zholty Memorial Volume*, Jerusalem 1987 (Hebrew)

Post-biblical Hebrew Literature: An Anthology, ed. B. Halper, vol. II, Philadelphia 1921

Scholem, G., "A New Document for the History of the Beginnings of the Kabbalah," in *H.N. Bialik Memorial Volume*, Tel Aviv 1934 (Hebrew)

Shlomo Yitzhaki (Rashi), *Commentary on Psalms*, facs. ed., Jerusalem 1972 (Hebrew)

Solomon Ibn Verga, *Shevet Yehuda* ed. A. Schohat, Jerusalem 1947 (Hebrew)

Ya'ari, A., (ed.), *Travels to the Land of Israel*, Givatayim 1976 (Hebrew)

Ta-Shma, I., "The Attitude to *Aliya* to Eretz Israel (Palestine) in Medieval German Jewry," *Shalem*, 6 (1992) (Hebrew)

The Mamluk Period

Casola, P., *Canon Pietro Casola's Pilgrimage to Jerusalem in the Year 1494*, ed. and tr. by M. Margaret Newett, Manchester 1907

Eshtori ha-Parhi, *Kaftor va-Ferah*, ed. A.M. Luncz, Jerusalem 1897 (Hebrew)

Ish-Shalom, M. (ed.), *Christian Travels in the Holy Land: Descriptions and Sources on the History of the Jews in Palestine*, Tel Aviv 1965 (Hebrew)

Meshullam of Voltera, *The Journey of Meshullam of Voltera to the Land of Israel*, ed. A. Ya'ari, Jerusalem 1949 (Hebrew)

Neubauer, A., "On Matters Relating to the Twelve Tribes," *Kovetz al-Yad*, 4 (1898) (Hebrew)

Obadiah of Bertinoro, *From Italy to Jerusalem: The Letters of R. Obadiah of Bertinoro from the Land of Israel*, critical edition with introduction and annotations by Emanuel Hartom and Abraham David, Ramat Gan 1997 (Hebrew)

Ya'ari, A. (ed.), *Letters from the Land of Israel*, Jerusalem 1943 (Hebrew)

The Ottoman Period – The First Centuries

Hagiz, M., *Sfat Emet*, Amsterdam 1707 (Hebrew)

Sandys, G., *A Relation of a Journey Begun in 1610*, London 1615

Van Egmont, J.A. & J. Heyman, *Travels through Part of Europe, Asia Minor, the Islands of the Archipelago, Syria, Palestine, Egypt, Mount Sinai, & c. Giving a Particular Account of the Most Remarkable Places ...*, 2 vols., London 1759

Illustrations

Abbreviations of Repositories

Acknowledgments
Repositories and Photographers

Israel Nature & National Parks Protection Society 99

Jewish National and University Library, Jerusalem 140 (upper), 165, 215 (lower), 249, 252

Jewish National and University Library, Jerusalem, Laor Collection 20, 58, 167, 205, 209 (upper), 243

The John Rylands University Library, Manchester 173, 184 (upper)

Nissim Krispil 156, 174 (lower)

Gabi Laron 91, 109, 116 (lower)

Leeds University Library, Brotherton Library, Cecil Roth Collection, Leeds 172

Ya'akov Meshorer 44 (lower), 46 (lower), 63 (lower), 71, 79 (upper), 82,

Musée des Beaux-Arts de Tours 104

Musée du Louvre, Paris 37

Museo U. Nahon di Arte Ebraica Italiana, Jerusalem 224, 238 (lower), 241, 244, 245

Museum of Islamic Art, Jerusalem 157

National Library, Lisbon 46 (upper)

National Library of Russia, St. Petersberg 137 (upper), 144 (upper), 145, 160

National Museum, Damascus 44 (upper), 85 (lower)

National Photo Collection, Government Press Office, Jerusalem 297, 299, 300 (lower), 301, 302, 310 (upper), 312 (upper and lower), 313 (lower), 314, 315, 319, 320, 321, 323 (upper)

Photo David, Jerusalem 57, 304 (lower)

M. Pollak Gallery, Tel Aviv 47, 240

Private collection, New York 155

Zev Radovan 24 (upper), 26 (lower), 28, 36 (right), 45, 49, 51 (upper), 53 (upper and lower), 55, 63 (upper), 66, 73, 79 (lower), 85 (upper), 89 (upper), 98, 102 (upper and lower), 103 (lower), 114 (upper), 117, 118, 119 (upper), 120, 123, 126, 179, 187 (upper), 212, 234 (lower), 318

Real Biblioteca de San Lorenzo de El Escorial, Madrid 182 (upper), 192

Abraham Rosenthal 68

Shalom Sabar 152, 158

Sarajevo National Museum 39, 112

David Silverman 216

Staats- und Universitätsbibliothek, Hamburg 26 (upper)

Ilan Sztulmann 78, 134, 144 (lower), 237 (lower)

Tate Picture Library, London 203 (upper)

Topkapi Palace Museum, Istanbul 227 (upper)

Tower of David Museum of the History of Jerusalem, Jerusalem 21, 106, 147, 199

Ezri Uval 195

Sarit Uzieli 250

Menahem Ron Wexler 289

Moshe Wexler 62 (lower), 175

Yad Izhak Ben-Zvi, Library, Jerusalem 142 (left and right), 150, 161, 180, 183 (left and right), 193 (upper), 208, 209 (lower), 215 (upper), 239, 242, 246, 255, 260 (upper), 266

Yad Izhak Ben-Zvi, Photo Archives, Jerusalem 78, 105, 134, 143 (lower), 144 (lower), 175 (upper), 235, 236, 237 (lower), 254, 256, 257, 259 (lower), 272, 318

Authors and Publishers

D. Ben-Gurion et al., *The Jews in Their Land*, London: Aldus Books, 1966 [p. 111] 43, [p. 230] 225

L.F. Cassas, *Voyage pittoresque de la Syrie, de la Phénicie, de la Palestine et de la Basse Égypte*, vol. III, Paris 1798 [no. 25] 69

O. Eliashar, *The Book of Hebron* (Hebrew), Jerusalem: Keter, 1970 [p. 183] 260 (lower)

Encyclopaedia Judaica, vol. IV, Jerusalem 1971 [col. 733] 84

History of the Jewish People, vol. II: *The Middle Ages* (Hebrew), Tel Aviv: Dvir, 1969 [facing p. 47] 143 (upper)

Illustrated London News, 18 December 1858 263

J. Kelman, *From Damascus to Palmyra*, London: Adam and Charles Black, 1908 [facing p. 280] 97, [facing p. 108] 174 (upper)

E. Kühnel, *Nordafrika*, Berlin: Wasmuth, 1924 162 (lower), 166, (upper and lower), 170 (© by Ernst Wasmuth Verlag, Tübingen, Germany)

L. Mayer, *Views in the Ottoman Empire…*, III: *Palestine*, London: R. Bowyer, 1804 [p. 47] 232 (lower)

D. Nicolle, *Armies of the Ottoman Turks 1300–1774*, London: Osprey Books, 1994 [pl. B] 227 (lower)

Picturesque Palestine, Syria and Egypt, vol. I, New York: D. Appleton, 1881 [p. 248] 138, [p. 44] 210 (upper)

Ludwig Preiss, *Palästina und das Ostjordanland*, Stuttgart: Verlag Julius Hoffmann, 1925 [pl. xvi] 139, [pl. xviii] 261, [pl. xi] 267 (lower)

J.M. Rogers, *Empires of the Sultans: Ottoman Art from the Collection of Nasser D. Khalili*, London: The Nour Foundation, 1995 [p. 153] 233 (upper)

H. Schedel, *Liber chronicarum*, Nürnberg 1493 184 (lower)

M. Soloveitchik, *Biblical Ornaments* (Hebrew), Berlin: Dwir-Hamikra, 1925 [pl. 3] 27 (upper)

Syria, the Holy Land, Asia Minor… illustrated by W.H. Bartlett [a.o.], London 1836 [v. 2, opp. p. 92] 237 (upper)

The publisher wishes to acknowledge all sources of illustrations appearing in this book which remain unidentified

Index of Names

350